The Walls of Badajoz

Martin McDowell

Published in 2018 by FeedARead.com Publishing – Arts Council funded

First Edition – ISBN:9781788762625

The author, Martin Andrew McDowell, has asserted his moral right under the Copyright, Designs and Patents Act, 1988, to be identified as the author of this work.

A CIP catalogue record for this title is available from the British Library.

Dedication

To my wife, Doreen, and children, Amy and Steven,
who are so indulgent of my tedious
Napoleonic obsession!

And Dave Wood, History teacher colleague; ever in our memory.

Acknowledgments

The History of the Peninsular War-
Volumes IV and V - Sir Charles Oman

In Hell Before Daylight – Ian Fletcher

Waterloo - Mark Adkin

Costello. The True Story of a Peninsular War Riflemen
Eileen Hathaway

An Atlas of the Peninsular War - Ian Robertson

During the Campaigns described in this volume:-
The 105th are in place of:
  the 71st Glasgow (Highland) Regiment of Foot,
- for the advance from Santarem, part of Erskine's Brigade, Spencer's 1st Division.

The 1/45th Nottinghamshire Regiment of Foot – "The Old Stubborns",
- for the advance through Redinha, Cazal Novo, Foz Do Arouce, Sabugal, El Bodon, and the siege of
  Cuidad Rodrigo. All part of Mackinnon's Brigade, Picton's 3rd Division,
  For the siege of Badajoz, part of Kempt's Brigade, Picton's 3rd Division.

Books by the same author.
                105th Series   - Worth Their Colours
                                      - Close to the Colours
                                      - The Plains of Talavera
        A Question of Duty – a novel set in Nelson's Navy, post Trafalgar

Cover Picture
The 88th Connaught Rangers storm the Castle Walls of Badajoz – by Chris Collingwood

List of Characters

105th Privates and NCOs
Regimental Sergeant Major Cyrus Gibney
Light Company – 1st Section
Snr. Sgt. Ethan Ellis, Cprl Ezekiel Saunders, Chosen man John Davey,
Privates - Tom Miles, Joe Pike, Nat Solomon, Len Bailey, John Byford, Bill Turner.
Light Company – 2nd Section
Sgt. George Fearnley – Company Surgeon's Assistant
3 Company (Colour)
Colour Sgt. Jedediah Deakin - Regimental Colour. Colour Sgt. Harry Bennet - King's Colour.
Sgt. Obediah Hill, Sgt. Henry Nicholls, Cprl. Toby Halfway. Private Neet Barker
Grenadiers – 1st Section.
Sgt. Arthur Bennett
Grenadiers – 2nd Section
Sgt. Luke Ridgway

Colonel's Staff
Sgt. Herbert Bryce – Colonel's Clerk.
Corporal Herbert 'Bugle' Bates
Reverend Thomas Albright – Regimental Chaplain
Servants
Private Percival Sedgwicke – Chaplain's Assistant.
Private Sidney Morrison – Servant to the Light Company Officers
Private Arthur Binns – Servant to the Genadier Company Officers

Followers
Mulcahey family
Bridie Mulcahey 'Army wife' to Jed Deakin. Mother of - Eirin Byford (nee Mulcahey) 19, married to Pte John Byford, Kevin 16, Sinead 14, and Grandmother of Jedediah Byford – Eirin's baby son.
Nicholls family
Nellie Nicholls, wife to Henry Nicholls. Mother of - Sally 16. Trudie 14, Violet 12.

Consuela Saunders – wife to Ezekiel Saunders
Betty Barker – wife to Neet Barker.

Soldiers' families in England
Mary Pike (was O'Keefe – Bridie's youngest sister), married to Pte Joe Pike – son Thomas.
Molly Davey, wife to Chosen Man John Davey. Children - Tilly Davey 14. Babies John Davey and Rachel Davey.

105th Officers
Lt. Col. Bertram Lacey. Senior Major Padraigh O'Hare. Junior Major Henry Carr.
Grenadier Company – Cpt. Lord Charles Carravoy. 1 Section, Lt. Royston D'Villiers.
2 Section, Lt. Simon Ameshurst.
3 (Colour) Company - Cpt. Joshua Heaviside. 1 Section Lt. Lionel Farquarson.
Light Company - Cpt. Nathaniel Drake. 1 section, Lt. Stuart Maltby. 2 Section, Lt. Richard Shakeshaft.
Ensigns. Barnaby Rushby - King's Colour. Ensign Patrick Mulcahey - Regimental Colour
2 Company – Cpt. Reginald Charters
Surgeon George Pearce

Women in England
Jane Carr – wife to Henry Carr

Cecily Drake – wife to Nathaniel Drake
Lady Constance Fynings – Aunt to Jane.

Cavalry
General Stapleton-Cotton – Division Commander
Col. Slade's Brigade
1st Dragoons (Slade's own) and 14th Light Dragoons - Col. Dodds.
Col. Frederick Arentschildt's Brigade.
16th Light Dragoons and 1st Hussars King's German Legion, Col. Durnfeld.
16th Light Dragoons:-
Colonel George Withers
Major Arthur Johnson
Captain Lucius Tavender – One Squadron Commander
Servant Ted Robinson
Cornet Harry Smythe – A Troop Leader
Sgt. Ned Shelby
Cornet Ben Faversham – B Troop Leader
Captain Lionel Vigurs (later Captain Oakwood) – Two Squadron Commander
Cornet Willoughby Carr – C Troop Leader
Sgt. Septimus Baxter, Cpl Jim Makepeace, Troopers Len Spivey, Percy Nunney.
Cornet Douglas Peterson – D Troop Leader
Sgt. Desty
Captain Vaughan Somers-Cocks – Three Squadron
Captain Myers – Four Squadron

Regiments involved in Major Engagements

Santarem - Spencer's First Division
Erskine's Brigade – 71st (105th), 1/50th (Cadell), 1/92nd (Locke),1Co. 5/60th (Capt Twyford)

Redinha, Cazal Novo, Foz Do Arouce - Picton's Third Division
Mackinnon's Bgde – 1/45th (105th), 5/60th (Capt. Twyford) 74th (Dewey), 1/88th. (John Wallace)
Colville's Bgde – 2/5th, 77th, 2/83rd, 94th.

Sabugal - Picton's 3rd Div.
Mackinnon's Bgde – 1/45th, (105th), 5/60th, 74th, 1/88th
Colville's Bgde – 2/5th, 77th, 2/83rd, 94th (Walter Blakeney).

Cuidad – Picton's 3rd Division
Mackinnon's Bgde – 1/45th (105th), 5/60th (Capt. Riley), 74th (McArdle), 1/88th (Wallace)
Campbell's Bgde – 2/5th (Major Ridge), 77th (Fanshawe), 2/83rd (O'Neill), 94th (Harper)

Badajoz – Picton's 3rd Division
Kempt - 1/45th (105th), 5/60th, 74th, 1/88th
Campbell's Bgde – 2/5th, 77th, 2/83rd, 94th.

Chapter One

What kind of army?

Tom Miles sighted along the barrel of his Baker rifle, sighting forward to a doorway, then up, to a window. From behind him, from a sheltering corner, Joe Pike sprinted past him and beyond, to the nearest doorway, to then train his weapon menacingly forward, as had Miles before him. John Davey, next, appeared from behind, both to take his turn and run ten yards up the street to menace any possible enemy vantage point further up, then Miles, once more, moved forward to do the same. In such manner, they progressed up the wrecked street, each advancing never more than ten yards and always under the protection of the weapons of their two file mates. A mangy dog, carrying something appalling in its mouth, crossed the street and gave Miles but the same scant attention as Miles gave it. The 105th Light Company were progressing through the wrecked town of Santarem, the town that they had sat watching for the Winter months of 1810 and early 1811. All through that period they all had sat wondering when the occupying French would finally move, probably from sheer starvation and now, in early March, that had finally happened.

Henry Carr, Junior Major of the 105th, followed close on the heels of the 105th Light Company Section, it commanded by Lieutenant Stuart Maltby, him a tense figure just ahead, sword in one hand, pistol in the other. Carr's companion was none other than his own Brigadier, General Sir William Erskine, each was concentrating partly on the fluid movement of Maltby's men and partly on the condition of Santarem. They shared a look, not as superior to inferior, but simply as two decent men, both utterly aghast at what they were seeing. The town was a wreck, merely a collection of gaping buildings, all wood having been stripped from all doors, windows and roofs and the streets were full of half burnt smashed furniture and shattered tiles, these the result of their roof timbers being pillaged. However, what was worse were the sights in almost every alleyway, piles of bodies, most naked and decomposing, food for scavenging animals, piles of French dead and civilians also, who had stayed too long and failed to provide the French occupiers with the food they needed. Thus, many had died not from violence, but from sheer starvation throughout the long winter months. A few remaining near-starved citizens flitted across the road, too traumatized by a brutal military occupation to pause at all to examine the nationality of these newcomer soldiers wearing red. What had been a thriving city of between four and five thousand Portuguese souls was now a shattered and eerie monument to five months of French occupation, of an army that lived off the land and cared little for how their sustenance was procured. Of living souls, there were now pitifully few, most of the occupants now were the dogs and cats that had once been family pets, but who now scavenged a meagre living from amongst the awful evidence of brutality and extreme deprivation.

The Light Company Redcoats progressed on, never once relaxing from their drill, subconsciously stepping over the rubbish and wreckage in every street, each always tense and wary of any potential ambush. Finally, on reaching the town outskirts, the streets grew wider and the buildings further apart, until they were staring out over empty fields and trees, these poorly attempting to produce the first signs of Spring. Maltby ran back to his two superiors, pistol lowered, sword sheathed. He saluted and spoke to Erskine.

"No sign, Sir. Just odd bits of equipment, but not long left abandoned. The rain has done little damage, so they could not have lain there for very long."

Erskine nodded and then turned to Carr.

"Right. It's us chasing them."

He paused for thought.

"Carr. Get back to Lacey and tell him to send runners to Cadell and Locke. I want all three Battalions on the road ready to march through. Twyford's Rifles to remain out on the right, where they are now. I want us through and out of this place in half an hour."

Carr saluted and ran back through the noisome streets, keeping his eyes fixed firmly ahead. Soon he was at the opposite outskirts where his own 105th Foot were stood in line abreast in columns of companies, facing the town and ready to advance should any frontal attack be needed. The other two Regiments of the Brigade were formed up to the left of the 105th, the 1/50th Queen's Own and the 92nd Gordon Highlanders. The Brigade Company of the 5/60th Rifles were no-where to be seen, having matched, using other routes, the advance through the town of the 105th Light Company. Carr ran up to his two superior Officers, Lieutenant Colonel Bertram Lacey and the Senior Major, Padraigh O'Hare.

"The French have gone, Sir, but what's in that town beggars belief. The place is in utter ruin, buildings all but destroyed, bodies all over. The Brigadier wants us formed up to march straight through as soon as possible and so Colonels Cadell and Locke need to be told."

Lacey turned to O'Hare.

"Can you see to that?"

As O'Hare ran off, Lacey turned back to Carr.

"Where is the Light Company now?"

"Far side of the town, Sir. With General Erskine."

"Very good. So, get ours formed up. Colour Company first. I think we'll march through giving demonstration of who we are."

Carr hurried away to address each Company Captain and soon his Regiment was fully formed as one column of fours on the road to march into Santarem. The Colour Party was in the lead, Colour Sergeant Jed Deakin on the far right, outside of Ensign Patrick Mulcahy, him carrying the bright green Regimental Colour, next to him Ensign Barnaby Rushby carrying the King's Colour, a huge Union Jack with the numerals CV in the centre, and on his left Colour Sergeant Harry Bennet. Between them and the three Senior Officers furthest ahead stood the lugubrious and deeply religious Joshua Heaviside, Captain of Number Three, the Colour Company, the outline of his Bible conspicuous in his greatcoat pocket. Lacey led the Brigade forward into the town, but soon all formation was lost as the men were forced to pick their way through the rubble strewn streets. Perhaps this was a blessing for the simple act of marching diverted all their attention away from the sickening sights in the alleyways either side. However, little escaped the attention of Joshua Heaviside and, as they emerged onto the good trunk road that led North, from his own thoughts he found the quote that he muttered to himself as, at last, they entered the clean air of the trees and fields.

"Their feet run to evil, and they are swift to shed innocent blood; their thoughts are thoughts of iniquity; desolation and destruction are in their highways. Isiah 59, verse 7."

Subconsciously, he eased his sword in its scabbard, whilst behind him Jed Deakin turned to his good friend Corporal Toby Halfway, marching immediately behind.

"Johnny's lost none of his nasty habits, Tobe."

Halfway could only shake his head and lower his head into the collar of his greatcoat.

They marched on further in silence, past wrecked farms and hamlets, each with not a living soul nor creature to give evidence that this was once a worthwhile place of livelihood. With the dying of the day they were forced to halt before the wrecked bridge at the river Aviella. Their Followers soon came up and food was prepared, but little was said and that night there was a larger than usual group for Evening Prayers around the Reverend Thomas Albright, the Regimental Chaplain and his Assistant, Private Percival Sedgwicke.

oOo

Lord Frederick Templemere, late of the 16th Light Dragoons, 'late' for the reason that he had been taken prisoner by the French and was now under parole, for the first time approached the yawning portico of the House of Lords, one notable feature that gained his brief attention being the huge chimney oddly vertically aligned with the centre of the door. However, without pausing, Templemere strode forward through the ornate stonework, confident and full of good prospects. On this day, Black Rod himself was acting as Doorkeeper, behind a huge desk with an Assistant, and he soon spied the dapper figure, dressed in the height of fashion, who strode forward and spoke first, in a very confident, even superior, manner.

"Good-day. My name is Lord Frederick Templemere. To whom do I have the honour of speaking?"

Black Rod fixed Templemere with a look that was blank and unwelcoming, but he spoke in a clear authoritative manner.

"Sir Francis Molyneux, Gentleman Usher of the Black Rod."

He then bowed his head.

"At your service!"

Templemere grinned at the words. This was becoming more enjoyable by the minute.

"I live in the hope that you are aware of my letter informing the Lord Chancellor of my intention to take my seat. Here!"

Sir Francis turned to his Assistant.

"What do we have?"

The Assistant opened a Register that seemed to have a permanent place on the desk and turned the pages, alighting upon one, down which he ran an inky finger.

"Yes. Lord Frederick Templemere. Eldest son of the late Lord Joshua Templemere, the holder of a Hampshire Estate of that name."

Sir Francis turned to Templemere, disapproval growing by the second, as registered by the lowering of his prominent eyebrows. As he spoke he placed an emphasis on the second word.

"You are registered my Lord and I take it that this is your first time here?"

Templemere grinned and flicked his gloves onto the front edge of the ancient desk, speaking in the clipped tones that were the mode of the day.

"That's it! Just got back from the Peninsula, or more like France. I was taken prisoner and have given my parole. Had to or I wouldn't be here. Given as an Officer, you understand! Taken just before we got into The Lines. Got too far forward and the damned Troopers wouldn't follow me. If you have a knowledge of that sort of thing?"

Sir Francis drew himself up to his full height and frowned down his nose at this overly cheery, overly self-regarding sprat who stood in front of him.

"Yes, I believe I do. Seen enough of that sort of thing myself!"

Templemere nodded and grinned further.

'Well. If that's all, I would like to take a look at the place. Choose where I may wish to sit, sort of thing."

"You may, but first would you consider yourself a Whig or a Tory?"

Templemere essayed mock outrage at the question.

"Why, Tory. Of course!"

Sir Francis remained impassive. He felt no humour to be justified with this one.

"Then you take a place on the right, as you look from the Royal Throne. There is a sitting at 11.00 am tomorrow, my Lord. You may wish to be introduced then. Do you have friends to introduce you to the Lord Chancellor?"

Templemere leaned forward on his cane.

"Indeed I do. Yes, to be sure. Lords Mahon and Hopgood. As I'm in town, may as well do the proper deed."

Black Rod bowed ever so slightly.

"As you choose, My Lord. I will inform the Lord Chancellor of your wish. Now, my Assistant here will show you to the Chamber."

The Assistant left the desk and gestured for Templemere to follow him. The walk was quite brief; through a door, down a short corridor and then through another door and into the Chamber itself, with the Woolsacks prominent in the centre and the Royal Throne at the far end. As the Assistant bowed his own dismissal, Templemere took a deep breath to smell the ancient benches, the thick carpet, and the tapestries, these an expanse of faded green on both sides, now barely able to display their subjects which seemed to be taken from the time of the Spanish Armada. Templemere eased himself forward, pausing but a moment for a cleaner to avoid him. He oriented himself to the 'right' and took a seat on the polished red leather of the Tory benches. He stretched forward, luxuriating in his unassailable place at this consummate seat of power, of which he was a permanent Member.

oOo

Jed Deakin had given himself the luxury of studying the efforts to mend the broken bridge over the river Aviella. Some timber had finally come up from somewhere and one stout length had at last bridged the gap over the turbulent waters of the river, this now loud and menacing, swollen by the February rains. He made a final professional judgment; they would not be crossing that any time soon, probably not even tomorrow, only when the repair could take the weight of guns, heavy cavalry and supply wagons. He muttered the same conclusion to himself as he walked away.

"Nosey won't take no chance of moving infantry forward alone, not without the guns and cavalry."

He walked further through the crowded mess lines, the whole of his own 1st Division under General Spencer and also the Light Division were crammed into the narrow fields beside the river, but soon he came to his own mess camp and he sat on the low wall that bordered one side of their area. All around was quiet activity, men cleaning and checking equipment, their Follower women cooking and preparing, the children doing small chores. Deakin looked up at the sky, the sun was breaking through; things could be a lot worse, especially as rations were up and regular. He searched his mind for a topic of conversation and found one, and so he turned to the intellectual 'gentleman ranker' of their group.

"Here, Byfe! You heard from Eirin?"

John Byford looked up from his book.

"No. Only that letter which we received before we moved towards Santarem."

Tom Miles cut off the thread with which he had been repairing his French back-pack. All had one, being better made than British issue.

"The one as said that you was now a Dad! Though not one."

Nelly Nicholls, the harridan nemesis of Tom Miles, looked up from preparing the salt pork for their stew.

"Now, don't you be startin' on that subject, Tom Miles. Sure, was it not a good Christian thing that John here did? Marryin' Eirin whilst she was expectin'. An' the babby not his!"

Tom Miles, never slow to anger when Nelly Nicholls was involved, threw down the pack.

"Now, for why are you startin' in on me? All I did was speak the plain truth!"

Nelly pointed the wicked looking knife at him.

"Have you never heard the sayin', 'Least said, soonest mended'? Sure, is Eirin not in a good place, safe, fed and well cared for?"

The harmony shattered, Jed Deakin wished that he had not raised the subject at all. Eirin was his 'step-daughter' by custom, his 'Army wife's' eldest daughter, and her welfare was of no small concern, if only for the peace of mind of his Bridie, who just then handed him a mug of tea and a dough cake. Deakin was both the sage and de facto leader of the group and not just because of his rank as a Colour Sergeant.

"Let it go, the pair of you. Let's just hope that she and the babe comes back to us safe and well, that's all. It's a long way up from Torres Vedras."

Bridie looked at him.

"Now the babe's born, for how long will they care for her? Those Nuns?"

"Albright only said 'whilst the child is small', so, six months and they'll shift her out? Your guess is as good as mine."

"But she'll be safe, you think, on the way up?"

"Oh, no fear there. They'll sit her on some supply wagon and that'll be that. When the time comes."

Nelly looked away from giving Tom Miles the 'evil eye'.

"Well, we made the most of a bad business. Thanks to the Blessing."

She looked at her own three daughters, busy peeling vegetables, these being Sally, Trudy and Violet, 16, 14, and 12 respectively and fixed them with a look that would have shivered even Tom Miles.

"Now just you three learn from this, you hear? 'Specially you, Sally. You're now of an age when more than one man is lookin' at you more than once. You watch what you're about!"

The three nodded their heads and gave answer in unison.

"Yes Ma."

Jed Deakin grinned as he turned to John Davey and Joe Pike.

"You heard from Tilly?"

John Davey, Chosen Man, also grinning, gave reply.

"No, not since that letter as came this Christmas just gone. All was well then, with the babes and the small-holding. Can only hope that things is still holding together in the same way"

Deakin nodded.

"More chance of that back home, than with the doings here. I rate this for a tough year what's coming. Johnny's bein' pushed back an' I don't see him givin' best too easy."

Bridie hit him with a spoon.

"Well, aren't you just the body for cheerin' up all the souls here around!"

Which brought a wide grin to the faces of 'all the souls here around'.

Further down the wall was the camp of the now cheerful group, but excluding Jed Deakin and Toby Halfway who were Colour Company, were their Light Company Officers. These Officers, Captain Nathaniel Drake, Lieutenants Stuart Maltby and Richard Shakeshaft were all sat with Major Henry Carr, for the simple reason that he had once been Captain of the Light Company and he and Drake were good friends. They were all seated, sharing a bottle of wine, whilst their servant, Corporal Henry Morrison did his best to provide a wholesome stew. Conversation was sparse, Shakeshaft was busy sketching, Drake adding to his diary like letter, Maltby cleaning his pistol, and Carr just brooding. Nat Drake, noting the inactivity of his good friend and Major, looked up from his writing.

"You could begin a letter to Jane, or even continue it, if you have taken my constant advice. We'll be here for a good day more and we don't even have pickets to worry about, with that river between us and the French."

Carr nodded and felt behind him for his pack that contained paper and pencil. There could be no argument not to begin a letter; for him to at least write something to his newly wed wife, even though the topic uppermost in his mind was the ordeal that he expected to have to endure as they followed a beaten, demoralized and starving French army. However, with paper now arranged on his back-pack, he began, although his attention was often drawn to the overheard conversation of the next group of Officers along, close to them, these being of the Grenadier Company; Captain Lord Charles Carravoy and his Lieutenants Royston D'Villiers and Simon Ameshurst. D'Villiers was worrying at a topic that often concerned him, this being exchanging into another Regiment. Ameshurst was wholly unconvinced.

"What good will it do? We're out here for another three years, two at least. All of your fashionable Regiments, as you call them, are out here with us. The Guards are all in our Division, in Stopford's Brigade, so you'd just be marching in our footsteps!"

The countenance of D'Villiers took on a pained expression, as though the decision weighed heavily upon him.

"I was thinking of the Fusiliers, perhaps."

Lord Carravoy lowered his glass of wine, fine glass of course, no tin mug for him.

"That would be even worse! They're off with Beresford down to Badajoz, in Estremadura, where we all ended up after Talavera after almost starving to death! A more obscure and Godforsaken place I cannot imagine. And one where we all got that weird fever."

D'Villiers became defensive, even a little more resolved.

"Well, the next time we get a Gazette, I'm going to take a serious look at what's being offered."

At this point Carr intervened, having overheard and searched the contents of his own pack.

"Royston! Here!"

He threw a closely folded newspaper, a Gazette, over to him.

"But I doubt you'll find much in there to interest you."

D'Villiers retrieved the newspaper from the damp earth between them.

"Thank you, Sir."

Carr returned to his letter.

"Think nothing of it."

At that point D'Villiers began to ponder if the gesture on the part of his Junior Major held any significance regarding Carr's opinion of him as a worthy brother Officer within their Regiment. The question still in his mind, he began to scan the creased pages.

With the arrival of the late afternoon of the next day, the Division crossed the bridge. The Engineers had found themselves under the constant scrutiny of Wellington himself, which injected no small amount of speed to their efforts. He was plainly impatient to be after the French. The 105th, following the 1/50th and 1/92nd of Erskine's Brigade, strode across the stout timbers with the weak sun westering on their left. A forced march left the Followers behind, this pushing on through the growing gloom that increasingly hid the desolation and destruction either side of the road. Their efforts brought them to the village of Alcanhede and, in the full dark, they marched straight through, the village buildings merely dark, brooding shapes either side, and they camped in the fields beyond. Immediately Senior Sergeant of the Light Company, Ethan Ellis, began touring the mess-camps of his Company.

"Campfires is alright, but we'n marching before dawn, so keep all things handy."

He looked at Miles, the one soldier in his Company for whom he had a serious dislike.

"You hear that, Miles?"

Miles looked up from kindling the fire.

"When was the last time you saw me late for muster?"

"I asked, did you hear!"

It was Chosen Man John Davey who answered,

"I'll have him there, S'arnt. No fear."

Ellis gave Miles a last cold look, which was returned with interest and he left.

Pickets were out, one of which was John Byford with his good friend the giant Ezekiel Saunders. They were close enough to talk, but far enough apart to keep good watch. It was Byford who was first startled by odd sounds and shouted as he swung his bayonetted rifle from his shoulder.

"Halt! Who goes there?"

He could see nothing ahead as Saunders came running up. Then Byford felt something touch his leg. He looked down to see several crawling figures.

"Por favor, Senors. Comida por favor."

Saunders gave judgement.

"Either these poor buggers is crawlin' to beg, or they'm too weak to stand. What they want?"

"Food!"

"What've you got?"

Byford reached into his haversack at his side.

"Just some biscuit and dried peas."

Saunders had conducted his own search.

"Same here."

Saunders knelt to dole out the contents of his haversack, for the items to be immediately consumed, the dried peas being crunched up with the biscuit. With nothing more forthcoming the figures crawled off. Byford shook his head.

"Whatever kind of war is this? Everything and everyone, wrecked or killed."

The answer came the following morning as the 1st Division marched on, the 105th taking their turn to lead, with their Light Company scouting in front. The French were now but a day ahead and the bodies of their sick and wounded, horribly mutilated, hung from trees by their feet or were spread-eagled and tied against fences. As many among them were Portuguese peasants, equally mutilated and killed in the most sadistic manner. Ragged, emaciated figures were emerging from the woods and ravines when they saw the Redcoat column on the road, but all were too weak to manage any form of greeting. With the arrival of the afternoon the 105th could smell smoke and the source began to grow on the horizon, soon revealing itself to be the village of Porto de Mos and they arrived to find every house alight, some more than others, but all on fire. Ellis, in the lead, waited for Maltby and Carr to come up.

"What are your orders, Sir? Go round, or get through?"

There were thick woods either side, on steep hillsides, which Carr had noticed.

"No way around. It's through. The main road looks wide enough to avoid those fires. Close up and push on."

Ellis saluted and walked off, shouting the orders and they marched in. Carr followed until they came to the village Square, which had a large Convent on one side, this also burning, but with only thin smoke moving across the statue of a female Saint above the door and the huge cross topping the portico. He looked around for any figures of authority that may be of use and he saw Jed Deakin and Regimental Sergeant Major Cyrus Gibney, a thorough Yorkshireman.

"Deakin! Gibney! We need to go in there. There may be women in need of our help. This is, was, a Convent, would be my guess."

They entered the main archway, its door missing, then into the interior and the air inside smelt of both fire and putridity. All was destruction, the floors were torn up, several pieces of cut up mattress lay along the corridor, along with smashed china, glass and scattered kitchen utensils. Carr led them on, to a door at the end.

"Try here, we need to find their cells, where they sleep."

The door led not to a dormitory but into a Chapel which had a wide fireplace on one side, in which was a large fire, still burning, on which had been heaped broken pieces of the altar, wooden images, picture frames and some ornamental woodwork, probably from the organ which had been thoroughly smashed.

"This is not what we want."

Carr turned to leave and Deakin followed but Gibney was stood in a side door of the Chapel, his face leaning on his forearm which was up against the stonework of the door entrance.

"Sir. Tha'd best see this! Tha'll need a light, 'tis fair dark."

Deakin pulled a piece of burning wood from the fire and Carr and Deakin walked over. What was inside took their breath away. The side chamber was full of partly fire-consumed bodies, some lying, some kneeling, some leaning against the walls. The floor was covered in ashes, in many places still red-hot. The higher each body was in the room, the less consumed it was by fire. Carr, horrified himself, placed a consoling hand on Gibney's shoulder.

"Get some men in, Sar' Major. The least we can do is get these outside."

As Gibney left, Deakin went further in, to find a bag at the upper end of the chamber. He opened the bag and let out a cry of anguish. Inside was the dead body of a child, strangled, the ligature cord still in place. He lifted the bag and carried the body outside himself. Soon, on Gibney's orders, all the bodies, both whole and part, were outside in the Square and covered in whatever fabric could be found: carpets, curtains, bedding, even tablecloths, although all were scorched and charred. The 105th were formed up in a column of fours, ready to negotiate the burning street and all saw what was being brought forth. Some citizens had arrived, ragged and emaciated, to kneel at the rows of bodies and begin keening and praying. They knew full well whom the French had herded into the Chapel. The 105th, all grim faced, marched on and that evening Carr added to his letter. 'I cannot begin to describe the sights that I am witnessing in these Portuguese towns and villages, nor would I even wish to try. We are following a French army in retreat and anyone who holds any sympathy for Napoleon should come here and observe for themselves what his armies inflict on local civilians who will not or even cannot, give up the food demanded of them. The men are very incensed and are eager to come up to the French, which will happen any day now. Massena, who is their Commander, must make a stand sooner or later.'

At this point in time Chaplain's Assistant Sedgwicke took it upon himself to thrust his distraught and dissolving Chaplain back into the interior of their small cart.

"It would be better that you stay back here and just rest, Sir. Were you not composing a hymn and a prayer, Sir? You could continue with that."

He arranged some blankets for his Chaplain.

"I strongly advise you not to pull back the canopy, Sir. You know how disturbed you were by what we saw during the advance up to Santarem last year. This is much the same."

Reverend Albright, his mind in anguish, obeyed without demur and Sedgwicke continued.

"We will soon catch up with the French and this will be at an end."

However, it was not to be. The 1st Division hurried on in pursuit of the fleeing French, to spend a night at the large town of Thomar, mercifully not thoroughly wrecked, and then they turned West on the good road towards Leiria. Albright was kept strictly inside the cart as they passed by the great and ancient Monastery of Batalha, now pillaged and burning. On the same day, the 10th March, they found Leiria to be a copy of Santarem, wrecked, sacked and on fire in several places. Albright was given a bottle when they finally came to pass through, the spirit emerging from a store secretly hoarded by Sedgwicke, but not for his own exclusive use.

"Here, Sir. It will take your mind off things."

The next day the 105th took their turn to lead and, as for almost every one of the previous days, they passed yet another appalling sight, such as with which they had now become all too familiar, but always it tightened jaws and raised anger. Then Davey, in the lead of Maltby's Section, hurried back to find Ellis.

"Sarn't, there's some live French up ahead. Though 'live' b'ain't quite the right word, as you'll see."

Curious, Ellis hurried forward to find two wounded Frenchmen, although their original wounds were indistinguishable from what had recently been inflicted on them by vengeful Portuguese. Their faces, their hands and their feet were all a bloody mess.

"What happened?"

Miles pointed up the hillside.

"We chased off about half a dozen Portugee, then found these two."

The two French soldiers, both of the 4th Leger, the number still legible on their collars, could hear the English voices around them. One managed to raise himself up and pleaded, through a broken mouth.

"Messieurs. Nous tuer. S'il vous plaît, nous tuer!"

He fell back, exhausted. Ellis turned to Byford.

"What he say?"

"They want us to shoot them!"

Ellis spat.

"Not us! Leave the bastards. They following might, but not us."

He pointed forward.

"Move on, we should be further on up. We'n not doin' our job."

His men prepared to move on.

"Oh! And I've got some news. We've won a battle at a place called Barossa, down South, and the French have captured Badajoz, on the border. On top, we're leavin' the 1st Division. The 3rd's arrived, that's Picton's, and Mackinnon's Brigade of it is under strength. We've been moved."

The response was blank looks of utter disinterest, then all turned to walk off.

"Miserable bloody shite-auks! I'll keep it all to meself next time."

As he finally moved on, he heard the Portuguese scuttling back down the hillside. What happened next Ellis never discovered. That afternoon they made camp at the next village up, Canheira, each house a blackened shell, with no inhabitants to be seen, either living or dead.

oOo

Senior Captain Lucius Tavender, of the 16th Light Dragoons, veteran of Vimeiro, Talavera and the retreat to Torres Vedras, sat wearily on a weary horse. For the tenth time that day he pulled out his telescope and focused it forward, but this time it was different. He turned to his nearest Troop Leader, Cornet Harry Smythe.

"Looks like, at last, we may have finished chasing them around and them chasing us off when they feel able. Take a look. I do believe that town to be Pombal and I do believe that to be about eight Squadrons of French Light. Two Regiments, more than twice us."

Smythe produced his own telescope and was focusing it as the second Cornet arrived, this being Ben Faversham. Soon both were peering through their instruments at four squadrons uniformed in light blue and another four in mid green. Both came to the same conclusion, but this spoken by Faversham, in his broad Cumberland accent.

"He's wanting to do something serious, Sir, and that's some town set behind."

Tavender nodded.

"Harry, get back and ask Colonel Withers to come up, and Ben, get to the Hussars and bring up Brigadier Arentschildt. What happens next is up to him."

As the two rode off, Tavender turned to the nearest Troop Sergeant, Ned Shelby.

"Shelby!"

"Sir!"

"Have the men dismount. We could be here a while."

Soon came the sounds of a whole Squadron dismounting and then came the sounds of cheerful conversation as the Troopers stood down and relaxed, then Tavender used his glass again. The French had not moved, remaining static in their line of Squadrons. He had just snapped the glass shut, when Colonel George Withers galloped up, accompanied by the Senior Major Arthur Johnson. Both reined in their horses and pulled out their own telescopes and scanned back and forth, when the Brigade Commander, Colonel Frederick Arentschildt, of the 1st Hussars, King's German Legion, arrived. After his own scanning, the first words were spoken by him.

"It would seem, George, that the French at last wish to play, nicht war?"

He scanned the French line further, which occupied two thirds of a broad defile.

"We must not disappoint them."

More studying ensued.

"I'll take mine in first. Four squadrons, right at their centre. You split yours either side, 300 yards back. Stop them closing in behind me. Then we'll take it from there."

He looked at Withers. The respect between the two as cavalry commanders was absolute.

"I'll bring mine forward immediately. Deploy behind me. Good luck."

Withers nodded.

"You too, Fred."

With that Arentschildt was gone, followed by his own Major. It did not take ten minutes before the whole of the KGL Hussars, resplendent in royal blue and gold with a distinctive brown busby, rode forward at the trot, and their four Squadrons to then deploy into one line and slow to a walk. Meanwhile, Colonel Withers had given his own orders and Tavender took his Squadron away to the right with that of Captain Somers-Cocks and Major Johnson in command of both, whilst Withers took the other two way off to the left. Once in place, Johnson judged the distance as they advanced and decided that Tavender was in error. He called over.

"Lucius! You're too far up. Drop back. 300 yards on the KGL right shoulder."

Tavender felt his throat tighten at the simple rebuke from a man he had scant respect for, him being a native of the far Fenlands and sounding like it, but he had no option but to slow his men to the merest progress. Meanwhile, the KGL had broken into a canter and Johnson now did the same and drew his sabre, a signal for all to do likewise. The scrape of steel on scabbards was lost in the drumming hooves, but Tavender was concentrating ahead on the French in plain sight and making no move.

"It's a damn fool in command there if they meet us stood still!"

As if in response, the French did move, but backwards, their Squadrons turning away and cantering for the central road. Tavender drew his own conclusion.

"Too late! He is a fool."

Arentschildt had come to the same conclusion, for the KGL immediately spurred into a full gallop. Within a minute was heard the clash as the KGL crashed into the last French squadron and then came the familiar sounds of screaming men and horses. The pace forward of the KGL against the French had barely diminished, obviously they had spurred the French into a full gallop away, which continued for several hundred yards down the road. Signs of combat were passed by, shakoes, busbies, weapons and the occasional casualty from both sides, both dead and wounded, but very few. Johnson was shouting across.

"Lucius. Hold the line. We may be needed here. It may be a ruse."

Tavender raised his sabre in acknowledgment, but it was no ruse, nor any kind of trap. Remaining hundreds of yards ahead, the KGL finally halted, the task complete. Now individual buildings of Pombal could be seen and so Arentschildt had prudently halted his men and both wings of the 16th did the same; they also halted and waited. Arentschildt quickly turned his men around, as they were now vulnerable to a counter-attack and they trotted quickly back. Tavender could see several light blue and green uniforms amongst them, evidently prisoners had been taken. Johnson trotted over, but it was Tavender who spoke first.

"What was that all about? They didn't hold us back for even a minute!"

"Who can say, but when have French cavalry ever stood head to head with us? No change here, so just get yours back. I'll ride over to Somers-Cocks. I expect he's as bemused by this as we are."

Leaving his Cornets and Sergeants to arrange the men, Tavender walked his horse back. He had been involved in no more than an ineffective gallop and was in no good mood. As he approached their original line he noticed a knot of horsemen on the low ridge, all in 16th uniform. The question immediately arose, "Why had they not come forward?" Angered yet again, he spurred his horse into a canter to approach the group, which he could now see numbered about 20. One figure has placed himself in front, him wearing a Cornet's uniform, this distinctive with its tilting cap. Tavender went straight up to him.

"Explain yourself, Sir. Why did you not join our advance?"

The Cornet saluted.

"Sorry Sir, we've only just arrived and managed to find you. We are a reinforcement draft, just come up from Lisbon. Sorry we missed it, Sir. Just too late. We arrived just as you were turning back."

Such an explanation left Tavender with no more argument to make. He sat forward in his saddle, intending to re-establish some level of superiority.

"And you are?"

The Cornet saluted again.

"Name's Carr, Sir. Willoughby Carr."

Tavender's teeth and eyebrows came together, each to the other.

"Is one Major Henry Carr known to you?"

"Yes Sir. He's my brother. My elder brother."

His face plainly showing his discomfiture, Tavender pointed to Colonel Withers, him now visible and riding back.

"That's the Colonel there. You'd best report to him."

Then Tavender pulled his horse away, conflict arising within him regarding which attitude or even emotion to adopt, but he was certain that the idea of a Carr in his Regiment was a development which did not appeal at all.

On the same road into Pombal, but a mile back, the 105th stood waiting. The rest of the 1st Division had marched back for their own re-organisation, but the 105th now stood waiting for Picton's 3rd to come up to them. Wellington was clearly assembling his army. The prospect of re-joining the 3rd occupied the minds of both Nat Drake and Henry Carr.

15

"Picton again! No love lost there!"

Nat Drake grinned.

"No love lost between Picton and anybody."

Drake turned to him.

"But! He was fair to you during that enquiry after Casa de Salinas and Talavera. He gave short shrift to all that rubbish brought up by Perry, dismissing the whole sorry gamut."

Carr nodded.

"He did. I really cannot complain, but I've never seen a man so quick to temper."

Drake looked down the road.

"Well, here's your chance to view any change, such as what's coming can ever reveal. I doubt he'll have much to say to the likes of us."

Picton was riding at the head of his Division. If anything, he appeared to be in one of his better moods, the face still temperamental red, but the corners of his mouth not so far turned down. First to greet him were Lacey and O'Hare, each reaching up to shake Picton's hand whilst he remained on horseback. That done, Picton rode on, but then he did notice Carr. Both him and Drake had sprung to the attention as Picton began to pass by, but he did not. Instead, he reined in his horse.

"Ah, Carr!"

"Sir!"

"Got over that boo hoo business back after Talavera?"

"I like to think so Sir. A lot has happened since."

Picton nodded, but made no reply, simply urging his horse back to a walk. Picton's first Brigade, led by Brigadier Colville, passed by, then came his second, led by Brigadier Mackinnon. The greeting between Lacey, O'Hare and Mackinnon was utterly different. Mackinnon dismounted and all then observed much hand shaking and back slapping. At Busaco, the three had stood together to hold the line at the crisis point on the vital ridge. The last words came from Mackinnon.

"I'll send for you. We'll all have a drink!"

It was much the same when he came to Carr and Drake. He stopped his horse and returned their salutes.

"Carr, Drake, good to see you both again."

Carr grinned.

"Good to see you again, Sir."

With grins all round, Mackinnon moved on. However, the atmosphere was nothing like so convivial as the Battalions passed each other. First came the 74th Foot, all in their kilts and quickly dismissed by Miles as 'Scots girlies', but then came the 88th Connaught Rangers with whom the 105th had the deepest mutual antipathy. Before Talavera the 105th had been duped into a wrestling match between Saunders and the Connaught's all Irish Champion and that was followed by the 88th Lights complaining bitterly at the 105th Lights not making a share-out of the booty garnered from a skirmish before Busaco. Stoney looks were exchanged from the road to the roadside and returned with interest in the opposite direction. However, this was in sharp contrast to O'Hare and the 88th's Colonel John Wallace. The pair had together led a desperate charge against a whole Divisional French column at Busaco, and they exchanged handshakes of appalling ferocity. However, when all had passed on, the 105th sullenly formed up on the road, where Miles had the last word.

"Back with they bloody Irish diddykites again!"

It was not long before one of Mackinnon's Aide-de-Camps came galloping back to rein in his horse before Lacey and O'Hare, him doing his best to salute whilst sat on a wheeling horse.

"His Lordship wants to take a crack at Pombal, Sir, just up ahead. He's sent a Battalion of Cacadores and two Companies of Rifles to try to get over the bridge and take the town, with the Light Division following immediately. Our Division is to go left and try to cross the river below the bridge. Brigadier Colville's Brigade will try first, we'll be in reserve. Please to come up on the right of the 88th, Sir."

Lacey grasped the horse's bridle to steady the mount and asked his question.

"What do we know of the French?"

"They are in the town and up in the Castle. That's all we know, Sir. You can see the Castle from here."

Lacey released the bridle, which signaled the Aide to ride off. Both Lacey and O'Hare peered into the distance and, as had been stated, the Castle was very visible, high on its hill, behind and above the town.

Lacey turned to O'Hare, but the question had to wait, as the 88th moved off, just ahead. Lacey simply waved his arm forward and all progressed down the good road.

"I was going to ask, how are the men?"

O'Hare continued to peer ahead.

"All with rations and full cartridge boxes. And hating the French!"

Lacey nodded, as they wheeled left off the road and at that moment the sounds of combat reached them. The bridge was being attacked, but for them the only action was to take position behind Colville's 94th and beside the 88th.The sounds of combat intensified, then waned and then intensified again. Carravoy had found a high wall and was atop it, using his telescope. He called down to O'Hare.

"Johnny's coming down from the Castle in force, Sir. I think they're contesting the town."

O'Hare nodded, but the 94th were moving leftwards, as were the 88th. He turned to Lacey.

"I think we are about to get wet!"

Fifteen minutes later, Carr, his face screwed up against what was to come, felt the cold mud squeeze between his toes and then the chill water rose up his legs, over his groin and up to his waist. His boots, with his hose inside, all hanging ludicrously down from one end of his sabre, his pistol in its holster balancing at the back, all portraying anything other than a dignified Commissioned Officer, but he pressed on. The ford was being marked by the men and horses of the 16th Light Dragoons and, seeing the Regimental number on their saddle-blankets, he fully expected to see Tavender and there he was in the middle of the line, boots held out of the water by shortened stirrups. Carr gave him a nod, but Tavender had no greeting for him, rather a piece of information, delivered in a very blunt manner.

"Someone at the end of this line, Major. Someone you may recognize. Sir!"

Puzzled, Carr waded on, and studied the end of the line and the final figure did become familiar, albeit difficult to recognize in standard Light Dragoon uniform. He waded over and then was sure.

"Good Heavens, Willoughby! By all that's Holy. I had no idea. No-one said."

He halted and waded a little closer.

"What are you doing here? No, stupid question."

He could get no closer, because the water was approaching his chest, but his younger brother was grinning from ear to ear.

"Hello Henry! We heard you'd got married and been made a Major. Heard it on the grapevine, Father will allow no discourse with you as the subject. But I hope you are well!"

Carr grinned.

"It all depends if I can dry out. But let's hope that we can meet up some time. Should be possible."

Young Carr grinned.

"Yes, let's hope."

However, further conversation was now impossible. Away from the ford, Carr was struggling to keep his feet and the rushing waters provided their own noisy hindrance. Both could now only wave as the distance between them increased. Finally, with all across the river, and with Carr's thoughts anywhere other than the situation in hand, all Picton's Battalions formed line again to the East of the town. Picton arrived to tour his reserve line and impart some intelligence, which any could see with unaided sight.

"Nothing doing here, Lacey. The Frogs have fired the town and took themselves away."

All sounds of infantry conflict had now ceased, all that could now be heard was a careful cannonade coming from the British side, but no gun smoke was visible in the growing darkness. They saw Picton ride to MacKinnon and the same Aide as before then rode back to stop at Lacey.

"Into columns, please Sir. We're marching past the town. Please to make camp and post double pickets. The French have not retired very far."

Using the last of the light, the seven columns of Picton's Battalions picked their way up a steep hillside and made camp using the light from the burning town, all buildings alight save the Castle and, through the hours of darkness, the town was to be allowed to burn itself out. With all settled and food being cooked, Nat Drake took the trouble to visit his pickets, all from One Section of his Company. He found Byford and Saunders stood in a 'double' and looking Northward. Both came to the attention as he approached.

"What can you see men?"

It was Byford who answered.

"Not a great deal, Sir, nor have we heard anything, but Zeke climbed up into a tree a while ago."

Drake turned to Saunders.

"And?"

"Campfires, Sir. About five mile up, I'd say."

"Right, well done. That's Johnny at a place called Redhina. It'll be tomorrow's dancefloor, I shouldn't wonder."

Both soldiers grinned and Saunders answered, he being of the superior wit.

"Long as it's a dry floor, Sir. Not like today!"

Drake grinned himself.

"Let's hope!"

Elsewhere on the hillside, Tavender found whom he was seeking, Cornet Carr, sat with his fellow Squadron Cornet, Douglas Peterson. Both rose to their feet on the approach of a Squadron Captain, albeit not their own.

"Evening Sir."

Both spoke in unison and Tavender nodded in reply.

"So, young Carr, did you spot your brother, this evening?"

"Yes Sir, I did and it was good to see him."

Tavender kicked a biscuit box into position and sat on it, and so the pair resumed their place on their log. Tavender convivially warmed his hands at their fire, vigorously rubbing his hands together.

"So, you've not see him in a good while. Since after he joined the army?"

"No, Sir. He went into the 6th Foot and that was about the last we saw of him, but letters did arrive."

Tavender nodded, studied the fire and then looked up.

"Something of a family rupture, was there?"

Young Carr was immediately on his guard at so pointed a question.

"Nothing terrible, Sir. He just left home and became caught up in the army."

"He's the eldest?"

"No, Sir. James is. He'll inherit the estate. Both Henry and myself were packed off to the army."

"Willingly?"

"Yes Sir. For my part."

"And your brother's?"

The suspicions in Willoughby Carr now came thoroughly to the surface. He did not wish to be less than open with his superior Officer, but he discerned that Tavender was searching for something.

"He made his choice, Sir, between the family business and something else. He chose something else."

"And what was the family business?"

"Coal and timber, Sir."

"What kind of a brother was he? A good example, you'd say?"

"Yes Sir, I'd say he was. He always looked out for me and as to a good example, well, yes again, except at school where he was a shocker. Father always having to travel up."

"In trouble? What sort of trouble?"

Young Carr stood up, bringing to mind the excuse he needed. This conversation could be doing his brother harm.

"Excuse me, Sir, but I need to check on my pickets. I should have some time ago, Sir. So, if you'll excuse me."

Tavender rose as well, realizing he would get no more.

"I should, also."

Carr thought for one horrible second that Tavender would accompany him, but he turned and left in a different direction. Carr walked to the edge of their camp to find Sergeant Baxter, of his own C Troop, his short carbine in the crook of his arm.

"What can you see Sergeant?"

"Campfires, Sir. About five mile up."

"French, I assume?"

"Not ours, Sir. Be certain of that. We'll be looking at each other come tomorrow."

"Not with any affection, eh, Sergeant?"

"No Sir, not with what we've all seen on the way up, there'll be little enough of that!"

oOo

Redhina could not be seen, it being beyond a long, significant ridge, but the defending French on the ridge's summit could just be made out, three Regiments in line abreast and, as was the French system, each Regiment of three Battalions, formed in column of Battalions, one behind the other. All observers thus concluded that nine in all holding the French position. Lacey, O'Hare, and Carr were at the head of their own 105th column, with the six other Battalion columns of Picton's Division divided either side, all advancing at a brisk march. Picton was ahead with his Brigadiers, Mackinnon and Colville and always one of the three was making use of a telescope. Before them was the Battalion Company of 60th Rifles and a whole Battalion of Portuguese Cacadores, their brown uniform almost blending with the dark earth of the empty fields. As these advanced to the foot of the ridge, the French columns became hidden behind the thick woods on the slope above and Picton sent an Aide forward to halt the Rifles and Cacadores. On his return, he was then joined by another and both Aides then rode back across the seven Battalions, giving orders. One came to Lacey.

"General Picton wants all Light Companies to lead, Sir. As you know we have to turn the French left and the Light Division to turn their right, before the 4th Division can attempt their centre."

Lacey nodded.

"Yes, that's well understood."

Lacey turned to his Corporal Secretary, Corporal Bryce.

"Get Drake's Lights up here."

Bryce hurried away, but Lacey noticed that the Aide had not gone. He looked at him, quizzically and received an answer.

"General Picton would like Major Carr to command the centre of the skirmish line, Sir."

Lacey looked at Carr, stood by his side.

"There you are Henry. General's orders. Good luck!"

Carr nodded, subconsciously eased his sword in its scabbard and walked forward to soon be caught up by Nat Drake and his Light Company.

"Picton wants us up with the 60th and the Portuguese before we enter that wood. That's our job, to clear it and get through so that the rest can follow. Wellington wants the French left turned. By us."

Carr walked on, to pass Picton sat motionless on his horse. Carr received a hard stare in return for his salute, but Mackinnon spoke his good wishes. The 60th and Cacadores remained far ahead, as the 105th Lights split into their skirmish formation of files of three and then advance forward. The wood was unkempt, thick and often overgrown but with some clearings. Soon all formation was lost and the British Light troops caught up with the Cacadores. They could hear artillery fire, but the sound was muffled and so who was firing and who was suffering was impossible to tell. Joe Pike found himself to be one of the furthest forward after struggling through the undergrowth and up the slope. He joined a Cacadore who was kneeling behind a fallen tree on the edge of a clearing and drinking some wine. He offered it to Pike, who, his convivial nature always to the fore, took it, spoke his thanks and then drank. At that instant came a musket shot and the Cacadore lost part of his left ear. Pike dropped the wineskin and sighted forward to see a French Tirailleur, an elite skirmisher, running back. Pike sighted on him, just as another French ball splattered the log by his right elbow, distracting his aim. He sighted again, but the Tirailleur had gone. The French drill to retire matched that of the British and Portuguese, but their own drill was now rapidly being applied by the Allies, at least by his Company and the Cacadores, all advancing quickly, gaining shelter and only leaving cover when their comrades were ahead and protecting their advance.

First to bring down a Frenchman was John Davey, his Baker rested perfectly in the crook of a sapling. All along the line, both sides were engaging, the French deployed in a thick screen of Voltiguers and Tirailleurs. Miles felt the need to pass some comment, even though he found himself filing in with Company Sergeant Ellis.

"Tassle swingin' bastards and they red-decked gamecocks!"

Ellis made no comment to Miles, only to John Davey off to the right.

"John, you loaded? Can I go?"

Davey was sighting forward.

"Yes. There is one, but he's reloading. Go now."

Davey fired and there came a scream from further on in the woods. Ellis ran forward, leaving Miles to reload and bring his rifle up to cover.

"John! I'm loaded. Go on."

Davey ran forward, just as Ellis, just ahead, fired at a Voltiguer, newly appeared. The man fell, wounded, and he was in Miles' path as he ran up, but Miles was in no mood for mercy. As he ran past, he swung his rifle butt viciously into the side of the man's head.

"That's for what we seen, on the way to yer, followin' you bastards all the way up! Evil toad shite!"

A trumpet sounded, the call unrecognized by any on the Allied side, and many blue uniforms rose up and began to retire, but always with good discipline and following their drill to hold back their pursuers. The French were falling back and, to hurry this on, Picton had sent his Grenadiers forward to reinforce his Lights. Carr could see the trees thinning and growing expanses of grey March sky and the ground was now sloping away from him, plainly they were now over the ridge. He looked to either side to see his men advancing carefully, but steadily. The sounds of combat were dying away, but nothing was coming from the direction of the 4th Division who should be in the centre. Soon Carr's men would be in open fields and he did not want the advance to be continued as a straggling mass. He shouted to each man either side, one of whom was Ellis, never far away.

"Two lines, advance on."

The lines were formed and Carr led his men forward, to hear someone running up behind. He turned and found Carravoy hurrying forward to catch up with him. The Captain Lord of the Grenadiers could never bring himself to use 'Sir' when addressing Carr, but Carr found little motive within himself to enforce such military etiquette.

"Where are we now?"

"That's Redhina, Charles. And it looks to be full of French, all trying to get over that bridge. They've given up the fight!"

He looked again.

"Get yours together in a firing line to follow me in support. I'll take the Lights on quickly."

He looked at Carravoy to see a blank look, but no objection.

"See you at the bridge!"

He took a deep breath and ran forward, waving his sabre.

"One Oh Five! With me!"

The whole line joined his rapid advance, which was wholly unopposed, until they came to the river. There they took fire from French sharpshooters attempting to cover their retreat across the bridge, this narrow structure now being badly jammed with fleeing French soldiers. Drake was one of the first into the houses near the bridge and he quickly decided that the French upon it were too an easy target for Baker rifles and what was needed was to suppress the fire of the Tirailleurs beyond the river, this designed to ease the passage of their comrades over the river. He shouted to any 105th he could see. These, with their more accurate weapon, were the men for the task and Saunders was easily spotted.

"Saunders! Leave the bridge. Take those the far side of the river, keep their heads down, pass it on."

Saunders saluted in acknowledgment, but many had revenge on their minds and instead found cover to then pour fire into the mass struggling on the bridge. Many French fell, both dead and wounded to be trampled underfoot on the narrow stonework. The Light Division came up on the downstream side to add to what was becoming a massacre, but the final French crossed, many by crawling over the bridge beneath the protecting parapet. At this point, Campbell arrived to order cease fire, but for much of Picton's Division, the affair was ending in frustration, this being very obvious in front of O'Hare, stood on the bank of the river upstream from the village.

"This'll not serve, men. Come out."

He looked up from the sight of his men struggling to wade over the river, the Soure, to then see crowds of French fleeing up the road out of the town and over the hills either side, then Picton arrived. The men were in the water obeying his orders to find a ford that would enable him to cut off the French. O'Hare saluted.

"We've tried here, Sir, but it's too deep and fierce."

Picton reined in his horse so fiercely that his ears almost touched Picton's uniform. He looked at O'Hare, then at the men struggling to help each other out of the water, with a look that could almost be taken to mean that he blamed them for the task being impossible, against the depth and current of the Spring nourished Soure. He finally managed to speak.

"Get yours down to the bridge. We'll soon be crossing."

O'Hare called to his men to 'form fours' and when they came to the bridge, they found men of the 4th Division clearing it of the last French dead and wounded. They also found Lacey with some other 105th

Companies, all equally wet from their fruitless efforts at fording the river, but all was not yet finished. Picton himself, now in slightly better mood, came up to issue further orders.

"The Light Division are going over first, then us. Mackinnon's first, then we all move right again. His Lordship's afraid of the French forming on the other side and wants them pushed off and further."

Lacey, O'Hare and Carr gathered their Companies and formed on the road to be the first over the river of Mackinnon's Brigade, followed by the 88th and the 74th. This meant passing across the front of the 88th and 74th, both waiting at the side of the road to follow on. Insults were exchanged between the Irish and the 105th. From the 88th mostly of the nature of, "Well, have you got yourselves a little bit damp, now, boys? Sure now, 'tis no good thing to go too near the water if you can't trust your feet to stop you falling in!", to which came the reply, "We didn't see too many of you bogmen at the bridge. Got your dim-witted selves lost in the woods?" Cold and sullen looks were exchanged, but luckily the 74th were between the two as the Brigade column marched through the tangled hamlet of Redhina. Once through, the seven columns of the 3rd Division took themselves over to the right, again led by Picton, him forever peering forward through his telescope or questioning his Aides for what they could see. He received one reply amongst many that proved useful.

"There, Sir, there, by that windmill, but they're pulling back. They can see that we'll be around their flank again."

Picton followed the direction of the outstretched arm and then found the windmill, in time to see the final ranks of the French columns disappearing over the back of a low ridge. He snapped his instrument shut, again in foul mood. He turned to Colville, his other Brigadier, him sat his horse beside Mackinnon.

"He'll not want me any further forward. Best to hold here."

He again studied the empty landscape before them and then turned again to his nearest Brigadier.

"Colville. Go tell his Lordship that I'm holding here and spending the night. Observing the French!"

Colville grinned and rode off. Soon all Picton's men were seeking the meagre shelter of walls and hedges, but the woods nearby provided ample firewood and parties ran back to the Soure to gather water to prepare food, mindful to take from upstream, for downstream below the bridge was a French charnel-house. No-one felt the need to enter the water and bring them to the land for proper burial.

The first Jed Deakin knew of the arrival of the new day was when he was being shaken awake, but not too roughly. He pulled his blanket back from over his head to see his 'stepson' Patrick Mulcahy, peering anxiously down at him.

"Uncle Jed. We've all got to form up, on the road, ready to march off. Soon!"

"Sir! I'm not your Uncle Jed, not no more. You're an Ensign, meanin' you'm an Officer and I'm just a Sergeant. You calls me Sergeant, I calls you Sir."

Deakin sat up, checking the state of the stubble on his jaw, then he took a deep, weary breath.

"Are those your orders, Sir? To rouse the Company?"

"Yes."

"Very good, Sir."

Deakin rose, quickly rolled his blanket and strapped it to the top of his pack. He took a quick swallow of water, picked up the Regimental Colour, secure in its leather case and then began touring the Company, nudging with his boot those who were not already awake. The dawn light was just strong enough to see other Companies of their own Regiment, along with those of the 88th and 74th gathering on the road. It was still dark when Picton led them forward and Carr and Drake marched side by side at the rear of the 105th column. Drake took a swallow from his water bottle and spoke as he replaced the cork.

"Glad he's not pulled us out, to scout up front. Who is up there?"

Carr delayed his answer until he had swallowed a biscuit.

"Our 60th and the Cacadores."

"Good. What've you heard?"

"Massena's left Ney at Condeixa, next town up. It's Ney we're against, we've learnt that from prisoners. So, expect more action on the flank. Wellington wants to keep pushing Johnny Eastwards, to keep him out of Coimbra, just to the North. The word is, that if we get them quickly out of Condeixa, up ahead, then the job's done and they'll have to cross the border into Spain."

Drake found his own biscuit.

"So, more right flanking."

However, as the light grew, so did the signs that the French army was falling apart. Almost by the minute they found themselves stepping over discarded equipment of all types, but worse was the growing frequency of French dead, horribly mutilated when their wounds had caused them to fall so far behind their columns that the Portuguese peasants could descend on them with impunity. After four hours hurrying along the road, all in the 3rd Division were grateful when Picton allowed an early midday meal, but immediately after eating, he took them off the road, to begin to climb a mountain path which took them off to the right of their previous direction. Drake had predicted correctly, but his self-satisfaction soon evaporated when he saw Lieutenant Simon Ameshurst running back down their column, evidently with a message.

"Sir, Captain Drake. The General wants you out in front as a skirmish screen."

Drake nodded and turned to Ellis.

"Double forward!"

Within minutes the 105th Light Company were up with the 60th Rifles, who were leading the way. Once with them, Miles sidled up to a Rifles Private.

"What you got?"

There was no need for explanation.

"Some brandy. That's it. These Frenchers is in a poor way and the peasants strips 'em of anything of use, before we can get near."

"How you off for baccy?"

"Bit short! You got?"

Miles nodded.

"Some. How's a tip into my canteen for a handful sound?"

"'Bout right!"

The exchange was completed and the Rifleman moved off, for Miles to take a swallow of brandy and water, 'half and half'.

Another Rifleman had noticed him.

"How come you've got a Baker."

Miles gave him a malevolent look.

"You complainin'? They'n just as handy with us, as they is with you!"

Miles was staring forward.

"'Sides, take a look. Seems a few of them tassel-swinging bastards is up ahead."

The Rifleman took a glance for himself, saw what Miles had seen and checked the priming of his own rifle. They advanced up, but the Voltiguers disappeared, allowing the 3rd Division to march further on across their mountain, through the thinning smoke blowing across them from Condeixa, now abandoned by the French and thoroughly on fire. Once past the burning town, the 3rd Division came off the mountain and regained the road. Carr was now at the front of the 105th column and as weary as anyone after their tiring flanking march over the mountain which had forced the French into further retreat. He was almost closing his eyes as he marched when he heard the jingling of harness coming up on his left. He looked up to see the command party of the 16th Light Dragoons, which included Tavender, who did not lose the opportunity to continue the subject of Willoughby Carr as he passed by.

"Had a chat with your brother, the other night, Major. Got a bit of family history!"

Carr was puzzled and so he could think up no reply and Tavender was soon gone. Carr watched the Squadrons trot past but saw nothing of his brother and so he returned to somnambulant marching as the daylight faded. Had he known the truth he would have immediately brought himself wide awake. His brother was far ahead of the whole army, progressing along the road, with orders to make contact. What would have re-assured Carr was who he was with, the veteran Sergeant Baxter, who was not in the slightest bit impressed with the order from his Squadron Captain Lionel Vigurs to young Carr to scout forward with his C Troop to 'make contact'. These two words could mean anything up to a full scale 'stirrup to stirrup', their vagueness concerned him greatly and so he was imparting good advice to his Cornet Officer, who seemed altogether too eager to follow his orders to the letter.

"Best ease up, now Sir, what with the light fading and who knows what's just ahead. When we sees lights up ahead, that'll mean Frog campfires and there'll a cavalry screen out 'tween us and those. These is veterans and they knows how to go about their business."

Cornet Carr looked quizzically at his very experienced Sergeant, but Baxter had more to say.

"If they've stopped and made camp, that's all our Officers wants to know, nor needs to know. No sense in us blunderin' into some French patrol and gettin' captured or wiped out. Then no-one will get back to say what needs to be said!"

22

Carr absorbed the good sense of his Sergeant and slowed his horse to a careful walk. Then came another worry as the darkness closed in and the road was almost indistinguishable from the churned-up fields to the side.

"We could lose our way Sergeant!"

"We could, so when you're not sure, Sir, 'tis best to stop. There's no point in makin' a report when you've small idea about where you're making it for."

"Yes, Sergeant. There's truth in that."

Some minutes passed as they walked on, then Cornet Carr spoke.

"Are those lights, Sergeant?"

Baxter rose in his stirrups.

"I'd say a village, Sir, with a few of them in there holding it, that's the group of fires low down. The main army is them higher up, probably back on some ridge. That's them, Sir, so job's done."

"So we ride back?"

"I'd advise not, Sir. Let them come up. There's been many a good man shot when he's come ridin' out of the dark and met some nervy pickets. There'll be an Officer on his way up to us. That's the drill."

Carr absorbed the truth of that also and Baxter had a better solution.

"I'll ride back a small way with a couple of lads and get a fire going, such as'll light things up. They'll see us then, whilst you holds here, Sir. Observing the enemy. As an Officer, that's your job. Sir."

"Very good, Sergeant. Sound idea."

oOo

A meagre breakfast was barely over, when Major Carr approached his immediate superior.

"Sounds as though things are getting a mite hot over there, Sir."

Carr was looking in the same direction as Lacey and O'Hare and neither spoke to disagree. Through the poor dawn light, the sounds of a fierce combat were coming to them on their left, from about half a mile away, whilst they again made what was now their standard flanking march to the right of where the French were believed to be, another small village. The sounds were mostly continuous cannon-fire, pushing the sound of musketry into the background, the huge horizontal blasts of cannon smoke coming off the ridge behind the buildings.

"Do we know who's in there, Sir, for our side, that is."

Lacey turned towards him.

"According to Mackinnon, Erskine's taken the Light Division straight at this place, Casal Novo, despite the fog earlier. The Johnnies will clear out as soon as they see us, marching past to get in their rear. Be certain that he can see us from where he is, back up on that ridge."

This bland statement had a very different meaning for the members of the 105th Light Company, up ahead alongside the Rifles, with the Cacadores on their left and closer to the village. Relations with these elite soldiers had become very respectful and convivial over the past days, the Rifles recognising veteran and capable soldiers the equal of themselves. However, at that moment it became clear that each was going to need all the skills they possessed. French Light troops were pouring out from behind Casal Novo, with a whole French Regiment forming up in line behind them. The Rifles Senior Captain called Drake over.

"I can't see these advancing any further. They've come out to keep us back, whilst the rest make good their retreat out of that place. It sounds as if there's a fair old set-to happening in there."

Drake studied the French line behind their skirmishers.

"I daresay you're right, but it's still our job to keep those Voltiguers and whatever, away from our main column, coming up behind. It'll be a poor show if we let these get close enough to take pot-shots at Picton and whatnot. I'd say we keep edging forward and push those fellows back onto their line, but stay out of range of a full volley. Perhaps by that time, Ney'll feel threatened enough by us coming around the corner and he'll withdraw anyway."

The Rifles Officer nodded.

"Agreed! Move on, nice and careful, with careful aimed shots."

"Agreed. Good luck!"

Drake ran over to his men, calling Maltby, Shakeshaft and Ellis to him as he pointed to the French skirmish line.

"Move forward onto those. Keep outside 100 yards, but inside 150. Use the advantage of the Baker,

23

aimed and careful."

When John Davey heard, he felt inside his pack for the leather patches and the small hammer. For aimed shots the ball needed to be wrapped in leather and the ball tapped down with a hammer hitting the ramrod. That done he advanced forward, judging the distance carefully to 120 yards. French musket shots hummed around, but inaccurate. Davey pulled Miles in front of him, then they both knelt and Davey took aim resting on Miles' shoulder. He had already picked out an Officer, waving his sword. He adjusted his sights, took careful aim and squeezed the trigger. The verdict on his effort came from Miles when the smoke had cleared

"You gott'n John. That's some silver buttons! Now 'tis my turn."

Davey lowered his rifle to see his previous target now a blue and white shape stretched on the turf. The positions were reversed and Miles brought down another leading soldier, probably a Sergeant. This was happening all along the French line as the British and Portuguese held their distance, quickly downing any Frenchman who came too close. However, by now the column of the 3rd Division was coming up behind, its arrival heralded by Picton himself, coming first to Drake and plainly none too impressed with what he could see.

"What are you about, Captain? Why are you not up into their faces?"

Drake turned and saluted.

"We thought it sensible just to keep their skirmishers back, Sir, but not get within range of those Battalions behind."

The distance between Picton's jaw and his eyebrows lessened considerably as his face screwed up in anger.

"They'll not give you a volley whilst their Lights are out across their front! Get up to them I say."

Drake saluted and obeyed the order, leading his men forward and shortening the range. He looked behind to see the newly arrived 3rd Division forming into line to advance, he was not fully reassured, but what did considerably ease his mind, was the sudden silence from the village and the French before him beginning to fall back. He quickened his pace, their role now being to harry the retreating French and so he urged his men on. Their rate of fire increased, no need for leather patches now.

That evening Carr slumped down with the three Officers of the Light Company, all with barely enough energy to eat, however, when Morrison did bring the pork stew, all found the energy to partake and all sat up. Drake looked at his Major, eating with his eyes closed.

"And how many times today were we required to march around Johnny's left-hand pocket and winkle him out of yet another ridge or cluster of hovels?"

Carr opened one eye.

"Three! We've gained 14 miles and lost a dozen men, four severely wounded. Two killed."

Shakeshaft dropped his stew bowl onto the ground and lay back, head on his rolled-up blanket, before reaching out to his pack, fishing out a pencil and a small book, sitting back up again and beginning to write. All had noticed, but Drake was the most curious.

"What's that, Richard? Some kind of journal? Thought you were the sketcher amongst us."

Shakeshaft continued writing.

"Yes, but this also. I may have it published when all this is done."

"And what will you call it?"

"I was thinking 'Memoirs of an Infantry Officer'. I think that conveys the subject."

"Could you not think of something rather more specific? Or even just add on 'in the Peninsula', sort of thing."

Shakeshaft's intent scribbling continued."

"You may be right."

Then he looked at Carr.

"Where did we start this morning, Sir?"

"Casal Novo."

"And where are we now, please?"

"Miranda de Corvo is about two miles ahead. Tomorrow we push up to it. For us, same as usual, I would expect. Flanking out on the right."

Carr dropped his own bowl and lay back himself, drawing over his blanket. Morrison then came forward to collect the empties.

Drake was now busy writing himself, adding a few lines to his continuous letter. When he spoke, his voice was full of irony.

"Why, thank you Major. That makes everything absolutely clear. For a change!"

However, Carr did not hear, him now being sound asleep.

The following morning found Drake stood before his paraded Company, with Maltby, Shakeshaft and Ellis close by. It was Ellis who most wanted the key question answered

"What's the job, Sir?"

Drake pointed with his sword.

"Push through those woods alongside every Light Company Picton's got. So, pass the word, nothing rushed. I want a steady advance, follow the drill of threes."

Ellis hurried away and began bellowing orders. Then the three Officers led their men forward, all immediately spreading out into skirmish order of files of three, with their fellow Light Companies of the 3rd Division deployed far out on either side. They approached the wood and at 100 yards came under fire. Drake was not prepared to casually walk up to the wood as an easy target and so he raised his sword.

"Double!"

All his men broke into a run, as did all the Light Companies either side. The French firing ceased before they came to the trees and they entered into what was a well-spaced wood, clearly well maintained. Drake shouted in both directions.

"Advance by drill!"

The trio of Davey, Pike and Miles found themselves advancing with Ellis nearby, him and Davey often in conversation.

"Take it slow, John. These'll be falling back, even if we downs many or even if we don't."

Pike was in the lead and staring intently ahead. He was the first to see a significant collection of blue uniforms. He turned back to Ellis.

"Line up ahead, Sarn't."

Ellis nodded.

"Right. Up to 120 yards. They won't stand long."

His men opened fire for some minutes, then Ellis watched as his words came true. Outflanked from elsewhere in the wood, the French skirmishers fell back. Thus, it continued through the morning to the afternoon when the trees gave way to fields containing dangerous walled enclosures, each of which could act as a small fortress, perfect for skirmishing troops conducting a retreat. The potential for heavy casualties was clear. Ellis hurried to Drake, the men now halted within the trees for cover.

"Sir. What are you orders?"

Drake did not like what he could see amongst the open fields, all the stone pounds built to serve as enclosures for securing animals at nighttime.

"Find the Lieutenants."

Ellis hurried away and soon brought back Maltby, then Shakeshaft arrived.

"Advance by Sections in open order. Twenty yards at a time. Then kneel to give covering fire, whilst the other advances."

Shakeshaft studied the nearest.

"Are any French in there?"

Drake rose up.

"We'll soon find out! Stuart, yours from here, Richard off to the right. Sergeant, go with Lieutenant Maltby, I'll remain here with you, Stuart, and we'll start."

Whilst they were speaking the whole Company had remained within the trees, Saunders was standing with Byford and both could see the danger that lay before them.

"That is not good, Byfe!"

Before Byford could reply, Maltby arrived and the orders came soon after. Maltby checked his pistol.

"Forward. Out! Come on!"

They ran forward as Shakeshaft's men open fire on the enclosure from the trees. Some French heads appeared and set up a stuttering reply. Drake heard a man grunt as he was hit, but Maltby's Company made their twenty yards, then knelt and opened fire. Shakeshaft then took his cue.

"Out! Come on!"

He led them forward, sword aloft. Twenty yards on past Maltby's men, the sword was lowered to indicate their line.

"Kneel and open fire."

All was repeated twice more, leaving five red-coated shapes lying on the turf, one very still. Then Maltby's First Section was over the opposing wall, with many French skirmishers, both Tirailleurs and Voltiguers, vaulting out over the back wall. Needing no orders his men ran to the back wall and those with loaded weapons opened fire to bring down several. Drake saw Shakeshaft's men running up.

"Straight on! Don't let them get into another."

Drake now turned his attention to these fleeing Frenchmen running to the next enclosure, then a look right showed that the 88th had taken a farmhouse, whilst the Rifles and the Cacadores were disputing possession of a wall to the left. He looked again to the next stone enclosure and his mouth fell open in astonishment. Several of the fleeing skirmishers were attempting to climb the wall of the next enclosure but they were being prevented by occupants already in there. A Tirailleur Officer was screaming at those inside, but the reply was several muskets being pointed in his direction. The Officer and his men had no choice but to run on to the next enclosure. Drake vaulted the wall.

"Come on!"

All ran forward, but there was no opposing fire. They reached the wall to be astonished. Under the stonework, sheltering, were about 25 Line Infantry, all with shakoes bearing the number 27. On seeing the British faces appearing, all cast down their muskets and sat sullenly against the wall. Saunders, one of the first over, picked up a musket and examined it.

"Sir. This is loaded and ready to fire."

Drake looked at one, who seemed to have some kind of rank.

"Ne vous se rendent?"

"Oui Monsieur. Nous rendons."

Now assured of their surrender, Drake looked around.

"Byford!"

"Sir."

"Ask them why their guns are loaded."

Byford looked at the man.

"Pourquoi vos fusils chargés?"

The soldier made a cutting motion across his throat.

"Les paysans vont nous tuer horriblement. Nous protéger nous-mêmes, jusqu'à ce que nous ne pouvons céder à vous."

Byford turned to Drake.

"He says that the peasants will kill them horribly and so they keep their weapons loaded until they can surrender to us."

Byford studied the soldiers.

"Seems they are wholly terrified of falling into the hands of the peasants. Sir. Surrendering to us makes them safe."

Drake now had two concerns; one, to continue the advance and two, what to do with the prisoners? He looked at Chosen Man Davey.

"Davey! You, Miles and Pike. Guard these until the Division comes up, but I do not think they will give you any trouble."

Davey came to the attention.

"Sir!"

Drake found Maltby and Shakeshaft.

"Right! Forward. Same drill as before."

Both Sections continued forward, leaving the three to study their prisoners. One looked at Miles.

"Vous avez de aliment, Monsieur?"

He pointed into his mouth, which was the worst thing he could have done. Miles was onto him in an instant, seizing his epaulette and punching his face.

"Food, you bastard? I know what you've been up to today and what wickedness did you get up to on your way here? We seen plenty of it. Just what did you do? Eh?"

By now John Davey had a hand on Miles' shoulder.

"Enough Tom! Leave him. There's no way to know. Stand away, 'til the Colonel gets here.

Meanwhile, help Joe stack their weapons."

Miles gave the man a final shake and let go of his tunic.

"I'd string you up, you murdering sack of shite!"

The remainder looked wholly cowed by Miles performance and few met his malignant eyes as he helped gather their weapons. That evening, with the French so near at Miranda de Corvo, double pickets were set, one pair again being Saunders and Byford and, with full night, Ellis found the pair staring intently ahead at a glow on the near horizon. Corporal Saunders was the first to speak.

"The Frogs are up to something in there, Sarn't, and them fires don't look like burning buildings, more like a lot of bonfires."

Ellis climbed a wall to obtain a better look for himself.

"Daresay you're right, but there's a hell of a hullabaloo comin' from just this side. Like a lot of animals upset over something. Something pretty dreadful."

Their first understanding of what had happened during the night in the village came in the early morning with the sight of Picton returning from reconnaissance with Campbell and Mackinnon, all escorted by Brigadier Slade and a Troop of his Heavy Dragoons. The group were heard first, more than seen, because a dense fog had arisen during the night, thickened by the smoke of the fires started by the French during the night and the village was now burning. All had faces as though each were soon to vomit. Picton turned to Slade.

"Get your Farriers up here. Arentschildt's too."

Then to Mackinnon.

"Stand yours down."

Mackinnon rode over to where his Colonels Lacey, Wallace and Dewey were gathered.

"Johnny's took off, he must have made a night march. There are fires everywhere and the town's burning from end to end. That must've been the last thing they did as they quit the place."

He drew a deep breath.

"But prepare yourselves, when we do go in. There's something dreadful along there, you can hear it."

It was well into the morning when the fog lifted and Mackinnon gave his orders to form up and march. The bellowing that had gained the attention of the picket had not diminished and grew louder as the 105th followed the 74th and the 88th on towards Miranda de Corva. They were not so long on the road before they saw the first signs of what had so nauseated Picton and his party. Either side of the road was a sprawling, heaving, mass of horses, mules and donkeys, all struggling to rise from the blood-soaked earth, but all failing because they had all been hamstrung by the French before they began their night march. Carr turned to O'Hare with whom he was marching, both aghast at what they were seeing and hearing.

"There must be 400 here!"

O'Hare shook his head.

"More like five! And look ahead, there's your answer for why. He's no need for these, he's burnt all his transport, destroyed everything that would slow his march and left nothing for us."

O'Hare was pointing to the smoldering remains of the fires, all with enough unburnt timber to tell the story that the fuel for the fires had been wagons, carriages and artillery limbers. Destroying these had rendered the draught animals redundant. Carr now had his own opinion.

"But this is just shocking cruelty. For the Love of God, he could just as easily have shot them!"

"He could've, but anything to slow us up."

The Light Company were now at the centre of the hideous sight on either side. None spoke, until Nat Solomon.

"My Grandfather was a Jewish butcher. Meat had to be slaughtered the right way to make it Kosher. He just cut their throats and they were gone in seconds. That was that! But this, this is beyond all ....!"

His words tailed off as the cavalry Farriers began to arrive and mercifully to begin to dispatch the kicking, struggling animals. All turned away to study the pack of the man in front, spirits thoroughly lowered by what they had just witnessed. The final words were spoken by Tom Miles.

"Issue of horsemeat tonight, then!"

From all directions came two words.

"Shut up!"

Once into the town the heat was oppressive and came at them from all sides, many unbuckling their blankets and draping them over their heads to protect their faces from the glowing embers and still burning fires. Emerging on the far side was a blessed relief, but there was no relief from Picton, who rode back and forth up and down his column, ordering his Officers to urge the men on. Relief came with the Midday meal and Jed Deakin sat around their fire with Toby Halfway and Harry Bennet, waiting for the water to boil for their tea, to help wash down the biscuit and dried beef. Bennet was feeding the fire.

"You ever seen the likes of what we seen on this campaign, Jed?"

Deakin shook his head.

"Not on what they calls the continent. I've chased natives around in India, and saw bad stuff there. But these is French and same religion as us and whatnot. And on just the other side of the Channel!"

There was no reply and all studied the steaming water, hoping to bring it quicker to the boil, but their studying was interrupted by one of Picton's Aides, galloping along the column.

"Form up in fifteen minutes!"

The three looked at each other, then at the half-heated water. Deakin looked at Halfway.

"Best chuck in the leaves now, Tobe, or there won't be no tea at all."

There was no time for the tea to brew nor did it, the tepid water not hot enough, so the three sat there drinking weak tea and chewing their food, all done at the best possible speed. Captain Heaviside arrived, chewing dried meat himself. There was some tea left and Deakin produced a spare mug.

"Last of the tea for you? Sir?"

Heaviside nodded his thanks and the tea was given.

"Midday break's a bit short, Sir."

Heaviside nodded again.

"Make the best use of the time, because the days are evil. Ephesians Five. Verse 16."

With that he swallowed the last of his tea and moved on, leaving the three to pack their camp. Very soon they were marching again with the same urgency, but the short March day was defeating them, which fact transferred itself even to Picton and the pace slowed. However, there was daylight remaining enough for all to see the next village, with a prominent ridge behind and Picton halted his men on the road. Mackinnon joined Lacey and O'Hare.

"Now we'll see some fireworks. The Light Division is up with us. Erskine's got them and wants to consult with Picton. What to do now? For sure, there's no love lost between those two!"

He looked in both directions.

"Seems like we're the audience!"

Coming from behind was Erskine under whose command they had served in Torres Vedras, but his face showed nothing like the cheeriness that they remembered of him. A similar mood was coming the other way, Picton, in the lead of a few Staff. Erskine halted first and nodded a curt greeting.

"Picton."

"Erskine."

"What do you know?"

Picton sat up in his saddle.

"His main strength's up on that ridge. With a good glass you can see them. He's also got some this side of the next river, with a rearguard holding the bridge, both left and right of the village."

Erskine nodded.

"What do you think? Do we give it a try?"

Picton's face darkened, him now thinking that Erskine was transferring the decision to him, one that was finely balanced.

"What do you think?"

Erskine sat back in his saddle.

"Take positions for camp, and wait. Wellington's not far behind."

Picton nodded. Whatever his feelings for Erskine, that made sense.

"Very good. I'll move right, as usual, if you'll go up on our left to face what he's left behind."

Erskine nodded and wheeled his horse. Picton looked down at Mackinnon.

"You heard, Mackinnon. Take yours over rightwards. I'll tell Colville what to do with his bastards!"

Orders rang out along Mackinnon's Brigade and the 105th followed the 74th and 88th off the road and onto the fields, but Mackinnon was worried.

"Carr! Get a horse and find the Johnnies. I don't want to go blundering into a whole French Division."

He turned to one of his Aides, mounted behind him.

"Phillips. Give him yours."

Carr re-occupied the saddle vacated by Captain Phillips and cantered over the open fields, angling away from the road, but he soon slowed to a walk. He pulled his telescope from his pocket and focused it on what had aroused his suspicions. The course of the river he took to be a line of trees, but before that he could see at least six blue uniformed Battalions in position, but not formed for combat. Before them, were several pickets strolling up and down. Carr snapped the glass shut and spoke aloud to himself.

"I don't think he knows we're here! He's set up for the night."

He turned his horse to see his own red lines just over half a mile back and he cantered back in their direction. He had not far to go when he saw an unmistakable party cantering down the line he was heading for, with the immediately distinguishing cocked hat worn 'fore and aft' in the lead. This notable personage noticed the lone rider that was Carr and halted his party as Carr drew up and was recognized.

"Ah, Carr. What do you know?"

Carr pointed back towards the river.

"He's back there, my Lord. Six Battalions this side of the river. In camp, my Lord. I don't think he knows we're here. At least those this side of the river."

At this point Picton arrived with Mackinnon and Colville, precisely when Wellington would have wished.

"Picton! Get your men up and drive at them. They're this side of the river. We can do them some damage. There's enough daylight left. I'll tell Erskine the same."

Without waiting for any reply, Wellington wheeled his horse and rode off to find Erskine. Picton looked at his two Brigade Commanders and wasted no time.

"Mackinnon. Yours first. Colville in reserve."

Mackinnon mounted his horse and rode to each of his Colonels. The 105th were the final Battalion he came to, on his right, having been forced to march further away from the road to find unoccupied camp ground.

"Advance as ye are Lacey, on the right. The 88th are centre, the 74th the left."

Within minutes Colour Sergeant Deakin was suffering an even quicker disturbance of his tea making as Ensign Mulcahy came running up.

"Uncle Jed! They're calling for The Colours."

Deakin sighed, but there was no time for the correction of titles. Both he and Bennet picked up their precious charges, still in their cases and ran to their positions in the centre of the 105th line. Captain Heaviside was stood before his Company, with Lacey and O'Hare out before him. 300 yards beyond all, were all the Light Troops of Mackinnon's Brigade, supported by Picton's Rifles and his Cacadores. The advance had already begun, but Lacey turned to his line, with something to say, that matched the feelings of all under his command.

"Men! We're up with them at last. We've seen what these Devils are capable of over the past days and now, finally, we can get right into their faces. I say we pay them out for what we've seen them do!"

The response was shouts of agreement and muskets being brandished in the air. The need for revenge was undiminished, ever since the convent at Porto de Mos, now over a week ago. Heaviside turned to his own Company and raised his own sword.

"He does not bear the sword in vain. For he is the servant of God, an avenger who carries out God's wrath on the wrongdoer. Romans 13. Verse 4."

He looked at his Colour Party.

"Uncase!".

Both Colour Sergeants pulled off the long leather cases and the two huge Battalion Colours fell free as both Ensigns set their shaft in their holster and, with that, Lacey led his men forward. Before them, Drake was advancing forward with Richard Shakeshaft, his Section out in skirmishing order. Drake called to Ellis.

"Fire when you see a target. Pass it on."

Shakeshaft was worried.

"Shouldn't we warn their pickets, Sir? Before we make an attack. We usually do, seems only fair."

Drake's mood reflected that of his men.

"Not this time."

The first to fire was John Davey, kneeling to fire at maximum range with his rifle carefully loaded. His target twisted and fell. Other good shots did the same and then Drake raised his sword.

"Double!"

His men ran forward to close the range and all began to bring down the French sentries, but these soon ran back into their camp where the French were rousing themselves at the sound of gunfire. Drake ran forward another 30 yards and raised his sword.

"Firing line!"

His men, still in open order, began to send aimed shots into the forming French ranks, but soon these French veterans had their own line in place and began to return fire. However, Drake was keeping one eye on what was coming up behind and he saw his own Battalion, merely 50 yards behind. Once more he held his sword aloft.

"Re-form!"

This was the signal for his Company to split, each Section in opposite directions. His men turned and formed on the ends of the 105th line that was moving inexorably forward. Captain Lord Carravoy, out before his men, with D'Villiers and Ameshurst either side, stared intently at what was happening 100 yards in front of him. The French had quickly responded and were forming their three-deep line on a three Battalion front, with another three-deep line held in reserve, this second line also of three Battalions. His stomach turned over, he concluded that this would be nothing other than a bad firefight. He looked at D'Villiers, whose face seemed to reflect his own feelings, then at Ameshurst, whose face, in contrast, was set as grimly as those of his men.

Lacey kept up the pace forward, he wanted to hit the French before they were set. He could still see many running to their positions and the French line was far from steady. He judged when his line had advanced to well under 100 yards and he raised his sword. His line came quickly to a halt.

"Volley by ranks!"

His men brought their muskets to the vertical 'make ready'.

"Lock on!"

The second rank moved slightly to their right to see between the heads of the first.

"Present!"

All muskets came to the horizontal.

"Fire!"

Then came the appalling crash, but only from the first rank, close on 250 muskets. Within the 105th those in the second rank knew to count to three, 'to give the first hit time to fall over and get out of the way'. The three seconds seemed like an eternity, but then it came, the same appalling crash. Lacey raised his sword.

"Advance 20!"

All came forward 20 paces. Lacey knew that the shock of seeing a solid line emerging from the smoke to close the range further was almost the equal of receiving a full volley. His front rank were already reloaded, they had been trained to load whilst advancing.

"Make ready!"

All muskets in the front rank came to the vertical.

"Fire!"

The same crash and then came that of the second rank, ragged, but all eventually fired. Lacey raised his sword again.

"Advance 20!"

Again, his men came forward to repeat their volleys at a range now less than 50 yards. Stood beside The Colours, Jed Deakin and Toby Halfway went through the motions of loading without thinking, their jaws grimly locked closed, except to bite open a cartridge. Deakin especially carried in his mind the image of the garroted baby he had found at Porto de Mos and every shot into the stumbling blue ranks before him, was aimed with hatred.

Still stood before his men, Lacey considered a bayonet charge, the French were much in disarray, but he soon rejected it. There was a fresh French Battalion behind this one and he remembered the debacle of Talavera. His volleys were pushing the French back and so he decided to continue in like manner and it was not long, after suffering the appalling punishment of the 105th's volleys, that the French did began to fall back. However, over on Lacey's left, the 88th Connaughts had charged and shattered both Battalions before them, sending both streaming to their own right to reach the bridge. The 88th at the river meant that the 105th's opponents were cut off from the bridge and panic soon set in with them, especially when some of the 88th, looking for more combat, began to attack their right-hand companies. The 105th continued to press forward, sending continuous volleys into the dissolving French ranks, until the French retreat became a rout, but Lacey kept his men together.

"Hold the line, boys! Hold the line. Press on, but keep together."

His men advanced still firing, to find the French disappearing into the river, which was shallow and wide in some places, deep and narrow in others. The advance at a slow walk of the 105th had caused them to be outdistanced by the running French and, therefore, when the 105th reached the river bank, most of the French were over, but the 105th firing continued at any that could be seen, now as fast as individual soldiers could reload. On the left of the 105th, where Maltby's Section had re-formed, the river was deep and there, many French were struggling almost shoulder deep and even drowning, but even in the growing gloom within the trees individuals could still be picked out. At the extreme end of the 105th line, the river became shallower and Corporal Saunders, between loading, was looking for the next target, when his gaze fixed on a man in elaborate uniform wading across with difficulty. Saunders dropped his rifle.

"Byfe. Tom. We'll have that one prisoner! That's their Colonel."

Saunders jumped in first and, with his considerable strength waded quickly through the water. Then he stopped, something brightly coloured was being carried downstream beneath the surface and it had bumped into his leg. He reached through the water, his fingers closing on a wooden shaft which he pulled up to find himself holding a French Eagle, with the soaked Standard beneath it, wrapped around the shaft. Byford stopped to examine the prize with Saunders, but Miles was intent on the Colonel, who, on seeing the precious Eagle of his Regiment in the hands of the enemy, was equally intent on the hopeless task of rescuing it back. He was met by a battle-maddened Miles, who crashed a left-hook into the man's face and then seized him to push him under the water and keep him there. The scene had not gone unnoticed by Drake, seeing the French Eagle first and then the struggling figure of a French high Officer being held under the water by Miles.

"Miles! Let him up."

Tom Miles decided that there was no reason why he should have heard and continued to hold the now almost limp figure under the water. Seeing no response, Drake drew his pistol and pointed it at Miles.

"Miles! Let that man up, or I will bloody well shoot you!"

That order Miles decided he had heard and he released the man, for him to float down-stream, seemingly lifeless. Byford was now holding the Eagle, but luckily for the French Colonel he floated past Saunders and the wrestler seized the prominent epaulettes and hauled him up out of the water and dragged him coughing to the bank, where Nat Solomon helped Saunders drag him further to safety. Meanwhile, Drake was still taking issue with Miles, him now stood dripping on the bank.

"Miles. I gave you an order."

Miles sprang to the attention. It could mean lashes on the triangle.

"Sorry Sir. Didn't hear you first time. Got a bit beside myself. Sir."

His face still dark with anger, Drake leaned forward towards Miles, their faces almost touching.

"Disobey another order from me, Miles, and you well know what comes next."

Miles had remained rigidly to attention.

"Sir!"

"Right Miles. Get your rifle and run and tell the Colonel what we've got over here!"

"Sir."

Miles ran towards The Colours where he most expected Lacey to be and he was correct. He came to a halt at the attention, rifle against his right boot.

"Sir. We've captured a French Officer, Sir, we believe him to be a Colonel, and got one of their French flags. The one with a bird on the top. Sir."

Lacey immediately looked at O'Hare, who was stood nearby.

"We must see!"

Both started forward, then Lacey remembered his Regiment and turned to shout at Carr, also by The Colours.

"Henry. March the men back, if Mackinnon's agrees, that is."

With that, they both ran across the front of their left wing to find Captain Drake pulling out the now unfurled Colour, both him and Maltby reading the central words, almost in unison, Drake's pronunciation being markedly superior.

"L'Empereur Napoleon. Au 69th Regiment D'Infantry de Ligne."

Saunders was kneeling beside his prisoner, feeding the Colonel some of his own brandy between taking a few pulls at the Frenchman's flask himself.

"There's some more words on the back, Sir."

The elaborate and heavy cloth was turned around for Drake alone to read.

"Ulm. Jena. Eylau. Friedland. Essling. Wagram."

Drake turned to Lacey.

"Those are French Battle Honours, Sir. This 69th must have been real veterans!"

For a full minute and more, the four of them studied the trophy, noticing the brass Eagle with the number 69 prominent on the base. It was something from another world, another culture, until Lacey remembered where he should be and that his Regiment was now marching back to its camping ground. All through their studying of the Standard, they had not noticed that combat was continuing downstream from them, at the bridge, but the sounds of infantry warfare had now been replaced with an artillery exchange. They marched back, Drake carrying the Eagle, Saunders the Colonel.

As soon as their campfires were burning nicely, night finally arrived, but their mealtime was then disturbed by a large explosion beyond the town. Drake, from looking in that direction, returned to his stew of horsemeat and beans.

"That's the bridge gone! Seems that Johnny managed to keep hold of it."

All nodded agreement, then Drake noticed Shakeshaft busy in his diary.

"Something special to write about this evening Richard. You'd agree?"

Shakeshaft looked up.

"Yes. A Colonel and a French Standard captured."

Drake's brows came together.

"Well perhaps not captured. More like rescued, the Colonel from the attentions of Miles and the Standard rescued from drifting down to the Bay of Biscay. All the same, both something of note."

Shakeshaft nodded, before adding the finishing touches. He looked around, hoping for an answer from anyone, but it was Carr who was the provider.

"And this town is called?"

"Foz de Arouce!"

"And the river?"

"Ceira."

"Thank you, Sir."

Carr raised a hand in acknowledgment.

In the mess-camps of Davey and Deakin, the topic of conversation was much more mercenary, Saunders looking at Deakin.

"Getting hold of something like that Eagle thing, well, that's got to be worth a few guineas in prize-money. Fair reward so to speak."

Deakin was already wrapped in his blankets, hoping that soon the Followers would catch up, if only so that he could enjoy much better cooking.

"Don't count on it, Zeke. I've heard of the like, but as soon as they're wavin' it around in their mess-halls and palaces, they soon forgets about the likes of you."

He turned over, before sleep claimed him.

"Still, you never knows. 'Tis not beyond experience, even though the thing found you, rather than the other way round."

oOo

The blown bridge meant that the advance was halted and few below the rank of Brigadier complained. The Followers did indeed arrive late the next day and Bridie Mulcahy had no sooner kissed her common-law husband in greeting, then she was off to find Ensign Mulcahy to check on his health and completeness. Satisfied that he was whole and hearty, she brought him back to their camp to make sure that he was well fed that evening. Despite his being an Officer, no-one felt inhibited, because it was too common a sight over the past years for him to be sat with them, especially when his Drummerboy friend, Henri Rasenne came and sat near him, and from kindness, Byford sat and talked to him in his native tongue. Henri was a captured French Drummerboy from the Battle of Corunna, but now amongst the Drummerboys of the 105th, however, retaining his French drum.

With the Followers came supplies and rations and Toby Halfway took it upon himself to give out the meat in the time honoured way, stood facing the barrel, with the representative of each mess stood behind him, unable to see what he had speared with his bayonet in the barrel now drained of salt water. He secured a piece.

"Who wants this?"

Nellie Nicholls spoke.

"I will. I'll take that."

The piece was given and greeted with delight. It was almost all lean, with little fat nor gristle.

"Sure now, that's a grand piece. 'Twill make good eating this night, will it not now, for sure?"

In triumph she bore it away, many other Followers looking on enviously. One was the wife of a new replacement in the Light Company, she being Betty Barker, wife of Neet Barker, both from London. Her brows came together on seeing the piece, but it had been arrived at fairly. The next came out of the barrel.

"Who wants this?"

She spoke up.

"I'll have that. Give it 'ere!"

The piece was dropped into her apron from the end of the bayonet and her face registered her full disapproval. It was mostly gristle and tubing, there was even some skin. Grumbling she walked off, thinking of whom to blame, but could think of no-one.

The following day at Noon, there was enough timber over the ruined bridge for cavalry to walk their mounts over and Captain Vigurs came to Cornet Willoughby Carr in the 16th's camp, half a mile back from the village.

"Get your Troop mounted. We're scouting forward."

Young Carr was grateful to see his Sergeant Baxter nearby, who had heard Vigurs' order and set all that was necessary, quickly into motion. This brought Carr's Troop first onto the road, his Regiment to follow the 1st Hussars of the King's German Legion through the village. Before moving off, Vigurs reined in his horse next to Carr's.

"Be vigilant! He's sending us forward and we're the first with the KGL. He has no idea what the French have done, whether they've gone or stayed."

They walked forward to soon dismount at the bridge, the wrecked stonework scorched from the recent explosion, now spanned with some timber, but too precarious to ride over and so they had to lead their mounts across the waters containing many dead from both sides. Once mounted, the KGL having crossed before them, set off North, whilst they took the road North-East, leaving the river Ceira behind. After barely a mile, Vigurs, riding beside Carr, felt justified to give a verdict.

"Looks like the KGL will soon be turning back!"

The justification was obvious, it was the 16th that were following the French. Their road was strewn with dead horses and mules, abandoned equipment, and the occasional group of French stragglers who threw down their muskets when the 16th approached, holding on to their weapons until the last moment in case peasants and even guerillas should come upon them before they could surrender and be safe. It was not long before Major Johnson cantered back and reined his horse next to Carr.

"Four men and you take the prisoners back. We'll not be long coming back ourselves, there's no sign of any serious Johnny, apart from the fact that he's marched this way. The Colonel thinks he must have made a night march, which would account for so many stragglers. When your prisoners are delivered, come back out."

Baxter had heard all.

"I'll choose you men, Sir."

He turned his horse and called out the names of the men he trusted most, the first a Corporal.

"Jim, Harry, Len, Perce. You're with Cornet Carr, escorting prisoners back. Keep them together, they'll want questioning."

The four wheeled out of the line and Carr followed them, back to a group of about 30 prisoners, all sat by the roadside in a state of utter dejection and exhaustion, their once proud French infantry uniforms filthy and torn on their emaciated bodies. Carr and his men were left alone as his Regiment moved on, so he rose in his saddle and shouted.

"Marche! Vite!"

There was little movement, two stood, one came to his knees. Corporal of Horse, Jim Makepeace, looked on.

"Perhaps if you promised them food, Sir."

Carr nodded.

"Aliments. Au village."

At that promise, all dragged themselves to their feet and began to shuffle back. The pace was dreadfully slow and soon Carr was daydreaming in his saddle, barely awake. He was in the lead, with his four men either side of the sorry column, when he was roused by a shout from behind.

"Cães assassinos! Cães assassinos!"

He turned, just in time to see a man crash the edge of a heavy spade into the skull of one his prisoners, before turning and making his escape into the trees. The column stopped and Trooper Len Spivey dismounted to examine the victim. Almost immediately he looked up to Carr.

"Dead, Sir."

Carr sighed with exasperation. He had been charged with getting all the prisoners back and he had failed. Corporal Jim Makepeace saw the look.

"Not your fault, Sir. There's nearly 30 of them and only four of us. These Frenchers is really hated and if some peasant is wound up enough, he'll get through. Just hurry 'em along, Sir. That's all we can do."

Carr nodded and rose up in his saddle.

"Marchez! Vite!"

After the frightening incident, the pace quickened and after a minute, Carr turned to the Trooper behind.

"Any idea what that peasant shouted?"

The Trooper was Corporal Makepeace, who had not a clue, but he shouted to the Trooper on the opposite side of the column.

"Percy. What he say?"

"Something akin to assassin dogs, Sir. Cães is Portuguese for dog."

Carr nodded and it was with great relief that he finally saw the roofs of Fos de Arouce. The village was fully occupied on their side of the river, not just by Allied soldiers, but also by Portuguese peasants who had come down from the hills where they had gone for safety. Many picked up stones and began to throw them at the prisoners and Carr feared again for the safety of his charges, but Officers amongst the Allied soldiers ordered their men to push the Portuguese back. Thus, all were able to cross over the now augmented bridge to the safety of the far bank. Once there, Carr handed his prisoners over to the Provost cavalry, who were there for just such a purpose.

Then events took a turn towards the more cheerful. Henry Carr had seen the return of some of the 16th and had taken himself to the bridge, hoping to gather some news of his brother, when he saw the person himself, sat his horse and now watching the French march away. Carr jogged over, a smile covering his face.

"Willoughby!"

Young Carr turned at the sound of his name spoken by his brother's voice, beamed himself and dismounted. Both hugged each other for a brief moment, before Elder Carr placed his hands on his brother's shoulders.

"Why, you're now the same size as me!"

He looked him up and down.

"Have you heard from home? Are they all well?"

Young Carr grinned.

"No, I have not heard, but they were all well when I left."

"And Mother?"

"She's well too. Beatrice has got married, but James isn't, although there are plenty of girls around on the scout with so many away in the army. We heard that you'd got married."

"Yes. I'm very lucky, but not so much with my Father-in-Law, who wishes me in the fires of Hell! But I'd love you to meet her, you, James and Beatrice. She's called Jane and she's living near a place called Taunton, in Somerset. But whom did Beatrice marry?"

Young Carr grinned again.

"The local Vicar."

Carr grinned back.

"So we've now Clergy in our family. Good to have God on your side."

Young Carr's face became serious.

34

"I'll write and tell them I've seen you. Perhaps even Father will have mellowed."

Carr let out a sharp breath.

"That I doubt. But you look after yourself. The Light Cavs are always involved somewhere."

Young Carr, nodded, embraced his brother once more and remounted. Seeing his four men drawn up in a line reminded him that he had been ordered to get back. Elder Carr now looked at the four and saw four stern and capable faces, then he saw Corporal Makepeace salute.

"We'll take care of him, Sir."

Carr was moved to hear the re-assuring words and he returned the salute perfectly, to then stand and watch the five ride away until they were out of sight.

As Spring was now marching on, each dawn was now less chilly but all still paraded in greatcoats preparatory to marching off. The dead had been buried, the bridge repaired, time to follow the French, with the Followers on the road, once beyond any danger from the retreating French. Picton's men crossed the Ceira first and kept up a good pace along the correct road as discovered by the 16th. The road was still covered in the now decomposing bodies of animals, but most of the French abandoned equipment had been gathered by the peasants for their own use. The only sign of live French were the larger and more frequent groups of French prisoners being marched back. Then it began to rain, harder, when Picton himself, wrapped in oilskin, directed them off the road to begin the climb of the ridge that separated the Ceira from the next river, that being the fierce Alva. Carr and Drake were marching side by side, hands in pockets, oilskins on the side of their shakoes totally folded down. As the path became arduous, Drake turned to Carr.

"As a Major, do you have any idea why we are doing this?"

"But a vague one! This river Alva is a considerable barrier and so one can only suppose that we are making a huge flank march to get around some impossible crossing point held by the French."

Drake's head sunk deeper into his collar.

"Hope it's worth it."

Two days later he was answering his own question at the village of Avo as he dried his breeches wet from the ford over the Alva before a decent bonfire made from French wagons, carts and tumbrils.

"We're pushing Johnny out of Portugal and barely needing to fire a shot. Do you think we'll catch him?"

Carr examined the damp in his own socks by pressing them to his cheek.

"Not a chance. Word is, so we're hearing from the cavalry, that he must be making forced marches, including at night, 20 miles a day, through this tangle of hills and valleys. We're taking hundreds of prisoners who have been left behind whilst out foraging. They come back to find their army gone."

At that point, O'Hare wandered up to warm his hands at the fire, immediately amused at the sight of Drake, in long-johns, holding out his breeches, still not dry. Drake was the first to notice him.

"Hello, Sir. We were just discussing the chances of catching the French."

O'Hare rubbed his hands together in the warmth.

"And your conclusion?"

"We won't!"

"That's where I'd put my money. They're falling apart and we're running out of rations, both for us and the mounts. Wellington's dropping off Divisions so that they can be fed when supplies finally come up. Three will be chosen to push on and keep him moving."

Drake now felt able to pull on his drier breeches.

"Well, it shouldn't be us! We've been in the vanguard since Santarem."

However, at that moment their fate had already been decided and it was being communicated to those involved, in the form of Picton talking to Mackinnon and Colville.

"It's us that he's pushing on with, us, the 6th Division and the Light. The Lights are moving out as we speak and they've been given the rations that's left. Barely enough for us three, never mind the six he's got up here. One thing, I've no mind that we do this with forced marches of our own. Johnny's way ahead, we've heard nothing that matters from our cavalry out there following them since crossing at Foz, but that's orders, so get your men ready."

An hour later the Third Division were parading on the main road. The one consolation was that they were marching on a good road and in weak sunshine. Miles looked at Saunders peering into his haversack.

"What've you got?"

Saunders moved the sack around, then held it horizontal, the better to see the contents.

"Biscuit. Peas. What looks like figs."

Miles' face became even grimmer.

"And we're the ones what's winning!"

The following days did nothing to improve Miles' mood, these being but a monotonous blur of marching along a road that never seemed to leave a valley of some kind, with French wreckage and dead animals before and French prisoners left behind. The one source of relief was watching the villagers returning to their homes and often baking bread for the passing soldiers, one occasion being at the village of Pinhancos. As they sat resting, trying not to think about their hunger, a girl emerged from a building with the word 'Padaria' above it and set a tray of bread on the wall outside. The group rushed over, whilst a man emerged with a flour stained apron and he began cutting the loaves into quarters, which he gave to the members of the queue that had formed. Once given his portion, Miles noticed the comeliness of the girl. He turned to Byford.

"Byfe! What's Portuguese for 'My name's Tom'?"

Davey immediately butted in.

"Never you mind what 'tis! And we gives some buttons to these. This must be about the last of their corn."

Davey looked at the girl.

"'Sides she wants bugger all to do with you. 'Tis Joe she has eyes for!"

The merest study of the girl told that Davey was right, she, now staring at Pike, who was stood beside Davey, but Miles' was not finished.

"You're wastin' your time there, girl. He's well-spoken for and a Father on top!"

Then came the bugle call to fall-in and within minutes the last of the houses of Pinhancos had passed by, to merge into a memory of so many more that had come and gone.

Four days after leaving Foz de Arouce, Mackinnon and his Colonels marched into Picton's billet. On his table was a plate with a few cubes of bread and some dried fish. Mackinnon spoke first.

"Sir. The lads cannae keep this up. There's been nae food tae speak of, not for three days now, we have tae tak' it slower."

Picton looked up, but said nothing and so Mackinnon continued.

"Sir, we cannae risk marauders leavin' the ranks tae go out looking for food, like before Coruna. The French are 20 miles ahead! More than a day's march. We'll only come up to him when he chooses to stop and then we'll have tae stop ourselves and wait for Wellesley and the rest tae come up."

Picton looked at his plate and then at his Colonels, his face somewhat sad, but definitely resigned. He trusted each implicitly and he knew that they would not be there without good reason. He nodded.

"Lads'll soon be dropping out. I know. March ten, then rest. At least then there'll be daylight left for them to go out shooting for rabbits and whatnot. But make it clear, any looting or stealing will mean the rope!"

The four waited for more, but none came and so they saluted and left. The next day the sun was well up before they took one step on the road and, come mid-afternoon, the Division halted and camped. The messes of Deakin and Davey went straight to a dying mule, which Nat Solomon immediately dispatched with his clasp knife. The meatier parts, even from a starving animal, were cut up and boiled. Local peasants arrived with some husks of corn and so that became their meal, which even Bridie Mulcahy and Nellie Nicholls could not make any more savoury. Picton toured his Division and decided to use another day for rest, on the pretext of obtaining food from whatever source. His men slept, it took their mind off their hunger. Others spent their time cutting up musket balls and then trying their luck with the local rabbit and bird population, and of these Davey, Pike and Miles were more fortunate than most which brought onto their heads the sincere blessings of their two Irish cooks.

oOo

It was a mood of deep contentment, both for his status and recent situation that buoyed the spirits of Lord Frederick Templemere, newly 'Introduced' to The Lord Chancellor, as he took his seat for the second time on the worn but thick red leather bench in the House of Lords. A most excellent lunch of roast quail and a bottle of good claret now sat easily in his stomach to the extent that he began to feel somewhat drowsy. The debate after his introduction had been concerned with conditions in Poor Houses, a topic that held no interest for Lord Fred at all and so on that occasion he had absented himself early, but today's session had a distinctly military flavour. He was brought back to full consciousness by one of his two companions, Lord Charles Hopgood, leaning across him and pointing out the entrance of the Lord Chancellor.

"That chap is the 'Top Dog' around here. The Lord Chancellor. Name escapes me for the moment, but we all have to defer to him."

From his other side, Lord Mahon interrupted.

"Lord Eldon"

"That's the chap!'

At that moment, Black Rod entered, progressed with measured tread to the Woolsack and then turned to face the entrance. His Rod of Office was allowed to slide down his hand to the floor at which point he spoke, his voice echoing in the now established silence.

"All stand."

All did and both Templemere, Hopgood and Mahon then observed the stately progress between the benches of a portly figure, topped by a heavy bell-bottom wig, that almost covered a full white lace collar. Both of these covered the upper portion of a black gown heavily embellished with dark gold stripes, which in turn then stretched down to cover the upper portion of yellow socks secure within bright black shoes with huge silver buckles. At Lord Eldon's entrance all fell silent, even more so when he stood before the Woolsack that was his traditional seat.

"My Lords, I call upon Lord Lyndhurst to begin this session to celebrate the most glorious achievements of our armed forces in Spain and Portugal. Lord Lyndhurst."

The named Lord stood and began the topic to which Frederick Templemere felt he had sufficient involvement, enough to justify giving up some of his precious leisure time.

"My Lords, I call upon all in this House to join me in celebrating the glorious victory of Barossa of 5th March this year, during which our General Graham, heavily outnumbered, defeated the forces of Marshal Victor and, what is more, captured the Eagle of a French Regiment. In addition, I call upon all here to also celebrate the success of our forces under General Lord Wellington, who are, as we speak forcing the French from the soil of our noble ally, the Kingdom of Portugal."

As the speech wore on, Templemere lost interest as the same words, in a different order, were repeated time and again. This continued until his other companion Lord Anthony Mahon, stood and received the nod from the Lord Speaker. Mahon turned to look at Templemere.

"My Lord Chancellor, we have amongst us, one, recently sworn in here, who was part of that very campaign we now speak of, that being to drive the French out of Portugal. A hero of our armed forces! May I point out Lord Frederick Templemere, of the 16th Light Dragoons, present at the glorious victories of Talavera and Busaco and taken prisoner during the retreat to Torres Vedras? He now sits here under a wholly honourable parole."

Caught up in the mood of overblown patriotism burning brightly from that most volatile of fuels, military success, many stood and began to applaud. After almost a minute of this, Hopgood nudged Templemere.

"Fred. You should stand and say something. Begin with My Lord Chancellor."

His meal now feeling distinctly uncomfortable, Templemere rose.

"Lord Chancellor."

He managed that and then to frantically search for words. In actuality he need not have worried, the pause added to the drama.

"What my good friend Lord Mahon has said is perfectly true, it was my great honour to serve as a Captain in the 16th Light Dragoons who are, continue I should say, as we sit here, to serve and give good service in our army in Spain and Portugal commanded by Lord Wellington. What we speak of today gives me great pleasure to hear, that we are defeating the forces of the hated tyrant Napoleon."

He paused for breath, during which came several cries of 'Hear, hear!'.

A start made, successfully it would appear, Templemere became emboldened and somewhat light headed.

"I say the French now know what it means to stand against us and I saw the result at Talavera and Busaco. We beat them even against the odds and, even when the odds are too great, we have in Wellington a General who can plan and outmaneuvered the best that Napoleon can send. I talk of the Lines of Torres Vedras from where we held off twice our number of French. I myself was captured during the fall back to those lines, but make no mistake, our men and my Regiment gave a very good account of ourselves and made them pay dearly for every yard. Now they are being pushed back and back themselves, over the border and back into Spain and so I say, we have every reason to celebrate these victories and confidently expect many more in the future."

The House erupted with applause as Templemere sat down and all from behind that could, reached forward a hand to clap onto his shoulders and those before turned in their seats to look back up at him whilst continuing to applaud. Templemere beamed all round and was still in rapture when the House rose and the three exited onto Parliament Square, Westminster Cathedral looming up before them. Lord Mahon turned towards the other two, but really addressed Templemere.

"I say, Fred, that was a jolly fine rant you gave there. It will be remembered, I can tell you. I think we should go somewhere and open a couple of bottles."

Templemere nodded, feeling thoroughly superior, in command and wishing to exercise it. However, he had other ideas, that being the delights of an exclusive bordello just over in Pimlico. This was infinitely superior to the idea of sharing a couple of glasses of highly suspect wine with these two. He had not forgotten how they had both abandoned him when he had been dismissed from Horse Guards Parade by the Prince of Wales himself, after a confrontation with the hated Henry Carr. There would be a reckoning one day, with this pair, and the Prince, if he could manage it.

"I think not! That's enough celebration for one day. I think I'll retire to my club. Be in touch."

With that he took himself across the Square to the cab rank and he placed his hand on the door handle of the first, but it immediately pulled away. More than a little annoyed, he waited for the next to pull up, which it did and Templemere shouted the destination and then he got in, to find himself confronted by another man joining him through the door on the far side. Templemere's annoyance increased.

"I'm afraid this cab is mine. You'll have to get out."

The man did the exact opposite and took a seat. That done he hammered his cane on the roof and the cab began to move, forcing Templemere to sit whilst his door slammed shut from the momentum. The stranger sat back and smiled calmly at Templemere, which he found to be both annoying and rather discomfiting. The stranger spoke first.

"My Lord Templemere. My name is Michael Granger. That is not my real name, but that does not matter."

Templemere's brows came together. He was both puzzled and intimidated.

"What do you want with me?"

His voice was very much less than steady. Gone were the confident tones of the House of Lords.

"Where are we going? I ordered Pimlico."

The man smiled confidently.

"Oh, just roundabout. When we have finished, this cab will take you wherever you wish to go. No charge!"

The confident smile remained as the man continued. Templemere noted that the man had the slightest accent, but from which region or even country he could not discern.

"But I must now explain my business with you."

He pulled a black satchel onto his lap, but did no more.

"The people that I represent are very grateful for the information that you supplied, in the days prior to them reaching the Lines of Torres Vedras."

The image surged into Templemere's mind, of him sat at a table with Marshals Massena, Ney and Reynier, on the far side and Templemere answering their questions in order to obtain a swift parole, but he did not like the notion of returning memories of Portugal. At this point, the man opened the satchel to withdraw a plain but very well made wooden box, about 15 inches by four and three deep. He placed it on the seat between them both and opened it to reveal a solid gold bar, totally plain, with no markings visible. This the man proved by tilting the box so that the bar fell out into his hand, which subsided with the weight. The man turned the bar to show all sides and then replaced it. Templemere's eyes were wide open, his mouth also. With the price of gold as it was in such uncertain times, he calculated that the bar must be worth something approaching £400! The man noted the astonishment on Templemere's face and continued.

"If you can help my Principals further, then you can expect more of these. Many more."

Templemere looked again at the bar, it now back in the box, then at the man.

"What help?"

The man took a deep breath.

"Wellington has divided his forces. He has a force in what we call the Southern corridor at Badajoz. He has another that has reached the Northern containing Cuidad Rodrigo. He will advance accompanying one or the other, but obviously not both. One force may even remain in place, whilst he advances with the other. My people need to know which he chooses and whichever it is, they needed to be certain that Wellington himself will direct the advance. They need to know which force Wellington will accompany. My people hope that you can help. The recompense for this information, well, I have already made clear the form it will take."

He paused, his eyes level and now malevolent as he looked at Templemere.

"Also, I'm sure that you would not wish it revealed just how helpful you were to Marshal Massena in order to obtain a swift parole. Just before he came up to The Lines, to make it clear."

Templemere's face darkened considerably, his mouth a stretched line of anger.

"How do you know of that conversation?"

Granger smirked a little.

"It is my role in such affairs as these, to know everything."

Having no effective answer, Templemere reverted to the original topic.

"Why do you want to know which 'corridor' as you put it?"

"That is not your affair and it is best that you do not know why. My suggestion to you is this. You now have influence in the House of Lords, a heroic veteran I have just heard you described as. Your Wellington is proving himself to be successful. You could suggest a mission to Wellington out there in Portugal to find out what further help he needs; what he needs to achieve his ambitions. All you need to do is to find out where the location needs to be, for this help that needs to be given. Given in the right place! My people think it safe to assume that where improvements will be made and resources made available, that is where Wellington will place himself."

"What kind of improvements?"

"Anything of use! Improve a quayside, improve a road, build a bridge. Anything!"

He smiled.

"And this is but a small thing, yes? Anyone dressed as a peasant could wander around and observe such a thing. The recruiting of a large workforce, for example."

Templemere's face lost its sheen of anxiety. The man was correct. Such as that for many gold bars!"

"Let me give it some thought."

The man nodded.

"Of course and we will know of your decision by what you say in the House. If we hear of your suggestion for a mission to Portugal and it is accepted, then we will be in touch. A letter will arrive. Memorise its contents and then burn it. For you own security."

He beat his cane on the roof of the cab and it began to slow.

"So, my Lord, we await your words in the House of Lords."

He picked up the box and placed it back into the satchel, then he handed Templemere the strap.

"A token of good faith!"

The cab stopped and the man quickly got out, leaving Templemere holding the strap, his mind in a turmoil, but he was brought back to reality by the cover of the small speech hole sliding open and the cab-driver speaking through.

"Where to, Sir? Still Pimlico?"

"No. Ruddle's."

All thoughts of the delights of the bordello were now gone. He needed to get back to his room at his club, collect his belongings and return to his estate to think. He now lifted the satchel, it was, indeed, very heavy. He withdrew the box and took out the bar, to turn the shining metal over and over again until the cab drew up at his destination.

oOo

Captain Nat Drake was sat at a table in an upstairs room examining the soles of his boots by pressing his thumb into the centre. It was worryingly thin. He leaned back in the chair to address the open door that led downstairs.

"Morrison! Who do we have that can repair boots?"

A shout came back up the stairs.

"The Farrier of the 1st Dragoons, Sir. He can stitch another sole on."

Drake sat back.

"A crude job, I don't doubt. Using a bit of old saddle."

Major Carr was stood at the window, examining the busy Square outside, Redcoats and townspeople mingling side by side – a very peaceful scene. He added his own comment.

"What does that matter as long as you no longer feel the stones!"

Carr turned away from the window and sat on a spare chair. The room was plain and stripped of anything that could tell of its time as part of a family home.

"So we're here, and hopefully for a number of days. Celorico, about as noteworthy as any of the other damn places we've had to chase Johnny out of."

Captain Shakeshaft was sat on the floor in the corner, working on his journal. Carr turned to him.

"Give me the facts, please, Richard, of our journey here. The days, I mean. It's felt like months. The month of March being most apposite, in view of what we have been required to do so much of."

Shakespeare thumbed back a few pages.

"Why not really months, Sir. We left Santarem on the 5th, got to Alcanhede on the 7th, Porto de Mos on the 8th, Thomar on the 9th, Leiria on the 10th."

More page turning.

"Pombal on the 11th, Rehina on the 12th, Casal Novo on the 14th, Miranda on the 15th, Foz de Arouce same day. We crossed the Alva at Avo on the 18th and then marched unopposed to here, to arrive yesterday, the 25th, here, at Celorico."

He looked at Carr.

"About three weeks, Sir."

Carr nodded.

"It's exhausting merely to hear it spoken. And I cannot remember being this hungry since the retreat from Talavera."

He turned to the same stairs as Drake.

"Morrison!"

"Sir."

"Have the rations come up?"

"Yes Sir. And the Followers. Seems we can all now enjoy better food and better cooking!"

"Deeds will speak louder than words, Morrison!"

"Yes Sir. Water's just boiling now, Sir."

Drake was tying his boots together with an awkward length of string, using the pull loop at the back, this preparatory to receiving the attentions of the 1st Dragoons Farrier.

"Do we know where our noble foe is, at this moment?"

Only Carr could have any idea and he did.

"Yes. Guarda."

"How far away is that?"

"About six miles."

"Only six and we are still at peace?"

"Make the most of it. It won't last long."

Whilst military peace was holding, another kind of warfare was breaking out, at the rations barrel, again with Corporal Toby Halfway using his bayonet. A piece was speared and brought up, but hidden by his body.

"Who wants this?"

Betty Barker was stood almost beside Nelly Nicholls and she thought it to her advantage if she spoke before her.

"That's mine! I'll have it. Give it 'ere."

Halfway turned and dropped the meat into her apron. It was not a good piece at all, very comparable to the disappointing piece some days ago. She stood examining it, when Halfway spoke again.

"Who wants this?"

Now Nelly spoke.

"I will."

The piece was dropped into her apron and it was another quality piece, which fact was soon observed by Betty Barker when Nellie walked past her. Her anger found a subject.

"You two are cooking summat up between you!"

She turned to Nellie.

"This 'appens too often, for you, you Irish baggage, you always gets a fine piece whilst I gets not much better than offal. You've got some scheme between you!"

Nellie took a pace towards her. Both were of equal weight, Betty taller, but Nellie broader.

"You needs to watch your mouth and who you're accusin' of what!"

The two were now face to face and Halfway turned to defend his honesty, speaking to Betty Barker.

"Now just how do you think I can get it across to people behind my back, just how good each piece is what I'm calling out for?"

She was now thoroughly enraged.

"I don't know, but something's happening and this Irish toe-rag gets the best of it! You've got some scheme. Where your feet are, your left elbow is, anything!"

Stood in any other place, they would soon have come to blows but that would mean dropping the precious meat. They had to settle for glaring daggers at each other, until Halfway stepped between them.

"Get on off, ladies and get that cooked. Your men are hungry."

Betty Barker turned sideways to walk off.

"This isn't finished yet, not by a long way!"

Nellie stood her ground.

"And that's all you've said so far that's the God's honest truth!"

Halfway gently eased her on her way, but each managed to turn their heads and exchange a mutual look of pure hatred.

oOo

41

Chapter Two

Sabugal

Cornet Willoughby Carr was giving himself specific instructions. "This is our job; scouting! Not serious combat. That's for the Heavies. Scouting is our job!" That decided, he resolved to do it well. There were risks, obviously, but the Army must know, particularly Wellington himself, now known to Young Carr as 'The Peer' or 'Nosey'. Whatever it was, at that moment himself and his Troop had been sent forward down the Guarda road to see what could be seen. Riding just behind the 'off' side of Cornet Carr's horse was his Sergeant, the estimable Septimus Baxter, Seb to all of equal rank. This worthy had almost zero concern for the Army Staff's opinion of what the true role of Light Cavalry was, but what he did know was that this Cornet, likeable and receptive to good advice as he may well be, was, nevertheless, utterly green. He could lead his Troop of veteran Light Dragoons into the utmost peril through simply not knowing the care and caution necessary. It was not that Cornet Carr was reckless, it was simply that he did not know. Therefore, whilst his Officer was debating within himself his proper role in military life, Baxter was considering where they were at that moment and where they were on their way to. On top, concern within him was growing that Tavender, being the Senior Captain, would slightly too often send Carr's Troop out on such a mission, if Vigurs was not available to consult or even object. There was such a thing as Troop rotation, but the rotating seemed to come around too often, for his peace of mind, to fall upon his Troop,

With that thought, Baxter was of the opinion that blithely continuing down this road in the direction of a French army was becoming a mite too perilous, but the opportunity to stop had now arisen. They were on the main road from Celorico to Guarda, with open country either side. No-one was going to come at them out of any woods and ahead was a small hillock. He eased his horse up alongside that of Carr's.

"Perhaps take a look from that small hill off to the right there, Sir. Seems a good place to see what's up ahead. Shall I call a halt, Sir?"

Carr was jolted from his internal debate and brought back abruptly to where he was.

"From where, Sergeant?"

"That small hill there, Sir. Shall I call a halt, Sir?"

"Yes. You and I will go forward."

The Troop halted and both rode forward, but not alone. Baxter had motioned four trusted Troopers from the front rank to follow. Thus, six came to the hilltop, but only Carr and Baxter came up to the skyline. The four veteran Troopers knew enough to hang back out of sight. Immediately Carr saw the merit in stopping to take a look. Half a mile further on, there was a French column, marching quickly on the main road. Carr spent a minute with his telescope and then handed the instrument to Baxter.

"That must be their rearguard, Sergeant, moving back to Guarda. Would you say that town up there on that high hill was Guarda?"

"I would, Sir, and this means we have made contact. That town is about two miles on."

42

At that point, Cornet Carr rose up in his stirrups.

"And what have we here?"

He pointed with the telescope.

"There, Sergeant. Coming out of that collection of buildings. Out of what must be a big farm."

Baxter looked and saw for himself a large group of infantry, around 20, hurrying from the farm, not running, but carrying boxes and bundles which could well be sacks, the distance from them being about 500 yards.

"We should attack, Sergeant!"

"Yes Sir, we should, 'specially as them French is making off with what is probably food, but first we should check for any enemy cavalry nearby that could come down on us, Sir. Taking us unawares."

"You're right, Sergeant, and I will do that immediately."

He scanned all around with his telescope, but could see no enemy of any description, nor any place on the open plain where any could hide. However, he did see something which could greatly help.

"I see no cavalry this side of what looks to be a river, up ahead, and only one bridge. If we cut them off from that, then the job's done."

"Are there any cavalry on the far side, Sir. As could cross and oppose us?"

Carr used his telescope again and was re-assured.

"I see none."

He turned to Baxter.

"We have to do this, Sergeant. And we should hurry!"

"Yes Sir, as you say."

"Bring up the Troop."

Baxter had no need to ride back. He had left Corporal Makepeace at the head of the column. He drew his sabre and held it aloft, which meant to Makepeace that they would be going into combat and then Baxter circled his left arm forward. Makepeace immediately brought the Troop forward along the road at a canter, while Carr's group came down off the hill and took position before them. The Troop then automatically formed into two lines and within a minute they could see the French foraging party. Carr's Troop was a strong one, 47 men and they immediately broke into a gallop. The French saw them and ran for the river, dropping their forage, but the bridge was a hopeless ambition. They came to the river and stopped, this was the fiercesome Mondego, at this point down within a deep chasm. No sooner had they discovered this, than the 16th were upon them and they all threw down their weapons, including an Officer, who threw down his sword. For them it was hopeless, with the 16th now drawn up in a confining semi-circle and so all captives now stood forlorn along the bank. Baxter rode forward, creating a gap in the line and he motioned the French to march back. All complied; they were now prisoners and the Troopers, now well practiced in herding such, arranged themselves as escort, but the French were allowed to pick up their gains from the farm, before marching away. However, before they rode off, Baxter pointed to the Officer's sword.

"You should have that, Sir!"

Carr looked at the sword, then at Baxter.

"You really think so, Sergeant?"

"Yes Sir. That's how it works, Sir."

Baxter then dismounted and picked it up, to hand it to Carr, who swished it around and then looked at the blade.

"Anything on it, Sir."

"Yes."

Carr brought the blade closer to his eyes.

"Boutet. Klingengthal."

"You don't say, Sir. I've heard that those are a cut above. If you forgive the use of words, Sir."

Carr grinned at the pun.

"I bow to your superior knowledge, Sergeant, and I'd say 'job done'. We've found the French and taken some prisoners. Who could complain about that?"

"No-one Sir, and don't forget your own quality capture!"

Carr gave the elegant blade another downward swish before lodging it carefully in his belt.

"Yes Sir. Best get back now and report what we've found."

43

oOo

Simultaneously, back in London, as Wellington digested the news as discovered by Cornet Willoughby, Lord Templemere drew up in a hired coach at the gates of the House of Lords for a Post-Noon Sitting. Three Lords alighted and these, Templemere, Mahon and Hopgood, signed themselves in with the Usher and then went to the changing room to adorn themselves with their robes. They entered the Chamber and took their places, Templemere now in a state of supreme self-worth, confident in the success of what he was about to attempt. He leaned forward, the better to see Lord Mahon, him sat beyond Lord Hopgood.

"You did give that note to Black Rod, did you not, informing him of your wish to speak?"

"I did Fred, and so, if the system is working, then the Chancellor will ask me to rise and address the House."

"And Spencer's been primed?"

"That Pimlico establishment you have made us all aware of, now awaits him. If he delivers!"

Templemere grinned.

"Very good. So, here's hoping."

Black Rod then entered, the signal for all conversation to cease and he strode forward to his place at the Woolsack.

"All stand!"

All did and they only sat when the Lord Chancellor John Eldon had taken his own seat, having walked his own 25 paces from the entrance arch. The debates began, all of utter tedium for Lord Templemere as they ranged across conditions in mines, to port duties for Russian ships and then some unfathomable Irish question. Templemere was fighting the effects of earlier glasses of port and claret, when the Lord Chancellor turned his head towards the Tory benches, the long appendages of his bell-bottom wig swinging outwards from the generated centrifugal force.

"My Lord Mahon. You have some business to put before this House?"

Mahon rose and waited for all eyes to turn to him that were in a position to. He opened his notes.

"My Lord Chancellor, it was but days ago that we were celebrating in this House, the glorious victory of Barossa and the capture of a French Eagle. Also, expressing our sincere hopes and good wishes towards our noble General Lord Wellington in his efforts to drive the French from the soil of our worthy ally, the Kingdom of Portugal. I wish now to put it to this House that our good wishes should be augmented with more practical help."

He paused to hear what he had hoped for and several Lords cried "Hear hear" from around the Chamber. Thereby encouraged he continued.

"What that practical help should be, is impossible for us to know, sat here in this House, and so I propose a fact-finding mission to Portugal whereby the participants can talk to Lord Wellington and his Generals to find out exactly what they require and then to judge whether or not it is possible in the light of the financial constraints that we are now under. I further propose that this mission should come under the guidance of Lord Frederick Templemere, who, as we all know, has military experience and has recently returned from that very theatre of war. I would commend him as the Chairman of this fact-finding mission and I now commend this proposal to the House."

The Lord Chancellor lowered his head to regard the benches before him.

"Are there any here who would wish to speak on this matter?"

A hand went up.

"My Lord Spencer."

Lord Spencer rose and adjusted his robes before grasping the edges before his chest in both hands.

"Lord Chancellor. I would speak in favour of this proposal, that our noble Lord Templemere should go out to the Peninsula. This House owes Lord Wellington and his courageous forces any help that can be afforded, within reason, of course. Further, I would leave the matter of who accompanies Lord Templemere on his mission to his own good judgment, him being, as has been said, well acquainted with the issues facing our forces out there."

Spencer sat as another hand went up, this time from the Whig benches, to receive the nod from the Lord Chancellor.

"Lord Brougham and Vaux."

A slight figure stood, in far less elegant robes than those displayed so far, and begin to speak immediately, in a clear Scottish accent.

"I see no cause to dispute the good sense in actually going out to Portugal and gather what facts as can be ascertained and after that point, deciding on what can be done. However, my Lord Chancellor, the key point is, what can be done with the resources that are available? I would urge this House to require Lord Templemere to include in his party someone of proven experience in matters of military planning and its execution. With all due respect to the heroic service given by Lord Templemere, he has no background in such matters, meaning supply and command. What we decide to do that will aid Lord Wellington requires careful consideration, this being judged using criteria gained from knowledge and experience. Therefore, I would wish to see the inclusion of our current Secretary to the Commander in Chief, General Sir Henry Livermore. He has held that position for several years now, is a wounded veteran himself and has deep experience of taking important decisions at a strategic level "

He sat down to several "Hear hears" as Lord Chancellor Eldon paused for thought.

"I have two proposals here, which I see no reason not to combine, that a mission be sent and that mission should include both Lord Templemere and General Sir Henry Livermore. Do I hear any objections?"

None came.

"Then I put the motion. Those content?"

Almost all raised their hands.

"Not content?"

There were none.

"I declare the House content."

Eldon looked up at Templemere, the latter no longer so sure of himself.

"Lord Templemere. The House has placed this matter in your hands!"

Templemere and his two companions rose, as did the House and they left the Chamber. Once disrobed and in the corridor, Templemere turned to both.

"Who the Hell is General Sir Henry Livermore?"

Black Rod was intent that Templemere would soon find out.

"Lord Templemere. If you would care to wait a few minutes I will furnish you with a letter to carry to Sir Henry at Horse Guards, informing him of the wishes of this House."

Within 30 minutes the three were progressing up Whitehall to the squat entrance of Horse Guards. The three strode straight up, for their progress to be halted by crossed muskets and bayonets across their path, placed there by Coldstream sentries. Templemere immediately flourished the letter, the Corporal read the name of the addressee on the front and the weapons were withdrawn. Once inside, Templemere turned to look, by chance, into a dark room, where sat a melancholy and cadaverous man, his own darkness submerging him further into the gloom of the interior. From inside, a grandfather clock chimed the hour. Templemere completed his turn and went straight in.

"We have come directly from the House of Lords. It is vital that we see Sir Henry Livermore immediately. Are we in the correct place?"

The use of the word 'immediately' had no impact on the man at all, him slowly sitting back in his chair.

"I am Sir Henry's secretary. My name is Benjamin Wilson. May I know the nature of your business?"

Mahon immediately piped up.

"Ho! Secretary to the Secretary. What!"

This had no impact on Wilson, other than to further darken his features as he waited for an answer. It came from Templemere breaking the seal on the letter and spreading it before Wilson, the correct way up so that he could read it. Wilson leaned forward and did so. Even he could not delay a communication from such a place and so he rose with the letter in his hand.

"I will take this directly to Sir Henry."

He turned left and knocked on a very solid door in the wall behind his desk. None of the three heard any reply, but Wilson, nevertheless, opened the door and entered. To stand waiting was too much for Templemere and so he followed Wilson through, to then place himself almost in front of Wilson, there to see a large, broad-shouldered, late middle-aged figure sat behind a large desk. The leonine head was already raised to inspect the commotion, which included Templemere striding forward towards him.

"We have come from the House of Lords and that is our introduction!"

Templemere pointed to the letter that Wilson was placing on the desk, having manoeuvred himself around Templemere, Wilson now conscious that he may have failed in his duties as guardian of the door.

"I'm sorry, Sir Henry."

Livermore waved his hand in dismissal.

"It's nothing Benjamin. Return to your desk."

Wilson bowed and withdrew and Livermore picked up the letter, but before reading it, he scanned his three intruders.

"Gentlemen. Be seated!"

There were three chairs in the room, but only two at the desk, and so Hopgood had to bring one forward. Whilst that was happening, Templemere, from his central position, could see that most of Livermore's left ear was missing and there was a furrow down that side of his head leading directly to the injury. Whilst they sat, Livermore read the letter, but Templemere felt the need to speak first, whether or not Livermore had finished reading.

"The letter is clear?"

Livermore delayed his answer until he had completely finished reading and then he placed the letter carefully aside and looked at Templemere, grinning.

"Perfectly. Their Lordships wish me to accompany your Lordships on a trip out to Portugal where we pester Lord Wellington to tell us of his plans, if he knows them himself. Then we see what help can be given by spending the odd bit of money that The House will see its way clear to make available."

Templemere was horrified for two reasons; firstly, Livermore's levity and secondly his stating, in terms of difficulty, exactly what Templemere was to be paid in gold to find out. Would such information be forthcoming that he could pass on?"

"Is this unconscionable?"

Livermore shook his head.

"No! Indeed, some good may come of it. Whether or not it will tip the balance significantly in our favour, I doubt, but doubtless it will help."

He grinned further as he looked at the three, dismissing Mahon and Hopgood as know-nothing aristocratic idiots and Templemere as an over-blown, self-regarding, rather nasty piece of work. Nevertheless, he was a soldier and he had his orders.

"How do we get there and when?"

Templemere relaxed. This was going to happen, under his direction and with the full authority of the House of Lords.

"Day after tomorrow, I propose. Mahon here has a fast vessel, moored in the Thames as we speak, at Deptford Hard."

"Very well. I will meet you there at the time of high tide the day after tomorrow."

He sat back, having no wish to shake their hands.

"I will see you then. My Lords."

The three rose and took themselves outside, where Templemere dismissed his companions.

"Deptford Hard. Day after tomorrow."

Then a thought.

"Your ship, Mahon, or whatever. She's up to the mark?"

Mahon's brows came together.

"Oh yes. Ex-Excise cutter and armed as such, with new copper sheathing. She fast!"

Templemere nodded.

"Right. I'm off to Hampshire to make my preparations. Until then!"

He walked off to hail a cab. Within an hour, he was in his own fast curricle drawn by a matched pair and three hours after that he was in his own mansion, well pleased with the positive outcome. His mood was further uplifted with the arrival of a letter early next morning. He broke the blank seal and read the brief words.

"Massena will have withdrawn to the line of the River Agueda by the time you arrive. He will hold Cuidad Rodrigo, but withdraw from Almeida, leaving a garrison within. North-East of there is a village called Barba del Puerco, with a Chapel alongside a track which leads down to a Roman Bridge deep in the chasm. The Priest is sympathetic to us. Leave your letter behind the Altar, marked Para Frade Estaves. He will look each day. In your Coach-House is a further gesture of our good faith."

Templemere spoke the name of the village and the Priest to himself several times, then he burned the letter and hurried to his Coach-House. No thought came to him that the information that was in the letter would be of the highest importance to the British military and that perhaps he should pass it on, as a patriotic duty. His mind was elsewhere and the briefest of searches revealed an innocuous large rough wooden box. He levered it open to find two more of the well-made boxes he had been given four days previously. After seizing each and forcing open the lids, he found a gold bar within each identical to that which he already possessed. He then spent some time turning them over in his hands, the lantern light accentuating the orange lustre of the pure gold.

oOo

On that same day, further discussions were taking place merely forty miles from the village mentioned in the letter, but with not so strategic a span. Sat in the upstairs room of their Headquarters, discussing the condition of their men, Lacey, O'Hare and Carr had no need of servant's forewarnings to know that Brigadier Mackinnon had entered the building. The three stopped their discussions immediately on hearing from below, "Your Officers here?" and Bryce answering, "Upstairs, Sir." After seconds of stair clumping, Mackinnon came through the door and wasted no time.

"Arentschildt's boys have found Johnny. He's over the Mondego and now in Guarda, so we can assume, and is no doubt pillaging the place. He's there with a large force, so peasants tell us, who saw them pass by. So, Himself is sending us out tomorrow, the whole led by Picton, us being our three Regiments. And two Battalions of Portuguese, Colville's are being left behind."

It was then that the three noticed the map under Mackinnon's arm, which was produced and spread over the table. His forefinger came down on three points in succession.

"We are here, in Celorico, we cross the Mondego here at Mizarela, get onto this ridge above Prados, then see what to do about Guarda, which will be in view."

Carr looked at the route.

"No easy march, Sir!"

"Don't complain, Carr, he's sending Erskine's Light and Arentschildt's Cavalry by an even longer route to the North to come down the far bank of the Mondego. Campbell's Sixth drew the long straw for the shorter route, they're crossing at Quinta de Ponte to come at Johnny from the centre, with both of his flanks enveloped. We fear that he has two Corps in the place. It could be a tough fight, so get your men up to the mark. You're leaving this evening!"

He noted the shock on the faces of the three, caused by the thought of a night march over a Sierra, and leaving in about three hours, but he said no more on that subject.

"Now! What have you to drink?"

O'Hare reached behind him for his bottle of special Irish and Carr found the glasses. An hour later Carr was outside, the spirit still warm in his stomach, as he toured his Captains to warn them of their imminent departure. He had just left the Colour Company with one of Heaviside's quotes ringing in his ears, something about, "Whatever you do, work heartily...." when he saw a Trooper of the 16th Light Dragoons, on foot, walking towards him.

"Trooper!"

The Dragoon stopped and came to the attention.

"Sir!"

"Is your Headquarters nearby?"

"Yes Sir. Just back there, two hundred yards or so. A white and pink building. Sir."

With such a clear description, Carr felt he could afford five minutes to check on his brother and so he hurried in the direction in which the Dragoon had pointed and he soon saw the building, obvious in its lurid colours. He hurried towards it and entered to find two Cornets stood talking. Both sprang to the attention.

"I don't suppose Cornet Carr would be close by?"

The nearest spoke.

"Willoughby? Why yes, Sir. I saw him upstairs, first room, but a few minutes ago"

Carr climbed the stairs and entered the first room to find his brother, another Cornet and a Captain drinking wine as poured out by a pretty servant girl, who sashayed around Carr as she left. Elder Carr grinned and nodded.

"Why am I not surprised!"

47

Meanwhile, all three had sprung to their feet at the sight of a superior Officer and introductions came first, conducted by Cornet Carr.

"Captain Vigurs. This is my brother, Major Henry Carr."

Carr held out his hand.

"Pleased to meet you, Captain."

"And you, Sir."

Young Carr turned to the Cornet.

"And this is Cornet Douglas Peterson"

Peterson saluted before taking the hand as offered by Carr, who then spoke to all three.

"Thought I'd drop round to wish you well. You've the long night march off to the North, I understand."

Vigurs nodded.

"Yes Sir. We're to leave soon with the Light Division."

He turned to young Carr.

"Your brother here, Sir, has done rather well. He came back yesterday with a parcel of prisoners, having also discovered that Johnny had crossed the Mondego. A very neat job!"

Elder Carr grinned as he studied his brother.

"Well done! Well done."

Younger Carr then dropped his hand to his sword hilt.

"And I got this!"

He pulled out the blade and handed it to Carr, who tested the weight and then read the words.

"Klingenthal! My word, this is a bit special. And it goes into your scabbard?"

"Well, no. I had to relieve the French Officer of that as well, but he was happy enough when I passed over a length of sausage. Which did not fit into the scabbard!"

Everyone laughed, but they all turned at the noise coming from the direction of the door to see Captain Tavender stood just inside the room, a cold grin arriving on his face when he recognised Elder Carr

"Major Carr. Pleasure to see you, Sir."

Carr nodded, his expression cold.

"Captain."

"Just doing my rounds. Sorry if I'm interrupting something, but we have to be ready to march soon."

Carr nodded, then turned to his brother's two companions, offering his hand to each.

"I should be getting back. A pleasure to meet you. Good luck to you both."

With that he slapped his brother on the arm and left with not a glance at Tavender, who, nevertheless spoke to Carr's disappearing back.

"Brotherly affection would appear to be strong characteristic in your family, Major."

The embarrassing, oleaginous tone of the remark was not lost on the three observing from across the room, particularly young Willoughby Carr and so they quickly departed themselves, leaving Tavender to his own affairs.

Formed in close column, in the lead of their Brigade, the 105th hurried forward, darkness having thoroughly closed in around them by the time they felt the gradient of the Sierra resist the push of their marching feet. Deakin and Halfway were marching together, their heads deep within their collars and shako oilskin turned down. The higher they climbed, the more it rained and the more the wind blew.

"We can only hope that those up front knows where they'n going."

Deakin chuckled.

"I saw some Portugee locals go up front after we crossed the river, so here's hoping. Must be a guide of some sort."

Captain Heaviside was merely two yards before the Colour Party and turned to impart his usual verbal gift.

"Now faith is the assurance of things hoped for, the conviction of things not seen. Hebrews 11. Verse 1."

Deakin spoke into the darkness, wholly unconvinced.

"Yes Sir. I'm sure all the lads sees it that way Sir."

They slogged on, the one reassurance being that they were on a decent road, albeit of pounded gravel, which crunched under their feet. The hours passed and there was no sign of dawn when they finally did come

48

to a halt and were given the order to rest, but no fires. All found whatever shelter they could, against walls, under trees and hedges, even ditches. However, there was no sleep for Lacey, O'Hare and Carr, stood behind Picton, him stood with Mackinnon. The only comfort was O'Hare's depleted stock of Irish whiskey, the last of which had gone into his hip flask. Picton was pacing about and Mackinnon left him to it, sometimes talking to the Officer group of the 88th, sometimes that of the 74th. Picton began studying his hand held out before him, hoping to see more details of his palm. He managed to convince himself and he turned to Mackinnon, stood now with Lacey, O'Hare and Carr.

"Who have we got, that can sneak forward somewhat and see what's in our front? Some kind of poacher!"

Carr thought immediately of John Davey, but he was at the back of the column, probably asleep, as was the rest of his Company and therefore very difficult to find.

"I'll go Sir."

In his dark greatcoat, Carr felt the task neither too onerous nor dangerous and the answer from Picton was a finger pointed in the right direction. Carr unbuckled his sword and would have dropped it on the ground, but O'Hare took it from him before it fell.

"Good luck, Henry!"

Carr walked forward, passing through a final, baleful look from Picton, which aroused no small degree of resentment in Carr.

"If you hear muskets going off, Sir, you'll know they're not too far and that I've found them and they've seen me."

Something between a growl and a grunt emitted from Picton as Carr passed and then began to buffet his way through the heather and the long grass. He counted the steps, hoping for each to be a yard through the dense covering on the exposed hillside. It was growing lighter and all was utterly silent, he was out of the wind on the lee side, but the ground remained level as Carr, still counting, placed his feet carefully and, with each ten steps, he stopped to listen. Twenty more brought him to two hundred and he stopped again. Silence, twenty more, then something loomed up on his right, certainly a French picket, but there came no challenge. Carr dredged up a smidgen of French, because it would help if he spoke first, as would an Officer.

"Tout va bien?"

"Oui Monsieur. Tout va bien."

Carr stepped away, hoping for the remaining gloom to hide him

"Bon. Bien."

Carr hurriedly retraced his steps, and found himself not far from Picton.

"Well?"

"I bumped into a French picket, Sir, at about three hundred yards out. I could go no further forward. I would assume there is a force there, Sir. It remained too dark, so as for numbers that we could cope with, that I cannot say."

Picton grunted.

"That's for me to decide, Major!"

Carr saluted.

"Yes Sir."

Picton turned to his sole Brigadier then present.

"What do you think, Mackinnon?"

"Ah'd say he was reet, Sir."

"So, we do what? Day's breaking."

"We get our five Battalions across this ridge, each on a two Company front. Light Companies out as a screen. Then we can fight on a ten Company front or advance, as we choose."

Picton paced some more, hand flexing on his sword hilt. Then he stopped and faced Mackinnon.

"Do it!"

All Picton's Colonels and Majors fell back to their men and, within 15 minutes, each of Picton's battalions was part of a ten Company front, each Battalion showing two Companies facing towards where the French were most likely to be. The two Companies fronting the 105th were the Third, Colour, and Carravoy's Grenadiers, all staring ahead, apprehensive as to what the rapidly dawning day would bring. Carr was stood with Drake, 150 yards further even than the Lights screen out in front, each using his telescope, which, as yet yielded nothing but heather and gloomy murk. They could only stand and wait, chewing biscuits, dried beef

49

and drinking water. Suddenly, amazingly, the dawn sun found a gap in the clouds and fully illuminated the plateau. Before them, at no more than 300 yards, was a single Battalion of French in camp, who, on seeing them, sent bugle-calls up and down their line. Immediately, blue coated figures began to spring out of the heather and form their line, three deep, as was their custom. That done, nothing happened. French Officers walked up and down, studying the British, but there was no further move on their part, not even a screen of skirmishers emerging. Picton gave the order.

"Show The Colours!"

All along the line the leather cases came off the Battalion Colours and all were lifted aloft by their Ensigns, the ten points bright on the ridge, this now clear in the Spring sunshine. Every man on both sides studied the other, but the minutes passed and there came no orders, whilst the sunlight scanned across the hillside and even penetrated the valley below. Carr, still with the Light Company, spoke to Drake whilst continuing to study the scene now revealed way down beneath them on the main road.

"Well, this is a turn-up!"

A whole French Division was marching to the East, whilst two more were camped in a deep valley outside Guarda, at the base of the hill they were on. Carr drew out his own telescope.

"Would that we were stronger. Advancing from here, we could do untold damage to a whole Corps of them. Oh, for a battery of guns."

"Will Picton attack?"

"No. If we do that, those opposite, will just fall back onto their supports below, and they see us as too strong for them to attack. So, we stay here, both sides ogling each other!"

He turned left.

"Take a look left, can you see any sign of Campbell or the Lights?

Drake used his own telescope, for three minutes.

"No. Nothing. No sign."

He folded the telescope.

"So, what do we do? Just stand here and look, like a bunch of schoolboys at an end of term dance? Confronted by actual girls?"

"If it keeps Picton happy!"

The minutes passed, then the hours. From three hundred yards, both sides stared at each other, but they exchanged no musketry. The Light Company of the 105th stared forward, many indulging in lingering two fingered salutes for those opposite, but this was wholly insufficient for Miles.

"Byfe, Zeke, Nat, Len. Gather round."

With the four gathered around, forming a screen, Miles turned his back on the French, dropped his trousers and began slapping his bare backside at the observing French. The laughter from the four masking the spectacle drew the attention of Sergeant Ellis, who ran over to see Miles busy with buttons.

"What the Hell were you up to, Miles?"

"Sorry Sarn't. Got took short."

There were grins all round, except from Ellis, but Carr and Drake were now calling Ellis over and he had to obey. The two Officers had resumed studying the French in the valley below and Drake handed Ellis his telescope and pointed down into the valley.

"There, Sergeant, just passing that white cottage. On a horse. Does he look in any way familiar? He has one arm, I do believe."

The image swung into the lens as Ellis found the subject, it was a one armed General.

"You think that's him, Sir. That General Loison what we had a run in with, down in Lisbon, back in the year eight? The one as we got out of there, before the Portugee tore him apart."

"I do."

"I told him to look for our Colour, Sir. Up on some hill. I can only hope he's seen it, up here, like."

Meanwhile Carr was studying the countryside over left, looking for their supports and seeing them, both the Sixth and the Light Divisions.

"He may well take another look up here, Sergeant, because our other two Divisions have arrived, and it looks as if our Light Division may well get in behind him."

Ellis looked back down into the valley, still holding out the telescope.

"With your permission, Sir."

Ellis refocused the instrument on Loison. He was pleased to see French riders approaching their Divisional Commander who, just at that moment decided to check for any movement by the Allies on hill above him, now that two threatening Allied columns had just arrived. Loison's telescope pointed directly up at them. Ellis mumbled under his breath.

"I hope you can see us, you lopsided, murdering bastard. You come on up and take a crack. You've got 15,000 down there."

However, it was not to be. More French bugle calls sounded and the French Battalion opposite turned and ran down the hill, accompanied by many catcalls from the Allied skirmishers, to then form on the end of the final French column that was rapidly quitting Guarda. Carr, Drake, and Ellis watched for some minutes, as three French Divisions marched on the road heading South East at their best French marching pace. Drake let out a sigh.

"Well, that's that, then. Wish all our successes were gained in such a manner! For now, though, some food wouldn't come amiss."

At that point, Lacey and O'Hare came to join them.

"Any orders, Sir."

"No, Henry. Picton says stay here and wait and see who Himself decides tae send after the French. My guess is that will be Erskine's Light. They have guns and cavalry."

However, as all casually studied the disappearing French, orders did arrive soon, as carried by Mackinnon.

"Picton's lost his temper. We're going down. He's convinced that we'll be spending at least one night in this place, so why should Campbell's Sixth get first pick of the billets?"

O'Hare snapped his telescope shut.

"Can't argue with that, Sir."

"No! So. Back with your men. Column of fours. Picton's a mind tae let our two Portuguese Battalions lead in, tae give everyone a bit of a lift, y'understand? As liberators."

Obeying Picton's orders, the 105th were the last to march off the ridge and down into the town. Guarda had suffered nothing like the depredations of Leiria and the larger villages around it and almost immediately the population of the lofty town returned to their homes and streets from the hills above and, as the 105th approached, they could hear wild cheering as the Portuguese Battalions entered, all Colours flying and drums beating. Halfway leaned forward from behind Deakin.

"Any chance of the Followers comin' up, you think, Jed? Bit of decent grub."

Deakin turned his head back.

"Not much, Tobe. Later in the day, perhaps yes, but too late to make much difference to the present."

Deakin's last statement was incorrect, but for the wrong reason. The good citizens of Guarda made every effort to feed and house this newly arrived, liberating army and so the Followers would have made little difference to the quality of their meals that evening, there being bread, dried fish and sausage aplenty. Having fully eaten their fill Davey, Pike and Miles now sat apportioning the leftovers into each other's haversacks.

"How'd they keep all this out of the hands of the French? D'you think?"

Davey threw Miles a fillet of dried fish.

"Who cares, Tom? What matters is that we've got plenty to see us through the next couple of days."

Miles stowed the fish into his haversack and sat up.

"You listen to that! There's a fair old barn dance goin' on, all round here tonight. Think they'll let us do a reel or two?"

His messmates laughed before Davey answered.

"You must be bloody jokin'. They've let the Portugee loose on the town and good luck to 'em, but thee, me and Joe here, no chance!"

Joe Pike gave a rare opinion.

"I'll settle for this billet, the food and that nice lady who keeps bringing us soup."

Davey looked at him.

"Most wise and sensible, Joseph. It's not for responsible married men such as ourselves to go gallivanting about chasin' young Portuguese womenfolk."

Miles frowned.

"You sound like bloody Byford! And you speak for yourself! I wouldn't mind my arm round some doxey!"

Davey looked at him.

"B'ain't no doxies here! You treat one of their women wrong and you'll get the whole family on your neck and a few neighbours too."

Miles grumbled but made no reply. They were all in a large townhouse with Redcoats in every room and soon came Sergeant Ellis, him in good mood, chewing bread and sausage, a mood so good that even the proximity of Miles brought no change. His words were clear and simple, almost comradely.

"Dawn muster, boys. We march straight out of here."

oOo

True dawn found Picton's Division on the straight, flat road out of Guarda, following in the footsteps of Loison's French, both armies following signs that pointed to Sabugal. The turn of the month brought more intensive sun and the road, over a level plain, now began to throw up dust. Marching together, Drake turned to Carr.

"Do you know what today is?"

Carr adopted a bored expression to his weather-beaten face, his eyes sheltering under the short peak of his Shako, this tilted forward against the sun rising in the South East.

"Do tell! First day of Lent?"

"No. We are well into that."

Carr looked away and mumbled.

"Can't say I noticed! Seems we've given up most things whilst treading in Johnny's footsteps."

Drake continued.

"All Fools Day. April the 1st!"

Carr turned towards him.

"Right, and so that gives you until Noon to play some tedious trick!"

It was now Drake's turn to pull his face into a resigned expression.

"Thought that might cheer you up a bit. Something to raise the spirits, I hoped."

Carr nodded, feeling somewhat chided, but his serious mood persisted.

"If pressed, I'd say that Johnny is coming together again. There's not much abandoned and discarded French kit on this road and no stragglers or wounded at all. I suspect a battle in the offing, either tomorrow or the day after. The next town's Sabugal. M'sieu's going to make a stand either there or someplace nearby, and the Peer's gathered us, the Light and the Sixth, with the 1st, 7th and 5th Divisions close up behind. He suspects Johnny'll try something, of that I'm certain. He's concentrating."

The detailed military information and the serious tone transmitted itself to Drake.

"We need to get letters off, then."

Carr nodded, whilst pulling out his pistol to give it a brief examination.

"We do!"

The flat plains gave way to low hills, which taxed them but little and their tree covered slopes provided ample fuel. When a halt was called the messes of Davey and Deakin lay under the shelter of the trees, enjoying their stew of a large variety of ingredients, some army issue, some from the generosity of the grateful citizens of Guarda. Ellis passed amongst them, giving his Company warning that a battle would soon be upon them.

"Equipment check in the morning. Johnny's just ahead, so they think. We could be in for a set-to come Noon tomorrow."

Davey looked up at him, a look on his face that could be described as friendly.

"You bin fed, Sarn't?"

"No, not yet."

"Well, we've got plenty. So, if you've a mind."

Whilst Miles looked daggers at Davey, Ellis paused for a moment, almost in surprise at the offer, then he sloughed off his pack and pulled his pannikin from between the straps, to then hold it towards Davey, who spooned in a portion of the stew. Ellis found his spoon and knelt to consume the food. After a few mouthfuls, he looked at Davey.

"This is alright. Who cooked it?"

Davey grinned.

"Miles here's the cook, with Nellie and Bridie still in the rear."

Ellis looked across to Miles and nodded.

"Well, it's a decent lash up, I'll give him that."

Miles said nothing as Ellis cleared his plate, but Davey now felt able to question their flinty Sergeant.

"You fought the Frogs before? Before Maida, that is?"

Ellis took a swallow of water.

"No. Not before then."

"What do you reckon to them?"

Ellis worked his jaw to recover a scrap of food from his cheek.

"Nasty, cruel, selfish, murderin' bastards as don't like the bayonet. I for one have not forgot what we seen on the way up here, worst I've ever heard of, and if tomorrow we gets a better chance to pay 'em out, you'll get nary a complaint from me!"

Ellis reached behind him to take a handful of grass with which he cleaned his plate. With all his eating utensils now either in or on his pack, he stood up.

"Thanks for the food. See you all come dawn."

The back-pack then went on.

"You've got hidden talents, Private Miles."

With that, and in silence, he took himself off into the darkness.

The next soldier of any rank that they saw, came at dawn, this being Sergeant Ellis again touring his Company in his usual brisk manner.

"Fall in, on the road. Ten minutes."

Miles watched him continue his tour.

"Hope that stew gave him bellyache!"

It would seem not, for soon Ellis was marching beside them, saying nothing, but keeping step with the relaxed, easy gait that had taken him across the countless miles of several campaigns, more than he cared to remember. Mackinnon's Brigade of Picton's Division were following that of Colville's and not long into the day, they found themselves directed off the road and away to the right, where they were required to slog their way over rough farmland. Drake and Carr were marching together, but not so much marching as placing their feet carefully in the ploughed ruts.

"I'd call this taking positions."

Carr looked over to his right to see the whole Light Division with a large body of cavalry making their way over the same rough country.

"I'd not disagree! That's Erskine with his whole command."

Had he known that his brother was part of that force, he would not have been so sanguine. There were both Brigades of cavalry, Slade's 1st Dragoons and 14th Light Dragoons, leading Arentschildt's 16th Light Dragoons and the 1st KGL Hussars. Erskine also commanded the Light Infantry Brigades of Beckwith and Drummond. Towards the rear, rode Cornet Carr, at the head of his Troop with Sergeant Seb Baxter just behind. Young Carr was both anxious and excited, looking around at the long column of both Brigades from the Light Division close by and the long column of the Third Division, further over to his left. All were now advancing on a wide front up a long ridge. He turned to Sergeant Baxter.

"Would you say that we are forming up for a major battle, Sergeant?"

Baxter had no need to make any sightings of his own.

"I'd not bet against it, Sir. It has all the makings."

He paused to chuckle at the next thought.

"And if they gives us a rum ration, Sir, then you can take that as a signal that all will soon get very lively!"

However, it was not to be that day. A Brigadier from Wellington's Staff rode across the front of all and bid them halt, on the slope of the ridge from where Sabugal was hidden from view. Thus, they stood for some time, until Carr and Drake heard the sound of cantering hooves and jingling harness to see Wellington himself and his Staff ride to the crest of the ridge, pull out their telescopes and begin to consult. Drake drew his own conclusion.

"I think we can safely say that Sabugal is just over that ridge."

"I'd say that you are correct. Perhaps later, we can take a look, if we are not required to go marching straight over within the next couple of hours."

In predicting the latter, he was incorrect. The same Staff Brigadier rode along the line and ordered them to make camp, there would be no battle that day. Therefore, with their men settled, both wandered up to the top of the ridge to take a look in the last of the daylight. The slope from the ridge summit dipped sharply down to a river and Drake felt the need to state the obvious.

"That's the Coa and that town down-stream there, that must be Sabugal."

Carr gave the town but a glance, quickly noting the Castle of obviously Moorish origins and the narrow bridge beneath its walls over the Coa. He was far more taken with the long ridge opposite, on the far side of the river, the height of which was populated with French troops, starting from the town on his left to about half a mile over to his right.

"Johnny's going to make this a serious business. He means to stop us here, and he has a strong position. It looks like the Peer wants us to cross here and go for their centre. That track, up and down, both sides of the river, must mean a ford, where we will be required to cross."

Drake exhaled a long breath.

"That's why Picton's here, with both his Brigades."

Carr let out a sigh of his own.

"As you say!"

In the fading light both walked back to their men, their campfires now prominent in the gathering gloom. They passed Chaplain Albright moving amongst the mess areas accompanied by his Assistant Sedgwicke.

"What's he about, this evening?"

Carr gave him barely a glance. He already knew the answer to Drake's question.

"Administering unto his flock, would be how he'd describe it. It does no harm and I know the men appreciate it. Hopeless cove that he is, they give him credit that he means well. And the Followers are up. That'll give the men a bit of a lift on top!"

As they spoke Albright was entering the mess area of Deakin and Davey. At the sight of an Officer all began to stand, but Albright waved them back down.

"As you were men, no prayers this evening, unless you wish to come to the Service that I hold at my personal transport. A sort of Evensong, to which you are all welcome."

A mumbled "Thank you, Sir", came from many directions, whilst Albright took his place in the centre of the group, hands clasped before his chest, slightly leaning forward, as though dispensing profound Scripture to one of the more devoted of his following flock.

"Are you all well? It has been a long, hard march, with much to disturb our spirits and Faith in the Good Lord."

Deakin spoke the reply for all.

"All well, here Sir. 'Specially now that our families is up with us."

Albright beamed

"Ah, yes. What comfort to dwell in the company and the bosom of those we love, before such a time of peril, as awaits us on the morrow."

Deakin now did feel the need to stand.

"Yes Sir. There's much truth in that!"

Bridie looked up from spooning an extra portion in the direction of her son and his friend Henri Rasenne.

"Yes Sir, and to hope as well that we all comes through it, Sir, with The Blessing!"

Albright beamed further, despite the Catholic reference, but Sedgwicke was now touching his sleeve.

"We have many more to get to, Sir, before your Evening Service."

Albright brought himself back to the present.

"Indeed yes, indeed! You are right."

He leaned forward even further, hands still clasped and then rotating his body in the direction of all.

"I commend you all to the protection of our Good Lord, Jesus Christ."

Bridie and Nellie genuflected, whilst came several more 'Amen. Thank you, Sir' from various directions. Albright turned and glided off followed by Sedgwicke, whom Deakin addressed with his usual familiarity.

"How goes it, Old Parson?"

Sedgwicke smiled at the warm greeting as he followed his Superior.

"Well, I thank you, Jedediah. Very well."

Nellie shouted after him as he disappeared into the gloom

"You'll come round soon for a doughcake and a drop of tea, now, Parson, will you not?"

"I will" came out of the darkness beyond the edge of their firelight.

Dawn brought the dire portend of the rum ration, the distribution of which by the Orderly, him carrying his swinging buckets like a milkmaid, was carefully watched by Tom Miles, in case a swindling thumb found its way into the measure, but there was none. Miles held out his beaker for the pungent, dark brown liquid."

"Good luck, Tom. Come the finish, eh?"

"Thanks, mate. Come the finish!"

The dawn brought not only rum, but also thick fog and Picton's foul language could be heard from yards around, heard especially by his two Brigadiers. Finally, Picton gave a decision.

"What else, Colville, but to march straight down some small way? The ford's down there. Get them closer and then wait for orders!"

The sounds of vigorous skirmishing came from the direction of the town far over to their left, presumably at the bridge, as Picton lead his column forward, the three Regiments of Colville's all in column of Sections, around 20 men wide, the 5th Fusiliers in the lead. Satisfied with the small advance, he then halted. Mackinnon's Brigade remained on the ridge, also in columns a Section wide, but side by side, the 105th on the far right, now seeing nothing after the last Section of Colville's 94th had disappeared into the murk.

For Cornet Carr, deep within the leading 16th Light Dragoons of Erskine's column, it was also a trip into the unknown, the fog was so thick all around them. His Squadron was in the lead, with his Troop at the front, therefore he could see and hear all that took place in the leading group before him. Erskine, Slade and Arentschildt were the leading three, with his own Colonel, Major and four Captains just behind them. Erskine was in a very animated mood. He called a halt at a road which all assumed ran parallel to the river and turned to Arentschildt.

"Have those Light Brigades, Beckwith and Drummond, crossed yet?"

After a pause, Slade gave the only possible answer.

"Impossible to say, Sir. Apart from the fact that we can hear no sounds of combat from that direction."

Erskine flexed his fingers impatiently on the pommel of his saddle.

"We must cross at our ford, Drummond at his and Beckwith at his."

Now he began pounding the pommel.

"Where are we?"

Arentschildt looked at Slade in disbelief, whilst Erskine stared into the fog. Again, Slade answered.

"On the main road, Sir, about half a mile alongside the river, would be a reasonable guess."

Erskine nodded.

"Right! We go down and find our ford. If we cross, then Beckwith and Drummond must also. We can assume they are halted on this road if they've not already crossed. If they have, all well and good."

Erskine turned to Arentschildt.

"Who do you have? To send across to Beckwith. He is to lead and Drummond to follow."

Arentschildt could hold back no longer.

"Sir. Would it not be best to wait? At least for orders. Our Commander may have called everything off, owing to this damned fog! There's a whole French army over there, who knows what we may blunder into or even miss altogether and go marching off into the unknown."

Erskine's tone conveyed both his irritation and uncertainty.

"I asked who do we have?"

Resigned, Arentschildt turned to look behind him at the Officers of the 16th.

"A Senior Captain, Sir?"

Erskine was still staring forward, only half listening to the answer.

"Agreed. Send him."

Arentschildt looked at Tavender.

"Lucius, go along this road, back to Sabugal. If you see Colonel Beckwith, tell him General Erskine orders him to cross and advance as planned."

Tavender nodded and wheeled his horse left to then canter back along the road to Sabugal. After five minutes through the static fog he found Colonel Beckwith at the head of his own column, formed and waiting. Beckwith was sat his horse, as static as the fog, as Tavender rode up and saluted.

"I have come from General Erskine, Sir. He wishes to know why you have not crossed!"

Beckwith's mouth fell open in astonishment.

"And that's from General Erskine?"

"Sir."

"Has he crossed?"

"He was about to, Sir, when I left him."

"Tell General Erskine, if you can find him, that I am crossing directly. Colonel Drummond is behind me and will find his own ford upstream and cross there to my right, between me and General Erskine."

Tavender watched the first files of Beckwith's 43rd turn down the slope, then he pulled his horse away. After five minutes, he found himself with the 14th Light Dragoons, the last of Erskine's cavalry, all now moving towards the river. He rode to the head of the column to find a very exasperated Erskine, sat with the front hooves of his horse just above the water, his hands flexing constantly on the pommel of his saddle, his head turning both left and right. A Captain whispered to Tavender as he slowed his horse.

"We can't find a ford."

Tavender reined in his horse just behind Erskine.

"Sir!"

Erskine did no more than turn his head once and so Tavender continued.

"Sir. Colonel Beckwith is now crossing the river, with Colonel Drummond crossing further upstream from him and towards us. Sir."

Erskine did no more than flick a hand in Tavender's direction and so he returned to his Squadron. They sat for half an hour and then they heard the sounds of very heavy fighting from in front and to their left. Withers turned to Johnson.

"That's Beckwith and Drummond over there. All on their owny-oh, with us stuck over here, trying to find a way over to give support."

Then Captain Somers-Cocks returned and rode up to Erskine.

"Further downstream, Sir. We think it's practical."

Slade now spoke up.

"Sir, that's too close to the infantry. We'll not be able to get out beyond the French flank."

Erskine gathered his reins.

"Can't be helped. We have to cross. Lead on Captain."

The ride downstream along the bank began and within two minutes they were all making a slow passage through deep water, deep enough to reach and soak their horse blankets.

From their own position at the head of the 105th column, Lacey, O'Hare and Carr themselves listened to the sounds of ferocious combat, even though deadened by the fog. O'Hare looked at his watch.

"That's been going on now for over 30 minutes and all we've got over there is two Brigades of infantry and there's no way of telling if they're both engaged. It could be just one, against awful odds. And Picton'll not move!"

Lacey was hoping that he could see the backs of Colville's 94th who had disappeared forward some time ago, through the fog now slightly thinned, but he could see nothing.

"No! He won't. Not Picton. He'll want to, but he won't!"

Not so Erskine, who was now leading his men up the slope away from the river, which he decided must be the required direction. The more they climbed the louder the sounds of combat from their left. Erskine turned around in his saddle.

"Where's that Captain we sent to Beckwith?"

Tavender was called forward.

"Drummond was following Beckwith, you said. Correct?"

"Yes Sir, but not by the same ford. He should be between us and Colonel Beckwith, Sir."

"Very good. Ride over now and, if he is not already engaged, inform Drummond that he is not to support Beckwith, not, you hear, but to continue forward and get behind the French line."

Tavender saluted and rode off, in what he hoped was the correct direction, it was at least over to the left where Drummond should be. Then he was hit by driving rain which came as a heavy shower, but after some minutes, to his huge relief, he saw red uniforms appearing through the fog. He approached the nearest file.

"Who are you?"

A Corporal answered.

"The 52nd, Sir."

"Is Colonel Drummond leading?"

"Yes Sir, just ahead."

As Tavender cantered forward and the sounds of conflict redoubled from his left, he soon came up to Drummond at the front. At Tavender's arrival, Drummond turned from staring in the direction of the sounds of combat to study the new arrival.

"Where have you come from?"

"General Erskine, Sir. He's off to your right, by about half a mile, and his orders are that you do not engage with the combat that we can hear, but continue to march forward and threaten the French rear, Sir, by getting around their flank."

Drummond gave Tavender a blank stare.

"You may tell General Erskine that myself and my men will now march to the aid of the 43rd that we know are engaging the French and have been for some time and must be under some pressure. I will march to their aid and I am prepared to answer for the consequences myself, afterwards."

He turned away from Tavender and began shouting orders.

"Two Company front!"

Within minutes the veteran 52nd were in five double lines, one behind the other, each of two Companies, and one minute later they were marching forward into the fog behind their Colours. Tavender sat nonplussed until he found himself alone in the murk and then he turned his horse back to where he hoped General Erskine would be, by now. He heard shouting and turned his horse towards the sound. The sounds of hooves and harness grew louder and then he could make out riders and horses. He spurred his horse to the head of the column, to find, to his great relief, Captain Vigurs with his Squadron and he asked his anxious question.

"What are you doing here?"

"Erskine sent us off to scout. How we'll find him to get back and tell him what we find, God only knows!"

Tavender grew anxious.

"I'd better had. Drummond has refused Erskine's orders and gone off to join the fight. I'd better try and let him know."

"Indeed you had and good luck. I'll witness that you tried. Methinks our Erskine will not come out of this too well and there could be some questions. As for me, I think I'll head for the sound of guns myself. Must be something there worth scouting for."

With that, he spurred his horse on and waved his men forward.

Back on their ridge, Lacey could now only utter two words.

"Good God!"

The fog had suddenly risen like a theatre curtain and O'Hare and Carr were altogether uncertain as to the cause of Lacey's exclamation, either the speed of the fog rising or what he could now see on a hillock over to their right front. All three pulled out their telescopes to see one Battalion of Redcoats, with one of brown uniformed Portuguese Cacadores and four Companies of Rifles, all now mixed in, and perilously beset by greatly outnumbering French. They came from above them, from the hillock, and also came from their left what looked like fresh French reinforcements, these a count of seven Battalions. What was happening on the far side of the hillock was impossible to see, but what could be seen was sufficient to cause disquiet enough. Picton also had seen quite enough and was already in the ford, on his horse and waving his sword above his head, constantly yelling foul expletives. The 5th Fusiliers came on behind him, in a column one Section wide, narrow enough to cross the ford. Lacey watched briefly, he was more interested in, and anxious about, what was happening on the ridge, because the French were making changes. With the lifting of the fog the French Commander could see 10,000 men about to cross the Coa, 5,000 at the bridge and Picton's 5,000 now coming over the ford. To Lacey's great relief he must have given orders to the seven Battalions, who drew off from assaulting the embattled British and Portuguese on the hillock and then re-formed to face the oncoming Legions of Picton, these now advancing up the slope towards them. Mackinnon was stood with Lacey.

"Best cross, Colonel. Nae point remaining here!"

Lacey ran to the centre of his men, drawing, then raising his sword.

"Uncase The Colours! We're going forward!"

With all set, he led his men down the slope to the ford, now much churned up and reluctantly releasing muddy water downstream, all the result of the continuous passage boots worn by the advancing Redcoats.

Beyond the hillock, visibility was now almost perfect. Vigurs halted his men and took a moment to decide his next move. The 52nd, remaining in column of double Companies, were thoroughly engaged with the French, fighting at the hillock above Beckwith's Brigade. However, what looked like two Squadrons of French cavalry were closing on the right flank of the 52nd but being held off by their controlled volleys. He called up his two Cornets, Carr and Peterson.

"Peterson. Your Troop to lead. In line. Carr, yours behind and in line. Be quick!"

The Troop Sergeants had heard all and quickly orders were ringing out and men were urging their horses into position, each Troop in a double line. Vigurs waited until all was ready and then drew his sabre. This was the signal for all to do the same and it was Cornet Carr's first experience of the eerie scrape that came as all sabres left their scabbards. Baxter, realising the need for some encouragement, spoke from just behind Carr.

"Now's your chance to try out that fine sword of yours! Right, Sir?"

Cornet Carr turned to him and managed a weak smile, but now Vigurs was leading his men forward at the canter. At 100 yards' distance, they were finally noticed by the French cavalry, who had been too intent on the 52nd and only a small proportion then turned to meet them. At this point Vigurs stood up in his stirrups and raised his sword, to then let out a long shout.

"Charge!"

He regained his seat and crouched low, sword extending forward. His men took up the shout, which made young Carr feel quite intoxicated as he took up the cry himself. Petersen's Troop crashed into the French, the men fencing with their swords and doing little damage, but most of the impact on the French was inflicted by the 16th's superior horses, who barged into their French equivalents, sending many to the ground and their riders sprawling. Carr's men crashed into the melee with the same result, where he, now thoroughly hot-blooded, looked for an opponent and he saw a green uniformed Chasseur stood still in the midst of the conflict. Carr was lucky, he had come upon the Chasseur on his bridle hand, meaning that his sword was on the far side. Carr spurred his horse at him, rose in his stirrups and, before the man could bring his sword over, he crashed his own sword down onto the top of his shako. To Carr's astonishment, the blow only penetrated four inches and Carr's sword was stuck in the headgear which immediately left the Chasseur's head, the chin-strap having parted. The Frenchman was now wheeling his horse to get within distance to deal a blow of his own, when Baxter crashed his horse into the right flank of the Frenchman, just behind the horse's neck. The horse was hit left, and so the Chasseur was thrown over right, within range of Baxter's left hand, which seized the green tunic and dashed him to the ground. Baxter then wheeled his horse over the squirming body to leave him battered and incapable. For Carr, that ended the conflict, as it had for all. The French Light Cavalry, now charged from the side with such force, soon turned and made off back along the ridge. A Captain of the 52nd, blood issuing from a face wound, came over and offered Carr his hand.

"So glad you could join the party. We are wholly grateful, believe me."

He looked around.

"Seems were moving, following the French. Hope you can join us!"

Carr released the hand and nodded blankly, but Vigurs had the same idea as the Captain and, on a Troop front, they joined onto the right flank of the 52nd. Baxter came up beside Carr, just before they moved off.

"There's a lesson Sir. You couldn't get through a French shako with a hatchet. Go for cloth, every time."

Carr, now in a state of mild shock, nodded, but said nothing. Corporal Makepeace then handed him his sword, having levered it out of the Chasseur's shako, needing his foot to hold it down, before it finally came free.

At this moment, Elder Carr was now leading a wing of his own Regiment up the slope, five Companies in column, one behind the other, each on a double line Company front. The leading Company being Carravoy's Grenadiers, but no words were spoken between the two Officers and besides, speech was useless as the 5th Fusiliers poured volleys into the centre French Battalion. Colville's remaining two Battalions had swung leftwards to meet their own French opponents, meaning that the 105th would need to move up on the right of the 5th Fusiliers to meet the French line. As they were, their front would not be wide enough and so Carr doubled behind the Grenadiers to Company Two. He ran to their Captain, Reginald Charters.

"Reginald. Double yours up beside the Grenadiers."

As these increased their pace he came to the next Company to give the same order to their Captain.

"Double up alongside Two."

The 105th line was extending right, until he came to the final Company, which Carr led himself. The other wing of the 105th was already in action, led by Lacey and Heaviside. Soon the half Company volleys were pounding the French opposite and their line soon began to crumble. The 88th had come up on the right of the 105th and they gave one volley and then charged, emitting an unearthly howl. Lacey gave the inevitable order.

"Fix Bayonets!"

Firing ceased along the line as the bright and vicious weapon was drawn out of every belt sling and attached to the muzzle of every musket. Lacey raised his sword.

"105th! Follow me!"

A shout went up all along the line and the 105th surged forward. Heaviside turned and bellowed at his advancing Company.

"With God we shall do valiantly. It is He who will tread down our foes. Psalms 108. 13!"

His men heard but gave no reaction, their faces grimly set in the direction of the French, seen beyond the wicked points of their extended bayonets. Their opposing battalion, seeing their brother Battalion on their left broken and running before the 88th, soon did the same, leaving many dead and wounded remaining on the ground, caused by the 105th volleys. As his men pressed on, Lacey grew anxious.

"Keep the line, boys. Hold the line!"

His men strode forward, holding their line, with bayonets extended. Soon, they had crossed the ridge and were descending the far side. Half way down the slope they came to the French rear-guard, drawn up in line to face them, but at the sight of Picton's 5,000 men and more coming down the slope with every advantage, their Officers quickly ordered a withdrawal before either side could exchange any fire. Picton galloped along his line, sword raised, battle-madness full on his face and in his voice and words.

"On! Get onto them. Onto them, ye fighting villains! Whore's melt scum! Forward! Why do you wait? Don't let them stand."

After such a blandishment, his men surged forward again, holding their line and pushing to the lower slope. The French had stood again and at 100 yards, Lacey called a halt.

"Load!"

Many already were and came immediately to the 'make ready'. Lacey saw that the French were already pulling back, but all his men now stood with their muskets pointing upwards.

"Present!"

He counted two seconds.

"Fire!"

The first rank fired, then did the second with the three second gap, but the French were far back and few casualties were inflicted. Then it came on to rain, heavy and persistent, so heavy that visibility fell to little beyond 100 yards. Lacey held his men there as had the Colonel of every other Battalion of Picton's Division and they were soon proved wholly correct to do so. Lacey looked in the direction of Sabugal, his eye had caught the sight of a splendidly mounted and elegant Aide de Camp riding along Picton's line, secure from the rain in an expensive riding cape. He reined in at Lacey.

"This from Wellington himself, Sir. Halt the pursuit and return to the ridge."

"Which? Ours of this morning or the one we've just taken from the French?"

The Officer looked puzzled.

"Why the latter, Sir. The one you've just come down from."

He saluted and rode on, leaving Lacey to turn to Carr and O'Hare.

"Back up. Column of Sections."

The two ran off and soon, each Company in four ranks, they were marching back to the ridge above. Mackinnon came to join them and Lacey asked the obvious question.

"What now, Sir?"

"Make camp and let the men cook."

The mention of cook gave rise to the next question.

"Bring up the Followers?"

"Aye. Nae reason why not and they can help wi' the wounded."

Lacey looked around and saw a Captain, that of the Fifth Company.

"Michael. Get one of these horses that are loose and ride back to bring up the Followers."

The day wore on, as did the rain, now falling steadily on the 105th, all back on the French ridge.

The messes of Deakin and Davey all produced their pieces of dry kindling from their rucksacks, and managed to start a fire large enough to cook and boil, so a decent fire was available when their families arrived. Deakin was the last to arrive after his duties as Colour Sergeant and he immediately looked around at all the faces.

"Everybody alright? Where's Tom?"

Zeke Saunders looked up from cleaning his Baker rifle.

"Where'd you think? Him and Len both together."

Both these villains were at that moment harvesting the battlefield despite the rain, Miles going about his business under a very serviceable French Cavalry Officer's cloak, Bailey making do with a French greatcoat. Pickings were worthwhile, but less than good, as voiced by Miles.

"We didn't kill enough of the bastards! Too many got away."

Bailey looked up from rifling through an Officer's pack, having tipped all out onto the ground.

"And here come the scavengers from the town!"

Miles looked over to see tens and scores of Sabugalese and others, edging their way onto the battlefield, with much the same hopes that had brought Miles and Bailey onto it. Miles looked into his swag-bag.

"I'd reckon there's not much more gainin' from here and those bastard diddykites has the next plot over and they Portugee comin' up will be all over the rest. We ain't done too bad. I've got some coin, about two dozen buttons and a few other silver bits and pieces. You?"

"Bout the same, and brandy."

"That'll do. Best get back. Stew's not long off, I needs my portion and means to get my fair share."

Thus, was the day spent and with its end, they slept in the rain, under whatever form of shelter could be found, mostly French blankets and greatcoats. Dawn brought a dry day, but no orders came to move and Carr and Drake summed up the reason.

"Today's a day for the cavalry."

They were correct, however, this did not involve the 16th Light Dragoons, as conveyed to a group of its Officers by Colonel Arentschildt, who was pleased that Captain Vigurs was there.

"Owing to the glorious efforts of Captain Vigurs here, the job of finding the French today has been given to Colonel Slade and his Brigade."

Many grins in the direction of Vigurs, but Arentschildt had more.

"And by the way, under our Brigadier Erskine, we did do some good. My Hussars captured the private baggage of Generals Reynier and Soult. It was Reynier who commanded our opponents yesterday. I do believe it's all now with Stapleton-Cotton, but, for today, we rest. And drink!"

From his saddlebag, he produced two bottles of brandy and all rushed for their tin mugs.

The better night that then fell was followed by a day's march that tracked the French retreat and they overtook many signs of a beaten army, again this conclusion arrived at by Drake to Carr, but Carr had the supressing answer.

"Massena still has more than us, so I've heard, further up country. Sabugal was just to buy himself time to get his army back together after their long retreat from Santarem."

However, his men were in excellent spirits, seeing the French abandonments all along the road and especially so when they reached Alfayates, where Wellington himself watched them march past and, more to their liking, the locals threw them food; bread, sausage, oranges and wine, all to the cry of "Viva Ingleses!" This was all very much to the good, because their own supplies had failed; they had outmarched their supply lines again, which was evidenced when they left the village and there saw two Battalions of Portuguese slumped by the roadside. Saunders was the first to draw attention to them.

"What ails these?"

The cries of 'Comida, por favour", gave the answer. The Portuguese had no food at all. Their supplies from their own Government had completely failed. They were starving and could move no more, so they were

60

forced to remain there until supplies, hopefully, came up to them. Later that day, the subject and issue of rations brought renewed hostilities between Nellie Nicholls and Betty Barker. Once again Toby Halfway stood at the barrel and this time Mrs Barker made the correct call, obtaining a piece of salt pork not only of better quality than that called by Nellie Nicholls but also of superior size. Mrs Barker wasted not the opportunity to brandish the piece in Nellie's direction, which brought an Irish response from Nellie.

"Now, careful you don't spoil that good piece. Sure, I'm thinkin' the likes of a gobshite like you would not know one end of a spoon from the other! Nor a knife for the trimmin' off."

Luckily Nellie's husband, Henry, Sergeant of the Third Company was on hand to usher her away. Luckily, although both were at the rear for the marching column, the circumstances of the next day kept them apart within the group of Followers itself. Bridie and Nellie with all their children, were, as was their habit, walking beside the small cart carrying Chaplain Albright and driven by Chaplain's Assistant Percival Sedgwicke. As usual the conversation began with the issue of time and, as usual, from Nellie.

"For how long have we been on the road, now, Parson darlin'?"

Sedgwicke drew out his watch, the only item now that reminded him of his time as a country Vicar, given by his sister.

"Three hours, Mrs. Nicholls. Just over."

"So, how long does that give us to the Noon break?"

Sedgwicke looked down.

"Another two. Just under."

Then came the real subject.

"Have you any idea what's up ahead of here? For us? Is it a town with a decent billet or another night in the trees?"

"Well, Mrs Nicholls, I am no authority on such matters, but we are hearing that we are to prepare to man a picket-line before the French. Ahead are the big fortress towns of Almeida and Cuidad Rodrigo. We will be opposite them for some time and so I think you can reasonably expect a decent billet. At least for yourselves, but who knows what for your men; if we begin the likely sieges."

Bridie had been listening.

"Now that makes good sense, Parson, your Honour, but would that be tomorrow or the day after, now?"

Sedgwicke smiled down. In common with many, he had a deep affection for Bridie Mulcahy.

"As far as I can judge, Mrs. Mulcahy, I'd say the day after tomorrow."

That day came and the 105th, as part of Mackinnon's Brigade, found itself spread North-South along a ridge that centred on the village of Aldea do Obispo. The ridge sloped down before them to the course of the Agueda, now having flowed past Cuidad Rodrigo. Spring was gaining pace and the day was almost warm. Their first turn as picket came when a wing from each of Mackinnon's Battalions, five Companies of the 105th, with the same of the 88th, and the 74th, were all spread in a thick skirmish line along the ridge. Carr was stood with Major O'Hare.

"'Tis a fine day, Henry!"

Carr turned and smiled at his fellow Major, for whom he had the deepest liking and respect.

"It is and would you agree that, over to our right front, on the far horizon, is Cuidad Rodrigo?"

"I would and that's in Spain."

"Of less than happy memories!"

"True, so let's hope for better this time, when it eventually comes."

The fact that they were in close proximity to the French was made clear to them within the next five minutes. They were the furthest right of Mackinnon's pickets and fully across their front came a whole French Division, arriving up from their right, at first sighting, somewhat over half a mile due South. O'Hare pulled out his telescope.

"And what's their plan? Don't they know we're here?"

He passed the instrument to Carr who made his own observations.

"I count nine Battalions, all marching along as content as you please. Each on a double company front. We should send a runner back to Division."

O'Hare was looking left.

"That may be superfluous. Look right."

61

Carr did, to see a whole Brigade of cavalry, two Regiments strong, almost 800 men, galloping in the direction of the French, accompanied by a much more serious threat, a six-gun field battery.

"This is not going to be nice!"

The whole picket line stood to watch the unfolding events. The cavalry attacked first whilst the battery pulled ahead to unlimber and cover the future route. However, as the cavalry approached, within a minute the French were in Battalion squares ready to fend them off, which they achieved easily, the British cavalry being forced to withdraw and re-group. With that, the French quickly resumed their columns of double companies and marched on, but then they came under fire from the battery. However, the battery's round shot, which was all that could be used at that range, mostly combed harmlessly through the spaces between the ranks. The cavalry attacked again, and again the French formed squares to successfully fend off the attack, then the field guns tried again to again be almost nullified by the double company formation, for the same reason as before. Carr and O'Hare stood in admiration.

"Whoever is running that show, he damn well knows his business!"

O'Hare nodded.

"But my hat comes off to those soldiers who can change their formation that quickly."

Twice more the cavalry and field-guns tried, only to be frustrated twice more by the sheer professionalism of the French Battalions. Finally, they were left unmolested when the cavalry rode off to capture some baggage and inspect the very few dead and wounded of either side stretched on the ground. As for any more attention from the field-guns they were now beyond effective range. Then Carr and O'Hare had to turn and grin at the sound of their own men cheering. Many had grounded their weapons to applaud and clap, many had placed their shakoes on the muzzles of their muskets to raise them in the air. O'Hare laughed again.

"The mutual affinity of the foot sloggers, one to the other. I always thought that there was little love lost between the infantry and the artillery and cavalry. Now I know."

He studied the French again. They had either heard or seen the appreciation from the British ranks, for many had placed their own shakoes on their muskets in reply. He watched in great amusement until the French disappeared into the valley of the Agueda. O'Hare had the last word.

"I never thought I'd see the like and I needed to see it to believe it."

Their Relief came in the shape of the remaining wing of the 105th with Captain Carravoy in command. In a light-hearted mood, Carr spoke as they passed.

"You'll never guess what we've just seen Charles. Next chance I have, I'll tell you about it."

Carravoy did little more than salute as he passed.

"As you choose."

Carr did not react, he was in a good mood as was O'Hare and they spoke before they parted.

"Well, after that little entertainment, back to a decent billet and a more than halfway decent meal."

O'Hare nodded.

"I'll settle for that. Johnny's over his river and we're all snug sat around Almeida. Can't be long before he gives that place up, one way or another."

oOo

The less than welcome news reached the Officer Corps of the 105th via Brigadier Mackinnon, pleased to find all Captains and all ranks above sat in one room.

"We've received a visit from the House of Lords. They presented themselves at His Headquarters and now it's come down from above that they are tae be afforded every courtesy. The word is that they're here tae find out what we need, or more like what the Peer needs and they will do their best to provide it. However ineffective it may be, they must be given credit for that. They haven't spoken together yet, them and the Peer that is, but that will soon happen."

Lacey, the only one standing, asked his question.

'Do we know them?"

Mackinnon pulled out a piece of paper.

"Thought I'd better write the names down."

He found some spectacles.

"General Sir Henry Livermore. Lord Frederick Templemere, in charge, and Lords Mahon and Hopgood."

Mackinnon looked around.

"Anyone here? Have their acquaintance?"

Lacey was beaming.

"Livermore and I served together in the Americas. I hope we can meet."

Mackinnon beamed. Duty required him to be as welcoming to the Lords as possible. That was a good start.

"Anyone else?"

Carr raised his hand and it was clear that he was anything but pleased. Drake looked at him sympathetically, whilst Carravoy plainly relished Carr's discomfiture.

"All three are known to me, but for the wrong reasons. There's been a lot of dirty water under the bridge between me and those three. If it's all the same to you, Sir, I'd best keep out of their way. Little good can come from our meeting again."

Mackinnon became downcast.

"As ye choose Major. If you think it for the best!"

He pocketed his list of names.

"Right! Best get around tae the others."

As Mackinnon left, another meeting was assembling at Wellington's Headquarters in Freneida, the four of Templemere's party now climbing out of a carriage to be greeted by Wellington himself and his Senior Divisional Commander, Lieutenant General Sir Brent-Spencer. Introductions were made, handshakes exchanged and the four visitors were led by Wellington up a small flight of stairs to a gallery from which they entered a small room, already prepared with two chairs behind a desk with four arranged in front. The room was cool and low-ceilinged but clean with fresh whitewash and smelling of empty wine bottles. Wellington and Brent-Spencer sat behind the desk, whilst the others took their seats and Wellington sat forward to place his fingertips together, smiling pleasantly. He looked at Brent-Spencer, who was not, then he spoke to Templemere.

"Lord Templemere. How can we assist you?"

Templemere pushed across the same letter that he had presented to Livermore. Somewhat askance at the reply being merely a gesture, rather than the spoken word, Wellington looked at Templemere before picking up the letter and quickly reading it. He pushed it back to Templemere.

"My Aides have informed me of the contents of that and so I ask again, how can we help? What can we say that will help you fulfil your mission here?"

Temlemere had planned his questions carefully.

"As we speak, your forces are divided, are they not, between here and Estramaduria, namely Badajoz, to the South?"

Wellington sat back.

"You are well informed, Lord Templemere."

Templemere sat back.

"It pays to be! Now, I'm sure you appreciate that funds are limited. Whatever it is that needs doing and can be done, can only be done for one of your forces. Either here, or at Badajoz."

"That is most likely true, but as I'm sure you are aware, I am responsible for both, as Commander in Chief. You would allow me to choose. General Beresford is at Badajoz as we speak. Assistance for him may well tie up, or even draw away French forces from here, which would assist my efforts here."

"But your main effort will be here? At Cuidad?"

"It may be, it may not. I have my own sources of intelligence and, when these arrive, then I can make a better-balanced decision. I have my own Intelligence Officer still out there, beyond the Agueda and a very useful guerrilla character called Julian Sanchez. He's already cut off Cuidad from support from Salamanca and sends me all sorts of interesting stuff that he hears and intercepts."

"A balanced decision as to which area of operations you concentrate on, that is?"

"Yes, but surely you are here to find out what I need, rather than what I intend to do?"

Templemere interrupted.

"Surely, these are linked?"

"Not necessarily, Lord Templemere. What I need is a siege train. Tomorrow is Easter Sunday, before this year is out, I will be laying siege to both Cuidad and Badajoz, I hope. Which comes first, I do not yet know. Two, even three, dozen 24-pound naval guns will be much needed. Also, a Brigade of Pioneers, men skilled in the art of trench building, redoubts, revetments, roadbuilding and suchlike. At the moment, I have to rely on the good sense of my fighting infantry. If you can provide me with either or even both, then your mission here will have been more than accomplished."

Templemere was thwarted. That was an answer and a clear one, but Templemere had another dice to throw.

"Naval guns are easily obtained. Our Navy bases are full of them. So, if we obtain such, to which port should they be sent? Lisbon or Oporto?"

Wellington sat back.

"That also, as yet I cannot say. It may be that the circumstances facing Beresford afford a better opportunity. As we speak, I cannot say. He is already at Badajoz, whilst I am still some way off from Cuidad Rodrigo, with the French in between."

He stood up, wishing to end the interview.

"My Lords, here at this moment, that is the best answer I can give you."

He turned to Brent-Spencer.

"Unless you can add anything nor suggest an alternative?"

Brent Spencer shook his head.

"I cannot. My view is that you have the right of it. Sir."

Wellington turned back to Templemere.

"There you have it, my Lord, but I may be able to add a thing or two later. You have almost a week here, I understand?'

Templemere nodded.

"Good. During that time feel free to move amongst my men and go where you choose, but please, not too near the Agueda. The French are still sending patrols over and, Lord Templemere, I understand that you are on parole and the French may regard it as a breech if they find you back at the front!"

Templemere spoke through a clenched jaw.

"You are well informed, Lord Wellington."

"It pays to be! Now, refreshments are available downstairs and so, if you will allow me, I have army business."

All four stood and began to file out, but Wellington had not finished.

"Sir Henry! Could you stay for a moment? It has been some time."

Livermore returned to his seat as did Wellington and then Brent-Spencer produced a bottle of whisky and three glasses. He poured three measures in a silence which was not broken until they heard the last footfall on the stairs. Wellington pushed a glass towards Livermore.

"So, how did you come to be mixed up with those three jackanapes?"

Livermore drank the measure and then pushed the glass back for a re-fill.

"You saw the letter!"

When it arrived, this he sipped.

"So, do you have any plans?"

Wellington had drained his own glass and slid it across to Brent-Spencer for his refill.

"As far as any plans last for more than a week! I have some idea, strategic, you know how it must be, but I'm damned if I'm going to share that with that trio of pumped up fops!"

"And that was a serious answer? A siege train and pioneers?"

"It is, and if you could push for that, you will be doing me a great service."

Wellington took a drink from his own glass, then peered inside, unsure of the pedigree of the liquid, but spoke instead about his guests.

"Is that what they have in the House of Lords these days? One even had an ear-ring!"

Livermore laughed.

"Did you notice the scarring on Templemere's right cheek?"

"I did."

Livermore grinned.

"Put there by Carr."

Wellington's glass came down on the desk, loudly.

"Carr!"

"Yes. They fought a duel, back in the year five. Templemere accused him of cheating at backgammon, of all things. Carr resigned his Commission in the King's Royals to take him up. Carr won the duel, sort of, by cracking Templemere on the cheek with the pommel and then knocking him out by a punch with the bell-guard. He was black-balled by the King's Royals because of it."

At this, even Brent-Spencer started grinning. Livermore continued.

"That done, he came to me at Horse Guards wanting to re-join. I got him a place with the 5th Detachments, as the 105th then were. Best not to mention Carr in the presence of our Lord Fred."

Livermore then stood up and turned towards the door, leaving the pair still grinning.

"Right. I'd better get out and continue with their Lordships commands. Although I think I've already heard enough from what you said earlier. Be certain that'll do for me. Good day to you both."

The both were still grinning as Wellington drained his glass and Brent-Spencer returned the stopper. With that, Livermore left the room and the building, mounted his horse and rode off in the direction of Almeida to take a look at the provisions for a siege, now built all around what he had heard was a mighty fortress and about which he was immensely curious.

It seemed to Cornet Carr that the path he was on simply did nothing except get steeper and more perilous as they descended into the first reaches of the steepest, deepest gorge he had ever seen in his life. Craggy towers of rock rose up of the gorge below, their source remaining hidden further in the depths. Mercifully, as the path became worse, Vigurs called a halt.

"This'll do, we can see all from here. In fact, more from up here than going any further."

They all stopped, with their Squadron in line behind, to take in what could be seen before them. It was a veritable canyon and they had descended enough to see all the way down, where a narrow but well-built bridge spanned the gorge. Even from there, they could see the quality. It was Peterson who had the most classical appreciation.

"Roman. I'd say."

Vigurs nodded.

"Roman! Well good luck to those old lads who had to slog their way up here from that, wearing full armour and carrying their kit."

"Darius' mule!"

"What?"

"Darius' mule, invented by Emperor Darius. A sort of cross staff that they hung all their kit on, Sir. They didn't have back-packs like us."

Vigurs looked askance at him, his eyebrows together.

"Right! As you say. All I know, is that the French Division that crossed our front yesterday crossed over the river here and, did you know, there was a fearful set to here back before Busaco, last year. A Company of Rifles managed to hold off six times their number, down there, back in the March of that year.

They all studied the depths further, before Vigurs spoke further.

"This is the only crossing point downstream from Cuidad, apart from some very desperate fords, too close to Cuidad to be of any use for us. So, any Johnnies that come over at any point, are very, very likely to find themselves caught with this Agueda at their backs, if they stray too far from any crossing point."

Carr was now studying the track that led up the far bank, away from the bridge.

"Looks like someone's coming to take a look, Sir. On the track to here, opposite."

Vigurs looked and saw what had attracted Carr's attention, before using his telescope. On the track and all mounted, was a very well-ordered column of riders, almost military, were it not for the variety of their clothing. He passed over the telescope.

"I think we are about to have our first encounter with these so called Spanish Guerrillas. Best we wait and do the proper thing. Could be Johnnies in disguise!"

They did wait and watch, as the column crossed the bridge and began the ascent, all now being forced to dismount and lead their horses up in single file. It was over fifteen minutes before the first figure emerged from around the nearest hairpin bend. This man saw them stood waiting, but he came confidently on, breathing hard from his climb, but nothing like exhausted. In fact, he had enough breath to turn and shout behind him.

"Mateo! Acqui!"

A bespectacled, academic figure appeared around the bend and hurried forward, pulling his own mount.

"Les cuento que estamos."

The figure overtook the leader and came up to Vigurs.

"Good mornings. We are the Lancers of Castille and this man, here, is Julian Sanchez, our Commandante."

The leader, hearing his name, bowed slightly in his saddle, whilst swinging his right arm out to the side in a gesture of obeisance. He never took his eyes from the British Officers and what drew their attention away from the proud moustache, were the fierce eyes above and the mouth set tight below, as though humour never caused any change nor indication of mood. However, now he turned towards his interpreter.

"Digales por que estamoes acqui."

The interpreter nodded before turning back to Vigurs.

"We are here because we have news of the French, where they are. Also, we need supplies. Food and ammunition."

Vigurs looked at his two Cornets.

"We can't just let them ride through. And they might get lost."

The interpreter had heard all.

"You just tell us the name of the village you want us to get to, and we will find it, Senor. Up there is Barba del Puerco. No?"

Vigurs had decided.

"I hear what you say, but we will take you to the best place for you to conduct your business with us. We have a Headquarters nearby."

He turned to Carr.

"Go with these as escort to Aldea. Picton's there, he'll know what to do."

"Not Gallegos, Sir? That's where our Erskine is."

"No, that'll not serve. He'll probably have them all locked up and questioned before he does a thing. Assuming he's woken from his afternoon nap, that is. You heard that a French supply convoy got into Cuidad because he was too damn slow to react. These Spanish are the genuine article. What they know, the Peer will want to know soonest. Douglas' Troop can stay here with me, continuing the picket."

Carr saluted.

"Very good, Sir. I'll turn mine around."

With that he rode off, leaving Vigurs to address the interpreter.

"That Officer will guide you to our General Picton. Your mission will best be taken on from there. That's the best place. Good luck to you all."

The man beamed.

"Mucho gracias, Senor!"

He turned to Sanchez.

"Ellos nos guiaran a General Picton en la Aldea. El puede ayudar con lo ques necesitamos. El nos desea buena suerte."

Sanchez nodded.

"Bien! Mucho gracias, Senor."

He led his men forward and past, with no more than a nod in the direction of Vigurs, despite having been wished good luck by him. Then, his Troop came up, all hard-eyed men, grimly guiding their mounts up and past with not one sideways glance at the stationary British. Closed, blank faces told their own story; mercy did not come easily into the thoughts of such as these.

Lord Templemere was now in somewhat of a quandary. Wellington had given him a good answer with which he could satisfactorily return home and report to the House. On the other hand, he had gained little in relation to the gold bars that he wished to earn. His only justification for remaining was that he was there for some more days and perhaps there would be something more to be gained that was useful, by way of his House of Lords' quest. Perhaps gained by looking around and talking to those who may have an informed opinion or even some useful knowledge, especially old acquaintances. Therefore, to this end he was riding to the picket lines of his old Regiment, the 16th Light Dragoons, specifically to find Captain Lucius Tavender. However, on arriving at their camp, the first Officer he came upon was Captain Somers-Cox, stood feeding his horse himself, with some rather suspicious hay. He did not notice Templemere walking his horse up.

"Vaughan!"

Somers-Cox turned from his hay forking.

"Good Heavens! Templemere! We heard you'd been paroled, yet here you are. Here!"

Templemere nodded, a confident smile on his face.

"Yes, well, that's all by the by, now. I'm here as Chairman of a House of Lords mission, of which you may have heard."

"Yes, we've heard!"

Somers-Cox continued his pleasant expression, trying not to think of the reaction of Colonel Withers on hearing the news, "Damn well keep him out of my way".

"You'll be looking for Tavender?"

"Yes!"

"His Squadron are at the far end. Best try there."

With neither a nod nor a thank-you, Templemere urged his horse on, leaving Somers-Cox to stand and silently agree with the verdict of his Colonel. Templemere rode on, acknowledging no-one who recognised him, until he came to the lines of what was clearly the final Squadron. He stopped when he came to the first NCO, whom he recognised.

"Shelby!"

"Sir!"

Sergeant Shelby spun around, came to the attention and saluted, then realised his mistake, he was looking at a civilian, but the face was familiar. He relaxed as the newcomer spoke.

"I'm Lord Templemere. I was a Captain with you. I'm looking for Captain Tavender."

Shelby pointed behind him. He felt no inclination to exchange any pleasantries.

"He'll be in one of those tents there, my Lord, but I cannot say which one."

Again, with no acknowledgment, Templemere urged his horse on. Once at the tents indicated, Templemere motioned for a Trooper to come and take the reins of his horse, which he did, somewhat reluctantly, him not really understanding why he should, whilst Templemere dismounted.

"I am looking for Captain Tavender."

The Trooper still holding the reins, pointed to the horse-lines.

"Last time I saw him, he was up there, Sir. Looking after his horse."

The description puzzled Templemere, but he made the short walk to find Tavender piling unpleasant looking fodder for his own horse. Templemere approached to mere feet before calling attention to himself.

"Lucius!"

Tavender looked around and immediately ceased his hay piling.

"Templemere! We heard that you'd arrived and I can't say that I'm surprised at you wandering over. You have some mission, we understand?"

Templemere ignored the question.

"Why are you feeding your own horse?"

Brought back to the subject, Tavender forked some more material within muzzle range of his mount.

"Because up here, on this damn plain, it's all we can do to keep them alive. There's no grazing, just dead grass and old hay from the abandoned farms, so, if you want your own horse to get a share, you have to do the job yourself. Mounts are dying every day! We've lost most of the spares."

Templemere pulled a face.

"Sorry to hear that, but I was hoping that you could help with the reason why I am here."

He had carefully rehearsed the next words.

"We are here, us Lords that is, to find out what Wellington wants and needs and where. He's got forces both here and down at Badajoz."

Tavender ceased his piling.

"And you expect him to know! If you ask me, I'd say he's making it all up as he goes along. Damn Sepoy General!"

Templemere was taken aback by so negative an answer, but he hoped for more if he could get Tavender to talk further. He must have some intelligence about the army's situation and so Templemere continued.

"Well, he's mentioned a siege train but, when we get it, where will he want it? Surely that's important. I mean, he may want a dock improved or something similar, to get such as that unloaded. At Lisbon or Oporto, but the man won't give any kind of answer."

Tavender stopped and leaned on his pitch-fork, but said nothing, therefore Templemere continued some more, with what was a basic untruth.

"For the House of Lords, 'where' is as important as 'what', if we are to get things going."

"As I say, I doubt he knows himself, but one thing that may force him to choose Cuidad to receive his siege train, is the simple fact that he has twice as many men up here, as down South. 40,000 here, 20,000 with Beresford. And half of those down there are Portuguese. God only knows how they'll conduct themselves. There'll be a battle here before any siege work starts to take Cuidad, because Massena's regrouped over the border. Beresford's just down there to try his luck with Badajoz, top drawer strategy that! Wellington won't send men off to reinforce Beresford, which means leaving less than 40,000 to face Massena up here in the North and he won't go down there himself with more men to try anything different, because it includes the risk of not being in charge when things kick-off, up here, and you don't get much change out of two weeks to march a force down South. It's too big a risk. Three or even two Divisions caught marching on the road when Massena advances and so no use either here or down at Badajoz, would be a disaster. Even he can work that out!"

Within himself Templemere jumped for joy, that was a key fact. He pulled a silver hip flask from his pocket and passed it across.

"A drop of proper French. Not the acid they give to their own."

Tavender unscrewed the top and drank.

"Where now? For you?"

Templemere regained the flask.

"Well, if we are talking siege trains, I would suppose that I must go and talk to the artillery. Could you give me a pointer?"

Tavender shouldered his pitch-fork and walked towards the Officer's lines and so Templemere followed.

"They're up at Almeida. Get on the road you used to come down here and just ride back up. Keep going and you cannot miss it. A huge place, surrounded by our men."

Tavender walked on. Templemere now caught up and Tavender looked at him, his face grim, before speaking.

"There's more."

"What?"

"We have a younger Carr with us now. A Cornet and our despised Major Carr's younger brother."

Tavender looked at Templemere to gauge his attitude and saw that his face bore an even more irritated scowl, as Templemere mused over the situation.

"A Cornet, you say. The youngest is often the most cossetted."

Then Templemere paused, as if for thought, before delivering his verdict.

"But often in dire danger are Cornets, as we both know, pity if something were to happen to him. It would depress the whole family, I should say. Carr and that wife of his, she who turned you down to marry him. Whatever, we are all subject to the fortunes of war and we must all take our share of the dangers thereto, even Cornet Carr."

Templemere paused again before fully speaking his mind.

"We both have a score to settle with that family, don't we?"

Tavender turned to look at him, but said nothing on the subject and now they had reached the Officer's tents.

"As I say, keep to the main road and you'll get there."

He halted at the first tent, but did not offer his hand, instead he leant on the pitchfork.

"Good day and good luck."

Templemere appreciated that there had been no invitation to spend some time with his old Regiment, for dinner or anything, but he was unconcerned. He was now eager to return to his own quarters, his quest satisfied, or so he felt. He now had enough to give to the Friar, even if it did not come directly from Wellington himself. After all, thinking about this intelligence gathering business, a clear answer from the Allied Commander-in-Chief was more than that Michael Granger and his French masters could expect. What he had, they would have to make do with and if not, then they could withhold the rest of the gold bars. He was well up in the stakes with the three that he already had. He mounted and rode North at a fast trot and after some minutes he saw a column of infantry crossing the road going down into the valley of the Dos Casas, the stream that ran through the village of Fuentes de Onoro, the centre of the British position. He noticed that they had the lurid green cuffs and facings of the 105th and perhaps a pointed exchange with Carr would add to the day's work, but him he did not see and, in any case, he was well satisfied with the outcome of this day. Visiting Almeida could wait until tomorrow.

The subject of Templemere's thoughts was at that moment leading his Regiment past the Fuentes de Onoro Church, the highest building in the village and he was now far enough past it to see the village itself, much further down the slope. He shook his head, it was like no village he had ever seen before. It looked to be little more than piles of carefully placed rocks and boulders, with little to distinguish the appearance of the walls and stock pens from the houses themselves, all being made of carefully crafted, but wholly irregular, natural stone. However, if there had been care in the placing of the stones to make the structures, there seemed to have been little care in their positioning. The village itself was a maze of small alleyways and cul-de-sacs, a random tangle of walls, paddocks and store-houses, but the villagers themselves had not deserted their homes and had made the Redcoats welcome with wine, cheese and bread, all these now sat in the open air, contentedly indulging in the fresh food. Soon all the 105th were placed within the village and setting up their mess areas as best they could. The Officers went back to the Church, whilst the men made good use of the barns, sheds and hovels, their mess-fires adding to the smoke issuing from the village chimneys, each of these very solidly built, as though to serve as a look-out tower. It was not long before Ellis arrived at the mess-area of Deakin and Davey, for once looking cheerful to the point of happiness, as he placed himself in the centre.

"I've got someone here that I've a mind you'll be pleased to see!"

All heads soon turned to the figure that was just behind him, this a female form carrying a bundle, and the first to recognise the newcomer and jump up was Bridie Mulcahey.

"Eirin!"

Bridie immediately had her arms around her daughter, closely followed by Nellie and then came the Mulcahey children, all wanting to touch their sister. It was not a minute before the top of the bundle was pulled aside to reveal the face of an infant, asleep and evidently very healthy, which fact immediately occupied the thoughts of all stood around, as Eirin displayed the sleeping babe. The men made no move, content to study and be amused by the tight-knit, chuckling and cooing group, knowing that, in any case, they could not gain a sight of the child until the women had finished. Finally, Jed Deakin stood up.

"What's the name you've given, Eirin?"

The group split apart so that Eirin could walk towards him.

"Jedediah. If you've no objection, Uncle Jed?"

Shock and surprise came to Deakin's face and he soon needed to pass the back of his hand across his left eye, in case any should see the tear that was forming there. He shook his head, whilst nodding at the same time.

"Why no, girl! 'Tis your infant, and, and ...."

He then ran out of appropriate words, but Zeke Saunders had thought of some.

"Well, now that makes you a Grandfather, Colour-Sergeant!"

Laughter came from all around which further discomfited the good Deakin, but he soon recovered.

"John's just over there."

The 'John' in question was not Davey, but Byford, who was, strictly in the eyes of the Church, her lawful husband. Byford stood, to him good manners required it and Eirin went over to him. Byford held out his arms to take the child and Eirin passed him over. Byford smiled down at both Mother and child, but Eirin could not meet his eyes, which fact was not lost on either Bridie or Nellie.

The following day, all remained at peace, particularly in the village of Fuentes de Onores which now housed both the 105th, the 74th Scots and also the three Companies of the 60th Rifles of the Third Division. Mackinnon's 88th were at the top of the village, with just enough distance between them and the 105th Light Company to prevent any strife, which suited the mess of John Davey perfectly, Tom Miles specifically. Carr was supervising the fortifying of the walls and houses that were immediately adjacent to the Dos Casas, at that time of year now a significant river, flowing along the Eastern, French, edge of the village. The whinny of a horse drew his attention and he saw both horse and rider stationary at the ford there. The rider he soon recognised as Sir Henry Livermore and Sir Henry soon noticed him. Carr went over and saluted.

"Sir!"

Livermore peered down with some measure of approval, but nothing too obvious.

"Carr. I trust I find you well. And congratulations on your Majority. After Corunna was it not?"

"Yes Sir. It was."

Livermore peered forward, then he used a telescope.

"Who's out there?"

"Our Light Company, Sir, and two Companies of Rifles. A third Company of the Rifles and that of the 74th are held in reserve, back here, Sir."

"Can they see the French?"

"Sometimes, Sir, but mostly cavalry patrols."

Livermore shut his telescope.

"Hmmm. Right, tell me where your Colonel is. Time we renewed acquaintance. We were in the Colonies together."

"You probably passed it, Sir. The Church at the top. All Officers are in or around there, and our Headquarters also."

Livermore turned his horse.

"You know Templemere's around."

"Yes Sir, I've heard."

Smiling slightly for the first time, Livermore rode off.

The other subject of his amusement was at that moment approaching Almeida, dismounting from his horse at a revetment, this manned by Riflemen of the 95th. As Templemere arrived, some were returning from duty closer to the walls. He waited to hear a Sergeant question his returning men.

"Did you down any?"

"One, Sarn't, and perhaps wounded another, but they let loose their big guns at us. Grape! We had to take cover."

"Anyone wounded?"

"Ben. Got one that scored down his back!"

The Sergeant became immediately angry, slapping his left hand to his side.

"Another wounded and one dead yesterday. Sending us out there to shoot the bloody cows belonging to that place is costing us men!"

He looked along the group.

"Well done lads, but I'll pass this on."

Templemere walked forward to peer over the earthwork, to the consternation of the Riflemen, them seeing a civilian so exposed and, more importantly, attracting enemy fire in their direction.

"Sir, that's dangerous. They loose off their heavy guns at anything they see."

Templemere saw no reason to conform to the advice from so lowly a source and he remained standing to observe what was before him, seeing a low, squat wall pierced by many gun embrasures and a large French flag flying from the Cathedral within. He remained there but attracted no fire, concluding that the French could not be bothered to load one gun to fire at a single figure wearing a top hat. He turned to the Riflemen.

"Perhaps not today!"

The men nodded in acknowledgement, but scowled as he walked away, for him to then steer a course towards another revetment further back, only this was manned by artillerymen. He went straight up to the Officer.

"I am with the House of Lords' party. Perhaps you have heard of us?"

The Officer saluted.

"Yes Sir."

Templemere looked towards the fortress and thought it best to begin with some cheerful small talk.

"Much happening today?"

"No Sir, not really. This is Easter Sunday and I'd say it matters more to the Frogs than it does to us."

"Hmmm, despite their Revolutionary habits."

Templemere allowed a pause, whilst he smiled at the Artilleryman as amiably as he could, then he began.

"Do you have the calibre of gun to tackle such a place?"

The artilleryman shook his head vigorously.

"No Sir. Nothing like. We're here to starve the place out, Sir. I suspect they have bigger guns in there, than we have out here."

"We're hearing that a siege train may be useful. What are your thoughts?"

"Absolutely, Sir. Sooner or later we'll be tackling Cuidad. If we beat Massena badly enough in the forthcoming battle that would force him back to Salamanca."

Templemere studied the man, then placed an ingratiating smile on his face.

"So this, you would say, is the main area of operations? Here in the North.'

"I'd say so, Sir. Yes."

"And the siege train could land at Oporto?"

"It could, Sir. Easily. They have docks there with heavy tackle for loading large wine barrels. That's its main purpose, trading in wine."

Templemere grinned openly, took one last look at Almeida, smacked his riding crop against his boot in delight and re-mounted his horse. He had enough; his conclusion of the previous day was confirmed, and what did the French want, a signed letter of confirmation from Wellington himself? He cantered back to his quarters in Freneida to find Mahon and Hopgood drinking wine as poured by a local girl, whom both were trying to maul at any point of her person within reach, were it not for the fact that she was too alert, supple and quick with an iron spoon, which she had learnt to bring with her. Templemere ignored the pair, went straight to his room and wrote the letter. He had no sealing wax and so he flattened the paper, wrote 'Para Frade Estaves' on one side and then further established the creases. He opened his jacket and shirt to place the letter carefully inside. It was approaching Noon, but food could wait, he would deliver the letter immediately. He left his room just as luncheon was arriving, carried by the girl's Mother. Also arriving was Sir Henry Livermore and the two passed at the entrance to their dining room where Templemere was spotted by Lord Hopgood.

"Fred. Lunch's here. Come and have some!"

However, Templemere had thoughts only for his mission.

"Perhaps later. Later."

He hurried away, his back being studied by Livermore, who heard Mahon remarking.

"Funny! Not like Fred to turn his back on good food."

All three sat, to hear the sound of Templemere's horse's hooves as he hurried away. Mahon spooned out the fish stew, whilst Hopgood looked longingly at the girl, which fact went not unnoticed by her Mother, who was bringing in bread and, in the doing of this, placed herself between them both, but Mahon spoke further.

"Wonder what's got into him?"

Livermore wondered also, but perhaps more suspiciously. What could be so urgent about their mission that could not wait until the cool of the late afternoon?

Templemere had over an hour's ride ahead of him, which he set about at a fast canter. He took the road North, back to Almeida, which took almost an hour before he turned off when he saw the wreck of Fort Conception, blown up by Crauford the previous year. This was his guide to Barba Del Puerco and, in some haste, he passed the tragic, wrecked bastions to take the road North. All was going well, when he saw a column of British cavalry coming towards him from the opposite direction. It would be suspicious to leave the road and so he rode on, intending to brazen it out. The cavalry turned out to be a Squadron of the 1st Dragoon Guards led by their Brigadier and Colonel, Sir Henry Slade and it was he who halted the column on noticing Templemere riding towards him. Templemere was forced to halt.

"Sir. My Lord. What are you doing out here? It really isn't safe. We're out on picket because Massena regularly sneaks men across, two's and three's, to see what we are about. Especially what is happening at the fortress, as those we capture tell us."

He studied Templemere, very concerned.

"It isn't safe!"

Templemere sat back in his saddle, adopting his most confident pose.

"You may be right, Colonel, but I was cavalry once myself, you know. I think I learned enough to keep out of trouble. I'm just taking the chance to take a look at the ground, as it were, before we take ourselves away and back to England."

He stood up in his stirrups.

"Is that Johnny land over there?"

He pointed to across the valley.

"What's that village over there, on the horizon?"

Slade did not need to look.

"San Felices, from where Massena sends out his scouts."

Templemere sat back.

"Well, I'm inclined to take a look. That's what I'm here for. You've heard of our mission here?"

Slade nodded, his face careworn at the thought.

"Yes Sir, I have, and if you must go on, then I must give you an escort."

Templemere shook his head.

"No, no, absolutely not! There's no need."

Slade shook his head.

"I'm sorry my Lord, but I must insist. You have met us now and think of the scandal if you were to be taken or killed and I had seen you and allowed you to ride around here, this dangerous place, without so much as a single man as escort. They'll not get in your way, Sir, and they know the way. You'll not get lost. I'll give you four men."

He turned to his nearest Captain.

"Tell off four of yours to accompany his Lordship here."

Whilst the Captain called out names, Templemere knew that any further argument would look suspicious because Slade was absolutely correct. Besides, he felt confident that he could shake off the four when the need arose.

"Very well, Colonel, I cannot argue with the sense of what you say. I'm told that this place Barba del Puerco is the crossing point between us and them. It's there I wish to take a look."

With no more words, he swung his horse to the right of the column and rode past. The column moved off with a clatter of hooves and harness, then he was on his own, but soon hearing the sounds of his four escorts close behind when they caught up. A village appeared over the many stone walls, at which point he slowed his horse to a walk, allowing the Sergeant to close up.

"Is that Barba del Puerco?"

"It is, Sir."

Templemere nodded and urged his mount on. Remembering the words in the letter, 'a Chapel alongside a track that leads to a Roman Bridge deep in the chasm', he looked over to the right where the chasm obviously was and, to his relief, he saw that the Chapel was quite prominent on the edge of the village, above where the slope evidently began. He continued on to where the road entered the village and stopped, with his escort just behind.

"Does this place not have an inn of some sort Sergeant, where I can treat you all to a glass of something, whilst I take a bit of a look around?"

"It does, Sir, but that would be against our orders, Sir. 'Twas only yesterday we caught a couple of Frenchers dressed as peasants comin' up the slope. They'd crossed by the rocks, Sir, not needing the bridge. Orders are to stay with you, Sir. At all times."

He paused.

"If anything happened to you it would cost me my stripes, Sir, and a dozen on the triangle."

Such an argument could not be countered. Templemere could only nod and turn his horse onto the track that led past the Chapel and down into the chasm. He rode far enough down to enable him to see the bridge and then halted, not so much to admire the view, as to think of a way to get into the Chapel alone. Finally, the sheer scale of the view forced its way into his thoughts and also the presence of the Sergeant alongside him.

"So that's Johnnyland, over there!"

"It is, Sir, but he hasn't got things all his own way. The Guerrilla characters dispute everywhere, we often hears sounds of combat and find bodies, all messed up, of both sides, floating down the river."

"So, things are pretty vicious over there?"

"Yes Sir. This is a very nasty war. Sir."

Templemere turned his horse back to begin the ascent. He was close to abandoning his mission, when, seeing the Chapel, came the idea that would salvage everything. He turned in his saddle to see the Sergeant.

"We return to England soon, Sergeant. Perhaps tomorrow. I was raised a Catholic and I think it right that I say a prayer in there, before we leave."

"Very good, Sir. I'll just sit at the back."

"No Sergeant, that I do not want. I prefer to make my devotions alone."

"Very good, Sir, but I'll need to take a look first. Could be a couple of Frencher scouts hiding in such a place."

They both dismounted and entered the small Chapel. It was small, old and now somewhat uncared for. Dust showed on most surfaces, the floor was dirty and the smell was an unpleasant combination of damp, unwashed bodies and powerful incense. The Sergeant strode up the short aisle to the only place where anyone could hide, which was behind the altar, where he took a look and then returned.

"I'll leave you to it then, Sir. Your prayers. We'll be just outside. Say one for the lads, if you would, Sir."

Templemere ignored him and walked up to the altar and sat on the front pew, this cleaner than most. When he heard the door close behind him, he rose, looked back at the door to check, then at all the windows, then, now content with seeing no-one, took himself behind the altar. There was a small recess with a shelf, built into the back. He unbuttoned his jacket and shirt, extracted the letter and placed it carefully on the shelf, writing upwards. Excitement welled up in him; what an adventure, to be so fully bound up in such events and such fulsome payment for so small a risk. He buttoned his clothes and returned to the pew to sit and while away the time that should lapse for anyone at prayer. The silence closed in on him, but his thoughts were far away at the Templemere estate, considering how to spend the money that would come from the gold bars. Suddenly the door opened and the Sergeant came half way in.

"We should be getting back, Sir. Evenings coming on and 'tis some way back to our lines."

Templemere stood and was more than content to now leave. The Sergeant held the door open.

"Finished your prayers quickly then, Sir."

Templemere was puzzled.

"How do you mean?"

"Well, you was back sitting down. Me and the lads, Sir, in Church, says our prayers on our knees."

Templemere was somewhat taken aback.

"Oh, yes. Well, I'm sure you do, but I took a moment for quiet contemplation, you understand."

"Very good, Sir, just as you say."

Both mounted their horses and turned them West towards the lowering sun. "Was there anything in that?" Templemere thought. "No, couldn't be!"

oOo

Mackinnon hurried from Wellington's Freneida Headquarters at his best speed, the words of an incandescent Brent-Spencer assaulting his ears, even across the corridor and out through the windows. Lacey and Wallace, his two Senior Colonels, were waiting for him.

Wallace asked the question.

"What's got Spencer into a lather?"

"Erskine's allowed another convoy into Cuidad! Nothing less than being plain slow tae react tae the news that one was on its way. When it arrived and he had the chance tae intercept, he refused tae send a force over the Agueda fords and they all just sat and watched the Frogs file in."

All three mounted their horses as Mackinnon continued.

"It's a blessing The Peer took himself down tae Badajoz yesterday. Tae take a look, but I wouldn't give a rat's backside for Erskine's chances of keeping the Light Division when he gets back. Brent-Spencer will give it tae Crauford and move Erskine somewhere. The Peer will confirm and no give it back!"

He urged his horse forward.

"One blessing though. Their Lordship's mission has gone home. Early! They're off our back, having heard enough, so I hear. Siege guns and pioneers they're going away with, so let's hope. Both would be a boon tae us, and that's a fact"

Once at Fuentes de Onoro, Wallace parted from their company and the remaining two continued down to the river, to find Carr and the Captains of the occupying Companies staring across it, listening to the sounds of combat. Mackinnon looked down at Carr.

"Who's out there, Carr?"

"The 88th Lights and Number Three Company of the Rifles, Sir. Captain Riley of the Rifles in command. I must say that sounds some way off, Sir. It may be cavalry, we see a lot of both theirs and ours. The Light Division is far out on our right front, Sir, beyond our men. I saw General Crauford ride out with them."

Mackinnon turned to Lacey, stood nearby.

"He's got his Lights now, and perhaps he's let some of his men out of their band-box, eh, Lacey?"

Lacey managed a small smile.

"That may be, Sir. If I know the Light Division, they'll not be too impressed with any kind of lid closing over them."

That evening, not ten miles from the Officers of the 105th dining on salt beef and Spanish beans, Massena sat with his Corps Commanders, Reynier, Loison and Drouet at a table replete with roast saddle of mutton and fresh vegetables, to be washed down with a very acceptable Spanish wine brought from Salamanca. The main topic of conversation was the content of Templemere's letter, now translated and transcribed into four copies. The meal finished, Massena gave his orders, for three Couriers on good horses to ride, using different routes, to Navalmoral where existed General Godinot's Brigade of almost 4,000 men. They were to march to join Soult for his advance on Badajoz, to swell his army to 24,000.

A week later Wellington, now returned from Badajoz, called his own meeting of his Divisional Commanders, including Picton. There was no hospitality of any kind and soon Picton was calling his own Commanders to Fuentes de Onoro to forewarn them. He was brief and to the point.

"The Peer's got intelligence that the roads from Salamanca are blue with French columns. Massena's coming forward with the aim of relieving Almeida. Prepare your men, we'll be trying conclusions with M'sieu within a few days. Fuentes is our pivot and must be held at all costs."

Whilst Picton was preparing his men for battle at the vital village, Wellington, alone with Brent-Spencer, was poring over a translation of an intercepted despatch, the original somewhat stained with blood. He passed it to his companion who immediately adorned his face with a monocle before reading the translation. That done he looked at Wellington and passed the letter back.

"It speaks of reliable intelligence being obtained, giving details and numbers about us. From where? How did they come to their conclusion, that we're making our main move up here?"

"Who can say? I certainly cannot. Pass it onto Colonel Waters will you. This is a puzzle for him to solve."

"Waters of Intelligence?"

"The same."

Brent-Spencer pocketed the letter, then returned to the main subject.

"4,000 men extra men going down against Beresford. Will he hold?"

Wellington looked worried.

"He'll have to. He's beyond our help, and we've Massena's hordes to contend with up here. There's plenty enough on our plate!"

At that moment Godinot's men were two days into their march. Two of Massena' couriers also marched with them to join Soult, the third was now a naked, headless corpse hanging from a tree, suspended from his ankles nailed to a suitable branch with the still smouldering remains of a fire beneath the mutilated body.

oOo

Chapter Three

"Had Boney been here, we'd have been beat!"
Lord Wellington after the battle of Fuentes de Onoro

"So, what can you see?"

The fourth word was heavily emphasised, spoken whilst the two Officers both used their telescopes to study events playing out almost a mile before them. All events were taking place out beyond the Dos Casas, this river adding its own sounds to the tense scene, as it surged between the stones of the ancient narrow clap bridge, standing alongside the main ford that led into the village of Fuentes de Onoro. Carr had been quickly able to focus his instrument, but his companion, always requiring spectacles, was experiencing some trouble with the same task. Carr took the time to study further, whilst his companion decided to now try without spectacles, but only after cleaning the lenses of both scope and spectacles with a huge blue handkerchief. Carr's companion was Colonel Thomas Williams, a Lieutenant-Colonel of the 5/60th Loyal Americans and the commander of a substantial force pushed forward into Fuentes de Onoro by Wellington himself, consisting of the Light Companies of six Brigades, British, King's German Legion and Portuguese, with the Battalion of the 2/83rd, minus its own Light Company, in reserve further up and back towards the Church. After the pause, Carr felt able to answer, because the strong Allied picket, a mile out before them, could now clearly be seen, falling back before a strong French advance.

"It looks like the whole of the Light Division is coming back in, Sir. In good order, I hasten to add."

His telescope now better focused, Williams felt better able to judge for himself.

"No need to add that, Major, now that Crauford's returned and back in charge."

He studied further, now that all was much clearer.

"A slow withdrawal, would you not say, Major?"

"I would, Sir, Crauford's making them pay for every yard."

"Again, Major, no need to add that, not in the case of Crauford! So, in your judgement, how long before they are back with us?"

Carr still had his telescope up to his right eye.

"I'd say 30 minutes at the absolute earliest. More like an hour. They seem to be almost enjoying themselves, Sir."

Williams gave a snigger. He could see for himself the smooth fall-back of each of Crauford's Battalions, both Redcoats and Rifles, to quickly reform behind the holding Battalion and open fire at the advancing French when their turn came, this proven by the clouds of white gun-smoke easing away in the gentle May wind. Perhaps it was the balmy wind against his cheek that put the next thought into William's head.

"What is the date? Today?"

Carr had just added substantially to his ongoing letter to his wife, Jane, and had the answer immediately.

"May 2nd, Sir, and over half-way through the day."

Williams nodded.

"Right. We'll get some Captains to keep a thorough watch and, with all thereby secure, perhaps you'd like to join me for some coffee with our Midday meal. Just arrived, I had it sent out."

Carr grinned with pleasure at such an invitation.

"That's very good of you, Sir. I'd be delighted."

The pair walked to the rear of the roof and Williams shouted down to one of his own Captains to watch developments and keep them informed. That order despatched, Williams set about orders for food and a small table with two folding chairs arrived at the roof-top for the pair to enjoy some food and good coffee, whilst not being so far from the ongoing action that they could be described in any way as negligent. In the event, Crauford gave himself the rest of the day to finally bring his elite Division back across the Dos Casas. Carr and Williams took the trouble to welcome him back to the village, but his only reply to the salute he received from the pair, was a dark glower, down from his huge horse as the mount splashed back over the river, Crauford the final man, as he followed his superb Battalions back up through the village.

In their place back above the village, were the remaining nine Companies of the 105th, including the Colour Company, this numbering in its ranks Colour Sergeant Deakin and Corporal Toby Halfway. The pair were stood together in the now deepening darkness, smoking and staring out towards the French position, noting the lighting of more and more bivouac fires as more French Battalions arrived to add to the force already there. More staring and more points of light from the French finally drew an opinion from Corporal Halfway.

"This is going to be a bad one, Jed."

Deakin withdrew the pipe from his mouth and tamped down the tobacco to achieve a slower burn before answering.

"That's a fact, Tobe. Here's another veteran French army, so I've heard, as've come here to sort us out."

He replaced the pipe, took a puff and then removed it, the smoke issuing forth as he spoke.

"This'll be as bad as Talavera, you wants my prediction. The Frogs have had enough of us having things all our own way, pushing 'em about after they quit from afore The Lines. They've come to settle accounts."

Halfway merely shifted his pipe to the corner of his mouth.

"Well, at least us, placed here, we'll have some walls to stand behind. Not like Talavera."

"True, but even walls won't help that much, when there's a whole army determined to come marchin' up through this village and over us. This'll be a bad one, you mark my words."

By now, both pipes were exhausted and so both extracted a small knife to scrape the bowls clean. That done, both walked back to their mess fires, and Deakin, as his last act of the day, held his Bridie tight in his arms under their blanket. Orders were for 'stand-to' before dawn.

The dawn came, May bright, the rising sun in the East slowly revealing the French position, it now being eagerly studied by both Carr and Williams, this time with the naked eye, with both perched on a convenient roof-top.

"Nothing yet, Sir. I'm surprised they didn't come whilst it was still dark. It's not as if they can get lost!"

"No, but let's be thankful for small mercies. They'll come today and it'll be here, where we are."

He turned from his studying to look at Carr.

"What are the men doing?"

"Taking breakfast in turns, one file eating, another stood to."

Williams nodded.

"Very good. There won't be much time for eating once it starts."

He turned to Carr.

"Would you be so good as to check on our dispositions, as we agreed? Mackinnon's Lights and Colville's of Picton's are at the river. Positioned further back in the village are Power's Portuguese of Picton's and all of Brent-Spencer's 1st. When the Rifles come in, they will add to Picton's here, at the river."

Carr saluted and descended from the roof, simultaneously tugging from his pocket the piece of paper on which were written all the Regimental numbers of the Light Companies in William's command and an almost useless description of where each one was, all buildings and paddocks looking so very much alike. The previous day, Williams and Carr had toured the village and Williams had quickly come to the simple conclusion.

"There is no discernible defensive line between the river and the Church. We can hold the line of the river, but after that, I propose to give each Company their own building or paddock to defend, then to fall back from it, if circumstances require, covered by the next defended whatever; building or paddock. You would agree?"

Carr had and so now he was touring the river bank calling out the Regimental numbers of the Light Companies there, which was simple compared to the complexities of finding the rest further back in the village within their own barn, byre, building, or paddock. With each finally found, he was at least re-assured that any French force attempting to advance up through the village would have a very tough task, with each prominent point held by elite troops, either British, Portuguese or King's German Legion. Furthest back up was the easiest task, to find the remaining nine Companies of the 83rd, with their Colonel, Walter Blakeney, with whom Carr merely exchanged salutes, before hurrying back to join Williams, still up on his roof.

Beneath their feet in the room below, were the Light Company of the 105th, holding that house and a walled paddock immediately downstream of the ford, with the ford road on one side and the river in front. Carr would not have been pleased to see what was happening at one particular window, the men of two files disobeying his breakfast orders, these being all mixed together and all wolfing down their corn porridge, fortified with bacon and sausage. Miles was the main instigator of the disobedience.

"I got a bad feeling about this one, and I b'ain't waitin' no time afore I gets to eat. Whilst I'm stood yer, just watchin' an' still hungry, Johnny could show up and that'll be that!"

Ellis arrived and noticed the rank disobedience, but said nothing. He knew that weapons could be exchanged for spoons in an instant and the men being fed mattered, as he knew himself from long experience. He came to the window next to Davey.

"Anything?"

"No. But Carr's up on the roof with the Colonel. We'll know when he does."

"You done a weapons check?"

Davey nodded.

"All's well. We're ready."

Ellis stood back, now assured by Davey's words, whom he thoroughly trusted.

"Right. I'll get round."

He left the building to then look up at Carr and Williams and see the two suddenly point out over the river, then to see Carr running to the rear of the roof and descend. Ellis stood and waited as Carr came out from behind the building.

"Stand to!"

Ellis took a brief look of his own, to see at least three columns of French infantry coming over the slight rise, this 500 yards beyond the river. It was not long before the Riflemen of the 60th and 95th, all lodged in the more scattered buildings and enclosures on that side of the river since well before dawn, began to open fire, immediately causing French casualties in their own advanced Light screen. Ellis ran into the house held by the 105th, but ordering 'stand to' was superfluous. All in there were at their chosen places, three deep at each firing position, each man to take turns, thus sending continuous fire out from their lodgement. It seemed to Davey, studying events on the far side of the river, that each Rifleman fired three shots and then retired, because soon, in their green uniforms, all were running back and splashing through the Dos Casas. Their orders were to take any position in the line that they came to and one came tumbling through the window manned by Davey, to then reload his Baker rifle. Davey gave him one glance, before returning to study his own ground before him.

"How many?"

The Rifleman was by now using his ramrod.

"A lot! Three columns, two of 'em two Battalions strong."

Soon, he had joined Davey at the window.

"What're your orders? No hand-to is ours. Hit 'em with shots, but if that don't stop 'em, file back through the village to the next strong point."

"Ours are the same. No bayonet work, but file back onto supports. Same drill, to file back."

The Rifleman looked at Davey.

"You been trained in that? You're only Line."

Miles was next behind Davey and immediately took umbrage. He had little regard for Riflemen.

"Never mind only 'Line', you cheeky bugger. You go teach your Granny to suck eggs! You want to file in with us, that's your choice, but you'll not find us wantin'!"

Davey had not heard. His attention was thoroughly taken by the solid columns of French, the first ranks of whom were now within range, just beyond a small Chapel, this curiously detached from the village, 100 yards beyond the Dos Casas. He nudged the Rifleman, now disengaged from Miles.

"Dead in front. Two Officers. Mine's on the left."

Both men brought their weapons up to their shoulders, each barrel resting on a nail, especially hammered into the wooden window frame for the purpose. Davey fired first and his Officer, in the act of waving his sword whilst turned and facing his men, jerked from the small of his back and collapsed. The Rifleman's target, in a more elaborate uniform, slumped to his knees to be absorbed into the column. Immediately, Davey fell back for Miles to take his turn and he downed an animated Sergeant. Carr, meanwhile had run to find Drake, finding him stood with Lieutenant Shakeshaft. His Section were holding the paddock alongside the house, the noise from their filing and firing now almost continuous. Carr took the quick opportunity to look over the wall and look both ways along the line. Smoke obscured much but the noise and flame from both directions, both left and right, told him that the French were being hit by a severe weight of shot, but the question came to mind, "Would it be enough?" It was a powerful attack on so narrow a front, a whole French Brigade, probably 2,000 men. He had seen three columns, but the worry was that each column appeared to be two Battalions in strength. Williams' command could take a fearful toll on the advancing French, but not enough to stop them from entering the village, not without artillery support and of that there was none, not even from the ridge crest behind them.

Carr peered through the smoke. He could see the Dos Casas, as yet empty of French, but one more minute changed everything. French uniforms began entering the water, many falling under the weight of fire, but as many advancing on. At the paddock wall was a solid line of 105th Light Company, the smooth changeovers creating a continuous volume of fire, but it was not going to be enough. As soon as a continuous line of French was formed on their far bank, Carr knew that the time had come. French shot was buzzing above and around them, also smacking into their wall with increasing intensity. He turned to the Captain of the Light Company.

"Nat! Fall back to the next wall. Get reloaded there and give them a volley as they come over this wall!"

Leaving Drake to shout his orders, Carr ran into the 105th house to find the process of evacuation already underway. Maltby had read the signals the same way that Carr had. Reassured with these events, he felt the need to check on the main route into the village, this up from the ford. He exited the rear of the building to run left to the ford road, cross it and find the wall of the paddock forming the upstream corner at the ford being defended mightily by the Light Company of the 88th Connaught Rangers, firmly supported by that of the 74th. Against this Celtic bastion, the French were making no progress at all, but Carr knew that the British line was falling back, probably on both sides of the ford road, therefore these doughty defenders risked being cut off. He recognised Captain Sennet from their efforts together at Busaco, the previous year.

"Sennet! Get them out, yours and the Scots. Get back and re-form!"

Orders were shouted and all quickly left the enclosure, but many of both Companies, not so much from training, as from the sheer indignity of falling back before the French, fired, fell back, loaded and fired again, all giving ground with the utmost reluctance. Carr ran back another 50 yards. The Celts were retiring up towards him, but he was judging what was happening on either side, both left and right. He could see the Companies that had held the first line at the river, all now running back through the alleys and passages that led upwards. More reassuring was the sight of the second line of Companies coming to readiness within their own bastions, as their comrades ran past and up. Carr spoke out loud.

"Here's where we stop them!"

It was not a difficult conclusion to come to. The French could cross the river in a solid body, but, once into the village, the maze of small plazas and narrow streets would create treacherous killing zones, where numbers would count for little, especially against the elite Light Troops such as he had, each capable of well over three shots a minute. By now Sennet, his 88th and the 74th were back up to him.

"Sennet! Fall back further and find something you can defend. Make a stand there."

The 88th Captain saluted and waved his men further back up into the village. Carr ran with them, but just a short way, where he dived through a window of a building held by Riflemen and some men of the 5th. There he received news that gave his high optimism a severe knock, this from a Rifleman of the 60th, when he asked the question.

"Have you seen your Colonel?"

"He's wounded, Sir. Bad. Like to die."

The breath went out of Carr. He was now in command!

"Has he been taken back up?"

"Yes Sir. I was one as took him, Sir."

Carr nodded.

"Very good. Now take your place."

The Rifleman ran to a window, cocking his rifle fully as he went. Realisation now came fully to Carr; he now commanded the equivalent of a small Brigade! Nothing for it, but to get around, show his face and encourage the men. That decided, he ran out of that building to the next Company, these holding a barn and a paddock. He found the Captain.

"Carr. 105th."

The Captain saluted.

"Burridge, Sir. 83rd."

"Are you holding them, Captain?"

"Seems so, Sir."

Carr looked at the wall, noting with satisfaction the smooth rhythm of the 83rd, each man firing and falling back to reload, to then be immediately replaced by another closing up to the wall. Carr smiled.

"Well done, Captain. Now praise your men for their efforts. Give them encouragement."

With that blunt ending, Carr left and ran on, to enter a barn and climb to the loft, this held by the 94th Foot. Burridge had been right, any effort by the French to emerge from between the buildings was being blasted back by the continuous fire from the second line of strongpoints. The assault was faltering, evidenced by many French now occupying the buildings they had taken and returning fire, rather than attempting any further advance. The second line would be held, the French would get no further, and they had suffered severe casualties advancing even this far. The belligerent, combative side to Carr's nature, came to the surface. "Why should the Frogs keep any part of our village?" It came to mind that there was still the 83rd in reserve, back above the village, and the Companies of the river line were now back there with them. He leapt more than walked down the barn stairs, ran out of the back door and then up the first alley that led upwards, where he passed through the two Portuguese Companies of William's command. Despite twists and turns the alley ran all the way up, where he soon came to the 83rd, drawn up in readiness. He saw their Colours and ran to them, where he found their Colonel. He came to the attention and saluted.

"Carr, Sir. 105th"

The salute was returned and the Colonel allowed Carr to continue.

"Sir. Colonel Williams has been badly wounded. You are now in command, Sir. May I recommend a counter-attack? Our casualties have been light and our men are still in their units. The French have been stopped and I'd say they were not steady. Not at all. Sir."

The Colonel nodded, then looked down from his vantage point to see the smoke of the ongoing combat and register its sounds.

"Very well, Major. Where would you recommend I take my men?"

"Veer over to the left, Sir, and you will gather with you those Light Companies holding there as you descend. As you choose, Sir, but I will take the right and attack down the road to the ford. We are strong down through there."

"Very good, Major. Begin your advance and be sure of my full support."

Carr came to the attention and saluted before running off, tending to the right to reach the main road down to the ford. His aggressive mood was undiminished and the first Company he came to was his own, that of the 105th, now back and holding a long garden wall. He ran to stand before it, draw his sword and wave it above his head.

"Come on, you bastards! The Frogs are on our land. That we don't allow. Not now, not ever!"

First over the wall were Drake and Shakeshaft, followed by the whole Light Company. As they careered down the road, they were soon joined by Mackinnon's Lights of the 88th and 74th. From their position in reserve, the two Portuguese Companies on the left sprang forward at the sight of Carr and his men beginning their counter-attack. With the attack from his three Companies now well under way, Carr left to join the Portuguese. They would descend to where Burridge was commanding his 83rd, him with several more Companies holding either side. If Carr led the Portuguese into the French, all these would join the advance. He ran to the head of a likely alley and put himself in the lead, with a Portuguese Captain alongside. Carr had directed correctly; the Portuguese came to Burridge's enclosure, charged across it and over the wall. Now led by their own Portuguese Captain, they crashed into the French in the alleyways opposite. Carr had halted amongst the Redcoats of the 83rd, to shout two words.

"Bayonets! Charge!"

In seconds the 83rd Lights had fixed their bayonets and were over their own walls and out of their buildings to pitch into the French. It was not long before the Captains of the other Light Companies ordered their own men forward and Carr found himself advancing with the 94th Highlanders, Scottish curses rising above the sounds of the hand-to-hand combat in the narrow spaces. Simultaneously, on the right, the three Companies of Mackinnon's Brigade, led by Drake and his 105th, were now back within sight of the river and the ford. The dreadful quartet of Saunders, Miles, Solomon and Ellis, were wreaking appalling havoc in the French ranks, which were crumbling before them as the four used their bayonets, butts and boots to deal out death and injury to any within reach. Soon they were at the river and Miles waded in to continue to the pursuit, but Ellis stopped him.

"Miles! Miles! Halt."

The maddened Miles halted and turned to face Ellis, who pointed to their original building.

"Enough! Get back to our posts. In there."

Miles waded back and followed his Sergeant to what had been their post at the day's beginning. Soon they were back inside the building, but not before Miles and Bailey had relieved two French Officer uniforms, one occupant dead, the other wounded, of many of their silver buttons. By now Carr was back to the 105th original paddock wall, studying the retreating French. He came to a quick conclusion, "They won't give best this easily. Not just with one Brigade." The French on the far side had left Tirailleurs in the buildings, paddocks and Chapel and so the occasional shot buzzed past or slapped into the stonework. This dissuaded

Carr from returning to the original roof that he and Williams had used and so he continued to study the scene from where he was. What happened in the next half-hour, he knew was crucial, hopefully nothing, because his men had fought hard, twice. They would be tired and worn down and would need at least that time to settle back to their original posts.

The minutes ticked by. His own 105th were busy carrying back their dead and wounded, away from the scene of any future possible conflict. It would be some time before they came to man their wall again, or when Carr could justifiably give them an order to do so. However, after no more than 10 minutes Carr saw something and he drew out his telescope and focused it beyond the thin veil of smoke from the Tirailleurs' fire. His worst fears were confirmed, another French attack was coming over their low ridge, bigger than the first. The French were sending down fresh Battalions, supported by the rallied troops of the first. This his command would not hold. The Companies of the first, the Dos Casas line, were possibly in place, but the Companies of the second line were almost certainly not back in their strongpoints, which had been crucial for holding the first French attack. This would have to be a fighting withdrawal, holding them back as best they can, until this attack also ran out of steam, mostly because of the tortuous nature of the village. He levered himself from the stonework and slammed his glass shut. It was no use despairing over retreating again, this was just one act in a major battle and this was how the thing played out.

"Stand to! Stand to!"

The whole Company picked up their weapons, many had not even had the time to clean them, but they nevertheless ran to man their positions. He looked across the paddock.

"Nat!"

Drake ran over.

"Don't expect to hold these for much time at all. File back through the village when things become too hot. If we can man the strongpoints as we did before, we can absorb the blow, but we must keep hold of some of the village."

Drake nodded, then ran to the wall to study the French for himself. Carr ran to the 88th and 74th, back at the ford. He found Sennet, although changed somewhat, with a bandage over half his face.

"They're coming again, stronger and reinforced. So, same as before, fall back, and hold any good position for as long as you can. Don't get cut off. Don't!"

Carr ran off, leaving Sennet's salute circling in the air. He took himself back into the village, yelling to all he saw to return to their positions and when he came to the buildings where the Rifles were gathered he found the nearest Captain. There was no time for introductions.

"Get yours above those defending the ford, find a position and hold there to support. They will be retreating back up to you. Deny Johnny from using the ford road to get up higher into the village, make him move between the buildings."

Orders were shouted and the three Companies left immediately, many carrying their equipment in their hands and hurrying to secure the various belts around their waist and shoulders. Carr then left the building to watch from a higher road that ran across the village centre, parallel to the river. Musket fire erupted all along his front when the French columns came within range, but it was not long before he saw all his Companies filing back, all following their drill to retreat, for a retreat it now was. The French had come on at a run and were now over the walls and issuing between the buildings. They looked to be led by Voltiguers, elite assault troops. He looked behind to see that the building there was well defended, but it was clear, that when the French arrived their attack would have sufficient momentum to carry it on up and further into the village. His first serious command would end in defeat, but there was nothing for it, other than to conduct the retreat in as controlled and effective a way as possible and make the French pay for their gains. At least, there would be no headlong retreat, of that he was determined. What was re-assuring was the manner in which the men fell back, all Captains of the elite Light Companies taking good decisions on when to abandon their position, and the men falling back in good order, holding off the French with musketry whilst their comrades ran back to the next usable position.

What mattered was the road up to the Church, up through the upper half of the village, and so Carr decided that was his place. A short jog took him there to find the Rifles slowly giving ground, also that the 74th and 88th had passed through them and were further up and forming in their own position, prior to making a stand. All here was re-assuringly in good order, however, for the men of the 105th Light Company the situation was anything but. They had run into a second building to continue their orderly retreat, but the French were now on both sides of it and their only route to safety was from the back of the building, into a narrow alley at right angles to the back wall and it would take precious seconds for all to issue through. Thus, they were still having to defend the front doors and windows, where Saunders was at the door wrestling with a Voltiguer, whilst Miles, Davey, Ellis and Solomon were holding the windows with butts and bayonets. Pike, Bailey and Byford were at the back of the room, all furiously reloading. With all three loaded and at the 'present', Byford called out.

"Loaded. Fall back!"

Saunders sent his opponent backwards with a vicious head butt, before sending a heavy trestle out through the door to further discourage the man. He retrieved his Baker, then him and the other four retreated to the back wall containing their exit door. However, almost immediately five Voltiguers came through the five doors and windows. Three were downed by the trio waiting with loaded rifles, but two came on. Ellis sprang forward to astutely push aside the man's guard, slice his bayonet across his face and then bayonet him, all in one movement, but the second landed a heavy blow on Ellis' shoulder with the butt of his musket. He was knocked sideways, but Miles was close and used the butt of his own weapon to smash most of the man's face back into his skull. Ellis could now carry his musket only in one hand and so he was first to follow Solomon, Saunders and Davey out through the door, whilst Byford, Bailey, and Pike defended it from inside, now using only bayonets. A musket fired from the window and Byford reeled back, spinning sideways. Pike and Bailey remained 'en garde', holding back two Voltiguers with the long 'sword' of their Baker, whilst Solomon dragged Byford out. Davey and Saunders, now outside, had quickly reloaded and Davey called out.

"You three! Back!"

Pike and Bailey turned and passed between the two, who sighted into the room from outside the door and fired in through the opening, downing two of their assailants. Miles, the last, tried to follow, but a Voltiguer was too close and he had to defend himself. Having deflected a thrust from the Frenchman's musket butt over his left shoulder, his own weapon was then in the perfect position to use the butt of his own to then dislocate the man's jaw practically out of his head. Outside, Saunders now picked up Byford and threw him over his shoulder to then run up the escape alley, followed by Davey. The final three of Miles, Pike and Bailey, now held the back door, but their troubles were far from over. The alley running along the back of the house was, in peaceful times, closed by a gate, but now it was being held closed by Shakeshaft and two men, whilst French Voltiguers on the other side demolished it with their boots, musket butts and shoulders. Whilst Pike reloaded, Miles and Bailey menaced any approaching Voltiguer from the house with their bayonets. Pike now fully cocked his rifle and shouted to the three holding the gate.

"Sir!"

Shakeshaft took his shoulder away from the disintegrating gate and pulled his two men back with him. Seeing Pike sighting along the back-alley wall towards the gate, the three had the sense to close to the left, leaving Pike clear to put a bullet into the Voltiguer Officer who was first past the wreck of the gate. All six then sprinted up the escape alley, passing Davey who was knelt ten yards along it, his Baker loaded and sighted back, waiting for the first Frenchman. When he came, Davey collapsed his chest with the half-inch lead ball and then ran back, to what proved to be the end of the alley, where Saunders was waiting, with his Baker loaded, and he downed the next Voltiguer, after Davey had run past.

All were now out and so Saunders picked up Byford again and with Ellis at least completely mobile they all ran up the next alleyway, which thankfully had a marked turn left, this hiding them from any French musket fire. In addition, the adjacent walls were held by the formidable Light Company of the 5th Northumberland Fusiliers. Now feeling at least safer, Davey examined Byford, who was grimacing with the pain. The ball had hit the muscle of his shoulder, just below his armpit. There was no exit wound so he had to ask himself, had it smashed his shoulder-blade? However, there was no time to discover that, because the 5th were now engaged with the oncoming French, their advance still having some momentum. Saunders produced a clean rag which was thrust inside Byford's shirt to staunch the bleeding and, with Byford now at least able to stagger if supported by Saunders, they came to the very top of the village where stood the Church, surrounded by its graveyard. Although in a state of complete confusion, with all Companies mixed up, the Light Infantrymen had rallied and were holding whatever strongpoint they could, under whichever Officer was nearest. However, it seemed that the tide of the French advance had at last spent itself. Some sallies were made against the British line by French Officers leading groups of men, these either trying their Gallic luck or simply intoxicated by their success, but they were soon beaten back. Carr, now stood by the Church, took stock of what had happened and the conclusion was inevitable; almost all of Fuentes de Onoro was now in French hands. He told himself that he could have done no more, but, nevertheless the defeat rankled.

Stood alone just above the Church, he must have struck a forlorn and dejected figure, for at that moment Wellington arrived with his Staff.

"How now, Carr! What have you to report?"

Carr turned and sprang to the attention at the sound of the distinctive voice.

"I'm afraid most of the village is lost, Sir."

The mournful tone was not undetected by Wellington, who surprisingly grinned.

"Be of good cheer, Carr, this is no more than I suspected. This is a game of who can wear down whom and still be here at the last. By the end of today, in this village he will have lost a Division to no gain and it will still be ours."

Carr's brows came together in puzzlement.

"No gain to them, Sir?"

"None! I'm sending in three Battalions from the 1st Division, led by Cadogan and his 71st."

He paused to study Carr.

"I understand he's short of a Junior Major. You may wish to offer your services."

He turned in his saddle to look back up the road.

"I do believe that they will be arriving just about now, if those are their wailing bagpipes that I can hear. Do you have a pistol?"

Carr pulled his from his waistband.

"Yes Sir. This."

"Then, if you wish to accompany Colonel Cadogan, I suggest you get it loaded."

Wellington turned in the saddle, to see the 71st, now plainly in view with bayonets already fixed, led by a Colonel, on foot, his face seemingly more quarried than born of woman, and brandishing a sword in one hand, a Dragoon pistol in the other.

"Cadogan!"

Cadogan halted, and so did his men, whilst Cadogan used his sword to salute his Commander in Chief, who had words of his own.

"You are short of a Junior Major, I understand. Carr here is offering his services."

"As he chooses, Sir."

Wellington turned to Carr.

"There you are Carr. As you choose. So, I'll leave you to it."

With that, he wheeled his horse to walk it back up the road, followed by his Staff. Carr walked the few steps to Cadogan.

"Where do you want me, Sir?"

The reply was terse and almost impatient.

"Your experience?"

"Mostly Light Company, Sir."

Cadogan turned away and continued to lead his men along the level ridge at the back of the Church

"At the rear."

There was just time for Carr to ask a question and to receive a reply.

"Who are our supports, Sir?"

"79th on the right. Left rear, the 24th."

Carr stood waiting for the 71st to pass by and then he joined in, when their final Company, the Light, came up. He fell in alongside their Captain.

"Carr. 105th Foot. I've been invited to join. I understand you are a Major short."

"Beamish Sir. Yes Sir, pleased to have you along. I understand this has been pretty desperate?"

"Yes. This place has changed hands four times. As we speak, the French have it."

Beamish gave a half smile.

"Well, we'll soon change that, Sir."

Carr smiled and then looked along the marching column. The 71st was a Scottish Regiment with a distinctive dark blue tartan, the kilts swinging with the rhythm of their marching. It was not long before Cadogan called a halt and his Regiment formed up as separate columns of Companies. Cadogan had halted his men directly above the centre of the village, just down from the brow of the ridge. French bullets began to arrive and the 71st suffered its first casualty, the Captain of Nine Company collapsed with a shattered shin bone. "That's my place", thought Carr, and he took himself over, just as two Highlanders dragged their

Captain back to the space between the columns. Carr had just enough time to face his front, when Cadogan raised his sword, screamed some unintelligible Gaelic and then he and his men charged forward, over the top wall of the village, across the top road and into a series of paddocks. Immediately they came under fire and many fell from the first French volley. Carr felt a bullet buzz past his face, but he kept on, leading his Company from the front. Cadogan and the centre Companies soon disappeared into a major alleyway that served as a secondary route up from the village, but Carr, on the right, had to choose what looked like a courtyard, with, hopefully, a route downwards from it, if only through the house.

Their timing was fortuitous. They came to the back of the house just as French muskets, now reloaded, appeared through the windows, but they were just too late to fire. Many of the Highlanders threw their muskets in through the windows as if they were spears and followed them through. Carr and three Highlanders were battering at the door, which was giving at the top, but immoveable at the bottom. Two of the Highlanders took a step back.

"Gi' us a space, if you please, Sir."

Carr stepped aside and the pair launched themselves at the top of the door which splintered but did not give. However, one boot more and two shoulders caused its final demise and they were over the wrecked remains and into the house. The room was already cleared of French and so those Highlanders first in through the windows were now the first out, through the front door, this mean dwelling having but one downstairs room. Carr noticed movement on the stairs. Two French Voltiguers were at the top, but before Carr could raise his pistol, four Highlanders fired and the pair were thrown back against the wall, to then topple forward into the room. Carr looked at the four Highlanders.

"Reload and then follow. You'll need loaded muskets."

Carr was the last out through the front door and he was in a narrow alleyway, with another just to the right and slightly opposite, which led further down into the village. He ran to it and then on down, trying to lead the advance and passing Highlanders battering at doors and firing up at windows. Any form of order was impossible. Men simply joined whichever fight was nearest, but the French Voltiguers, supported by the Line infantry of the first French assault were not giving ground easily. As had the British retreated up in good order, so did the French retreat down, holding any likely strongpoint, but, as had happened for the British, such strongpoints were soon outflanked by some alleyway that threaded through the tangle of the village. Thus, although now in the opposite direction, the fighting remained of the same nature; house by house, paddock by paddock, wall by wall.

Carr estimated that he was about half way down to the river. He saw a group of 71st looking for employment, then noticed another group of Highlanders, but these with a different tartan, this dark red and blue. Carr pointed to both groups.

"You! With me!"

Carr kicked open a wicker gate into a back garden and led his men to the back of yet another crude cottage. French fire came from both the ground and upper floors, but Carr's men were now too close to the wall and only two dropped. Some extra men had joined from both Regiments and so now Carr had around thirty. He noticed a Corporal.

"You! Take fifteen around the side. Hold that alley and the road beyond."

The Corporal's hand came up to his tartan headband and he led his men off, these deciding for themselves which of the two parties they should be in, to go or to stay. He allowed his own group to gather.

"Right lads. We're going in here and kick 'em out of our parlour. They're being too free with our womenfolk! And our stew!"

Many grinned at the absurdity as Carr pointed to six men.

"When that door goes down, be ready to fire through it."

Carr grabbed the crossbelts of a Highlander.

"With me!"

He looked at another.

"You grab him!"

Locked together the three launched themselves at the door. It gave way about a foot and a musket fired from inside, the ball just showing through the splintered wood.

"Once more!"

The three took a pace back and again charged the door. This time the hinges gave and the door collapsed backwards, but Carr carried his two companions down to the floor, as above them, the French fired out and Carr's six fired in. With that now passed above them, Carr was on his feet, where he drew his sword and pistol and charged through the smoke. A bayonet came forward out of the gloom which Carr deflected, this causing a moustachioed face to appear, which Carr immediately assaulted with the iron bell-guard of his sword. The man fell and Carr had the fleeting impression that he was immediately bayoneted, but he had no time to discover either way, because he was immediately engaged in combat by an Officer. The two locked swords and stood transfixed, one against the other, until a Highlander, coming up behind, buried his bayonet up to the socket between the Frenchman's ribs. Carr saw the pain cross the man's face and then his eyes glazed before he finally slumped to the floor. Now that the door was down, more of Carr's men were coming through it and also through the windows. It was clear that the French were abandoning the building, because Carr could see bodies falling into the street outside as they jumped from the upper windows, but few escaped. Carr's Corporal was now at the front and his men either shot or bayoneted almost all that attempted to flee after falling into the street below.

Carr emerged into the street. He had his sword, but where his pistol was he had no idea, in fact he had no memory of firing it, but his men now gathered to him once more.

"Well done, lads. Now to the river, where we can all have a wet!"

A Scottish voice came from behind.

"Better wi' a dram o' French brandy, Sir?"

Laughter came as Carr replied.

"Any you find is all yours, but come on. Keep them moving back."

He led them over a wall, which proved to be part of a double paddock, the middle wall being held by some French, but as Carr and his men advanced, a French Officer screamed at them and they fell back. Once over that wall, a short run at the last half paddock brought them to the wall beside the river to find that it was as crowded with French as was the far bank, but all in headlong retreat, the river also now full of retreating French. Several of Carr's men began to climb the final wall of the double paddock to continue the pursuit, but Carr ran along his short line pulling them back.

"Reload! Reload and hold here. Give fire, but hold here!"

His men began to do just that, firing and reloading to cause the French their final casualties. Soon there came an eerie silence where they were, it broken only by the cries of the wounded, of which there were many, but more French than Allied. This was ignored by Carr, he was looking over the river to see what caused an anguished tightening of his throat. He remembered the disastrous charge forward at Talavera, which was why he had held his men back, but many other Highlanders had crossed the river, in force, and were pursuing the French through and beyond the last of the buildings by the Chapel. Carr felt a tap on his shoulder to turn and see a Captain of the 71st, with almost a whole Company. He looked no more than 17.

"What are your orders, Sir."

Carr could have kissed him.

"Hold here, with your men and these. Hold this wall. All those out there will soon be running back with perhaps Johnny cavalry at their backs. Hold here!"

With that, Carr was over the wall and through the stream. He was determined to gather some men and man a strongpoint that would delay any French, so he ran up and arrived at the Chapel, which had a small graveyard. Any men within voice range, he ordered into it, but Carr's worries soon fell away. Cadogan was there and had good control of his men. He was already ordering them back and, as the acting Brigadier, he had sent runners to the Colonels of the 79th Scots and 24th who had come down with his own command to do the same. Like a tide receding, the wave of the two Scots Battalions and the Warwickshire 24th, began to fall back, in good order and facing the French as they did so. Carr stood on a headstone and became doubly grateful for Cadogan's firm grip. He could see that another four French columns were now advancing over the brow of their own ridge, but Cadogan's men were running back and out of range. Cadogan himself came to Carr in his graveyard.

"What are you doing there? Carr, isn't it?"

"It is, Sir, and I thought that holding this may be a good idea, Sir. To cover any retreat,"

Cadogan's face darkened.

"Not needed! Get back."

Carr saluted and led his men out of the graveyard gate, but they were not the last over the Dos Casas, this was for Cadogan, as he studied the oncoming French. Then he gave his orders.

"Firing line. All three Battalions."

The order was directed at Cadogan's Senior Major, who stared back, incredulous.

"Sir?"

Cadogan stared straight back, his manner challenging.

"Yes! The 71st don't need stonework to skulk behind. Walls and whatnot! Firing line. And show The Colours."

Carr was as bemused as the Senior Major, it seemed absurd to ignore the cover afforded by the walls and buildings of the village, but Cadogan then turned to him.

"Get any of yours you can and use them to extend my line!"

The orders rang out and soon all three Battalions were in a two-deep firing line, stood between the lowest walls of the village and the near bank of the Dos Casas, with a complete mixture of Light troops extending to the right. Carr now studied the French, there was not much daylight remaining but enough for one more assault on the village, which could take the French back to where they had been before Cadogan and his Brigade intervened. Almost immediately, he saw the French skirmishers emerge from their columns and run forward, then Cadogan came riding up, now on a captured French horse.

"Carr! You know something about Light Infantry work. I'm sending out all three of my Lights and putting you in charge."

Behind Cadogan, Carr could see the three Light Companies named already crossing the Dos Casas and so he had no choice but to salute and agree.

"Sir."

Carr gave himself the luxury of crossing the Dos Casas using the ancient clapp bridge and then found Captain Beamish at his side.

"Do yours understand fighting in files of three?"

"Yes Sir, they do."

"Then give the order."

All across the British front the Light troops spread out into skirmish order and Carr began a walk across his line and give his orders.

"200 yards out from the river. No further."

The range between the two sides' skirmishers barely approached 100 yards and, after little more than 10 minutes of exchanging fire, casualties remained minimal. Carr had noticed that the French columns had halted, but he concentrated on managing his men, until it dawned on him that the threatening French columns had not resumed their advance and, he then concluded, they would advance no further. He turned to look at his own line beyond the river and saw what the French saw, a long, intimidating, Redcoated line, each Battalion with their Colours in the centre, brazen and challenging. Besides the Union Colours of each, was the buff of the 79th, the washed pink of the 71st in the centre and finally the green of the 24th. Amid the stuttering skirmisher exchange Carr looked again at the French columns and he saw them turn and withdraw, their skirmishers disappearing behind the nearest convenient stonework. The French were calling it a day, but, had Carr known it, the columns were of General Marchand's Brigade who had stood in reserve at Busaco and watched two British Battalions, such as those opposing him now, practically annihilate three times their number. Cadogan had been correct to make the challenge, Marchand had no wish to try conclusions when the odds were only four to three in his favour and his side had already lost almost a whole Division in a futile attempt to secure Fuentes de Onoro. As the sun dipped beneath its own horizon, so too did Marchant's Brigade disappear behind their own ridge. As the last French shako disappeared, Cadogan came forward.

"That'll do, Carr! Take your Lights back into the village and hold the river line. I'll see that you get relieved."

oOo

"How long, mate?"

The Surgeon's Assistant looked around at the casualties arranged in the wide, square tent.

"A good hour. He's got three or four amputations to do before he gets to your mate there. And some extractions."

The man hurried off, carrying armfuls of blankets, leaving Miles to look down at the fevered face of John Byford. He turned to Zeke Saunders.

"He don't look good!"

"No! A bullet in the shoulder is one thing, but I've heard of what they calls shock, that's the hit and suddenness of the thing. Some can die just from that. The sooner that bullet's out the better."

Saunders looked from Byford to Miles

"Didn't George Fearnley get a bullet out of you after Talavera?"

Light came into Miles' face.

"He did and he got one of Shakeshaft's shoulder during that set to we had with them cavalry after Catanzaro."

"Well then, he can't be much worse that what any Surgeon will do. And probably be a sight more careful. He can take more time, like."

Miles nodded agreement.

"Right! I'll go fetch 'im."

He walked off, but his face fell somewhat when he heard Saunders next instruction.

"And brandy!"

Saunders knelt beside his good friend and placed his hand on his chest, now heaving for breath.

"Hold on, John. We're fetching George Fearnley, he'll get that Frog ball out of you. That done, we'll get you back to Bridie and Nellie. They'll take better care of you than this chop and cut crew. Then you'll soon be up and about."

Byford managed to turn his head and place his right hand on Saunders' forearm, but a slight nod of his head was all he could manage. Saunders knew that if there was smashed bone inside the shoulder, then it would be just a matter of time. He pulled forward his own canteen containing a weak mixture of brandy and water and gave Byford a drink, then he squatted on the floor, trying not to dwell too much on the sights all around, these being bloody bandages around heads and torsos and the worst being those around stumps of legs and arms.

It was not long before George Fearnley arrived, the Sergeant of the Light Company who had some medical training and knowledge. The first question he asked confirmed this.

"Where's his jacket?"

Saunders, still on the floor, passed it up. Fearnley examined the hole and was pleased to see that the sides of the bullet hole came together perfectly. He then knelt himself to examine the shirt and his face lightened to see the same for the hole through that.

"No cloth was carried through. That's good!"

He looked up at Miles.

"I'll need a scalpel, a pair of forceps and two reverse-clamps, if you can get them. If not two flat blades'll do."

However, Miles had his own question, blunt and simple.

"What do you think, George?"

Fearnley twisted his mouth.

"Well, fired from only across a room, 'twill be in deep. Regarding bone, well, behind there is ribs and the shoulder joint. And there weren't no cross straps, such as saved Joe, taking much of the force. Now get what I need."

Miles was off and hurrying over to a table covered in surgical instruments, all of which Miles knew had names, but none that he could lay his tongue to, by way of identification. He seized the arm of the nearest Assistant, who was busy hanging lanterns on the tent poles.

"We needs a scalpel, some forceps and two reverse-clamps."

The Assistant jerked his arm away, obviously annoyed.

"All these belong to Surgeon Pearce!"

Belligerence soon surfaced in Thomas Miles.

"Think I don't know that? Think I'm goin' to steal 'em? Our own Surgeon Sergeant just wants a borrow, is all. He can do the job as well as your Surgeon an' that's one less for him to have to worry about!"

The Assistant made no move, so Miles leaned forward to within inches of his face.

"Listen you! We've got a mate as've got a bullet in his shoulder and we needs some kit to get it out. You takes it onto yourself not to help and you'll find yourself behind some tent some night with a few teeth missin' and a few bits bent or broke!"

He paused as deep concern spread across the man's face.

"Now, those bits of kit!"

The man turned to the table to quickly pick out the four instruments needed and hand them to Miles, who nodded and almost smiled.

86

"When we're done with 'em, where'd they go?"

The Assistant pointed to a trough of water, from which another Assistant was extracting instruments and wiping them clean. Miles now actually grinned, but malevolently, before nodding and hurrying off. Back with Byford, Fearnley had already prepared the wound, by covering it with brandy, but that seemed to have no impact on Byford. John Davey had arrived, with Len Bailey and Joe Pike, so now Fearnley gave his instructions. First, the gag, which he tied himself, the wood going between Byford's teeth and the leather thongs tied behind his head, then he organised his helpers.

"Each of you on an arm or a leg, but Zeke, you push down on his chest. Len, get a lantern and hold it up."

Within a minute, all was ready and Fearnley took the scalpel and cut three inches vertically, each side of the wound. Byford's body arched, but Saunders was ready.

"Here John, take a drink of this."

He tipped some brandy into Byford's mouth and he managed to swallow most of it. Meanwhile, Fearnley had inserted both reverse-clamps into the cuts above and below to hold the wound open. He then took the forceps.

"This is the worse bit, John, but I'll be as quick as I can."

He inserted a flat blade from his own kit and also the forceps to hold the wound open. Blood welled up and Saunders wiped it away. Fearnley went deeper but could see nothing and Byford's body arched even more, but the four pressed down on him. Fearnley could now see a rib and he slid the forceps down beside it and felt something stop the forceps from going further. Now guided only by the feeling he gained from the forceps he probed for the location of the ball and closed the jaws where he thought it was. The forceps held something but could not withdraw it. Twice more he tried, but with no success.

"I'll have to cut deeper to see."

He did and Byford screamed over the gag. There was less bleeding and Saunders wiped away what there was, but now Fearnley could see.

"It's lodged in a lot of tendon."

He looked at Miles.

"I need a hook of some kind."

Miles was immediately up and over to the instrument table, rapidly scanning all to see anything that had any kind of hook. There was nothing, but when he looked up he saw the handle on the nearest lantern. He took it down from its nail, wrenched off the handle, and took it over to the washers at their tub. Then he thrust it at the nearest.

"Here! Wash this."

The man took it, even though utterly bemused, dipped it into the water and then wiped it, before handing it back. Miles then ran back to Fearnley and handed it to him and he studied the small right-angle bend where the handle went into the lantern. He bent the whole almost straight, then tipped brandy over one end before carefully inserting it behind the ball. A strong tug and it came free, then Fearnley returned to the forceps for the final extraction which was but the work of a moment. More brandy was then tipped into the wound and Fearnley then produced his own sewing kit, but once again the key question came from Miles.

"What d'you think George?"

Fearnley answered whilst threading the curved needle.

"Well, I've never done anything deeper and the ball may well have fractured that rib. With all that cutting his left shoulder'll never work quite the same again, but my worry now is that he'll take with a fever. Some men can take a ball hitting them, some can't. 'Tis just down to how they'm put together, by Mother Nature."

He inserted the first stitch, but Byford did little more than wince. A dozen more and some more applications of brandy and Fearnley pronounced himself satisfied.

"Right. Get a stretcher and let's get him over to the women. It's all down to good care now."

Miles and Bailey quickly found one and Byford was lifted onto it. Four now on the handles left Miles redundant, but he gathered the instruments and took them to the washers. The lantern handle he took to the original Assistant.

"Here, mate. A very useful bit of kit. Tell your Officer."

The man looked at the disfigured lantern handle with astonishment, but Miles was gone.

Ten minutes carrying of Byford got them to their mess fires at the rear of Fuentes ridge where Bridie rose at the sight, her apron being raised immediately to her face in deep concern. Nellie was busy with Sergeant Ellis, him with his jacket off and his sleeve rolled right up. Eirin was nursing her baby, but she continued even when she saw that it was John Byford who was wounded. The stretcher was lowered to the ground and Bridie hurried over to examine the patient, but Miles was more concerned with the sight of Ellis in their camp.

"What's he doing here?"

Nellie had resumed stirring something in a cooking pot but looked up at him, her stare at Miles as challenging as his own.

"Now don't you be startin' trouble, Tom Miles. Sure, is there not enough grief around here, now, without you addin' to it all?"

Miles had no reply and so Nellie continued.

"The Sergeant here has taken a nasty clout on his arm, but 'tis just bruisin', nothin' broken, and so I'm just boiling up a good poultice to ease the stiffening."

Still no reply.

"As if it's any business of yours!"

Ellis grinned at the demolition of Tom Miles, but his expression changed when the thick, glutinous substance was applied to his arm. His face screwed up in pain, which altered Miles' mood, especially when Ellis gave his verdict.

"It's hot! And it stinks!"

Nellie took no notice but continued to wind bandage around the muscle of his arm and over the poultice.

"Sure now, what's that? 'T'as to be hot to carry the goodness down in and don't you know that if any medicine doesn't smell bad or taste horrible, then it can't be doing you any good. You'll be right as rain in a day or two. Come back at the end of tomorrow and we'll put on another. There's plenty left."

Ellis nodded, his face betraying his uncertainty, pulled down his sleeve and put on his jacket. That done he flexed the arm and winced a little, before picking up his Baker and walking past Miles.

"I'll say thank-you for your coming forward in that fight back in that house, but that's all!"

However, he then stopped.

"But don't get too comfortable. We're back into the village, like we were start of today. I'm going down now; you get some food and come on after."

Davey, as Chosen Man and hearing all, knew he had the responsibility to see that all was carried out.

"The same Lights as this morning?"

"That's right, with Carr in command."

With that he departed, but Miles said nothing, he was now thinking about food. He turned to Bridie, still kneeling over the prone figure of John Byford.

"Any food going, Bridie?"

Bridie made the briefest of turns towards him and, with the briefest of gestures indicated the pot hanging above the fire. Miles went to his backpack, pulled out his pannikin and began spooning out what was mostly vegetables. The others joined the queue, but all sat in silence as Bridie continued wiping Byford's face and his wounded shoulder. Whilst the newcomers ate, Jed Deakin and Henry Nicholls took themselves over to the stretcher. Both looked at Byford, then at each other and Henry Nicholls spoke the thoughts of both.

"He's going down for a fever."

At those words, Bridie looked up at Jed and he answered the anxiety he saw there.

"You know how it works, Bridie. Keep him cool or keep him warm as the fever takes him. He's young and he's tough. He'll pull through. Let's just hope the Frogs don't force us out of here. On a retreat, things'll be different. Bad!"

Before the night closed in thoroughly, Reverend Albright arrived at their mess area but did little more than bid all a good night with God's Blessing before moving on. He missed all those of the Light Company who had left to hurry back down to the village and, in the dark, pick their way over the hundreds of bodies, whilst avoiding the bandsmen carrying back the wounded. As they descended, the sound of a bickering exchange between both Allied and French marksmen grew louder.

"No peace down here, then?"

Saunders chuckled in the gloom.

88

"Especially for a wicked bugger like you, Tom!"

The six found their way to their original position, not easily, but eventually they arrived at the ford to find Captain Drake stood by a wall. Davey walked up, came to 'Order Arms' and saluted.

"Reporting, Sir. We've been attending Private Byford who's been wounded Sir. S'arnt Ellis gave us the word and so we've eaten and come down. S'arnt Ellis was wounded too, and he's also had some treatment. Sir."

"Very good Davey. How is Byford?"

"Not good, Sir. It was a struggle to get the bullet out. He's took with a fever and being cared for now."

"Right, I'm sorry to hear that, but get into our building, to the upper floor. We have to answer this French fire, if only to let them know that we are still in here."

The six turned towards to the back of their original building and went in through the back door, after clambering over a pile of French bodies, blocking the alleyway. On the top floor, they found Fearnley.

"How's John?"

"Fever!"

"As I thought. Right, John. Half and half, at the windows and at the back getting some sleep. You're in charge here. Ellis is down in the paddock with Maltby, Shakeshaft's downstairs. Drake, you found. Carr, I don't know where."

With that he left, leaving Davey in charge of two dozen men and so, in the light of two thick tallow candles, Davey divided them. That done, half tried to sleep and the rest took position at the windows. Pike and Miles were at the same window and Pike peered through, his rifle loaded and ready.

"How do we see to shoot, Tom? It's black as pitch out there!"

Miles, thoroughly ill-tempered because of where he was yet again and with little prospect of any decent sleep, felt the need for sarcasm.

"Just noticed that, have you boy! Well, take a look out and you'll see the flash in the pan when they fires. You fire where you saw it and you can't do no more, but we has to send some their way. You heard what Drake said, to keep the buggers back."

With that, he drew out his bayonet and hammered it into the wood of the window frame with his small mallet.

"You do the same and rest the barrel on that. That way, you'm always at the present, like, and you've a better chance of sighting quickly on the light of their pan sparkin' and hitting something. If those buggers out there has any brains they'll fire and move, so you needs to be quick."

Pike did as he was told and the pair sent shots regularly out into the French position, but with the turn of midnight, and in the darkness, both sides recognised the absurdity of any prolonged conflict of that nature and, even before Pike and Miles were relieved, the sounds had died away. However, both were allowed but a short time rolled up in their blankets, before they were woken by Highlanders of the 71st clumping up the stairs, led by a Corporal.

"We're taking over. You're for back up."

Soon, all of the Light Company of the 105th were gathered on the main village road and, led by Drake and Carr, in the chill of the remaining darkness, they made their way back up through the village, past the Church. They eventually arrived at their mess areas, but to gain little respite, before Ellis was rousing all to wakefulness.

"Form up!"

Wellington had ordered his army stood-to well before dawn. When full daylight finally arrived, placed out before their men, Lacey, O'Hare and Carr, made continuous use of their telescopes, but to neither purpose nor gain. Eventually all instruments were collapsed and stowed in jacket pockets. Lacey shook his head.

"Nothing! I've seen no movement at all. Yesterday gained him nothing, so he'll not try the village again, but this is Massena. He may be a pounder most of the time, but he can come up with a trick or two."

O'Hare nodded.

"He pounded us at Busaco and took a beating, but still pushed us back when he got around our flank."

He turned away, to be followed by the other two.

"He's up to something, but I'm for some coffee."

As they walked back, Carr spoke of what was now obvious.

"What about the men, Sir? They're still in line."

Lacey nodded.

"Yes, but we've no orders to stand down. We can allow them to sit and perhaps one in five bring up some food, but they must stay there."

Carr's concerns were fully addressed when eventually just before Noon, Staff Officers rode along the line ordering stand down and the placing of pickets. However, the Staff Officer that arrived at the 16th Light Dragoons ordered no such thing. The sight of an Aide-de-Camp galloping into their camp brought all Officers to the Headquarters tent, where Colonel Withers and Major Johnson were sat outside enjoying their own coffee. The messenger dismounted and approached the pair.

"Sir. Lord Wellington is convinced that the French are attempting a serious manoeuvre against our right, at Pozo Bello and Nave de Aver. His orders are for all cavalry to create a screen between here and Nave, Sir. He has also detached the 7th Division under General Houston to occupy Pozo Bello. Brigadier Slade will be making your dispositions as you march. This should be done with some urgency. Sir."

Withers took a final swallow of his coffee and then threw the rest onto the ground.

"Thank you, Major. We will be riding out directly."

The Aide saluted, mounted his horse and rode off. Withers looked at his Captains.

"You heard! 15 minutes formed by Squadrons."

All ran off and within 20 minutes the column of the 16th Light Dragoons was riding South, following the valley of the Dos Casas over on their left, with the remaining Regiment of their own Arentschildt's Brigade, the 1st Hussars King's German Legion, in column behind. To their right was the column of Slade's Brigade, the 1st Dragoons, with their tall, almost ludicrous helmets and the 14th Light Dragoons with their contrasting blue uniforms and high curved busby with its distinctive white plume. Soon both overtook the long column of the 7th Division, this with a full six-gun Field Battery at its side and so they trotted on across a high, bleak plain with no sign of any agricultural use, the whole dotted around with clumps of rocks. Cornet Carr was riding at the head of his C Troop with Sergeant Baxter just behind.

"This could be the moon, Sergeant!"

"I'll take you word for that, Sir. Never been there myself, but if Boney were to invade that, I daresay we could find ourselves up there."

Although, strictly speaking, Baxter's words bordered on insolence, all grinned at the idea, which maintained their spirits until they came to the hamlet of Pozo Bello, which proved to be a tight collection of squat hovels grouped close around an almost equally squat chapel, seemingly for both protection and spiritual succour. Slade galloped across to converse with Arentschildt at the head of their column, but he soon galloped away to re-join his own column which progressed on towards Nave de Aver, this now being visible at two miles' distance further on, mostly because it was built on the only discernible hill for miles. The order came to halt, shouted down the column, but not to dismount. A bugle sounded 'Officers Call' and Cornet Carr saw his own Vigurs gallop off and then Captains Somers-Cocks and Myers pass by on either side, from their own Squadrons at the rear. Within five minutes all were back, Vigurs with unwelcome information, spoken immediately to Carr.

"The 7th Division have this Pozo Bello, namely Houston's 85th and a bunch of Portuguese. Cacadores, I believe they are called. We're out in the Campo."

He waved Cornet Peterson towards them.

"We've got to cover three miles. Us and the KGL, all the way back North, back up to Fuentes and a bit South from here as well, towards Nave de Aver. Too grand a name if it's the same kind of dung heap as this place."

Peterson's brows came together.

"Three miles, Sir. The Brigades hardly big enough to cover one!"

"I know. Can't be helped. Slade's holding the space South between where we'll finish and this Nave place. We're doing the bit that's South. And I mean 'we', our One and Two Squadrons, South from this Pozo place. At least we'll be able to get water for the horses, assuming this place has a well. So, even allowing for that minor comfort, we are out in the fields. Your Troop out there at day's end."

Within an hour, the horse lines were in place and some mess-areas had been established, some 300 yards before the village of Pozo Bello, with Troopers taking turns to mount picket on a line that overlooked the valley of the Dos Casas. The day drew on, the short Spring day soon succumbing to the creeping gloom of evening. Cornet Carr's C Troop rode out to man the picket line, which meant his men tying their horses to a piece of scrub or to a stake hammered into the ground, such that the man could then keep watch whilst the horse made the best of the poor grazing. The only two mounted, to ride the length of their line, were Carr himself and his Sergeant. Carr had three concerns and he voiced both in order of anxiety.

"Are there any of ours out in front of us, Sergeant?"

"Yes Sir. In the wood. The Lights of the 85th and some Portugee."

Carr changed the subject.

"I feel we are spread rather thinly, Sergeant."

"You're not wrong there, Sir, but what matters most is the foot-sloggers holding the village behind. Johnny won't come any further until he has that. It'll be our job to hold the flanks of that place."

"You're confident about that? Our job, that is?"

"I am Sir."

"Next. Can you hear anything?"

The pair reined in their horses and all became quiet, bar a strange shuffling sound. The near silence held for half a minute before Baxter answered.

"No Sir. At least nothing that I could put a definite name to."

"But you can hear something?"

"Yes Sir. The sort of odd sound you get from being close to a gang of navvies building a canal. A kind of shuffling murmur, if the wind's right."

oOo

The urgent notes of a bugle call cut down through the layers of sleep that had claimed Cornet Carr and his men, but immediately both NCOs and Officers were kicking their men awake. It was Baxter who woke Carr.

"Sir! It's started. We have to form up, alongside the village."

Carr sprang up, leaving his blanket spread on the ground as he ran to his horse. Within three minutes he was pulling tight the final strap and mounting up. Once in the saddle he felt he should do something to gather his men, there was enough daylight for him to be seen. He rose in his stirrups.

"To me C Troop! To me!"

His men gathered and formed up into fours to trot forward and join the gathering Squadrons of the 16th. Carr saw Vigurs detach himself away from the group made up from their Colonel, their Major, Brigadier Arentschildt and their Captains. At a canter, Vigurs reached him and Peterson soon arrived as well. Vigurs was a little breathless.

"The Frogs have attacked Nave de Havar, in Brigade strength, at least. Sanchez' Guerrillas, who were holding the place, had no chance to make any difference and have taken off. Some 14th are doing their best to hold the Frogs back, but first reports are that this is a huge attack and part of it is coming our way."

No sooner had that been said than Colonel Withers arrived and immediately gave Vigurs his orders.

"Lionel! Get yours formed to the right of the village and forward. Two ranks, C Troop behind D. A KGL Squadron will be on your right. You must hold until the 14th get back, or they'll be cut off. You'll have two Battalions of the 7th Division in front to your right, the 7th Division's furthest right flank. Good luck!"

Orders rang out and Vigurs' Two Squadron formed as ordered, each Troop in a double line. Once formed and from where they were, Carr had only to look to his right towards Nave de Haver to see a desperate rear-guard action being fought by what looked like two Squadrons of the 14th, these gallantly showing a front more than once against greatly superior numbers, before being outflanked on both sides, requiring yet another fall back, before they bravely turned to show front again. Relief came at last when they passed the first Regiment of the 7th Division who dealt the pursuing cavalry a punishing volley, which halted their advance. However, the grins on the faces of the 16th and the KGL on witnessing this, soon disappeared when hundreds of French cavalry appeared on their own front, coming over the low hills beyond a stunted wood. The weak sun shone on brass helmets and steel breastplates, informing every observer that they were all Dragoons, meaning Heavy Cavalry.

Vigurs and his two Cornets were in advance of their men, Vigurs studying the ground. He pointed forward.

"There! That defile through the woods, with that track. We can stop them there!"

Peterson looked at Carr and mouthed a single word.

"Stop?"

However, Vigurs was now giving orders.

"Narrow our front. Two double ranks. Be quick!"

As Withers had ordered, Peterson's D Troop were in the first ranks and Carr's C in the second, and so both split to then form a narrower column with each Troop in four ranks. Carr could now only look over the heads of Peterson's ranks, but he saw Vigurs lift his sword above his head. Carr presumed that this meant that the French were now in sight and this signal caused all other swords to be drawn and the Squadron began to walk forward. Carr could see nothing, which added greatly to the level of his anxiety. He could also hear nothing above the beat of the hooves and the jingle of the harness. Peterson's Troop broke into a trot and soon into a canter. A trumpet sounded from some way ahead, then came the shout of "Charge!" and Peterson's men spurred their horses into a gallop and Carr's did the same. The shock, when it came, was appalling, a crashing din of neighing horses, clashing steel and screaming men, but what was worse was that it seemed as though the Squadron had ridden into a brick wall, Peterson's Troop had come to a sudden halt and Carr's had cannoned into the rear of them. Carr's men urged their horses forward, but before them was a dense mass and it was not long before the men of the 16th were forced to give ground, from the sheer press of the far greater number of French cavalry, also larger men on heavier horses. The cry of "Fall back" began to be heard from the British ranks, and heard more often, as their pace backwards increased from the solid press against them. Carr took his own decision.

"Fall back to the village. Reform."

His men turned and galloped back, soon followed by Peterson's Troop. Carr slowed his horse to monitor and judge events and, thus, he saw the single Squadron of the KGL charge forward to hit the flank of the oncoming French column.

"That's suicide!"

Baxter was beside him.

"Come on, Sir. We've got to get back together. There's a lot more of this to come. Back to the lads, Sir."

Carr turned his horse to the right direction, but nothing more, he had to watch. The clash, when it came, was no different from what they had just experienced, but no better for being heard and seen from a distance. The KGL Hussars crashed into the front left corner of the French column. Men and horses of both sides were thrown to the ground and then the front stabilised as men hacked at each other urging their horses forward to push against those of their opponents, but the outcome was inevitable. Now through the defile, more French Dragoons came onto the flank of the KGL and this and the press from in front, sent men and horses slithering back over the loose turf until they also were forced to retreat. This was done swiftly, leaving the French to re-form before they came on. The 16th and the KGL Hussars had heroically bought time for everyone.

Once returned to Pozo Bello, Carr found both Troops reforming, with both Peterson and his own Sergeant shouting orders. Carr rode up to Peterson.

"Where's the Captain?"

Peterson turned from examining the line of his men.

"Captured I'd say! Now a prisoner."

Carr's face fell. He had realised the full importance of the development.

"That makes you Acting Captain. You're Senior."

"Thanks for that, but I feel but little elation, strangely."

"So, what are your orders?"

"Form here and wait for some, but I'm pleased to say that may not be too long."

British cavalry, such as there was, were arriving from all directions. First to arrive at the 16th's line was the Captain of the gallant 14th Light Dragoons, who had fought their way back from Nave de Aver. His men formed up beside the 16th.

"Brotherton. 16th."

Both Carr and Peterson saluted and introduced themselves, before Peterson spoke.

"We've lost our Captain and about a quarter of our force, Sir."

Brotherton nodded.

"I've lost a third of mine!"

He pointed down to the slope before them.

"Are those KGL coming back up?"

"Yes Sir. They charged after us."

92

"Seems they've also lost a good few."

He turned to the pair.

"Right, I'll hold things here. Now, Carr, isn't it?"

"Yes Sir."

"Get off back. See if you can find Arentschildt or even Slade. They may have some idea what can be done next. When you know, come and find me."

"What shall I tell him, Sir?"

Brotherton looked forward, his face grim.

"Tell him that French cavalry are coming out of the woods in overwhelming numbers, enough to outflank us, and I can also see two dense columns of Frog infantry advancing on Pozo. Go now."

"Can I take my Sergeant?"

"You may. You may need him."

Carr wheeled his horse and galloped around the ranks of the 16th into the wide space beyond, followed by Sergeant Baxter and two Troopers whom he had motioned to follow him, these being Corporal Jim Makepeace and Trooper Len Spivey. They emerged into a scene that was all a confusion of galloping horsemen. The one solid British force that he could see, was the remainder of the 7th Division, formed almost a mile away, these minus the 85th and 2nd Cacadores, who were still in the village. Carr rode 300 yards and then halted.

"Can you see anything or anyone that looks like Command, Sergeant?"

"No Sir, but that looks like a Squadron of ours over there, Sir. Some way back from the village. You might find the Colonel or the Major there, Sir."

With no viable alternative offering itself, Carr urged his horse towards the visible Squadron of the 16th. They were halfway over their journey, when the sounds of ferocious combat came from the village of Pozo Bello just over to the right of their route. They looked over but could see little as yet, only red and brown uniforms between the houses. They came to their Squadron to find Tavender as the only Officer.

"Sir. I've been sent to try to find Brigadiers Slade or Arentschildt. Have you seen them, Sir?"

Tavender ignored the question.

"Sent by whom?'

"Captain Brotherton of the 14th, Sir. He joined us with his men just after Captain Vigurs was captured."

"So, he's commanding both Squadrons?"

"Yes Sir."

"Right! I've lost Cornet Smythe of A Troop. Missing! You stay with me and take his place."

Carr was aghast.

"But Sir, I've been tasked to take some orders back to Captain Brotherton. He's holding at a forward position, alongside the village."

Tavender exploded with anger.

"Take a look around you, Carr. It's a shambles. No-one knows where anyone is! Brotherton, just like the rest of us, must make up his own mind, based on what's in front of him. Now get over to A Troop. There!"

Carr and his three went in the direction of the pointed arm and placed themselves on the right of the single rank. They had no sooner settled their horses when the roar of combat increased in Pozo Bello and the two garrison Battalions emerged from the alleyways and over the walls in headlong retreat, the red uniforms of the 85th and the brown of the Cacadores much mixed together. Almost all were soon out, but now closely pursued by the blue uniforms of masses of French infantry. The two British battalions were broken and confused, but then Carr looked to the right of the village and his face froze with horror. A whole Regiment of French Hussars was galloping towards the broken infantry, with very obvious, very serious intent. Carr urged his horse forward to reach Tavender.

"Sir! We should attack and give what help we can."

"Not yet. Await developments. When the French are broken up by their attack, then we'll move."

Carr choked back the words he next wish to say and rode to his Troop, now being A. Baxter's face was grim, as was the expression of all, as they sat and watched. The men of the two Allied Battalions saw the approaching danger and quickly formed defensive groups, just as they were swamped by hundreds of French Hussars. The Hussars halted and all of the 16th saw their swords rising and falling. More and more red or brown shapes could be seen prone on the ground. Then Baxter spoke.

"Look left, Sir. What do you think of that?"

Coming in from that direction were two Squadrons of KGL Hussars, riding in perfect order and within a minute they were into the French Hussars. Arriving in formation, they quickly pushed back the loosely formed French and, almost by a miracle, many groups of Allied soldiers were seen still standing. Their Officers began shouting orders, they picked up their wounded and began to form their columns. Meanwhile, the two Squadrons of the KGL had pushed on as far as was possible against the four of the French. Tavender at last decided to move forward and menace the flank of the French cavalry. He drew his sword and signalled his men to advance at a walk, but they had advanced no further than 100 yards before the French drew off, yet the KGL did not follow. Plainly their Commanders had grasped the new role now forced upon them, that being to fend off attacks and defend the inevitable retreat.

At last Command arrived, in the shape of General Slade, galloping up, to fiercely rein in his horse alongside Tavender.

"Name?"

"Captain Tavender, Sir."

"You stay close to those two Battalions trying to get back to the 7th. All other Squadrons will engage further out to help. When they're safe, join in against all this Frog cavalry, but first you cover that infantry."

He paused to stare at Tavender. No-one could be certain if Slade had seen the Squadron stand idle during the French cavalry attack, but if he had, he said nothing on the subject. Simply one word, before galloping off.

"Clear?"

Before Tavender could answer, Slade was gone and so Tavender looked over to see masses of French cavalry emerging from the valley of the Dos Casas, therefore it was obvious that they form on the left of the 85th and Cacadores column, now limping its way to safety. He spurred his horse to the far end of his two ranks. At each end was an NCO.

"As we are, come around and form column."

He trotted forward and the two lines followed him, now strung out in pairs, with B Troop riding between A and the infantry column, these on the right. There was not a man in the whole Squadron who did not frequently glance anxiously to his left in between holding his own mount on the tail of the horse in front. A forty-odd column, even of mounted men, did little to hide the column of infantry marching exposed over the open plain, which was now a kaleidoscope of the many different uniforms worn by many clusters of charging cavalry, all holding and retreating from larger assemblages of equally multi-coloured uniforms. Each minute the scene changed, as Slade's Hussars and Light Dragoons, fought to hold their Heavy French counterparts away from the alarmingly exposed infantry that Tavender was escorting, these hurrying to reach the 7th Division, now drawn up at the top of the long, shallow rise that marked the watershed between the Dos Casas and the parallel stream of the Turonne.

It was not long before the inevitable happened and what appeared to be half a Regiment of French Dragoons emerged from the confused melee on the plain to menace the lone 16th Squadron and their two Battalions. Immediately the order came down the column from Tavender.

"Face left. Draw sabres."

Thus, the Squadron halted, whilst the infantry marched on, but, now exposed, they also saw the menace for themselves and halted to show a front. Tavender appeared before the centre of his men, sword drawn and resting over his right shoulder. The French were formed for the charge and coming on, it seemed intending first to deal with the British cavalry, before attempting the infantry. Tavender waved his sword forward and urged his horse into a walk. The French were coming on at the trot and the gap was closing to under 200 yards, when suddenly there came the roar of cannon from the right. The first thought that came to Cornet Carr was "Whose?", but the sudden destruction of men and horses in the French ranks made that very obvious. He turned to see a British battery to the right of them that had unlimbered and sent what must have been grape-shot on ball into the French ranks at short range. The double munition had cut swathes through the two French Squadrons and Tavender saw his chance. He urged his horse into a canter and his men followed, then, 50 yards from the struggling French ranks, he spurred his mount into the gallop and his men crashed into the French, many easily penetrating the gaps in their front caused by the cannon-fire. Carr and his Troop, arriving second, barely had time to land a blow before the French turned their mounts and fled. With superb discipline, the 16th pursued for little more than 50 yards before halting, no orders being possible nor needed. Every man knew that their task was to shepherd the infantry to safety and not to become embroiled in the confusion of the cavalry combat. This was now progressing up towards the position of the 7th Division, as Slade's men were pushed back, despite so many controlled and effective assaults against their heavier opponents.

Within minutes, the Squadron was reformed and back in their place alongside the infantry column and so it was not long before they came up to the battery of field-guns. Tavender was at the head, with Cornets Faversham and Carr close behind. The three swung their horses out of the route of their own column as they progressed on beside the marching infantry. Tavender approached the Battery Commander, his men now limbering up the six guns preparatory to moving again, and Tavender saluted the now mounted Major.

"Tavender, Sir. 16th Light Dragoons."

"Bull!"

"We've been ordered by General Slade to escort this infantry back to the 7th, Sir."

"And I've been ordered by the same General Slade to cover the same, with my guns, as best I can. And I don't mind telling you that a battery stuck out alone in the middle of this barren acreage with cavalry all around, is not the most comforting order I can think of."

Tavender thought for a second.

"No Sir. That I can appreciate, but if we've both been ordered to act as escort, perhaps I can help. If I give you a Troop to cover you, then that makes it more likely that you can cover the infantry. Sir. As you've been ordered."

Bull thought for the briefest second.

"Yes. Give me a Troop and get on and I'll reform closer to the 7th. It's down to under half a mile now."

Tavender saluted and turned to Carr.

"Carr. Your Troop to serve as protection for Major Bull's battery. I'll continue with the infantry. Give him what protection you can, his guns will be very useful."

Sergeant Baxter and Corporal Makepeace looked daggers at Tavender. Tying Carr's A Troop up to a battery of field-guns was a task extremely hazardous, practically suicidal. He did not give the guns a Cat-in-Hell's chance of getting off the plain. Cavalry could ride out of danger in seconds, a formed battery took minutes to re-limber which was all a Squadron of Dragoons would need to annihilate the crew of every gun. However, Cornet Carr was naïvely saluting as Tavender took the remaining B Troop on after the still marching infantry. Carr now turned to Major Bull.

"Where do you want us, Sir?"

"Out on our left. Screen us as best you can until we un-limber again. There'll be plenty of work for us around here."

Carr led his 44 men out to the left of the battery, these now trotting forward, traces taught against the bouncing limbers and guns. It occurred to him that, with both involving horses, both would appear as cavalry to any observing French. After 500 yards further progress they had pulled ahead of the marching infantry escorted by Tavender's single Troop and Bull called a halt for his men to un-limber their battery, which was set up for action with commendable speed. Bull called to his Battery Captain, whilst he studied events ahead.

"Ramsey! Grape on ball, as before. I'll direct one to three, you take four to six. Loose off a couple and then limber up. The smoke will do us as much good as anything we send in their direction."

A shout of "Sir!" came from a fresh face under a bright bronze helmet, this decorated with a thick, high curve of black fur, front to back. Fascinated as he was, Carr soon came back to reality and turned to Bull.

"Where do you want us, Sir?"

Bull pointed beyond the end of the battery line.

"Out alongside me, but back a bit. One more jump and our job's done."

As Carr's Troop, led by Baxter, formed to the left of Bull's battery, Bull rose in his stirrups. He had seen a worthy target.

"Gun layers! Quarter left. Five elevation."

The crews jumped to the gun wheels to train their pieces slightly left, whilst two gunners raised each gun trail to swing it around. Once in place, the gun-layer set the elevation of the barrel, signalling to those on the trail to adjust the barrel for the five degrees of lift. Bull waited a few seconds. Carr could see a group of French Dragoons together, crossing their front at about 400 yards.

"Fire!"

The three guns crashed out, followed closely by those of Ramsey. He had seen the same target, then all was smoke, billowing back on the slight breeze, covering both them and the infantry now marching behind them, having now caught up. The smoke cleared and Carr looked for any signs of French casualties, but none seemed to have been added to the many already scattered over the plain. The target still cantered on.

"Once more, Ramsey."

Within less than a minute the guns were re-loaded and re-set and again they roared out. However, this time, when the smoke cleared, it seemed that their target had veered away. They must have inflicted some damage, so Bull closed his telescope.

"Time for off, Ramsey."

The six horse teams were brought forward and again, with astonishing speed, the guns and limbers were hitched up and the battery trotted on to once again over-take the infantry. These had increased their pace, their comrades of the 7th Division being now within shouting distance and Carr could hear cheering as the two Battalions closed up to where a Staff Officer was directing them to form, on the end of the 7th Division line. Now that they were nearer, Carr could see that General Houston had placed his men, exposed as they were on the open plain, in a position of considerable strength. They were not in squares, despite the French cavalry, instead secure behind groups of rocks and lengthy stone walls. However, the gallant men of Slade's command had at last been driven back upon them and Carr could only conclude that Slade had decided that his men had done all that they could. They were now, as he watched, withdrawing behind Houston's position, to re-form in his left rear.

Houston's men were now alone to face the onslaught of the mass of French cavalry, but even the inexperienced Carr could see that the whole mass was a complete jumble of many uniforms. The French had lost all formation. Meanwhile, Bull's men had once more lined up their guns, all now loaded and waiting for orders. Carr brought his men to the same position and watched, as did Bull. They were now able to fire across the front of the 7th, a very powerful addition to the fire-power of the infantry.

"As before, Ramsey. Fire when you think it worthwhile."

It soon was. Waves of cavalry surged up to the line of the 7th, but these, mostly British Battalions, met the onslaught with a heavy concentration of fire from behind their walls and boulder fastnesses. Bull's guns kept up a steady fire of their own and it soon became clear that the French Dragoons would fail to break into Houston's position, at least from the front, because all in the 16th could see the frontal attacks fall back. However, at a distance through the smoke could now be seen a mass of cavalry assailing Houston's right, but his men again stood firm behind their walls and boulders. The infantry action died away significantly, but Bull maintained fire against any cavalry that he could still see. After some long minutes, Baxter came up to Carr and Bull.

"Sirs. Coming up behind. There's something you should see."

Both Bull and Carr turned to look and saw a long column of British infantry advancing along the ridgeline, five British Battalions and two Portuguese, with a screen of green uniformed Riflemen out before them. Bull spoke first.

"Looks like Wellington's invited someone else to the Ball!"

Carr, meanwhile, was now looking in the other direction.

"Seems like the French have seen them, too, Sir, and they are pulling back."

Bull now turned his attention to the same direction.

"Pro tem, Carr. They're just sorting themselves out. This is perfect cavalry country and can you not see the columns of Frog infantry coming up behind? We're not done here, not by a long chalk!"

Baxter was stood just behind them and again felt the need to address his superiors.

"Sirs. I think we've got someone important coming to visit."

Both 'Sirs' now turned to see five horsemen cantering towards them, in the lead a man of average stature, but on a huge horse. However, what became more noticeable as he approached were the very dark features under his bi-corn hat, this worn 'fore and aft'. Bull recognised him immediately and came to the attention long before the horsemen arrived.

"That's Crauford!"

Carr sprang to the attention also, just as Crauford arrived.

"Names!"

"Major Bull, Sir. Royal Horse Artillery."

"Cornet Carr, Sir. 16th Light Dragoons."

The next question from Crauford came as a challenge.

"Another Carr?"

"Yes Sir. My brother's in the 105th."

The response was a growl from somewhere back in his throat.

"Right! Major, I'm here to cover Houston, who'll soon drop back down into the valley of the Turonne behind him. That done, we then have to get back ourselves. Slade will be staying with us. Wellington's turned half the army at right angles to hold the ridge behind us, where safety lies. So!"

He leaned forward in his larger than average saddle.

"How're you fixed?"

"A bit down with ball and grape, Sir, but plenty of canister."

"Right! Houston's falling back already I see, now that Johnny's drawn off a little. We'll go back as Battalion squares, with your guns in the intervals. Slade's men will still be needed I fear, as will yours Carr, but it cannot be helped. This is a desperate business."

"Yes Sir. But where do you want me, Sir."

"Remain here with this battery. These guns matter."

He now looked fully at Carr.

"Are you a betting man, Cornet?"

Carr smiled, whilst Crauford did not.

"I like the occasional wager, Sir, yes."

"So, what odds would you give on us getting back?"

"Better than evens, Sir."

"You're wrong! Long odds against, so keep your money in your pocket! We're talking about nigh on a two-mile point to point."

With that he swung his horse away and cantered quickly back to his column. Bull sprang into action.

"Ramsey! Limber up. We're to support infantry squares. Those just come up. They're here to get us all back home. Some hopes!"

Crauford's Light Division had already wheeled left and were marching to cover the width of the barren plain, this area, as yet, with no casualties to break the sweep of the ground, merely several clumps of rocks. However, the Crauford's Riflemen were already running to lodge themselves in the first of these, and soon his Light Division Battalions, the elite of Wellington's army, were formed in squares, a first line of four squares with, some 200 yards back, three more behind, coinciding with the intervals. With mixed feelings Carr watched Slade's much tried and, by now, exhausted cavalry, ride across their front to place themselves before Crauford's first line of squares and await the now re-organised French cavalry. The battery and Carr's Troop cantered back at a leisurely pace, to pass through Slade's cavalry, many with bloody faces and hands and all with the haggard and anxious look of men unable to give much more. They arrived to unlimber in the space between the two formations of Crauford's men, in line with the centre gap between the first four and the centre square of the back three. Carr was puzzled.

"Can't we just walk back, Sir, sort of ease ourselves away?"

Bull shook his head.

"No Carr, 'twon't serve. You have first to knock them back apiece, then, whilst they're pulling themselves back together again, you take off, for a few hundred yards more. One act at a time, in this drama."

He looked at the youngster.

"And I'll tell you one more thing. 'Tis wholly pleased I am that it's Crauford's boys all around. Marching back, whilst under attack and holding your square, is something only the very best can do."

Carr nodded.

"Right, Sir. Understood."

Bull now gave his own orders.

"Ramsey! One and two train full left, three and four forward, five and six full right. Three and four canister, the rest load grape. Double shot all."

Bull's guns now formed their own square, albeit only three sides, with their horse teams behind and Carr's Troop behind them making the fourth. Bull pulled out his watch.

"What time have you got, Ramsey?"

Ramsey fished inside his own jacket to pull out a watch then hidden in his palm, but connected by a huge chain.

"Five after seven, Sir."

"Carr?"

97

Carr had by now retrieved his own timepiece.

"Same Sir."

"Well, the next hour is going to be a very long one!"

They all looked up to study the ground before them and it was not long before the sights and sounds of cavalry conflict began again. Seen between the middle two squares in front, Slade's men, now with much reduced Squadrons, charged forward against the French mass of cavalry that was advancing upon them. The balance held for minutes and then the inevitable happened, the Light horsemen were forced to fall back. They galloped between the first line of squares to also pass through the next and re-form in the far rear. The French were now at the first four squares and each erupted with musket fire, while those that passed between, had Bull's guns waiting for them. The central guns, three and four, fired first, then the remaining four, two either side, fired at any Dragoons that emerged between the intervals of the outside squares. It was a severe check, French Dragoons and their horses lay all over, whilst the rest pulled back.

"Time to go, Ramsey!"

The front four squares began their withdrawal, at first walking back, bayonets still showing, but soon running back to pass by Bull's guns about to make their own retreat. All passed through the next three squares, but the British cavalry were again gallantly coming forward to make a front. All the time, the French cavalry were being peppered with accurate rifle-fire from the Greenjackets and Cacadores that Crauford had placed on the clumps of rocks and behind the stone walls that were now more numerous the closer they came to Fuentes. The French had been knocked back, as Bull had described it, but such was the flanking force that Massena had sent around Pozo Bello that hundreds of hardly tried Dragoons were still available. Back in their second position, Crauford came to inspect.

"All well Major?"

"Yes Sir. All to the good so far."

"So far, yes, but well done, nevertheless."

With that he was gone, off to lodge himself in the next square behind, where his men opened their ranks and he walked his horse in. The French came on as before and, as before, they were checked severely. The cavalry did what they could, then the British squares showing a front against the renewed assault, opened fire and then fell back, covered by those behind and again, now closer to safety, Crauford's men reformed to set their faces against Massena's onslaught. Showing admirable control, discipline and steadiness, twice more the Light Division repeated their manoeuvres, so that, finally, the lines in red that could be seen on the ridge behind, which was their goal, became individual figures. Bull looked behind at the ridge.

"Once more and we're done. I never would have thought it, Carr. I never would! Whoever the Frog General is, who's running things for them, he must be getting desperate. He should have scattered us long ago."

Bull was correct. The General was Montbrun and so, with his last chance before him, he sent forward everything he had, concentrating on the flanks. In addition, the trials of combat, exhaustion and casualties amongst the British infantry, but mostly amongst the cavalry, spread confusion, with many men separated from their Squadrons and their Officers. The controlled, but hitherto, effective, British cavalry charges no longer had such an impact and so, the French Dragoons, making their final throw, found themselves now more able to penetrate between the squares and attempt to break them. Thus, Bull and Carr found themselves in the company of many more French Dragoons than before. Their situation was becoming increasingly perilous and Bull had had enough.

"Ramsey!"

Ramsey's five and six, pointing right, had just been loaded, whilst the four pointing forward and left were at that moment empty. Therefore, these began to be limbered up immediately, whilst five and six took the time for a final discharge at the Dragoons, milling around on their front. After that, the infantry squares that had been making a front at that time, were by then already running past them, leaving the battery badly exposed. Bull looked around at the French cavalry on both sides, soon to close behind them and he took the inevitable decision.

"Ramsey. I'm pulling out. Follow when you can."

Ramsey may have heard but he made no reply, now busy connecting a limber to a field gun. Bull shouted at Carr.

"Carr! Your Troop come out with me. Cover my flanks. If you wish to help Ramsey, well, God's Blessings on you!"

Bull's four guns galloped off. Carr saw a Corporal that he did not know of his Troop and pointed to him.

"Take the Troop back with those guns."

He could say no more, time was urgent, but the purpose was obvious. The Corporal shouted to his men and they followed Bull's four guns away. Baxter looked at Carr.

"What are you going to do, Sir?"

Carr's face became grim.

"Help Ramsey!"

So also became Baxter's. He flexed his hand around the handle of his sabre to test the grip.

"As you say, Sir!"

Makepeace and Spivey, close behind, had heard all and they looked knowingly, one to the other. Meanwhile, Ramsey's two were limbered and ready to go, but the French Dragoons had closed in behind them, albeit not a thick screen but enough to make the point that they were surrounded. Before they could begin to move, a Dragoon Officer rode up to them, his face bloody and sweat streaked, his sword drawn and threatening.

"Vous devez abandoner!"

Ramsey turned towards him, pointing defiantly at him with his sabre.

"The Hell with you!"

Then back to Carr.

"Carr! The Frogs are not getting these guns!"

He spurred his horse forward as did his gunners on their own teams, whips rising and falling. Immediately Ramsey was at their head, sword extended, whilst his gunners urged their teams up to maximum speed. The Dragoons barring their way were now more numerous, but Ramsey and his guns were now at full gallop. Baxter was just behind on his outside, just ahead of Carr, whilst Makepeace and Spivey had placed themselves on the far side of the two-gun teams. The Dragoons were now in a loose line, up ahead, but static and faced with two careering gun teams. Ramsey aimed for the space between two horses where no sabre could reach him effectively and he hurtled into the gap, fending off weak blows when he entered the press. Behind him came the first gun-team, an intimidating sight for anyone, large, galloping horses stretching out at maximum, those of a gun-team being larger than most heavy cavalry mounts, with their following guns and limbers bouncing head high over the rough ground. Many French horses shied away from the sight, making a gap which the gun teams hurtled into. Baxter, just behind Ramsey stretched out his sabre to deflect a thrust from a French Dragoon. That done, he hammered the hand-guard into the man's face as his mount dealt a glancing blow to the fore-quarter of the Dragoon's mount. Ramsey blocked another sabre, the impact of both the galloping rider and the heavy Royal Artillery sabre, taking the Dragoon weapon from the Frenchman's hand. A repeat by Baxter, then they were through. Carr was following Ramsey and Baxter, but the pair, along with the guns and Makepeace on the far side, had acted like a battering-ram, this working powerfully on the minds of both Dragoons and their horses, more than any significant impact with their weapons.

However, the French were not done. Many turned their horses to ride alongside the still galloping teams, but for Ramsey, Baxter and Carr it was easy fencing. The French Dragoons had to reach across their bridle hands and their blows were weak, such that Baxter was able to cut two across the face and throat. Carr saw Makepeace and Spivey, these at the bridle-hand disadvantage, simply block whatever came their way with their sabres in their left hands, but then they were surrounded by red cavalry uniforms and the multi-coloured French had gone. The main British line was just ahead and all lined up there were cheering the rescue. Now surrounded by their own cavalry, the teams slowed to a trot and an Officer came across to Ramsey.

"Brotherton. 14th Light Dragoons."

Ramsey extended his hand, releasing the reins of his sweating mount.

"Ramsey. Royal Horse Artillery. It goes without saying that we are unbelievably grateful!"

Brotherton nodded and then noticed Carr.

"Carr! Pleased to see you still in one piece. All in all, a fairly desperate business. You'd agree?"

"Indeed Sir. Yes."

Bull now arrived and was almost speechless with emotion.

"Damn!"

Baxter, Makepeace and Spivey had come around to join Carr, who now addressed Bull as the senior.

99

"I'd best get back to my Regiment now Sir."

Bull could now speak, but was still somewhat engulfed in sentiment.

"Of course, Carr, but the Royal Horse Artillery will not forget the 16th. Be certain of that."

Carr saluted and urged his mount to a walk, then he turned to his three other-rank companions of the 16th.

"Thank-you for that men. You could have gone with the rest of the Troop."

Makepeace grinned.

"I made a promise to your brother, some time back, Sir, and anyway, a bottle of something will cover the whole thing nicely."

Carr grinned, as he steered his men towards what looked like a large group of his own Regiment, their bright yellow facings making the journey look very promising and he was correct. In fact, Withers and Johnson came forward to meet him, but Withers was as stern as ever, speaking in his usual gruff, flat tone.

"Well done, Carr. We saw the whole thing. You did well."

However, Johnson extended his hand.

"Well done, Carr. And you, too, men. A credit to the Regiment."

"Thank you, Sir, but you've heard, I take it, that Captain Vigurs has been captured."

"I have, but now get back to the lines. Get a drink and something to eat, then rejoin your Squadron. This affair still has a long course to run."

Cornet Carr and his men rode up the slight rise of the ridge and he took the time to look around. As Crauford had said, Wellington had turned half his line through ninety degrees, a long line now stretching East, crowning the ridge, to face this new onslaught from across the plain from Pozo Bello. The French who had pursued him were still massed before them, but making no serious move, even though the sounds of conflict could still be heard from various points. A moment's thought caused him to realise that the point of the newly created right-angle in the British line was Fuentes de Onoro, this but half a mile over to his right and, just at that moment, the whole area erupted with gunfire, as if a volcano.

oOo

Nat Drake now had his hands over his ears. Stood with his Company in the line of the 105th, they were just behind the six, six-gun, batteries that Wellington had placed there during the lull of the previous day. Now all 36 were fully in action and the noise was deafening, as each was served to the maximum. Major Carr, stood more to the centre of the 105th line and therefore more knowledgeable because of less smoke, could see the reason for the sudden action. The French had moved their own batteries forward to batter from close range the houses containing the holding British garrison at the river houses, firing in support of what was plainly a whole Divisional French assault on the village. However, Carr could see that the French gunners were at some disadvantage. Not only were the Allied guns 300 feet above them, but they were also more numerous. In fact, during the minute or two that it took for him to come to that conclusion, two French guns were wrecked by Allied roundshot. Stood next to O'Hare, he lowered his telescope.

"For once we've got them outgunned!"

O'Hare was still looking through his.

"True, but not in troops, it would seem. I estimate he has three Divisions opposite here. One just going in and two waiting in support. It's here that it'll be decided. If Johnny takes the village and then gets up here in force, well, the thing's done."

Now anxious, Carr raised his own telescope, to quickly lower it and then look behind.

"What's he put here? Behind us?"

O'Hare folded his arms and continued to look forward, as, from halfway down the slope of the village, the sights of infantry combat came into view, white musket smoke, and the occasional sound of musketry from there, between the cannonading. The French were already in the village.

"Well, we're first reserve to the village, and the rest of McKinnon's Brigade and Colville's are behind us, as second. After them, there's the whole of the First, but down there, in the village it's just the Scots 79th and 71st in there again to hold up Johnny. The 24th are in reserve of them, that's them formed on the road beneath our feet."

Carr now studied the events that could be seen between the houses, barns and paddocks of the village. It was not long before he saw the Highlanders of the two much tried Battalions, once more being forced from

100

their positions and retreating back up through the roads and alleyways that led to the Church just below him. Behind came the blue masses of the Divisional French assault. Carr turned to O'Hare.

"It won't be long, will it?"

"No. We'll be back into that pile of rubble again, soon enough. It's just a question of when."

Instinctively Carr began to walk to the left, where the Light Company were and so he soon came to Number Three, The Colour Company, where stood Captain Joshua Heaviside.

"Hello Joshua. Seems we're going to be needed again, and not too far off."

Heaviside nodded, his face grim, his black eyebrows now close together, his chin rapidly becoming in need of another shave. He slowly nodded agreement.

"Yes. This is becoming as bad as Talavera, but I feel, that if we win this, then the balance of this whole war will be tipping our way. This is a major judgment on who stands superior. 'Blessed is the man who remains steadfast under trial, for when he has stood the test, he will receive the crown of life.' James One. Verse 22."

Carr smiled.

"I hope we can all look forward to that one, Joshua! But, good luck. Come the finish, as the men say."

"Indeed, and good luck to you too, Henry."

Carr walked on. From his vantage point above the highest road, with the Church and its cemetery immediately below that, he could see that soon the French assault would be once more back in the upper half of the village, just as when he had command the Light Companies two days previously. Formed on the road below, were the ten Companies of the 24th. He continued on, warning his Captains of impending action, as the smoke of the combat containing the two Scottish Regiments took itself higher and grew thicker above the dull orange roofs of the village, but nothing could be heard of that, the six batteries of their own line, were still bellowing their defiance. The two Battalions now in the village and the 24th just above it, were all from the First Division and their own Divisional Commander, Brent-Spencer was himself beside the 24th's Colonel, albeit the former on a horse. However, from that height, he could see what Carr also could, that the Scotsmen would soon be forced back to the Church and the French had to be stopped. Carr saw Brent-Spencer say something and almost immediately the 24th's Drummers beat the advance. The Battalion split into Companies and the Companies into Sections in order to negotiate the droves and alleyways at the top of the village. The 24th passed through the Scots retreating up and then began firing Section volleys from line. The Scots rallied and joined in, the counter-attack now moving forward, which continued back down the slope, clearing the village by disciplined fire-power alone. The assaulting French had not had time to secure the important buildings of the village and so, all crushed together in the narrow spaces between the buildings, they were an easy target for the very destructive musketry of the British Brigade now descending upon them. Within minutes the sights and sounds of combat were back amongst the lower houses. Thankfully, with the repulse of the first attack on the village, the Allied cannonade had ceased, as much to replenish ammunition as for a lack of targets and the French batteries had now pulled back some 200 yards, but leaving many wrecked guns behind. By now Carr had reached Nat Drake.

"Well, there's a lesson, Nat. You can send too many men into a place like this. So many, they could barely move to reload, nor fix a bayonet."

Drake smiled grimly.

"One can only hope that they will continue to make that mistake …….."

He pointed forward.

"……. but now you can see as much as I can. He has two more Divisions, at least, in his reserve, waiting for their turn. Johnny wants this village, very, very badly!"

From the lowest houses of the village, alongside the river, came only the sound of musketry being exchanged, which Carr now commented on.

"He's still got the lower houses."

Carr pulled out his telescope and focused it to just below the French ridge.

"You were saying that he wants this village, very badly! Well, you could well make a living from such predictions, because some of those you saw, are coming forward now and it looks like a whole Brigade, three Battalions of the best he's got. And all Grenadiers!"

Drake looked anxiously at Carr, as he pulled out his own telescope to focus it on the main road down to the ford from the French side, and then on both sides of the road. What he saw confirmed what Carr had said. Striding confidently forward he could see what looked like Napoleon's Imperial Guard, but these were merely Grenadiers from Massena's Ligne and Leger Regiments. However, the word 'merely' did not accurately apply, these all being tall men, this accentuated by bearskin hats with a huge red plume in the centre and shoulders appearing wider due to the large, red epaulettes on each. Drake lowered his telescope.

"We'll soon be part of this!"

At that moment, Picton arrived with a number of Staff. The pair sprang to the attention and saluted, but Picton gave them hardly a glance, being far more intent on events in the village. It was at that moment the cannonade began again, with the Grenadier columns as their targets. Conversation was now impossible and so Picton continued to stare forward, as did Carr and Drake, with Picton merely two yards away on his horse. When a usable reduction in the cannonade came, but not a cessation, Picton felt inclined to lean over.

"Get your men ready, Carr. You'll be in this, with the rest of Mackinnon's Lights. You're going down first."

His face took on a disgusted look.

"I've never seen a fuss of the like, over such a pile of badly joined up stone in all my born days!"

With that he wheeled his horse right and walked it back to the higher ground behind. Drake turned to Ellis, stood just behind.

"Load. Very carefully."

Ellis saluted and walked back to the line.

"Careful load. Pass it on."

The first to hear were the group of Lieutenant Maltby's One Section. These, all carrying Baker rifles, took this to mean wrapping the ball in a small piece of leather, the better to grip the rifling of the barrel. All silently began the careful process, whilst occasionally glancing up to see exactly what they had expected, the British once more falling back through the village in the face of another determined assault. Davey and Miles, amongst the first to finish, were the first to see Mackinnon arrive and go to Carr, who simply drew his sword. Drake walked back and drew his, to then stand before his men and say one word.

"Forward!"

Drake led his men, over the wall, across the road and then he positioned his Company behind the stone wall on the road's lower edge and some also occupying a barn which had a large door and a window facing down towards the village. From previous conflicts, the door was already blocked by an old cart, lumps of stone and items of ancient machinery. Carr had remained back at the battery gunline and what he saw confirmed Picton's words, the Light Companies of the 88th and 74th, with the Company of the 60th Rifles, had also crossed the road and were occupying their own positions, these being walls and barns, with the 88th and the Rifles holding the Church and the cemetery. It was not long before the Light Companies of the 1st Division began to arrive in the rear, as a reserve, but it was now plain that the Scots of the 71st and 79th had given all they could, also the 24th. Forced back twice in a dangerous retreat, they now passed through Mackinnon's four Light Companies for the final time, with haggard faces, eyes sunk back with fatigue, stuck to the sweat around their mouths and over their chins was lodged gun-powder from biting open cartridges, their faces black from dirt and musket smoke. The men of the 105th Light Company reached over the wall to pull the tired men up and over. Miles grasped the wrist and hand of a bearded Corporal of the 79th Cameronians and hauled him up.

"Come on over, mate. We're on the job now."

The Corporal croaked a reply through his severe thirst.

"My thanks tae ye!"

Miles swung the strap of his canteen over his head.

"Here! Take a swig of this. Mostly brandy. Take a pull and leave it there."

The Cameronian took a long drink and then replaced the stopper before dropping it on the ground beside Miles.

"If ye're ever in Lennoxtown, come an' look me up. Macphearson's the name."

"Fat chance! Anything North of Gloucester's a foreign country to me."

There came a croaking laugh, but with that the man had gone, falling back with his comrades, but Maltby had seen and shouted his annoyance with Miles, as he re-hung the strap of his canteen around his shoulder.

"Miles! Stand to, damn you!"

Miles brought his musket forward to rest on the stones and mumbled to himself.

"All right. All right. These turkey-cocks is only just now in range. I'll get my share. Don't you worry."

At this point Carr was behind Davey.

"Can you see one?"

The 'one' meant a high-ranking Officer, which Davey had also been looking for.

"Nothing like a General, Sir, but there's plenty down there as looks like Colonels."

"You choose. Just bring one down."

Davey brought up his rifle and fully cocked the hammer.

"Sir."

He sighted, held his breath and eased back the trigger. The weapon went off with its customary flat bark and Carr saw a leading Officer flung backwards by the half-inch lead ball. Davey taking his shot was the signal for the rest of the Company to open fire and each aimed shot inflicted a casualty, but not enough to even slow the Grenadier advance. With bravery born of supreme confidence, the dense masses of Grenadiers clambered over the walls and simply marched around the buildings using the droves and alleyways. The firepower of four Light Companies would not be enough to stop them. Although their casualties increased the closer they came to the defenders, their advance barely slowed.

Anxiety grew in the minds of Carr and Drake as the French tide flooded up closer and closer. The Grenadiers were now answering their fire and their own men were falling. All this must have been seen by someone, perhaps Wellington himself, because Drake sensed movement behind to see another Light Company coming to re-inforce them, their Captain holding out his hand.

"Fellowes. 30th Foot. 1st Division."

"Drake. 105th."

Fellowes peered over the wall.

"Not good!"

"No!"

"Fire by files?"

"Agreed!"

Both Captains shouted the order and their men split into their threes, to maintain a continuous fire over the wall, one firing, one falling back, the last reloading. The increase in the amount of lead being sent into the ranks of the Grenadiers had an effect, because their Officers now bellowed orders that could be heard from the wall and the French began to form their own firing lines, mostly from cover, but some in the open. Carr looked rightwards and felt slightly more confident. Yet more Light Troops were being sent down, including many brown uniformed Cacadores, but the Grenadiers had pushed the French advance to within 50 yards of the Allied gunline behind him and he knew, that beyond these guns, there was little that could hold another determined attack such as this. The French still had one Division, at least, unused, or so he believed, which did nothing to boost his confidence, and it now seemed that the Grenadiers had made most progress over at the main road, so much so that they were now surrounding the Church and were into the cemetery, fighting desperately with the 88th over and around the tombs and gravestones.

He climbed back to the gunline and found his concern very justified. All the Light Companies facing the Grenadiers were maintaining a ferocious fire, but theses elite French soldiers were holding their ground and it would require a serious attack on the part of the Allies to send them back down to the lower reaches of the village. What really heightened his concern, however, was that the next attack would plainly come from the French, not a counter-attack from his own side. The Corps Commander, or even Massena himself, had plainly decided that just one more heave would send his men over the top of the slope and then the key to Wellington's position would be carried. In confirmation of this, from his vantage point Carr could see four distinct columns, three of two Battalions, but the one column aiming furthest right, for the main road and the Church had three. There was no possibility of the Light Companies currently holding the line to resist an attack of this magnitude. He ran to the head of his own 105th, to find Mackinnon stood with Lacey and O'Hare. All three turned towards him and all three immediately caught the anxiety of his tone as Carr spoke to none in particular.

"Sir. Have you seen what they're now sending up?"

Mackinnon's face was as grey as granite and equally grim.

"Aye Carr, ah can see as well as ye! Tak' yersel back tae yer men and hold as best ye can. I'll see what we can get from Himself!"

Very much less than assured, Carr hurried back to the line of the 105th to find that the situation was unchanged apart from the fact that two of the French columns, albeit in no real formation, were advancing up through their half of the village, one to their left, the other straight for them. Plainly, both would soon pick up the Grenadiers now holding the top of the village and then advance on. Deep anxiety welled up with Carr, now almost certain that the French were on the brink of a significant victory. He ran into the barn in the centre of their front. Holding that would be vital.

Remaining before his men, stood with O'Hare and Mackinnon, Lacey could see for himself that the French columns had gathered the Grenadiers and all were now advancing forward. The Light Companies were still holding, but most were now ceasing to reload; they were fixing bayonets for the final defence. Then Mackinnon tugged at his sleeve.

"Lacey. Wi' me."

Over to their right, were a group of mounted Staff Officers, but they did not contain Wellington.

"There's Packenham. Perhaps he can give an order. If not, we'll have tae go anyway, yours and Wallace, and damn the consequences!"

Mackinnon reached Packenham and saluted.

"Sir! The line won't hold. Should mine advance? Sir?"

General Sir Edward Packenham, one of two of Wellington's most senior Staff Officers, rose in his stirrups and looked forward. The French now had the Church, most of the cemetery and were now pushing over the road beyond to take the groups of rocks beyond it. The Light Companies were fighting with both shot and bayonet to hold the very last of the slope and, what was worse, the three Battalion column, with the longest route, was now advancing up past the Church on the main road, now almost unopposed and in perfect formation. Packenham wheeled his horse to turn back.

"Give me a minute."

With that he was gone and Mackinnon turned to Lacey and Wallace, who was now part of the group and also seeking orders.

"Minute be damned! Wallace, where are yours?"

"Still on the main road, not too far back."

"Right. Bring them forward and hit that column coming up, I'll be with ye. Lacey, yours down that other back alley, over on your side. Hit one of the columns at least. The 45th will have tae stay here, as some kind of rearguard, if all goes wrong. Now, Lacey, awa' and Wallace, let's get on."

However, at that moment Packenham returned and the three halted their departure.

"He says you may go. Come along!"

The first sentence the three understood, the second made no sense, but Mackinnon held his place only long enough to shake Lacey's hand.

"Good luck, Lacey!"

Then the pair were gone and Lacey ran back to his own men, only 100 yards away, to find O'Hare waiting.

"We have to go in! Down that drove."

He pointed to what was little more than a wide cart-track, now full of French line troops.

"Column of Sections. Colours first!"

O'Hare was horror-struck.

"But there's another column beyond them. Who takes that?"

"I know. We can only do what we can. Please give the order."

O'Hare ran off and soon the drums were beating out 'column by sections'. Lacey looked over the slope to the road, where his men and the 30th were holding the wall, but the French were around the barn. Inside that barn, Carr may have heard the drums of his Regiment behind him, but they did not register. His men were fighting to hold the building, both back and front. He was at the main door, stood atop the cart, his sword in one hand, a small axe in the other. From the loft door above there came a continuous stream of fire as his men and those of the 30th filed up to the opening to continuously bring down any Frenchman about to use his musket against those defending the main door below. Thus, with Saunders, Solomon, Ellis and Shakeshaft, Carr defended the main door. Yet another Grenadier came to the cart intent on using his bayonet on Carr, but he used his sword to deflect over the bayonet, then his left hand swung the hatchet into the side of the man's head, the chin strap parting as the hatchet bit into the man's temple as far as the bridge of his nose. However, next came an Officer with a pistol, which was immediately aimed at Carr who was frantically trying to disengage the hatchet, but Saunders had a French musket in his hand, complete with bayonet, and he hurled it as a javelin, to pierce deep into the man's chest. Then came relief, however temporary, in the form of their own men with loaded muskets, who came up to the barrier and fired across it, between the legs of Carr and his men.

At the back of the barn, beside the road, Fearnley, Len Bailey and two others were doing their best to keep the back door closed from the assault of what must have been over half a dozen musket butts. The door was a half and half stable-door and, although they had blocked the half below with heavy chains and a plough, the top half could not be so well supported and eventually the locking hasp gave way to reveal the mustachioed faces of many Grenadiers and French line infantry. The door top-half swung back even further inwards and the defenders saw several French muskets come to the present to fire in, but Bailey had the presence of mind to swing the door back closed just as they fired and the wood on their side splintered as the many balls penetrated, to only disfigure the inner surface. The door swung back inwards slightly with the impact, but there was no hurt to Fearnley and his men. However, the door swung fully open again, pushed by the French outside and two of Fearnley's men fired through the opening, but just before the smoke obscured all, Fearnley's spirits lifted. He could see a column of his own Regiment, their bright green facings very prominent, coming down from the crest of the ridge. With such as that merely yards behind them, the French melted away. Fearnley ran to the main door to see Carr, still battling atop the cart with sword and hatchet.

"Sir! The lads are coming over."

Carr made no reply, still fending off bayonets, but Saunders was unengaged at that moment and could turn momentarily.

"Good!"

Up on the slope, beside the Regimental Colour held up by a very excited and grinning Ensign Patrick Mulcahy, Colour Sergeant Deakin marched forward with Toby Halfway to his right. Deakin needed only to look at the scene before him, desperate Redcoats holding a wall against what seemed like many hundreds of French, a blue tide, to realise that his own chances of surviving the day alongside The Colour were not of the best.

"If we don't both get through this, Tobe, I can only say it's been nice knowin' you. If you comes out an' I don't, take care of Bridie. She's a fine woman and've got sense an' she'll take you on."

Halfway took a deep breath.

"I'd say we'll both be for layin' out after all this is done! We'll soon be chargin' on through that crew t'other side of that wall an' may the Good Lord preserve us both."

However, his thoughts were interrupted by a loud, but eerie howl, coming from over on their right, at the main road.

"That's them Irish bastards goin' in. Heathen diddykites!"

At their head, merely yards in front, marched Lacey, sword drawn, leading his Regiment to the top of the drove, with O'Hare just behind. The French actually in the drove, intimidated by the sight of the solid column, were spreading either side, over the wall, and O'Hare realised that, from behind the drove walls, they could pour fire into the flanks of the 105th column. O'Hare ran back to the second Company in the column, the Grenadiers, where he saw Carravoy.

"Charles! Pull yours out and double up on our left. Clear the French from the drove walls on that side. Protect our flank!"

With that he was gone, leaving Lord Carravoy stunned by the magnitude of what he had been asked to do, but Lieutenant Ameshurst had heard all at the head of his Section marching immediately behind.

"I'll take mine now, Sir."

He turned to his Sergeant.

"Ridgway! Double out and follow me."

Ameshurst was off at a sprint, with his men following. Now in the rear of a whole Section of his own men, Carravoy had no choice but to run beside D'Villiers when he came up to him with his Section. Meanwhile, Lacey was at the point of no return, of full commitment or nothing. He raised his sword.

"Charge, boys, charge! Hurrah for the King! Hurrah for the 105th!"

His men surged forward into the drove and the French parted, but there were still hundreds either side in the adjoining enclosures. O'Hare had taken himself rightwards, to the wall so desperately defended by his own Light Company and those of the 30th. He knew that both flanks of the 105th needed protecting and with the 105th Grenadiers holding the left, he must ensure the right. He climbed up onto the wall and waved his sword so that many would notice him. A French bullet whipped back the tail of his jacket and another set his shako at an odd angle.

"Come on now, boys. Sure, 'tis no kind of a good thing, to be lettin' a little bit of stone like this be holdin' youse all up!"

With that he jumped down onto the French side and the men of both Regiments poured over, but leaving many dead and wounded on their own side. The French in the paddock beyond, many being Grenadiers, gave but a little and held there, so both sides now stood their ground and fenced across the disputed ground with swords, butts and bayonets. O'Hare found himself facing an Officer, who had obviously singled him out for single, honourable, combat. The Officer stood in a classical fencing pose, sword extended. O'Hare waited for the blow and when it came, deflected it and sprang forward against the man to head-butt him on the nose. The man staggered back, blood pouring over his chin, but with a horrified look on his face that his opponent had committed so unchivalrous an act. O'Hare swore at him, but held back, to hold his place in the line, whilst his men slowly inched their way forward. Then suddenly their opponents were falling back. The outcome was being decided further over on the left, by the 105th column penetrating deep into the French at the drove and threatening the flank of those confronting O'Hare. Carr, still in the barn adjoining the wall, felt, rather than counted, that the French at his doorway were now less numerous. Still holding his sword and hatchet he leapt down from the cart, encouraging his men in a very 'Picton', fashion.

"Come on you whoreson bastards! It's our turn now!"

As his men followed him from the doorway, Carr noticed, lying on the ground, the pistol of the Officer that Saunders had 'javelined'. He dropped the hatchet and picked it up, to then check the priming. Satisfied, he shouldered his way through his own men to get to the front, his rightful place, however dubious he was about the whole idea. There he raised his sword and pointed it at the French, now in full retreat.

"Forward! Get to the Colonel."

Carravoy ran on with D'Villier's Section on opposite side of the drove, however, the de facto leader of the Grenadier Company at that moment was Ameshurst, two paces in front of his men. Either side of him were the close line of his bodyguard, who downed with musket fire any Frenchman who presented their weapon with the intent of harming their much-esteemed Section Lieutenant. Carravoy's Grenadiers, in solid order were pushing the French back, as much by the intimidating front they presented, as by the amount of firepower they dealt out, although the 105th Grenadiers were firing and loading as they advanced at walking pace. Seeing this French retreat and thereby feeling more confident, Carravoy finally came to the lead, just ahead of his men. A wounded French Officer lay on the stubble before him, attempting to raise his sword. Carravoy stood on the man's forearm and brought back his own sword for a coup-de-grace, but he saw the look of abject terror spread across the Frenchman's face. He could be little more than a teenager and Carravoy stopped himself. This was murder and so he lowered his sword and contented himself by kicking away that of the Frenchman. Then he was on forward, pressed on from behind by the close ranks of his men.

The whole issue facing the 105th had been decided by Lacey's column on the drove. Their flanks protected from serious assault they charged down the narrow space, not in a headlong sprint, but more a controlled, yet rapid advance. What mattered, Lacey knew, was the appearance of a solid and intimidating formation, seemingly unstoppable and that was what he had, himself just in the lead of the Colour Party, both Colours up and prominent, with Colour Sergeant Deakin continuously doing his best to hold back his Ensign, who seemed intent on leading the whole charge himself. The French were falling back on all three fronts, beyond both walls and in the actual drove. Through the spaces between the backs of the fleeing French, Lacey could see that some kind of line had been formed by them where the drove ended and entered the village. Despite his own breathlessness, he knew he had to arrive at that line at the same time as the fleeing French. They would give him both cover from their fire and disrupt the line as they passed through. He raised his sword to use the last of his breath.

"On boys, on! Into them. Don't let them stand."

He was soon overtaken by those fitter than he in his first ranks, which included Ensign Mulcahy. Led now by Heaviside, the column of the 105th, now only a dozen men wide across the narrowing drove, increased their pace and, on the heels of the French they were chasing, crashed into the disrupted line. Heaviside brushed aside a bayonet and sent a left-hook into the face of the man wielding it, before finding himself trampling on the struggling figure of a French Grenadier who had been felled from some other source. The line was overwhelmed and so, with barely a pause, the column of the 105th entered the village. Then, astonishingly, from several houses and hovels came men of the previous Regiments who had fought in the village but minutes before, all 71st, 79th and the 24th, also several Greenjacket Riflemen. All had been holding out in various defendable places, holding out because the last two French assaults had not had time to clear these groups of enemies remaining in their rear. All these now joined the three points of the 105th assault, led by Carravoy, Lacey and O'Hare.

The column was now in the village proper and Heaviside, now in the lead, knew the dangers of the maze of paddocks, byres and hovels, that they were attempting to clear. All over, in any space, lay heaps of dead, many in the uniforms of Highlanders and French Grenadiers and Line troops. He held his sword across the rank of his men. They were deep into what had been the French position, yet few of these could now be seen and the sounds of musketry and close combat were becoming less intense in their part of the village, whilst from further over on their right, from the main road, still came the sounds of utter mayhem. He urged caution on himself, but the advance needed to be maintained whilst, at that moment, they were stood at the entrance to what looked like the village Plaza. A few French were still emerging from buildings on the far side, to run back between their alleyways to the river. He decided that the 105th must advance on and so he took a deep breath.

"Let caution be our watchword, but let fortitude steel our hearts."

A voice came from behind.

"Is that in the Bible, Sir?"

Heaviside led his men forward.

"No, but perhaps it should be!"

"Yes Sir."

They crossed the Plaza and entered the widest alleyway from where, 100 yards further on, they could see the river, with scores of French pouring across it. Many in the column now began to fire their muskets. 100 yards was effective range enough and several French began to fall, some into the waters of the Dos Casas.

Lacey had now taken himself over to the left. He was mindful of the final French column, that furthest left, unopposed as far as he knew, with only his Grenadier Company on that side. He turned left along the first street he came to and immediately bumped into a party of his Grenadiers, who immediately presented arms.

"We've done well, men, but who's on this side? Are your Officers still alive?"

A Corporal spoke up.

"All are still alive and unwounded, Sir. Captain Carravoy and Lieutenant Ameshurst are up front."

"So, what are you doing here?"

"Sent over by Captain Carravoy, Sir. To make contact with you. Sir."

"What was the situation when you left? Were you in the village?"

"No Sir. We cleared our paddock and then Lieutenant Ameshurst sent us to man the wall, far over. A lot of French were falling back across us."

Lacey felt immediate relief. The final French column was not about to fall on his flank and rear.

"Right! Good! Lead me to your Captain."

The Grenadiers turned to trot back, at 'double pace', and Lacey, now recovered, followed. Soon they were just up the slope above the village and he saw the paddock with its far wall being held by his Grenadier Company, all pouring fire into a mass of retreating French, who were being pursued, more than pushed, by what he took to be Power's Portuguese Brigade from his own Division. Soon the French were gone and all that was left to do was for the Portuguese and British to congratulate each other by cheering and shaking hands over the wall. Lacey trotted up to the three Grenadier Officers, all sharing some brandy, probably newly obtained. Ameshurst was in possession of what looked like a flask covered in very fine filigree work of French origin.

"Take a pull, Sir?"

Lacey took the flask and then a long drink. It took some seconds before he regained his breath.

"Well done to you, all three. Now. Get some men into the village, but not right up to the stream. The buildings there are well covered by Johnny's guns. Hold at halfway, I want no more to die today. I'm off to see what has happened further over. Give it fifteen minutes and then, Royston, come over yourself to find me and we'll go on from there, when we know more."

At that exact minute, far over on the 105th right, things had come to much the same stand, but closer to the river. The Light Company were further downstream from their original ford, there using the windows of a large and well-appointed building to send aimed shots into the fleeing French masses. Davey, Saunders, Pike et al were at the first-floor windows, when a very Irish voice shouted from the stairwell.

"Any of youse French bastards up there, you'd best surrender yourselves and quick!"

Miles was the first to answer, as he was at the top of the stairs, reloading.

"Diddykites! Sod off! There's nothin' 'ere for you!"

The reply was what seemed a multitude of heavy boots pounding on the ancient stairs, but it turned out to be no more than a Corporal and four men, all clearly Connaught Rangers identified by their bright yellow cuffs, collars and facings. It was the Corporal who spoke first.

"Ah now, don't be like that. Sure now, shouldn't we all be gettin' a share of the good pickings to be had in a place such as this?"

Saunders turned on them, his sheer size halting their progress, leaving them where they stood.

"There's no pickings here. All here was as poor as church-mice and anything handy has been took off by Johnny and is in some Frog back-pack by now."

Miles, now reloaded and on his way to a window, took the time to agree.

"S'right! So, if you'm lookin' for pickings and've got no orders, then get down to some of they Frogs lyin' all over. But just Frogs, mind! There's Scots lads amongst 'em too. That's for their own boys."

The Corporal essayed a look of mock affront.

"The very idea, now! How could youse be sayin' such a thing?"

However, at that moment a French cannonball came through the front wall and straight out the back, showering all with dust and rubble. Rubbing his eyes and coughing, the 88th Corporal took his leave.

"You may be right. This is no place for any kind of careful look-round."

He turned to the stairs and shooed his men down, but that was the end of their scavenging, for at the bottom of the stairs, an 88th Captain was introducing himself to Major Carr.

"O'Dowda, Sir, 88th."

"Carr. 105th."

Carr turned to see the five Connaughts descending.

"These are yours, I take it."

O'Dowda looked up at his men and gave a stern order.

"Back two buildings and hold. Tend left and you'll find our men."

He then turned to fully face them.

"But what are you doing here?"

The Corporal answered from the top of the stairs.

"Just chasin' French, Sir. Got a bit lost."

O'Dowda's face showed that he wasn't at all convinced, but this was no time for an enquiry.

"You now have your orders. I'll be there in five minutes and expect to see you there."

The men hurried off, giving Carr the chance to interrogate O'Dowda.

"So what happened at your end? On the road?"

The 88th Captain let out a deep sigh.

"I would never have believed that we could do it, but I have to credit the men. They're untrustworthy villains and scoundrels, everyone, but the very Devil in a fight."

Carr looked quizzical.

"But that column had three Battalions?"

"It did, but we demolished the first, bayonet to bayonet, which sent them back into the second and then the third. We carried on pushing forward, they all took off and that's them you can see from the windows of here."

Such a simple, bland statement had Carr shaking his head. For one Battalion to so thoroughly defeat three had him more than a little amazed, but, as before, there was no time for an enquiry.

"Right. A few parting shots and then back from the river. Johnny's got these under his guns. There's enough good men died this day. Any more, will be to no gain."

O'Dowda saluted.

"Yes Sir. I couldn't agree more."

O'Dowda left and Carr ascended the stairs to halfway, where his men were still sending shots into the retreating French. Than another French cannonball passed through, creating a fog of plaster dust.

"We're done. Out and fall back two houses. Hold there and get something to eat. There's plenty of haversacks with rations now orphaned. This is done!"

oOo

Chapter Four

First Siege

After any major conflict, the most noticeable change in any Battalion camp is the sudden arrival of white amongst the uniforms worn around the camp lines. It could almost be described as a cheery sight, were it not for the connected sounds emerging from the Surgeon's tent and, therefore, those in need for any amount of white bandage in any form about them would most certainly settle for what fortune had dealt them. Much rather that, to be thankfully whole, albeit 'holed', than have the need to wait for the attentions of any Surgeon or his assistants. Therefore now, all over, white bandages could be seen, around heads, hands and as arm slings, and some around ankles, these soon not so white, and many hidden, yet fattening sleeves and trouser legs. Such as this was about to happen to Ensign Mulcahy, if his Mother, Bridie Mulcahy, could bring herself to concentrate on the task of bandaging his thigh just above his right knee, rather than occupy her mind with berating her 'Army' husband, one Colour-Sergeant Deakin. Her voice rose in inverse proportion to the amount of bandage she was applying.

"Sure, is it not your job to take good care of such as him? To not let the Heathen French get at him with their wicked bayonets and knives and whatnot. He could have been kilt, sure as God's above!"

Jed Deakin was sat on a biscuit-box, head down, hands between his knees, a picture of weary resignation. He looked up to see the fierce Irish eyes of his 'Army' wife.

"Now, what on earth can I do, in the middle of a battle, if this half-wit youngster goes charging off, wanting to lead the whole affair on his own? I was pulling him back by his cross-belts, more than using me own musket!"

The eyes became even more incandescent.

"He's no kind of a half-wit, sure he's not! It's your job to teach him and show him what's what!"

Deakin gave a sigh of complete resignation and George Fearnley grinned and chuckled as he closed his medical kit, having just finished, minutes before, stitching the bayonet wound in young Patrick's leg. All around were giving rapt attention to the tirade being heaped upon the head of their de facto leader, Jedediah Deakin. He looked at Patrick, stood with his trousers around his ankles, whilst his Mother applied the bandage, now tying the final knot, but Deakin did not wait.

"Patrick. Come here!"

An Ensign was far superior in rank to any Colour Sergeant, but, having suffered the severe ire of his beloved Bridie, he was in no mood for niceties. Patrick, breeches still around his ankles, shuffled over. Deakin did not wait for anything to be hoisted up to achieve propriety, before he began.

"You are not the Colonel! He leads, you follow, with your Colour. One of them! Did you see Rushby prancing about, wavin' his Colour like it was some kind of Mayday carnival? You did not and that's because he stays in the line, 'cos that's his place and there he can be looked after. If the Regimental got taken, 'cos you decided to go off cuttin' capers out at the front an' the Johnnies got hold of you, it'd be a disgrace to the Regiment. D'you hear? A disgrace to lose our Colour! Any Colour! So, from now on, you holds your place in the line, 'tween me and Rushby. That's where you'm safest, both of you, meanin' you and the Old Bit of Rag what you carries."

He paused for breath.

"Now. Has that sunk in?"

Ensign Mulcahy, thoroughly chastened and still with his trousers at half mast, for his Mother was only now pulling them up, looked down at the ground, but this was not good enough for Deakin.

"I'm here, not down there!"

Patrick looked up to meet the fierce gaze of the worthy Deakin.

"Yes, Uncle Jed."

"Right! Now kiss your Mother and bugger off to where they've put the Officers' tents. An' don't forget what I said!"

Bridie Mulcahy, now fastening her son's side buttons, looked at Deakin with an expression of merely mollified anger, but she was inwardly satisfied. She nodded her satisfaction, received her kiss from her Officer son and then rose to attend to the evening meal. All around were hungry, weary men. It was now late afternoon and the only sounds of conflict that echoed of the brutal battle earlier were the distant exchange of long-range musketry across the Dos Casas. All that any of the 105th wanted to do was to eat and then sleep.

Many, but not all, looked up at the sight of their Commander riding along his lines, assessing the state of his army, the Third Division in particular. Mackinnon and Picton were with him and they halted at the three Colonels of Mackinnon's Brigade, Wallace, Lacey and Dewey. Wellington gave no time to dispensing congratulations.

"Massena's still there! With plenty of reserves."

In the ensuing pause, all could hear the ongoing skirmishing across the river alongside Fuentes which confirmed Wellington's statement, then he turned to Picton.

"I'm moving you back. The First will come up into the line here, in your place. Your Third, Picton, will go back to hold the ridge between here and Freneida, The French who pushed Houston and Crauford back across the plain from Poco Bello are still there in force and I need you to face them."

He looked down at the three Colonels.

"Get some rest into yours during what's left of the daylight. You're moving back as soon as it's dark and then you'll be digging trenches through the night. This is not yet over and all may well begin again tomorrow. As far as Massena's concerned, Almeida's obviously not relieved, so, ..."

He took a weary breath.

"...... we fortify our position ready to meet what may come."

Picton was fuming.

"Damn it, Wellington. Didn't I hear some talk, sometime back, about a Battalion of Pioneers? It was the Third that stopped the French in that filthy maze of a village, but the next night after, it's them that's got to pick up the shovels!"

"You may have heard about the possibility of Pioneers, General Picton, but they are not here now and we need to fortify our position. Needs must, and that's that."

He turned his irritated gaze away from Picton to the Brigadier present.

"You've got your orders, Mackinnon!"

With that, he swung his horse around and rode slowly away, Picton going with him, on their way to Colville's Brigade of the Third. Mackinnon was left with his three Colonels, him sighing deeply, Scots accent returning with any emotion.

"Sorry, boys! I'll try tae get some food sent up during the night. He's reet! Johnny's still got plenty beyond the river, not used and he's got three Divisions and cavalry right now, facing the ridge, hardly tested. We've nae choice!"

The three Colonels saluted and walked off. Hours later, with the rising of a sliver of moon, the men of the 105th found themselves taking turns with picks and shovels along the defensive ridge. However, when Sergeant-Major Gibney came along the lines asking for those with any level of woodsman experience, who could be sent to the valley of the Turonne for just that kind of work, Davey, ex-poacher, was identified plus his two companions. Joe, in an earlier life, had been in charge of all the fences on a large estate and Miles pleaded his skill with a knife for detailed woodwork. In this way, the three found themselves with hatchets in the woodland behind the ridge, felling saplings in a darkness relieved only by the light of guttering candles in unsound lanterns. Miles, typically, was the first to grumble.

"What if I hits my leg, in the dark? Or someone else's leg? What then? Am I on the triangle for self-inflicted wounds?"

Davey paused briefly.

"So, you'd rather be back on the ridge, wielding a shovel in total dark, 'cos if they needs to light any lanterns, they can be seen by the Johnnies and then they'll get fired on with shot and grape. That French General's got thousands waitin' out there for mornin'!"

Miles let out an irritated, sharp breath in the dark.

"What's all this timber and brush for anyway?"

At that moment Captain Drake came by carrying his own lantern.

"The answer, Miles, is that we must block the valley of the Turonne, which penetrates our ridge. With an abattis, as it's called. Basically, a lot of trees and bushes lashed together."

At that moment came the sound of intense fighting from over on their left.

"There! That's at the Turonne gap and, I suspect, that's the Rifles I saw there, putting a stopper on another French attempt to get into our position. They must still be around, having tried once already, early this evening. Without the abattis, they'll try again in the morning. Try seriously."

Davey paused from felling a small sapling.

"Right Sir, Understood, Sir. Then we'll gather up what we've got and get ourselves over there."

The last tree felled, they lashed together what they had and dragged all towards the valley of the Turonne. By the time they arrived, the fighting had died away and they found the men of the Rifles, overseen by Crauford himself, dragging dead and wounded French Voltiguers away from the narrowest part of the valley, where the abbatis needed to go. Miles picked up a discarded French shako and began swinging the yellow cord attachments to the side peak, signifying a Voltiguer.

"Uh! Tassel swingin' bastards!"

He was interrupted by Davey.

"Tom! Get over here. I've got us in the building party. No more tree chopping for us."

Thus, was the night spent and it was before dawn that their construct was in place, a massive tangle of branches and brush, completely denying any advance down the course of the Turonne. All now as Crauford desired, the three returned exhausted to their mess area, where they found all others asleep in the trenches that they had just dug, but within an hour, Ellis was kicking them awake.

"Stand to!"

Cold, unfed and tired, the 105th filed into the trenches, grateful for the half-light of the early dawn in which to find their way. Carr was stood with O'Hare behind the 105th trenches, on a high part of the ridge. He looked along the ridgeline, to see a continuous line of Allied trenches and at least three, there were probably more, dug in batteries, with their guns already installed. He turned to O'Hare.

"He must have ordered two whole Divisions to build all this, during one night!"

O'Hare nodded.

"Must have! And you can bet Johnny'll not be too pleased to see all this, when he takes a look in full daylight."

Fifteen minutes more and full daylight revealed the sight on the plain before the pair, there were French encampments all over, of artillery, cavalry and infantry. However, what the Allied Officers on the ridge were now looking for, were French Officers examining the Allied position, these looking to examine the over-night developments. Also, they could not have failed to see such as Carr and O'Hare within their French lenses, both these now making good use of their own finely ground glass, regarding those focused on them.

"There, Padraigh! There, just left of dead-ahead."

O'Hare swung his small telescope over to focus on what Carr had seen.

"I see them. A bunch of French 'high-ups', all taking a look."

"Massena?"

"Could be, who knows. Could be that during the night he planned to try here, come daylight, having failed in the village."

Carr lowered his telescope and grinned.

"Then we can only revel in his disappointment."

111

They watched the group mount their horses and walk them away. They had seen what Carr had identified himself along the ridgeline, an open glacis before the trenches, the slope having been cleared of all cover, and all exposed to the potentially murderous fire from British firing lines, secure in trenches and supported by well-placed batteries. With the stalemate established, the hours of the early morning now passed, with no movement from either side. At 10.00am Lacey came to Carr and O'Hare.

"Post sentries. Let the rest sleep. Send one in five back to get some food. They've not eaten since yesterday."

Carr nodded.

"I'll see to it Sir. This reminds me of The Lines at Torres Vedras. Us in trenches, basically alright, Johnny out there, hopefully starving."

Lacey chuckled.

"You may be more than half right with that, Henry. From what I hear, that Julian Sanchez character is once again in behind Massena, pillaging his convoys."

Within an hour, Zeke Saunders and Joe Pike were returning to their mess area to obtain the cooking pots full of hot stew. Food was plentiful and there was even a choice, one of beef stew, the other of fish. Both men hurried back, the sooner they arrived back in the trenches, the sooner they could eat themselves. Now unoccupied, Bridie and Nellie sat drinking tea and Nellie poured a mug for John Byford, lying prone under a pile of blankets, and took it over.

"Are you feeling any better, now, John, at all?"

The answer was a shake of his head, possibly from fever chill, and also a quivering jaw, that definitely from the fever. Her face took on a deep concern as she offered him the tin mug of hot liquid.

"Well, here you are now. Get that inside you and it'll warm you up. There's a spoonful of sugar in there, is there not?"

Byford raised himself on one elbow, reached out a pale hand from under the blanket and took the mug. He drank half, but then lay back exhausted, so that Bridie saw the need to come over and help him drink the rest. That done, she pulled the blankets back over him.

"There now, John, you rest now. You'll be right as rain bye and bye."

She returned to Nellie and both sat together.

"Where's my Eirin? She should be doing this, and there's not been altogether too much of it, to my recall."

Nellie's jaw tightened as her mood blackened.

"You'll not like this, but I've a mind that you'll want to know what I think and what I've heard tell of? 'Tis no happy tale, that's for sure?"

Bridie nodded her agreement and Nellie drew a deep breath.

"Well, I've seen her but once this mornin' and if I had to guess where she is now, she's off moonin' around the Officers' tents, hopin' to see that Lieutenant Maltby. She'll be thinking that, if he sees his child, he'll want to take up with her again. And properly."

Bridie sat bolt upright.

"You really think that? That's what's in her mind?"

Nellie turned fully towards her, her own anger rising.

"Well, she's not here now, is she? And there's her husband over there, him as made an honest woman of her, now at death's door and despaired of. Why's she not here and carin' for him? My guess is, she's traipsin' round the camp like the lovelorn fool she is, hopin' to catch the eye of her beloved Lieutenant, curse the day that he was born! He'll only take advantage again, so he will, sure as Heaven's up above!"

Bridie rose from the box she was sat on, her mood now as black as that of her friend's.

"I'm off to find her! And what I say, depends on where she is."

With that, her shawl went around her shoulders, then around her back, for the ends to then be tied by the corners, before her waist and then she hurried off, leaving Nellie to tend the fire. At that moment, Chaplain's Assistant Sedgwicke arrived, to stand before the seated Nellie.

"Mrs. Nicholls, good morning. I understand that you have someone here who is not in the best of health."

He turned to look at the wan Byford beneath the pile of blankets, the top one a French saddle blanket with 22CN on the corner, obtained after Sabugal.

"Clearly I am correct, a fever of some sort. Well….."

His hand went into his pocket and produced a small folded packet of greased paper.

"My sister gave me this, before we left England. It's a physic of some sort, but prepared to help with agues and fevers. I wonder if you would like to give it to your patient, here?"

Nellie reached up and took the paper. She had seen such before and had no need to open it, so she smiled up at ex-Parson Sedgwicke.

"'Tis a good, kind man that y'are, Parson darlin'. A good, kind man. Now, sit you down and I'll get you a drop of tea and you can have the first dough cake, nice and hot from the griddle there."

Sedgwicke quickly sat himself in Bridie's vacant place and then eagerly awaited the treat that so often accompanied a visit to the mess area of Bridie Mulcahy and Nellie Nicholls. Meanwhile, Bridie was stalking the tent-lines of the 105th and soon she came upon Sergeant-Major Cyrus Gibney and, on seeing her approach, he drew himself fully upright and saluted. There were few who did not have a soft spot for Bridie Mulcahy, but Bridie spoke first.

"Mr. Gibney, have you seen my Eirin? You know the one, do you not?"

Gibney frowned, the suspicions that had entered Nellie Nicholls head had entered his own.

"Ah do, lass, aye."

"So, do you know where she might be?"

"Ah knows that, an' all."

He took a deep breath.

"There's some trees over yonder, beyond our tents. 'Tis often ah sees her in there, with the bairn, sat beneath."

"Whose tents are closest to there?"

Gibney paused before answering. The answer was as explosive as gunpowder.

"Those of th' Officers."

Bridie's face became blank, as she looked straight up at him, her head tilted back.

"Sure, but 'tis grateful I am to you, for telling me the truth. Now, good-day to you, Mr. Gibney."

Bridie took off, as Gibney saluted, heading for the trees which were very obvious some 200 yards away. The sun broke through the scattering clouds and light shone into the small copse, where she saw both what she wanted to see and what she did not. Eirin was sat on a log, with Lieutenant Maltby beside her, him very close, with one hand holding open the blanket at the child's face, the other arm around Eirin's shoulders. Eirin's face was alight, whilst the expression on his, she condemned as a leer. Bridie pounded up and first dealt with Eirin.

"You! Back to our fire, now!"

"No, Ma, I wish to stay here."

"You bring shame on us all! Get back, or I'll throw you out and we'll look after the child ourselves, on our own, without you, 'cos sure as tomorrow, you'll not be able to. And you think then that this tripehound will take care of you, when he did nothing first off, 'till your Uncle Jed and the good Colonel forced him to?"

At this point, Maltby stood up.

"Woman! You need to remember who you are talking about. I've seen Followers like you on the triangle before now."

Bridie ignored him, she was still looking at Eirin, who had not moved.

"You've got a good man as a husband. Of the best, but like to die for want of care that should be comin' from you. Now you go from here, or, as God's my witness, you're gone from any family of mine! And alone, 'cos I'll see no Grandchild of mine off to starve in the gutter, 'cos that's where you'll be. And you can count on it that you'll get nothin' from this gombeen. Nothin'!"

Eirin was stunned by the strength and vehemence of her Mother's words and so she did stand, adjust the baby in the supporting shawl and then, with one last look at Maltby, she walked away, past Cyrus Gibney who was stood some way off and now worried for the outcome. So, he approached near enough not to have any effect on it, but near enough to hear what would be said. Bridie, meanwhile, had turned her attention to Stuart Maltby, fixing him with a fierce gaze from her burning green eyes. For the moment, Maltby was shocked, which gave Bridie her opening.

"You, you are the very Devil! You had your way with her once and the result now sits in her arms, so now you're fixin' to do the same and don't tell me you're not!"

Her voice rose with the final words and a deep breath allowed her to continue.

"She's a married woman! Church married, because you'd have nothing to do with her, once she was with child and, now that she's not, you're fixing for more of the same. She's a ring on her finger and a husband and a bairn to go with it. Were you any kind of a decent man you'd send her back to her husband with your blessing, but I find you here, all over her once again."

Maltby was now thoroughly incensed at being spoken to in such a fashion by such a person as a mere Follower.

"I said you could end up on the triangle, and I meant it!"

"And who do you think has the say so to put me there? Not you! 'Tis the Colonel and he'll remember the story as it was told to him, by my good man Jed. You'll not get very far with any complaint, is what I'm thinking'. Rather end up dirtying your own nest when your foul intentions come out in the open! Out again, what's more!"

Maltby tried another tack, to justify his attention to Eirin.

"Do I not have the right to see my own child?"

Bridie took a step forward but she just restrained herself from hitting him.

"And did you not yourself put a question over you being the Father, like she was some kind of easy slattern as will go with any man as comes along? And look what it took to get some coin out of you to help with her time in the Convent! Without what was said to you by our good menfolk, you'd not have given over one brass farthing."

"Your man told me I'd be killed if I didn't!"

"So, now, doesn't that just sum it all up! It took a thing such as that to get anything out of you and, on top, a good dressing down from the Colonel was needed, is my understanding."

A pause came, time for some more shriveling from the fiercesome gaze.

"You leave her alone, or I'll be off to the Colonel, so I will, and then we'll see what's what!"

With that final salvo, she turned and hurried after Eirin, who was making slow progress due to the several times she had turned to see what was happening. Bridie passed by Cyrus Gibney who sent an appreciative nod in her direction but, after that, he delivered a prolongued, stern and condemnatory gaze in the direction of Lieutenant Maltby, fully conveying the fact that he had heard and agreed with every word Bridie Mulcahy had spoken. Gibney stood for some time, his critical stare unwavering, until Maltby, thoroughly discomfited, quit the small copse and disappeared behind a tent.

Eirin hurried on before her Mother and arrived at their mess area before her, but it did not save her from the next tirade that Bridie was intent on delivering. She stood over her sitting daughter.

"Your Father and me, we raised a fool! You think the sight of a babe's face will change the mind of a man like him? You let him have his way with you once, the result is on your lap and now you still go mooning up to him, making all so very clear that he can do it all again until the same result comes along."

Eirin managed to glance up at her fuming Mother, but could not hold it for long. By now, Bridie was pointing at the prone figure of John Byford, now with no blankets, because with the change in the fever, he was now so hot.

"There's your man, there! As good a man as you'll find. As stood with you at an altar, in a Holy Church and spoke Holy Vows before a true Priest. There's your man, and he's sick! Sure as Heaven's above, 'tis your Holy duty to care for him and nurse him back to good, not to go off, hoping for a glance or two from that heartless, womanising Devil."

She paused and Eirin did now manage to look up at her Mother as Bridie delivered her final words.

"Now, your name is Eirin Byford, you're wedded to that man there, so you care for him and do what you promised in front of an Altar of the Lord Jesus to do. In sickness and in health!"

Eirin stood and gave the child to his Grandmother. The she went and knelt beside the prone figure of John Byford. He sensed her presence and opened his eyes to smile weakly, but warmly up at her. There was warmth also in his hand placed on her forearm, but Eirin could only look at him blankly, but at that moment, Nellie came over with a bowl of warm water, which she thrust at Eirin to the extent that some spilt on her dress.

"Here! He needs a wash!"

Eirin began to wash and bathe the fevered face and after a minute Jed Deakin arrived and quickly sensed the atmosphere.

"What's been goin' on here? Some kind of ruction?"

Bridie presented him with a mug of tea.

114

"Nothin' At least nothin' that needs to bother you!"

Deakin shook his head and allowed nothing important to enter it for the short remainder of that day and the following night. The next day, curiousity did come upon him concerning cavalry passing by, as he drank his tea and spoke his thoughts aloud to his companion, Toby Halfway, sat nearby.

"Well, don't they all look cheerful! A day off's done wonders for them. What would they look like if they had to fight a battle, spend the night diggin' trenches and then man 'em for a day and more, waitin' for the Frogs to start all off again?"

Halfway volunteered no answer, he merely finished his tea. Deakin was right, in the cavalry column all was, indeed, of good cheer. The 16th Light Dragoons were being moved up towards Almeida, this now being a third focal point of concern, the equal of dire possibilities on the ridge and in the village. At the head of Two Squadron, now commanded by Major Johnson, rode Cornet Carr heading his C Troop, privileged to be riding alongside the Regiment's Senior Major. All was indeed well within the ranks of the 16th Light Dragoons, because they had performed well during the retreat from Pozo Bello, suffering merely 27 casualties; killed, captured or missing, which did not include Cornet Smythe, who had returned with Houston's cavalry. In addition, some of their number had been very much involved with the rescue of two field-guns, which, if captured would have been the equivalent of a Regiment losing their Colour. The 16th had been thoroughly and even gloriously involved and so it was no surprise that they all rode North in high spirits.

However, one of their number was not so buoyed up and this came to the surface when they dismounted at the village of Villar Formosa on the Portuguese/Spanish border. This being Captain Lucius Tavender and he lost no time in delivering sarcasm in the direction of Cornet Carr, when Carr led his horse up to the hitching post, prior to obtaining a cup of coffee at the local canteena.

"Ah! The hero of the hour!"

Carr felt disinclined to salute.

"We all did our best, Sir. I'd say we all had some measure of success in what was a very tight business."

Tavender said no more and neither did Carr, as he entered the hut where coffee was available, this refreshment halt being set up by an enterprising Portuguese and his wife, who needed to bake non-stop many batches of her delicious pastries, such was the demand. Soon, Carr, now joined by Peterson, had pastry crumbs all over his chin and uniform, as did his companion and, when the call came to remount, both grinned at the predicament they were in, as they brushed away all vestiges of pastry as best they could. Carr was grateful that, when they returned to their horses, Tavender was no-where to be seen and so he took his place at the head of his Troop with Major Johnson. However, within an hour, on approaching Almeida, they came upon a disturbing sight close to the road, where two, of what appeared to be Portuguese peasants, were stood before a wall in front of a firing squad. Withers halted his column at the sight and Johnson enquired of a nearby Lieutenant of the 36th Foot.

"What's this? Executing two locals who've thieved from us? Usually, it's the other way round."

The Lieutenant grinned.

"No Sir, they're not Portuguese. They're French caught trying to sneak into the citadel. They were dressed as you can see them, Sir, out of uniform and so they're being shot as spies."

Johnson nodded, whilst Cornet Carr, just beyond, looked on horrified as the hoods were placed over the men's heads. One immediately cried out.

"Vive la France! Vive l'Empereur!"

However, Johnson was still interrogating the Lieutenant.

"As spies, you say. When were they caught?"

"Last night, Sir. Seems like Johnny is trying to get a message into the citadel, to the garrison."

Johnson nodded.

"So it would seem. Perhaps things are happening?"

He steadied his horse by patting its neck.

"Thank you."

The Lieutenant saluted and Johnson looked up to see the execution climax. Eighteen muskets fired at once and the front of the men's shirts became a bloody mess as they were hurled backwards, to then slide down the wall. That finished with, Colonel Withers, at the head of the column, wasted no further time.

"March on!"

The column resumed its march and soon the squat walls of Almeida came into view, at a distance, with the distinct towers and gate-house rising above all. Everyone in the 16th allowed themselves a minute or two to study the vital Citadel, but soon it disappeared behind the low hills and the 16th spent another half hour before they arrived at their billet, this identified by a name-board, Malpartida, which all attempted to pronounce, but Peterson probably came closest.

"Hymalparteeda."

Cornet Carr grinned and nodded.

"As you say, Douglas. I'll have to try it out on some locals. Create some amusement if nothing else."

However, Carr had no opportunity, for Colonel Withers soon arrived, aiming straight for Carr, who was still mounted.

"A Night patrol's needed, orders are to patrol alongside the Agueda, and you know that part of the world. It's 7pm now, come back at Midnight. Keep alert! Staff are worried that the French are trying something in the Citadel. They're stuck in there with no hope of relief, so it's surrender or do something suicidal."

Carr dismounted, undid the strapping on his roll and other possessions and gave them to the Officer's Servant. Sergeant Baxter was nearby and had heard all.

"Us two and ten, Sir?"

Carr nodded.

"Yes. See to it, please. I'll try to get some food for us all. This looks to be a village that the French overlooked."

He was correct and, within fifteen minutes, some biscuit, salt fish and dried fruit had been obtained by Carr and portions were spread around the patrol. That secured in their saddle-bags, the patrol departed with Baxter, as usual, riding just behind Carr's off-side. He turned to Baxter.

"I hope that, between the pair of us, we can remember our way around this place. It's utterly dark, but I feel a ride over to Barba del Puerco will be as good as any."

"As good as any, Sir. And this half-moon will do no harm, the more it rises."

"Very good. So, as I recall, ride East, cross the Turonne, then get on the road up to Barba."

"Yes Sir, but it's all wild country. Gently does it. Sir."

"Absolutely, Sergeant. Where's the need to hurry?"

An hour's walk brought them to the banks of the Turonne, in May it being barely a flow, and they splashed through, barely dampening their horse's fetlocks up to the knees. More rough country for half an hour brought them onto the familiar road up to Barba del Puerco, a turn left and Carr raised the pace to a trot. Even in the poor light of the moon, on arrival the silhouette of the village was familiar and Carr took them right, past the Chapel and some 200 yards down the track into the gorge. There he called a halt and raised his hand for silence. Each Trooper stilled his horse and all listened, but all that could be heard was the faint murmur of the Agueda as it peevishly assaulted the many rocks and boulders that hindered its course into Portugal and to the sea. Carr sat for a good ten minutes, then turned to Baxter.

"Nothing here, Sergeant. I think a slow ride home."

Carr led the turn and they rode back up, to turn left above the Chapel and re-take the road, now South out of Barba del Puerco. It was not difficult to find the place where they had joined the road after crossing the Turonne, because Baxter had marked the spot with a branch to which was tied a ration bag. They now turned right and all were off the road, when they saw a sudden flash of light on the far horizon, followed seconds later, when it reached them, by what they took to be the accompanying sound. Carr called a halt.

"What was that, Sergeant?"

"A heavy battery, Sir. Quite a few and from the citadel."

Carr pulled out his watch and, with just enough light from the moon he was able to read the time.

"Ten o' clock, exactly. Is there any significance in that, do you think?"

"Hard to tell, Sir, only that it was loud enough to be heard on the Frog side of the river."

Apprehensive, Carr led his men on, to soon see and hear a repeat, and again he looked at his watch.

"Five past! It's got to mean something."

"Looks that way, Sir."

After five more minutes riding came a third duplicate event and, again, out came Carr's watch.

"Now ten past. It's got to mean something!"

"No argument Sir. That's got nothing to do with calling the Faithful to Midnight Mass."

"So, you think it's a signal of some kind?"

"Yes Sir. That loud at exactly ten, with exactly five minutes between the next two, it can't be anything else. Sir."

"Well, let's get back and leave the worrying to those given the rank to do it."

"You're learning fast Sir!"

Many grinned in the dark as they rode on and within the hour they were back at Malpartida in time to see another night patrol get on its way. It was Colonel Withers who greeted them.

"Anything?"

"Nothing human, Sir. But we heard the guns."

"From the Citadel?"

"No doubt Sir, and it was all very carefully timed."

"Yes, we came to the same conclusion ourselves."

"Yes Sir. Are we dismissed, Sir? The men are tired."

Carr's question pulled Withers away from his distracted thinking about cannonfire.

"Yes, yes. Of course. Stand down and get some rest. With those guns we've just heard, I've a feeling it'll be a busy day tomorrow."

Withers was correct and the first that Cornet Carr knew of the following day's 'business' was when Major Johnson came running up during first daylight, sword scabbard held safely at his side by his left hand, a rolled map in the other.

"Carr! Get yours out and down South. It seems that Johnny's pulling back to Cuidad and Himself wants all the news that we can give. Look here."

He unrolled the map on a barrel head and immediately stabbed his finger down on the first turn of the big bend of the Agueda.

"Start there, it's about five miles South of Barba."

He then ran his finger to follow the course, upstream, of the almost straight canyon holding the Agueda.

"Then down to here, Seranillo. No further and after it's done, just get back at your best speed, but send a galloper over to Villar Formosa with your findings. It's central to our position and all findings are being co-ordinated there."

He rolled up the map and gave it to Carr.

"Have you a good glass?"

"No Sir. Not what I'd call a good one."

"Alright. Get around to my servant. Tell him to give you my spare. It's a decent French capture. And make notes on whatever you see, however insignificant you may think it is. The place being empty is as significant as it being full of Johnnies. You understand?"

"Yes Sir, but there's nothing concerning the Citadel, after the signals of last night?"

"No! Now get on."

Carr saluted and jogged his way to his Troop. Sergeant Baxter, now seated, saw him coming and immediately discerned that there was some urgency, this being caused by some task of some kind, he had no doubt, and he rose to meet his Troop Commander, who soon arrived.

"Get them mounted, please, Sergeant. We've been given some more country over which to exercise the horses."

"In daylight this time, Sir?"

"Yes. Command believes that our foe may be pulling back from the river and it's our job to confirm or prove otherwise."

An hour later, Cornet Carr was admiring the clarity afforded by a good spy-glass, as he studied the scene on the far side of the Agueda, stood at the most Northerly point of its unusually straight North-South course. Further North from that point, the big bend of the Agueda was sweeping around behind his right shoulder. Beside him was Trooper Percy Nunney, who had some skill with pencil and paper and Carr spoke whilst still focusing the glass on various features.

"Write this. At big bend, cavalry and artillery on road South to Cuidad."

Nunney busied himself with the instruction until he came to the final word.

"How do you spell 'Cuidad', Sir."

Carr unrolled the map, to find that it did not go that far South.

"Don't know. Just write a big C, then dash d."

At that moment, there came the sound of cannonfire, as loud as that of the previous evening and obviously from the Almeida Citadel. All in Carr's Troop looked back, but Carr soon brought their attention back to their task.

"That's not our worry! Ours is to take a look over the river all the way down to this Seranillo place, and then get our findings over to Villar Formosa."

It was well into the afternoon that they finally arrived at the small Seranillo hamlet, this having buildings built right up to the beginning of the chasm, above which any construction had halted in terror. Carr led his men in, to find it held by a Company of Rifles and so he rode up to their Captain, who was at the highest point above the gorge. The Rifles Captain turned on hearing the approaching hooves and out of respect to a superior rank, Carr dismounted and saluted.

"Carr, Sir. 16th Light Dragoons."

"Uniacke. 95th."

"How do you do, Sir? We are on patrol to discover the situation beyond the river. With the French that is. Have you anything that you can add to our report, Sir? From opposite you."

Uniacke nodded.

"Yes, include this. Over from us, Johnny has been pulling back infantry and artillery. All day."

Carr turned to Nunney, just behind.

"Got that, Nunney? Start the sentence with 'opposite Seranillo.'"

At that moment, as Nunney began his careful lettering, there came another loud boom from the direction of the Almeida Citadel. Uniacke looked at Carr.

"Do you know anything about all that?"

"Only that yesterday evening there were three carefully timed salvoes, starting at 10.00."

Uniacke nodded.

"I do hope that those placed over us have worked it out. Those were signals last night, but what we hear now is the garrison destroying what they can before either attempting some lunatic break out, or they're destroying the place prior to surrendering. It's not exactly higher mathematics."

"No, Sir, but I need to get over to Villar Formosa, with my findings."

Uniacke nodded again.

"Of course, off you go, but don't try cross country. It's a mad house of bogs and valleys designed to mislead even the Divinely Guided! Take the road North-East and that will loop around and down to the main road from Almeida to Formosa. Good luck!"

Carr saluted, re-mounted and led his Troop the recommended way, through villages seemingly just coming back to Portuguese occupation, judging by the number of carts full of furniture being unloaded at dwellings of a variety of size and quality. Everywhere they were greeted by laughing children, often running beside the horses, and also waving adults, many shouting "Viva Ingleses!" On that journey, they heard two more 'booms' from the Citadel, evidence of French destruction as opinioned by Captain Uniacke. They came to the main road and Carr called Baxter forward.

"Get them back to Malpartida, Sergeant. Best I deliver our findings myself, I feel."

"Best take Makepeace and Nunney with you, Sir. You never know."

"Very good, Sergeant. I'll see you this evening."

Whilst his Troop departed North to skirt around Almeida and return to their base, Carr set off South, in the lead of his double escort. At Villar Formosa, he found himself in a tangle of buildings and alleyways, but instinct required that he maintain his direction South and, with much relief, he came to the main chausee that crossed there from Portugal into Spain. A left turn soon brought him to the familiar coffee and cake canteena, this doing extraordinary business from all the British Officers now in the village. Carr approached a Captain of Provosts, still mounted but enthusiastically munching a Portuguese pastry.

"Excuse me, Sir, but I have a report on French movements over the Agueda. Do you know where I should take it?"

The Captain swallowed a mouthful and then pointed further on.

"There! The house next door to this."

Carr saluted and dismounted to hand his reins up to Makepeace.

"I'll not be long, but buy something from here, if you wish. I'm sure we have time."

Makepeace saluted.

118

"Thank you, Sir."

Carr entered the building, which was plainly once important for the local municipality, having many self-important windows both above and to either side of an imposing door, but it now gained its prominence for military reasons and Carr joined a queue of Cavalry Officers. However, within minutes he was at the desk and handing over his report, the contents of which were immediately examined by the Major in charge.

"Right. Good. Who, date, times and places, all very clear. Well done Cornet! Off you go."

Carr saluted and left, to then buy his own coffee and sweetmeats and wander over to three Cornets stood nearby, two from the 14th Light Dragoons, one from the 1st Royals. They halted their conversation and one of the 14th Cornets spoke first.

"What do you know?"

Carr delayed a second bite of his cake.

"Only that Johnny's pulled right back to Cuidad, he's sent signals last night and now he's wrecking the place, Almeida Citadel that is. What about you?"

"Not much more, only that the Peer's confident of taking it, plus garrison. He's sending all sorts up to strengthen the ring surrounding it. Shouldn't be too long now."

Carr nodded, then took his last mouthful, as did the other three, but Carr finished first.

"I spoke to a Rifles Captain who thinks the Johnnies inside may attempt some crazy break-out."

The Royals Cornet chuckled.

"They'd be mad to try. There are thousands up there ringing Almeida."

All nodded and the group broke up, each wishing the other good luck. Once back in the saddle and heading North, Carr let the horses have their heads and they loped along at an easy canter, but less than an hour on the road brought them up to an infantry column marching rapidly in the same direction. Carr addressed the first Officer he came to of equal rank, a Lieutenant of the Light Company at the rear.

"Good evening. Carr, 16th Light Dragoons. Who are you?"

"36th, marching up to Malpartida."

"Our destination also."

"See you there in a while, but a word of warning. General Campbell of 6th Division, no less, just overtook us, with all his Staff. Don't be surprised if he makes that his HQ and that you've been turfed out of the best billets."

Carr frowned.

"Hope not! It's quite comfortable."

The Lieutenant laughed.

"You've been warned!"

With some mild anxiety, the three completed their journey to find that the 36th Lieutenant's prediction was indeed true. Campbell had moved the 16th's Headquarters out of the best-appointed building which nudged everyone else down to the next worst. Carr eventually found his new accommodation, pronounced it as 'not too bad', and then strolled off to find the Officer's mess, hoping for some food. He was again very hungry.

oOo

Tavender strode through the door of the Officer's billet of 1st and 2nd Squadrons and threw his scabbard, containing sword, his paillasse and busby into a corner, from where it was quickly rescued by their servant, him anxious that it would get too dirty piled there and he would have to clean it. Meanwhile, Tavender was sat in a chair.

"Much more of this, and all I'll need do is keep myself in the saddle. My horse knows the exact route himself, the number of times we've ridden it."

He reached for the bottle of local red wine.

"Three patrols in three days, each discovering less than the one before."

Peterson pushed a glass across to him and Tavender poured whilst continuing his polemic.

"Well, this nonsense can't go on much longer. Things are pretty much done here, and I hear that it's hotting up down around Badajoz."

Tavender stopped pouring, but continued.

"And that's a one-act play I'd choose to keep out of. It's either a slog over that dreadful Sierra de Gata or the very long way round through Castelo Branco. I've been talking to some KGL who've been up and down and it's a trek!"

One of his own Cornets, Harry Smythe, spoke up, to perhaps mollify his Captain.

"Well, it's not us yet, Sir. And at least we've heard no more booming from the Citadel. When they've finally turned it in, then perhaps we'll be given something different. I also know every inch of my patrol route. Tedious isn't the word for it."

Tavender glowered at him, but said no more. Instead he took the bottle, still half full and took himself off to his own billet. Soon, the others followed as darkness descended and Carr made his way to the room he shared with Peterson, where he took off most of his uniform, then sat on his cot-bed to add some more to his letter home. Sleep came easily, until it was shattered by a huge explosion. Peterson was the first to the window, to see a massive flash of light from the direction of the Citadel, quickly followed by a second colossal rumble when the sound of the explosion arrived, but not as loud as the first. Transfixed, he saw and heard a third, when he was joined by Carr.

"Something's up! We'd best get dressed."

Carr was on his way back to bed and now yawning.

"You really think so?"

"I do! There'll be 'stand to' any time now."

"What's the time?"

Peterson lit a candle using his tinderbox and found his watch.

"11.30!"

"Oh God! I've not been in bed two hours!"

Peterson lit another candle.

"Stand to' coming up!"

He was right. Within ten minutes bugles were blowing and NCO's were shouting. Both Cornets were now dressed and Peterson led the way to their Headquarters building, there to find General Campbell himself, prominent at one end of the room. It seemed that a one-sided argument was in progress between himself and their own Colonel Withers, who was speaking as they arrived.

"But Sir, if this is a break-out then the only way across the Agueda is the bridge at Barba del Puerco. Should we not, as a precaution, get across to hold it, both mine and the 36th?"

Campbell's face became thunderous, he found it insufferable to be argued against by a mere Colonel, two ranks below him.

"No! At present, we know nothing and it could be that we'll hear nothing, and if it is nothing after two hours, then we'll all go back to bed."

At this point, Carr noticed Colonel Cochrane of the 36th prominent in his red uniform amongst the blues of the cavalry.

"That may be, Sir, but I also feel a break-out to be more likely. Why is this happening at night? If the garrison wanted to surrender, they would do it during the day. Surely? They like to sleep as much as we do."

Campbell turned his ill-tempered gaze in Cochrane's direction, another impudent Colonel.

"We wait! I can see the sense in forming up, yours and that of Withers, but we make no movement. Not until we hear more. That's final."

With that, the assembly slumped down onto the chairs and benches, to at least close their eyes as a poor substitute for sleep. Some went to check on their men, which group included Colonel Cochrane and his Major.

Time passed, as did the atmosphere of excitement. Three hours after the explosions, Carr and Peterson joined Major Johnson on the roof of a building on the edge of the village nearest to Almeida. He had ignored Campbell's wait of two hours and then do nothing, he was convinced that something was happening and it was not the garrison surrendering. It was a still night and he turned one ear in the direction of the Citadel.

"Can you hear anything? A sort of crackling, like musket fire?"

Both Cornets listened intently, but Peterson spoke first.

"I can hear something, Sir, but what it is, I cannot tell. Sounds like a fire of dry sticks."

"Yes! Musket fire."

Meanwhile, Carr was studying the road, barely lit by the thin moon.

"I think something's happening that will soon tell us everything, Sir."

On the road was a galloper and soon he passed directly under their observation perch. Johnson walked back to the steps down off the roof.

"We'd best get back to Headquarters."

They ran down the outside stairway, just in time to see the messenger disappearing through the doorway of their Headquarters. They hurried in themselves to see the message now in the hands of their own Colonel, General Campbell having gone back to bed an hour ago. Withers read it quickly, he then looked at Captain Somers-Cocks.

"Fetch the General, quickly!"

The 16th Captain ran from the room as Withers looked around at all the Officers there, including many from the 36th.

"This is from General Pack. It says the garrison have blown the place up and are making for Johnnyland. He's chasing them with about 80 Portuguese, directly East."

He lowered the paper.

"Get your men together and ready. We'll be leaving soon."

There was a mass exodus, which included Carr and Peterson, and soon the narrow streets were full of mounted Troopers and files of infantry. Anxious Portuguese opened their upstairs windows and called down.

"Os franceses estão voltando?"

The answer they received was very much less than reassuring, almost always a shrug of the shoulders, for two reasons, either the Ingleses could not understand the language or, they could understand, but had no idea of the correct answer. Carr and Peterson were also accosted, by an anxious shopkeeper. Peterson understood, but could only answer in English.

"No, the French are not coming back. All will be well."

The shopkeeper understood enough and shook Peterson's hand before ushering his wife and children back inside to then close the heavy door. The pair of Cornets were on their way back to Headquarters for orders, where they found Withers, Cochrane and General Campbell, him reading the note for the tenth time, one of his shirt-tails still hanging over his waistband. His face betrayed his confusion.

"He says they're heading East. Damn obvious! That's where Johnny is."

Withers had fetched a map and had spread it on the table. He jabbed a finger down onto it.

"We are here, Sir."

He slid the finger down the map.

"Directly East of the Citadel is here, Sir. In the area of the village of Villar de Ciervo."

The uncertainty in Campbell's face did not disappear and so Withers continued.

"Sooner or later, Sir, even in the dark, they will come to the Agueda gorge and the only way over is the bridge at Barba. He will turn North to get to it, Sir, he has no choice. May I respectfully suggest that Colonel Cochrane, here, and myself march there now and hold it?"

Campbell's mouth became a thin line. To agree now would concede that he had made a bad mistake three hours ago.

"No! We must support Pack. He may well be outnumbered."

Withers grit his teeth and then sighed.

"Very good, Sir, but may I send a message to Reigada, North-West of here. It is my belief that there are Portuguese Dragoons and infantry there. You could order them to Barba del Puerco, Sir."

Light came into Campbell's face.

"Yes. Draft the order now. I'll sign it directly."

He returned to studying the map, now feeling much more in command, but it took him a good minute to find Villar de Ciervo again.

"Right. It's now dawn. I will personally lead the 36th to this Villar place, whilst you, Withers, will take yours due South and try to cut them off."

He looked full at Withers.

"Is there any kind of road, from here to this Villar?"

"Not a road, Sir, but a decent track."

"Right. Withers and Cochrane, you have your orders!"

Within fifteen minutes, Withers was leading his men South, in columns of Squadrons, all four in line abreast with 300 yards between each. Johnson, leading Two Squadron with Carr in close attendance spoke his approval of their open formation.

"This'll do, it's the best we can do. We're covering 900 yards and we can see for a mile either side, but it's terrible country."

Carr looked before him and could only agree. They had been up and down, over gullies and hillocks, all crowned with large copses of trees these now adorning themselves with their Spring foliage, which did not help with their view in any direction. However, it was not ten minutes before they came upon all the signs they needed; dead and wounded men, some Portuguese, but mostly French, the latter begging to be taken up before the Portuguese peasants came along. In addition, which would not ease the mood of any peasant, were numerous items of plunder, which the escaping French hoped to make off with. Withers rode across his line, soon coming to the three Officers of Two Squadron.

"The wounded Portuguese say they've been there two hours, almost. We've well and truly missed them. We'll ride East to Villar. Column of Squadrons."

Withers immediately rode off to lead One Squadron and the remaining three Squadrons immediately formed a single column behind. The ground was even worse, it seemed that every gully cut across their path, with crumbling banks that were difficult to climb. However, no-one doubted that they were in the correct direction, as more dead and wounded of both sides were sorrowfully passed by and much discarded booty and equipment littered their route. This was endured for six miles and the following of this depressing trail proved by the minute that they were too late to cut off the escaping French from reaching the Agueda, and all knew that it would be at Barba del Puerco where they arrived. The experience of the tedious recent patrols of the Agueda valley told them that there was no other viable crossing. It was well past 11.00 am when the squat rooves of Villar de Ciervo came into sight, to soon disappear when they were forced to descend into a valley, more deep and wide than most hitherto. The trail of bodies and booty continued East, but it missed Villar by about half a mile and soon they were on the familiar North to South road that ran along the chasm of the Agueda. Withers called up his Squadron Leaders and soon he was sat with Johnson, Tavender, Somers-Cocks and Myers. The route of the escaping French remained obvious, the same left-overs were now on the road that they were on themselves and all led North. Withers stated the obvious.

"He's making for Barba!"

He pulled out his telescope and focused it on the furthest horizon, hoping to see some evidence of a French column, but he could not even see an English one. He snapped the glass shut, now very angry.

"Remain in column. At the canter."

The words were orders enough and the Captains had only to wait for their Squadrons to arrive up to them before re-joining the column. Johnson came in beside Carr.

"What's happened, Sir?"

"Johnny's way up the road. To Barba. And, what's worse, the 36th did not intercept them."

"Why not, Sir, do you think?"

"Pure conjecture, boy, but my thoughts would be that our esteemed General led his men along some deep valley, like the one we just crossed, for the convenience of the march and then missed them on this road alongside him for lack of look-outs on the levels above!"

He sighed.

"Or, the 36th haven't even arrived here yet, being still on that God-awful track, with enough gullies and valleys to hide a fleet!"

In silence, they cantered on, then after about five miles, the detritus on the road changed, most it was now British packs and knapsacks. Someone had ordered British Troops up ahead to discard their heavier equipment, presumably to enable them to run faster. Johnson came back and shouted over at Carr.

"This was your patrol. How far now to Barba?"

Carr looked over.

"No Sir, it was not, I was further South, but I rode it several times. I'd say about two more miles."

At the front, both Withers and Tavender were straining their eyes forward and it was not long before they saw a line of red on the road at the furthest distance, but it made neither feel any better, especially Withers, who spoke his thoughts out loud.

"They've not caught up. They're still marching."

However, after another mile came the sounds of combat, with the white houses of Barba del Puerco now as a backdrop. Within minutes both could see that two British Battalions were forming on the edge of the gorge and firing down. Then the leading Battalion disappeared over the edge. Withers shouted over to Tavender.

"Ride back. Get Johnson up here."

Within minutes Johnson arrived with Tavender and Withers pointed forward.

"We're no use in the fight going on down there. String us out along the road as a screen to pick up any escaping French. Seems that we've caught up with them at the very last moment."

Johnson saluted, but just before he rode back, he warned his Colonel.

"As you say, Sir, but I think there's a visit coming from our General."

Withers looked forward to see Campbell approaching and soon he could see that the General was in a state of extreme vexation, which he plainly intended to take out on Withers.

"Colonel! Why did you not cut them off?"

"Our route due South was too far East, Sir. Too close to Almeida. They were long past by the time we picked up their route."

Withers said no more and the atmosphere in the ensuing silence was charged with accusations that Withers could not speak of, much as he would wish to. Campbell, on the other hand, looked at him with daggers, but he could say nothing more on the subject. Instead he changed it.

"Spread you men as a screen to pick up any French trying to sneak back up."

Withers saluted.

"Already done, Sir."

Campbell's expression now changed, as though he had just taken a mouthful of vinegar. Campbell's shout of "Carry on" was accompanied by him wheeling his horse back up the road to the village. Withers turned to Tavender.

"Get yours up behind the infantry. We'll string back from there."

Tavender saluted and called his men forward. Soon they were spaced out on the road leading back the way they had come, close to the edge of the gorge. However, with his men placed, Tavender eased his horse forward to a cliff edge with a sickening drop, but giving a clear view of the scene below. A French column was already crossing the bridge, but behind was a broken crowd of French, being fired on by two British Battalions from the several good positions alongside the twisting track down. A third British Battalion had arrived from somewhere, ordered by some other General. There were many French both prone and struggling at the bottom of the gorge and Tavender saw many fall, either from losing their footing because of their extreme haste or being felled by a bullet. However, the British were not having things all their own way. On the far side were three Battalions of French infantry and a half battery of field-guns, sending their fire across the gorge to hold back those who were pursuing their own countrymen. Tavender spoke his thoughts.

"This was planned. All along."

The first French column was now across, followed by a disorganized crowd from what must have once been a second column. Then Tavender gasped.

"No! Don't do it!"

A British Officer was at the very bottom, and was waving his sword to gather men on the path that led immediately onto the bridge. When he felt that he had enough, he led them over the long stone structure and up the path on the far bank. There, they were met immediately with a volley by the first French Battalion and then a bayonet charge. The volley downed about fifteen men and the bayonet charge captured fifteen more, one being an Officer. The rash effort quickly withdrew back across the bridge, dragging many wounded. Johnson had now arrived beside him.

"Damn foolish effort!"

Tavender turned to look at him, but said nothing and Johnson added his next opinion.

"This was planned!"

Tavender looked at him and grinned.

"My thoughts entirely, Sir."

"Pleased you can find some humour in all this. Anyone of us could be hauled up before a Court Martial when the Peer hears about it all."

He paused to study the rapidly escaping French.

"How many, would you say, have got across to safety?"

Tavender studied the now united French column, seeing many demonstrating insulting gestures back at the impotent British.

"Somewhere around a thousand."

Johnson nodded.

123

"I wouldn't argue. There'll be the Devil to Pay for this!"

He turned his horse away from the gorge and Tavender followed, both leaving the playing out of the final scene, this being the Allies collecting French wounded, mostly with broken limbs, all needing to be pulled out from the dreadful piles of bodies at the foot of the precipitous slopes.

oOo

Captain Drake and Major Carr eased their horses onto the road that led from Villar Formosa up to Almeida. There was little to do and therefore both had decided on an excursion up to the Citadel and, to that end, they had borrowed some horses and set off for the day or at least part of it. Mostly they rode together in relaxed silence, but their passing through Villar had brought forth a thought in Drake's mind.

"It seems that the whole army is walking on tip-toe!"

Carr let out a sharp breath, but not in humour.

"A most poetic way of putting it. From what I hear the Peer's in an utter fume at the escape of a thousand French. That's more than a Battalion."

"We saw Campbell go past to Freneida yesterday and that was Erskine we saw just now in Villar. From what I hear those two are the chief culprits. What happened? Do you know?"

Carr took a drink from his flask before answering.

"The impression I've got, is that both placed their men too far back, this for reasons of easy roads and comfy billets, so that the only force of ours stood in the way of the break out was a picket of Portuguese. All others were too far away to respond in time to a quick French run-out."

He took another drink.

"There it is, but I wouldn't give much for the chances of the wallpaper in the Peer's Office once he gets hold of Erskine. It was his Division that was mostly given the task of blockade."

"But Erskine seemed capable enough when we were in his Division during Torres Vedras and the advance."

"So he did, but who knows, ill health, the rigours of campaign, the weight of command, all can take its toll. He made an utter hash of Sabugal! Two Brigades of infantry nearly wiped out, sheer luck and good management by their immediate Officers ensured that they weren't!"

Drake sighed. There was no answer and so he changed the subject.

"Have you written?"

Carr's face took on a pained expression.

"No. At least, not since the battle."

Drake's expression became stern, even determined.

"Right, When we get to the Citadel, we'll take the time to pen a few lines."

They rode on for an hour, passing endless military traffic, but when they came to Almeida, the shock it delivered took some time to recover from. Every building within 200 yards of the Citadel was badly damaged and few windows remained beyond that. The yawning gaps in the walls told their own story of the violence of the explosions that were set off by the French just prior to their escape. The pair stood and wondered at the wreck that was once a proud and impregnable fortress. As usual Drake was the first to speak.

"Well, that's the end of this place as anywhere useful!"

Carr shook his head, but in agreement.

"It'll take years to put this back together, but, if my feelings for it all are correct, Johnny's time in Portugal is very much a thing of the past, although he may manage a toe from time to time. When we've got him out of Cuidad and Badajoz, then it's onward through Spain."

Drake looked at him.

"You think things have turned?"

Carr nodded.

"I do. Not significantly, just a little, but Fuentes was a major throw of Johnny's dice and he lost. Things have tilted, just a little, in our favour."

Drake's face lit up somewhat.

"Right. Good. I hope you're right. So, now a few lines."

Both walked to a place where the wall was still intact and there they brushed away some rubble to making sitting more comfortably and both spent a pleasant hour in the May sunshine, writing to their wives.

124

That done, they gave their horses their heads and within two hours they were back at their own camp, where their mood was immediately dampened by Major O'Hare.

"I've been looking for you. We've got movement orders. We're off to Badajoz, our 3rd and the 7th Division also, so prepare for a long march, day after tomorrow, the 14th."

Drake was the first to react.

"Do we know the route?"

"Sierra de Gata!"

"Oh joy!"

oOo

Over 800 miles away, in his Westminster office, Colonel John Waters moved his chair, the better able to read yet again a letter, using the strong May, London, sunshine for illumination. He held it up above his head, hoping that the umpteenth reading would this time provide some helpful inspiration, but first he dwelt for a second on the stain where a fold, two thirds down, showed the origins, that of an intercepted French Courier, plainly done to death either during or after the letter's capture. Then he looked at the signature, that of Massena himself. There could be no doubting the provenance. He read through the attached translation and then lifted his head.

"Radipole! Get in here, if you would be so good!"

The door was half open and in came a young man, dressed as would an undertaker, the only white visible amongst the black being his clean, plain cuffs and snowy-white neck-tie. No-one ever used his first name, this being 'Redeemed', and Waters could only request, not order, because Radipole was every inch a civilian, but it was his demeanour that made him stand out. It was as though, via his pale, unblinking eyes, he was taking in, analyzing and filing away in a well-ordered mind, every detail of the world as it presented itself to him. He sat himself carefully in the chair before Water's desk and studied his superior with the usual level, but enquiring, gaze. They had only come together the previous day, this being Waters first full day back from the Peninsula. Waters handed the letter across, with the translation pinned to the back.

"What do you make of this?"

Radipole read each paper, one sentence at a time, checking the translation. Finally, he placed both on the edge of Waters' desk.

"I would challenge the translation. The French uses the word 'forni' which has been translated as 'obtained'. It doesn't mean that, it means 'provided'. Someone provided, that's the correct word, the French with the information that Wellington's main effort on the border would be at Cuidad. Which provided the justification for the French reinforcing Soult with Godinot's Brigade in the Badajoz corridor, giving them the opportunity, as they saw it, of outnumbering and destroying one of our forces on the border."

Waters reached for the letter, took a pen and made the alteration, then he read the whole sentence again.

"So, this is intelligence on Wellington that someone obtained, somehow, and then passed onto the French. A spy! Which means a French spy network."

Radipole folded his pale hands over his waistband.

"It's the only possible conclusion, Colonel."

Waters stood up, taking the letter with him.

"Get your coat! We're off to see Livermore."

Within ten minutes they were saluted, rather than impeded, by the sentries and were invading the sanctity of Livermore's Outer Office, Wilson being given no more attention than it required for him to answer a simple question.

"Is he in?"

However, Waters was a familiar visitor and so he received a simple nod of approval. Waters went straight in, closely followed by Radipole. He strode up to Livermore's desk and placed the letter before him, this done before he sat down.

"Sir! There's a spy in Wellington's camp. I think that proves it."

Livermore scanned the French version, noting the signature and the bloodstain, then he read the translation. Then he nodded.

"Plainly someone was either told or worked out Wellington's intentions and then passed them onto the French, which set Godinot off on a trek South. This is smart strategy on the part of Massena. If Beresford's

125

beaten in the South, that corridor is open and Wellington would be forced to pull back or perhaps be cut off from the coast. He would be cut off from Torres Vedras, even. Soult would get there first and, if Soult and Massena combine, then who knows, evacuation may be necessary."

Livermore studied the pair sat before him, both now rather downcast.

"However, it's just come in, you won't have heard. We won at a place called Fuentes de Onoro, but it was a damn near run thing. We can only wait for news of Beresford down at Badajoz and hope that Godinot's contingent did not tip the balance down there in Johnny's favour. It could mean that whole army beaten and scattered and what I've just described set in train."

He sighed deeply, then he picked up the top letter, the original, to look again for any helpful detail, then he noticed one thing. With that he reached across for his own diary and flipped back a number of pages. With that finished, he looked at Waters, his expression betraying his deep concern.

"The date! Massena's letter was written in Cuidad on the day after I left Wellington in the North. Bar one day, this letter overlaps with my visit. So, this is the likely sequence, as I see it. Massena receives the intelligence, probably on the day after it's passed over to the French side, after, take note, and he writes the movement order immediately. So, it was passed over on the previous day, when I was there, my final day! Or during my last days, at least."

Waters looked steadily at him.

"You can read too much into that, Sir. It could be no more than coincidence."

Livermore's eyebrows came together as he stared back at Waters.

"We never make assumptions like that, Waters! Coincidence doesn't appear in our dictionary. I had three companions there, none of whom I would trust any further than I could throw them. My Lords Hopgood, Templemere and Mahon. Idle fops, the three of them. It's either them, or some traitor on Wellington's Staff, to know such information as this, this describing his intentions for the next six months!"

Waters looked at Radipole.

"Your opinion?"

The young man treated each of his companions to his detached, level, gaze.

"It's plain to me, that information was certainly gathered, passed over and acted upon by the French. Whoever this person is, they have now done this once and will almost certainly be prepared to do it again. We cannot rule out the three you have named. They were there; that it could be one or more of them is very possible. On top, it is likely to have been someone with the freedom to roam, away from any point of duty, in order to deliver the information, which was very likely in written form, to Massena. That points to your three. Army Officers are more constrained. Or, there is the possibility that it could have been given to some civilian close by, to cross over with."

At these words, both Waters and Livermore sat back in their chairs, very thoughtful, then Livermore looked at Waters.

"He's right, Officers do have some freedom. As for the civilian, that I doubt. To be found wandering towards French lines with a military document means death, and our patrols were extensive. Whoever organised all this, needed to be more certain that the information would arrive."

Livermore drummed his fingers on the desk and fingered what remained of his left ear.

"I've got to leave this with you, but we've nothing else to run with. I'll think about the Staff, you do the fops. You know you can count on my help as you need it, but someone did this and was, presumably, paid for it. With what, we do not know, but do your best. We cannot let this go. In the absence of anything more promising, start with those three that I came out with."

The payment end of the bargain, arrived the following day, in the same manner as the previous two. Clutching the letter informing him of its presence, Templemere hurried to his Coach-house to find a rough wooden box, somewhat larger than the previous occasion, which, when prised open, revealed within the straw packing three more gold bars. Each was carefully examined for weight, colour and markings, of which there were none, before being transferred one at a time, held inside his coat, to be safely lodged in the safe within his study. Before closing the safe door for the final time, he ran his hand over each of the six and thought of possibilities; certainly a new carriage and possibly a new town-house, in a more fashionable area of London than where the current one now stood. He pushed the door closed, swung the heavy handle up into place and allowed himself a small smile of contentment.

There were no contented smiles on the faces of any of the 105th Foot. The Prince of Wales Own Wessex Regiment as they pushed forward to achieve Wellington's required 20 miles a day and cover the 180 odd miles, by the shortest route available, from Fuentes to Badajoz. Two days of flat plain brought the jagged peaks of the Sierra de Gata within sight and, on the third, they began their ascent and it was not long before the order they had been expecting, but dreading, came along to them, in the shape of RSM Gibney, speaking first to Sergeant Ellis.

"Ethan! Thy Company's turn. Get on back."

This meant returning to their supply wagons at the rear of their column and hauling on the ropes to aid the horses up the gradients. They were gratefully handed the ropes by Number Nine Company and so they took their turn which would last for the rest of the day. Ellis noted grimly that the Grenadiers were on the ropes of another wagon, with Lieutenant Ameshurst at the head of the rope for his Section, whilst Carravoy and D'Villiers were nowhere to be seen. However, more cheerfully, bringing a half smile to even his grim visage, he saw Sedgwicke walking between the heads of his two mules, leading them on, whilst Albright walked beside and the Nicholls and Mulcahey children sat on the cart's front bench and step, oblivious to the effort around them, all playing pat-a-cake.

That evening, fully tired, they slumped down under the trees of the deep woods either side of the road. However, John Davey, the poaching expert and Tom Miles, the handy craftsman, made off into the trees to see what could be trapped or shot and they returned with three almost decent rabbits, even though not all as plump as Davey would like. He threw them down beside Nelly Nicholls.

"Not as good as I'd of liked, Nelly, they'n still winter thin."

Nelly Nicholls picked one up.

"They're good enough, John, to add a fair bit of meat. Three's better than two!"

She shared a mildly antagonistic look between herself and Tom Miles, but then, to delight all round, John Byford arrived at their camp, and this time he had some good news.

"Surgeon Pearson says I'm off the wounded wagons, and back with the Company."

From his place on the ground Miles looked up at him.

"Does that included pulling on the ropes?"

At that Nelly took immediate umbrage.

"It certainly does not! How could you ask such a thing? He'll be marchin' along with us, carryin' what he can, the dear love!"

Miles' face contorted in perplexity.

"I was only asking! And I don't see you tailing onto a rope when the time comes."

Nelly stood up with her arms akimbo, now very angry, something easily achieved when required to deal with Tom Miles.

"And how am I supposed to do that now, what with all the stuff we've got to carry? All the pots and pans and whatnot, as provides the food for the likes of you!"

Jed Deakin, then checking a boot, had had enough.

"Shut up the pair of you. This march over these mountains be vexing enough without you two adding to it all. Begging your pardon, Henry."

Nelly's husband grinned.

"You just beat me to it, Jed."

Whilst Nelly looked daggers at her husband, Deakin looked at John Byford.

"What'd he say about your wound?"

Byford lay down his kit in a vacant space.

"He says it's healing well enough, but has to be kept clean for the time forward. Washed and fresh bandage."

"So, what's on there now needs changing?"

Byford nodded and began to remove his tunic, his face wincing with pain as the flesh around the cut was stretched. Deakin looked accusingly at Eirin, sat cradling her baby. He gestured with his head towards Byford and Eirin passed the child across to Zeke Saunders, him sat beside her. Then she rose and went across to her husband who was now doing his best with his shirt, this being more awkward, having no buttons, being simply a regulation 'pull up and over'.

"Best if you kneel down."

Byford did and the shirt was pulled up and off, to reveal the grey, much used bandages.

Bridie now spoke up.

"They'll have to be bathed off. Sure, will they not be stuck on there, by now?"

Eirin looked at her Mother and, without speaking any agreement, obtained a pannikin and tipped some warm water into it from the pot on one of their fires. Then she took it back to Byford and began to bath off the bandage which had indeed stuck to the wound. Whilst he looked fondly at her, she met his eyes but twice, but the second time there came the ghost of a smile. The bandage eventually came off and Eirin gasped at the red, ugly wound, merely half healed. Deakin heard and came over to examine, whilst holding Byford's left shoulder.

"'Tis still weepin', but it don't look what I'd call 'angry', nor nuthin'."

He turned to Tom Miles.

"Fetch George."

Irritation immediately came to Miles' face, but an order from Jed Deakin was rarely questioned. He rose and left the fireside, to soon return with Sergeant George Fearnley, who immediately knelt to examine the wound. However, he did not shake his head, rather he nodded in satisfaction, before pronouncing his verdict to no-one in particular, but all listened.

"With a cut as deep as that, I had to leave off the bottom stitch, to give it all a chance to drain. And from there 'tis running clear, which has to be to the good. And it looks no more than the healing of a bad cut, no sign of infection."

He looked directly at Byford.

"When the runnin' out stops, John, tip me the word and I'll put in the last stitch. Now, how far can you swing your arm back, like?"

Byford gingerly raised the muscle part of his arm parallel to the ground and pushed it back behind him about six inches before he had to stop, but Pearson was satisfied.

"I'd say that's not too bad at this stage. I'd say you've pretty much got away with it!"

This brought smiles and grins all round, but positive action from Nelly Nicholls.

"So now you'll stay for a drop of tea, will you not, George, darlin' man?"

Pearson grinned himself.

"I will, Mrs. Nicholls, that'll be most welcome."

Saunders and Solomon immediately moved up on the fallen log to give him room to sit and Pearson was soon indulging in the hospitality and good provender from the two 'Queens' of that mess.

The days of the march South all merged, one into the other, each a wearying trudge up the endless slopes on a road whose surface hindered rather than aided their purpose. When the gradients lessened out as they neared the summit, it began to snow, May sunlight influencing nothing at those altitudes. Eventually they came to a point at the summit that looked familiar, especially as they were allowed to camp there. Miles shouted across to Byford.

"John! B'ain't this the place where we camped Christmas afore last? Where you read out that letter from Tilly?"

Byford had no need to look around.

"Yes Tom, indeed it is. And we all took our ease under his very overhang of rock. And it was snowing then, if not a bit warmer now."

Miles now turned his attention to Davey and Pike, each arranging their blankets against the biting wind.

"John! Joe! 'ave you heard from Tilly since?"

Davey nodded.

"Yes, we got one last April, when we arrived at Fuentes, just after that Sabugal caper."

"All's well?"

"Yes, all's well. The babbies is doin' well and so's the smallholding. They built more onto the cottage, one up, one down."

Saunders looked up from examining the contents of his back-pack.

"Sounds like you two'll be goin' back as well-to-do farmers!"

Miles gave a loud chuckle.

"Ah! If they stays alive, but I wouldn't give much for the chances of any poacher as tries to take off him. Squire Davey! Tricks he knows!"

That set a cheerful mood and then the stew arrived, which added to the good cheer, merely salt-pork and Spanish beans, but it was wolfed down against the cold. The time came to sleep and Byford looked across at Eirin, holding her baby close against the cold, her back to the wind. He went over and felt inside the blankets wrapped around the tiny form.

"Eirin! He's not warm!"

She looked up anxiously, but said nothing.

"Right. He goes inside my greatcoat with me, and my blanket over us both. I'll be against the wind, you on the other side and with Jed between us. That'll keep him good until morning."

The arrangements were made and the three huddled close beside each other. Eirin, facing Byford, released a hand from her blanket and touched his face, then she kissed him briefly, on the chin, before lowering her head into his chest. Soon, Mother and babe were warm and asleep, but it took Byford a little while longer than usual. Not so Jed Deakin, who had noticed all and pointed it out to Bridie, she and he now under the same pair of blankets. She, as pleased as himself, delivered him a kiss, before they both fell asleep.

The next day the road was all downward and, on the Southern slopes that caught the sun, the snow soon disappeared and warmth came to them all, but of equal relief was the end of duty on the hauling ropes. All the transport now trundled down, greatly helped by simple gravity. At the villages of Coria and Caceres supplies were waiting for them and although most could only manage a gross mispronunciation of the names, the gratitude of the Spanish was obvious and manifest. In fact, the reason for their thanks became clear at Caceres, with Shakeshaft running into the Officer's Mess of the Light Company, which included, as usual Major Carr.

"Have you heard? About Beresford? There was a dreadful battle at a place called Albuera, South-East of Badajoz. He held the French and they've pulled back, but his army was almost destroyed. The Buffs were practically wiped out, and many others Regiments suffered over 50 percent losses. The French were commanded by Soult and he's now way back, but the Peer heard about it a couple of days ago and he's in a dreadful buzz. He went on ahead."

Carr put down his glass of the rough Spanish red.

"Destroyed, you say. Nothing left?"

Shakeshaft subsided somewhat.

"Well, all I've heard is that casualties are appalling. They were dreadfully outnumbered, but held on. Somehow."

"And you got this from whom?"

"Well, I know a Lieutenant in the 5th, who knows a Major on McKinnon's Staff, who's well in with a Major on Brent-Spencer's."

Carr looked knowingly at Drake, but Drake did not match his mood of cynicism.

"Whatever, from wherever, it sounds a pretty tight and desperate affair."

However, Shakeshaft's perspective on the conflict at Albuera was much confirmed when they reached Elvas, the massive Portuguese border fortress, the equivalent of the Spanish Badajoz. Wellington kept his two Divisions out of the town and all made camp in the fields around, so it was a day later before Carr and Drake could break off from their duties and come within any close distance of the town. The first thing they remarked on was the huge aqueduct that carried water into the town over the main chausee.

"We'd better mention that in the next letter."

Carr nodded.

"Yes. There's nothing like that back home. What's today's date?"

"22nd."

"Right. This evening, then. Meanwhile, we find Picton's Headquarters and try to find out what's what. I'd like some idea of what they have in store for us. We might find someone who can tip us the word, unofficial as it may be."

However, the nearer they came to the titanic structure, the more they saw that under every arch there were about 100 wounded and they had a struggle to enter the main gate, such were the number of carts, full of maimed and wounded men, all now beginning their sorrowful and painful journey to Lisbon and thence to England, where many, despite the fact that the Surgeon had done his best for them, would not survive, either the journey or the finding of a new livelihood. Inside, the streets were also full of wounded men, of all three Allied armies, British, Spanish and Portuguese, and many French also, some awaiting the Surgeon, some recovering from his attentions, before they could themselves be placed on the painful carts of wounded. Both Medical Orderlies and Spanish civilians bustled around, doing their best with the acres of wounded men. Drake looked around.

"This is as bad as Talavera!"

"You'll get no argument from me! I'd say worse."

They progressed carefully into the town and came upon a Major on horseback, doing his best to pick his way out through the wounded lying everywhere. Carr stopped him, although the Major was barely moving.

"Any idea about Picton's Headquarters? The Third?"

"Alongside mine, of the 7th. Get up to the Cathedral, top end of the Square, when up there you can't miss it."

Carr patted the horses neck and held the rein at the bit.

"Do you know anything? What's in store?"

The Major looked downcast, even as he nodded his head.

"Now that Beresford's pushed Soult back, at a cost that you can see all around you, Nosey's going to have another crack at Badajoz. Beresford made a start, but got distracted. Obviously."

"So that's the word?"

"Yes. That's why he's brought us down here."

Carr nodded.

"Fine! A siege. Therefore, any point in struggling up to the Cathedral?"

"No. None. You'll know the details soon enough. So, were I you, I'd have a drink and get out. Disease hasn't hit yet, but I'd say it will, sooner rather than later, with the crowds of wounded we have in here."

Carr released the rein.

"We're obliged to you. We're Carr and Drake of the 105th."

The Major saluted.

"Chelwood. 51st."

The Major rode slowly on and Carr and Drake immediately looked for the nearest Estaminet. One was within yards and so they entered to see a lone Captain sat at a table, his leg heavily bandaged and a crude crutch leaning against his chair. Drake went straight up and offered his hand.

"Drake. 105th. Mind if we join you? Me and my Major here, Henry Carr?"

The Captain lifted his head and managed a welcoming smile up at Drake, before offering his hand and raising himself slightly using only his good leg.

"Stokes. 31st."

Both Drake and Carr sat and Carr signalled for the waiter, who hurried over.

"Una botella de vino tinto, por favor."

Drake looked at Stokes with plain and evident sympathy.

"Were you there?"

He nodded.

"Yes, in the centre and we were lucky."

"How so? We'd like to know. Wouldn't we Major?"

Carr nodded.

"Yes. But only if you feel up to the telling of it."

Stokes smiled.

"It's alright. If anything, it helps."

He took a deep breath.

"Well, Beresford marched us out to this place named Albuera, and drew us up on a ridge facing the Frogs when they showed, but Soult sent only some at us and at the town, the rest, all he had, he marched around our right flank, which was held by the Dons. They turned their flank to face up and made a decent showing, but there were too many Johnnies for them to hold, but it should have been alright when Colbourne's Brigade, including us, were marched up to face the Johnnies by Stewart, 'Auld Grog Willie'."

Both Carr and Drake smiled encouragingly. All knew of General Stewart's proclivity for giving extra rum to the men of his Division, and Stokes continued.

"He came in alongside the Dons, formed line and began to hit their left column. Then it rained, a downpour and, as if that wasn't bad enough, the end of our line was hit by cavalry, murdering Polish Lancers. Where they hit, they had no time to form square, you couldn't see them coming anyway. They came out of the rain and rolled up the Buffs first, then the 48th, then the 66th. We were lucky, we were on the far end of Colbourne's line and we had time to form square, but Colbourne's right and centre were wiped out, nothing

130

left there. That left just us facing the Frogs in front, and some Dons, who'd stood, stood well, but suffered badly."

The wine arrived and Carr opened it and he poured Stokes a generous glass and he took a good drink from the measure.

"Then Houghton's three came up to replace the Dons, with Abercrombie's three next to them on their left. That put us in the middle between the two, and then it started, us seven against God knows how many of them. We'd got there at about 10.30 and, including the cavalry attack, from then on we stood that hill for two hours. Just standing, firing and closing into The Colours. Houghton's, on our right got it worst, for some reason Johnny concentrated his guns on them. Then Soult sent up another Division to try and get around our right, where Houghton's were stood in shreds, and another Division to hold off the Fusiliers just arriving, but they fought their way up to us, there on the ridge, and they saw off their Division, completely. With that defeat there, Johnny gave best in front of us and pulled back. What saved us, really, were some guns, two batteries side by side, one Don, the other KGL. If there were any heroes, it was that Don battery, they held their place there from first shot to last, the KGL came up after with Abercrombie. It was them that held back the French for us. Houghton's was furthest from the artillery support and got it worst."

He took another long drink.

"Then the smoke cleared and then you saw the worst of it. I've seen cricket pitches bigger than that battlefield and the dead were piled all over. Ours in rows, theirs as heaps! Walls even!"

He shook his head.

"But those Don gunners! When the Frogs pulled back, we went over, to shake their hands, pat them on the back, anything, but they'd collapsed, like puppets whose strings had been cut. We couldn't wake them up. I've never seen men so deadbeat. Not that ours were far behind."

Silence fell and all took a drink, before Drake asked his own question.

"It was a big attack then? By the Frogs?"

Stokes was almost angered by the question.

"Massive. You couldn't see the end of them, whichever way you looked, they just stretched away, front, left and right."

He looked carefully both Carr and Drake.

"It sounds stupid, I know, but I have nightmares of that battle, each the same. I see us bringing down the front rank, but then another just steps up, over and on. No end!"

He paused and took a deep, sad breath, to then speak each word very carefully.

"How we held them, I will never know!"

With that he finished his wine and stood up, to gather up his crutch.

"If you'll excuse me, I must get back to my men, both sound and wounded."

Carr and Drake stood also, as Stokes continued.

"I'm not too bad, just got a lance thrust in my leg."

Then he paused, his face very serious.

"Just remember those Polish Lancers. The worst bastards I've ever heard of. Many of Colbourne's tried to surrender, but they took no notice, just carried on stabbing and killing. If you get the chance, get one back for all of us, the Buffs, the 48th and the 66th!"

He shook the proffered hands of both, who were nodding vigorously and then hobbled off, whilst Carr and Drake watched him go. Both sat down and ordered another bottle. During its arrival, both sat in stunned silence, a reverie that was broken with the arrival of the waiter with the wine. Whilst he poured, Drake voiced his own conclusion.

"Seems like Johnny made a special effort down here."

Carr nodded.

"Something extra, that's for sure."

They drank another glass, paid, left the Estaminet and then the town, picking their way between wounded men, attendants and carts of wounded. Once in camp, Drake summoned Ellis.

"Sergeant. We will soon be involved in a siege. Have you any experience?"

"Yes Sir, in the Lowlands."

"So, you know what's involved?'

"I've a fair idea, Sir. It'll involve work gangs, workin' day and night. Farmin' lads are the best, as knows about ditchin', revetments and whatnot. Each gang needs a few, to see that the work gets done right. Each Section usually equals one work gang."

"Right. Good, but see that the skills you spoke of are spread over our two. We cannot be accused of shoddy work."

Ellis came to the attention and saluted.

"Sir. I'll get onto it right away."

On that day, back in London, the news of Albuera had arrived and Livermore sat through the early afternoon, reading a copy of Beresford's report. One phrase he read several times, 'It is impossible, by any description, to do justice to the conduct of the men.' Another described the French attack on his right flank as 'the biggest attack, so far, of the whole Peninsular War'. He sat back, both saddened and angered, then he picked up a copy of Wellington's report to note that Beresford had been replaced by General Hill, but Livermore had nothing but sympathy for Beresford. He had been out-maneuvered, partially, but what General had not? Much the same had happened to Wellington at Fuentes! He returned both into the cover, placed this into a drawer and rose to leave his office.

"Wilson! I'll be two hours. Perhaps more."

Wilson looked up, startled, but said nothing.

Feeling no need to button his great-coat, Livermore took the back way, across Horse Guards and Birdcage Walk, to pass between Westminster Hall and Westminster Abbey, to soon find himself entering a well-appointed doorway of an ordinary townhouse in Great Smith Street. All was familiar inside and he climbed two flights of stairs to enter a room where he found Radipole reading some papers, outside the sanctum reserved for Waters.

"Radipole. With me!"

The young man rose and followed Livermore into the inner room, where sat Colonel Waters. As Waters looked up, Livermore spoke.

"You've read it, I take it? The Albuera report?'

Waters sat back and nodded, but said nothing.

"Anything on Massena's letter?"

Then Waters did speak.

"Well, yes, a possibility. I've been studying a map of our front at that time and, to get a letter over, well, there were only three places, North to South; Barba del Puerco, the ford below Seranillo, and the village of Carpio de Azaba on the main chausee between Villar Formosa and Cuidad. At that time, it was inhabited, but held by neither side. Our forces at those three places may have seen something, but it's a long shot."

Livermore's face remained grave.

"I'll try to make some enquiries about those three, but I'm here, those men are out there. So, what of our three Peers?"

"Nothing! I've had them watched, but nothing unusual. Templemere is the one with the most active nightlife. Seems he entertains quite a lot, with overnight guests."

Livermore allowed himself a moment's thought.

"Let's start with him. See if we can't shake him up a little; by showing him the captured letter and what it says."

He turned to Radipole.

"Any thoughts?"

The unblinking eyes turned to Livermore.

"Three things! Unless their motive was pure French patriotism, someone benefitted from this in some material way, as you have pointed out, Sir. That is worth watching out for. Secondly, I'll be interested to hear what Templemere has to say about the other two, Mahon and Hopgood. He may think that questioning their movements whilst out there, diverts attention away from him. Last, if he has any motive to deflect attention from himself, then he may try to move our attention onto one or both, by revealing certain disobliging facts about each, perhaps some that can be revealed by us as untrue. If it is one of those three, I doubt that he has the experience or guile to understand the subtleties of such as this."

He allowed his audience to absorb that before continuing.

"Also, was it not Templemere who stood up in the House of Lords and advocated the visit in the first place?'

Livermore nodded.

"Right. Let's get hold of him. Write him a letter inviting him over here, speaking of a matter of some concern to us that he may be able to help with."

Waters sat forward.

"No need! He's here, in town. Now, or at least very likely to be! The House of Lords is holding an emergency debate on both Fuentes and Albuera. Both were very close calls and they want to know why. Beresford himself was there this morning, and General Erskine. Both are back in England."

Livermore's face brightened considerably.

"Right. Get the letter written and Radipole, you take it to the House and get Black Rod to give it to Templemere. Request his attendance as a matter of urgency."

Within half an hour, Radipole was alighting from a hired carriage at the gate of the House of Lords. He came to the door, but stood politely at the entrance, advancing no further. Black Rod was at the Usher's desk and noticed him. He was more than a little impressed with the restrained and businesslike appearance of the young man, nothing ostentatious, everything sober and carefully measured. His manner wholly respectful.

"Can we help you?"

Radipole strode forward, holding out the letter.

"If you please, Sir. If Lord Templemere is present, might it be possible to deliver this letter to him?"

Sir Francis Molyneux, Gentleman Usher of the Black Rod, took the letter.

"Who is it from?"

"General Livermore, Sir. There is a matter of some urgency that he hopes Lord Templemere may be able to help him with."

Molyneux looked sternly at Radipole.

"Livermore?"

"Yes Sir. Yes."

Black Rod passed the letter to his Assistant stood beside him.

"Get this to Templemere. I saw him pass though myself."

Within the Chamber, Lord Templemere was thoroughly enjoying himself, having now spoken twice in the debate, once to be heavily critical of the retreat to Torres Vedras, forced upon the army after the victory of Busaco and secondly, to exaggerate the supply problems before the battle of Fuentes de Onoro. His final sentence within both had been to question General Lord Wellington's competence to manage and command a campaign of that scale and that having his flank turned causing near disaster, was now becoming a regular occurrence with this current Commander. He had just retaken his seat and was now looking forward to an hour's pleasure in Pimlico before a good dinner at his club, therefore it came as a shock when suddenly a letter was passed to him by his companion, Lord Mahon. He broke the seal and read the brief request, "Would you please be so good as to attend immediately with Colonel Waters and General Livermore at their premises? They request your aid on a matter of some national importance. A carriage awaits at your convenience, with our good servant, Mr. R. Radipole, who awaits your pleasure."

Templemere looked at Mahon.

"Livermore wants to see me!"

Mahon's eyebrows went upwards and the corners of his mouth downwards.

"Then you'd best go."

Templemere re-folded the letter and lodged it in his inside pocket, then he rose and shuffled his way along the bench, disturbing all the other Nobles at that moment contentedly sat there. Now free, he walked the corridor to the entrance where he first spied Radipole, who immediately came to a kind of civilian attention, but said nothing. Templemere was slightly discomfited by the ordered and immaculate appearance of the young man, but also his by confident, self-assured bearing. However, Templemere's natural character soon surfaced and asserted itself in the form of a desire to establish some form of superiority, even though he knew the answer.

"And who might you be?"

"Radipole, my Lord. As your letter has informed you, I have a carriage waiting. As are Colonel Waters and General Livermore at Colonel Waters' offices."

The smooth conjunction of the last two sentences did nothing to make Templemere feel that he had achieved his objective. As for the half smile on Radipole's face, that made Templemere feel that Radipole knew something that he did not, which also did nothing to move the situation in his favour.

"The carriage is just beyond the gate, my Lord."

Radipole led the way and went straight to the carriage to open the door, thus allowing Templemere to enter first. Templemere took one corner, but Radipole, when he entered, took his seat in the corner diagonally opposite, the furthest away possible. There he sat in silence, which Templemere found insulting. Something should be said to ease his mind as to what this was all about. He became more than a little irritated.

"Why have I been dragged out of a very important House of Lords debate?"

Radipole slowly, even indulgently, turned his head towards him.

"Did not the letter state a matter of national importance, my Lord?"

Templemere's irritation grew.

"Yes, but that could mean anything!"

The disconcerting half smile returned.

"Yes, my Lord, I suppose it could, but, as I'm sure you appreciate, such things should only be discussed within the confines of a private office."

With that Radipole turned to look out of the window, leaving Templemere feeling doubly annoyed at having his enquiry so effectively dismissed. Great Smith Street was less than a five-minute ride from the House of Lords and the carriage soon pulled up. Radipole alighted first and gestured Templemere to follow him and climb the four marble front-steps and enter, which he did, still irritated by the absence of any deference from this inscrutable young man.

"Two flights up, my Lord, then the first door you come to."

Templemere, now fully appreciating that nothing would be forthcoming which would help explain the nature of his summoning, climbed the stairs and entered the room without knocking. There he found Waters and Livermore waiting in the outer office, both leaning against Radipole's desk. Livermore immediately levered himself vertical.

"My Lord Fred! I trust I find you well. Please forgive our summoning you here, but something important has come up."

Templemere did no more than stare at him and so Livermore continued.

"May I introduce Colonel John Waters?"

Waters offered his hand, which Templemere shook briefly, as Waters essayed a slight bow.

"You servant, my Lord."

By now Livermore was standing at the door of Waters' inner office and gesturing for Templemere to enter, which he did, to find a desk with two chairs before it and one behind. There was another in the corner. Templemere took one of the two, whilst Livermore occupied the desk chair and Waters came to sit beside Templemere. Thinking that he was settled, he was discomfited to see that Radipole had followed them in to occupy the corner chair. He turned to Livermore.

"Why does this messenger boy have to attend, if all this is so private and confidential?"

Waters turned to him, a warm smile on his face.

"Be at peace, my Lord. Young Radipole will be taking some notes, merely to keep a record, you understand?"

Templemere did not, but things were happening on the other side of the desk which pulled his attention in that direction. Livermore was pushing what looked like a high-status letter towards him, with another piece of paper pinned to the back. He withdrew his hand and left the letter in place, to await a reaction from Lord Fred, who simply stared at it, appearing to be perplexed, whilst really, for the moment at least, he wished to express his annoyance at being there. He raised his eyes to stare at Livermore.

"This means what?"

Livermore stared back.

"The top copy is a letter from Marshall Massena, written whilst he was in Cuidad, instructing one of his Generals, Godinot, to move his Brigade to reinforce Soult down at Badajoz. Massena acted upon intelligence received, provided even."

Livermore was staring hard at Templemere. Was there just a flicker in his eyes when he spoke the final sentence? He continued.

"The letter was intercepted by Spanish guerillas. The courier was tortured to reveal that there were two more couriers, carrying copies. Events at Albuera bore this out, that Godinot had indeed received this order. Some men under his command were captured after the battle. We are hoping that you can help. Please read the translation on the accompanying sheet."

Templemere picked up both, gave the top sheet a quick glance, then folded it back to reveal the translation. This he read, whilst both Livermore and Waters studied him hard, but there was no reaction, until he attempted to speak, when he had to clear his throat. He had noted the alteration of 'obtained' to the significant 'provided', but he soon recovered.

"In what way do you expect me to be able to help?"

Livermore leaned forward, his demeanour quite cheerful.

"Look at the date, Lord Fred. It was written immediately after we left, the day after. Whoever sent the information across to the Johnnies, did it whilst we were there, probably our last day. It makes sense that it was the day before Massena wrote his letter."

Templemere's eyebrows came together, he had reacted well enough so far, relying on demonstrating sheer puzzlement, when that was far from the case. Waters now spoke up, causing Templemere to twist in his seat to face him.

"You were there, my Lord, you know, riding around and looking around, more than most. Perhaps you saw something? Anything at all might help. That letter proves that Wellington is operating with a spy in his camp who may still be there."

Templemere merely stared blankly back at him and so Waters continued.

"The main point, my Lord, is, as I've said, that you and your two companions were there. I have to say that no-one can be above suspicion. Even Livermore here!"

Both men grinned, whilst Templemere did not. He had recovered enough to think of what best to say.

"Wellington has an army of thousands! It could be any one of them."

Livermore now sat right forward.

"Agreed my Lord, but we know that somehow the letter was got across the Agueda, at one of only three possible points, Barba del Puerco, the ford at Seranillo, and some village called Carpio de Azaba on the main road. Almost certainly by someone with licence to go where they pleased. We think a mere civilian unlikely, the three points were very difficult to penetrate. Only someone with the right to be there could have delivered. Massena would have acted on that intelligence very quickly and so it was probably delivered one day before he wrote his own letter. You are here, Lord Fred, Wellington's men are not. We now hope for some answers to questions sent to them, but that will take time. We are hoping that something might jog your memory. Please take some time over the next few days to re-live your movements and what you saw. Anything might help."

Templemere felt relieved and secure. This was something that he could agree to.

"I will do that, gentlemen, most certainly, if it may help. Such would be no more that my duty as a patriotic Englishman!"

Livermore nodded.

"Just so, my Lord, but you see, and to reiterate, the fact remains that it happened during the time of our party being there. What of your other two companions? Can you vouch for them? Assuredly?"

Templemere took a moment to think. This was an opportunity, but it required a measured response.

"I have known both for some time, but I know little about the family history of each. Hopgood has some ground in Dorset, Mahon some in Essex. All I can say is that Mahon has some 'émigré' in his background, they came over at the time of what we call 'The Terror', and I believe his Father or Grandfather married into our aristocracy, they being French 'aristos' themselves. How strong those French connections remain, I do not know."

He looked at both, turning from one to the other, rather pleased with his careful words, and then he continued, equally carefully.

"I'm afraid, that, in that direction, that is the best I can do."

Livermore stood, as did Waters and Radipole, Livermore extending his hand and Templemere briefly taking it.

"Well then, thanks you for your time, Lord Fred, and, as we have said, please do dredge through your memory of our time out there and see what you can recall. We are determined to get to the bottom of this and expose the traitor."

This last phrase gave Templemere momentary disquiet, but he soon recovered and bowed in the direction of Waters, whilst Livermore spoke a brief farewell.

"Radipole will see you out."

Templemere was now retrieving his gloves and cane.

"Not to bother. I can see myself out."

With that he turned towards the door, taking the time to deliver a disdainful look at Radipole, but, for all the reaction he got, he may as well have been staring at a blank wall. With him gone, Waters held the door open to be certain that Templemere had descended into the street, then he gestured for Radipole to sit in the now vacant chair.

"Radipole, investigate this Mahon. Find out how far what he said about him is the truth. Was it worth saying or just a ruse to deflect our attention, as you pointed out?"

Radipole nodded and made some notes, whilst Waters looked at Livermore.

"What do you think? About Templemere, that is?"

Livermore pursed his lips before speaking.

"He's a 'runner and rider'. We cannot discount him."

He turned to Radipole.

"What do we know about him?"

Radipole flicked back a few pages in his notebook.

"He served in the cavalry for a year, going out with Wellington's second time out there. He was at Talavera and part of the retreat down, but captured before they reached Torres Vedras, then paroled. Prior to that, he was a bit of a rake. He fought a lot of duels and killed quite a few. He gambles a lot; backgammon and the horses, but is not popular with the ladies. Inherited large estates from his Father in Hampshire. Is not held in high esteem anywhere, neither with the local nor the town gentry. He was beaten, illegally, in a duel with an Officer of the 105th. You saw the scar. Back in 1808 he was humiliated by the Prince of Wales after a Colours ceremony at Horse Guards. His main associates are Mahon and Hopgood."

Waters nodded.

"One of whom, Mahon, he wants us to shine a light upon."

Livermore then sat back, to adopt his usual pensive pose of elbows on the chair arms, fingertips opposed from each hand.

"On Mahon, certainly, but, as we've agreed, someone was paid for this, probably handsomely. Keep an eye on their spending, all three!"

oOo

"So that's what this is all about, it would seem."

Captain Ned Drake eased the straps of his pack as he marched beside the Lieutenant of his Second Section, Richard Shakeshaft. In the distance, but very discernable in the clear May sunshine, could be seen the towers and white to grey walls of Badajoz. It had taken them a long time to come within sight of the vital border fortress, having forded the River Guadiana close to Elvas to then take a long sweep to circle Badajoz to the South, but now, finally, they were approaching their objective with serious intent. The pair halted whilst their line marched on behind them, and they drew their own telescopes to better study the squat town, squat that is, apart from the Castle at the right of the town, on its hill, thereby making the Castle tower the most prominent feature of the town, it being high above the walls and the walls of that area being high above the town. A high church tower rose up from the town centre. No answer from the Lieutenant to the original question being forthcoming, a singular feature now captured Drake's attention.

"Strange! What are they?"

With Drake's exclamation, the pair fixed on an odd and what appeared to be triangular fort, now almost opposite them in line with the town and another over to their right. Both were obviously fortified with as many gun emplacements as their short walls could accommodate. It was Shakeshaft who gave an opinion.

"Outworks! To protect something. I'd say that the ground on which they are built is higher than the town walls and so they are there to restrict any siege-works that are placed in that position to bombard the town walls, which will be lower, relative to there! Quite an advantage."

Drake lowered his telescope, folded it and returned it to his pocket.

"You really think so! We'll have to make you our siege and fortification expert."

Both laughed until they realised that the Followers had now come up to them and that they must hurry on. Had they but known it, hostilities had already begun, but of a different kind. The ill feelings between Nellie Nicholls and Betty Barker still smouldered and, on this occasion both were marching close together, Betty firing the opening salvo, but speaking loudly to her walking companion, Sally Prinsett.

136

"I hear that all them in Ireland has webbed feet. The better for crossing all the bogs and wet moss and whatnot."

Nellie immediately bridled at the comment, which had been directed not only at her, but at many of her friends, and she shouted, but did not turn.

"Better to walk on webbed feet than broken legs!"

Then she did turn to face her enemy.

"Nor to try and see through two black eyes!"

Both Betty and Sally were Londoners and had grown up within families always at, or just above, starvation, therefore neither were the same size as Nellie Nicholls, but the two together were a different proposition. Sally weighed in.

"You start on her an' you'll have me to deal with, an' all!"

At that point, Bridie joined in.

"Don't you think that I'll be stood idle! Pair of gobshites you both. Useless and ever all for yourselves."

She warmed to her subject.

"Sure, and have we ever seen you helpin' with the wounded, at all. You've not the stomach nor the strength. Useless, shirking gobshites! More like out robbin' the dead. And wounded!"

Betty could think of no other reply, than a plain insult.

"Irish bog-totter! Stupid and dirty."

At this point, hostilities could well have become more open, had not Chaplain's Assistant Sedgwicke intervened and, after him, the French.

"Peace ladies, please. Be at peace. Are we not all, each of us, in the same circumstance and would it not be better to resolve to help each other, rather than to hate and hinder?"

If this made any difference it was impossible to tell, because a salvo of cannon-fire came from the outwork on the far right of the two, much too far off to cause any serious harm, but a spent cannonball came bowling over the ground in the direction of the Followers. Sedgwicke immediately held out his arms to halt those behind him and create a lane for the ball to pass through, which it did, with an alarming hiss. Sedgwicke took his cue.

"There, is that not a sign from our Good Lord to emphasise the perils we must all face together."

Bridie and Nellie obediently genuflected, whilst Betty and Sally merely scowled. Up ahead, Lacey and O'Hare grinned at each other.

"Welcome to Badajoz, Padraigh, but make sure you keep away!"

"Love to! I've no good memories of this place, and I fear that nothing in the future will change that."

Two hours later, Zeke Saunders, with two shovels on one shoulder and a pickaxe on the other, looked down into the scummy, green water of the ditch in front of him, then he looked up at the far walls of Badajoz, these crowned with the Castle, then over to the Guadiana, some 200 yards to his right. He dropped his tools where he stood and waited there for orders. The rest of his messmates soon came to join him and all stood to study their new situation. In front were the formidable walls of the Castle, whilst the other remarkable feature was the single fort, someway over to their right, isolated on its hill, on the far side of the Guadiana.

"Well, this I don't like!"

Byford, his constant companion grinned, leaned on his own pair of tools, a shovel and a crude soil hack.

"Well, Zeke, you are not alone in that. A lot of us caught a fever last time we were here, but perhaps this is a little early in the year."

"Here's hopin'! Meanwhile, we can count on this bein' our camp ground, so let's get set up."

The making of a fire was by the simple action of using cartridges broken open and soon there was a cheerful blaze that they all gathered around, hoping to be ignored, but it was not to be, for soon their Section Commander, Lieutenant Maltby arrived, him carrying three six-foot poles, each with a small flag. They all stood and waited for what was to come, knowing that it would not be pleasant, and it was not.

"Who's a good judge of distance?"

Saunders was a Corporal and as entitled to speak as any there, in fact more so, but he confined himself to one word.

"Sir?"

"We start our first entrenchment tonight. The Engineers want it 800 yards from the castle wall that you can see there. So, as we're digging at night, there have to be markers placed during daylight. 800 yards from the wall, that is where our first parallel will be. And our batteries."

Maltby spoke with some authority, because he had been selected as one of the Officers from the Third Division to be trained by the Engineers in the arts of fascines, redoubts, revetments and gabions and he was fresh from his single day's induction. He looked around.

"Any volunteers? Or do I begin my own selection?"

Byford then spoke up.

"I'll volunteer, Sir. About five cricket pitches. I can judge that. How many more men do you need?"

Maltby was somewhat taken-aback and more than slightly unsettled. Here was the man who had legally married the woman whom he had hoped to take as a mistress again and was now bringing up his son. Therefore, he answered as minimally as possible.

"Two more, besides yourself."

Davey then stepped forward.

"Cricket pitches, be buggered! 800 yards is nigh on half a mile, just under."

Then came Miles, more than happy to take the chance to look the likes of Maltby right in the eye.

"With me, I'd reckon you've got your three. Sir."

Although Miles' final word had been spoken with some venom, Maltby smiled, more from relief than genuine gratitude and he handed out the markers.

"Right! 800 yards. Off you go."

Miles hefted his over his right shoulder.

"Any chance of a rum ration when we gets back, Sir?"

Maltby pretended that he had not heard and watched the three walk forward. First, they had to cross the noisome ditch that had preoccupied Saunders, using a suspect bridge of double logs, then they walked forward. The daylight was still strong and the white-grey walls of Badajoz were clear in the distance, with the French Tricolor blowing out straight in the stiff breeze above the Castle. Miles was beside Davey and they had now walked 200 yards. Many others from the 3rd Division were spread out to the left and right, each carrying their own marker.

"When do you think they'll give us a gun? 'Tis not like them to let us just stroll up, as and when we pleases."

The answer was several gushes of white smoke from the battlements, the 'whoosh' of the passing ball and then the reports, each sounding like a large man clearing his throat. Davey turned to Miles and grinned.

"You were saying?"

The answer from Miles was a noise not dissimilar to the gun going off, but then Davey called across to Byford.

"What's your thinking John?"

"That piece of fence, dead ahead. That and 50 paces further."

Davey nodded.

"I'll go along with that. A bit less than 800, off the walls, but that'll do me."

More cannonballs sang past, one ploughing the dark earth 50 yards off and level with them. With that, all guns on the battlements opened up at their best speed, because now they had the range of all these approaching flag carriers. Davey had had enough and they were sufficiently past the vestige of fence.

"Right. 20 yards apart between us and get gone."

All three pushed the ends of the poles into the earth, with difficulty, they had not been sharpened, which brought a torrent of expletives from Miles which began and ended with the word 'Maltby'. Then they ran back and the cannonade lessened, but Byford ran over to help a man from the next Regiment, who was being helped by the next man beyond. The man could barely walk and his comrade explained.

"Winded! Shot came too close and took the breath out of him."

The man was carried back to his own lines and Byford ran back to his, where Maltby was waiting.

"Well done, men. Now get some rest. We dig with the darkness!"

Such a poetic conjunction achieved no reaction, appreciative or otherwise, from his men, as they moved back to their mess-fires. There the Followers were close to applying the final touches to their meal, but Bridie knew what was required.

138

"You sleep now, boys, and I'll wake you at the sunset, so's you can eat and have something inside you for your labouring."

They obeyed without a murmur and, at the due time, they were woken to eat the hot salt-fish stew, peas and Army biscuits. By then the town walls were enveloped in darkness and the whole Battalion was ordered forward with some form of agricultural tool to dig the first parallel. At the 800 yards' distance, the town walls could just be seen but few paid them any attention. Maltby marked the line of the back of the trench, showing the 150 yards that was to be dug by the 105th, this to be their contribution to the total 1,200 required for the parallel. The remaining length to be produced by the remaining six Battalions of Picton's Third Division. As Maltby walked with his bag of crushed chalk he repeated the litany,

"Three foot deep, three foot wide, parapet three foot high."

"All the threes then!"

This from Saunders, as he sank his soil hack into the soil of good pasture, but there was no such equanimity from Miles as the 3rd Divisions Riflemen passed through them to mount picket 600 yards from the walls. He looked up after no more than a half-dozen spade fulls, most indignant as they trod on the parapet bank that he had started.

"And just wer' be all you cossetted sods goin'? Don't you get to take a turn on the tools?"

A Corporal, bringing up the rear, felt inclined to answer.

"Seems not! Seems someone is needed to mount picket out yonder, to stop any nasty Frenchman coming along and spoiling your nice piece of landscaping."

All the Riflemen laughed which did nothing to improve Miles' mood, but Ellis was near.

"Keep digging, Miles. They wants this trench finished afore dawn."

Thus, they laboured through the night, thankful that the soil, all part of the Guadiana flood plain, was easy digging. The French on the walls knew that something was happening and sent howitzer shells fizzing through the night, but all were too short or misdirected. However, apart from the odd shell exploding well short, all their practically uninterrupted efforts were accompanied by the noise of incessant cannon-fire from the direction of the isolated fort on the hill beyond the Guadiana, resulting in all from time to time ceasing their digging and shoveling whenever there came a particularly loud volley from that point. Saunders, as curious as anyone, wanted to know of events up there and used the arrival of Maltby to try to find out, him checking on depth, width, height and the general adherence to his chalk line.

"That place up there got a name, Sir?"

The answer came down from the darkness.

"Fort San Christobal."

"Have we got men up there, Sir, doing what we're trying down here?"

"Yes, but it's all rock, no soil. Up there they have to make a parallel out of gabions."

"What are they, Sir?"

"A big wicker basket, four foot across and five foot high. You put the basket where you want it, then fill it with soil."

"Seems like the Frogs up there are taking great exception to our efforts, Sir, to do that."

"I'd say you were correct, Corporal."

The cannonade, intense at the fort, sporadic from the Castle, continued all night, but in the case of the latter, with the light of dawn the French could see the first evidence of the siege they were now to endure, a parallel well over 1,000 yards long with a high parapet of over three foot in most places. The 105th, with all the other Battalions of the Third Division were withdrawn with the daylight and so all took themselves off to the Guadiana to wash, prior to sleeping. This gave them a good view of the slope in front of the San Christobal fort where work had taken place during the previous night to begin the siege there and the cannonade from the Fort in reply was now continuous. Miles drew the obvious conclusion.

"Well, that must have been one long wasted effort!"

All others had come to the same opinion, because where there should have been a neat line of solid gabions, there was instead a mess of shattered wickerwork and spilt brown soil. The gunners in the fort continued to batter the line, even though it was a wreck with no Sappers nor soldiers to be seen. It was only 400 yards from the walls, well within accurate range and it provided no shelter for any Troops that could be placed behind it. The whole had been an obvious failure. With that established in their opinions, the 105th collected their clothes and returned to their mess areas, for a brief meal and then sleep, but only after tending to open blisters with vinegar, but most often salt-water. They slept until the Midday meal, when they were woken by the arrival of teams of mules and men pulling the guns that would go into their parallel. All sat up to watch the teams and guns being detached from each other, but even the inexperienced Joe Pike felt qualified enough to pass comment, as he sat with Tom Miles and John Davey.

"Some of those guns look over 100 years old! Especially the biggest, those we need the most."

Tom Miles grinned.

"Don't be too unhappy, boy. They're here to make a breach in them walls and if they hasn't the power, then there's no breach that the likes of us has to scramble up through. There's nothin' worse they can ask us to do, than to go attacking some breach in a city wall. No! For the likes of us, nothin' worse!"

At that point, Lieutenant Maltby arrived with the order for the coming night's digging. He motioned over Sergeant Ellis and showed him the plan.

"Our job tonight is two communication trenches into the centre of the parallel. Zig-zag so that the French can't fire along it. There will be two more close by and the four will lead into the battery that will take all these guns just arrived."

Ellis frowned.

"Does it have to be at night, Sir, it being this side of the parallel?"

Maltby rolled up the plan.

"Orders, Sergeant, and thank our good fortune that we are down here and not up there at San Christobal. Casualties have been severe to very little gain. So far, all we've got is blisters!"

Miles turned away for a pointed grumble.

"Ah, but not on his pretty hands!"

So, whilst the continuous crash of counter-fire came from the Fort high on their right, they settled to an afternoon of rest, many making crude palm gloves from old blankets and canvas. In the last of the daylight they found the flags put there by the Engineers to mark the beginning of their work and they began to dig, gradually increasing the depth until finally they had a three-foot zig-zag trench that matched the floor level of the battery when they finally came up to connect with it, the interior having being fully completed at the same time by Artillery Engineers. They had finished way before dawn, but all hopes of an early return to their camp were dashed by the Chief Engineer Colonel Fletcher, him approaching Maltby.

"Get your men on the far side of the parapet, Lieutenant, and dig from that side to increase its height and thickness. We must make full use of the time we are given. It's June now and the short nights are upon us."

Thus, the rest of the night was spent on the French side of the battery, building up the parapet's strength before the siege guns came into place. Dawn found them trudging back through their own communication trench to again use the Guadiana for a wash and to again see that Maltby had been right. Nothing could be seen on the San Christobal slope that in any way resembled a battery line, but the 105th settled down to their own affairs and the day was spent with sleep and food. The afternoon revealed what would need to be done that following night, as ropes were attached by the artillerymen to every gun. Throughout the night they would all be dragged up the four communication trenches and set in place at their embrasures. The one relief was spoken by Tom Miles.

"Well, at least we'n done with shovellin'."

However, with the arrival of darkness he came to regret his words, at least partially. Mackinnon's Brigade were given the task, two Sections to one gun, of dragging fourteen, 24lbs. brass guns, along the 500 yards of communication trench, it being barely wide enough. The pieces were 17th Century siege artillery with huge metal wheels and metal trails, to be hauled over the difficult surface of the trench, it being no more than compacted soil. The larger and stronger, including Zeke Saunders and Nat Solomon were given a length of stout timber to thrust into the barrel of the gun, with which to lever the gun straight when it slewed sideways, as it so often did. Half-way along it began to rain and the men on the ropes slid and toppled every which way as the trench became slippery. In addition, the floor of the trench softened with the rain and the metal wheels dug deep into the soil and became clogged with mud which added to the weight so that each zig-zag turn in the trench presented a major obstacle, the guns having to be swung around to face the new direction, largely by hand. When they finally arrived at the battery, the men were utterly exhausted, soaked and caked in mud, but the task had not ended. Each gun then had to be dragged to its embrasure, but at least the rain had stopped and, whilst they had laboured along the zig-zags, the artillerymen had laid boards throughout the battery and, although the 105th and the others were sent over to the French side of the earthwork to drag the final yards up to the embrasures, now the guns moved less reluctantly over the stout flooring. With each gun in its final

140

place, their work was done and the artillerymen set about securing the gun tackles to the stout spikes driven into the earth beyond the embrasure. As tired as anyone, Miles had the final word as the gunners worked.

"There you are, boys. All yours and welcome."

Back to the Guadiana, the river was soon full of naked men, washing both themselves and their mud-caked uniforms. Few bothered to deflect from the task of washing both themselves and their heavy woollen and canvas clothing to look up at San Christobal, where there was no change to be seen. It was during their return journey, wearing only cotton underwear, still wet, that their own guns opened up and Pike looked at the pillars of smoke and spoke his fears.

"All that will keep us awake!"

Davey put his hand on his young companion's shoulder.

"Somehow, boy, I don't think so!"

Davey was correct. All slept the sleep of the exhausted, warm in the early June sunshine. Another blessing was that there was no more night-duty and so they stayed awake long after sunset talking around the fire, or each taking a turn to cradle baby Jedediah, especially Deakin, for some reason. Nelly and Bridie had soon got over their spat with their Cockney rivals and all were of good cheer as they sat and joked and talked of old campaigns. Most of this was provided by Deakin, Nicholls and a rare visit from RSM Gibney, these all being ex-9th Norfolk before the formation of the 105th. Even Sedgwicke arrived, now that his charge was bedded down with a lantern and a Bible, him being welcomed by Deakin with the usual, "Hello Old Parson! Come and sit down!" However, what pleased Bridie and Nellie most was the sight of Eirin and John Byford sat side-by-side and that, when the baby required nursing, it was Byford's tunic that went across her to preserve her modesty.

The next day, all guns before the Castle began an incessant bombardment and Carr decided to walk forward to see if he could engage some Artillery Officer in conversation and discover anything. He soon found one, stood on the parados at the back of the battery, frequently using his telescope, on both the Castle and Fort San Christobal. Carr walked forward, offering his hand.

"Carr. 105th. How do you do?"

"Hawker. Brevet Major. Royal Field Artillery."

"So, how are things?"

Hawker lowered his telescope and sighed.

"Not good. Anywhere."

Carr frowned slightly.

"That depressing?"

"Well, were I a raving optimist, perhaps no, but it's pessimism that tends to run in my family and I cannot seem to shake it off."

He pointed to the battery just below him.

"All these guns should be in a museum; each would not be out of place in our own past Civil War! Perhaps Cromwell sold them off to the Portuguese as a job lot."

He pointed at the gun immediately below, just then being sponged out by its crew.

"Each has its own oddity, except perhaps that one. That is beyond odd! It should be in an experimental artillery school. It can practically fire around corners; it puts such a bend on the ball. With all the others, it's taken us the day so far to achieve even a semblance of concentration on one point."

Carr nodded and studied the wall alongside the Castle, noting that no impression seemed to have been made by the bombardment so far, exactly as Hawker had stated. He changed the subject.

"What of San Christobal, up there?"

Hawker shook his head and released an even deeper sigh.

"Awful! Simply awful. Up there, poor souls, they can only make a battery out of gabions, but there is no soil up there to fill them. Johnny's cleared most of it away. Their guns are no better than ours and many have been knocked over having no protection. The Peer's spent £400 on wool packs that are arriving now to make some kind of protection, but Johnny knows that San Christobal is the key to all this and he's doing all he can to hold it."

He raised his telescope again to observe the result of another ball crashing into the castle wall. Carr was not unimpressed at the result, but Hawker shook his head,

"It should be 10 foot higher and 20 to the right."

He lowered the telescope.

"Where was I?"

"Johnny knows the Fort is the key."

"Ah yes, and what makes me think such, is that from the castle walls there in front of us, he keeps dropping mortars on our men up there at the Fort, instead of dropping them on us down here, as counter-battery fire."

Hawker raised his telescope as another gun fired and he shook his head at the result whilst allowing the telescope to fall on its sling suspended around his shoulders.

"And this 'key' thing. It's true up to a point. If we get into the San Christobal, with decent guns, decent mind you, we can drop cannon-fire on him from a height, but it's long term. It just moves us to the next stage of the siege. Just because we're in the Fort, doesn't mean we can walk into Badajoz the next day!"

"Anything else to cheer us all up?

"Yes, to be effective down here, there should be a second parallel, 400 yards closer. Then, we could do some real damage. And you're infantry. How would you fancy mounting an attack from here, 800 yards out and across that open space, with that tributary to the Guadiana running across your front?"

"The Rivellas, I believe it's called."

Hawker nodded.

"The same! Wouldn't you want to begin your advance from closer in?"

Carr screwed his mouth sideways. He had no argument.

"Well, if San Christobal's the key, as you say, let's hope for better fortune and a trot across your 400 yards may not be needed."

"Yes, let's hope."

They shook hands and parted, but on the way back to his camp-lines Carr looked up several times at the Fort where all guns, both French and Allied were blazing away at each other. The wool packs must have arrived, he decided, but the greater volume seemed to come from the Fort and Carr could see for himself the fizzing mortar shells arcing across from the Castle to land on the San Christobal slope. He passed through the mess-camps of his men and into the tent that served as Headquarters, where he found O'Hare and Lacey sharing a bottle of wine. Both saw the depression in his face and so O'Hare found a glass and poured Carr a measure.

"How now, Henry! Why so far down in the mouth?"

Carr took a drink.

"I don't think we are going to manage this!"

O'Hare looked at him with mock surprise.

"Really, you've worked that out! Let me tell you, this is a doddle. Early Summer weather, and the bad stuff going on up at the Fort; not down here. I could tell you about the siege of Alexandria, now that was a siege! 10,000 unwelcoming French, heat, flies, thieving Arabs, nothing but sand. Scorpions! Now that was a siege!"

Carr finished his wine with one big swallow.

"If it's all the same to you, perhaps some other time!"

Carr left to take himself to his tent, leaving both O'Hare and Lacey laughing and finishing the last of their bottle.

A night's sleep did nothing to improve Carr's mood, awaking to the rumble of guns in the distance and the sharp crunch from those nearer. He wandered over to the tent of the Light Company, where at least the coffee was good and two cups and two fresh baked rolls made him feel better. However, the day progressed with sitting and telescoping the Castle and the San Christobal, where guns roared throughout the morning and into the afternoon. Sat beside him, Drake had a sudden thought.

"What about letting the men bathe? In the river? I can't see us being called forward for any reason."

Carr nodded, but the height of his eyebrows also gave full assent and so Drake turned to call for Sergeant Ellis, his mess-fire always being nearby.

"Pass the word, Sergeant, to all Companies. The men can bathe, if they have a mind to."

Ellis rose and saluted and, within the hour most of the 105th were bathing in the shallows of the Guadiana where the water spread over firm gravel. The Followers took the invitation to include themselves, but they went much further upstream, with one of them acting as a sentry in between the two groups armed with stones in case some soldier took it upon himself to see what could be seen.

142

However, whilst fun and frolics were paramount in the Guadiana, there was nothing in any way so uplifting at the main battery, as Carr found when he took it upon himself to wander up the zig-zags again, to find Hawker still there and equally as fretful. Carr did his best to be cheerful.

"Afternoon, Hawker. Anything that could be called progress?"

Hawker halted the raising of his telescope which was in the act of being raised for the hundredth time that day.

"Afternoon Carr. Well, progress of sorts, I suppose. Our Artillery Colonel, Dickson, is now well aware of how practically hopeless this is from here. Him knowing that, has done some good, at least he has influence, and there will be a new battery tomorrow, on the right and closer, but still filled with more of these Armada relics. However, I hear that we have six decent iron ships' guns on their way, all to go into a third battery which will be closer still."

He pointed to an area about 100 yards closer.

"So, there'll be this new battery tomorrow over there, and things may improve still further when we complete the battery beyond that, ready for the Navy guns, but I cannot ignore this fact!"

He handed his telescope to Carr.

"Take a look at our point of battery."

Carr focused on a point being consistently hit and noteworthy because there was now no stonework there.

"Behind the stonework is sheer cliff! The stonework of the castle wall is just cladding. A facing, if you see what I mean, in front of solid rock. You cannot knock a breach in a whole cliffside!"

Carr could clearly see what Hawker meant. The stonework had indeed all been knocked away, but the vertical seams of the living rock were resisting all the shot sent against it. He lowered the telescope.

"And what of the Fort?"

"Some progress. The wool packs have helped and they have a sort of breach up there and they've demolished Johnny's parapet above, but they've the same problem with the guns that I have."

He pointed to several guns in turn.

"On those two, the carriages have fallen apart and we are trying to lash them back together. Those two have 'unbushed', this being that the core at the touch hole has blown out and so we have to make two more."

He paused, for more exasperated breath, but he continued to point.

"Those two, being brass, get 'muzzle droop' when they get hot. It is so alarming that we have to wait over five minutes for the thing to cool before the next re-load. If we put in a charge too soon, it goes off under the rammer!"

He paused again.

"Oh, and the French have knocked one over, but right now they aren't bothered with us. They're busy enfilading our works at the Fort."

He turned to face Carr, intent on venting his spleen completely.

"I don't expect to have above nine guns working tomorrow out of the original fourteen!"

Carr pulled out his brandy flask.

"Take a drink! From what you say, things are better at the Fort and there is some hope of progress up there."

Hawker handed back the flask.

"You may be right, because there is very little here!"

Carr decided to take his leave and wander back, wondering who would be building the new batteries for the extra guns, but that night they were not called upon, and so, in the morning it was the Portuguese Brigade of the 3rd Division who could be seen making their way back to the river to wash off the dirt and sweat of hard work throughout a warm night. One of the new batteries had been constructed and filled and so the 'Armada' guns roared out as soon as there was light enough to see. Many Officers brought their chairs and their telescopes to the beginnings of the communication zig-zags to watch the heavy fire of the extra guns pound the rock exposed on the castle cliff, but all were disappointed. The living rock suffered little erosion. Mackinnon arrived and took himself over to sit with Lacey, O'Hare and Carr, his old Busaco comrades, these all sat with little more to do than place idle bets on the next fall of rock, however small, in one hit's time, or two, or three and so on, but Mackinnon totally interrupted their mild amusement.

"He's going tae try the Fort, the night after this. Today and tomorrow should now be enough work with the guns."

Lacey turned to him.

"And for us, there in front?"

Mackinnon exhaled a huge breath.

"Dickson, our Siege Engineer, is o' the opinion, that come tomorrow night, those in front will have widened a rock seam enough for one man tae clamber up and in."

Lacey and O'Hare turned to him and spoke in unison.

"One man!"

Mackinnon nodded.

"One man."

He paused.

"One man. And we've been hitting that wall now for three days and I'll be damned if I can see this 'widened' seam."

At that point several telescopes were raised, the result of which was much shaking of heads, at which point Mackinnon rose.

"Well, that's the best I can say, I'd best get round and see Wallace and McArdle. They need tae hear the good news too."

With that he mounted his horse and was gone. Many telescopes were re-raised and focused, but there was nothing new to see, therefore O'Hare reverted to their previous activity.

"One lump in two hits time. One shilling!"

He lost, it took three.

oOo

The following day, the 6th June, was one of growing tension as the guns, both above at the Fort and below at the Castle, continued to pound their targets. Carr decided to wander forward once more to consult his new acquaintance, Major Hawker, whom he found at the same place as on the 5th. Carr came straight to the point.

"An assault up there tonight, we are hearing."

Hawker nodded.

"Yes. His battlements are now all down for several yards. They're going to give it a go and have called for volunteers."

Carr turned towards him.

"Volunteers! That won't be enough. You send whole Battalions against breaches. Volunteers, that's absurd."

Hawker shrugged.

"Who am I? Who are we, to comment?"

Carr returned to the wall before them.

"And what's this we're hearing about a rock seam, now wide enough for one man?"

Hawker passed over his telescope.

"Just to the left of the darkest grey. The seam there."

Carr focused and could just make out what looked like a narrow, open chimney at the point described. He shook his head.

"One man who is a skilled ascender of rock-faces and has no-one up above to cause him any bother."

Hawker nodded in agreement.

"And one who has not been required to advance under fire over 800 yards, ford a river and then scramble up a steep slope before he can even begin the climb."

Carr turned to walk back.

"I think I feel a headache coming on!"

Hawker grinned and descended into the battery as Carr began his journey back through the zig-zag trench, returning to the position he observed from the previous day, listening to the bombardments and watching the results whenever the gentle breeze managed to disperse the smoke, especially that of the French guns at San Christobal, still making a spirited reply to their besiegers. The rumour of the British assault had circulated and the watching crowd grew as the daylight faded. Soon it was full dark and every eye was on the point in the blackness where they knew the Fort to be. Watches were consulted by lantern light and the comment became more frequent, with Shakeshaft amongst the first to voice it, him now as fearful as anyone.

144

"They should be in by now. This is giving Johnny time to do all sorts; clear away the rubble that ours need to climb on and to fill up the space beneath with obstacles. All sorts."

Carr looked at his own watch.

"Five minutes to Midnight. I suppose that the Witching Hour is the one which has been chosen!"

Within that choice of timing, he was proved correct. Flashes, as from muskets, could be seen and the sound came down to them, accompanied with the deeper sound of cannon-fire. Someone spoke the single word 'grapeshot' and then the sound and the flashes intensified, many now throwing light further than mere musketry or cannon-fire, even against the night clouds. It was Lacey who identified the probable source.

"Johnny's throwing grenades. They use them, we don't."

O'Hare answered from the darkness.

"Yes, but some are bigger still, those are whole shells thrown over."

The minutes progressed, but it was plain that the assault was not. There was no change, the sound and flashes of explosions went on and on. Drake pulled out his own watch and held it to a lantern.

"12.30. Whoever it is, trying to get in there, they are giving it one helluva go!"

For fifteen more minutes the display continued, flashes of explosions, both large and small, with their ominous sounds reaching the watchers on the plain below in waves that carried only despair and disappointment. Just before 1 o' clock everything ceased, the darkness returned and so did the silence. They were too far away to hear the cries of wounded men, but O'Hare drew the conclusion.

"If they were in, we'd hear cheering!"

However, there was none and everyone, apart from a hugely optimistic few, returned to their tents. Dawn supported O'Hare's conclusion, the French Tricolour still flew over Fort San Christobal, and with the light of dawn the cannonading was resumed, both on the Castle and at the Fort.

Carr remained by his tent. Depression had settled on the whole army and he knew that another conversation with Hawker would provide no relief. However, this mood had descended more on the Officer Corps than on the men, who spent the day, as with the previous, eating, bartering, singing and dancing and generally arguing over a variety of subjects, not least what would come next. The most authoritative discussion was between Jed Deakin, Henry Nicholls, Ethan Ellis and Cyrus Gibney.

"They'll try again, most probably fail and then we'll be marching out of here."

"How long then, Jed?"

This spoken by Henry Nicholls.

"Two, three more days. He'll try again on the third night. What do you think Cyrus?"

Gibney folded his mighty arms and thought.

"Ah can't say any different. We've not the guns as is needed for a place like this. The Fort's the best chance, but really no chance. We're in this place to get into Badajoz, yonder, not that bird's nest up there!"

However, this was not what was worrying Ethan Ellis.

"Three days more! That's enough to make them think there's a chance with what's straight ahead. That Castle there. That'll be for us!"

All four looked at the Castle, the small gap in the wall, the intact battlements either side, the steep slope before and the French Tricolour standing out stiff in the breeze. It was Gibney who answered.

"That'll not be something as ah cares t'dwell on!"

With that, mugs of tea arrived carried by Trudie and Violet Nicholls and all stood and drank in silence. The arrival of the six ship's guns did little to improve their mood as they watched them being hauled down to the newly prepared, third battery and, within two hours, despite the attentions of the French, all were roaring out their effective fire.

The following day, Lacey and O'Hare were called to Picton's quarters, a farmhouse a half mile back up the Guadiana. They entered to find every Colonel and Senior Major of Picton's Division crammed into the largest room of what was only a middle sized Spanish dwelling. Picton came straight to the point.

"The Frogs have re-grouped. Soult's moving from where Beresford pushed him back to and Marmont's moving to join him with a whole Corps. They're at Llerena, just under 100 miles away and we all know how fast the Frogs can march. We know all this from those Guerrilla brigands that roam about and watch and intercept couriers."

He took a drink of brandy.

"Wellington's going to give San Christobal one more try, the night after this one. We haven't the men down here at Badajoz to fight a pitched battle if we abandon the siege to go out and meet him and we musn't be caught in the trenches. We either get in and laugh at him from off the walls or get ourselves back to Elvas. So, if the attack fails, in all likelihood we'll be going back and it may have to be quick, so make pre-arrangements."

He took another drink.

"That's all!"

However, it was not, because Colville, one of Picton's three Brigadiers, put up his hand.

"Sir. Is he going to send us against the Castle?"

There were several murmurs of approval at the question, but Picton scowled over at his questioner.

"I'll say this. Six more iron guns have arrived and have gone into our parallel. That you probably know. They may make enough of a difference to this chimney flue they've been talking about, they may not. What I do know is that Wellington wants to keep the initiative after Fuentes and if we have to abandon here, that initiative will go back with the Frogs. How anxious he is to prevent that, well, your guess is as good as mine! Now, away, the lot of you."

They all filed out and most walked back to their lines. On the road, Lacey asked the pertinent question.

"How long before we can start to move if we have to, between receiving the order and finally moving out?"

O'Hare screwed over his mouth.

"As we are now, two hours and we may have to abandon some items, water wagons, perhaps."

"Right. I want one hour, so get all lined up, just off the road and ready to move, with mule teams handy. Tell our Officers."

The order circulating at Noon did nothing to ease the tension within the Officers of the 105th. Plainly there was some threat from somewhere and the rumour arrived concerning a re-juvenated Soult now back maneuvering and thereby posing a growing threat. However, the anxiety within Carr was of a different kind, what of the 'breach' at the Castle. He took himself forward to see for himself and perhaps find Hawker. At the main battery, however, he was not there, but there was now the third battery with its good iron guns, firing at a rate far more in excess of that from the main battery at his feet. He pulled out his telescope and studied the rock wall. The cannonade had certainly deepened the cleft back into the rock face, but he quickly concluded that it would be a most desperate and almost reckless enterprise to use it to get into the Castle. In addition, he did not need his telescope to see that every embrasure on the walls either side was still intact and containing the black mouth of a cannon. The 800 yards from where he was to the foot of the wall would be murderous. Just how desperate was Wellington? At that point Hawker arrived, from the battery to the right of the main one. He saw Carr stood pondering.

"Hello Carr. Are you in Wellington's shoes, judging if it's practical?"

Carr turned to meet him, both now standing on the parados.

"If it were left to me, I'd say no, but I don't know the mind of our illustrious Commander."

"Nor I, Carr, nor I, but I cannot see anyone risking such a disaster. I've always held the impression that The Peer is more careful with the lives of his men than most."

However, Carr shook his head.

"Let's hope that pertains."

He turned to face him.

"I assume you are pleased with your new additions."

"Absolutely. Six good naval 24 pounders!"

"In a new Battery. When did that come about?"

"Yesterday. The Portuguese again did the job. Johnny wasn't too pleased and sent a few shots our way, but too far for the small stuff he's got up there."

"As you say, but large enough to do a lot of damage to any force crossing that ground."

"True Carr, but that's for the likes of you footsloggers to worry about. My worry is that of the 26 guns that I could have, of all types, mortars, howitzers and naval, I've only 21 that could be used and, as we speak, there's only 19 actually in action. 13 of those only from the past three days!"

Carr shook his head.

"Not good! And not good last night!"

"No, and from what I hear, through those early hours of darkness, Johnny had all the time in the world to make the breach, if it can be called that, absolutely impossible. Ours ran up and down their wall, trying to use ladders, but when all those were broken, they had to give best and pull back."

146

Hawker shook his head and looked from the Castle up to the Fort.

"Ah well, what else? Just keep on, keeping on. They're trying again tonight."

At that both men grinned and Carr then descended into the zig-zags and returned to his tent to find something to do. He sat for some minutes, but his spirits sank with every minute, as he remembered the struggle, shock and sacrifice of Fuentes de Onoro and Albuera, and now, in all likelihood, the French were to be allowed back to the border from which they had been so bloodily ejected. At a low ebb, he reached into his portfolio and retrieved his ongoing letter to his wife, Jane, then for some 30 minutes he wrote to her the most profound and heartfelt letter he had ever written in his life. The spilling onto paper of his deepest feelings for her, lifted his mood, but only somewhat. The idea of the possibility of being sent against the castle wall, still weighed heavily with him, because failure at San Christobal could mean exactly that. However, feeling marginally better, he wandered out to join the crowd waiting for the day to end, telescopes all fixed on the section of the San Christobal Fort that was still under bombardment. Each decent hit that dislodged masonry was greeted with a cheer or some other expression of glee and it was true that the Fort now had the appearance of a battered heap and the besieged could only manage merely the occasional gun in reply. However, few there would describe themselves as overly optimistic.

What the watchers, including Carr, did not know was that as they sat there, Senior Engineer Colonel Fletcher and Colonel of Artillery Dickson had just left Wellington's Headquarters and they had reluctantly told him that they could not advise an attack on the Castle. The reasons being that the closest distance from the parallel was the 600 yards from the third battery, which meant that they would have to cross the Rivellas and that guns both from the Castle and the undamaged part of San Christobal could enfilade the attacking columns. Nothing could be done from the area before the Castle, until either the San Christobal had fallen or a second parallel, much nearer to the castle walls had been constructed. With that depressing report Wellington took himself to the camp of the Third Division, from there to observe events and hope.

The daylight faded from across a cloudy sky and with the arrival of the full darkness, the final gun in both areas fell silent. As with the previous occasion, three nights previous, all eyes were fixed upwards to the area of blackness where they knew the Fort to be. This time they did not have nearly so long to wait. When those consulting their watches saw 9.00, immediately came the flashes of musket fire, the sound of which reached them but a moment later, but it was plain from their alignment that they could only come from the walls of the Fort. Some flashes could be seen just to the right from what must be the Allied position, but these were feeble in comparison with what was coming from the French held battlements. For minutes on end, from what could only be the walls of the Fort came a continuous ripple of flame, then came the larger flashes of light from the now well-known grenades and live shells, but what was new were fire-balls dropping down obviously into the trench below the walls, seen for just a second before they disappeared into the depths. Many remarked, in a very sombre tone, that these would give light to aid the musketry of the French defenders. The attack did not last as long as the previous night and well within an hour all fell silent, which meant that no Allied force was atop the walls celebrating their achievement. As dispirited as before, the crowd dispersed and much hard spirit was consumed before sleep claimed many of them.

Carr woke sometime after dawn and hurried to their Regimental Headquarters, there to find Lacey and O'Hare at breakfast. He wasted no time.

"Does last night mean that we have to go against the Castle?"

Lacey sat back.

"No! We've just had a note from Mackinnon, saying that the Engineers and Gunners regard it as much too impractical. In our language, pretty much hopeless!"

Carr let out a long sigh of relief, something noticed by the pair and so O'Hare poured him some coffee.

"Here! And there's the sugar!"

Carr could not but grin, then he noticed the absence of something.

"No gunfire!"

Lacey answered.

"No, and a truce has been declared up at the Fort. Our casualties were very heavy, the 400 yards and the slope below the wall are covered in our dead and wounded. I'm expecting an order to withdraw, so, when you've finished your coffee, get outside and oversee preparations."

Within 30 minutes the rumour of withdrawal was all around the Third Division, but there was little cheer in the minds of Ellis and Deakin, they well knew what would come next.

"Them good guns down there, Ethan. They'll not leave them for the Frogs, they've got to be got out."

A Staff Colonel arriving at their Headquarters began the process of withdrawing the guns, then O'Hare emerged to send runners to all the Captains. Within an hour, Mackinnon's whole Brigade was filing down to the batteries, many carrying ropes, there to be directed by Dickson himself to the newest battery where were lodged the six precious iron guns. The artillerymen attached the ropes and then all began to haul the guns into the zig-zags and back to the road out. Drake stood on the parapet and with better hearing than most, spoke down to Shakeshaft.

"Those Frog bastards are mocking us!"

Shakeshaft came up to join him and both could see waving figures behind the Castle battlements, some with their shakoes on the end of muskets.

"You're right."

"I'm not bloody having that. When we get these back, I'm getting a sheet and a pot of paint."

It took longer than he had hoped but all was eventually achieved, the six guns emerging from the end of the zig-zags and to there be hitched up to the mule teams and begin their arduous journey back to Elvas. Then Drake began his task, with a sheet, a pot of paint and two of the poles used at the beginning of the siege to mark the parallel. Carr came along just as he was finishing, to mispronounce the French.

"Voir tous vous revoir bientôt! See you all again soon!"

"Damn right, yes. I'm not being laughed at."

Carr chuckled at his good friend.

"Well, you'd better get down to the battery quick. I expect our Artillery friends will still be there with the handy mallet you'll need."

Drake ran off, carrying his banner, leaving Carr still laughing. At the battery, Drake ran up to Hawker.

"Sir. With your permission, I'd like to leave a message for those damn cheeky Frogs up there."

When Hawker read the banner, Drake's intention became obvious.

"Be our guest. My men will help."

It took little time to hammer in the poles and a Gunner Sergeant stood back.

"What's it say, Sir?"

"See you all again soon."

"Damn right, Sir, We'll be back to try again with this lot. This b'ain't done. Not yet it ain't."

He turned to Drake.

"Do you think they've got telescopes on us, Sir. Right now?"

"I don't doubt it Sergeant."

"Good."

With that, he turned to the Castle and delivered a long and lascivious two fingered salute in the direction of the battlements.

oOo

Chapter Five

Test by Morale

"Look at that! Sure now, wasn't that a good sort of a King, back then whenever, to build such a thing for his people, to bring them all the water as they'd be needin'!"

Nellie Nicholls could only nod her head in agreement with her good friend Bridie, as both approached the mighty aqueduct at Elvas, this now close enough for each to appreciate its sheer height and scale. Nellie turned to her children and Bridie's, all tailing along behind and carrying their burden, be it pot, cauldron, tripod, or griddle.

"Now, youse all should take a look at that. You'll not see the likes of that when we get back home to Ireland. For sure you won't."

It was Sally, Nellie's eldest at 16, walking beside Bridie's Kevin, both of the same age, who replied, but not in the way that Nellie expected. Each had quickly released the others hand.

148

"Sure, Ma, but I've heard that there's something quite special, up North of ours, called the Giant's Causeway."

Nellie turned to face her daughter, whilst at the same time continuing to walk.

"Now who's been teaching you such as that?"

It was Kevin who answered.

"Parson Sedgwicke, Auntie Nellie."

Nellie's brows narrowed, her now being somewhat put out.

"Well, that may be true, but this here viaduct, as it's called, was all man-made. Men had to hoist up all those blocks of stone, all the way up there, to carry the water to this place. And this you'll not see again in a hurry. That Giant's Causeway place, so I've heard, is all natural and made by the Good Lord Himself, so it was."

With that she turned away and Kevin and Sally re-joined their hands. Bridie was studying the viaduct wondering if they would get any closer and perhaps walk through one of the arches, but at the head of their Brigade column, the 105th continued to march around the stark walls of Elvas. With this colossal citadel now behind them they continued just East of North, so that within an hour they were on a dry and dusty plain and all very grateful that they had taken onto themselves as much water as they had containers for, when they had forded the Guadiana at the dawn of that day.

At the head of the Brigade column, Mackinnon was now riding with Lacey and O'Hare, his Brigade at the rear of Colville's, him at the very head of the Divisional column, entertaining Picton, as and when their General seemed to be in one of his rare moods for idle conversation. With Mackinnon, things were far more convivial, but the subject was inevitably military, with Lacey and O'Hare listening, whilst Mackinnon explained, him on a mission to impart all he knew to the Senior Officers of his three Battalions.

"He's going tae hold a line from Elvas up tae a place called Ouguela. There's a river there, but the name escapes me. He's assembling all he's got. Spencer's Division is almost in line and he's even calling in Pack's and Barbacena' Portuguese Brigades. From what we hear, Soult's stripped other parts of Spain of French troops tae concentrate here. The Peer expects a serious trying of conclusions here with the Johnnies, now that Soult's pushed us awa' from Badajoz."

Lacey had been listening intently.

"So how strong is this position we're moving into."

Mackinnon sat back in his saddle.

"Very! It's got three fortresses, Elvas on the right, Campo Maior in the centre and this place we're goin' tae, Ouguela. And ye know the Peer, we're on a good ridge and placed all along it, with good communications behind. He expects a battle and that's how he makes his preparations."

O'Hare now had a thought.

"So, how long is our front, Sir?"

"About twelve miles."

O'Hare nodded.

"Understood, Sir, so as I see it, what matters is detecting Johnny's approach, when it comes. He'll not go for the whole line, it's my guess he'll concentrate on one part and so, seeing it coming, wherever it falls and then getting the message around, will be all important?"

Mackinnon nodded himself.

"Correct, which ye will be part of, out there on the far left. Picton's chosen ye tae occupy this Ouguela, by the way. He thought about putting in the Portuguese, coming on behind us, but he considers yours the better disciplined and ye'll no antagonise the locals. Quite a compliment, ye ken. Our allies are too likely tae thieve, being so poorly supplied by their ain Government!"

Lacey smiled.

"Yes Sir, we'll certainly take Picton's choice of us as a garrison, to be a compliment indeed."

Mackinnon continued, although the irony of Lacey's words was not lost on all listening.

"Do so, aye indeed, but back tae the point. Detecting, as ye say, O'Hare, is vital. On our front, on the border are several 'Atalayas', as they are called, these being old Moorish watchtowers. Ye'll have one tae man and signal flags tae fly from it if anything causes ye concern. Apart from that, the main job of eyes and ears is wi' the cavalry."

At that moment the said cavalry, at least three Brigades of it, were being led forward by their General, Stapleton Stapleton-Cotton, which odd name cause much confusion in many quarters. Their route brought them from the North-West, on the road that led directly to Campo Maior and in the lead, was De Grey's Brigade of Heavy Dragoons, then Slade's mixed Brigade of Dragoons and Lights and finally Anson's Brigade of two Regiments of Light Dragoons, the 14th and 16th. The sun was approaching its zenith and so their General called a halt for the Noon meal, at a curious collection of dazzlingly white buildings, grouped around what seemed like a Holy institution of some kind, identified by a small, rather apologetic cross upon the highest apex. However, the immediate concern for almost all was for their horse, the day was hot and so most tipped water into whatever receptacle allowed their mounts a drink, water then being replenished from the village well. That done, all sat or lounged to eat; fruit, sausage and army biscuits, this being washed down with plain water. However, lounging at ease soon became standing, when Stapleton-Cotton himself came back to where Anson, their Brigadier and also Colonel of the 14th, and his fellow Colonel, Withers, but of the 16th, were taking their own luncheon. He rode up, but did not trouble to dismount, as Anson now stood waiting with his Senior Officers.

"Anson. You're in reserve, about five miles due East of here. From what I've been told, you stop moving when you see a squat sort of fortress on a hill, that's where he wants you. It's called Ougella. Slade will remain here, also in reserve, whilst De Grey's come with me to be the reserve behind Campo Maior."

Anson, still holding his length of sausage had one question and it was a matter of deep concern.

"In reserve of what, Sir?"

"Madden's Portuguese. They are out patrolling in front of you between the two rivers that run through Wellington's line, the Caya through his centre at Maior and the Gevora by this Ougella place, Wellington's furthest flank Northwards. South of the Caya is the task of Long's three Lights, between Maior and Elvas."

That question answered, Anson continued with another major concern.

"Sir, this area is utterly barren, forage is sparse enough, but practically no water!"

His General sat forward, his face not unsympathetic.

"You're not wrong, but here is where he wants you, so you must make the best of it. If there's no rivers, there's probably streams, so do your best. If you have to camp slightly off to get closer to water, so be it, but no more than a mile. If you have to water your mounts in relays, you'll just have to put up with it. There's a huge French army on the Guadiana which he expects to advance against us. We must be ready. I'll supply you from this point, three days from now. Have your wagons waiting here."

With that he wheeled his mount around and rode off, leaving Anson to finish his sausage. Between mouthfuls he addressed Withers and Johnson.

"Right, being as we're in the middle of nowhere and need to ride sort of North-East to find this Ougella fort, we'd better find a compass and hope to find this odd sort of construction before dark. That done, tomorrow we find water! So, take all you can with you now."

All canteens, and more besides, were filled from the village well and they set off, leaving the road at a diagonal, envious of Slade's Regiments now settling into the village and they were soon out of sight of Stapleton-Cotton, him remaining with De Gray's, as their two routes diverged. Major Johnson, riding with Carr at the head of Two Squadron, soon felt moved to comment on their surroundings.

"This place is as dry as a Quaker funeral!"

Carr could not help but laugh as did the men immediately behind, Baxter et al, but Carr could see the seriousness of the statement. Poor forage was bad enough but horses would soon die from lack of water. However, after an hour's riding, Anson, at the head of his Regiment and holding the compass, called a halt and Withers rode up the column to consult. His arrival prompted Anson to point at a hill about a mile and a half away. It was, indeed, topped by a low, squat, noticeable but somewhat insignificant, construction.

"I'll call that the fort Stapleton-Cotton spoke of."

He looked around, then turned to Withers.

"Right, I'll go a half-mile that way, you go a half-mile in the opposite. That way we may keep our horses alive by being apart, but don't go too far."

He looked around.

"God awful place to spend any amount of time!"

He turned to face Withers again.

"Are your supply wagons in one piece?"

Withers nodded.

"They are, so at least we'll have food, and he made that promise about supply in three days' time, if Johnny doesn't have a hand in matters."

150

Anson nodded.

"That was his promise, so let's set about settling in."

He motioned his men to follow him and Withers returned to lead his men off in the opposite direction. Within five minutes, Withers called a halt on a piece of land that seemed to have more grass on it than elsewhere. He called over to Johnson.

"There's enough daylight left. Send Carr and Peterson off to find a stream or brook or something!"

Within five minutes the two Cornets were riding out of the temporary camp, but not, as yet, in any constructive direction. Carr halted his mount.

"How do you find a stream?"

Peterson shrugged.

"Keep going downhill, I suppose."

He studied the ground.

"That way!"

They walked their horses forward, always choosing a downhill route and casting their gaze around for greener grass. Carr pointed over to a small, but steep valley, which looked the most promising.

"Let's try there."

They did and there was water, but Peterson pronounced judgement.

"I've seen a better flow from my Mother's kettle!"

Carr laughed.

"So have I, but it's continuous and we could dam it up. I can't see anywhere more likely."

Their horses were busy drinking from the tiny flow whilst they talked and when they had drunk their fill, the pair pulled their mounts' heads around to return to camp. On hearing their report, Withers soon moved the camp to the source they had discovered and, as Carr had suggested, the stream was damned to create as large a pool as possible.

Simultaneously, the same odd fort that had been on Anson's horizon was now coming into full view for the 105th, still marching onward and it drew comment from Nat Drake.

"I think I could vault over those walls with an average walking stick!"

His companion, Major Carr, laughed but said nothing. The walls were, indeed, less than impressive from the road they were on, seeming to peek in great trepidation of what just might be out and threatening beyond the intervening hillside. However, that first impression proved to be deceptive, because on climbing the hill, on which the fort was built, it proved to be a small Castle, with impressive walls, gatehouse and flanking towers. Lacey led his men off the road and straight in, where they found the garrison to be two whole Companies of Portuguese. The Company on duty had paraded outside and presented arms, which Lacey acknowledged. Proceeding through the imposing square gatehouse, this proudly flying the Portuguese Royal Standard, revealed a large enclosure, between two long opposing walls and two short, the wall facing in the direction of the French the shortest of the four, but the highest tower was the gatehouse in the long wall beside the road. Lacey halted his mount and spoke to O'Hare without looking at him.

"Right. Settle in. First, does this place have a well? Second, this place will be Officers and administration only. We cannot turf the Portuguese out of their barracks. Battalion functions take place only within the walls. Portuguese Officers will have to mess with ours. Can't be helped, if this place is to function properly."

The process of settling in, immediately fell to RSM Cyrus Gibney, him soon touring around with Chaplain's Assistant Sedgwicke in tow, Sedgwicke being one of the few who could write quickly and fluently. Gibney pointed to the most imposing building, intending to run down the list which he had in his head.

"Raht, Percy. There's Headquarters and private quarters for the Colonel and the Major."

Sedgwicke identified the building by its colour and noted its new function, and in that manner, they continued, identifying Officers' quarters, stores, sickbay and guardroom until Gibney's mental list was complete. He then took the paper from Sedgwicke and hurried off to hand it to his Colonel so that the process could begin. Thus, was the rest of the day spent, organising and dispensing the domestic arrangements. That done, all that had shelter made use of it, because, even with the dying of the day, the heat within the enclosure was oppressive. The men made their camp outside in the fields to the South of the main curtain wall, and they were not put out in any way, because there it was cooler, they had as much space as they liked and the slope picked up the breeze. From that slope, they could look back along the road they had arrived along and see the

151

encampments of Mackinnon's other two Battalions, the 88th and the 74th. Seeing these, back there, the 105th counted themselves lucky. They, at least, had easy access to water, because there was a well in the Castle, but the depth of water within it soon proved to be sparse. Disappointed, Lacey decided that a supplement was needed and so, the following morning, RSM Gibney was given the task of exploring the village itself, this close grouped beneath the walls on the opposite side to the camp. Gibney chose his men.

"Jed, Henry, Davey, Pike, Miles, Saunders. With me!"

The seven trooped onto the road and proceeded around the walls, then into the village, where many curious locals had gathered for whatever reason, but all plainly grateful for the British arrival, some speaking, although not shouting, "Viva Ingleses" whilst several came forward to shake Gibney's hand, although many regretted it, once released from the iron grip. In the village, they searched but found nothing and Miles soon lost patience.

"If you wants to find something out local, Sar' Major, send Pike over to the nearest girl and get him to ask her. The Portuguese for water is agua."

Gibney treated Miles to his blackest frown.

"Ah knows the correct word. Thank-you! Miles!"

However, the idea seemed to have struck a chord. Gibney looked around to see who was close and it seemed that most of the young female population of the village had emerged to satisfy their curiosity over the 'Soldados Ingleses." He turned to Pike.

"Pike! Thee knows what to say?"

Pike nodded.

"Yes Sar' Major."

"Well, there's a group of lassies over yonder. Get over and ask! An' put a smile on tha' face, for a change."

Joe Pike, tallish, blonde, handsome and perfectly proportioned, walked hesitantly over to the group of young, teenage girls who would seem to be the most likely to respond. He stopped before them, but only one was brazen enough to meet his gaze.

"Excuse, Senorita. Agua, por favor. Agua."

All the girls began to giggle at Pike's dreadful pronunciation, but the boldest pointed down an alleyway.

"Hay agua allí. Abajo allí."

Pike turned to his companions, some yards behind, but Miles reacted first.

"Pretend you don't understand! Shrug your shoulders. Say agua again."

Pike did as he was told and shrugged his shoulders to repeat again.

"Agua. Por favor."

The girl giggled some more and seized hold of Pike's cuff, to pull him in the direction she had pointed, then down into a narrow street. Miles walked forward.

"It's worked! Told you it would."

Gibney ignored Miles' triumphant tone and they followed, the street descending alarmingly between two houses, to then turn left. There they found Pike, with the girls, stood at a large double trough. The whole was fed by a spring from the rock beneath the castle walls, and the girl was explaining the purpose of each trough, the first overflowing into the second, which was the larger by far. She was trickling water from her hand, taken from the first, the smaller.

"Esta agua es para las personas."

She then dipped her hand into the second, fed from the first.

"Esta agua es para los animales."

Miles had heard all, but understood nothing.

"Wish we had Byford here!"

Gibney rounded on him

"Thee can go teach tha' Granny to suck eggs, Miles. Ah understands well enough. Humans drinks from the first as doesn't get drunk from by the animals. They takes from the second!"

Miles knew enough to keep quiet, whilst Gibney turned to Pike, him now with his guide edging slowly closer, eyes wide open and gazing upward.

"Pike! Thank the Senorita, and let's go before t'Mother and Aunties all shows up, an' we has a family riot on our 'ands! An' they wants thee betrothed. An' bigamous!"

Joe Pike smiled and bowed.

"Mucho gracias, Senorita."

That said, Davey seized his shoulder strap and hauled him away, Pike giving a small wave, this returned by all the girls. Back in the Castle, Gibney went straight to his Colonel.

"Sir. The village has water, through the square, down over opposite and under t'Castle walls. Clean and plenty. Sir."

oOo

The next day Gibney was just as busy and he entered the Officers' Quarters. He found Major Carr there and saluted, because now he had a second duty, the first issue of water partly solved. He thrust his hand forward.

"Sir, this piece of paper, Sir. 'Tis for you. 'T'as come with three flags, Sir. They's all outside, Sir, by t'door."

Carr stood up and walked towards Gibney with his hand outstretched for the note, which he took and read.

"Has this been passed onto me by the Colonel?"

Gibney nodded,

"Aye Sir. It came from General Picton, not 10 minutes since."

"You say the flags are outside?"

Gibney began to walk to the door.

"Aye, Sir. Just outside."

Carr followed him, to see three coloured flags, each attached to a ten-foot pole. He manoeuvred one to enable him to pull out the flag, this one being yellow, its size roughly five foot by four. The other two were red and bright green. He consulted again the paper, on which were written the instructions. The first sentence said that they were to use their nearest Moorish Atalaya as a signal base. Carr looked back at Gibney.

"Do you know where our nearest tower is?"

Gibney nodded.

"Aye Sir. Abaht half a mile behind us."

The distance between Carr's jaw and eyebrows increased considerably.

"Behind us! As in away from the French?"

"Correct, Sir. Aye."

Carr read the instructions again.

"Fly green at all times whilst no French are in sight. Yellow for French cavalry on your front. Red for French infantry."

Carr nodded.

"Very well. It's clear enough, but we'll have to use the gatehouse tower, that's the tallest and we'll have to take down the Portuguese Standard. And keep it down! It's mostly red. Whoever made this up, didn't think of that."

Carr stood and thought for some minutes, then he turned to Gibney.

"This must be handled carefully. Ask Captain Lord Carravoy to come and meet me at the gatehouse, and then you get hold of Byford of the Light Company, he can speak a bit of Portuguese. And we'll need a dozen of our Portuguese soldiers as well, with one of their Captains or both of them. They've moved themselves to the local inn, and I can't say I blame them too much for that. Could you do that, get them? Better from you, rather than some ranker runner. Get Deakin to do the other stuff, like find Byford."

However, Gibney remained in place, wholly in shock at what he had been asked to do. Failure to carry out orders was simply not in his lexicon.

"But Sir, ah don't speak a word of this Portuguese!"

Carr's own brows came together. Gibney had a point.

"Ask Byford what to say. Twelve men and an Officer at the Tower. Por Favor. That'll do."

Gibney reeled off a salute and then hurried away. Carr called to a group of passing soldiers and pointed to the flags.

"Get these to the top of the gatehouse."

Leaving the men to do his bidding, Carr walked the 100 yards himself, whilst the men charged with the burden soon followed on. At the foot of gatehouse, he waited but minutes before Carravoy arrived.

"Charles! We have to lower that Portuguese Standard and replace it with these signal flags. For that we will need some kind of Guard of Honour, we need to be diplomatic about the whole thing. We do not want to offend anyone, least of all the locals who will see their Royal Standard replaced by a plain green flag. We simply cannot haul the thing down just to suit ourselves. They can be very touchy about such things. We'll need some of the Portuguese garrison there, as well, and some of yours, to do the proper thing, if you understand?"

Carravoy stood waiting for the direct order, but none came. Resentment still smouldered within him that Carr was the Junior Major and not he, and so he said nothing. Carr's face became quizzical.

"Is there a problem? A dozen of your Grenadiers should do it. Best to do the proper thing and avoid any ill feeling. You'd agree?"

There came a pause, thick with atmosphere, created by Carravoy's peevish expression, but it was Carravoy himself who broke it.

"A dozen, you say? We're going to polish the faces of these locals, for whom we are already fighting to free their country for them, when they can't do it for themselves?"

"Yes Charles, it's worth to take the trouble to maintain good relations. We could be here some while. So, get your men up to the mark, if you can. Here in half an hour, ready for a smart 'present arms', as we lower their Standard."

Carravoy spun on his heel and stalked off. Carr watched his back for a second, to see Byford passing Carravoy as he came the other way. Byford marched up to Carr and saluted.

"I understand you have need of me, Sir."

The aristocratic accent and choice of phrase was not lost on Carr. In all likelihood, Byford's family background matched his own, but he had joined as a ranker and that was that, so he dwelt on the question no more.

"Byford! We need to lower the Portuguese Royal Standard up there and replace it with our own mundane old signal flags. When our dozen Portuguese get here, do you think you could lash some of their language together, enough to explain?"

"Yes Sir, but why is that being done?"

"The signal flags are to warn of any approaching French."

"I'll give it a try, Sir. I have a Treatise on the Portuguese Language. It may not be perfect, but I'll give it a try."

Carr nodded.

"Well done, Byford. Back here in 20 minutes."

Byford saluted and turned to leave, but a kind thought had entered Carr's head.

"How's your wound?"

Byford turned back and came back to the attention and Carr regretted his question, but Byford smiled.

"Quite well, Sir, thank you. Not too stiff at all."

Byford saluted again and hurried off. At which point Carr became whimsical. He should try to do something for Byford, especially when he considered the beardless boys who led men in desperate circumstances simply because their parents could buy them a Commission. In addition, there were the wholly incompetent and the less snobbish, such as D'Villiers and the outrageously snobbish but not so incompetent, like Carravoy. Being an Officer meant mixing with such as them, so perhaps Byford knew that and preferred the company of the men? Carr felt disinclined to blame him for that, because he himself held the men in the highest esteem. He still harboured powerful memories of Talavera, where they had held tight to their firing drill amidst all the mayhem. They had obeyed their Officers and held off the French with little more than disciplined musketry, and also at Corunna, where they had returned to the fight singing, to come up and give support to the First Foot Guards, no less. Apparently, they now had a new nickname because of that, this being the 'Choirboys', but several other Regiments also rejoiced in that soubriquet. Personally, he did not much like being numbered amongst a body of men called the 'Rag and Bone Boys', but he had never heard anyone use the name in an insulting manner and that must count for something.

He decided to climb the tower, the first time for him, to study the ground that they were to watch over and he was amazed that from up there he could see for miles, the horizon being the low mountains that he recognized from their time at Badajoz. With a good telescope, they would be able to see any kind of French incursion. If they came, he thought, and the fact was that they should, if Soult had the 60,000 veterans he had heard about, whilst the Allies had merely 46,000 and only 29,000 of those were British. All the rest were

Portuguese, about whom he was much less sure. They had held a very strong position well enough at Busaco, but what about eyeball to eyeball on the open plain? Yet if Soult failed to take this chance of dealing a fatal blow on the Allies in the Peninsula, then the initiative gained by him at Badajoz would swing back. Perhaps their morale is not strong enough to face us, he thought, having failed badly at Vimeiro and Busaco, and also where they should have won, these being Corunna, Talavera, Fuentes, Albuera and that Barossa business. Perhaps facing British firing lines was now more than they had the stomach for, having endured it for three years and been beaten every time?

The inconclusive internal debate ended with the arrival at the foot of the tower of Gibney and the Portuguese soldiers, with their Senior Captain and a Sergeant. Carr heard their chatter and footsteps and hurried down to find that they were accompanied by the Mayor of the town, his Sash of Office well displayed over a very prominent bay-window of a stomach, and also by a few town dignitaries. Gibney came to the attention and saluted.

"Found them all in t'local wineshop, Sir. They were there with this chap, as looks like the Mayor and few of his cronies. He wanted to come along, to see what was afoot, Sir, ah'm thinking."

Carr nodded.

"I think you are right, Sar' Major. About the Mayor, that is. I'll just introduce myself."

He held out his hand to the Mayor.

"Major Henry Carr. How do you do?"

The Mayor beamed back.

"Paulo Gerondo, Senor."

Then Carr turned to the Captain, a new acquaintance, as there had been little chance to meet over the two days since their arrival. The Captain saluted and then offered his hand.

"Capita Ferrao Pereirra, Senor Major."

Carr shook his hand, somewhat concerned that he did not look a day over 20. However, he put that to the back of his mind and shook his hand, but then he did the same honour to the accompanying locals, nodding and smiling. Then to Carr's great relief Byford arrived, with a notebook, held open.

"Ah, Byford. If you could explain."

Byford turned to the Mayor and the Captain to then carefully pronounce the words.

"Relógio. Para o Francês. Na torre"

The Mayor and Captain looked slightly puzzled at the broken Portuguese, then realization came that the subject was all about using the tower to watch for the French and the Mayor nodded reassuringly to the Captain and so Byford continued with his next sentence.

"Sinalizadores para mensagens"

More nodding from the Mayor but more puzzlement from the Captain at Byford's words, but the Mayor understood that the tower was needed to send messages and he explained this to the Captain in rapid Portuguese. Byford pressed on, despite the increasingly concerned look on the face of the Captain.

"Norme Royale Portugaise. Para baixo. Por favor."

The Mayor turned to his companions, speaking rapidly and they replied in the same tempo, all with concerned looks, but nodding agreement, nevertheless. Finally, the Mayor turned to the Captain, who nodded, then did the Mayor in the direction of Carr.

"Sim. Para ajudar a bater os Franceses. Sim."

Byford turned to Carr.,

"He understands that we wish to lower the Portuguese Standard, Sir, and he agrees. I think he said whatever helps to beat the French."

Carr turned to the Mayor and again shook his hand.

"Mucho gracias, Senor."

Then to the Captain.

"Mucho gracias Capita Pereirra."

At this point, Byford touched his arm.

"Sir. It's obrigado in Portuguese!"

Carr looked rapidly from Byford to the Mayor, the latter still smiling, but Carr now unsure. Then Carr took his hand again.

"Obrigado, Senor Mayor. Obrigado."

The Mayor beamed even further and at that point the Grenadiers arrived, twelve, with Ameshurst in command and all absolutely immaculate, having been inspected by Ameshurst's Sergeant Ridgway, ably assisted by Colour Sergeant Deakin. The twelve came to 'order arms' and waited, at which point the Portuguese Sergeant began yelling at his men and they all lined up, to then begin polishing and cleaning as best they could in the time they had. Carr gave them three minutes and then led everyone up the stairs to the top of the tower and all paraded, the Grenadiers opposite the Portuguese, both in double ranks, with the Mayor and Corporation in the centre. With all in place, although all a little crowded, Carr untied the halyard and held it out for Capita Pereirra. He looked puzzled and turned his head to the Mayor, who nodded. With that irregular permission given, the Captain began to lower the Royal Standard, at which point, Ameshurst took his cue.

"Present arms!"

The Grenadiers came from 'order' to 'present' immaculately in unison, at which significant point the right marker of the Portuguese took it upon himself to yell his own order and the Portuguese followed, in a very satisfactory manner. The Standard now lowered, Gibney stepped forward to detach it from the halyard, and then, showing admirable diplomacy and sense of occasion, he draped the Standard over his arms and presented it to the Portuguese Officer, who took it over his own arms and solemnly bowed his head. That done, the soldiers returned to 'order arms' and the Portuguese Officers and soldiers, the Mayor and his compatriots, with all due dignity, turned for the stairs and descended, leaving Carr, Gibney, Ameshurst and his Grenadiers alone on the roof. Carr gave a huge sigh of relief.

"There! Done! And with all due respect and propriety."

He turned to Gibney.

"If something needs doing well, it's worth doing well! You'd agree, Sar' Major?"

Gibney nodded.

"Aye Sir. Ah think the sayin' does go something similar!"

Carr beamed. He was genuinely relieved. The British lowering the Portuguese Standard without a word of explanation and replacing it with a plain green flag could have caused all kind of local ill feeling, but that was now avoided. He rubbed his hands.

"Right! The Colonel has the best telescope. Let's hope he sees fit to deploy it up here."

Carr took the chance for a word with Ameshurst as they all descended.

"Simon. What happened to Captain Carravoy?"

"He found himself to be somewhat indisposed, Sir."

Carr looked puzzled.

"So, you came along yourself? With some of your men."

"Yes Sir. It seemed the only thing to do."

Carr nodded.

"I'm grateful to you."

Ameshurst allowed his Major to go first, with Carravoy's actual reply uppermost in Ameshurst's mind; "Major Carr can do his own greasing up to the local peasants." With that, Carravoy had stalked off, intent on some shooting of some description with Lieutenant D'Villiers. Handing the Standard to the local Mayor was not the only act of diplomacy that took place on the tower roof that afternoon!

Carr went straight to Lacey's quarters in the Castle and found him poring over a map.

"Sir. The Portuguese Standard is down, I'm about to hoist the green signal flag, meaning 'No French in sight', Sir."

Lacey looked up very briefly.

"Well done, Henry. Everyone happy, I assume."

"Yes Sir, the Royal Standard is now lodged with the Mayor, but we need the best telescope we have up there, Sir. I wonder if we may use yours?"

Lacey did not look up.

"Of course, get Bryce to give it to you."

"Very good, Sir. Thank you."

Carr continued to study his Colonel and he could see from the hunched shoulders and bowed head, that all was not well."

"Is everything alright, Sir?"

Lacey looked up to see the concerned face of his Junior Major.

"Nothing huge, apart from the fact that, if Soult comes, it's a pound to a penny, he'll come at us. Because! At the far end of our line is impregnable Elvas, in the centre is Campo Maior, almost as impregnable and then there's us, in what can only be described as the next one up from an earthwork."

He turned the map around to show Carr.

"Here's Badajoz, where he's concentrated, with plenty down as far as Olivenza. If he has any sense, he'll send his main force along the banks of this river Gevora, not half a mile to our left, which will bring them straight onto us. Then, as reinforcements try to come to our aid, another force can come straight up from this ford over the Gevora at this Valdebotoa and pin those reinforcements down on that section of the line, unable to move to aid us."

He shook his head at the thought.

"I don't think we're strong enough here."

Carr's brows came together.

"Perhaps Sir, but I'd back us, with the 88th and the 74th to hold this ridge against anyone!"

"Yes Carr. I do hope you're right, if it comes to that."

"Yes Sir. Does General Mackinnon share your opinion, Sir? About our vulnerability?"

"He does, yes, and also General Picton. He's going to see about some artillery support. At least one battery."

"Right, Sir, so the best that we can do is keep a very good watch. The best possible. Do you want a picket, Sir? A mile out?"

"We should, yes. A picket is at least permanent. The main scouting job is for the cavalry and it's Portuguese cavalry in front of us, another cause for anxiety and being cavalry of any description, they go roaming about. It's in their nature, they like riding their horses. However, we do have something decent in reserve close by, Anson's Lights, the 14th and the 16th."

Carr brightened up.

"My brother's with the 16th, Sir. The 16th were part of that business of saving the guns at Fuentes,"

Lacey looked up, somewhat cheered.

"Really! I did not know that he was out here. They are quite close, so perhaps you can ride over at some time to meet him?"

Carr nodded.

"Yes Sir, I'd like that."

Lacey returned to his map.

"Right. Good. Now get the telescope!"

At that moment, a water party was on its way into the village, hauling the water-wagon, basically a huge barrel on a wheeled frame. On another wagon was a pump, no different from the pattern used on Naval warships. Being the first visit, Gibney was taking his original party, with Miles leading the mules of the water wagon, whilst some new recruits, 'to show them the way', were pulling the pump wagon. They descended the steep alley between the houses with difficulty, at which point Miles, never slow with some comment concerning practicalities, especially any which could discomfit an NCO, spoke the obvious difficulty.

"Sar' Major! We'll never get a full water-wagon back up this slope. It'll be too heavy!"

Gibney nodded. Miles had a point.

"We'll try with us all tailing on, but we may have to tip some out, or get ourselves another way around."

The pump halted beside the troughs and the canvas hoses was inserted, one into the human trough and another to the water wagon. Then they began pumping to soon empty the human trough, despite the constant flow from the spring. Gibney stood in thought, with folded arms whilst studying the huge animal trough.

"We've all drunk worse than this in our time. 'Sides, t'as all washed through an' 'tis as clean in there, as 'tis for the people. What you think, Jed?"

"I've no problem with that, Sar' Major. None. Think of what we had to drink back in that Sicily place!"

Gibney nodded.

"Raht! We takes from the larger, an' all."

The hose was transferred and the water-wagon quickly filled from the much larger trough. Then they made the attempt to return and Miles was proven right. Even with the mules and all on a rope, they could not haul it up the very steep slope; the hard soil and gravel giving no grip to their feet. Gibney adopted plan B.

157

"Davey. Saunders. Get around the back of the walls. See if there's a way round there, back to camp. Ah can't see the point in comin' all down here an' then goin' back with but half a load. We'll not tip out, not just yet."

As the two hurried off, the rest took their ease in the shade between the houses, but in less than five minutes, Davey and Saunders returned, Davey speaking the conclusion.

"There is a quick way, Sar' Major, but there's an earth bank that we'll have to make a hole in. It holds up a terrace for a field on the far side."

Gibney looked at him.

"With tools could us lot do the job?"

"Yes, Sar' Major, but it'll need tools as cuts soil, like picks and mattocks, not just spades and shovels."

At that Gibney nodded sadly.

"'An we've no more than a half dozen latrine spades in the whole Battalion!"

At this point Miles spoke up, relishing the sight of their fearsome Sergeant-Major in such a quandary as to what to do."

"Wish we had some of them tools they gave us before Badajoz, Sar' Major. Pity they took them back off us."

Gibney turned on him.

"That's enough from you Miles. Why not set that nasty brain of yours to thinkin' about where we can get tools from? Raht now! An' 'sides, ah've a feelin' we'll be seein' them tools again soon enough. Too soon, with us set afore the likes of Roger's Town and that place, Badahoth."

Miles immediately shut up, but the cunning that Gibney had described soon lit on an idea.

"Well, Sar' Major. Most of these is farmers. Even in these houses, they'll have tools, as we can borrow. Or hire! A bit of tobacco always helps. From the Regimental stock, that is!"

Many looked down at the ground and grinned at Miles' effrontery, but although Gibney's face had turned to thunder, Miles did have a possible idea that might work.

"Raht. So, what's Portuguese for 'can we borrow some tools'?"

Davey searched his own capable memory.

"The Spanish is 'herramientas'. A remember a farmer shouting at us after Talavera when we needed tools to bury the dead. I think he was calling us thieves, but that was the word he used. The Portuguese can't be so different and Spain itself's but a mile away. If we just goes and says the word, that'll probably do."

Gibney nodded.

"Raht. Off and round, all of you. Say, herramientas por favor, an' let's see what that gets us. Goin' through the motions of diggin' and usin' a pick won't come amiss, neither! An' put Pike to the front if a lass answers door."

They all scattered, Saunders and Davey forming a pair. They chose a building on the very edge of the town with tended fields backing right up to it. Saunders gave his judgment.

"I'd say there's a decent smallholder here, as works his land to the full."

Davey nodded and was the first to knock on the door. The door was opened by one who could only be described as a Spanish beauty, tall and well proportioned, speaking of feminine strength. She looked at Davey, then at Saunders and her eyes remained on him, these smiling more than her mouth. Being so singled out, Saunders spoke.

"Senorita, por favor. Herramientas, por favor."

Then both went through the motions of digging and breaking ground with phantom tools. The woman's hand went to her mouth as she laughed at the pantomime playing out before her, but it came down soon enough to reveal good white teeth.

"Vou pedir meu irmão."

With that she disappeared back into the house. Davey looked at Saunders.

"Did that mean anything to you?"

Saunders shook his head.

"No, but I'm not sorry we picked this house!"

Davey grinned at the obvious reason for the comment, but within a minute a burly man had come around the corner of the house and was motioning for them to follow him. They followed him around the corner and he motioned some more and spoke.

"Soldados Ingleses. Muito corajosos homens bons!"

Davey looked at Saunders.

"I think that means he likes us."

By the time Saunders had nodded his head at the supposition of the farmer's opinion, they had arrived at a wide door in the back of the main building. The farmer opened the door and gestured the pair to look inside. When their eyes became accustomed to the gloom they could see all manner of earth cutting and digging equipment. There was even a scoop that could be pulled by a mule which was far more effective than men with spades. Davey looked back at the farmer, his face alight with pleasure.

"Muchas gracias, Senor. Bueno, muchas bueno!"

The famer grinned and motioned with his hands that what was inside, could be taken outside. Davey turned to Saunders.

"This lot'll just about do the whole job, I'm thinking. Best get back to Gibney and tell him."

Saunders nodded.

"Yes. You go. I'd best stay here and get acquainted with how this stuff works!"

Davey grinned.

"Of course Zeke! And that's the only reason, I'm sure."

Both grinned as Davey ran off. The farmer grinned, waved and took himself off to his other tasks, leaving Saunders in what he could only assume was the 'tool room'. He nodded at the racks of well-maintained shovels, spades and much else. A door opened at the back and in came a woman similar to the one that had answered the door previously, but with a baby in her arms and three more of varying ages around her feet. The eldest of the three carried a jug with two beakers and the woman looked at Saunders.

"Gostaria de um pouco de água, soldado inglês?"

The word 'agua', the jug and the beakers translated the words sufficiently for Saunders.

"Si. Yes. Gracias."

The child came forward, offered a beaker, which Saunders took and the child poured out the water. Saunders then drank, making much of the pleasure that it gave him, which produced grins all round. The child re-filled Saunders' beaker, set the other on the floor and filled it. Saunders grinned some more.

"Gracias. Muchas gracias."

Then an old woman appeared and began, in obviously angry tones, to talk to the younger woman who made short replies, which made the old woman even angrier, her words accompanied with violent gestures towards Saunders. By then the child with the jug had returned to the women and so the Mother and children turned and left, for the old woman to shake a fist at Saunders before she left. However, then the doorway was re-filled by the figure that Saunders most hoped to see again, her white teeth clear in the gloom. She came forward and Saunders felt obliged, by good manners to walk towards her, offering his hand which she took, although somewhat surprised at the gesture. Hands now released, Saunders patted his chest, all the while grinning and nodding.

"Zeke! Me Zeke. Saunders."

In response, she, far more decorously, merely pointed a finger at herself in response.

"Consuela. Peyroteo."

Saunders nodded some more.

"Consuela. Mucho bueno."

She laughed openly, whilst Saunders cudgeled his brain for something to say. He settled for the common topic, and pointed to the floor.

"Franchesi soldiers. Aqui?"

Her face fell and she nodded.

"Soldados franceses são homens muito maus!"

Saunders picked up on the tone more than the meaning.

"Si, yes, no bueno."

She grinned again.

"Soldados Ingleses vencê-los no Vimeiro. General Wellesley."

At the mention of Wellesley and Vimeiro, Saunders took the chance to assume that she was talking about that battle. His face lit up.

"Vimeiro! Si, yes. Me there. A Vimeiro."

He then went through the absurd motions of loading and firing a musket, which transformed her face back to mirth. He pointed to the chevrons on his arm.

159

"Corporal. Me Corporal. Zeke Saunders. Corporal."

At this point Gibney and almost his whole command entered the store and Consuela hurried away out through the door back into the house.

"What's all this, Saunders. Over familiarity is an offence. Tha' could find th'sen ont triangle, for any kind of dalliance wi' locals! Tha' Stripes gone, an' all!"

Saunders pointed to the beakers on the floor.

"They gave us water, Sar' Major."

"She, more like. Watch th'sen!"

Jed Deakin then intervened.

"We can't ignore those as wants to show thanks, Sar' Major. For keepin' the Frogs away from their door."

Gibney's face closed into a frown.

"Aye, 'tis true, that, but we all as to watch our 'sen!"

Deakin and Saunders shared a look, yet all was immediately forgotten as the tools were gathered, but outside Gibney insisted on a stock-take to ensure that all was returned. Then they set to work with piercing the bank. The work was progressing well when a party of locals arrived. Saunders looked at Davey.

"Here's trouble!"

At the head was the Mayor from the Standard ceremony and he did look concerned. Gibney could do little more than gesture whilst speaking the single word 'agua' and gesturing with his arms towards the big field that contained their camp, in between him pointing to the water-wagon. The Mayor pulled a face, turned to his companions and perhaps nodded slightly. With that, all left, but within ten minutes a substantial work-gang of locals arrived and joined in with the effort. Davey, working with Saunders, gave voice to his own conjecture.

"Seems like they've decided that a bit of a road up from the water to this field is no bad idea."

Saunders nodded as he sunk his mattock into the hard clay that they had now worked down to, but the necessary gap was soon created, but that was insufficient for the locals. A wagon with stone arrived to brace the sides and then another with slabs to make runways for the wagon-wheels. These were placed carefully to coincide with the width of the wheels and it was the water-wagon was the first up, towed by the mules alone and all looking on, to clap or cheer their satisfaction. With hand-shakes and gestures the two work-gangs parted and the Redcoats progressed on over the easy gradient into the camp. Carr was the first Officer to see them.

"That took some time, Sar' Major!"

Gibney came to full attention and saluted.

"Aye Sir, but we 'ad some road building to do if we was to get the wagon up t'here."

Carr's face showed his concern. Good relations with the locals still remained high in his thoughts.

"Road building! And the locals thought what, about that?"

"Well, Sir, seein' as they helped us with the building an' all, ah'd say they viewed it quite gradely, Sir. There's now a decent way from the water to this field that we're in. Ah'd say they was quite pleased about that. Sir. To help with their own farmin', Sir, like."

At that moment, Saunders, Davey, Miles and Pike arrived and Carr again frowned.

"And why are they late back?"

"Returnin' the tools as was lent to us, Sir, by one of the farmers. Ah checked them all back in m'sen."

Carr nodded his satisfaction.

"Very good, Sar' Major. Well done. Carry on."

Gibney reeled off a blistering salute.

"Yes Sir. Thank you, Sir."

This proved to be not the only instance of co-operation between the 105th and the denizens of Ouguela that day. Captain Heaviside was on watch that afternoon, sat on a chair before Lacey's telescope, this placed on some sandbags to achieve a comfortable height. In this he was disturbed by Colour Sergeant Harry Bennet.

"Beg pardon, Sir, but there's a set of locals, down below at the door. I think they've brought something that may be useful, Sir."

Heaviside withdrew his face from the telescope and looked at the nearest soldier, a Corporal.

"Keep watch."

The man took his place and Heaviside followed Bennet down the tower-steps. Just outside he found the Mayor, with three men, two carrying a huge telescope, the third a tri-pod. The Mayor shook Heaviside's hand whilst pointing to the instrument, it being splendidly magnificent, all polished brass, leather and wood, with an embossed leather cover over the lens at each end.

"O melhor para assistir o francês."

The word 'frances' and the telescope itself made it very obvious what the Mayor intended and Heaviside could only speak his thanks.

"Gacias, Senor, muchas gracias."

The Mayor grinned and nodded.

"Qualquer coisa para manter os franceses de nossas portas, sim?"

Heaviside had no idea what had been said, but, nevertheless, he grinned, nodded, and spoke his thanks again. With that, he and the Mayor carried the telescope carefully up the stairs, followed by the tri-pod and all was quickly set up. The Mayor checked the security of the instrument, took off the covers and focused it onto the distance himself, then he grinned and gestured to Heaviside to look for himself. The result was dramatic. What had been hidden in the distant haze and mist was now thoroughly revealed. There could be no movement of the French within five miles that could not be detected. Heaviside stood up and once more spoke his thanks, but the Mayor had more to say.

"Isto era uma vez no nosso atalaya para procurar os mouros."

Again, Heaviside had not the first idea what the Major had said, he could only repeat his thanks, shake the man's hand again, but then, being Heaviside, he instinctively added what most often concluded any conversation between himself and anyone.

"Every good gift and every perfect gift is from above. James One, verse 17."

Now it was the Mayor's turn to look bemused, but he copied Heaviside and spoke his agreement, several times, whilst Heaviside's soldiers grinned down at the ground. With that the Mayor and his men left the tower, leaving Heaviside to adjust the tripod to the correct height. It was not long before Nat Drake arrived for his turn on watch at the tower and he stood incredulous at the new, colossal instrument.

"Who brought this, Joshua?"

"The local Mayor. Take a look."

Drake sat and did and his face soon registered his astonishment.

"My Word! At 100 yards, you could tell if someone's had a shave!"

Then he examined the instrument as a whole, running his hand over the craftsmanship.

"But is this not a most splendid piece? It must be from the time of the Spanish Armada. Perhaps the ship with this in it got safe home?"

Heaviside nodded and spoke the usual before leaving the tower.

"Iron sharpens iron, and one man sharpens another. Proverbs 27. Verse 17."

Still bemused at the significance, or even relevance, of that quote, Drake once again set his eye to their additional, most magnificent, instrument of observation.

oOo

The first Cornets Peterson and Carr knew that something different was afoot was when Major Johnson came bursting into their tent, to rudely awaken the pair, with the sun not even edging over the horizon.

"Get your things packed. We're moving up."

Carr knuckled his eyes into something like functioning.

"Moving up? Where Sir? I thought the Portuguese were taking care of the front."

Johnson moved quickly to leave, to then halt half out of the tent opening, he was in a hurry, but he paused long enough to answer Carr's question.

"They are, or were, but they're totally unreliable! They spend all their time looking for food, getting nothing from their own Government. Picton went out yesterday and couldn't find one where they should be, instead he found most of them fishing in the Gevora! You can't really blame the poor Devils. They're being pulled back and us pushed up, us being Anson's. Picton wants us up there come daylight."

Peterson had now surfaced.

"Oh! No real rush then."

161

By the time the Regiment was moving forward, the sun had just cleared the horizon, but Colonel Withers took that to be good enough because at that point they crossed the road between Ouguela and Campo Maior to then set hoof on their patrol territory. Cornet Carr, riding beside Johnson, looked around for any signs of life. Of the Portuguese, whom they were replacing, there was no sign, but there was an obvious picket of Redcoats on a low hill, almost straight ahead, but slightly leftwards. Carr had two questions, and he voiced the first.

"What is our patrol area, Sir?"

Johnson did not answer for a short while, him studying the ground over on their right.

"A five-mile front, give or take, between this Ouguela and that Campo Maior place, where we will overlap with the 14th, but no bad thing that. We can manage that, but we'll be stretched. Keeping company with that bunch of footsloggers, in their Ouguela nest, that's the 105th, with the 88th and 74th in the open, back on the ridge."

Carr rose in his stirrups to get a better view.

"The 105th! Really! My brother's the Junior Major with them."

Johnson looked at him and smiled.

"Well, a visit should be possible, them being so close, and I don't mind telling you, that I have no qualms at all about having the solid 105th on my flank."

Carr nodded and smiled, then moved onto his second question.

"Where do we camp?"

Johnson now looked leftwards.

"I'm told that there is a decent field, with decent grazing, quite close to the river, that named the Gevora."

Carr smiled.

"Of that I approve, if only because we'll have an easy supply of water."

Johnson looked at him and nodded his agreement, but his voice carried mild sarcasm.

"Oh, you approve, do you, Cornet? Well, I'm sure we're all relieved at that, but yes, assuming it's a decent stream. It worried me, that back on the plain we were drinking from the same pool as the horses. Not good."

"No Sir."

In the event, the field was just beyond the 105th picket and slightly downstream. When they saw their new home, all in the 16th counted themselves fortunate to be moved out from the barren, desiccated uplands of the previous four days. They entered an extensive, well grassed field and all eyes opened in wonderment at the turnover in their circumstances. By the river sat the reason for their lush pasture, a water-wheel, powered by mule or donkey via a long lever, but now conspicuously idle. All was untouched by any Portuguese, military or civilian, and so the 16th soon settled into the area, it proving to be as good, or even better, than Johnson had described. The waters of the Gevora ran swift and clear, therefore was soon full of bathing men, washing both themselves and their beloved mounts.

All felt a lift in their spirits, even if it now required the tedium of constant patrols. To that end, Withers immediately sent out on patrol of both Troops of Somers-Cocks Three Squadron, even though they had no clear orders as to where. This changed that very evening. Withers called all his Officers to his tent and all 12 crammed inside. There they found themselves in the company of Brigadier Stapleton-Cotton no less and he did not mince his words.

"Soult's assembled upwards of 60,000 men, with over 4,000 cavalry, against our own three thousand. He's got the lot just the other side of the Guadiana, downstream of Badajoz. Our river Gevora swings across his front before joining the Guadiana and that's our patrol line. It's another barrier between us and them. The Peer's expecting a general action any time, with Soult now fully gathered. What we do not know is what Soult knows about us, that being where we are and what we are defending. We suspect that he is more in ignorance than knowledge and we must keep him that way, which means strong patrols, vigorous and aggressive if needs be, to keep his cavalry away from our line. Expect to be busy. Good-day to you, gentlemen and good luck to you all."

With that he strode out through their parting and saluting ranks, leaving them to share concerned and worried looks amongst themselves. Then they began to leave, but Withers called back Johnson.

"Arthur. Remain, if you please. We need to work out a rota and patrol areas. Bring that map over to the table."

At that moment, a gathering of the Senior Officers of the 105th, Captains and above, were also concerned over a piece of paper, but much smaller and altogether far less verbose and in the classic style of the author. It was from Picton, and Lacey read out a letter now just received.

"Soult has three armies the other side of the Guadiana, 65,000 men. Lord Wellington expects an attack inside the next three days. Be sure that you are ready."

It was Captain Lord Carravoy who spoke first, his voice not quite concealing the anxiety he felt.

"This could be another Talavera, Sir?"

Lacey looked at him.

"It could, Charles, yes, but I suspect not all along the full extent of our line, as it was there. We are the weakest flank. Here! If he comes, I would not bet against him coming against us. Elvas is impregnable, Campo Maior much the same. It is here that Wellington is most vulnerable."

Anxiety now showed, but only by Carravoy's left hand flexing on his sword hilt.

"Within the next three days!"

Lacey leant forward across his small table.

"Yes! You know, as well as I, that the French live off the land. Any army that size could only sustain itself from the countryside for a time close to that. He either uses it, or disperses it, before it starves."

"So, what should we do, Sir, in the light of this threat?"

Lacey stood up and folded his arms, evidently thinking.

"Well, I think it's time we polished up our firing drill. We've more ammunition than we can store inside, when you add in all that the Portuguese lodged here. So, include our two Companies of Portuguese. That will do no harm."

He looked over at O'Hare and Carr.

"Get that going, will you? Start this afternoon. Get Byford to translate 'First rank fire, second rank fire' he should be able to manage that."

Tension rose with each of the three hot June days that began to pass. The three day 'believe' soon became common knowledge and on the first day, the 25th June, two Squadrons of the 16th Light Dragoons set out at dawn to begin another patrol. The ground was bleak, barren and parched and clouds of dust rose with their passing. Major Johnson rode at the head of the column, with Captain Tavender at the head of One Squadron and Cornets Carr and Peterson leading Two Squadron and all followed Johnson South to their patrol area. Peterson and Carr had become good friends over the past weeks and chatted idly together, but, up ahead, Tavender said nothing, whilst Johnson concentrated solely on the ground ahead of the patrol. The only words that Johnson spoke had been at the start of their patrol, when they mounted up.

"Seems like your brother's Regiment is fighting a battle all on their own, Carr, judging by all the sounds of musketry coming from their camp!"

Carr had merely smiled sheepishly, but, after their brief ride, Johnson called a halt from a distinct hilltop, now that all that needed to be seen, albeit vaguely through the growing heat haze, was now in full view. He turned to Peterson and pointed leftwards.

"So, to be absolutely clear. Peterson, over there's for you and your Troop, within the bend of the Gevora where it turns South. Where it goes straight, you stop. You keep within the bend. No Frogs have been seen on our side around there, but there's one ford, deep inside the bend and that you need to keep an eye on."

He turned to Carr.

"Yours is from Peterson to the village of Valdebotoa, the straight run of the Gevora. You can just make it out, front right. Be wary, it has an easy ford over the Gevora. If these French bastards are going to come at us at our end of Wellington's line, then that ford will be their main route. What they are doing in Valdebotoa matters a great deal. Clear?"

Carr nodded.

"Yes Sir!"

Johnson then turned to Tavender.

"Your plot, with your whole Squadron, is from Valdebotoa to the main road that runs North-South between Campo Maior and the next village downstream, called Gevora, same name as the river. Don't go beyond Gevora village, there's no need, Long's Brigade of Lights are looking after that. Gevora has an easy ford as well, so be careful."

He sat back in his saddle, plainly unhappy.

"Johnny thinks this bank to be his territory and is disputing it. His cavalry are down there. On top of that, as you can see, closer to the river there are several stands and copses of trees. Many big enough to hide a squadron. So watch out. You are here to look, not to fight. Running away with good information is the right thing to do!"

He treated each to a final look, before wheeling his horse.

"See you all for supper!"

Without a word, Tavender then led his Squadron away, cantering swiftly off to the right to get beyond the barely discernable, distant village of Valdebotoa and reach their patrol ground. Peterson looked at Carr, before riding back to his own Troop.

"Well, like he said. See you for supper!"

Carr grinned as Peterson wheeled his horse, then he signalled for Sergeant Baxter to bring the Troop forward. Baxter was the first to reach him and Carr pointed to the river course before them.

"This is ours, Sergeant. From where the river comes out of its bend to run a straight course down to that village."

Baxter nodded.

"Right Sir. So, if you take my advice, Sir, you'd walk us from one high point to the next. Better for looking out and a walk throws up little dust, Sir, 'specially if we're on the edge of what the French counts as theirs. Again, my advice, Sir, only go as far enough into what the Frogs're claimin', so's we can tell what's what."

Carr grinned and raised himself by pressing down on the pommel of his saddle.

"Good advice, Sergeant. That makes sense to me, but pass it back to the men, to keep a good watch front and side. I don't like these groups of trees nor these dips in the land."

Baxter grinned himself.

"That's good thinking, Sir. Seems you might just be learnin' this here cavalry game!"

Carr grinned as he urged his horse into a walk, aiming for a high point on the undulating plain. Within ten minutes they were there and Carr took his decision.

"We split here, Sergeant. You take half and work left, but keep Cornet Peterson's in sight to link with him. I'll take the rest and cover the right and the village, keeping in touch with both you and Captain Tavender. Meet back here. Have you a watch?"

Baxter nodded and Carr grinned back at him.

"At 4.00. That's tea-time. You're turn for the cake!"

Baxter grinned slightly at the absurdity of such a statement, then the Troop split and Carr walked his men on, using a low ridge, but keeping just below it on their side, avoiding the skyline, of which ploy many veterans amongst his men thoroughly approved. They tracked their area for three hours until Carr called for the Noon meal, which was taken in a hollow, whilst Corporal Makepeace maintained watch from a group of trees.

Meanwhile, not so far away, Captain Tavender was keeping his own watch, but of a different sort and for different reasons. He was ever mindful of what Lord Templemere had said, during his visit to the 16th back in mid-April, prior to the battle of Fuentes, the words remaining clear, "Often in dire danger are Cornets, pity if something were to happen to him." Templemere was now a Member of the House of Lords and to enhance his favour with a Peer, no less, could do immense good in the future. Besides, an 'unfortunate event' befalling that odious 'darling of the Regiment' after his exploits with Ramsey's guns, would be most satisfying. On top, as Templemere had said, it would be a blow to the whole family, Elder Carr especially, or so he fervently hoped. His own Squadron was off patrolling, under both Cornets and therefore, or so he had told them, he had given himself a free hand to go as he saw fit, but 'fit' in this case meant looking for a possible opportunity to imperil Cornet Carr. He could see where Carr and his half Troop were, but as yet there was no opportunity and it would need some French cavalry close by to take advantage.

Johnson, another 'despisee', had talked of French patrols using the stands of trees. Why they should not be more forward towards the Allies and scouting, he could not imagine, but he used his telescope to examine the nearest copses, only midway between himself and the river. He was looking at the fourth, when he saw movement in its half-shade. He focused the glass more carefully and convinced himself that very probably there was a party of French Hussars within the dull green, high Summer foliage. All was confirmed, when a Hussar in a pale blue uniform came to the edge of the copse to relieve himself. He closed the glass.

164

Good, part one in place! Next, onto Carr. He spurred his horse into movement and cantered over, to find all there just packing up from their midday meal. He rode straight up to Carr.

"Cornet. Mount up and come with me."

Carr did so immediately and both rode to the top of the ridge which gave them a view of Valdebotoa. Tavender pointed down to the village.

"I've seen infantry down there. Within the houses."

Carr drew out his own telescope and quickly focused it.

"Infantry, Sir? The place looks deserted, apart from a few cavalry. I can see no infantry, neither in the place itself, either side of it, nor behind. Sir."

He closed the telescope and looked quizzically at Tavender, but he had his reply already prepared.

"Well I have! Get yourself down there and take a closer look. Take a couple of men, but if there are infantry in that place, that's serious. Johnson said so."

Carr continued to stare at him, but Tavender continued.

"I'd go myself, but this is your patrol area. My men are someway over and you and yours are right here above the village. I should rejoin mine."

He paused.

"We need to make sure, whether I'm wrong or right."

Carr took a deep breath and turned his horse back to his men. Once there he made his choice.

"Makepeace. Spivey. We need to get closer to the village. Captain Tavender thinks he has seen infantry moving there, and we have to be sure. It's why we're here and it's on our patch."

Makepeace and Spivey shared worried looks, but both mounted up and followed Carr to the ridge, where Tavender remained and he pointed down to the village.

"Also, that place and the woods behind could hide a Division. Find out. I'm returning to my men."

With that perfunctory statement, he spurred his horse into a trot, whilst Carr led men his forward at a walk. After half a mile, they crossed a gully and halted. They had come to the irrigated fields beside the river. Carr took out his telescope and again studied the village. He could see nothing between the houses. He passed it to Makepeace.

"You try, Corporal."

Makepeace took the instrument and used it as Carr had.

"Nothing, Sir."

Carr returned the instrument to his pocket.

"Well, we've got our orders. So, over this field and into the trees beyond, but we'll go no further."

Just over a half a mile back, Tavender was in a rage of frustration. The French Hussars must be lounging between the trees, totally neglectful, taking their ease or asleep. Something needed to happen. He drew his Light Dragoon carbine and cocked it, then his horse pistol and cocked that. He fired the carbine first, counted to five and then fired the pistol. The result was pleasing. Hussars ran out of the wood, looked this way and that and then one pointed to Carr and his small escort. Within a minute, the Hussars were leaving the trees and, even more pleasing, it appeared to be a full Squadron, well over 60 men.

Carr and his companions were almost across the field when they heard the shots and they reined their horses to a stop. Carr looked around.

"What was that?"

Spivey was looking behind as was Makepeace.

"Gunfire, Sir, and this is no place to stay until we knows what's goin' on."

They turned their horses and began the gallop back the way they had come. A minute passed and then Carr's throat tightened. From the left, a Squadron of blue uniformed Hussars were galloping across the path which led back to safety. The three steered their horses right, with luck they may just make it, trusting to their superior horses, and they may even be able to link with Peterson. That possibility sowed strong seeds of worry in the mind of the watching Tavender, but then, joy oh joy, another French Squadron came galloping out of another stand of trees, certain to cut off Carr. Tavender sat and watched events, with deep satisfaction. Carr, Makepeace and Spivey, with further flight now hopeless, slowed their horses to a trot. Carr drew his sword, but Makepeace bid him sheath it again.

"Best put that away, Sir. We're killed or taken. Staying alive is what matters now, Sir."

Carr halted his horse, as did the pair. He did not sheath his sword, instead he reversed it, offering the hilt in the direction of the French. An Officer walked his horse forward and took it. He grinned slyly as he spoke.

"Vous êtes nos prisonniers, M'sieu."

Carr nodded.

"Oui. Je sais."

The Officer nodded and examined the blade, his eyebrows lifting with both surprise and pleasure.

"Mon Dieu, un Clingenthal!"

Carr said nothing, then the Officer motioned men forward to disarm Makepeace and Spivey. As that took place, he turned to another Officer, evidently Junior.

"Tenir à Gevora. Latour-Maubourg est la. Il voudra mettre en doute ces. Soult, ainsi, plus tard."

Carr knew enough French to translate to himself that they were to be taken to Gevora and questioned. The Officer called out his orders and ten men emerged from the Squadron, to place themselves five either side. It was made obvious that the three were now required to move when the Officer slapped Carr's horse on the rump, much to the amusement of his men. They set the pace of a gentle trot, with one of their escort holding the bridle of each prisoner to prevent escape and, as they moved down river along the bank of the Gevora, Carr looked back to the now far off ridge to see his half Troop, now in silhouette, all sat watching the sad events. Inside Carr was seething, whilst Makepeace and Spivey were much more stoical, drinking from their water bottles and ignoring the taunts of the French either side. However, one Frenchman was not satisfied with mere insults, he made a point of frequently slapping Spivey on the exposed nape of his neck, whilst, to the great amusement of his comrades, repeating the same phrase."

"Vous êtes sans espoir anglais qui ne pouvait pas monter un cochon."

Spivey had no idea what the man was saying, but the process rankled more and more, but he was veteran enough to realise the need to stay quiet, suffer the insults and keep his head down. They were now hard alongside the bank of the Gevora and the village with that name was now coming into sight. The Officer turned to his men.

"Pour ces prisonniers, nous obtiendrons une bouteille supplémentaire de vin. Non?"

The distraction about extra wine cost them dearly. They were just passing a substantial copse, which suddenly disgorged about 50 mounted guerillas, immediately riding hard at them from a short distance that made escape impossible. Nevertheless, the Hussar escort cried out in horror and alarm and two rode their mounts into the river, even though there was no ford and they were thrown off as their horses bucked and twisted in the deep water. Whilst their horses swam away the two were stuck on the bank, neither could swim, but four guerillas, each with lances, came to the bank and speared both, several times, their grunts of anguish wholly sickening, until both were corpses being carried away by the current. Each guerilla had the same wicked lance and the remaining nine French Hussars sat their horses in shock and fear as many lances were pointed in their direction. Three began to weep, they all knew what happened if they fell into the hands of guerillas, and here it was, there worst nightmare now a reality!

The leader of the guerillas eased his horse up to Carr, seeming to recognize him.

"I am Mateo. I know you. We saw you at the Barba del Puerco, when we came up from bridge. I do the speak for Julian. We wait in trees for nightfall, to cross Gevora. Now we see you. Is luck for you, yes?"

Carr could only nod and grin. His mind was in a turmoil of relief.

"How are you, Ingles?"

"Better now that you are here. Thank you."

Mateo grinned, but the guerilla was pulling his horse away.

"Rápido, amigos, hacia los árboles!"

With a guerilla now holding each French bridle, Mateo led his men back into the security of the trees, where they could not be seen. Once there, each Hussar was hauled roughly from his horse and thrown to the ground, when the utter dread on the face of each contorting their faces into something almost inhuman. Mateo looked at Carr and grinned wickedly.

"These must be punished. Ingles!"

With that, he pointed with two fingers at his eyes, then he made a slashing motion across each wrist and then a final swipe across his throat. The message was obvious that the prisoners were to have their eyes gauged out, their hands cut off and then, finally, they would have their throats cut. At these gestures, each prisoner began to wail, several falling to their knees. Carr was horrified, not only at the fate of the prisoners

166

alone, but also, he fully realised, that they all could be questioned to obtain priceless information. Carr turned to Mateo.

"Sir. I ask you as a comrade and an ally to allow me to take these men back with me. They know important things. We must not waste the chance to find out what they know. Sir. Please, I beg of you!"

Mateo looked puzzled, but not annoyed.

"You are thinking that these dogs may know something good?"

Carr nodded.

"Yes, yes, indeed. What they know will help us rid your country of these invaders."

Mateo sat his saddle with folded arms, his head comically rocking from side to side as he debated the question. Carr decided that an example would help. He dismounted and went over to the Officer, also on his knees. The first thing he did was to pull out the Officer's own sword from its scabbard.

"This is mine anyway!"

Hope came into the Frenchman's face. He had understood enough of the conversation with Mateo to realise that this Englishman may have the power to save them from a very gruesome death, but Carr laid the point at the man's throat, yet he did not push it forward. Instead he began to speak.

"Infantry dans Valdebotoa. Oui ou non?"

Hope came into the man's face, him now being only too eager to please this English Officer, the only one who could save his life, or at least from death by torture.

"Non, m'sieu, non. Toute l'infanterie est de retour à Badajoz! Ou Olivenza."

He nodded vigorously, hoping that this would emphasise all his words, but Carr had turned to Mateo.

"There! What he just said is very, very important to us. He will know more, which will help us both, us Ingleses and you guerrillas!"

Mateo's jaw came together and he nodded.

"Very well, Ingles. You may take these dogs. We will find others."

He looked at his men.

"Camaradas, vincular a estos perros."

Rope was produced and the process of trussing up the prisoners began, but before it was far advanced, Spivey dismounted, took off his Light Dragoon shako and hung it by its strap from the pommel. Then he walked to the prisoners. The guerillas ceased their rope work and watched him, all very curious.

"Hang on a minute, boys."

He went straight up to his previous tormentor, seized the front of his uniform and then head-butted him with vicious force. The man collapsed to the ground, with blood pouring from his nose. Spivey stared down at him.

"That's settled you. Frog muck-rake!"

All the guerillas began clapping and cheering at the display.

"Bravo Ingles! Bravo!"

Immediately a wineskin was presented to him and one also to Makepeace. Spivey raised his up.

"Cheers boys! Thanks, and good luck to you."

Then he drank in Spanish fashion, pouring the wine from the spout some distance above his mouth and swallowing whilst still pouring. This encouraged even more shouts and clapping. Carr looked at him as he mounted.

"You've done that before!"

Spivey nodded as he handed back the skin.

"Yes Sir. A few times. In more than one cantina."

By now the prisoners' arms were tied and each neck bound back to the tied hands of the prisoner behind. There was no possibility of escape, all were on foot. The guerrillas herded the Frenchmen out of the trees, several using their lances with wounding force, but soon the nine prisoners and their three escorts were on a track which in all likelihood led up towards Campo Maior. The guerrillas followed them part way, until a British cavalry patrol could be seen, then Mateo came up to Carr, offering his hand.

"Good luck, Ingles, that you see again your country, I much hope."

Carr shook his hand.

"Good luck to you, Mateo. We may meet again."

"Si, Ingles, si. It can be so."

With that the guerrillas rode off towards Elvas, Gevora now forgotten, considering perhaps that their daily deed against the French had now been done. The cavalry patrol that had come into view was a Troop of Tavender's Squadron, commanded by Cornet Harry Smythe. He rode up with his men, smiles as wide as the band across their shakoes.

"You've made a good haul! How'd you manage that?"

Carr grinned.

"It's a long story and it will cost you a bottle of brandy, but I must get up to Campo Maior as soon as possible."

He pointed back to the French Officer.

"With this one! Have you a spare horse I could stick him on?"

Smythe nodded.

"Yes. A French one we found roaming about. Blanket all wet! With a number ten on it."

"Yes. We know how that happened!"

Smythe turned back in his saddle.

"Turner! That French nag we found. Get it up here!"

"And can I leave these on foot with you?"

The answer was another nod of the head as the horse was brought up and within minutes the Hussar Officer, tied to his saddle, was cantering up the track to Campo Maior, with Makepeace and Spivey just behind, on either side, and Carr in the lead. The fortress town was gained within fifteen minutes and it contained more Redcoats than civilians, as was evident when they entered the narrow streets. Carr saw a Major and rode up to him and saluted.

"Excuse me, Sir, but could you direct me to General Picton's Headquarters. I have a prisoner here, Sir, that he will want questioned."

The Major looked from Carr to the prisoner, then back to Carr.

"Get inside the Citadel, it's over to the left. Once inside, it's dead ahead."

Carr saluted.

"Thank-you, Sir."

The Major responded and Carr moved on. The Major was correct, the intimidating walls of the Citadel soon came into view, and the gate was easily found, so they entered and tethered their horses outside what was obviously Picton's Headquarters. Carr dismounted, as did the French Hussar, but with much less dignity, as Makepeace and Spivey hauled him out of the saddle with his hands still bound. All four entered the ornate and imposing doors to find, as luck would have it, General Picton himself in the hallway, arguing with another Officer. Carr went straight up to him, came to the attention and saluted.

"Excuse me, Sir."

Picton's face became even more thunderous, even though starting from a high base.

"What the Devil are you all about?"

"If you please, Sir. Cornet Carr of the 16th Light Dragoons. We have captured a French Hussar Officer."

He gestured back to the bound prisoner.

"He has told us, and I believe him utterly, Sir, that there are no French infantry in Valdebotoa and that they are all back near Badajoz, Sir, or Olivenza. I thought you would like to know that as soon as possible, Sir, and question the man further. Sir."

Picton turned to face Carr completely, his other opponent now forgotten.

"You are sure of this? What he told you?"

"Yes Sir. He said it to escape an unpleasant death at the hands of Spanish guerrillas. It's a bit of a story Sir."

Picton's face softened one or two degrees.

"Did he, by God!"

Picton looked again at the dejected French figure, then back to Carr.

"Right! Very well, Cornet. You did the right thing, coming here directly. You can leave him here. Dismiss!"

Carr took one step back, saluted and turned on his heel to leave, whilst Spivey gave the Officer one last shove forward, before following Carr out of the door. There Carr quickly mounted his horse.

"I don't know about you two, but I'm absolutely starving. Can't get back to camp quick enough."

However, once back in their camp, Makepeace and Spivey related the story to their messmates, but when they came to the part containing the orders from Tavender and the two shots, they were both thoroughly grilled by Sergeant Baxter and it was plain, when the story was complete, that he was not best pleased and now wholly suspicious.

oOo

Mackinnon sat on a chair at the top of the watch-tower. He had used the telescope there and pronounced it wondrous indeed, but he was plainly not well, drinking frequently from a jug of water, draining the glass and immediately refilling. His complexion alternated between sickly wan to ruddy flush, all within the space of five minutes. Lacey and O'Hare were at his side, both concerned, their worries being thoroughly aroused by the effort that Mackinnon had needed to make to get to the top of the steps. Lacey leaned forward.

"You're not well, Sir!"

Mackinnon shook his head.

"It'll pass. Remember what we called Guadiana fever back in 09. Dose of that again, ah fear, but it'll pass. It did last time."

He drank some more water, then looked up.

"Have ye anything stronger?"

O'Hare smiled and produced his hip flask from a side pocket. Mackinnon drained the glass of water and then offered it to O'Hare for a measure, which was duly poured. Mackinnon swallowed the spirit whole and seemed to be revived. He looked again out over the plain towards the Gevora.

"Tense times, Lacey. He's got tens of thousands over there. He must come or send them awa', tae forage elsewhere. What have you seen?"

Lacey took a deep breath.

"Well, Sir, through that telescope and from our own picket, a mile out, nothing bar our own cavalry, coming and going. Nothing that we would call French activity."

Mackinnon tugged out a huge handkerchief to ease the feel of perspiration on his brow.

"Today's the 26th. We've been sat here since the 17th, but he pulled all his together on the 23rd. These are worryin' times Lacey, but ah'll give this three more days. If he doesn't come within that, the games done. He'll have funked it!"

Lacey smiled.

"And you can get some rest, Sir."

"There's the hope, Lacey. Ah'll no say no tae that!"

With that, Mackinnon rose and went to the stairs, but after the third step he fainted and it was only the fact that O'Hare had gone first and managed to catch him, that prevented a dangerous tumble down the stone steps. Lacey seized an arm.

"Guard! Up here, all of you."

The guard of four dropped their muskets and then hurried up to take the burden of the swooning Brigadier.

"Take him to my Quarters and fetch Surgeon Pearce."

With full care and respect, the men carried their Brigadier away, then Lacey looked at O'Hare.

"This is no country for old men!"

O'Hare stared back.

"Do you include us in that?"

At that moment, oblivious to the higher issues that tried the nerves of their Officer Corps, the men of Davey and Deakin's messes were happily fishing in the Gevora, behind Ouguella. John Davey had been, as usual, far more successful, and so they were close to a good enough haul to provide a substantial fish and potato stew for their evening meal. They had spent the morning loosing off numerous ten rounds in half-Company volleys, then moving into square, then into open column by Companies, then back to firing line for more ten round volleys, then doing it all again. The Portuguese had hugely improved and could almost match their British neighbours, being motivated to match the awesome firepower that the British 'casacas vermelhas' could generate. Therefore, they proudly stood their place and followed the drill, their brown uniforms honourably placed beside the red, in 'uma linha de fogo Inglês', a British firing line! Now that all that was done, the men could take their ease and these had decided that some fish instead of the usual salt pork or salt

169

beef would make a welcome change. It was Jed Deakin, almost as successful as Davey, his skills learnt on the Somerset Levels, who pronounced the end of their sojourn.

"That's enough, boys! Any more will go to waste."

At his bidding, all wrapped their catch in whatever cloth or sacking they had, fixed the twine to the rough poles they all used, pushed the bent pin into the wood and then began the walk back to their camp, all except Tom Miles.

"Any extra of these we can trade! Tobacco or somesuch!"

Deakin stared contemptuously at Miles catch.

"You can trade them if you likes, Tom Miles, but I'll tell thee now, they tiddlers won't trade for much more than a pipe fill!"

All appreciated the humour, bar Miles, but almost immediately Deakin stopped and began to wonder.

"Zeke! B'ain't that the house up yonder of that lad as lent us his tools, t'other day? An' we used they to build the water road?"

Zeke was studying the house intently and he knew with absolute certainty that it was the very house, if only for the unassailable reason that Consuela was outside, washing some clothes in a large wooden tub.

"Yes Jed. 'Tis!"

Deakin began to point.

"Look yer. From this bank we'n stood on, that dip runs right into his land. 'Tis already fair wet at the bottom even in this June. I'd say we owes this lad a favour. If we pierced this bank, put in a sluice, then move on this dip about 50 yards further, then he's got water on his land, an' I'd say he could do with it, all here bein' so dry an' baked up."

Saunders' face brightened at the idea. As much in hope as in expectation, he had convinced himself that Consuela was doing the washing outside the house because of their, or, better still, because of his arrival, although they were 300 yards distant. Any further interaction with that household had his total approval and he answered with exaggerated enthusiasm.

"That's right, Jed, yes. I'd say we do owe them a favour, what with them making it easy to get water into the camp, like."

Deakin nodded.

"Right. Give your catch to Tom. Joe and Nat can take John's and mine. Drag up Byford, he might know the right words. We'll go up there now and see what we can work out."

John Byford and Eirin were walking to join them, Eirin carrying little Jed. They had been enjoying the sunshine together at the river, watching the fishing. Saunders motioned him over.

"John! You're needed. We're going up to the farmhouse yonder."

Byford passed the baby to Eirin and all three, Deakin, Saunders and him took the path that led to the house. Consuela continued her washing, but she had lifted her head to watch them approach whilst continuing to punish the sudsy clothes. Saunders put himself in the lead.

"Ola, Consuela!"

She beamed at him.

"Ola, Zeke."

Deakin looked at him.

"You've been takin' lessons from young Byford, here!"

Leaving the two to exchange furtive looks between themselves, Deakin called on their only interpreter.

"John. Ask this Consuela if we can see the man of the house."

Byford came forward.

"O homen de Casa, por favor."

She pointed the fields beyond some trees.

"Ele esta nos campos."

The answer was obvious and so off they trooped to the field beyond the trees as indicated, to find the farmer they sought. He had a companion, but both stopped their work as the three Redcoats approached. Deakin decided that he needed to take the initiative.

"Ola, Senor!"

The reply came back as cheerfully as the greeting, then Deakin turned to Byford.

"Ask him to come to the river."

Byford looked at him aghast.

"What?"

Deakin stared back.

"You heard! Give it a go."

Byford took a deep breath.

"Para o Gevora, Señor, por favor. Nos."

The accompanying gestures were more effective than the words and so the pair dropped their tools and began the walk to reach to the river. The next 15 minutes were a pantomime of odd Portuguese words, 'agua' being used most often, and gestures, such as indicated cutting through the bank, open a sluice, and then the motion of running along the depression whilst waving hands to signify water. The farmhand seemed to catch on quicker than the farmer and he spoke his impression of what the casacas vermelhas Ingleses were trying to convey.

"Eles querem fazer uma água vala no campo."

Byford immediately appreciated the two words for water and field, and he nodded.

"Sim, sim, agua para campo. Sim."

The farmer looked at his workmate, then at Byford, then at the bank and ditch. Then he decided.

"Sim! Deve adjudar. Sim. Gracias."

Deakin recognized agreement and offered the farmer his hand, which he took.

"Right. We starts after supper. There's plenty of daylight after that. We needs to get it done afore they moves us out."

They immediately set out for their camp, but there to encounter Captain Drake, who looked suspiciously at the three, who immediately came to the attention and waited for the inevitable question, which was spoken as Drake leaned forward, showing his concern.

"What's all this, Colour Sergeant? Why are you back so late? Your fishing party returned some time ago."

"Well yes, Sir, but me and the lads, Sir, we was thinkin' of a way to pay back that farmer as lent us his tools to make a way for the water wagon, Sir."

"And this would be in what form?"

"Well, Sir, rememberin' my time on the Levels, I could see that a rheen could be dug from the river to his crop field, Sir. To water his land."

Drake's face screwed up.

"A rheen?"

"Yes Sir, a water ditch. We could dig it easy and put in a sluice, Sir. Help him out and his people, Sir. Seems only right."

Drake paused to think. This could do no harm, but it would take them away from the ridge, their place in the event of any French advance.

"Very well, but only when duties are completed. Understood? And I want a signal set up to call you back if needs be."

"Yes Sir, that's understood, Sir, and we'll get Bugle Bates to sit up here, whilst we're working down over there."

Drake nodded.

"Very good, but you, Deakin, are Three Company. Captain Heaviside must also give his permission."

They all saluted and made off to their mess area, where the fish stew was almost ready. With food partaken of, Deakin himself went to Captain Heaviside and the reply was brief and wholly typical.

"Let brotherly love continue. Hebrews 13. Verse I."

Thus, for the next two days, after the Midday meal and through the light of the evening, almost 100 men dug and cut a deep 70-yard ditch, eight feet wide, from the bank into the farmer's fields. Joe Pike, ex-carpenter, with Davey, Miles and Saunders, constructed the sluice which was hammered into place at the end of the second day, with only two feet of solid bank remaining between it and the waters of the Gevora. Deakin hurried over to inspect.

"Right. 'Tis done, both rheen an' sluice. We'll open all tomorrow, 'tis too dark now. 'Spect other villagers will want to come. Seems like other fields could take the water as will be comin' through."

They began the walk back, with the farmhouse now more indistinct in the gloom, Davey and Saunders together and Saunders asked the question that had been uppermost in his mind for days.

"What do you reckon, John, to the way things is set up in that house."

Davey looked knowingly at his huge companion.

"Regardin' Consuela, no doubt."

There was no reply and so Davey continued.

"I'd be sayin' that she's the sister of the wife or the sister of the farmer. Nat Solomon saw her at the spring troughs and says that she don't wear no ring."

"No ring!"

"That's right, but be careful, Zeke. You get a complaint against you from the locals about messin' with their womenfolk and it can go hard. 'Tis not much short of lootin', especially if they decides to go for broke and call it rape or somesuch."

The harsh word caused Saunders to pause as they walked, but it was Davey who continued.

"Just be careful, Zeke, but I'd say you've caught her eye, and that's a fact."

Saunders let out a deep sigh.

"An' she've caught mine too, John, an' that's a fact."

The following day had two points of significance, firstly, the end of Mackinnon's prediction of the time period available to the French, which mattered not at all to the men, but what did matter to them, was the second point, the opening of the sluice. In the afternoon, after morning drill, the whole village gathered, with most of Three and the Light Company and all their Officers in attendance. Saunders and the farmer took a spade each and began to clear the last of the bank, lowering themselves into the water up to their knees to completely clear away the last of the soil and water flowed up against the sluice, which was now below the level of the water. That done, the last task was left to the farmer and his wife. The farmer used a lever on a peg in the sluice shaft to raise all up, this being Pike's design, and his wife inserted another peg to hold it up. At first all that came through was surplus mud and grass, then the Gevora poured steadily in. The farmer raised all up another peg and the flow became a flood. At this all around stood clapping and cheering as the water soon progressed to flow between the parched fields on either side and right up to those of their farmer. There was hand shaking and back slapping all around as the Redcoats dispersed, but the locals remained, to discuss the possibilities of the new supply of water, running far into their fields, hand gestures plainly indicating extra ditches. Deakin and his messmates, all with very satisfied looks on their faces, passed close by the farm and Consuela came running out with something in her hand. It was a human figure, made out of corn-stalks and she gave it to Saunders. He stopped to take it, saying 'gracias' many times, but she just gazed up, until Deakin called him on. He took the figure out of Saunders' hand.

"Seems like corn-dollies be somethin' what they makes yer, besides back home."

He then gave it back, but Davey had noticed the gift and was curious.

"A human figure! Could be a woman. Any meaning in that?"

Whilst Saunders continued to gaze at it in silence, Deakin shook his head.

"Blessed if I know, but there is one thing. She gave it to him, not no-one else!"

The day moved on and gathering clouds cut the daylight short, but Major Carr remained outside the good mood in camp, him now stood atop the Tower. He well knew that this was the last day of Mackinnon's prediction, which he shared, but the day was not done and he also feared a night attack. He was just making up his mind whether to go to the outlying picket now or after supper, when a Corporal sentry pointed out and off, far to the right.

"Sir. What's that?"

He was pointing to a new shape on the horizon, large and black, but it was changing as they watched. Carr took two steps to the telescope and trained it around to line it up. He was at the telescope, but then he stopped before he used it.

"Did you hear that?"

The Corporal looked at him.

"Sort of a rumble, Sir? But what called me to it was a flash, just now."

Carr nodded then studied the shape for a half-minute.

"Looks like smoke! You take a look Corporal."

The man did and studied the image for the same amount of time.

"Yes Sir. Smoke, now drifting away in the wind, but it's a fair size cloud."

"How far off would you say?"

"Hard to tell, Sir, but it has to be pushing on 20 miles."

Carr pulled a map out of a case resting against the battlement and he spread it open, to then look at the fast disappearing cloud.

"Pretty much due South."

He ran his finger down the map, past Elvas, then he stopped at the first and only significant town beyond that.

"It must be Olivenza! That's on his line. He's blown up Olivenza. He's on his way out! These bastard Johnnies are turning it in! Funked it, just like Mackinnon said."

oOo

Some form of conclusion dwelled in the mind of Lord Frederick Templemere as he hurried through the pleasant warmth of a London mid-morning, onto the gravel of Horse Guards, this crunching satisfactorily under his feet, the sound punctuated by the dropping of his brand-new silver topped cane, just before his right foot hit the surface. He had neither appointment nor invitation, but, in his mind, he was a Peer of the Realm and that gave him the right to call on any Civil Servant unannounced and whenever he chose. He entered the shadow of the classic portico of the Renaissance frontage and made for the tall, mirror-surface black door, for his progress to then be appallingly interrupted by the bayonetted muskets of the two giant Grenadier Guards on duty, this bringing Templemere to an abrupt halt. It was the Guards Sergeant who spoke first.

"What business have you here, Sir? If you please."

"No business of yours and I am a Member of the House of Lords. Allow me to pass. At once."

The muskets did not move, only the chin-strap of the Sergeant as he spoke yet more disrespectful words.

"Anyone could say that, Sir. Have you an appointment, Sir?"

Templemere had been brought to a halt in two ways, both physically and also plainly by lack of any prior arrangement. He was most discomfited by his assumptions being so thoroughly demolished, but he had no choice but to answer.

"No. I do not. However, I need to see Sir Henry Livermore on a very important matter."

The muskets still did not move.

"Very good, Sir. And you are, Sir?"

The more his status was denied, the more indignant Templemere became, his voice rising an octave, but, again, he was forced to answer this common soldier.

"Lord Frederick Templemere."

"Very good, Sir. I'll send in Appleby here to Mr. Wilson and we'll see where everything goes from there, Sir."

It was plain that the Guards Sergeant did not like Templemere at all and, for that fact alone, he was now seething. However, he was still forced to wait as Appleby turned to enter the deep shadow of the building, leaving the Guards Sergeant with his musket and gleaming bayonet still barring Templemere's way. The Sergeant stared down at him balefully, as though he were a thoroughly offensive recruit who had arrived on parade with a uniform at a most unsatisfactory standard. Appleby's words spoken in Livermore's outer office issued down the dark corridor, faint but audible, which did nothing to ease Templemere's mood.

"Mr. Wilson, Sir. We have a Lord Templemere outside. Can he come in? He says that he wishes to see the General."

The next sound, after some minutes, were footfalls in the corridor and the odious Wilson appeared, followed by the Guardsman. At the sight of him Templemere began to shout.

"Wilson! This is appalling. I demand to see Livermore!"

The lugubrious Wilson, black in every part, bar his white collar and cuffs, came to a halt, but his expression of calm disdain did not change one iota.

"Allow him through, Sergeant."

"Yes Sir. Very good, Sir. Go in, Lord Templemere, if you please."

The bayonet was withdrawn and Templemere stepped inside, still seething, now having been given permission from a mere Sergeant. As they passed each other, the returning Appleby broke wind, which caused Templemere to turn in double annoyance at the undoubted insult, but by now Wilson was far ahead. With ten more strides Templemere arrived at Wilson's domain, just as the huge clock, taller than either Grenadier, struck eleven. The thunderous chimes booming out, caused Wilson to simply indicate Livermore's inner door and the unspoken permission, somewhat contemptuous, prevented Templemere from venting his spleen, at least some of it, on Wilson. Templemere had no choice, but to enter the door indicated and he strode through, to find Livermore extending his hand in greeting, the first gesture of respect he had received since arriving.

"Good-day, Lord Fred. Sorry about the security, but we are at war, you understand, and everything thereto is a bit, ah, in the balance, as it were."

Templemere, still in a state of great agitation, did not take his hand, instead he took a chair, and he sat, with an ostentatious, ill-tempered flourish of his coat-tails as he sat. Livermore remained standing for a moment.

"Please sit down, Lord Fred. Now what is your business with me?"

Templemere had a full spleen to vent.

"You know damn well, Livermore! The last time you and I had a conversation, my name was being dragged into a conspiracy to provide information to the French. We parted with each of us promising to keep our eyes and ears open and myself to do my best to dredge my memory of our visit. Our visit, please bear in mind, to the Peninsula. I have some items which may help. What have you?"

"Nothing as yet, Lord Fred. At least not here in London. Waters is out there, rummaging around, he may yet come up with something. Which we'll know when he gets home."

Templemere felt better. He was winning.

"Well, whilst you have nothing, I do have something!"

He allowed the words to echo around the room.

"I have remained mindful of the question facing us."

Livermore nodded and sat forward, elbows on the desk, hands under his chin.

"Pleased to hear it, Lord Fred. What do you have?"

Templemere leaned forward slightly himself, one hand on Livermore's desk.

"It concerns Mahon. I should have said the last time. His household speaks nothing but French to each other, that for one, and for two, he is a devout Catholic, and this is the point, he expressed an interest in the village churches whilst we were there. I accompanied him into a couple, but then he rode off alone, and I can only assume he visited two or three more. He spent as much time alone as anyone. Finally, now that I have given it some thought, before we went out to Spain, he was a bit short of a shekel or two."

Livermore looked at him calmly.

"And now?"

Templemere sat back.

"Well. I've heard no more on that subject. From him."

Silence settled as Livermore sat thinking and Templemere sat bathing in self-congratulation. The clock in Wilson's office chimed the quarter-hour. Finally, Livermore placed both hands on his desk and pushed himself to his feet.

"Very good, Lord Fred. All you have said is very much grist to our mill. When Waters returns, we'll put it all through the stones, as it were, and see what comes out."

He offered his hand, which, this time, Templemere grasped.

"Thank you for your time, Lord Fred. If you have any more thoughts, then do drop by. Get Wilson to give you a note before you go, to help you get through the door next time. Unlike this time."

Templemere's face clouded as the memory returned, but the shadow soon passed when he later stood over Wilson's desk, having given this odious and disrespectful mere Civil Servant a clear order to write out the letter, which was duly penned and handed over. Livermore heard all and registered the tone, which annoyed him more than a little, but he said nothing and waited until the clock struck the half-hour. Then he levered himself upright again and hurried through Wilson's office. He was sure that, by now, Templemere would have disappeared, off to his Club or somewhere similar.

"I'm off to Great Smith Street, Benjamin. I'll not return today."

With that he took his hat and cane and made for the outer door, but he did not pass through without a comment to the Grenadiers.

"Good job, boys!"

At his coming, the two had presented arms in perfect unison, but the Sergeant mumbled his thanks at the compliment, as Livermore headed for the sunshine. A fifteen-minute walk found him ascending the stairs of the premises in Great Smith Street and then through the door of Waters office. There he found Radipole at his desk.

"Is there anyone with him?"

Radipole put down his pen and sat upright.

"No Sir."

"Right. With me."

Both entered to find Colonel Waters, not in Spain, but at his desk poring over a map. He stood immediately at Livermore's entrance, but Livermore had no time for niceties.

"Sit, both of you."

With both settled, he looked from one to the other.

"I've just had Templemere with me, spinning some stuff about Mahon. That his family speaks nothing but French in their household, that he roamed around the Fuentes area, alone, looking at churches, which is an interest of his and that, before we left, he was short of a bob or two. What do we have?"

Waters turned to Radipole, who opened the folder he had brought with him, it always remaining atop his desk.

"All three bank with Coutts. I have a contact there, he was with me at Cambridge. On Hopgood, no marked change in his financial affairs for some time. On Mahon, but two weeks ago he took out a loan for £300 pounds. On Templemere, no real change, bankwise, but he continues to gamble and for higher stakes than usual, so I am told, by my own acquaintances of the tables. The races also, as has been observed by our men."

Livermore looked hard at Waters.

"So, Mahon was short of finance before Albuera and still is. He must be, who'd borrow that amount with interest rates as high they are and they'll not fall whilst Boney is in the middle of Prussia and Austria's just declared herself bankrupt. Hopgood, no change, you say, so the only change being with Templemere? Upping the stakes at the tables! So, here's the question, is this a man secure in his own finances and content to risk heavy loss gambling? And why all the dirt on Mahon? Another question, is that an attempt to divert our attention? So, Radipole, see just how much of an interest this 'Churches' thing is. Waters? You're just back, what do you have?"

Colonel Waters nodded.

"The Peer has other concerns right now, such as what is Soult going to do at Elvas? I spent much time on that, but I did ride around the Almeida area, where you were and, as we identified last time, there's only three places where a meeting or a message exchange could happen. North to South; Barba del Puerco, then the ford, if it can be flattered as such, below Seranillo, where, if you haven't broken your neck getting down, you'll drown trying to cross, and finally the village of Carpio de Azaba on the main road between Villar Formosa and Cuidad. I'd say the first and the last are most favoured, but a ride to Carpio would have taken all day. Also, to finally scotch the civilian thing, none could have got through, in my opinion. That was our de facto front line and heavily patrolled."

Livermore shook his head.

"None of the three was away all day, ever, which takes out the Carpio place.!"

Radipole sat upright.

"Forgive me, Sirs, but are we sure that the information was delivered in the locality of Almeida? Could it have been discovered elsewhere and delivered elsewhere?

Livermore scratched his head.

"You may be right, apart from two things. Spain is a God-awful place to get around and so the general information that Wellington's main effort was to be on the Almeida to Fuentes line was only to be gathered there and could not have spread so very far, as soon as that became clear in anyone's mind, including Wellington's, at Cuidad itself. I'd say four days before it could arrive with Soult by any other route, too late to make any difference to him at Cuidad. Any message had to be got over there, and not by some roundabout route, if he was going to react in time to do himself any good, almost certainly the movement of Godinot. Second, the only place where anyone could gain any inkling that his main effort was to be in the Cuidad corridor, was there, at that place, as I've said. I suspect that whoever it was, looked around, listened to gossip, stuck his finger in the wind and decided that our main force would remain in the North. He then sent the letter or whatever and got lucky, because he was right."

Livermore paused to think and consider the logic of what was possible or not.

"Soult wrote his letter on the 19th to order Godinot South. I don't see how the information causing that could have arrived from any other area of Spain. Everything points to the letter to Soult, from our informant, being written on the Almeida to Fuentes line and crossing there."

However, Radipole was not satisfied.

"What about the Commisariat, Sir, back in Lisbon and Oporto? Could they have been told something by someone, which generated Soult's order, such as extra supplies to the North, because that will remain the bigger army? I'm sorry to be so pedantic over this, Sir, but it is possible."

Livermore nodded.

"It's alright, you are asking the right questions, but I cannot see how what you suggest is possible. Divisions put in requisitions for supplies, because they know the size of their musters. More being sent to Cuidad rather than elsewhere, does not come from Wellington. Because that's where I'm going to invade, so get more supplies North."

He sat back and sighed.

"What do you think. Waters?"

The face of the Intelligence Officer became stern. He looked from one to the other before giving his judgment.

"You both know the game we are in. It's all probabilities and conjecture. The most likely, I say most, is that the information that Soult acted on was concluded at the Almeida-Fuentes line. It was written between the 15th and the 19th and it crossed over at Barba del Puerco. Who was it, is our question. One of your party, Livermore, is clearly possible, but there were plenty of Spanish and Portuguese around at that time, who could have strong sympathies for France. Napoleon does have a Spanish Division in his army and there are plenty of Portuguese sympathisers!"

Waters took a deep breath before voicing his conclusion.

"We can do no more than watch Templemere and Mahon and await more information from Spain. What makes me favour Templemere is the fact that he keeps trying to pile suspicion onto Mahon. Whatever, I want this traitor, because that's what he is! He may do something of the like again and because of what he did do, a lot of good men lost their lives."

oOo

Cornets Peterson and Carr splashed through the ford of the Gevora, this inside the long bend of Peterson's first patrol.

"How many times have we done this now? It used to be out of bounds!"

Peterson grinned.

"Don't know. Lost count. It must be at least half a dozen by now."

Johnson had made him Senior, for now, in preference to Carr, because, "He has a better idea of the length of his nose and where to put it!", but Carr had no concerns. Peterson had more experience and always seemed to talk good sense. Carr had also noticed that Baxter, as Squadron Senior Sergeant, seemed to take no issue with Peterson's decisions, which most effectively confirmed the Cornet as Acting Squadron Commander.

"On top, I could ride this with my eyes closed. I know it by heart and it doesn't get less boring. Cross the Gevora to meet another river, the Zapaton. Ride the bank until we see a Church tower on a hill. Ride West 'till you come to another river. Ride down it to Ouguela and home. Look for French, all the while."

They were over the Gevora, but now the humour was gone.

"Have we seen any French. No! Not anywhere. Yet I'm ordered to keep the Squadron together, in case we meet any French incursion. If we could split into Troops, we could do less riding and do more watching."

Carr sighed and looked at his friend.

"Well, we don't meet anyone, including guerrillas. They're brave chaps, right enough, but what they do to their prisoners is appalling. I prefer not to be reminded, when I see the trophies tied to their saddles and their horses' mains and tails. It seems they've claimed the far bank of the Gevora, which is why we see so little of any of them."

"Well, guerrillas saved your bacon a while back, so don't be too hard. This is as nasty and vicious a war as any that our noble nation has ever been involved in."

Carr perked up.

"Yes. We must look on the bright side. What we are required to do whilst conducting it, is good for the horses!"

Later that day, looking on the bright side was paramount in the 'mile picket', as it had come to be known, of the 105th, this now being manned by Davey, Saunders, Pike, Miles, Solomon, Bailey and Byford, with Sergeant Ethan Ellis in command. As usual Miles was complaining, but he had chosen his moment whilst Ellis and Davey were out of earshot, both now sharing the telescope on something that had their attention.

"How many more damn days have we got to hang about down yer. And 'tis usually us, as has to take the watch, out in this hole in the ground."

Saunders, as usual had the answer.

"You give me out here anytime. There's worse! A lot worse. You'd rather we was back in camp, going through endless drill, kit inspections, uniform inspections, weapon inspections and anything else that the Officers can dream up, anything rather than let us sit quiet and content around our own tents."

He allowed the words to sink in, but Miles did have an answer.

"Well, out yer, there's not too much time left for you to spend time with your new Spanish acquaintance!"

Saunders was unmoved.

"Oh, that comes around often enough."

Byford had sat listening.

"What's your intention? There?"

Saunders took off his shako and rubbed his sleeve across his brow.

"I don't know. I don't want us parted and that's stating it plain. Soon we'll be off out, so, I either stays, or she comes with us."

Byford sat up.

"Stay means desert! The Provos will be onto you and that'll mean the rope. The only alternative, for you, is that she comes with us, meaning you."

Tom Miles now imparted his worldly wisdom.

"An' they don't do 'Follower Wives'. Not out 'ere. 'Tis either proper spliced or nothin'!"

Byford nodded.

"He's right. It would need a proper marriage for her to take up with us, Bridie and Nellie and all. How can she know how tough it is, to be a Follower? And what about the farmer? What's he going to say?"

Saunders took a deep breath, which came out as a sigh. He was in a quandary as to what to do.

"Well, as far as I can make out, he's her brother-in-law. She's the sister of the wife. I suppose he has a say, but 'tis her Father and Mother as counts the most, but I've no idea where they are. The old crone is the farmer's Mother."

More worldly wisdom from Miles.

"Could be the farmer just looks on her as another mouth to feed. The Mother too! She could be thinkin' the same."

"That's possible, with four already born."

"Well Zeke, you have to make your mind up, either ask her, or let it go. She'll not come with you without a ring on her finger, of that I'm sure. She's a devout Catholic, I'm sure of that also, which can cause other problems, but then, so are Bridie and Nellie, so that will help there, if she joins our Mess."

"He's right, Zeke. We'll not be here much longer. Johnny's buggered off or thrown in the towel for this time being. Soon, we'll be on our way back up North, that's my guess."

It was Byford who threw in the dampener.

"There's another thing. For her to come along as a Follower, wife or not, you need the Colonel's permission. Without that, there's no point asking. Gibney will go in for you. But that's where you start."

Silence fell and they left Saunders to ponder his fate. However, the silence did not last long as Ellis and Davey returned and Miles made his usual blunt enquiries.

"So you saw what?"

Ellis returned the telescope to its support, which was merely a pile of sandbags.

"Just cavalry, probably ours. We couldn't tell, what with theirs and ours having much the same fancy uniforms, but I'd say they were ours. Put it in the log, John."

Byford opened the book, picked up the pencil and began writing, but first he looked at his watch, a present in his mid-teens from his Grandfather. He had barely written the time, 2.30pm, before Miles noticed movement and pointed, back and to their right.

"Well here comes some more cavalry and I hopes to Christ that they'm ours!"

Ellis seized the telescope and turned to focus on the approaching horsemen, now less than half a mile away. He soon put everyone at ease.

"16th Dragoons. They've been riding around these parts for almost all the time we've been here. They must be as cheesed off as we are!"

Within ten minutes Peterson's and Carr's Squadron trotted past, soon to reach their own camp and the eight saw their own Relief party from the Second Company trudging their way out towards them. Once on their way back, Saunders had made up his mind.

"I'm going to ask her."

"When?" came from several directions.

"One evening soon."

"Where?", came from the nosey Miles.

"There's a seat in the square where we meet. Seems that's alright, because with all the neighbours being around things is kept proper, as they likes it around here. But only if the Colonel says it's alright. I can't marry her and then march off, taking her with us without his say so."

Byford was walking beside him.

"Right. So, if you're going to ask her, you're going to need the right words. I'll see what I can do."

However, the first words that mattered, were spoken late that afternoon, by Cyrus Gibney to Colonel Lacey in his office inside the castle, with both of the 105th Colours propped against the wall behind him. Padraigh O'Hare was also present. Permission to enter having been gained by Sergeant Bryce, Gibney was stood rigidly to attention, waiting for his Colonel to address him, but it was not long coming.

"You wish to see me, Sergeant-Major."

"Yes Sir, It concerns one of the men, Sir, Corporal Ezekiel Saunders. He wants permission to marry, Sir. A local girl."

Lacey sat back, looking puzzled.

"He can marry whomsoever he likes. He needs no permission from me."

Gibney cleared his throat.

"Ah yes, Sir, but if he marries her, he'd like to bring her along as a Follower, Sir. We, he, needs your permission for that. Sir."

Lacey looked at O'Hare.

"Saunders? Do you know him?"

"I do. A good soldier and a Devil in a fight. A good wrestler too."

Lacey nodded.

"What's the position with Followers."

O'Hare thought for a second.

"We've lost a few. Disease, casualties at Fuentes, and two just walked off. One went off with a local. There's room for more on the Roster. They all play their part to make us effective; cooking, mending and caring for the wounded."

Lacey looked at Gibney.

"Is he there?"

"He is, Sir. Just outside."

"Bring him in."

After much shouting, stamping and spinning on heels, Saunders marched in, came to the attention and saluted. Lacey studied him.

"So, you want to marry a local girl Saunders?"

"Yes Sir."

"Have you asked her yet?"

"No Sir. Seems pointless to marry her and then march off to leave her behind, if she can't come with us. Sir."

"Hmmm. Would she be part of the family whose fields we irrigated a few days ago?"

"Yes Sir. She's the sister-in-law of that farmer, Sir."

Lacey looked at O'Hare, who nodded, then Lacey looked at Saunders.

"Go ahead and ask, Corporal. She can join us if she wishes, as a Follower. And good luck to you!"

"Thank you, Sir."

Both NCOs saluted and marched out, but, outside, Gibney had something of his own to ask.

"How will you tell her what her life is going to be like? Remember what it was like on the way back to Corunna."

"I'll do my best and if she hates it, she can come back home and be the sister-in-law again. I'll not stop her."

Gibney nodded, almost sadly, and Saunders hurried away, back to his camp. As the news was divulged around their campfire and Saunders and Byford went off for their tutorial, Nellie and Bridie, with Eirin too, could hardly contain their excitement, Bridie tugging at Jed Deakin's sleeve.

"So he's going to ask this Consuela? Where?"

Deakin looked at her sternly.

"In the market square, but don't you go sitting on the other side, like some crowd at a fairground attraction. You give the man some air. This has to be done careful."

"But Jed, we want to see."

Deakin's face remained stern.

"Well, up on the wall of the Castle, you can look down into the Square. We can get you up there, but you keeps quiet!"

After the evening meal, Saunders stood ready for inspection, his uniform as bright and his buttons as shiny as could be managed. Nellie gave the final word.

"Well, I'd marry you, if I didn't have me own eejit husband in the way!"

With the laughter at Henry Nicholls expense sounding in his ears, Saunders marched off and all went in a different direction to enter the Castle and ascend the walls. When they arrived, Saunders and Consuela were already sat together, with Saunders doing all the talking, doing his best with the words that Byford had taught him, most often using his hands to help. Finally, she nodded, about four times, Saunders looked astonished, then he grinned. At that, they both stood up and disappeared around the corner which would lead to her brother-in-law's house. Bridie turned to Jed.

"That was a good sign, Jed, was it not? Them both going off together?"

"I'd say it was, but it looks like, to me, that they've gone off for a talk with the family. We'll have to wait."

They did, for about 30 minutes, then Saunders re-appeared alone. His face blank, if in shock or in sadness, they could not tell. He disappeared down the alley that led to the water-trough and all hurried down the battlement steps and back to their camp. There they found Saunders, sat by the fire. They hurried on, Nellie arriving first.

"Well?"

Saunders looked up, with a half-smile, but not one of joy, more of resignation.

"She said yes, but it has to be in their Church, and we went to see the local Priest to ask for a quick job."

He paused and took a deep breath.

"And he said no. Too quick."

Miles walked forward and looked at Bailey, Miles' fellow scavenger and of an equally reprehensible character.

"What's in the kitty?"

Bailey thought for a second.

"A decent haul. About 20 dollars, 30 silver buttons and eight silver buckles. Several rings. We did well from Fuentes."

Miles turned to Saunders.

"Right. Tomorrow we'll go see this Vicar. You, me and Byford."

With the arrival of full daylight, the three filed in. The Church was dark, dusty and reeked of incense, both old and new. It was plain that some early morning confession was in progress and the they waited until all had been shriven and emerged mumbling their penance. Then Miles and Byford crammed into the confessional, whilst Saunders remained outside, but close. By now the Priest was almost comatose from the unvarying ritual so early in the day and so he sat slumped behind the screen, waiting for the Portuguese words for, "Forgive me, Father, for I have sinned." Instead he had Miles knocking on the screen and Byford speaking something very different.

"Consuela Peyroteo. Case-se amanhã. Soldado inglês"

179

Something stirred behind the screen.

"Não. É muito rápido. Eles devem esperar o momento adequado."

Byford turned to Miles.

"He said no!"

"I guessed that. Say some more."

Byford took a deep breath.

"Soldados ingleses sair muito em breve."

"What did you say?"

"I told him that English soldiers will leave soon."

Miles felt into the kitty bag, for five silver buttons and two silver buckles. He lined them up in the space at the bottom of the screen and Byford said his piece.

"Para os pobres, Señor."

'Money for the poor' had no effect.

"Não. É muito rápido."

Miles found five more buttons and added them to the row, plus three dollarcoins. A thin hand came through the aperture to take the valuables but Miles seized a finger and held it tight.

"Amanha? Yes?"

The voice spoke, through what was probably no small amount of pain.

"Sim. Amanha. A tres horas."

Byford grinned in the gloom.

"He said yes, tomorrow, at 3 o' clock."

Miles released the finger and the silver collection was scooped up by two boney hands, whilst Miles delivered his verdict, spoken close to the screen.

"Don't you let us find you out alone, you bloody chiselin', double-bent, old Devil Dodger!"

The three hurried out of the Church, Saunders parting company with them to go to Consuela's house, Byford and Miles back to camp carrying the news. For the rest of that day and the following morning, in between duties, drill, guarding, on watch and being inspected, the group prepared for the wedding, mostly cleaning, washing and mending. At the due time, 2.45, the Bridegroom's side of the small Church was filled with Redcoats and Followers, whilst on the Bride's side were her family and some friends and neighbours. Saunders, sat at the front with Bestman Byford, asked the standard question.

"Have you got the ring?"

"Yes."

"Where did you get it?"

"The kitty bag. There was a smallish one. Miles was sure it will do."

"Miles! Well there's the kiss of death for that! It was off some battlefield, I suppose."

"Don't ask! What matters is that it has a better purpose now."

Consuela was late, by 20 minutes but she proceeded up the aisle on the arm of her Brother-in-Law. Saunders turned to look and the warm, loving smile that came over his face moved the Followers immediately to tears. The cadaverous Priest, dark eyed and disapproving, stood in Vestments that seemed no better than worn second-hand and also too big for his penitential frame, but, by rote, he took them through the ceremony. He kept it brief, there was no Communion, merely the repeating of words that Saunders did his best to remember and pronounce as they were spoken to him. Then the Priest spoke, with little solemnity, the final words that mattered.

"Eu os declaro marido e mulher."

The Portuguese began clapping and cheering and at the realisation of what the words meant, the British joined in, for the couple to then progress back down the aisle. Outside, was the best surprise, the villagers had laid on a Wedding Breakfast, assembled whilst the ceremony was taking place. All sat and the food arrived, all Portuguese dishes, but Miles looked askance at one.

"Is this bloody sheep's eyes?"

Deakin leaned forward.

"No, it b'ain't and if t'were, then you still bloody well eats it! Won't do you no harm. Wash it down with the good vino laid on."

"Tis all very different to what Bridie makes!"

"And where's the surprise in that? She's Irish, not Portuguese. Get it inside you. Moanin' sod!"

Miles did as he was told and he found it palatable, as were the subsequent dishes. Then came the speeches, if they could be flattered as such. Byford stood up to make the toast.

"Salud, boa sorte para Consuela and Zeke."

They all drank, after which Saunders stood up to stumble over his words of thanks.

"Obrigado por sua ajuda e boa vontade"

Nobody minded and then the dancing began, all of it communal with the Redcoats making a horrible mess of the moves but the wine and the evident good-will from one side to the other, all added to the enjoyment and the bursts of genuine laughter. The highlight of the evening, however, was Consuela, to the accompaniment of two guitars, an accordion and her own castanets and hard shoes, dancing a fandango, which had the Redcoats spellbound and Zeke Saunders in a trance of admiration. Lacey and O'Hare had come to the festivities to take a drink and try some local food, but mostly to wish Saunders and his new wife every happiness. It was all very formal, until Consuela whisked Lacey off for a dance, at which O'Hare could not stop himself from laughing.

"That's some wife you've got there Corporal!"

The trance had returned to Saunders' eyes.

"I'll not argue with you over that, Sir."

The evening broke up with much back-slapping and hand-shakes, for the couple to finally retire to a room prepared for them in the Castle. Then, in the dead of night, with the sentry at the road gate already briefed and bribed, Miles and Bailey inched their way into the town and around the back of the Priest's house. A dog barked once, but Miles fed it some salt beef and a bone and it was thereby quelled, whilst Bailey eased open the small back window to the Priest's dwelling. That done, he listened for some minutes to reassuring silence, then both eased themselves inside to look first in the bedroom, to find it empty and the bed unused. Another three minutes of easing around doors proved the house to be empty and then the search began, which, when they opened a box by the Priest's bed, retrieved all the buttons and buckles, but of the dollars there was no sign.

oOo

Chapter Six

Once More the North

"So, this is Castello Branco? A bit of a hole, but I'd rather this, than a trek over the Sierra de Gata, even with the season in our favour. And talking of favour, in its alternative meaning, I do hope this place improves with further acquaintance."

The pair of Cornets were riding side by side, but it was Peterson who, having the greater experience of Spain, was best placed to make comparative statements. Castello Branco began on its outskirts with dwellings that resembled not much more than a hole in the ground, as did most small Spanish towns, then on to dwellings composed of whole, or parts of, carts, carriages and stolen fencing, then wooden hovels and cottages, until finally came those of the centre, which were of good stone and mainly of Moorish origin. Both friends were in the centre of Stapleton-Cotton's Cavalry Division, the column being Slade's mixed Brigade at the front, Anson's Light 16th and 14th in the centre, and Alten's Light Brigade in the rear. They had left the Elvas to Ouguela line two days after the infantry and had now caught up with Picton's Third Division and Campbell's Sixth. However, it was perhaps Carr who had a better head for strategy and manoeuvre.

"What puzzles me is the fact that we are allowed a free passage North by the French, who only a week ago greatly outnumbered us and yet here we are now, wandering on as if merely enjoying some kind of leisurely Grand Tour."

Peterson grinned.

"You have no cause for complaint. This is equally as educating, far more exciting and it costs us nothing. In fact, we get paid to do this, from time to time that is, but your point about marching North, unhindered, at a leisurely pace does somewhat show you up as a bit of a Johnny Newcome. You see, Spain, being more mountains than flat, has only two areas that count, militarily that is. The Southern corridor guarded by Badajoz and Elvas, and the Northern, guarded by Cuidad Rodrigo and Almeida. There is, was, another citadel between those last two called Fort Conception, but Crauford blew that up in the year 10, to stop the French from using it. It is only in those two areas that anything of real military significance can take place."

Carr's face became blank.

"Thank-you for the lesson, all points well taken, pleased to have raised the subject, but as we speak, my major concerns are stiff legs, a parched throat and a stomach protesting at its emptiness."

They were entering what could be described as the 'wooden' or middle ring, the shanties were now behind them, and, to mildly add to their level of interest, they were overtaking a column of infantry, the steady rhythm of their feet matched by the rise and fall of their back-packs, topped with a swaying blanket. What next came to Carr's notice was the bright green of their collars and cuffs, which caused him to speak out loud.

"I think that's my brother's Regiment, just ahead."

He turned to Peterson, at that time his Commanding Officer.

"If my brother is just ahead, do I have your permission to fall out for a few minutes?"

Peterson looked at him and grinned.

"Of course! As your Superior, I grant you permission, of course."

Some hundreds of yards ahead, Carr Senior was marching, as was his wont, at the head of the Light Company, beside Captain Nathaniel Drake and Lieutenant Stuart Maltby. All three were hot, tired and longing for the Midday break. They had been on the road from Ouguela for five days and rumour had it, that their time at Castello would be a prolongued stay. Conversation was limited with both Carr and Drake thinking about their wives and their letters to them, albeit both now somewhat delayed, whilst Maltby's head was full of a whole polyglot of thoughts that ranged from his chances of promotion, to his next choice amongst the Followers. This required very little thought; he was thoroughly taken with Saunders new wife. However, the reveries of each was thoroughly interrupted by a cavalryman dismounting at their side, whom Carr immediately recognised, but it was the cavalryman spoke first.

"Hello, brother of mine. Sorry I could not drop by sooner."

Carr's face lit up. Here was probably the only male member of their family who would utter more than two polite sentences in his direction.

"Willoughby! You do look well. I'd like to say that campaigning suits you. A healthier complexion, but you are definitely thinner."

He slapped him on the shoulder and then remembered his manners

"You have not met my two companions here."

He dropped back a step to enable each to see the other.

"Captain Nathaniel Drake and Lieutenant Stuart Maltby."

Young Carr reached across and shook the hand of both.

"Your servant, Sirs."

"And yours!"

This last was returned in unison, but Elder Carr had his own question, this was, after all, his own flesh and blood.

"Well, come on! What's happened to you? All that we were doing back on that line was peering through a variety of telescopes, watching you and your sort exercising your horses. Anything to report?"

Young Carr grinned.

"Yes. I was captured!"

Three heads turned abruptly towards him, but it was his brother who spoke.

"Captured! How? How did you get away?"

He took a deep breath.

"Well. I was ordered up to the river to get a better look at some village on the far side. A bit close I thought, but orders are orders. Then there was some gunfire behind us and French Hussars cut us off. We were being escorted away as prisoners, but guerrillas rescued us and turned our escort into our own prisoners. That's about it, really."

What was close to shock registered on the face of each of his audience and so he disconsolately half withdrew his sword.

"Lost my Clingenthal, a French Officer took it, but got this one instead. If anything, I like it better."

Carr had recovered.

"Were you alone? You said 'we'."

"Yes. Two of my Troop were with me. Corporal Makepeace and Trooper Spivey. They were rescued too."

"Who gave you that order? To get that close?"

"Captain Tavender."

Carr's face darkened and he exchanged a knowing look with Drake, but at that moment Colonel Withers rode up and reined in his horse besides the group, but looked straight at Cornet Carr.

"Get back up with your men. We may be riding straight on to Sabugal. Nothing's certain as yet, but I need you with them."

Cornet Carr immediately reached for his saddle, but his brother held his shoulder for a moment.

"If you're still in this place, we'll speak some more. I'll come to you, the rank allows me to roam a bit more."

Carr nodded and swung himself up into the saddle. He waved to Drake and Maltby, who nodded back and then he was gone. Carr looked at Drake.

"Because of a Tavender order he was captured and it was only God's own luck that he got out of it."

Drake thought it best to be consoling.

"There may be nothing in it. You don't know of any malevolent intent on Tavender's part. Your brother was ordered forward, nothing wrong in that, but he got a bit too close. He is a bit green, still!"

Carr's mouth became a grim slit.

183

"If the orders came from anyone else, I shrug it off as part of the chances we all take, but it was Tavender, and that rings the alarm bells. There is more to be said and more to be found out."

At that moment orders were being shouted to halt the column. They were not being allowed into the centre of the town, the men were to disperse into the fields and the Officers to use the buildings such as were available, but Carr remained on the road as the column broke up and the men moved rightwards into their allotted fields. Carr always obeyed Lacey's central tenet and enforced it himself with the Officers of his Wing of the Battalion, 'First, your men!'. Thus, he would not allow any Officer to sidle off to their own tent, barn or house, without first checking on the situation of their men. This required Maltby to take himself to the mess of Corporal Saunders and Chosen Man Davey, who were, as usual, close neighbours of the mess of Colour Sergeant Deakin and Sergeant Nicholls. At his approach, the atmosphere immediately became strained as the men and their Followers began their arrangements outside their freshly erected tents. Bridie Mulcahy looked daggers at him, but she could say nothing and he chose to say nothing to her. In any case, his first concern was for the nearby men in his Section, led by Saunders and Davey, which was where he began.

"Davey! Is all well? Is there anything you need?"

"No Sir, apart from where we gets our rations from. We've been sayin' to each other that we hope there's a supply of some sort waiting for us here, Sir. In this place."

Maltby tried to be cheery and matter-of-fact, even though, sat on the dry grass, but yards away was Eirin cradling his own son. However, these he ignored and he turned to Saunders.

"Saunders! The same to you. Is all well?"

"Yes Sir. Only I have the same question, Sir. About rations."

"Well, I know little more than you, but I'll inform Sergeant Ellis when I have found an answer and he will tell you, I'm sure."

The cheery countenance was maintained.

"And how is your new wife? Coping well with the rigours of the march I hope?"

"I've heard nothing that sounds like a complaint. Sir. We're both getting better at the language, Sir, I'm picking up bits of Portuguese and she's picking up bits of English. Sir. We're gettin' by, Sir."

Maltby nodded.

"Pleased to hear it."

However, at that moment Consuela entered the area, with an armful of firewood and dried grass. Maltby turned towards her and saluted.

"Mrs. Saunders. I hope all is well with you?"

To Consuela, all Officers were automatically aristocracy, well above her social station. She dropped her load, lowered her gaze and curtsied, using the Portuguese for 'Highness'.

"Yes, Alteza. Is good."

Maltby leaned forward just enough to meet her eyes.

"Pleased to hear it!"

He turned to her husband.

"If I can help, Saunders, I'll make myself available"

With that he marched off, leaving Bridie and Nellie exchanging angry looks. They had no quarrel with Consuela, she carried her load and more, did her chores, helped with the cooking and gave no complaint, in any language. Also, and equally important, she was a good Catholic. It was Bridie who spoke first.

"I bet he will! He's found another subject for his dirty eyes! Not a word to Eirin from the gombeen, sat there with his own flesh and blood, but he'd been creeping round her not more than two months previous."

They both studied Consuela protectively. They liked her and Zeke Saunders was one of their own. Nellie sidled up to him.

"You saw the look he gave her."

Saunders nodded. His face severe.

"I did!"

"There's more grease in that one than a barrel of lard!"

oOo

Nat Drake entered the main downstairs room of their billet, to find his Major Carr sat at the table, poring over some documents. Drake took a glance and then turned away to fill a beaker from the bucket of water set on the dresser at the side. He took one gulp and then spoke.

"I thought for one reckless moment that those papers formed the bulk of a letter home. Obviously, a flight of fancy on my part."

Carr slid his own beaker across the table which Drake dutifully filled.

"No, and on that subject, I got a letter off yesterday. These are estimates of expected rations for the next quarter. Now finished."

He stuffed the documents into a leather satchel and drank from the beaker, but it was Drake who spoke.

"What of your brother and Tavender?"

Carr pre-occupied himself with the straps on the satchel.

"I've thought of little else, in my spare moments, but until I hear or find out more, I feel there is very little I can do. There is no evidence that Tavender sent my brother into a bad hole, that would be his riposte, and he would be right. I cannot say anything to the effect of 'if anything happens to my brother and you're involved, something bad will happen to you'. Threats like that will get me court-martialled!"

He held the satchel upright with both hands.

"But he's at the back of something! Of that I'm certain. He ordered Willoughby deep into Johnny's bailiwick and then there's gunfire to alert any Johnnies there roundabout. Tavender's a deep cove. He moves carefully, not like that noodle of a cocks-comb Templemere!"

Drake grinned as Carr stood up and cheered up, speaking more positively.

"Anyway, Willoughby is doing alright. I had a quick word with his Major, Johnson I believe, and they're pleased with him. He helped Ramsey get out of that scrape at Fuentes and brought in some prisoners to Campo Maior who gave up some useful stuff."

The satchel went over his shoulder.

"You do deeds like that and you make enemies. If only from jealousy, which would certainly apply to the likes of Tavender."

At that moment, the very same subject was exercising the mind of one Senior Sergeant of Horse, Septimus Baxter, as he groomed down his horse in company of Corporal Jim Makepeace and Trooper Len Spivey. He had been mulling over the incident at Valdebotoa. He had no particular affection for Cornet Carr, nor any particular dislike of Captain Tavender, both were burdensome Officers, the former he had to school himself. However, if Tavender was scheming to render harm unto Cornet Carr, then, just as with the case in question, it could mean himself and his good comrades being sent into danger, just to give a better appearance to it all. Everything he had learned from Makepeace and Spivey, both now close by, increased his suspicion, these facts being that no serious French force could be seen anywhere near the village they'd been sent to look at, they had been sent too far forward and some gunfire from behind had alerted the French. Something was wrong and he did not like it. He continued subconsciously brushing his horse's flank, whilst considering the possibilities.

However, with all that in the background, the final two weeks of July gave much opportunity for a Carr family reunion, with Young Carr and Peterson, often dining with the Light Company Officers. The most common topic of conversation was conjecture over Wellington's next move. Two facts were more than rumour, that a powerful siege train had been landed at Oporto and that Julian Sanchez had cut off Cuidad Rodrigo from Salamanca. The rumour was that the French were scattered along the border and would not be troubling them for some time. At the final meal, Cornet Peterson gave the reason why this would be the last of their pleasant social gatherings.

"Tomorrow, we're away! Two from our Division are to watch the passes East of here. One from Slade's Brigade, his 1st Dragoons, and one from ours, namely us!"

Drake turned towards him in surprise.

"Passes! What passes? There can't be anything worth a damn through the mountains East of us!"

It was Elder Carr who answered.

"I think we can assume that there are, passes of some degree, that is, or more like the odd mouse-hole that a string of emaciated mules could squeeze through. So, dear cavalrymen, welcome to the most of what soldiering is, for both of you. Sat watching and waiting."

However, in his mind he was not at ease. Here was yet more opportunity for Tavender to send Willoughby into peril, bar one thing.

"Do you not have your own Captain yet, of your Squadron?"

Peterson cheered up.

"Yes we do! A Captain Oakwood. He's come to us from the 11th on Stapleton-Cotton's orders. He's moved over and a Cornet moved up. He's a bit of a veteran, so we've been told. A good solid chap. We both think we're lucky."

Elder Carr relaxed. Seniority would be about equal, giving little opportunity for Tavender to give orders to an Officer with markedly less experience. He also cheered up and raised his glass.

"Well, give you joy for your posting to a mountain spa. I hope that both the air and the waters agree with you. We also are on the move, up to the Agueda again with, if memory serves, the 14th of your Brigade and Slade's KGL Hussars, to keep us company."

Thus, their parting was more formal than before and the following day Carr watched his brother's Regiment ride out and he did not waste the opportunity to exchange a cold and meaningful look with Tavender, him leading his own Squadron out along the mountain road.

The following day Wallace's Brigade, him still in the place of the ailing Mackinnon, led Picton's Third Division out of Castello Branco, with the 105th marching behind Wallace's own 88th. The whole column soon settled to silence along the straight, flat and dusty road, with little to relieve the monotony hour after hour, of following the man in front past the dry, brown scrub at the side of the road, broken only by stands of cacti. Conversation continued for longer within the Followers, until thirst and the exhaustion of topics quelled even their cheerful chatter. The Reverend Albright and Sedgwicke had their usual retinue surrounding their small cart and Sedgwicke lost count of the number of times he was asked if, from his marginally higher vantage point, he could see anything that would break the monotony. The answer was consistently negative until the late afternoon when they passed through an isolated village, where every inhabitant came to the main road to examine the wholly unusual sight of what seemed like a powerful army disturbing what had hitherto been their unbroken seclusion. However, Picton would not allow anything more than a brief, waterless stop and so he led his Division on, until the orange light of the dying sun caused even him to regard the march of that day to be done. For that he was roundly cursed, not least in the mess camps of Davey and Deakin, where even Joe Pike felt the need to voice his complaint at the lack of ready water, but Consuela came to their aid, by cooking cactus in the bottom of a cauldron, crushing it and then straining off the liquid. The taste was odd, but at least the salt fish could be boiled, with biscuit, into something edible and Bridie and Nellie looked upon her even more kindly than before.

The following two days merged into a single, blank memory of plodding feet and dry throats, until they found themselves marching down a slope to a town that was immediately familiar, this identified by Saunders.

"Sabugal! A lot more safe and peaceful than the last time we was here!"

Now the Coa provided plentiful cool and clear water and a supply train met them there, providing the rarity of fresh bread made from good flour. The slopes that they had advanced down into battle, four months previously, now provided an easy camp for the night, but the surprise came the following morning when they marched over the Roman bridge and through the town, the surprise being voiced by Zeke Saunders.

"Seems like having a battle just close by, did these a lot more good than harm!"

The cause of his comment was the sight of many of the inhabitants now wearing quality military clothing of all descriptions, the jackets being mostly blue, with all military insignia removed, bar the buttons. Many of the Portuguese, seeing the Redcoats, these being the soldiers who had killed the previous, thoroughly hated, owners, pointed to the good quality clothing and smiled and nodded their pleasure. However, Byford, having a better appreciation of commercial matters took a different view.

"Good perhaps, except for anyone who makes their living as a tailor, but on the other hand, what business is ever left intact after months of French occupation?"

With that philosophical and final note, they passed the final, poorest buildings, but then found themselves required to leave the good road, the junction off marked by a Troop of dour Provosts, to then begin a climb through dry and bleak hills, whose bare flanks stretched away on each side of what had now become a mere track, broken only by curious clumps of rocks, piled in odd and unfathomable shapes. When afternoon became evening, but with significant more daylight yet remaining, they began a descent into a deep, but gentle valley and, to the astonishment of all, Picton gave the order to make camp. No-one complained at the waste of daylight, least of all the Followers, because the valley contained a clear stream and soon there was a parade of women and children carrying pots and buckets to and from the welcome waters. The parade included Consuela, she carrying two buckets, one in each hand, and she was on her way back, a 300-yard uphill journey, when she was confronted by Lieutenant Stuart Maltby, him amusing himself by walking amongst the queue of Followers. He removed his hat and bowed.

"Mrs Saunders. Como esta?"

Having been asked after her welfare, she curtsied and replied.

"Estou bem, obrigado, Altzea."

Without asking, he smiled and took a bucket from her, then he indicated that they should walk on together. However, all had been observed by John Davey and he turned to Saunders, who was busy cleaning his Baker rifle.

"Zeke, look what's coming up."

Saunders looked up and immediately set down the weapon, unassembled, and sprang to his feet to hurry down the hill, almost at a run. The relief on his wife's face to see him was obvious and he went immediately to Maltby, to grasp the bucket rope, even though Maltby was still taking the weight. He stared down at Maltby with all the authority that his size and weight could give him.

"I'll take that now, Sir. Thank you for your help."

Maltby released the rope and halted, to again remove his hat and bow in the direction of Consuela, an ingratiating smile large on his face.

"Boa noite, Mrs. Saunders!"

However, Consuela did no more than nod and hurry on, for Saunders to take both buckets and walk with her. That done, Saunders looked back at Maltby remaining there to study the pair ascending the hill, and even Maltby could not fail to recognise the accusation behind the strong, level gaze sent in his direction from his Corporal, but it was Consuela who spoke.

"That man. Not nice!"

"Nao, meu amor."

The words of affection, learned from Byford, cheered her and she took his arm and smiled as they climbed to their mess area, where Miles, who had seen all, had the last word.

"Womanisin' shite-auk! Bunch of fives on a dark night is what he needs."

The following day's march was the same as before and once out of the valley, the poor track, now at its worst of all their days of march, meandered through bleak uplands. The bareness of the slopes was again relieved by the curious piles of stone, these the subject of discussion amongst the Officers, regarding how such odd constructions of huge blocks could possibly come about. However, the subject changed when, amazingly for the seeming remoteness of their location, they entered a well-appointed village. Drake, whose level of curiousity was always above the norm, asked the obvious question.

"So, what's this place? Must be something special to be out here, middle of nowhere, back of beyond!"

Carr, drinking water freshly drawn from the well by their servant, Corporal Morrison, lowered the beaker and answered.

"We'll know soon enough. Seems this is to be Brigade Headquarters."

What caused this conclusion was the sight of their Brigade's files and boxes being carried into the largest building and their Colonels, Wallace, Lacey and McArdle following them in. The night provided a good rest, at least for the Officers, all secure in their billets of the village, which they now knew to be called El Bodon. However, the following morning, Morrison disturbed Carr, still prone in his cot, but awake, with a message.

"From Colonel Lacey, Sir. We've been ordered to march on a few extra miles, Sir. Closer to Roger's Town to form picket."

Carr rubbed his eyes, then gave the same attention to a sore foot. He understood perfectly, the soldier's name for Cuidad Rodrigo was standard throughout the army.

"Immediately?"

"No Sir. They said at eight, Sir."

"Time for some breakfast then."

"Yes Sir. It's all ready."

The appointed hour found the whole Battalion again on the road ready to march off. Some of the 88th did not fail to waste the opportunity to stand at the roadside and grin, pleased that they, rather than the rival 105th, would have some days during which to recover from their hard march up from Castello Branco, resting idle in well-appointed billets. However, at the rear of the 105th column Tom Miles did not waste the chance to pass his opinions over in the direction of their smirking audience.

"Scavengin', tato chewin' diddykites!"

In the event, the road between El Bodon and the French held Cuidad Rodrigo was well made, straight and level, and so with little more than an hour spent marching, Lacey, O'Hare and Carr were on a hillock overlooking the walled town and, more importantly, also the road from Salamanca that entered at the Eastern gate. The first watch was allocated to the first Company that arrived, these being the Grenadiers and so O'Hare accompanied Captain Carravoy to decide on the placement of four picket areas. Two were set for overlooking the town, but the final two were set to oversee what mattered most, the vital road between Cuidad and Salamanca, until it disappeared Eastwards over the hills in the direction of the latter, and so the Major and Captain, with D'Villiers present, spent some time examining the landscape for the final picket lodgement. As the men gathered stones from whatever source to make a parapet, the three used their telescopes and it was D'Villiers who gave the first verdict.

"Nothing out there!"

O'Hare did not lower his own telescope.

"Then look harder. If you were leading a guerrilla band, set to watch the road, where would you hold your men?"

Thus chastised, D'Villiers tried again, this time focusing more carefully on clumps of trees or olive groves, these all somewhat scattered but cladding half of the sloping area above the far side of the road. Then he saw what O'Hare had seen, a whole Troop of Irregulars within the dark shadow of the dense groups of trees to the North-East of Cuidad Rodrigo. Beyond their position lay the city of Salamanca, some 40 miles away. O'Hare closed his telescope.

"Enter in the log. Road to Salamanca overlooked by guerrillas. In strength. 200 and more."

Carravoy opened the book, the first page clean and unmarked.

"What's the date?"

He turned to their servant, Corporal Binns.

"Binns! What's the date?"

"8th August, Sir. 1811."

Carravoy's mouth pursed at being so insolently told the year, but he said nothing, as he pulled out his own watch for the time, 10.48. After examining the quality of the point on the pencil, he wrote the title, 'Picket Four', made the entry at the top of the page and then closed the book. By then O'Hare had left and Carravoy turned to their servant.

"Binns! Make us a drink."

Binns already had a fire going and had set the coffee-pot alongside the flames. Carravoy gazed out into the void beyond their high perch.

"Any developments with that exchange that you were talking about?"

D'Villiers sat himself on the part of the parapet now finished.

"I've been looking, but I could see no point in pursuing what's there. The offers came from just another Line Regiment, much like our own. Where's the point? At least here I know who's who and what's what. All is at least familiar."

Carravoy scowled

"And who, from a society Regiment, would want to transfer into something known throughout the army as 'The Rag and Bone Boys'!"

He indulged himself with another deep frown.

"And chancy! Too much so for my liking. The fighting out here has been appalling and it seems that we're high on the list of Nosey's bright boys and likely to get chosen for the risky stuff or at least our Brigade. What about the Militia, back home? Are there not any that want to exchange from there? You would be out of this Hellish place."

D'Villiers nodded.

"There's merit in that, but no promotion. You know as well as I, how that depends on stepping into dead men's shoes!"

Carravoy scowled again.

"Meaning mine! I had no idea that I dwelt so high within your list of fond acquaintances!"

Evidence of being high on 'Nosey's list of bright boys' was at that moment coming up to them from El Bodon, carried by an Aide-de-Camp. He first found Lacey's Headquarters, out of courtesy, and then rode on to the one whom he sought, this being Major Henry Carr. The Aide-de-Camp was a Major of the 1st Royal Dragoons and he dismounted to hand over the note. Carr broke the seal and then read the single sentence, which so surprised him that he repeated it back to the messenger.

"My Light Company and myself are to meet this evening with Lord Wellington, just before dark, at Cuidad water mill. Which is where?"

The Aide-de-Camp smiled.

"Perhaps a bit of a stroll up to the top of that hill there, would help?"

Carr nodded, motioned to Drake to follow and then they began the walk of about half a mile. As the Aide-de-Camp rode whilst Carr and Drake walked, there was no conversation exchanged until they came to what was Picket One, manned by Grenadiers of Simon Ameshurst's Company. He was there and he and his men immediately sprang to the attention and saluted. Carr waved them back down.

"As you were, Simon. Remain on watch."

The Aide had moved to a position at the head of the slope and Carr joined him, for the Cavalry Major to then point downwards.

"There! Half a mile downstream of the bridge. You can see the mill lake. The overflow this side is easy to cross, there's not much to it."

Carr nodded. The mill was easily identified.

"Not much to it. Right, I'm sure, if you're on a horse! Have you any idea why we've been summoned?"

The Aide remounted.

"None at all, old boy. Need to know and all that! So, before you drop down there, best to make a good study of the lie of the land."

He kicked his horse into motion.

"Just be there when the sun's going down. It doesn't pay to disappoint El Douro!"

Carr turned to Drake.

"Right, let's go through what we can see from up here."

Drake nodded.

"Yes, but a bit of a map, drawn from up here, wouldn't come amiss."

"Good idea!"

Carr turned to Ameshurst.

"Simon! We need a page from your log."

From where they were, they drew a map, including everything in the area of the far side of the Agueda above the mill and the left of the town. It did not take long to draw the river, then two hills to the North-West of the town, that nearer to the town defences being lower, the higher having a manned redoubt on top, and then the fortifications themselves, big ravelins, wide triangular shapes projecting before the walls, designed to break up any assault on the main wall. The most distinct feature was an ornate, but barrack-like building, lodged between the Southern end of the lower hill and the river. Furthest North, there was a distinct change in direction of the wall where it turned right to cover the Northern approaches of the town. Drake drew the final line.

"Right! We take this with us. What do we call that building with all the decorations, between that smaller hill and the river?"

Carr took a careful look through his telescope.

"Call it a Monastery. Every town in Spain has at least three!"

He wrote the word, then Carr had a major concern.

"You included that road that runs between those ravellin things and the monastery? That's important!"

"I did!"

He turned the paper so that Carr could see it, and the latter nodded his satisfaction. Then Drake studied the completed drawing carefully

"Do you think I should sign it? As the commissioned artist, do you think?"

Carr gave him a look between contempt and total scepticism.

189

"Best not, not unless you turn it upside down. It'll probably look better that way!"

Six hours later, waiting in the Agueda valley and now close to the banks of the river such that they could hear it, Sergeant Ethan Ellis was harbouring no humour at all. This had all the hallmarks of a special job and that meant extra danger, cheek by jowl with the enemy. He had his Company all lined up before him within a wooded clearing, 76 men in two ranks and he was walking up and down before them.

"Loaded, but with frizzen closed and hammer down, off cock. We don't want nothin' goin' off by accident. 'Tis like to be a good moon, like last night, so a bit of earth over buttons and cross-belt plate won't come amiss. Cross-belts is already dirty, so we'll not worry too much about that. Last, wherever 'tis that we'n goin', all you clumsy buggers watch your feet. We don't want no-one tumblin' over somewher' an' cryin' out for help!"

He lowered his voice as he walked away.

"This I don't bloody well like!"

He walked up to Drake and saluted.

"All ready, Sir. As you ordered, Sir!"

Drake, with Carr beside him, nodded.

"Thank you, Sergeant. Very good. As they are, in two's, to follow us. We move when we cannot see the walls in front of us. Then it'll be too dark for the Johnnies to see us."

"Very good, Sir. Any idea what this is about, Sir?"

Drake grinned.

"None Sergeant, but we're about to find out, very soon, I feel."

Fifteen minutes later, the details of the main curtain wall of the town to their front right, closely observed from the edge of the wood, disappeared into the growing darkness and Carr led the Company forward. The mill remained distinct despite the gloom and soon they were splashing through the overspill, re-assuringly hidden by trees. Carr led them up to the mill building where several figures could be seen and he walked up to the one most likely to be an Officer, despite the indistinct green uniform.

"Major Carr. One hundred and fifth."

The figure immediately saluted.

"Captain Uniacke, Sir. 95th Rifles."

Carr extended his hand which Uniacke took, then Carr introduced Drake and handshakes were exchanged. Then Carr asked the burning question.

"Have you any idea why we are here, Captain?"

"Yes Sir. Lord Wellington wants to inspect the walls of Cuidad himself, Sir. With Colonel Dickson who ran the artillery during that abortive business down at Badajoz."

Carr took a deep breath at the implications of the news.

"And the plan is?"

"They both go forward with my dozen Rifles and myself as escort, Sir. You and yours, as I understand it, come forward, but not all the way, to hold a fall-back position, Sir. Should Johnny rumble our presence and get a bit excited, Sir."

Carr nodded, but said nothing and so Uniacke continued.

"We're just waiting for Lord Wellington now, Sir, and Colonel Dickson. They're a bit late."

At that moment the unmistakable figure arrived, on foot, to quickly hand the short cloak and bi-corn hat to a servant. Another, who could only be Colonel Dickson, was at his shoulder. Immediately the harsh voice barked out.

"Carr! Uniacke! Are you here?"

Both came immediately to the attention when Wellington came forward.

"Sir!"

"Carr. Do you understand what's required here?"

"Yes Sir. We are to go with you part-way to hold a fall back, Sir. In case needed."

He motioned Drake forward.

"We drew a map, Sir, looking down from one of our pickets."

They went behind the mill building and a candle was lit using a tinder-box. Drake opened the map out, and Carr spoke.

"I thought us remaining on this road, Sir, that runs past what we think is a monastery. It's along the base of the slope that has this major ravellin at the top."

Wellington studied the map and then nodded approval.

"Good enough Carr. That's sense. I'll be going around that nearest ravellin, to take a look at the wall behind as far up to this corner here."

He placed a finger on the distinctive change in the wall's direction, then turned to Uniacke.

"Are your Rifles ready?"

"Yes Sir."

"Right. We begin!"

The seeing distance was down to 20 yards, unless the half-moon emerged, which doubled it and so Carr indicated his own men, with Uniacke and two Riflemen, to move forward in front, but alone, without the two senior Officers, who were some yards back. On reaching the road, with the monastery wall looming to their left, he ordered all to stop and kneel down. Hearing nothing, Uniacke and his two then continued forward to soon disappear into the gloom and so now all waited again in silence. The wait brought on the full dark and then Uniacke returned.

"All is deserted and quiet, Sir."

From behind Wellington and Dickson rose up with the remainder of the Rifles.

"See you in a while, Carr. I estimate an hour."

Carr saluted, despite the near black of the night.

"Very good, Sir."

Soon the party were beyond sight and Carr and Drake stood together. Ellis was nearby and so Carr turned to him.

"Spread the men either side of here, Sergeant. Along this road."

Ellis departed without a word, he was not going to make any extra sound. As the dispersal took place, Carr spoke his hidden worry to Drake.

"We have our Commander in Chief in front of us and in the presence of the enemy, with 76 nervous men, all with loaded rifles. It would be a catastrophe beyond words if one of ours shot him, thinking him to be French, coming out of the night. It would not be the first time in history."

"So we do what?"

"Send three pairs, that should be enough, up the slope. The first pair to the point of this first ravellin, the two others up to the point of the final ravellin on this side, before the turn in the walls. One pair above its ditch, the last down the slope below them. I suspect that is where he will emerge. I doubt that they will come back the way they went. Most probably not. They'll go up as far as that corner turn in the walls and then drop back down the slope to return along the road, alongside the monastery wall."

"Right. I'll see to it."

"I want them unarmed! No rifle, just a bayonet."

Drake stopped, his silence speaking his astonishment, but Carr answered forcefully.

"Yes. When they see Lord Wellington, it is they who come back ahead of him to our line, to warn of his approach. They are unarmed so that they do not shoot him!"

Drake's reply was spoken softly, each word a question.

"But we have men we can trust, Henry!"

"I know. It's fussy, but it's not a chance I'm going to take."

Drake walked off to find Ellis and then explain. He could see Ellis' figure stiffen in the dark.

"I'll be one, Sir!"

"No you'll not. I want you here."

Fifteen minutes later, Miles and Pike were creeping forward, each feeling the slope that ran up to the walls become steeper under their feet. They were to be the furthest out, at the point of the last ravellin before the fortifications turned sharply right.

"This is one bad business and that's a fact. Roamin' about in front the Johnnies with no bundook, just a brummagem. This is no kind of soldierin' that I can take to!"

Pike was studying the looming structures to his right. They had been told to count three 'points', each a ravellin, then count 50 paces further and then go up the slope, which they did, to find themselves halted by the ravellin ditch, this identified not only by the deep darkness before them, but also by the finished stonework that formed the ditch edge. There they stopped, hoping that they were now at their allocated place, the structure looming beyond the ditch did seem to have a 'vee' shape where they were, signifying a ravellin.

They knelt and listened, but all was not quiet. Odd, but human sounds were coming from the bottom of the ditch. Pike nudged Miles's arm.

"Tom! What's that?"

Miles took in a deep breath. This was trouble.

"Well, you bein' a married man should have as good an idea as any about what's goin' on down in that ditch!"

Neither spoke as more amorous noises came up from the darkness below, then Miles pulled Pike back a few yards to whisper.

"We does not disturb! No noise from us, means no noise from them, an' Johnny stays none the wiser."

"Alright Tom, but where do you think they've come from?"

"If you wants my guess, some lover-boy 'ave come over the wall to meet his lass as 'ave come up from the houses down over. Best leave 'em be. Just stay here and keep watch, I'd say that here we'n favourite for Nosey to come strollin' up."

They settled to wait and time passed. From the depths below, there came the sounds of Spanish conversation in affectionate tones and Miles grew more anxious, wanting the couple to either disappear, or for Wellington to arrive, so that they all could disappear. In the event, what transpired was the worst possible. The girl, presumably pushed up by her lover, came over the edge of the stonework just as Wellington and Dickson came along it, still inspecting. The girl shrieked at the figures looming towards her out of the dark and two Riflemen escorts sprang from behind to push her to the ground. There she continued to scream, until one of them placed his hand over her mouth, but the commotion continued. Miles and Pike stood and Miles spoke, in a hushed voice.

"Lord Wellington, Sir, is that you?"

The angry voice came out of the dark.

"Yes! Of course! What the Devil is this?"

"A courtin' couple down in the ditch, Sir. We thought it best to leave 'em alone."

"And now this!"

"Yessir. She came up just as you arrived, Sir."

"And the male is where?"

"Must be back in the city, Sir. Now that he've pushed her up here."

The reply now came back more urgent than angry.

"Get down there and get after him. He could be questioned. Bring him back to our lines."

Pike now spoke up, worrying about the reason they were out there.

"But Sir, we're here to go ahead and warn our men that you'n on your way!"

The voice became even more testy.

"These Rifles will do that! You get after him."

Lights were appearing on the town battlements as Wellington and his party hurried off, having hauled the girl to her feet, with a burly Riflemen each side, practically lifting her off her feet, but she was now, thankfully, quiet. Miles and Pike jumped down into the gloom and Pike ran the short distance forward across the ditch to find the wall of the ravellin and follow it, but Miles pulled him to the ground.

"No further! Johnny's all awake now, so we stays here. Lover-boy's up over the wall by now and gone. Could even be some Frog soldier, they'm good with the ladies so rumour has it. So we goes no further, just wait a few minutes, then we'll go back. Things'll get very lively, very soon."

As if to confirm Miles' fears, burning torches arced down from the walls to illuminate the main wall ditch below, but the pair were far enough back to remain in shadow. More lights moved behind the battlements and French voices could be heard, then Miles pulled at Pike's shoulder.

"That'll do! We'n off, afore they sends out patrols."

Still in shadow, they eased themselves back the way they had come, remaining close to the ravellin wall. At the ditch wall, Pike gave Miles a boost up and Miles pulled up Pike, then they hurried back, down the slope and over to the Monastery. The first to greet them at their lines was Ethan Ellis, him somewhat advanced of their line.

"What's on with you two, Miles? You should have come in before Nosey!"

"Should've yes, but he sent us down into the ditches to chase some city lad who'd been courtin' his girl outside the walls. We was ordered to take him prisoner. No chance! He was back over the wall, quick as lightening."

Ellis paused to think, but there could be no argument with Miles this time.

"Right. Get yourselves to Major Carr and report. I expect Himself is still with him."

Ellis was correct and the pair soon found the Officers all grouped together. They approached and both stood at a respectful attention before Miles spoke.

"Beg pardon, Sir, if you please."

Wellington turned around.

"Ah, you two. Did you get him?"

At rigid attention, Miles spoke the best lie he could come up with.

"'Fraid not sir. He had a length of rope down over the wall and he was up it like a squirrel, Sir. We couldn't follow, Sir."

There was no reply and they were close enough to see that Wellington had turned his back on them. Miles pulled Pike back and they turned away, to bump into a Rifleman and Pike asked the question that was worrying him.

"What happened to the girl?"

"We let her go and she shot off like a scared rabbit. No idea where she went."

At that point Ellis arrived, much relieved at the safe outcome.

"Fall in, you two. We're out of this!"

oOo

The news was not welcome, as brought by Jed Deakin.

"Get packed. We're moving."

His Bridie sighed.

"Now there's a shame. This El Bodon place has all the makings of a fine billet. Friendly locals and all."

"You're right, but it can't be helped. On the road at nine."

"Do you know the name of where we're goin'?"

Deakin was walking away by now, he had his own concerns, but he turned and paused long enough to shrug his shoulders.

"Do we ever?"

Nellie had listened to all, standing annoyed with arms akimbo.

"And what use is that? All we wanted was a name and that would mean a village, as would give some comfort of sorts."

An hour later, Lacey, O'Hare and Carr were at the head of their Battalion, but all three electing to walk and they followed the 88th out of El Bodon, with the 74th behind and their single Brigade Company of Rifles was out at the van before the 88th. Wallace's Brigade were in the lead, with Colville's behind. The road was again the straight causeway towards the Brigade's picket posts, but these were passed through, now deserted. As they descended the slope beyond, the area they were marching into became clear, O'Hare voiced his opinion.

"This I don't like. You say the whole Division is being sent across the Agueda?"

Lacey turned to him, having formed his own concerns.

"Yes. The whole of the Third. We are to watch the road to Salamanca and intercept anything along it, but this looks like a complete wilderness and Division is far back at a place called Martiago, putting Picton not in the best of moods. There are no roads North to South worth calling such for us to use from where we'll be. We're to watch the Salamanca road whilst in the wilds and have to make the best of it."

They descended the gentle slope for a good mile further, then they were required to turn right onto a poor track, their diversion indicated by a trio of disgruntled Provosts. They were now on an open slope and Carr took a moment to stop and focus his telescope. He found the battlements of Cuidad and mused quietly to himself.

"This is the nearest we'll come to that place. At least for a while."

As if in answer, the whole battlement facing them suddenly erupted in white smoke, then he did speak out loud.

"Utterly stupid! We're almost two miles away. A complete waste of everything."

However, seconds later, back in the column, the first to see the rolling ball was Jed Deakin at the head of the Colour Company and he screamed in alarm as he saw some Grenadiers halt and point towards it.

"Don't touch it! Don't touch it. Leave it be."

One of the Grenadiers, perhaps a new recruit, plainly intended to stop the ball in some way, it rolling at much less than walking pace, but his comrade, hearing Deakin's cry of warning, pulled him back slightly, enough to take his outstretched foot out of the way, but not enough to prevent him placing the butt of his musket in the ball's path. The ball took away both the butt and the lock plate and continued on its way as if nothing had happened. The Grenadier raised his ruined weapon, staring at it stupidly, as his Captain, Carravoy, arrived to investigate the fuss. His face was distorted with anger as he gave his verdict.

"That will cost you three months' pay! Take his name, Sergeant."

Sergeant Luke Ridgway, of Lieutenant Ameshurst's Two Section, sadly drew out paper and pencil to write down the name.

"Well, Clerkenwell, you can throw that lot away and look on the bright side. At least there's a lot less on your shoulders now compared to the rest of us!"

As the column began to move again, both Ridgway and Jed Deakin shared a knowing look and many gave an extra look towards Cuidad, but nothing more came their way, presumably the overzealous Captain had been ordered to desist by his Governor, General Barrie, to save ammunition for the very likely siege to come.

At last they came to the banks of the Agueda at a point where they could cross and there they halted as each Battalion made their way over. As the 88th entered, O'Hare sat down on a convenient tummock.

"Both boots and hose are coming off. I know what a long march in wet footwear can do."

Then it was their turn and they entered the water, following the markers driven into the riverbed by their Riflemen. In the event, they were wading through a shallow mill overspill and then they had another, much deeper and well-defined water-course to cross, this being the leat of the mill, but this could be crossed via a narrow bridge, however, all within the mill to their left was still and silent, bar the now useless water running around the paddles of the slowly moving wheel. Up from the mill ran a reasonable road and now they were embarking on a climb as gentle as their previous descent. The more height they gained, the more that could be seen of the Cuidad to Salamanca road, on their left across a shallow valley with its own brook. In line with their march, ahead of them, the vital chausee eventually disappeared Eastwards into a fold of the hills.

After another half-hour of climb, Picton came riding back from the head of his Divisional column, accompanied by a mere trio of Staff. He had no real need to rein in beside a mere group of Majors and a Colonel of his 105th, but he did so, yet it was Lacey who spoke first and he did not mince his words.

"We're out on a limb here, Sir, in perfect cavalry country with none of our own. We'd be in trouble if we had to pull back before any kind of serious French advance."

Picton's nodded his agreement and for the moment remained silent. He felt no inclination on this particular occasion, to admonish Lacey for complaining about orders, although he was two ranks below Picton. He remembered Lacey rallying the Portuguese during the desperate affair at the crossroads atop Busaco ridge and, as a fellow front-rank soldier himself, Picton gave Lacey some credit and indulgence.

"You're not wrong Lacey, but Lord Wellington would have it. He wants that road watched, even closed if we can, although those guerrilla brigands seem to be doing that for us. Some cavalry will arrive. I've asked Alten to bring over his own 11th Light to join his KGL, leaving Slade with Crauford on the other side of the Agueda. Keep a good look-out, Johnny won't be letting us stay here, twiddling our thumbs and making life awkward for his 'amis' in Cuidad, down over there.'

He sat forward in his saddle.

"But to business. I want you up farther, on our flank, some farm's up there. Wallace's will be here in the centre and McArdle's 74th will be back down from him, to join with Colville, who holds from there back to that mill."

He stared down.

"But you're right, Lacey. I feel more exposed here than some Duchess with her drawers down. Anything you see, I want to know."

Leaving all around grinning and saluting, Picton rode off and Lacey turned to O'Hare, both still smiling.

"On we go then, up to this farm."

After 20 minutes, Lacey spoke again.

"This is our spot. We must make the best of it. Set up either side of this road, half down towards that stream to make life a bit easier."

194

Three days later, the Colour Company were manning a picket on the edge of their camp, Captain Heaviside visiting his men, Sergeant Henry Nicholls in charge of the picket and commanding the Watch. Heaviside, first stood just before the parapet, was allowing his mind to dwell on the composition of his evening prayer, always spoken out in a place of remoteness, but at that moment he was distracted by the shadows of the clouds scudding across the brown August hills beyond the road. Therefore, he stood in silence, his mind dwelling alternatively between manifestations temporal descending from the Heavens to matters spiritual, designed to ascend to it. It was at that moment that Henry Nicholls broke into his silent reverie.

"Looks like we got some visitors, Captain."

Heaviside looked at him and then followed his arm pointing across the shallow valley. Almost invisible, as they blended in with the brown landscape, could be seen a strong column of what must be guerrillas about to cross the ford over their local stream. Heaviside turned back to Nicholls.

"Company stood to!"

Nicholls immediately left the picket to begin shouting orders, as Heaviside watched the approaching column. The track they were using would bring them immediately past his position and so he only had to wait. It was not long before the sounds of mounted men came to him and soon after, the leader reined in his horse, merely yards from Heaviside, a wide grin from perfect teeth white in his brown face. He was certainly a striking figure, seeming to be as broad across the body as he was above the saddle, wearing a Hussar's jacket, probably French, this being of dark blue cloth but with multiple silver braid bars running horizontally either side of the central opening. However, what were even more striking were dark, deep set eyes, above a small nose that was in turn above a full moustache, extending either side of a still grinning mouth.

"Hola, Ingles!"

Heaviside nodded a greeting, then the rider continued, beating his chest as he spoke.

"Me, Julian Sanchez. El Charro! Enemigo de los Francheses!"

At these words, Sanchez' men began to cheer and shout, then he began to gesticulate, his left hand moving backwards and forward to indicate moving on up the hill.

"We, on, hasta, go. Si?"

Heaviside remained impassive.

"Por que?"

Sanchez reached down into his saddle pocket and pulled out a bundle of papers. These he held out to Heaviside, who gestured to a nearby soldier to descend and take them. The soldier took them from the outstretched hand and he examined them.

"There's blood on them, Sir."

Sanchez seemed to understand and he moved his hand over his throat in a cutting motion.

"Si. Sangre francesa. El mensajero está muerto!"

This brought more cheering from his men as the bundle came to Heaviside. The seal was already broken and he studied the writing to quickly see that the message was in cipher. He closed the packet.

"I will get this to Wellington. A Wellington. Mucho gracias, Senor Sanchez."

This signified to Sanchez that they were not to be allowed any further, which did not suit him at all. He turned in his saddle to bring forward the large saddle bags behind him, to then open the covers to show them to be empty.

"Necesitamos alimentos! Food! Si."

Then he opened his cartridge pouch and tilted it forward so that Heaviside could see that it was equally empty.

"Necesitamos alimentos! Necesitamos munición!"

Heaviside thought for a moment then he turned to Nicholls, stood before the Company, these all stood at 'Order Arms' across El Charro's path.

"Allow them through."

Nicholl's gave the orders and the double rank parted, for the now grinning guerrilla to spur his horse forward.

"Mucho gracias, Ingleses. Vaya con Dios!"

The Precious Word, being spoken from so Catholic a mouth grated somewhat on the wholly Presbyterian Heaviside, but he said nothing as the now cheerful Company spurred their horses up the hill, all waving and speaking their thanks. Nicholls came down beside his Captain.

195

"Did we do the right thing, Sir? Allowing them through? You know how light-fingered those coves can be."

Heaviside nodded gravely, but he had seen little that he could object to and the bundle of French despatches they had obtained and taken a risk to bring to them, could prove vital and for that he was happy to give them the benefit of the doubt. He turned to Nicholls to deliver the inevitable.

"You should not muzzle an ox when it is treading out the grain. Deuteronomy 25, verse 4."

Nicholls could only reply in the standard Deakin-esque manner.

"Yes Sir. I'm sure all the lads sees it that way, Sir."

Still utterly bemused Nicholls returned to the re-positioning of his men.

After three more days of watching and waiting, Wallace came into the 105th Headquarter's tent to join Lacey, O'Hare and Carr, their Brevet Brigadier somewhat breathless, despite making the journey on horseback, from Picton's Headquarters at Matiago, some ten miles back. He sat immediately, while O'Hare organised the glasses and the bottle of spirit.

"Things are moving. That despatch that came in through yours the other day, speaks of Foy's Division moving up to join Marmont at Salamanca."

Carr's glass was the last to be filled and so he was able to speak.

"So, Johnny's concentrating again, just as he did opposite us at Ouguela? He's going to try here what he couldn't do there?"

Wallace savoured the taste of O'Hare's good Irish whisky before answering.

"Seems so, Carr, yes!"

"What are his numbers? Have we any idea?"

"Yes. Nothing less than 53,000 up to 60. Perhaps."

Now all three of the 105th Senior Officer Corps looked worried and O'Hare asked the next obvious question.

"And us?"

"30,000! We've got 14,000 sick at the moment, which puts us down to about that, but Wellington won't give an inch at Cuidad unless he's got to."

"Sick?"

Wallace took another swallow.

"Yes. Guadiana fever did not hit us up at the Ouguela end of the line, but it did those at Elvas on the other end of the line. And all those reinforcements landing at Lisbon and Oporto served at Walcheren and the fever they picked up there is coming back out in this Spanish weather. Some arrived yesterday for McArdle's 74th and when they got here, most collapsed from the journey and he had to send for his Surgeon, rather than his Adjutant, to spread them over his Companies. It's a bad business!"

Wallace looked fully at Lacey.

"I know you look after yours, Lacey. Good latrines, fresh water and all, but don't let standards slip. As we speak, sickness is hitting us worse than any battle."

The glass went down on the table and Wallace seriously changed the subject.

"Right, but just as important, I want a far picket out along the Salamanca road. I know the guerrillas are out there, but they are as liable to bugger off and watch a bull-fight as they are to pillage a Johnny pack train. We'll share it between yours and mine, our Lights, that is. I've got some already up there."

Conforming to that order, within an hour, a dozen men of the 105th Light Company found themselves marching beyond the farm to begin a long climb up a sandy track to man a picket on the highest point of the ridge that overlooked the Salamanca road. It was dusk and they were to mount a 24-hour watch until relieved. At the picket, they were to replace a squad of the 88th and they found themselves looking at their old adversary Corporal Michael O'Donnell, who immediately recognised Saunders and Davey and he set about a usual greeting, although, as far as the two 105th NCO's were concerned, his words were utterly devoid of any sincerity.

"Well hello there boys, now. The top of this fine evening to youse all!"

Both Davey and Saunders nodded in his direction then at the state, or more like absence, of a picket wall and Saunders spoke his opinion.

"Doesn't seem like you've done much to turn this into a decent picket!"

O'Donnell grinned.

"Well, now. Couldn't really see the point. This being such a bird's nest of a place. But, feel free if you've a mind. There's plenty of rocks around."

With that he slung his musket over his shoulder.

"Well, must be getting my boys back down. See youse all in a while. It could be me, it could be someone else."

Saunders watched them walk off and he called out after them.

"That All Ireland Wrestling Champion of yours. How's he doing?"

O'Donnell turned but continued walking.

"Ah now, the saddest thing. Didn't we lose him at that Busaco place. An awful shame. It would have made a good contest now, between you and him, would it not?"

The unhappy news mollified Saunders' irritation somewhat and he felt the need to say something.

"I'm sorry to hear that. I'm sure he was a good man "

"That he was. A good man indeed."

With that the 88th were gone and the pair looked around at what was merely a natural clearing between the boulders, yet this was their picket and their responsibility. It was Davey who decided.

"Well. We can save the building for morning. Meanwhile, we're above the road and, I'd say, we can hear the most of anything happening from up here during the dark, but a couple closer, further down won't come amiss. You and I take first, Zeke, down there? Tom and Joe up here."

Saunders said nothing and so, assuming agreement from his superior, Davey turned to the rest, all the usual collection.

"Tom, Joe. Two hours, you're on now, up here. Len, John, you relieve up here in two hours' time. Nat, Bill, two hours' time you relieve us, down aways.

They descended for some time until they found the road and then went back 200 yards. Davey produced an hour glass, which he set next to himself and then he sat himself next to Saunders, just as stars appeared in the clear sky and it being the middle of the month, a decent half-moon. Both pulled out their pipes and shared Davey's tobacco pouch, then Saunders did the sparking with his flint and steel, whilst kneeling well down in their hiding place, at which point both settled and silence reigned for a few minutes, until Davey spoke.

"Your Consuela and Maltby. Anything?"

Saunders removed his pipe.

"He's tried, that I'm sure. When it comes to wood and water, one of the lads goes with her and if not them, Bridie or Nellie, or even Eirin, but he'll take any chance he gets to say a few words. He's a charmer, right enough."

Davey spat to the side.

"Thinks he is! Something needs to happen to that piece of shite! As though Eirin weren't enough."

The night passed peacefully, they were relieved on time and the following morning saw the welcome sight of a Troop of cavalry ascending the track to their high picket. When they arrived, the greeting was mostly in the form of gestures, but that did not worry the 105th group, for these were King's German Legion Hussars, and all in the British Army had the deepest respect for the quality KGL. However, the Officer spoke good English and he came to Saunders, as the Senior NCO.

"Anything Corporal?"

"No, Sir. Not from here."

"What do you suggest? We are new here."

Saunders pointed along the ridge.

"As you can see, Sir, this ridge line closely matches the road. Taking a look along it and finding out what you can see whilst holding this height, would be a sensible place to start. Sir."

The Officer smiled down.

"That's good advice. My thanks to you Corporal."

Saunders saluted and the Officer re-joined his men to lead them along the ridge track as Saunders had advised. Davey looked at them, then at Saunders.

"Now why can't all Officers be like that?"

Saunders clapped a huge hand on Davey's shoulder and then went over to their fire to get some tea. When their Relief came with full daylight and they had descended, Miles broke off from the dozen men to present himself at the door of the farmhouse at the foot of the path, carrying with him the tobacco ration of all of the picket. Above the door he read, but did not understand, the motto of the farm, 'Pedro Toro. Benecido en Cristo'. He used the huge, forged iron knocker as it was intended and soon the farmer appeared, as dark as the wood of the door and almost as broad. Holding the pouch open to the gaze of the farmer, Miles spoke four of the few Spanish words he knew.

"Huevos. Leche. Por favor."

Luckily the farmer understood and the tobacco was taken inside, for his wife to re-appear with a small canvas bag of eggs and a large earthenware jug of milk. Miles nodded his thanks which was responded to by some unfathomable Spanish and he hurried on to their mess area where he immediately handed all over to Nellie Nicholls, giving his order with a stern look and a similar tone.

"The milk is for the babby!"

Nellie Nicholls took both and her reply was an approving scowl, such as only she could accomplish. Miles nodded and hurried away.

Events seemed to take three-day intervals over which to transpire. On this occasion, it was Drake and Carr commanding the 105th picket above the ford and Drake spoke much the same words as Sergeant Nicholls had, six days earlier.

"Seems we have visitors!"

However, he only spoke to confirm what Carr had already seen and he was already pulling out his telescope to study what was still a half mile distant. After a moment's study, he snapped it shut.

"Guerrillas, with news or after supplies. My money would be on the latter."

Drake grinned, but he did not take Carr up on the bet, yet wished he had, when the leader reined in his horse at the picket wall. It was a relief that his English was better than that of El Charro's.

"Ola, Senor. You must get this news to your Wellington. The French are at San Munoz. One day ride, two days walk. They have taken food all from Salamanca. San Munoz is small place, they not stay long there, I think. I think they will march tomorrow, even today. Is possible."

"How many?"

The guerrilla leaned forward onto the pommel of his saddle, his face very serious.

"Hard to say, Senor, but a big army."

"Where are their guns and wheeled transport?"

"On and close the big road, Senor."

"Thank you. What will you do now?"

"El Charro will give up the road, but we will get behind them and do what we can to their messengers and mule trains."

He pulled the head of his horse around.

"We go North. Good luck, Senor. Vaya con Dios."

With that he and his men made haste back down the track to cross the stream and then the Salamanca road, but Carr was not there to watch them, he was hurrying back to the 105th Headquarters tent, where he found no-one but Sergeant Bryce, Lacey's servant and secretary.

"When you see the Colonel, tell him I've gone to Martiago to see Division. Guerrillas have come in, saying that the French are massed at San Munoz, about 30 miles off and could be on their way at any time. Our picket on the ridge should be warned."

Bryce had stood to attention as soon as Carr entered, but now he made to leave.

"Right Sir. Whilst you get yourself ready for the journey, Sir, I'll get you a horse. Will you go alone, Sir?"

"Yes. And you'll see that the picket is warned?"

"Yes Sir."

Once mounted and moving, Carr soon decided that any kind of a gallop was far too risky on that ground and so he alternated between a fast trot and a canter, as he crossed the bleak scrub-lands that formed his journey. He soon realised that he did not know the exact location of Martiago and so he needed to ask for the village from a well maintained small-holding down in a fold of the hillside by a stream, where he received a clear direction from a stiff arm, with a stiffer finger pointing over a nearby hill. More traffic going in his direction provided more reassurance and soon he was in the village and at the obvious Divisional Headquarters building. He quickly dismounted and handed the reins of his horse to a soldier stood on guard. Inside, the room smelt of damp and whitewash, but an Aide-de-Camp was sat at a small table, a Major, the same rank as Carr. He went straight up to him.

"Good morning. Carr 105th. I need to see General Picton urgently. Very urgently. I have just received news of the French. They have left Salamanca."

The Aide, possibly more intelligent than most, took but a second to digest the implications of Carr arriving so urgently and so he immediately stood up.

"Please follow me."

They went deeper into the building and there came the additional smell of onions and animals, but the Aide took him straight into a room where stood Picton, with Colonels Wallace, Colville and Alten, the last resplendent in the uniform of the 11th Light Dragoons.

"Excuse me, Sir, but Major Carr here has just arrived, bearing what he says is urgent news. I thought it right to bring him straight to you. Sir."

Picton frowned, but gave a nod of approval and the Aide took it upon himself to remain, as Picton turned directly to Carr, the frown having deepened.

"Well?"

Carr took a deep breath.

"Just over an hour ago, Sir, a guerrilla band came up to our picket. He could speak good English, Sir, and said that the French are now fully gathered at San Munoz, about 30 miles away. A large army he said and that they were giving up the road, that being the guerrillas, Sir. He added, when I asked him, that whatever the French have with wheels is on or near the main road, Sir. I thought that significant."

Picton seized a rolled-up map on his desk and spread it open, to place a thick finger on San Munoz. He turned his gaze to his two Infantry Brigadiers.

"What do you think?"

Colville answered first.

"The guerrillas have proven reliable. They don't tell lies and you cannot mistake a large army. Wellington's orders are to withdraw if threatened."

Wallace nodded.

"I agree."

Picton frowned again.

"But we are not yet threatened. 30 miles is a two-day push, even for the French, but get yours ready to move at an hour's notice."

He turned to Alten, who commanded Picton's cavalry.

"Pull your KGL back. Those are Wellington's orders, but slowly, give us what observation you can."

Then to Wallace.

"You have that far-out picket?"

Wallace nodded.

"Yes Sir."

"Keep that, I may get up there myself, but as soon as they see anything serious, then get down and pull everything out. Clear?"

Everyone in the room saluted and Carr left immediately, taking only the time to re-fill his water-bottle, then to begin his ride back, anxious to get up to the picket himself. Once back at their lines, he was grateful to see that Lacey and O'Hare were at their tent. He did not dismount.

"Sir, have you been told? I gave Bryce the message."

Lacey nodded.

"We have and what have you got from Picton?"

"Keep the ridge picket there. As soon as we see anything serious, the Brigade is to pull out. The KGL are on notice to withdraw before us, Sir, but to continue to scout for as long as they can. Wellington's orders are that they pull back and not engage."

Lacey looked at O'Hare.

"Hmm, seems he doesn't want to risk his cavalry, although we're not short, for once."

He turned to O'Hare.

"I want a Captain up there tonight and tomorrow with a whole Company. Carravoy for the rest of today and the night."

He looked up at Carr, still mounted and expecting to ride to the picket.

"Get some rest, Henry. I want you up there before dawn tomorrow. Can you think of any way to send a signal, if Johnny arrives?"

Carr nodded.

"Yes Sir. I'll get hold of a mirror or a flag of some kind."

"Good. I'll set a Watch here and they'll pick up what you send."

It took less than 15 minutes for Captain Lord Carravoy and his Company of Grenadiers to be sent toiling up the dusty track to what had come to be known as the 'high picket'. He would have complained to D'Villiers marching beside him, if anything like a complaint could be justified, but he knew that it could not. The 'high picket' was vital if Picton's Division were to be warned in time and had to be manned by someone. However, D'Villiers himself had a complaint.

"Why isn't this being done by the cavalry? At any sign of danger, they can ride off. What can we do? Run?"

"I blame Wellington. From what I hear, he's convinced that Marmont is only coming forward to re-victual Cuidad. So, according to our Leader Lord, the Frogs will throw a few months' worth of good dinners in through the back gate for their Garrison and scuttle off back to Salamanca for a few good dinners of their own."

D'Villiers shielded his eyes against the sun, the better to judge the distance remaining.

"And if he's wrong and this is a full-blown effort to send us back into Portugal?"

"Then we are in trouble and there could be a disaster for the whole Division and then perhaps he'll resign and the army will be rid of this damned 'Sepoy General'!

"And us?"

"Dead or in a French prison. Until we parole, which I fully intend to do. I'll not rot in some French hulk or somesuch, waiting for gaol fever to carry me off!"

They were approaching the top of the track and the picket of the 88th were already formed up and ready to march down, therefore the two Companies passed on the track, with only formal salutes being exchanged in greeting between the Officers. Once at the picket, D'Villiers set his men, whilst Ameshurst allowed his Section to rest and rekindle the 88th fire from dried gorse stems. A 12-hour picket made demands even on a Company of over 70 men. The day wore on and all three Officers took turns with a telescope, but only Ameshurst saw anything worth entering in the log, now well used, during his afternoon Watch and he made the entries himself: '2.22 – large body of guerrillas moving North and then East.' '4.16 – French cavalry patrol on far ridge. Halted for five minutes then withdrew East.'

With the coming of darkness all settled to sleep or sit and talk, to await their watch or to mount the Watch itself. When the merest of light appeared over the Eastern horizon, Ameshurst shook Carravoy awake.

"Sir! Sir. I'm sure I've heard something on the road!"

Carravoy had been deep asleep within one of the few comfortable positions within the picket wall, his slumbers brought on by half emptying his brandy flask. Slurring his speech, he managed to raise his head.

"What? And how loud?"

"I'd say mounted, Sir and you can just about hear it from the listening post down the slope"

Carravoy knew nothing about any 'listening post', that must be Ameshurst's own idea, but his mind was clearing.

"Can you hear it now?"

"Not from back here, Sir. Only from down the slope."

Carravoy could just about cudgel up enough military acumen to ask an important question.

"Any wheels?"

"No, Sir."

"Then it's a few horsemen roaming around. Probably guerrillas, they move at night, mostly. No need to alert the Regiment."

"It went on for some time, Sir."

"Same answer. Just keep listening."

"I think I should trot down, Sir, all the same and warn the Regiment."

"No. You're needed here. Just keep listening."

With that Carravoy's head subsided onto the rolled-up blanket, leaving Ameshurst in a quandary. He returned to Davey's original picket some 400 yards down the slope and found the Corporal who had sent a runner up to him.

"Any change?"

"Just finished, Sir. All is now quiet."

"I'd say it went on for five minutes, at least. What do you think?"

"It seemed to go on for some time, Sir. I'd say ten minutes, perhaps more. Sir."

Ameshurst decided. Within five minutes a whole cavalry Regiment could ride past.

"Keep listening, Corporal. Anything new, I'll be up above."

With that he was gone and soon back up, to awaken his Sergeant Ridgway within the picket.

"Get back down and find Major Carr. Tell him we've heard horses on the road below us."

Ridgway saluted, slung his musket and began a loping trot downhill. He knew where the Officer's tents were and luckily found Corporal Morrison already up, going about the business of preparing a breakfast for his Officers.

"Mornin' Sid. Carr about?"

The nearest tent opened and Carr's head appeared.

"Major Carr to you! Why are you here?"

Having been admonished, Ridgway came immediately to the attention.

"Beg pardon, Sir. Lieutenant Ameshurst sent me down, Sir. Says he's heard horses on the Salamanca road below our listening post. Sir."

"Where's Captain Carravoy?"

"Still up there, Sir."

"Does he know?"

"I believe so, Sir."

"Right. Get back up there."

Ridgway ran off and Carr turned to Morrison.

"I'll be dressed in five minutes. Saddle a horse."

Within ten minutes Carr had overtaken the hurrying Ridgeway and another five found him at the picket and one minute more found him beside the still sleeping Carravoy. He resisted the temptation to kick him awake, instead he ordered a Corporal to bring him to consciousness and then he took himself to the picket wall to look towards Cuidad in the growing light.

"Jesus!"

The plain beyond the road was covered by three Regiments of French cavalry, located, he thought, probably where they could not be seen from the camps of the 105th and 88th on the track below. At that moment Carravoy came to join him and his face, despite his eyes still heavy from sleep, registered his shock, but Carr spoke first, anger driving the words.

"Captain! You hear horses on the road, you send an urgent messenger and then you go back to bed!"

Carravoy was utterly flummoxed by the middle clause, but he had been found asleep by a superior Officer. He thought it wise to say as little as possible, but he was seething inside at being admonished in front of his men, especially by Carr.

"I thought it of little consequence."

Carr ground his teeth together. He also now appreciated that they were in the presence of the men and so he turned his attention instead to the military matters on hand.

"Then, Captain, I would fully appreciate it, if you would take that horse and ride to our Colonel and then to Brigadier Wallace and tell both that I estimate three Regiments of French cavalry to be outside the walls of Roger's Town, down there!"

Carravoy immediately turned away, mounted the horse and then was gone. Carr focused his telescope up the road towards Salamanca and was relieved to see that it remained empty, then, for some time he continued to study the new arrivals outside of Cuidad. Having reached a conclusion, he turned to Simon Ameshurst.

"Simon. How many colours can you see amongst those Frogs down there? Uniforms, I mean."

Ameshurst took the telescope and studied the cavalry in what was now bright sunlight. After a good minute, he turned back to Carr.

"I can see a sort of mid-blue, green and finally grey. Sir."

Carr folded the telescope.

"So can I. That's three Regiments. A whole Brigade!"

At that moment, the relieving Company of the 88th arrived and Carr was pleased to see a figure he recognised from a conversation in a wrecked house at Fuentes de Onoro. The figure saluted and Carr returned.

"Captain O'Dowda. Good to see you again."

"You too, Sir, but I understand that matters up here have become a mite anxious."

"Of that you are not wrong. Take a look to the right of Cuidad. Johnny's got his cavalry up in force."

O'Dowda slid off his back-pack to withdraw a telescope, which he needed to use for under a minute before he turned to Carr.

"A Brigade, I'd say, but not doing much. Very few are still in the saddle!"

"Let's hope it stays that way. So, it's all yours. Keep a good watch on those down there, but more important is whether or not anything comes along the main road to join them. We all need to know quickly, so use these."

He pointed to a large shaving mirror and a red flag, brought with them from Ouguela.

"If the sun's right, flash the mirror. That's best, but if not fire a musket and wave the flag. In fact, fire a musket anyway. There's a permanent Watch down there."

O'Dowda nodded.

"Tense times, Sir."

"Make no mistake about that, made more so by the fact that we are the furthest East of the whole of Wellington's army."

With that, Carr turned and began the walk down, following the Grenadiers by some 200 yards, but he was in no mood to catch up with Carravoy and exchange any pleasantries and so he took the excuse to turn around and accompany O'Hare who was on his way up and feeling the need to take a look at developments for himself. However, Carr soon left him to it and turned again, because as soon as O'Hare came to O'Dowda, the whole conversation between them was conducted in Gaelic. Once back in camp, Carr realised how tired he was and so he spent much of the day asleep.

In that state, Carr missed the growing tension throughout that day and in fact it increased further when the Third Division saw the KGL Hussars ride back in the direction of Martiago. Number Two Company went up to the picket to relieve the 88th, then a Company of the 88th relieved them and then it was the turn of the 105th again and Carr decided to accompany the Light Company on their night watch. In the dying light, he studied the cause of their anxiety one last time and was relieved to find one change, and that to the good; bivouac fires glowing in the gathering dusk all over the area that the French cavalry occupied. He turned to Nat Drake.

"He's cooking his Coq-au-vin down there, or whatever, but I want the listening watch down there, Simon set up markers for the route. Send your best, not now, but two hours before dawn. If he's going to send any along that road to join his cavalry, they'll be arriving then, with all of the day at their disposal."

"Do you think he knows we're up here?"

"Probably, but it matters not. If he arrives, he'll go straight at the whole Division. Anyone on that far ridge, his side of the road, can see that the Third is unsupported and on the wrong side of the Agueda!"

Thus, at the back end of the night, Davey, Miles and Pike found themselves feeling their way down, passing pieces of wood smeared in white pipe-clay. Once in the small enclave, the three incumbents already there, Saunders, Byford and Bailey, rose up and wordlessly began their journey up the slope. No-one spoke, each knew well enough that if they could hear the French on the road, then the French could hear them, but there was no human sound, only the sounds of the night, mostly predators despatching their prey. Finally, with the dawn growing on the Eastern horizon and the light improving by the minute, Davey tapped both his comrades on the shoulder and they made their way back up to the high picket, to then slump down by their mess-fire and, after a drink of tea that was waiting for them as prepared by Solomon, they took the chance for some sleep. Davey was the last to arrive at their fire having quickly reported to Drake the total silence of their watch. However, their sleep did not last long because what woke them was the inevitable noise of their Divisional Commander arriving, him having timed his leaving of Martiago to arrive at the picket with arrival of daylight. He dismounted and strode forward to the picket wall, where Carr had remained all night.

"Carr! What's the news?"

Carr came to the attention and saluted.

"There's been no movement on the road, Sir. All night. So, no change, Sir, unless those cavalry have left their bivouac fires burning whilst they get up to something.

"So, are the Frogs still there, back at their fires and cooking breakfast?"

"Yes Sir. Last time I looked, Sir, I'd say yes and the smell of garlic came wafting across."

Picton frowned deeply.

"'Fraid I don't appreciate your humour, Major!"

"No Sir."

"What's been happening before my immediate front? The other side of the stream before the Division?"

Carr craned his neck to peer off to his left and confirm what he already knew.

"Nothing Sir, bar those cavalry arriving yesterday."

"Very good. Right. Now get me some tea or something!"

The daylight grew and the sun warmed them all, even Picton, him now deciding to take a snooze in order to recover from the inordinately early start to his day and he was still in that state when events began to develop further. It began with Ethan Ellis stood to attention beside him, yelling "General Picton, Sir", very often. He dare not shake the General awake, to touch a superior Officer could see him on the gallows. Eventually, Picton looked up at Ellis, but said nothing and so Ellis delivered his message.

"Beg pardon, Sir, but there's a Frog column coming down the road."

Picton began struggling to his feet.

"How far?"

"A good mile, Sir."

Picton brushed off some gorse scrub and hurried to where he could see Carr and Drake, both using their telescopes. Carr handed his to Picton and he saw his General's jaw clamp closer together. Two French Divisions had already come into view, with the head of a third following out where the road emerged from the enfolding hills. Picton handed back the telescope to Carr.

"Identify that leading Division."

Puzzled, Carr took the instrument and focused it on the leading troops of the column, these now significantly nearer than when he first saw them. His own jaw tightened as he saw the high bearskins with a tall red plume, the broad white cross-belts and the black knee-length gaiters.

"That's the Imperial Guard, Sir."

Picton nodded and then turned away to yell at an Aide-de-Camp.

"Wakeridge! Get over to Wellington and tell him the French have arrived in force along the Salamanca road. At least three Divisions."

Drake had been studying the road and he now lowered his telescope and turned to Picton.

"A fourth's just come into view, Sir."

Picton swivelled his large frame in the direction of Wakeridge, him still organising the length of his stirrups.

"Wakeridge, it's four!"

At that moment, Stuart Maltby was pointing across the valley, far beyond the road.

"Sir. I do believe there to be more, Sir. Coming over from the North. You can just make them out, I believe, Sir."

Picton snatched Carr's telescope out from under his arm and focused it where Maltby was pointing.

"Give me a marker!"

"The corner of the forest, Sir, where it comes over the far ridge. Just beneath."

Picton peered into the distance and then focused to see four more French Divisional columns emerging from the tree line. His face turned red as he slammed the telescope shut, somewhat to Carr's consternation, him worrying for the continued wellbeing of his precious instrument.

"Wakeridge. Tell him I've got eight Divisions on my front and I am awaiting orders."

Wakeridge had sensibly waited for the final count and so now he hurried away on his horse and Carr came to the attention as the telescope was thrust back at him.

"Sir. Should I warn our Brigades below?"

Picton was now watching the column on the road, now having become four separate Divisions headed by the invincible Imperial Guard.

"Yes. Bring them to the alert."

Carr hurried away, as grateful to get his irreplaceable telescope out of Picton's reach as he was to warn the two British Brigades below. He found the mirror and began a regular signal, using the sun now risen sufficiently in the sky. Within a minute, he saw a flag wave from the Watch set beside the Battalion tent and so, warning sent, he returned to the picket wall. He found Picton still staring down at the French column on the road, a whole French Corps, now with its batteries of guns and transport bringing up the rear. He heard Carr arrive and frowned his acknowledgment of Carr's presence.

"What have you been in, Carr, during this Peninsular business?"

Although disinclined to boast, Carr saw no reason to be modest.

"Just about all of it, Sir, since we landed in Portugal in the year eight."

"And?"

Carr was flummoxed at the generality of Picton's reply, but decided it gave him license to reply in any manner he chose and so he gave his earnest opinion.

"We can hold them, Sir, at odds worse than three to two. They've got no answer to what we can deal out to them, but this, Sir, this is seven to one. Sooner or later, we'll be pushed back, Sir, if he comes at us."

Picton's frown lessened slightly, as Carr continued.

"If I know Johnny, that column on the road can, inside two minutes, face front to their left, form into their columns and come straight at us. Sir."

"Down below, Wallace and Colville. They've been warned?"

"Yes Sir and what we can see on the road, ours can now also see."

"Go take a look at what they've done."

Carr saluted and hurried to the top of the track to see all six Battalions of Picton's Division in a firing line, but held back, out of sight. Relieved he hurried back.

"All six formed up, Sir, and held back from the crest. I'd say that they cannot be seen from the road."

Picton's jaw again clamped together.

"That doesn't mean that they do not know we are here!"

"No Sir."

At that moment, the Relief Company of the 88th arrived and Carr felt justified in intruding on Picton's obviously worried thoughts.

"May I take my Company back down, Sir. The Relief's arrived and mine have been here all night."

Picton did no more than nod, but Carr continued, he had given his full opinion once, so he felt licensed to give it again.

"Our Commander's Headquarters is as Fuente Guinaldo. That's 20 miles from here, Sir. We won't hear back until late in the day, Sir."

"Wrong Carr. He's at El Bodon, we'll hear back come Midday. Wakeridge is well mounted."

Carr saluted and turned away, to soon lead the 105th Light Company back down the track. Far below them, the 105th were formed up for possible battle, any meal long past and Drake soon became concerned for the men of his Company following behind, which he imparted to Carr immediately they began their journey back down.

"They've had nothing decent to eat since yesterday evening, Henry. Can I give them an hour before they join the line?"

The question interrupted Carr's own thoughts regarding their predicament, but he turned to Drake and nodded.

"Yes, of course, but equipment stays on and weapons to hand. We could find ourselves muzzle to muzzle with the Imperial Guard within an hour and so the men remain in a state of readiness."

Once in camp, Carr and the Light Company went their separate ways. Drake's talk of food had reminded Carr of his own hunger and to he went straight to Morrison's tent and helped himself to what was in the pot, a weird combination of fish and Spanish sausage, but with army biscuits it filled him up well enough. That done, he took himself to the centre of the 105th line to find Lacey and O'Hare stood idle but talking together in urgent tones. Lacey noticed Carr first.

"Henry! Any news?"

"One bad, another a little better. Johnny's got two Corps in front of us, the one on the road and another's in the hills to the North, but Picton's sent word to Wellington about how perilous we are out here, kept out beyond the Agueda. He's at El Bodon and so we should hear reasonably soon."

"You're right, but neither is the best of news."

He turned to O'Hare.

"We cannot stand down. We just have to wait. Nothing else for it."

In the centre of the line Deakin was leaning on the Colour shaft, the precious cloth remaining uncased. He turned to Halfway just behind him.

"How long we bin stood 'ere, Tobe?"

Halfway was one of the few who had a watch and he dragged it out, it being large and of French manufacture, obtained during the Holland campaign of 1799.

"A good hour, nor more. Pushing two."

Deakin looked around to see what he expected, men running back from the line, often using the excuse to relieve themselves, when really it was to get back to their mess area for a drink and an army biscuit. Relief of the tedium came in the form of Colonel Wallace riding up over the ridge to halt before Lacey and O'Hare, both stood ten yards out before Deakin in the Colour Company.

"Stand them down, Lacey, but with kit still on. Colville's doing the same, standing his down for their Midday meal. Johnny's newcomes along the road have turned right and joined their cavalry at Cuidad. If Picton wants us back in line, he only has to say so. In fact, I'm going up to see him now. I've got my doubts if Johnny feels like starting anything, but Picton may disagree."

With that he urged his horse towards the high picket track and O'Hare gave the order for the 105th line to soon break apart as the men hurried to their mess areas. The stew was already prepared, being the type of food that could remain ready for some time. Tom Miles was the first to arrive.

"What's in the pot?"

Bridie answered.

"Salt fish and potatoes. With a bit of sage."

He sat down with Davey beside him and each removed the pannikin from the other's pack. To take off the pack for such a purpose contrary to orders would be a flogging offence. Both had wolfed down a biscuit and a length of sausage during Carr's hour of generosity, but they had remained hungry.

"Fish stew! My favourite."

Nellie Nicholls could not countenance Tom Miles giving any form of verdict on their cooking, complimentary or otherwise and so she looked up from spooning out portions to the others of the mess.

"Now don't you be speaking any of your miserable sarcasm, Tom Miles! Sure, have we not been doing our best with the Heathen French just over the hill? Giving us all the jitters!"

The first spoonful stopped halfway to Miles' mouth, his face amazed.

"What did I say? What did I say?"

Saunders was sat beside Consuela and now eating himself.

"You said fish-stew was your favourite."

Miles looked accusingly at Nellie.

"Yes! And so it is."

Nellie looked wholly unconvinced, but Miles was given an extra spoonful after his portion had quickly disappeared.

"Well. Fair's fair, I suppose. What with the milk and eggs you've been fetching down for us and the babby."

Deakin chuckled.

"Don't tell me relations have eased between you two!"

Saunders looked up.

"If they have, it's for the price of my tobacco! I've not had a smoke in days."

Halfway threw his tobacco pouch over at him.

"Take a fill from that. Supplies'll be up soon."

Deakin had other ideas.

"Ah! Or we'll all be marchin' back to meet 'em."

Deakin's prediction was not so far wrong, but it seemed remote when Wallace came back from Picton and entered the Headquarters tent of the 105th, to find Lacey, O'Hare and Carr sat drinking coffee. Wallace looked first at the coffee pot.

"Any of that spare?"

There were only three beakers and so Lacey poured some more coffee into his own and pushed it towards Wallace, who took a single drink.

"Picton's heard back from Himself and it isn't good. He's convinced that the whole Frog show is just to open the road to Cuidad and re-supply. He's not going to give an inch before Cuidad unless he's absolutely forced to."

The three of the 105th looked at each other before Wallace continued.

"That won't be long in coming. We've had a Squadron of Johnny cavalry up to take a look and gauge our strength. They got up to the 74th and then shot off back. They know how weak we are up here, compared to them down there."

By now Carr had finished his coffee and so he gave the discussion his full attention.

"Just what does 'forced to' mean, Sir. I take it to mean that we pull back, whilst still having a camp behind us and give Johnny all our tents and baggage? We should send the Followers off now, Sir, with our transport and tents."

Wallace remained thinking, but Lacey added his opinion.

"Henry's right. We can hold here, for two or three days, without the Followers. That's still obeying orders, but we won't be risking our camp."

Wallace stood up.

"Right. Do it. I'll persuade Colville to do the same. Picton's still up on his hill and he'll not complain if the men remain to hold the ridge."

Then Lacey had a disturbing thought.

"Which way? To send them back through Martiago still keeps them in danger this side of the Agueda. On top, they may get caught up with us in a running fight. Can we risk getting them back over at that mill, the way we came over?"

Wallace turned to O'Hare, the combat comrade with whom he shared wholly violent memories of Busaco.

"What do you think?"

O'Hare nodded. He had already thought.

"Johnny's only just arrived. It's worth the risk to get them quickly back over the river, even though his cavalry has been here some time. Get them away, if we don't, the men will only worry."

Wallace nodded.

"Yes. I'll send my Rifles with them as escort until they cross, Colville will include his, I'm sure. Once they are over, our Riley can bring them all back."

Carr jumped up.

"I'll get things moving."

'Getting things moving' involved telling off every Senior Sergeant, and so it was Deakin who came to Bridie and Nellie, both involved with cleaning, now that all their menfolk had been fed and departed.

"Get packed up! Your moving in 30 minutes, back over the river, the way we came."

"What about you?"

This came from Bridie and Deakin had his reply.

"We're to stay. Could be for two or three days, but you're to be got away. You and the wagons."

Sooner than 30 minutes the long trail of Followers was following the road back down to the river, with Colville's Followers some way ahead and Wallace's four Companies of Rifles strung out at their side. The ecumenical cart containing Albright and Sedgwicke, was at the head of the 105th Followers, with the inevitable Bridie and Nellie close by.

"Are you thinkin' that this will all work out to the good, now, Parson, do you think?"

Sedgwicke smiled down beatifically.

"I'm sure that it will, Mrs. Nicholls. I'm sure that the French will not take the trouble to capture or even molest a column of women and children."

Hearing such a question regarding the 'good and bad' in men, the Reverend Albright felt duty bound to offer an opinion.

"I'm sure that my servant here is correct, my good woman. Whatever they are, the French are of the Christian persuasion and I'm sure they will respect the status of non-combatant women and children."

By now they were within half a mile of the junction with the mill-road that led to the leat bridge. The head of Colville's column was already into the woodland that surrounded the mill, but a look over to the right made Sedgwicke's heart miss a beat. French cavalry were coming their way and a look forward almost caused it to stop altogether, the column of Followers had halted on the half mile of mill-road that led to the mill itself, because there was inevitable congestion at the mill bridge, it being wide enough for only a small cart. Wails and cries of distress and fear arouse from all around. Riley, the Senior Captain of the four Companies of Rifles, began yelling orders and his elite soldiers ran out to form a line between themselves and their charges,

206

who were at the early stages of panic now that everyone had seen the approaching French cavalry. Bridie was tugging Nellie's arm.

"That's nothing like enough soldiers out there to hold off all them French as is riding up. Nothing like, what'll we do?"

Nellie Nicholls shrugged off her pack which fell to the ground with a clatter of pots and pans.

"Well, I'm not standin' still to be letting those gobshites ride straight over me like I was some kind of scarecrow out in a field. I've handled a musket afore now and I can do so again!"

With that she ran to the 105th supply wagon to stand just below the two Waggoners.

"Youse! What kind of men are youse, to stay sittin' up there with Heathen French about to ride all over the women and children and commit all kinds of Devilry?"

The two, both well advanced in years, looked at each other and a resigned look came over both faces. Without a word, both descended and went to the rear of the wagon to pull out two muskets and bags of cartridges. Nellie was incensed.

"Not two! Three! One for me. I can load a gun and fire it, 'swell as youse. Probably better."

At that point, Consuela came around the back of the wagon and she pointed at a musket and then at herself. Nellie turned to the men now under her command.

"Four! Make that four."

The four, each with a musket and a pocket full of cartridges ran out to stand at the right end of the Rifles line. The nearest Rifleman looked over, somewhat amused, with Nellie standing nearest to him.

"What's this, Mother? You goin' to throw dough-cakes at 'em?"

Nellie was busy loading the musket.

"You can shut your gob and face your front!"

Now grinning even more, the Riflemen did as he was told. Nellie handed her loaded musket to Consuela and then loaded Consuela's for herself. Then both stood at 'Order arms'. Sedgwicke, back on the cart, had watched transfixed as the French cavalry approached at a fast walk. They were now under five hundred yards away and so he took a deep breath and turned to Reverend Albright.

"I'm sorry Sir, but I'm afraid I must do this."

Albright's head suddenly swivelled to his servant and away from staring at the cavalry.

"Do what, Private?"

"Join that line, Sir."

Albright's was aghast, his mouth falling open.

"I forbid you. It is not your duty to do such a thing."

Sedgwicke was already descending from the cart.

"I'm afraid that duty is exactly what it is. Sir."

With that he was gone from Albright's sight, hurrying to the back of the cart where was kept his own equipment. He pulled out his musket and cartridge pouch and hurried to the line where he joined in beside Nellie. She turned to him with a look of approval on her face.

"Well now, Parson, at least you've got enough in youse to come and face the French without the need for any persuasion."

She leaned forward to look at the two Waggoners.

"Not like some!"

Sedgwicke had been a hopeless Line soldier, but he knew how to load a musket and so that was done and then he stood to watch and await events. However, these played out in a very unexpected manner. The French cavalry, now plainly seen to be Hussars, were advancing on in two Squadron lines abreast, with their Colonel far out in front. The tension rose within the Followers and Riflemen with every step of his horse, then, at a distance of 150 yards from the Riflemen, he stopped and held out his sword horizontally to order his men to also halt and they did so, 50 yards behind him. He studied the scene before him for a full minute, plainly seeing about 200 Riflemen between him and a dense crowd of women, children and transport wagons. He was plainly comparing one course with another and even Sedgwicke could work out his choices. If he attacked, these very capable Riflemen, the 'Green Lice', would down many of his men at maximum range, then quickly form square, which he would not be able to penetrate, costing him more men. His men, angry and frustrated, would then go on to the easy target, to inflict death and wounds upon women and children, for little military gain and to utterly sully the reputation of his Regiment and French Hussars in general. Spanish civilians were one thing, all of little consequence, but massacring women and children Followers of the

British army, that was another thing entirely. It would create a scandal of huge proportions. Chivalry was generally well observed between the two armies, it was generally beneficial and was best preserved. On top, these Riflemen were escorting unarmed civilians to safety out of a battle-zone, not undertaking any threatening manoeuvre. He was directly opposite Captain Riley, who saw him smile, sheath his sword and then stand up on his stirrups to perform an exaggerated salute. Riley, in response, brought his sword across his face in a double sweep in reply. The French Colonel, then spun his horse around and led his men, in column, back towards Cuidad Rodrigo. Sedgwicke, stood between Nellie and Consuela, felt his knees go with the relief and he could barely stand, his hands releasing his musket. Nellie came to one side to prop him up and Consuela came to the other. With Sedgwicke dragging his musket by the sling they helped him back to his wagon, Nellie speaking encouragement.

"There now, Parson darlin', all's well now and when we gets across that gombeen river, I'm sure we'll be able to make a bit of a camp and get some tea and doughcakes goin'. Won't that be nice now?"

Sedgwicke lifted his head and managed to nod once.

oOo

Chapter Seven

El Bodon and Retreat.

For the 16th Light Dragoons each day after their arrival back from the passes to the Cuidad area, gave the opportunity for a more solid domestication of their position, which was very satisfying for them all. They were happily ensconced in Carpio de Azaba, a well-appointed village South West of Cuidad, with plenty of good billets, good grazing all around and water aplenty from the many wells and the river Azaba itself. They now had Colonel Anson as their Brigadier and were joined up with the 14th Light Dragoons, however, all was thrown askew when their most advanced picket, six of the 14th, came galloping back through the village. The four Cornets of One and Two Squadrons of the 16th were contentedly eating new baked bread, as bought from the local, now thriving, bakery, when the picket arrived. Peterson held out his arm to slow one of them, all hurrying on their way to the camp of the 14th, at the rear of the village.

"What news?"

The 14th Cornet slowed his horse to give just enough time to pass on their discovery.

"There's a big cavalry column coming out of Cuidad. We lost count of the number of Squadrons after we'd passed 12, but there were more behind. This is serious stuff. Expect to pull back. Us and you can't expect to hold that many."

With that he urged his horse after the rest of his picket, leaving the four staring at each other. At that moment, they were the only members of the 16th who knew what was transpiring. It was Smythe of A Troop, One Squadron who took the initiative.

"Right, I'm off to the Colonel."

He turned to Ben Faversham, his fellow Cornet of One Squadron.

"Ben. Get Jacobson to pack my gear with yours and saddle Roland. We'll be out of here very soon."

With that he ran off in the direction of 16th Headquarters and the remaining three ran off to their billets to assemble their own possessions, rather than leave them for the oncoming French. Within 15 minutes the 16th were following the 14th Light Dragoons out of Carpio along the main trunk road out of the village that led to Vilar Formosa on the Portuguese border. Within minutes of their leaving, Major Johnson fell back to inform all his Squadron Captains, soon arriving at Two Squadron, to give the relatively recent addition of Captain Oakwood, the chance to question him, but in the briefest manner.

"What's happening, Sir?"

"We're pulling back over the Azaba, back onto our infantry supports of the 6th Division. General Campbell commands them, so you can expect good sense from him."

They splashed through the almost insignificant stream of the Azaba and rode up the slope to reveal the wood at the top. There Johnson, on his way back along the column, turned to Carr nearby and grinned.

"There! Didn't I say we'd get sense out of Campbell?"

Carr looked either side of the column ahead of him, to see what looked like three Companies of Redcoats and one of Rifles lining the edge of the wood. Ahead, they saw the 14th move right, led by Anson himself, whilst the 16th swung off left. Very obviously, Anson was dividing his Brigade to each flank of Campbell's infantry line and soon Carr found himself sitting his horse alongside a Lieutenant of a Light Company. The Lieutenant look up.

"Who are you?"

"16th Light Dragoons. May I ask who you are?"

Strictly speaking a Cornet was of lower rank than a full Lieutenant, but not enough to require the inclusion of any 'Sirs', but the Lieutenant replied.

"Light Company, 11th Foot. What do you know?"

"Several Squadrons, over 12, have come out of Cuidad and are heading our way. We had to pull back from Carpio."

The Lieutenant nodded, hands folded over the pommel of his drawn sword.

"Time will tell."

The time in question was 15 minutes before a line of mounted green uniforms, about 25 across, appeared up from the valley of the Azaba. They were obviously the head of a column and the Lieutenant once again turned to Carr.

"You're cavalry. What do you make of that lot?"

Carr studied the line. They were obviously Hussars, French Chasseurs, with an almost ludicrously high red plume on each busby.

"Hussars."

The Lieutenant looked up at him, his expression ironic.

"Hussars! You don't say. I could have told you that!"

"Yes, but what I can say is that could be only the head of a long column."

The Hussars came on and, from where they were, far out on the British right, they could see a gap between the next French Squadron, this also Hussars. However, whilst Carr was studying events on his left front, the Lieutenant of the 11th was looking far left.

"Here we go!"

Carr looked over to also see a Squadron of the 14th advance at a controlled canter towards the leading Hussars, with what looked like Anson in the lead, all with swords drawn and sparkling in the sun. At exactly the correct moment, Anson raised his sword and swung it forwards, the signal to accelerate into a charge. The single Squadron of the 14th crashed into the Hussars who had made no change in their formation to receive the oncoming threat. The screaming of horses and men and the clash of steel came clearly across to them over the 300-yard distance. Given the extra impetus of charging downhill, the whole melee was soon moving backwards from the impact of the 14th Squadron, the Chasseurs rapidly giving ground and soon they were in full flight. However, Anson had his men well in hand and when a trumpet sounded the recall, his men broke off and cantered back to re-join the rest of the 14th.

Soon, everyone could see why Anson had broken off. Coming up the slope in support were more French Squadrons and it seemed that the first, defeated Squadron had rallied on their supports. The Lieutenant slapped his hand onto the top of his shako to set it more firmly and pulled the strap securely under his chin.

"Our turn now."

He turned to his men, in a two-deep line to his left.

"Make ready!"

All muskets were raised in the air, firelock beside each right cheek. Looking towards the French cavalry, Carr could see that, whoever commanded them, had now seen sense and his Squadrons were deploying left and right. The Hussars deployed to the British left, to Anson, whilst up to the right to be closely studied by the 16th, came Lancers, these having the only item in the line above the nonsensical plume of the Hussars, their lances, each with a red and white guidon at the top of the shaft. The question came up from Carr's left.

"That looks like four Squadrons. Can you see any more in support?"

Carr rose in his stirrups to gain an extra foot of height.

"No. That looks like it. At least for us."

"They're set to charge, you think?"

"I do."

Carr was right. The four Squadrons came on at a fast canter, not yet a gallop. From somewhere in the centre of the Redcoats and Rifles there came an order, shouted at full volume.

"Present!"

All the muskets of the 11th Lights came down to the horizontal. The Officer giving the order waited until the approaching cavalry were within 50 yards before giving the next, inevitable order. The muskets of the front rank crashed out and after five seconds came that of the second rank. As the smoke cleared, the order came down the ranks of the 16th.

"Draw sabres!"

Carr looked down at the Lieutenant.

"Here we go!"

"Well, good luck!"

The smoke cleared and it could be seen that the volley had brought the charge to a halt. All was a tangle of struggling horses and cursing men, many of both badly wounded or dead, with lances now up or down at all angles. Colonel Withers had arrived at the head of his two Squadrons that were formed on the left. He could see that the moment was now and he raised his sword.

"Charge!"

The two Squadrons of the 16th sprang into full gallop. In the space of what seemed to be no more than a heartbeat, they crashed into the confusion that was before them. Carr suddenly found Sergeant Baxter and Trooper Spivey either side of him as they battered their way into the Lancers' line, although progress quickly slowed due to the confusion of bodies on the ground, both men and horses. Whilst Baxter and Spivey hacked away to the sides, Carr ineffectually tried to stab forward, but within seconds the Lancers had broken and were turning their horses to retreat. Major Johnson appeared from seemingly nowhere and yelled his order.

"On! Push them on. Don't let them regroup."

The Lancers were now in retreat at full gallop, but the two of the16[th] held to a fast canter and from everywhere seemed to come the order, frequently repeated by Oakwood.

"Hold the line, boys! Hold the line. Keep together."

Soon the two Squadrons of the 16th were in a solid, intimidating line, with two of the 14th extending off to their left. The 14th had also pushed back their Hussar opponents and so all before Anson's men, only half of his Brigade, was a green confusion, topped by red plumes and white and red lance guidons. There was little for the Light Dragoons to do but to canter on, holding their line and preserving their horses for a possible late surge. After a canter of two miles the slope steepened down to the bed of the Azaba, where many Lancers were struggling to cross, owing to the steep bank and the exhaustion of their mounts. Carr's first instinct was to join them in the water to continue the fight, but Baxter placed his horse across Carr's.

"That'll do, Sir. Them's beat and we've lost no lads at all. No sense in losing any. That could be a real tangle down there. Joinin' that'll serve nuthin'!"

However, at that moment Tavender arrived, commanding the accompanying One Squadron, and obviously in a very aggressive and volatile mood.

"Carr! Continue the attack. Get some men and follow me!"

Where, was obvious, but then 'Recall' sounded and Anson's four Squadrons broke off immediately, including Carr and his Troop. Upon drawing back, the reason could be seen. Four more French Squadrons, all Hussars, were riding to the rescue of their beaten and stricken comrades. To go into the river would mean riding into a death trap when the French supports arrived. Baxter looked at Tavender, now walking his horse away from the river. He spoke, but was merely muttering to himself.

"I bet you saw them coming, didn't you? You treacherous bastard! And it wouldn't have been you as did go down into that river with Carr. Just a few of us lads."

oOo

At the same moment that the 16th Light Dragoons were crossing the Azaba in retreat, prior to their gallant action, the 105th were crossing their own watercourse, a tributary of the Agueda, but they remained on the wrong side of that major river. Captain Lord Carravoy was not in the best of moods and his temper was growing worse.

"If you want to know what I think, I'll say that this damned Sepoy General has made a complete pig's ear of the whole thing! Leaving us out to dry on the wrong side of the river and now pulling us back as odds and sods in different directions."

D'Villiers knew that he had no choice to hear, by being told in no uncertain terms, what his Captain's opinion was, but he had opinions of his own. What he did know was that they were marching to cross the Agueda and that at that moment they were wholly unmolested and, with that as fact, things did not seem to be going too badly. It made sense to him that Wallace's Brigade had split in order to use other crossings of the Agueda and he had seen the 74th and 60th Rifles swing right off the road to use what he assumed to be a ford. The crossing for the 88th and 105th was now coming into view as they marched in column of fours down a decent road for this part of Spain. He looked ahead and immediately counted his blessings further, no ford crossing for them.

"Well, if nothing else, we are seeing some sights on this retreat, if retreat is what it is."

Carravoy's mood had not tempered at all.

"Of course, it is and it's not over yet."

However, the 'sights' alluded to by D'Villiers were now before them, a chasm of the Agueda spanned by a magnificent Roman bridge, three arches each placed on a carefully constructed base that sat solidly in the river bed. D'Villiers felt his spirits lift considerably as they set foot on what was probably the original cobble-stones.

"Well, whatever, it's not often that you can say that you placed your foot in the exact same place as a Roman Legionary, so many centuries ago."

Carravoy was not appeased.

"And I don't doubt that he had a better General than the one we've got in charge of us!"

D'Villiers gave up and hitched his pack into a more comfortable position in order to enjoy the experience of setting foot on such a structure, but soon the bridge was behind them and now they had to set themselves for the climb out of the Agueda valley. Wallace, Lacey and O'Hare were at the head of the column and Wallace was relieved to see a Cornet of the 11th Light Dragoons waiting for them at a junction at the top of the main slope. The Cornet saluted.

"Good morning Sirs. I'm waiting for Colonel Wallace."

Wallace halted his horse.

"I am he!"

"General Wellington is at El Bodon, Sir. I am to guide you there."

"Very well, young man. Who else is at El Bodon, do you know?"

"As I left, Sir, three Squadrons of KGL Hussars and two of my own Regiment, Sir. And General Wellington with his Staff."

Wallace exchanged an anxious look with Lacey and O'Hare.

"If Wellington's come up, he must be worried. We'd best pick up the pace!"

The two nodded as Wallace turned to the Cornet.

211

"Lead on. I feel we must hurry. How far would you say?"

"Something short of three miles, Sir."

Half an hour later, they saw the familiar roofs of El Bodon and all in the 105th and 88th were more than a little fatigued after the forced march that now completed a long and hurried one. However, what was reassuring was the figure with the bi-corn hat and plain blue jacket riding out to meet them, although they were still some way from the village. The three halted and saluted as Wellington reined in his own horse.

"Wallace! Get yours up onto that ridge."

He pointed to an obvious horizon about 400 yards off the road.

"Cover the slope down. You'll be supporting Alten's cavalry and a battery. They will be out before the village."

"What are you expecting, Sir?"

Having given his orders, Wellington had turned his horse to ride back to the village, but he halted at Wallace's question.

"Marmont's sent a large cavalry column out from Cuidad, down the main road that runs through this place. Well over 2,000. It may be a push on his part, or it may be merely a look. Whatever, we'll hold it here."

"Yes Sir, but not just us?"

Wellington frowned at the pointed question, but Wallace, being Wallace, deserved an answer.

"Half of Alten's Brigade are already here, with two Portuguese batteries. Colville's 5th and 77th will be arriving soon, they're coming up from Fuente Guinaldo."

That now said, Wellington cantered off, leaving the three bemused, especially Wallace.

"Colville left the Salamanca road before we did! When Picton heard about the scare given to the Followers by roaming cavalry, he sent them off first!"

Lacey nodded.

"Yes, but he sent them to Guinaldo, in Wellington's main line, so now they've got to march back to here."

"Fine. Right. Enough! Get the men where he wants them, in line. There'll be some work to be done today."

O'Hare led the 105th rightwards from their line of march, across the flat El Bodon plateau to then form at the top of a steep slope that descended forward and then rightwards to the valley of the Agueda. Cuidad Rodrigo could be seen in the far distance before them. With his Battalion placed, O'Hare gave the welcome order.

"Brew and eat!"

Within minutes the fires were going, fuelled by the gorse stumps all around. Carr came up from the Light Company on the far right, to stand beside O'Hare.

"What are we faced with?"

"Two and a half thousand cavalry and I'd say that was them, emerging from that wood."

Carr extracted his telescope and had it quickly focused.

"It is. And what have we got?"

"Us, the 88th, about 500 cavalry and two Portuguese batteries. There's one of them, just below the village. Off to our left."

Carr craned his neck and he could just see the distinctive Portuguese Artillery shako, with its single plume and the rather ancient naval style tri-corn of an Officer.

"Anything on their way up to us?"

"Yes. The 5th and the 77th"

"Good! And not too far I hope."

It was not long before almost every Officer on the El Bodon position had his telescope to his eye to observe the French advance. Without halting, within a mile of El Bodon, the column split into three, but curiously, the right-hand column, from the Allied viewpoint, remained on the road, whilst the remaining two advanced to the left of the road. However, O'Hare did not dwell any further to debate the merits of the French formation, although it posed no immediate threat to them.

"Right! Fires out. Stand to. Three deep line."

It was Ellis who brought the message to the messes of Davey and Saunders, him hurrying around the Company and not halting to speak his order.

"Get that fire out and stand to. Three deep."

Unsurprisingly, Miles was put out, with tea only just brewed.

"Now? Right now?"

Ellis answered over his shoulder.

"Quicker than that Miles. There's Frog cavalry on their way."

Minutes later, the 105th were holding their position with the 88th on their right. It was with both puzzlement and relief that all three French columns of horse disappeared into the depression before the village and, clearly, they were attempting the left and centre of Wellington's short line, not his right where they were. As soon as they went out of sight into the depression, they came within range of the Portuguese battery close by, which immediately opened fire, the guns soon emitting a continuous roar. All in the 105th line were looking to their left, but their Officers had the privilege, almost the necessity, of edging forward to a vantage point where they could observe the events that could make a difference to their own well-being. For this Lacey commissioned Carr.

"Take Charles and a runner and get off left and as far forward as you dare. Keep a close watch."

Carr hurried off, scabbard held in his left hand, as he ran to the Grenadier Company who formed the far left of the 105th line. He had no confidence that discharging the role with Carravoy would be easy or pleasant, but those were his orders. As he ran, he could see what must be KGL cavalry, advancing almost at the charge down from the village, but their opponents he could not see. However, soon he was standing next to Carravoy.

"Charles! Lacey wants us, and a runner, as far forward as we dare, to observe what's happening."

Carravoy looked at him with a frown, as the sounds of cavalry conflict came to them between the volleys of the Portuguese battery.

"Now?"

Carr was already moving forward.

"Yes Charles, now. And bring that Corporal behind you."

At a distance of only 150 yards forward, Carr halted and Carravoy joined him. With so many French cavalry around, he wanted to give both of them a decent chance of running back to the safety of their line. Looking left, the smoke from the Portuguese battery hid most of what was happening, but they could see that the French were mounting a serious attack on the village, thankfully all so far repulsed by the 11th Light Dragoons and the KGL Hussars. However, the French Commander had so many Squadrons to call upon, that they could make almost continuous assaults against the front of the village held only by Alten's five, which was certainly happening, from where Carr and Carravoy were watching. As soon as one French Squadron was thrown back, another came on, the French Troopers urging their horses into as fast a gallop as they could manage up the steep slope. Carr was agog in admiration for what they could see.

"There's only two KGL Squadrons there that I can see, and look, each is taking turns to charge whatever comes at them up the slope. However many times. Superb!"

For many minutes the performance was maintained, each KGL Squadron, brown busby and blue jacket, charged every French advance, to withdraw in good order and reform, whilst their fellow Squadron rode forward in turn, to repulse the next, almost immediate, French attack. Carr took a deep breath and shook his head in admiration.

"That there is about as good as it gets! It'll take a lot before I say anything ill against any cavalry again. Especially KGL."

Carravoy was seemingly unimpressed.

"They have got the slope in their favour!"

Carr studied him, more than a little annoyed.

"And how many times have you seen each Squadron of ours ride forward, or have you lost count? Because I have. I'd say the Johnnies have ridden up at least 30 times. Slope or no slope!"

Carravoy changed the subject.

"But why aren't they coming our way? There's enough of a gap, where Wellington placed us!"

Carr continued to study the movements of the French on their side.

"A fair point, Charles, but give it time."

He paused, to try to make sense of the confusion before them, as the Portuguese guns continued to assault anything in range and the KGL continued their controlled heroics.

"I'd say there's another Johnny column lurking somewhere. I saw a fourth on the road behind the three he sent up as a front."

213

However, Carravoy had turned to look behind them and to their left.

"Help's arrived!"

Carr turned to see a Battalion of Redcoats, their column two Companies wide, aiming for the position that would fill the gap between Carravoy's Grenadiers and the buildings of El Bodon, but still some way off.

"That's the 5th or the 77th of Colville's. I think we can assume that the Colonel's seen them."

However, he turned back to observing the conflict, to then see something that immediately restored his anxiety. A whole column of French cavalry, in Brigade strength, were advancing to the right of the line of the road, straight for the Portuguese battery. These guns now gave this column their full attention and the destruction of their fire inflicted on this new target became more obvious with every yard they advanced, but advance they did. Carr spoke out loud.

"This is our business."

He turned to the Corporal

"Get to the Colonel at The Colour. Tell him a Brigade of cavalry are onto our left front, attacking the guns. Run!"

The Corporal ran off and Carr returned to the scene which was becoming more perilous by the second, the result becoming more and more obvious. Six guns could not stop 600 horse.

"We're going to lose those guns! Charles, get yours and Charter's Two Company down here. We must give those gunners somewhere to run to, for shelter, or they'll just be sabred."

Carravoy merely looked at him and Carr's anxiety burst into anger.

"Now, Charles, now!"

Carravoy's face twisted into anger, but he did then obey and hurried away. With that Carr drew his sword and alternated very uneasy looks between the all too likely and perilous events at the guns in front and the much-desired advance of the two Companies of the 105th from behind. The two almost coincided and, led by Royston D'Villiers Section, the Grenadier Company arrived first, with Number Two Company close behind and Carr led both forward. They were within 100 yards of the guns when the French Light Dragoons forced their way into the battery, forcing the gunners to retreat, most of them gratefully running up to the safety of the 105th line. However, on the far side, some gunners continued to fight the Dragoons around the guns, hoping to preserve these precious charges from capture, but Carr had little hope. Some French had already dismounted and had ropes in their hands with which they hoped to tow away their trophies. He spoke with despair.

"We've just lost six guns!"

However, Carravoy had been looking elsewhere, behind and to their left.

"Perhaps not."

Carr turned himself, to see the newly arrived British Regiment advancing at the run on what was now a four Company front and halt, less than 50 yards from the cavalry still milling around the guns. An Officer was out in front of the Redcoats and he yelled his orders, but these were barely heard by Carr and D'Villiers above the din at the guns. However, the result of the orders were three volleys being poured into the disorganised cavalry. Men and horses dropped at each discharge. The pair watched and D'Villiers voiced the question in the minds of both.

"What do they hope to achieve with that?"

The answer was immediate. The Officer raised his sword and led his men forward in a charge. Carr was astonished, infantry did not charge cavalry, but he could at least give support. If they arrived on the Dragoon flank it may make a difference. He turned to the Grenadiers and Two Company, in their three-deep line.

"At the double advance!"

They ran forward, but after the solid, three deep line of Redcoats, charging forward, had hit the French Dragoons, their bayonets stabbing upwards at their mounted opponents, but also many into several horses, causing them to buck and rear and unseat their riders. Within a minute, it was clear that the Redcoats were winning, the fought over guns beginning to emerge from the melee as the Dragoons were forced back. Carr brought his line around to where they could fire at the horsemen and they quickly re-formed. He held up his sword, calling the orders quickly.

"Make ready. Present. Fire!"

After the discharge of the first rank, the second and third obeyed their drill as taught and they each counted three seconds before they fired after the rank before. If it made any difference it was hard to tell, because by now their opponents were in full retreat, leaving many prone on the ground, either dead, or wounded and made prisoner. Many unhorsed Dragoons also stood with their hands in the air in surrender. The Portuguese gunners, who had advanced with the Redcoats, now ran to their guns and brought them quickly back into action, as if to exact revenge on those who had forced them to abandon their precious charges. The rescuing Redcoats were now reforming behind them and Carr felt the need to go over and at least say some words, if not all of congratulation. He headed straight for a tall, craggy, red-faced man, at that moment retrieving his shako, his sword still in his hand. As he sheathed it, he noticed Carr. His rank was that of a Major, but probably senior to Carr and he spoke first.

"Thanks for your support."

Carr took a deep breath.

"Well, I'm sure there are words to adequately describe what I've just seen, but for the moment they totally escape me!"

The Officer grinned.

"And I'm sure there are very few words that I could say in reply."

Carr closed the gap between them, extending his hand.

"Carr. 105th."

"Ridge. Just plain 5th!"

Carr laughed as they shook hands, but Ridge now had other concerns.

"Best reform, I'd say. Johnny's still about and also his Lordship, which is worse. Thanks to you, Carr, and good luck."

"Same to you Ridge, and well done, to you and to your men. Hoorah for the Fighting Fifth!"

Each waved to the other as they returned to their Regiments, all now back on the top of the ridge. Back with the Grenadiers, Carr found Lacey stood with Carravoy and it was his Colonel who spoke.

"Well done, you two. Six guns would have been a serious loss."

Carr bridled internally at the sound of 'you two', but he kept his silence. The Portuguese guns had resumed their fire, but the cavalry attacks had ceased. Lacey was now using his own telescope at events down the road, which could be seen from where they were.

"If I've got this right, I think Johnny's given best. I do believe that one of his Regiments is refusing to come forward. What do you think?"

He handed the telescope, already focused to Carr. Through it he could see Officers waving their swords forward for the advance and, just at the moment when the Portuguese guns ceased fire, French trumpets could be heard sounding the advance, but the line of cavalrymen remained stock still. Carr grinned.

"I do believe you are right, Sir."

By now, Carravoy had focused his own fine instrument and even he managed a grin, but at that moment Picton arrived, in no better mood than usual.

"Lacey! Get your bastards back on the road. Frogs are pulling back. Colville's have come together and are already on their way back out of here in column, so you and Wallace fall in behind them."

Lacey had only to turn and look at Carr to convey that it was he should obey Picton's command, but Lacey had a question of his own as Carr ran off.

"Sir. Who will be covering us, as a column on the road? Johnny's not half a mile away?"

Picton glowered down.

"Behind you will be the Portuguese guns and their 21st Line The 5th and 77th will march in square as cover and the KGL will be last out."

"Where are we going, Sir?"

"Fuente Guinaldo. The 4th Division are there in a fortified camp."

"How far, Sir."

"Six miles."

Picton noted the look on Lacey's face at the number, but said nothing more on the subject, he had lost patience. Conforming to Carr's orders, the 105th were now marching behind the last of Colville's battalions, along the ruler straight road.

"Best get to your men now, Lacey. Seems they form column quick enough when needing to march themselves out of some kind of a scrape!"

Picton remained just long enough to see the anger grow in Lacey's face, but then he was gone, riding towards the village. Lacey jogged up to the head of his men to where O'Hare was leading Lacey's horse. He mounted and joined O'Hare, still seethingly angry.

"When all this is done, if I call Picton out, don't be surprised. Our men have been marching since before dawn, with no break for any kind of meal and stood for hours in a battle line. You'd have thought that such as that would have perhaps tempered the kind of comment we're liable to get from our ill-tempered Divisional General!"

O'Hare gave a short laugh.

"Don't let Picton get to you. I recall a good line of Shakespeare, from 'Taming of the Shrew', "Thou art nought but a loud rudeby! Full of spleen!""

This helped, enough to cause Lacey to laugh and his mood was further eased when O'Hare passed over his brandy flask, but if anger subsided, anxiety increased when he saw the country through which the road to Fuente Guinaldo ran. For as far as the eye could see, the road stretched, almost straight, across a flat, open plain with a few undulations, these forming poor excuses for hills. Lacey turned to O'Hare.

"This is perfect cavalry country!"

O'Hare sighed in agreement.

"True, and Field Artillery also and Johnny's got plenty of both."

Lacey nodded his agreement.

"If ever there was a time for us to come up to Johnny's rate of march, this is it!"

The pace was set and it was quicker than usual. It was not half an hour before the sounds of conflict came from the rear and Lacey sent Carr, now mounted on a French Light Dragoon horse, off to the side to try to see what was happening. What he saw, was the rear-guard KGL riding back down towards him to join the end of column, plainly in retreat having been pushed away from El Bodon by overwhelming French numbers. Then he heard the firing as the squares of the 5th and the 77th defended themselves, these now being exposed to the full force of the French cavalry. However, the regular firing and billowing smoke continued for some minutes, which meant to Carr that these two good, steady Regiments were holding their square and dealing out severe punishment to the attacking French Dragoons. In fact, after that episode had passed, the KGL had reformed and then they charged back at the French besetting the two squares and within two minutes had driven them off. The firing ceased and the march of retreat continued unmolested. Carr clenched his teeth together and nodded in grim satisfaction, before speaking softly to himself.

"Hold that, French bastards! Who do you think you're dealing with, a Sunday School outing!"

With that satisfactorily voiced, he rode back to the head of the 105th column.

"An attack on the rear of column, Sir. Now beaten off."

"Thank you, Henry, but that's not the end of it. Be certain!"

The exact same certainty was uppermost in the mind of Jed Deakin and Toby Halfway, the third Company down the column, although being the Colour Company.

"I don't like this, Jed. 'Tis like we'n set up like some game of Aunt Sally at a fairground. With a couple of thousand Sally heads for the Frogs to shy at, 'stead of just one. Stuck 'ere on this road, I don't like it."

Deakin knew that his good friend of long standing was a natural worrier, but on this occasion, he could feel the full justification himself. The expanse of dry, burnt fields on either side defied the eye to find and then fix on any point of reference and he knew full well that soon there would be plenty to occupy his gaze both to left and right, this being French cavalry and horse-drawn guns. One crumb of comfort, at least, was Picton, still with them, riding up and down the column hurrying all along with a large variety of foul expletives. More comfort still, was the presence of their well respected KGL Hussars riding either side of the column, some occasionally coming to the column to beg a drink of water and always they had a wide choice from the many canteens offered up to them.

However, it was not long before the order came down the column.

"Load!"

Still marching furiously, each man of the 105th loaded their muskets, as did the other Battalions, leaving a trail of white paper cartridges on the road behind them. This, most surely, gave the French Light Dragoons an indication that their reception all down the column would be the same as they had received from the two squares, but first to appear was an escorted single six-gun field battery. It galloped up on the column's left, then set up far ahead, although challenged both on their way up and when in position by the gallant KGL

Squadron on that side. However, many French Heavy Dragoons protected the battery, and at their leisure, the Battery had been able to gallop up to the very head of the Allied column and beyond, to wait for them to pass by. Deakin, for one, could see the value of the KGL's efforts, him speaking to no-one in particular, but he had all around him listening.

"If I ever meets a German Hussar, I'll be buying him a drink and be lendin' the money if I has to. Makin' they Frenchers protect their guns, means that they'm in the way of 'em firin' at us. At least for a time."

'For a time', were the important words, because the KGL, vastly outnumbered, were soon forced to retreat back to the column, where they could obtain some protection from the its muskets. All along the column came the continuous sound of firing as men took shots at the surrounding French cavalry, keeping them off to a safe distance from the column. However, it was the field-gun Battery that the French Commander was relying on to break up the column for his cavalry. Soon, the six guns opened fire, at some 500 yards' range and at their best speed, their target being the part of the column passing across their front. It was not long before the 105th were marching over the gruesome results of the bombardment, but all they saw were the dead, not one wounded man was left behind, but the severed arms and legs and occasional shattered body disturbed them all. When the turn of the 105th came, to fully enter the arc of fire, instinctively all heads went a little lower into collars as shot of all kinds; solid, grape and canister whistled overhead and sometimes through their ranks, causing wounds both disabling and fatal.

A round-shot passed through the ranks of the Grenadiers, killing one man and taking off the arm of another. Blood and tissue was showered over their Captain, D'Villiers, who was promptly sick at the side of the road, but the remains of the dead man were dragged aside and the wounded man had his jacket removed and a belt wound around his upper arm. Then, supported by his comrades and although in shock, they all progressed on. Picton rose in everyone's estimation, always remaining in the line of the gunfire and foully admonishing the men over such banalities as the distance between the Sections of their 'closed column' and particularly the distance between Battalions. He wanted no gap in his column that the French could exploit and, if that was satisfactory, then he found some other criticisms of 'you whore's-melt bastards', such as the angle of their musket on several shoulders or a loosened collar button.

As the six miles and the two hours it would take to cover them ticked by, Carr saw the French battery ride up for the third time to re-deploy at the head of their column and his exasperation boiled over. He turned to Lacey.

"Sir, there must be something, surely, that we can do, rather than just march past and take it. What if we sat some of our Lights on the back of a Hussar and they rode over to those damn guns and sent in a few shots?"

Lacey could only laugh at that idea, but it did give him another. It was himself who had first introduced the effective Baker into the Battalion and he knew its potential.

"Bakers are inaccurate beyond 250 yards, but they can certainly disable at 500 if they hit something. On top, a few balls buzzing around the ears of those gunners will certainly slow their rate of fire. It may put them off somewhat, if nothing else. Get the Lights up alongside our column, in skirmish order. It may help, it can certainly do no harm."

Carr turned his horse back and quickly came to Nat Drake and the Light Company at the rear.

"Nat! Yours to fall out and double up the left side of our column. When you get opposite those French guns, send some shot their way. If we loose enough off, chances are we'll hit something. Give those damn gunners a bit of a headache, at least."

Drake turned to Ellis.

"You hear that, Sergeant?"

Ellis needed no other bidding.

"Fall out! Double up the column!"

The Light Company left the road and ran up alongside the ranks of the 105th. As chance would have it, Miles was close to Ellis as they ran up.

"So, what's this all about, then?"

"We're going to shoot at them Frog gunners, Miles, to show 'em that we're still alive. Even you!"

Davey overheard.

"S'arnt, that's 500 yards. The balls is spent by then."

"Think I don't know that, but that's what they wants."

Davey looked at Ellis as they jogged up.

"What about an extra half charge? Least it'll give the ball a flatter travel!"

His Company Sergeant thought before answering.

"It'll harden the kick and foul the barrel quicker, but it makes sense."

Soon they were up alongside Wallace's 88th and they slowed to a walk. When the 88th came under fire they halted and loaded, but Miles was not best pleased in any way, as the shot began to sing past, all around them.

"Oh, this is fine, just fine. Stood yer like a line of Aunt Sallies."

Ellis overheard and was none too pleased either, with both their situation and yet more insolence from Miles.

"Shut yer gob and get loaded, Miles. John's talked about an extra half charge. Get loaded and send a ball their way. Them, over yonder."

Ellis inclined his chin towards the toiling French gunners as he fully cocked his Baker and sent a ball off towards the French guns. At that moment, a scream came from behind him as a grape-shot found its mark.

"Keep firin', Miles. Now you knows why we're here and why we just might do some good."

At the end of the Light Company's line, Carr stood with Drake, each using their telescope.

"See that, Nat, did you?"

"What?"

"One of those gunners ducked instead of using his rammer. We're doing some good."

"Even better, I'd say."

"Why?"

"Look at their far right gun. There's a man down. Clutching his head."

Carr swung his telescope rightwards and saw a French gunner writhing on the ground with both hands to his head and his comrades grouped around him instead of serving their gun. For the next five minutes, they watched as gunners flinched and ducked from the Baker shot buzzing amongst them. It was not long before Picton rode up, fiercely bringing his horse to a halt.

"What the Devil's this all about, Carr?"

Carr gave him but a glance before returning to his telescope. At that moment, he had had enough of Picton.

"Doing our best to give those Gunners a bit of trouble, Sir. Anything to slow their rate of fire, Sir, and it seems to be working."

At the perfect moment, Drake confirmed this.

"That's another brought down!"

Picton's face contracted into a deep frown, but he did manage to growl a grunt of approval.

However, by then Drake noticed that all the 105th were now all past and it was the Portuguese guns that were now behind them.

"That's us done, Henry. Time to tag on at the rear. If Picton wants to replace us, he can use his own Rifles."

Carr closed his telescope and mounted his horse, whilst Drake gave the order. Within a minute all the 105th Lights were formed at the end of their own column and Carr noted that the 105th had left no dead on that section of the road. The whole circus progressed for another half-hour and Picton did indeed pull Wallace's three Rifle Companies out of the line to perform what the 105th Lights had done, which they themselves had to perform twice more to protect their own 105th. Then, the very distinctive Church of Fuente Guinaldo, high on its ridge, came into distant view, still a good mile away. Lacey rose on his stirrups to obtain a better view.

"That's home Padraigh. What's our bill thus far?"

"Four dead, six wounded."

Lacey turned in his saddle to face him, surprised.

"I'll settle for that, after a caper like this."

O'Hare did not reply, for he was looking off to their left beyond Lacey.

"This caper may not yet be over, Bertram. Johnny's got desperate and he's making one last throw."

Lacey turned to look the same way and he could see that O'Hare was correct. The whole cavalry force that the French had brought up to pursue them from El Bodon was now assembling 400 yards to the left of the Third Division column. Squadron after squadron of French Hussars and Light Dragoons were arriving up behind those already in place, to extend the line in the direction that spelt safety for the Allied column, all being formed parallel to the road still full of Picton's column. The scrape of sabres being withdrawn and the jingle of harness came across to the 105th, loud and threatening. When the final French squadron came into place, Picton arrived alongside the 105th, to sit his horse and study the French, who were equally as still and seemed to be studying him. Every man in the Allied column was alarmed at the sight alongside them, albeit at several hundreds of yards distant, but they continued to hurry along. Ahead of the 105th were the 88th and from somewhere in their ranks came a shout, clearly borne of deep concern.

"Should we not form square, Sir?"

Picton took off his hat to shield his eyes against the sun to study and ponder a while longer. Then he replied, loudly, without taking his eyes from the French, his reply as much for them as for his questioner.

"No! It is only a ruse to frighten us. And it won't do!"

For a further minute, Picton remained rooted to the spot, studying the French now walking their horses to match the speed of the column, whilst his men hurried along, on the road behind him. Finally, Picton turned his horse to ride beside his men, never taking his eyes off the French Light cavalry on his left. There was no noise bar the sound of marching feet and jingling harness, which significance soon dawned on Carr. The French six-gun battery was nowhere to be seen. The tension rose minute by minute, then Picton was proved correct. The French did not charge, in fact, in turn, each Trooper pulled on his left-hand bridle and turned his horse away, to return to El Bodon and away from the now very relieved column. Soon all in the British column could see what the French had seen first and caused them to turn away. Columns of British troops were coming out of Fuente Guinaldo, led by a whole Brigade of Heavy Dragoons, their breastplates glinting in the sun, a most welcome signal to the Third Division meaning that their awful ordeal was now finally over.

oOo

The Followers could not be held back when the battered column of the Third Division finally approached the fortified camp around Fuentes Guinaldo. Even with the naked eye and being stood at the Church high above the town, Bridie, Nellie, Consuela and Eirin could see the column of red on the single road and, to their dread, they could see the French cavalry milling around. However, much worse, they could also see the all too frequent billowing smoke from the field-guns sending cannon-fire into the column that contained their men. It was very rare for Followers to actually see their menfolk under fire and so when the British Dragoons rode out to affect a rescue, they followed, unstoppable, to run down the sides of the column. Once there, to try to identify their Regiment by the colour of their facings and then to peer into the ranks and enquire after their menfolk, if he could not be seen. Soon, the order of search for the 105th became Eirin in the lead, then Consuela, Bridie and finally Nellie, she being the least able to run, but still able to shout to those ahead.

"Eirin! Can you see the green, can you?"

"Not yet", was the reply and so the women ran on.

However, the Colour Company was first in the 105th column and so Bridie and Nellie, deeply relieved, came first to their men, Bridie seeing Jed immediately, as he was in the front rank and marching behind Captain Heaviside.

"Jed! Jed! Are you well? And whole? Not injured at all!

As the column marched on Nellie shouted much the same to Henry Nicholls, him two ranks behind. For the Followers to enter the ranks would be a flogging offence for them, but speech from the roadside was allowable and Heaviside was indulgent when Deakin replied.

"I'm fine, Bridie, just fine, and so's Henry, but I know nothing of the other lads, their Light Company and spent more time under cannon-fire than we did."

Hearing that, Bridie stood back anxiously from the column to look back down the road, but her view was blocked by Followers, all about the same business as herself and so she could see nothing of Consuela nor Eirin. However, these two were themselves surrendering sighs of relief, Saunders, due to his height, could be easily identified and Consuela smiled and waved at him and he replied in kind, even though supporting a wounded man. On the other side of their suffering burden was John Byford and Eirin surprised herself with the depth of her gratitude and relief that her own man had arrived back to her whole and uninjured. The column pressed on, with a moving cloak of Followers on either side, but all now needing to pass around the sad figures of women and children, prostrate with grief on the dust and stubble, who had found that their men were no-where to be seen, instead to be told that they were far back along the road, lying dead and unburied.

When they entered the town, and came to the narrow streets that climbed the hill to the Church, the Followers fell behind, the column of fours now occupied all the space available across the width of the main road up. In the square by the Church, Wellington himself sat watching and waiting as a valuable, veteran and whole Division passed by into safety, after the perils that he had himself placed them in. As events would have it, Picton was not heading his column but riding alongside the 105th, for no particular reason, but Deakin, with Gibney marching beside him outside the column, heard the brief, but chilly exchange, first from Wellington.

"Pleased to see you back, Picton."

The reply was an irritated look as Picton raised his battered top-hat and growled a reply.

"My Lord!"

Unusually, it was Gibney who made the only comment.

"Yon's none too pleased."

Deakin rightly assumed he was referring to Picton as they marched on, the whole Third Division, straight through to the fields beyond the town. There was no room within, it being fully occupied by the Fourth Division and so they emerged onto the flat, dry country behind the buildings, country identical to which they had just marched across. An Aide directed them to their transport, this having been sat waiting for them for some days after its crossing of the Agueda and so Carr and Drake sat wearily on the ground as their tent was pulled off from their transport wagon and erected. All around, the men of the 105th were about the same task of erecting their own tents, as well as lighting fires and shedding their equipment for the first time for days. Then, even as rations were brewed and stewed, the Surgeons got mournfully to work throughout the lines of the Third Division. Wallace, with his 88th nearby, felt the need to visit the Headquarters tent of the 105th. There he found both Lacey and O'Hare half-asleep, sat in their camp chairs, but both enlivened themselves when Wallace entered, particularly Lacey.

"No refreshments as yet, John! Sorry."

Wallace pulled up a spare chair, his pleasant face framed in his ginger whiskers, but as weary as anyone's.

"No matter! I'm pleased enough just to sit down."

However, Lacey was not quite correct, because the Headquarters transport cart, now parked outside, had included O'Hare's supply of Irish whiskey and a fresh bottle and glasses soon appeared on the table, searched out by him. When each had a measure, Wallace raised his glass.

"Well, here's to soldiers' luck!"

All drained their glasses, with O'Hare's first back on the table for a refill.

"And here's hoping there's still some left in the well!"

Regardless of whether the well was indeed dry or the bucket rope too short, with the arrival of dawn the next day brought little comfort to any of the Third Division, with Wallace again entering the same tent of the 105th to find Lacey, O'Hare and Carr at breakfast. This time there was no question of anymore refreshment for anyone, as Wallace made very plain.

"The Frogs have come up in the night. What looks like four Divisions, probably two whole Corps. He wants everything he's got lining the Guinaldo ridge, to put on a show at least. A bit of bluff, is how he put it."

Each of his audience took their final swallow, but Carr was the first to rise.

"So, what have we got here with us, Sir?"

"Only two Divisions, us and the Fourth, plus a Portuguese Brigade and three of cavalry, about 15,000. Orders for the nearest to concentrate here went out too late, although they are now on their way, the Light, the 1st and the 2nd."

Carr was still puzzled.

"But that's enough to hold off those four, at least until the others arrive, surely?"

"It would be, Major, were it not for the fact that guerrillas have told us that five more of Marmont's Divisions are marching this way. That confirmed by our own patrols. We could be outnumbered three to one! He's going to bluff and then move. During the night!"

O'Hare was making his own calculations after which he looked at Wallace.

"Then we need to break camp now and get it on the road back as soon as possible."

"Correct, Padraigh, and the first to get out on the road has the best chance of not being overtaken by soldiers making a forced march, back through the night."

"To where? Do you know?"

Wallace could only sigh.

"My best guess would be Alfayates. That was his Headquarters a while back."

"20 miles?"

"You're not far off!"

It was Lacey who had the last word.

"I don't think our illustrious Commander has been quite so sure-footed over the past week or so, as he would have wished!"

Within minutes the drums were beating for muster and there was urgency throughout the camp. The Reverend Albright, not yet dressed, protruded his head through the gap in their wagon cover to see Sedgwicke already disassembling their cooking equipment.

"Why all the haste and confusion, Private? What is going on?"

Sedgwicke did not look up as he wound the rope around their very important bundle of domestic ironmongery.

"We have to retreat back again, Sir. Very quickly. You need to get dressed, Sir. The Colonel hopes for us to be on the road within the hour."

"And the men?"

"They are to remain here, Sir, until tonight, when they will follow us."

At last he looked up from his tasks.

"Now, please Sir, do get yourself ready. We are ordered to move."

"No time for breakfast?"

"None, Sir. None at all."

Thus, in a very short time, the 105th Followers were moving one way in retreat whilst their menfolk moved in the opposite, advancing to possible conflict. A single crumb of comfort for Bridie was to see the parting of Eirin and John Byford, she with her arms around his neck and both kissing fondly. Nellie also witnessed.

"Well, at least that's goin' in the right direction!"

Then, even Nellie had some words of affection for her departing husband, Henry, although they were delivered in a markedly different form.

"Now, just you make sure that I'll be seein' your ugly face again in a day or two! Damn fool that y'are, like to get half of it shot off!"

There was laughter at this throughout the Colour Company as they marched up to the ridgeline to take their place amongst the ten Companies of the 105th, as they assembled together. There they found Wallace stood with Picton, with Lacey and O'Hare maintaining a respectful distance, but, as soon as Picton departed for elsewhere in his line, Wallace came over.

"Picton's last Battalion came in exhausted during the night, the 74th, having gone all around the houses to get here, but it's like I said, just us, the Fourth, two Portuguese and three cavalry, facing that which you can see Johnny's got out there."

Lacey and O'Hare had already studied what was on the plain before them and they did not need Wallace to explain the perils of their predicament. O'Hare had estimated 40,000 French arrayed within cannon-shot of their line and the lowest quality telescope could not fail to pick out additional French columns marching up along the road of their own ordeal of the previous day. The three looked at each other and exchanged wry grins, then Wallace spoke.

"Are you much of a card player, O'Hare?"

O'Hare grinned further, he knew where Wallace was going.

"Some, but bluffing at a card-table hardly compares with what we're doing in front of a whole French army!"

Wallace and Lacey laughed as they continued to study the French before them, Lacey's attention half on a battery of French field-guns galloping into position, whilst enjoying the banter. Eventually, he felt able to comment encouragingly, if only slightly.

"Well, if you're going to try to fool your opponent, you need some reputation as a winner and what M'sieu can see is a long line of Recoats holding a decent ridge, from which Johnny down there has never dislodged us before. They know that Wellington never makes a stand, unless he's confident. Marmont will be in a quandary, be certain, about what to do!"

Further along the line, the subject was much more mundane but equally urgent for such as those who were forming it.

"What've you got?"

John Davey opened his haversack to reveal it over half full with army biscuits.

"Got these last night. Pleased I did."

Tom Miles nodded.

"Same here, but what about Dopey Joe, stood yer behind?"

Joe Pike revealed himself to be not so dopey, because from his haversack he pulled out a large jar, the neck closed with cloth and string, this holding safe some kind of stew!

Miles was incensed at seeing such quality food, which he did not have, his own being composed of weavilly and even rotten, army biscuits.

"Where'd you get that?"

Pike returned Miles' vexed stare with a triumphant stare of his own.

"Auntie Nellie made it up for me!"

Davey laughed as he watched a Squadron of French Hussars canter along the base of the ridge.

"What's this 'Auntie Nellie'? She's no more Aunt to you than I am."

Pike's expression turned to hurt.

"Well! I like to show a bit of respect."

However, Miles had no patience with this discussion of family connections, he was interested in the stew, which he was now examining, having removed the cloth and string. There was no question that it would be shared out.

"Do you think they'll let us fall out and make a fire? Warm this up?"

Behind him Saunders laughed.

"No chance! Not with that lot ready to march up and say 'Good Mornin'. We'n stuck here all day, is my guess."

Miles therefore decided.

"Right, then we eats it now. Passing it around."

With that, he pulled his spoon out of his jacket pocket and ate three spoonfulls, before passing it to Davey, who began to spoon his share into his mouth. At that moment, Ethan Ellis passed and it was only something such as a jar of good-looking stew that could distract him from examining the French as he walked past

"What's that?"

Davey now knew, having eaten some.

"Fish and tatty stew."

Ellis peered into the jar and Davey, to the utter consternation of Miles, offered Ellis his spoon.

"Try a bit."

Ellis took the spoon and did so, obviously relishing the taste.

"Ah, that Bridie! She can work wonders with a few taters and a bit of fish! And the herbs! She's the one for that."

He handed back the spoon and marched on, but it wasn't long before Miles made his feelings known to Davey.

"That's our commons you've just given him!"

Davey took his last mouthful before passing it back to Pike.

"I don't see why that's so terrible. He's not such a bad old stick! Sergeants have to be Sergeants."

Miles gave him a look of utter astonishment. He had been a soldier since his mid-teens, whilst Davey was only a soldier because he was a convicted poacher.

"And how many Sergeants have you known? Bloody King's Hard Bargain!"

By now, Pike was passing the jar to Miles for the second round and, in a departure from his usual placid demeanour, he felt able to give Miles a piece of his mind. He found Ellis decent enough.

"Here! It's your share again. Take this and shut up!"

Davey starting laughing at the almost unique event of Joe Pike admonishing Tom Miles, but Pike was quietly incensed at Miles' first comment and he spoke further, but softly.

"I b'ain't no Dopey Joe!"

However, Davey's sharp eyesight had noticed something within the French ranks.

"Well, here comes something by way of French big-wigs. Perhaps they wants to talk."

The group that he saw, a lavish and numerous French Staff, rode 20 yards beyond their own lines and dismounted. Following servant soldiers, on foot, set up three enormous telescopes at that point, which the most ornamentally dressed of the party set his eye to, using the one placed in the centre. Two other, presumably Generals also, made use of the remaining two. The whole of the Allied army, drawn up and in full view, stared back at him and Miles became curious.

"So, who's that?"

Byford was just behind.

"Marmont, I would imagine. The French Marshall."

The whole Allied line, particularly those immediately opposite, could easily see a French Marshall studying them through a telescope and so, all along the Allied line, he was treated to ranks of derisory grins, distorted faces, 'V' signs and other lewd gestures, until a Staff Officer noticed and all were ordered to desist. Nevertheless, for ten minutes, they could see the French Commander swing the telescope to left and right, then he turned away to mount his horse and depart, as did his Staff, leaving the servants to dismantle the telescopes. Midday approached and then something occurred even more bizarre, in the place where the telescopes had been. A long table arrived, with chairs, then a mass of servants came forward to lay out the table for a midday meal. They all stood back when Marmont returned, with the same Staff as before, to sit and enjoy what appeared to be, with the use of Allied telescopes, a most sumptuous meal of several courses. Drake and Carr stood shaking their heads.

"Now just what can we deduce from that?"

Drake continued to shake his head in amazement.

"Who can say? Pure French display? Mere braggadocio? A demonstration of supreme confidence? Who can say?"

Then a thought.

"Shouldn't we be sending a few roundshot his way? He's well within range. We've still got those Portuguese guns that came with us from El Bodon."

Carr turned to him and grinned.

"It would be damn bad form, old boy, to interrupt a chap in the middle of his Midday meal! No kind of cricket at all!"

Whilst both grinned at the sarcasm, Wellington, merely yards away, remained impassive. Whatever the reason for Marmont's dining arrangements, it had no impact on the Allied Commander in Chief. The theatre from the French High Command induced no change from him, his show of strength remained stood in their ranks and were not allowed to sit, yet alone leave the ranks to cook. As the afternoon wore on everyone continued to study the French before them equally intently, watching for any change in formation, especially veterans like Carr, stood with Drake, who again spoke first.

"It's getting late. Surely he'd have come at us by now."

Carr had a ready answer.

"These can form column and come at us within five minutes. We can count ourselves likely to remain undisturbed as long as Mr. Frog there remains in line. If we see them form columns, then we'll know that Marmont's of a mind to try conclusions. If he brings his guns forward, needed to support columns, then we know we're for it."

He turned to face Drake.

"He's not faced us before, has he? Marmont? He may give it a go."

Drake continued to stare ahead.

"I really must confess myself to be not altogether too 'au fait' with the relative experience of our opponent French Commanders!"

Carr looked askance at him, mildly annoyed at the theatrical language of his good friend.

"Well, after that, and after all this, there must surely be a place for you on the stage as some kind of ham actor!"

Drake laughed, then Carr also, but tension remained high, because to be stood in full view of a huge French army, all within cannon-shot, played on everyone's nerves, until someone in the ranks of the 105th produced a penny-whistle and began to play the Regimental song, 'Brighton Camp'. The 105th began to sing, tentatively at first, expecting some Staff Officer to come, as before, and order them to remain quiet, but none came and so they gave it full voice. The 74th next to them joined in with the popular song. The 88th on the other side began to intone an Irish lament, until told to stop in various forms, from "Shut yer wailin' gobs" to "You're frightening the horses". The Scottish 74th then struck up with a pair of cheerful Highland tunes, which most thought well of, despite the bagpipes. Then from across the 500-yard gap came the sound of 'La Marseillaise', but little was heard of it on the ridge amongst the catcalls and hoots of derision.

The entertainment could not last for long, but the day was drawing to a close. Wellington rode along his line, accompanied by Picton, Lowry-Cole of the 4th Division and General Crauford, him recently arrived with the Light Division. Many tried to read their Commander's expression, but he remained as impassive and inscrutable as ever. As he rode back, the light was indeed failing, and the longed-for order came.

"Fall out and make bivouac fires!"

There were no rations to be had, but at least they could brew tea and all sat gratefully drinking, both Officers and men alike, all mildly content, until Picton arrived at the 105th Headquarters and Lacey, O'Hare and Carr sprang to their feet.

"We're pulling out at Midnight, leaving a Light Company from every Brigade behind, which'll be yours Lacey, and Crauford's whole Division. How long you stay is at Crauford's discretion, then the Light Companies leave first. His Light Division are to keep the fires going for another two hours before they finally pull out. My Rifles are staying as well, as are Lowry-Cole's of the 4th. Tell your men to keep their fires burning! We're going back over the border, somewhere called Aldea da Ponte. Count on twenty miles."

With that, he was gone and Carr looked at Lacey.

"I'll stay."

Lacey nodded.

"Very well."

Carr went to Drake to impart the unwelcome news, which was then transferred to the men of the Company via Sergeant Ellis and it was met with outrage by Miles.

"Why not them Diddykites next over? Them thievin' tripe-hounds can mooch about in the dark as well as anyone!"

Ellis jutted his face towards him.

"Well it's not them, Miles, it's us and you, but I'll send someone over to hold your hand just in case you gets a bit frightened of the dark! In case you gets a dose of the bugga-boos!"

Low laughter came from all listening, as always, when it was at Miles' expense, then Ellis was gone. When French bivouac fires began to appear, the Line Companies formed up and began to march away. The 105th Light Company now found themselves at the far-right end of the Allied line, all now commanded by Crauford, and he rode up to make inspections and found Carr. Unlike many Generals, he dismounted to speak.

"Ah Carr! We meet again. Haven't seen you since the bridge business after Talavera. Where was it?"

"Almaraz. Sir."

"Yes, that's the place. Are you well?"

Carr was more than a little astonished at a Major General enquiring after his health and welfare, but he found adequate words.

"Better now than I was then. Sir."

Crauford grunted.

"Aren't we all, Carr! Aren't we all. Now, I want yours as picket at the foot of the ridge. Barnard's 43rd will be above you, here. I'll send word to bring yours back up when the time comes, then we can all take our leave together. From what I hear, the route we take to this Aldea place is none too easy to follow. I've only one local guide, so we all go together. No sense in risking getting lost. You'd agree?"

"Yes Sir. As you say, Sir."

Crauford now placed both hands on his saddle pommel and his left foot in the stirrup.

"Right. Good luck, Carr. See you on the road."

Such easy familiarity from someone of Crauford's reputation left Carr mystified, but he saluted as Crauford hauled himself up into the saddle and rode off into the gathering gloom. Then Carr left to find Drake and Ellis to impart the disturbing news that they were to mount picket out in front of a skeleton force that was opposed by a huge army. Thus, when it was full dark the six of Davey, Miles, Pike, Saunders, Byford and Bailey found themselves inching their way carefully down the slope, hoping that no French scouts or pickets were that far forward. Saunders had been ordered to count 300 paces through the gloom, but at 239 they came to a deep gully which may have been a stream bed during the winter months and so Saunders halted there and placed his hand on Davey's sleeve.

"This'll do. Us three first, then you, Tom and Joe. Two hours each should do it."

Davey passed Saunders the hour glass and his two companions settled to some rest, whilst Saunders' trio stood and listened, their Baker rifles nestling in the crook of their arms. In their own silence, they could hear the distinct murmur from the French camp, although little could be seen of their bivouac fires that far below the ridge and also little could be seen anywhere in the poor light delivered by the sliver of the new moon. However, all was uneventful until the changeover came, which caused all six to be stood awake and their movements inevitably made a noise. A voice came out of the darkness.

"M'sieu! M'sieu! Rosbifs! Es tu la?"

The reply was six Baker Rifles being brought to full cock, but the voice continued.

"M'sieu. Anglais. Es tu la?"

It was Miles who answered, but not kindly.

"What do you want, Frog shite-auk?"

However, the voice did not take offence, probably because the reply was in Miles' own mother-tongue and it contained untranslatable words, but the Frenchman had been answered, and in English.

"M'sieu! Vous avez tout produit du tabac?"

Miles had now heard the vital word.

"He wants to trade!"

Saunders was suspicious.

"I don't trust the bastard. Byfe, ask him what he has."

Byford stepped to the edge of the gully.

"Oui, nous avons. Ce que vous avez?"

"J'ai cognac, M'sieu. Deux bouteilles"

Saunders was unimpressed.

"Could be like that last God-awful stuff we traded. Tasted like lamp-oil!"

"Est-ce bon cognac?"

"Oui! Des meilleurs!"

"Of the best, he says."

"I bloody bet!" came instantly from Miles. "Anyway, we're not short of baccy. We got a good ration yesterday. I say we can take a chance."

Byford turned towards the voice in the darkness.

"Très bien. Un seul homme, se manifester!"

"Oui. Tres bien. J'arrive vers l'avant"

Byford turned to Saunders to translate.

"He's coming, one man!"

"I'll go down. Cover me."

Saunders slipped down into the gully with his own, Miles', Davey's and Byford's tobacco pouches, for the last it was no great loss, he did not smoke. Soon a French shako appeared at the top of the gully and immediately five Baker rifles were pointed at the area beneath, but then two bottles of the type that indicated brandy, appeared over the edge. Saunders pulled out the stopper of one and tasted. He smacked his lips.

"I'm not sure."

He took another pull at the bottle, to which Miles took great objection.

"Never mind bloody well 'not sure', that's your ration you'm swiggin' off."

Saunders banged in the stopper.

"It'll do!"

Saunders took the other bottle and then a large French haversack appeared and Saunders tipped in the contents of the four tobacco pouches. That completed, a moustachioed face appeared over the edge.

"Merci beaucoup Rosbifs. Bonne chance!"

Davey was impressed.

"Well that was cheery enough!"

However, Byford had one last question.

"Quel est votre regiment?"

"La Garde Impériale!"

With that the face disappeared and Saunders was hauled up, but each said not a word, each slightly in shock at the named French Regiment. The bottles were stowed away in back-packs for distribution later, but

225

not before each had taken a good mouthful and they agreed with Saunders, that it was decent stuff. As they settled back for their period of rest, Saunders gave his opinion.

"Perhaps the Imperial Guard gets decent. Not like they poor sods they crowds into their columns to get mowed down!"

Silence descended once again, more total than before, as the card games, dice schools and songsters in the French camp finally parted company. Davey needed to turn the hour-glass twice more before Drake arrived and came forward, having been challenged sotto voce by Miles, then Drake asked the important question.

"Is all well?"

"Yes Sir', said his challenger. "We haven't seen a soul, nor heard nuthin'. Sir."

"Very good. Right, back up. We're leaving."

The three now on their feet shook awake those sleeping and equipment was gathered for Drake to then lead the way up. Even though it was the darkest hour of the night, the whole of the 105th Light Company that had formed the picket could easily be seen emerging onto the ridge, because all along the full length of the ridge, fires were burning brightly. Major Carr now arrived.

"Form up and march into the town. Crauford wants us to muster at the Church."

Soon, in obedience, they were traversing the ridge, marching from the light of one blazing fire to another, many fueled by furniture looted from the town. There were no inhabitants remaining to object to this, nor to vent their anger at the retreating Ingleses, as they formed up on the main road through the Church Square. The Rifles of the 3rd and 4th Divisions headed the column, followed by the four Light Companies from the four Brigades, with the 105th marching last. With all assembled and checked off, the order came to move off, which became a matter of absolute trust, because for each Battalion, in the almost complete darkness, there was no other course than to follow the Battalion in front, and for each man to march close enough to the man in front to maintain sight of his backpack. After almost an hour of shadowy marching they entered a village where all were awake, with all of the village loading their possessions and food onto carts, mules and donkeys. There was much crying and sounds of distress, because they knew that the French were once more in Portugal, the Ingleses were retreating and they must now go, and go quickly, before the Franceses arrived. The events of the past day and now the night, told them so.

However, there was no halt for rest allowed for the column, they pushed on through, still thankfully marching on a good road, and good progress was maintained. It was after some four hours that Crauford galloped past to the head of the column, his Light Division now following on behind. Drake was marching beside Carr, each in step with the men, all maintaining a good momentum.

"Any chance he'll let us stop to catch our breath? Perhaps get a drink of tea?"

Carr choked on a derisory laugh.

"Crauford! No chance. He's put together the toughest Division in the army and he expects it to behave as such. At this moment, we are roped in! A halt for a rest? No chance!"

Another hour on from the village that was being abandoned, they turned right to leave the road and march along a track which slowly became worse, as their feet told them, when they progressively stumbled more and more over loose rocks and into deep ruts. After almost an hour of difficult marching, they descended into a valley, which, so their ears told them, contained rushing water, but their fears of crossing a ford proved unfounded, when they thankfully felt the give and heard the echo of a wooden bridge. However, as again their feet told them, the track improved as they climbed out of the valley, to seem almost as good as a road. Soon, they passed through another village, this one thoroughly empty. Even in the dark, they could see doors and window shutters left open and abandoned and under their feet they could feel small items that had been dropped and never retrieved. However, once out through the buildings, they saw no evidence of refugees on the road, all then assumed that, in fear, they had taken to the safety of the hills, hoping for dense woodland or even caves. Dawn was upon the marching column when the road took a sharp turn and then they were into a village, thoroughly inhabited, but only by throngs of Allied troops. They halted on the main road and at last felt able to shed heavy packs from aching shoulders. Carr reached out a hand to stop a passing Lieutenant.

"What's the name of this place?"

"Aldea da Ponte, Sir."

Carr turned to Drake.

"So we're here. Now what has he in mind for us?"

226

"A good question, but first we find our Regiments and, second, once there we get Morrison to cook us some breakfast. Then a snooze, if allowed!"

They were joined by the two Lieutenants, Maltby, in relaxed mood, and Shakeshaft more creative, him writing in his Journal now that there was more light to see by. Drake was amused.

"Still keeping that thing up to date, Richard?"

Shakeshaft placed the last full-stop.

"Yes, each day, so far."

Carr smiled indulgently, but he felt inclined to make a test.

"Those two villages we just passed through. Did you write down their names?"

Shakeshaft held up the notebook triumphantly.

"Yes, I did. The first was called Casillas de Flores, the second......"

He hesitated over the pronunciation.

"...... Forcalhos."

Shakeshaft stood with a very satisfied look on his face and Maltby nodded.

"One day, we may come back, but never as soldiers, I sincerely hope."

Drake perked up.

"Well, I've an idea! We may well bring our wives and children back out. Show them where all the stuff we'll be talking about took place."

Carr's face darkened slightly.

"It'll need 20 years before this place will be worth coming back to, and I'm not so sure I'd want to show my loved ones the villages, bridges and hills where it all took place, much of it cruel or desperate. Too much that was too bad, would be recalled to my mind."

Drake grimaced at the morbid speech, which had thoroughly depressed their mood.

"Well, on that note, I think we should try to find our quarters. If you stay here, Henry, we'll go off, me, Richard and Stuart, then send someone back to guide you."

However, at that moment came the most unwelcome order to fall in once more. Packs were hoisted wearily onto shoulders that were very unwilling to receive them once more and they marched on, through the buildings of Aldea da Ponte. It took another hour almost, but at least on a good straight road, before they came to the next village, which was Alfayates itself, Wellington's Headquarters. Again, they were required to march straight through and only then the column halted and broke up, the Battalions of the Light Division to their own camp, but the four Light Companies of Picton's 3rd were left isolated and lost, where were their parent Battalions? The only crumb of comfort was the good light of a full dawn. Drake took a deep, weary breath.

"Well, as I was saying in the last place. We'll search, Henry, if you stay here."

However, they were spared a search, for Sergeant Bryce arrived, having been tasked by his Colonel to find them when they arrived and lead them to their camp.

"Morning, Sirs. Pleased to find you, Sirs. You need to come this way."

With Bryce showing the way, the four marched off with the Light Company following, on past Wellington, now in deep conversation with Crauford, although both still mounted and then they came to Picton, him now alone and walking on foot, examining his four Light Companies. The four Officers saluted, as Picton halted at their approach.

"You made it back then? Carr?"

"Yes Sir. It wasn't too bad. I think we fooled them, Sir."

Picton gave a grunt and then walked on, his hands behind his back and head down, leaving the Light Company and its Officers to follow Bryce to the 105th camp on the South-Western outskirts of Alfayates and then disperse to their tents to sleep and at that moment, for each of all ranks, the memory of a solid night's sleep far beyond ready recall.

oOo

The 16th were drawn up in line, the four Squadrons all abreast, all formed in two ranks, Officers to the fore, Cornets least forward, Colonel Withers and Major Johnson, the furthest. With the 14th alongside, they were to the East of Alfayates all studying the gradual populating of the far horizon with French infantry and cavalry, all very visible in the strong light of the Noon sun. Oakwood turned slightly to Cornet Carr, him but a horse length behind.

"Is this not the most perfect cavalry country, Willoughby?"

Carr could see for himself the bare, open fields that covered the flat open plateau.

"Yes Sir, it is."

Carr had quite taken to Oakwood. He reminded him of a Master Builder who had once worked on their estate, of similar square, burly stature and with large powerful hands. As with the Master Builder he spent little energy on idle talk, generally holding to the urgent business at hand and always trying to be reasoned and sensible. Oakwood's one sentimentality was a miniature of his wife and daughter, this he kept in his breast pocket and he took it out to study it during idle moments. However, at this moment, Carr was unsure if Oakwood was speaking from admiration or from anxiety and so he repeated his opinion.

"Yes Sir. Ideal for a good gallop at whatever. I can only say that I am comforted by the support that we have."

He was referring to the whole of the Light Division drawn up behind them, but extending beyond their right. These were alongside the whole of the 5th Infantry Division also drawn up, but behind the 14th Light Dragoons to their left. Oakwood nodded his agreement.

"Which explains why our friends over there are forming up side by side, but still remaining sat still to have a good ponder. Ourselves and two full Divisions must look like a serious bone to chew."

'Looking' became the order of the day as the sun rose and heated the ranks of both sides. With the arrival of mid-afternoon, when even Crauford allowed his men to make fires and brew tea, then so did Alten for his two cavalry Regiments and finally also General Dunlop for his 5th Division, far over to the left and covering Alfayates. When the sun began to make a serious approach to the Western horizon, the whole French line, both bayonets and sabres began to move leftwards, as the Allies saw them. By now, Alten's whole cavalry Brigade had dismounted to allow their horses rest and fodder and Alten was sharing tea with Withers whilst remaining mounted, when Dunlop rode up with what appeared to be two of his Colonels. He wasted no time.

"What do you think Alton? Crauford's for following, I'm for holding here, to maintain cover for Alfayates. What do you think?"

Alten eased himself in the saddle.

"Well, General, between you and me, it's well known that Crauford will always go looking for a fight rather than holding back from one, but I agree with you. We hold here. Johnny is not short of Divisions. Those yonder, taking their leave of us and marching to Aldea, I'd say, to perhaps join an assault on it, may be doing so because a whole Corps are coming up behind them to take their place. I say we hold here and follow his Lordship's orders."

Dunlop nodded, his face serious.

"What you say is very possible, Alten, I agree. I'll ride over to Crauford and tell him that we are both for holding and he should also."

As Dunlop pulled on his reins to direct his horse, Alten smiled.

"Good luck with that, General. If I know Crauford, he'll not like it!"

Dunlop gave no reply as he spurred his horse away, then Alten looked at the rapidly emptying horizon and turned to Withers.

"Stand the men down, George, horses back to picket lines. Make camp, what food we have we should eat. I suspect that we will be here even through the night. May as well get comfortable with those trees behind us for fuel. Autumn's coming on, even for Spain."

It was later on into that same afternoon that the sound of gunfire from the direction of Aldea da Ponte, two miles beyond their front, brought them back to the alert, giving Alten the difficult decision to either re-mount and re-form or await developments. He decided to trust the veteran qualities of his men to be able to complete the former soon enough in the event of a French arrival, therefore he allowed his men to remain at their campfires, but their horses bridled and saddled. Thus, they remained at their repose listening to the sound of gunfire from the direction of Aldea da Ponte.

It may well be, that to a veteran soldier, the sound of gunfire will intrude into the subconscious and bring him to wakefulness and so it was with Henry Carr, still asleep long into the afternoon of the day after their night march. His first thoughts were puzzlement over what had drawn him awake, but he quickly decided that it was the sound of guns, albeit some way off, and then his appetite reported in. He sat up.

"Morrison! What have you to eat?"

Morrison replied from the other side of the tent canvas.

"I can fry you some fat bacon, Sir."

"Please to do so!"

By the time the bacon had sizzled to perfection, Carr was dressed and outside the tent and at that moment O'Hare arrived and pointed to the bacon.

"Any of that going spare?"

Carr did not turn away from the distant sound of cannon fire.

"Absolutely not! It's all mine, but Morrison will cook you a portion, if you so desire."

O'Hare smiled.

"Now that would be a blessing."

Morrison needed no further orders and placed a thick slice of the bacon in the vacant section of the frying-pan after he had handed up a cooked piece to Carr within two thick slices of bread. After three mouthfuls and much studying of the distant, noisy, but unchanging horizon, Carr asked the question, now that O'Hare was distracted by the sight and sounds of his own frying portion.

"What's all that about? Do you know?"

O'Hare hesitated as Morrison handed up to him the second, now thoroughly cooked portion, also within bread. O'Hare answered before he took a bite.

"From what we hear, Johnny's followed us from Cuidad with just about all he's got. I'd say that was him taking a crack at that village in front of us, Aldea da Whatever and our Lordship not giving best there too easily. But it's here that matters, his line before Alfayates."

Both stood chewing as the sound of gunfire waxed and waned across the thick September air. Time passed, this time with coffee, then with almost full dusk now around them, the sound of fighting intensified, grew louder and nearer, then after some fifteen minutes, it fully ceased. Both looked at each other.

"That's that, then!"

Carr nodded.

"We can assume so. Well, being as I've not long woken up, I'd best take first turn around our night-pickets. We are not all that far back from his Lordship's main line and I would not be in the least surprised if Johnny now holds Aldea."

He wandered off to make his rounds, but some degree of confirmation for his opinion came with the arrival of wounded along the road from Aldea da Ponte, and so he halted his rounds for full confirmation by stopping a Captain of the 7th Fusiliers, marching back beside his Company.

"What was that all about?"

The Captain halted and saluted.

"Oh, not a lot, Sir. We just decided that Johnny would have to pay a price for what he wanted. He's got it now, but it cost him."

"Aldea?"

"The same, Sir."

"So where is he now?"

"About half a mile back, Sir, perhaps a bit more, if he comes no further out of Aldea."

The Fusiliers marched on and Carr continued his rounds, noting throughout the night the myriad mess-fires of his own army and the growing number out to the North-west, where the French were. Not long before dawn the half dark was filled with the sound of marching columns and Carr stood to watch and listen. The sun was just edging the horizon, when Sergeant Major Gibney came running up and saluted.

"Found you, Sir! Orders are to bring in our pickets. We're to march further back, Sir, full beyond this side of the village. We're in reserve, Sir. Front line's to be through the village itself."

"Very good, Sergeant. You go left, I'll go right to collect our men and then back to camp. Will that serve?"

"Aye, Sir, it will. Very good, Sir."

After cleaving the air with a wheeling salute, Gibney made off and within half an hour, all of the 105th were forming a column facing away from the new front line. Carr hurried up to a group of Officers that he recognised only too well, his own and Picton. Some way off all stood silent and idle as Wallace's 88th joined them on the road, where the 105th and the 74th were already formed up and waiting, with Picton's three Companies of Rifles formed in columns of twos at the side. Carr arrived and spoke first to Lacey, because to interrogate Picton seemed a step too far.

"Is he offering battle, Sir?"

However, it was Picton who answered.

229

"He is and I hope the Frogs accept! I for one have had enough of falling back at every sight of a blue jacket! Himself wants a battle. What we are holding is as good as at Busaco and not so long. I hope the Crapauds do give it a go."

Carr turned to him.

"We are in reserve, I take it, Sir?"

Picton glowered at him.

"Correct. With Colville's"

With that, he was gone to mount his horse. Wallace's 88th were now on the road and soon the 105th were marching around the Western outskirts of Alfayates, to wheel right and face the village some 500 yards distant. However, they remained in column, the 74th on their left, the 88th on their right, and Colville's whole Brigade were in the same formation to the far left, beyond the 74th. At Midday, Lacey became concerned for his men, they had been sat in formation all morning. He looked at them, then at O'Hare.

"I'm going to Picton. It's Midday and the men should have something to eat. They were not allowed any breakfast."

Picton was easy to find, sitting his horse with Colville, his Senior Brigadier. Lacey went straight up to Picton, him sat staring at the direction from which the French would arrive, even though the whole village of Alfayates blocked his view.

"Sir, the men haven't eaten all day. I think we should get some food to them, Sir."

Picton looked down, being reminded of his own duty by a Junior Officer did little for his mood, but he knew that Lacey was right.

"Break ranks and eat, yes. Remove equipment, no!"

"And the Officers, Sir?"

Picton looked down, now wholly irritated. He had made enough concessions.

"They can eat with their men. Let them get a taste of army salt-pork for a change!"

Then he seemed to relent.

"Or get their servants to bring them something up. But they remain in post! If the men do, so do they."

Lacey saluted and hurried off and set all in motion. Consequently, it was Ethan Ellis who arrived at the mess-fire of Bridie and Nellie.

"Can you get some food up? Picton's allowed the Midday."

The three, Bridie, Nellie and Consuela all rose up, with Bridie answering.

"'Tis all ready. They can eat it now. 'Tis all sat simmerin'."

Each took two heavy stew-pots from the fire and they followed Ellis, the children carrying sacks of bread and biscuits. As a consequence of that, not long later, Drake noticed the change in circumstances amongst his Company.

"The men are eating! What about us? The last food I had was last night."

At that moment, O'Hare came by and Carr turned towards him.

"The men are eating, Padraigh. Do we not get a Midday?"

"The word from Picton is, to go to your men and get a portion from them. We are not to return to our tents and servants. We can order them to bring something up, if we choose, but we stay in place."

Drake was aghast.

"That's unheard of! That we beg food from the men! What's Picton thinking?"

The answer was a shrug of Irish shoulders.

"You don't have to, if you're happy with bread, cheese and tea!"

Carr was already on his way over to the Light Company and he threw a comment back over his shoulder as he left.

"I for one have had enough of stuff between bread. I'm for something more solid."

He knew which mess to go to. At his approach, Deakin, Davey, Saunders et al, began to stand, but he waved them all down.

"Carry on, men. Get some food inside you. We could be chasing after the Johnnies come evening."

He looked at Bridie.

"Mrs. Mulcahy. Officers are ordered to remain at post and to not stand down for Midday. Is there anything left in that stew-pot you have there, which I may purchase? A mouthful or two?"

A look of consternation came over Bridie's face, that an Officer was about to taste what she had cooked herself, but she rose up with the stew-pot and tilted it to show Carr the remains of the meal.

"There's this bit here, your Honour. Perhaps with a bit of bread, it'll fill a corner, so it will."

Carr smiled.

"That will be perfect, Mrs. Mulcahy. If you have no plate, I'll eat from the pot, if you provide me with a spoon."

At that point, Jed Deakin did stand up, his face and voice serious.

"No need for that, Sir. We've spare of both."

These quickly appeared for the food to be scraped onto the plate and be handed to Carr, who remained standing, plate in one hand, spoon in the other. It was a decent portion and after two mouthfuls, he grinned at Bridie.

"Mrs Mulcahy! This is rather good. Salt pork, is it?"

Bridie blushed and smiled with embarrassment.

"Yes Sir, with some taties and swede, and a few herbs, Sir."

Carr paused from taking another mouthful.

"Well, it is rather good. We'll have to employ you in the Officer's Mess, when we get home."

It was Deakin who grinned ruefully.

"Home and eating in barracks seems a powerful long way off, Sir. From where we are now."

Carr nodded slightly but made no reply, instead he finished the stew. With that he pulled a shilling from his waistcoat pocket and offered it to Deakin.

"There's no need for that, Sir."

Carr pushed his hand forward a few inches, the gesture renewing the offer.

"For your grandson, there."

Deakin took the coin and nodded his thanks. Carr lifted his shako in the direction of Bridie and Nellie and walked off, leaving Deakin dumbfounded by the coin, but more so at the mannerly conduct of the normally stuff-shirt Carr. However, throughout the 105th, Officers were eating with their men, Drake with Shakeshaft's Company. However, there was one exception, this amongst the Grenadiers. Whilst Ameshurst sat amongst his men and D'Villiers stood to eat, Carravoy remained apart, sat in isolation at a small camp table, eating cheese and army biscuits.

The day wore on and became even further relaxed, despite Picton's Battalions being ordered to reform into columns, where the men leaned on their muskets and chatted happily. However, unlike the barter exchanges with the 74th on the other side, and despite now being fed and restored as neighbours, there was no friendly banter nor barter between the 105th and the 88th, between them there passed merely sullen, sidelong looks.

Eyesight also was the sole conveyor of aggression used against the French over on the Allied right, where Alten's Cavalry Brigade and the Light Division stood on the edge of the valley that overlooked the small village of Forcalhos. As a sop to his own aggressive instincts Crauford had taken his Division forward to occupy the ground of the French line of the previous day and he had persuaded Alten to also come forward to give him cavalry cover. Now they occupied a very strong position at the top of a long slope with Wellington's full accord, with the 5th Division placed on their left directly before Alfayates. All through the morning almost 4,000 pairs of eyes, excluding those of the horses, scanned back and forth for any sign of French activity around the village of Forcalhos below, or the ridge beyond it. The eyes in Crauford's head peered down and beyond much more intently than most, as he prowled up and down his line of cavalry and infantry, these all remaining perched at the top of his strong position. Finally, he came to Alten.

"I think Johnny's funked it! Just as he did at Elvas, but I'm uneasy about the gap between us and Dunlop's Fifth. Just for peace of mind, because there's obviously nothing to worry us here, send a couple of Squadrons, down and over, just for a couple of miles or so until they are in front of Dunlop and thereby certain there's no threat. French columns, couple or three, in that gap to try us out, could be our undoing."

Whilst Crauford continued to stare at the empty horizons, Alten turned his horse towards his left-hand Squadrons. The first he came to was Tavender's, the left centre. Oakwood's Two Squadron were far left.

"Lucius! Take yours down and work left. Make sure there's nothing down there in those trees to worry us. Oakwood's will be on your left, doing the same, but further over towards Aldea where Dunlop's front is. Keep in touch with Oakwood, he'll be closer to the French than you are. If he get's into trouble, I expect you to get him out of it. Go now, I'll brief Oakwood and then your Colonel."

Within 15 minutes, Two Squadron were easing their horses between the scattered trees of the valley that held Forcalhos, but always easing their way leftwards and down, this valley worn into the uplands by the small stream that watered the lower pasture as it made its way to the River Coa. On the far side, the top of the valley descended below theirs, whilst their own incline remained higher, covered with scattered woodland. Oakwood was riding with Cornet Carr.

"Keep yours high, Willoughby, keep them high. I don't like the idea of being anywhere in that valley, when we have no idea where the Johnnies are."

He suddenly turned rightwards in his saddle.

"One Squadron should be in touch on our right. Can you see anything, or more like, have you?"

"My impression, Sir, is that they remained closer to the top, but I saw them, Sir. They were there."

Oakwood nodded.

"'Were' being the operative word. The 5th Infantry is up above, that I know, so we'll scout over until we can see that Aldea place, which is Johnny's front and then get back, to report what we see. Makes sense?"

Carr grinned and nodded.

"To me, Sir. Yes!"

They maintained their height and held to the trees, walking their horses between the scattered pines. All was calm and tranquil until they heard the evident hurry of a rider coming rapidly between the trees. He reined in his horse before Oakwood and saluted.

"If you please Sir. S'arn't Shelby, Sir, A Troop. Message from Captain Tavender, Sir. He can see movement on the road East, coming out of Aldea, Sir, moving back to Portugal. He says it could be the whole French army. He advises that you send a Troop to take a look, Sir. He advises Cornet Carr's, because his has the most experienced NCO's. Sir."

Oakwood studied him hard.

"Why can Captain Tavender see this and we not?"

"We are higher up the slope, Sir, would be my guess."

Oakwood nodded. It made sense.

"Very good, Sergeant. Tell Captain Tavender that I am complying."

"Complying Sir. Yes Sir."

As Shelby rode off, Oakwood turned to Carr.

"So! Take yours over this valley and ease your way further up to this road that Tavender thinks he can see French on, until you can take a look. Take no risks, just take a look. I'll bring Peterson's down to the stream and hold there."

Carr saluted.

"Very good, Sir."

Carr rode off to Sergeant Baxter, sat nearby.

"In column of fours, Sergeant. We are to cross that stream and climb the far side, to take a look at a road at the top. Or beyond. Seems there may be some French on it."

Orders were shouted and soon the column of fours was splashing through the stream, but once over Carr halted, looking up the slope rising before them, seeing nothing but scrub and scattered trees. Baxter saw that Carr was thinking and was unsure.

"Best go up as a picket line, Sir. That way we sees more and if we're attacked by more'n a Squadron, spread out we has a better chance of most getting out, Sir. It'll be every man for hisself!"

His words struck Carr as describing a level of danger greater than he had realised, but for the moment he said nothing and so Baxter continued.

"Another thing, Sir, any Frogs seein' us all spread out and not much of a target, them seein' just one Troop, they'll probably not bother. Sir."

Carr nodded.

"Very well. Picket line, ten-yard gap."

Baxter shouted the order and the Troop, now on a 300-yard front, eased their mounts up the slope, progress being easier because this side of the valley contained far fewer trees. The gradient also eased and Carr raised his hand for a halt, when he turned to Baxter.

"Can you hear cavalry or perhaps marching men, Sergeant?"

Baxter listened for a half minute.

"Could be something, Sir. Carried on the wind, like."

Carr felt those words to be not much of a help and so he waved his men forward again. At the top, there was no road to be seen, they were on a wide, flat plateau and so Carr allowed his horse to walk on. They had progressed for two hundred yards, when a cry came from the left.

"Sir! Front left. Two riders."

Carr rose in his stirrups to see, some way off, yet very discernible, two horsemen in pale blue uniforms, now turning to ride away. Carr turned to Baxter.

"Right. Forward, at the canter. They're going back to something. We have to see what."

They cantered forward for not half a mile and then each man halted, there was no need for orders. On the horizon, well under half a mile beyond them, the view was filled with marching infantry and cavalry. Carr turned to Baxter.

"How many, Sergeant? What do you think?"

Again, Baxter paused to look along the full length of the column they could see.

"Two infantry Divisions and one of cavalry, Sir. Not far off that, either up or down."

Carr smiled.

"Right! Good! Job done, but they know we're here and probably won't tolerate our presence, staring at them. Time to go. Form column on me!"

At the order, Carr's men turned their horses and galloped or cantered to form a column as they hurried back to the safety of the valley and the waiting Oakwood. Baxter and Makepeace came together as they cantered back to the edge of the valley to re-cross.

"Ned Shelby told I that Tavender sent the message to come up here and to send Carr, not Peterson, who's Senior. Tavender saw that lot and suggested just one Troop, us, to go over. He hoped that Johnny would have a Squadron or two patrollin' this ridge on their flank and we'm bloody lucky that there wasn't. If Johnny knew his job, there would be, column or no column. That bastard Tavender! He don't let up, do he?"

Makepeace' expression now matched the harsh words of his Sergeant and both now shared the same opinion. Something needed to be done. Their Cornet Carr was plainly a target of Captain Tavender.

All throughout the Allied army, when the news spread of the French retreat, the most common order was to 'stand down' and so all returned to their tents, except the unlucky few required to mount a sparse picket on their ridge. From Picton's Division, this proved to be the 88th and so, as the Connaughts marched forwards through Alfayates, his remaining Battalions marched the short distance back, to their own camps. With all stood down and now going about domestic business, Lacey, O'Hare and Carr came together in the Headquarters tent to make an assault, supposedly minor, on O'Hare's bottle of whisky. Lacey provided the toast.

"So, here's to Johnny funking it every time! And a bit of peace!"

O'Hare understood, but Carr was a mite puzzled, after drinking his measure.

"Peace? How so?"

Lacey placed his glass on the table for another re-fill.

"Marmont's gone back with his 60,000, almost certainly to Cuidad, probably beyond. Winter's coming on and Himself will not risk taking the offensive against anything that size which Marmont's got that could end in a Talavera retreat or even a Corunna. We're for cantonments, close or near as may be, but we can expect a bit of peace. Of that I'm certain! And you Padraigh?"

O'Hare downed his second measure.

"I'm not quite so certain, but it'll be more in that direction that what we've been through in the last five days. I for one did not relish standing there at El Bodon, showing all bluff, daring Johnny not to think that I had no more than six high in a game of three card brag! That I can do without."

All three laughed, before downing a last glass and dispersing to their own tents.

oOo

My Lord Frederick Templemere was in the best of moods, this born of a high confidence that, by now, all the suspicious dust of Fuentes and Albuera had settled and it was time to finance a new 36 place dinner service, this to accommodate and further facilitate his slow, but steady rise up the social hierarchy of his home county. He had received, and gladly accepted, invitations to dine from the High Sherriff of Hampshire and various other Noble Lords and Judges and a reciprocal invitation from himself was now somewhat urgent. Time spent with Hopgood and Mahon was appearing more and more infrequently in his social diary. It was time to move on, leaving old cronies behind, although they were good enough company on the green benches of the House of Lords when tedium was the order of the day. The single gold bar he was now confident of turning into useful cash, weighed heavily upon his right shoulder, but the stout leather satchel suspended by an equally stout strap took the weight and enabled him to push open the heavy door of his bank 'Campbell and Coutts'.

He took himself straight up to the counter and was mildly annoyed when the Teller did not recognise him but merely greeted him with the standard, "Good morning, Sir. How can I help you?" Templemere did not reply to the greeting.

"My name is Lord Frederick Templemere. I wish to trade some gold, a bar in fact. Please inform your whichever colleague I require."

The Teller, pale, wispy and archetypal, turned to a more imposing figure sat at a desk behind him.

"Mr. Morgan. There is a Lord Templemere here, who wishes to trade some gold."

Mr. Morgan stood up and looked directly at Templemere, his outstretched left hand indicating that what needed to happen next would happen on Templemere's right.

"My Lord, if you would be so kind as to come to the door here, I will allow you through."

Templemere moved in the direction indicated and a door opened to reveal the complete figure of Mr. Morgan.

"Please step through, my Lord, and I will conduct you to our Mr. Marshfield, who deals with all of our bullion transactions."

Templemere was led across the Teller floor, then through a partition where there sat, behind a serious, walnut desk, a seemingly smallish man, late middle aged, somewhat portly, but immaculately dressed in black suit, black tie and white shirt and him definitely the bullion man of Campbell and Coutts, this evidenced by the array of scales, of different sizes, both behind, to the side and on his desk. Morgan held out his hand to indicate Marshfield.

"This is Mr. Marshfield, my Lord. You may conduct your business with him."

With that, he was gone and Templemere chose one of the chairs before the desk, his face blank, him feeling no need to create any form of convivial relationship with this mere 'banker'. However, Marshfield sat for a while, regarding Templemere, but eventually he spoke.

"My Lord. You have some business with us?"

Templemere opened the satchel and felt inside, to then bring out the gold bar, which he placed heavily on the desk.

"I wish to sell this gold bar. To convert it into cash."

Marshfield did not pick up the bar, instead he sat forward to study it. He may be on the wrong side of 50 and no oil-painting but his eyes described a sharp intelligence. Eventually he did pick it up and turn it over, more than once, then he looked at Templemere.

"Forgive my curiousity, my Lord, but your bar has no markings, no hall-marks of any kind!"

Templemere was slightly alarmed, but he quickly recovered.

"Oh, it's been in the family for generations. There's some family legend about it coming from some Spanish treasure ship, waylaid on its trip back to Spain from the Americas."

Marshfield sat back.

"Were that the case, my Lord, then there would be a huge Spanish Coat of Arms cast into it."

Templemere shook his head slightly. He was becoming irritated.

"Well, perhaps that's wrong. Whatever! I'm here to exchange it for money. Pounds, shillings and pence. It is gold, so please tell me what it is worth."

Marshfield looked at Templemere steadily, before turning slightly and bringing forward the appropriate sized scales. Templemere's bar went onto one arm of the scales and then Marshfield's weights onto the other, until the pointer met the mark at the bottom of the frame. Marshfield sat back, his face concerned once again.

"It is an odd weight, my Lord. I say that, because you see the Standard Gold Bullion Good Delivery Bar, as we call it, weighs 27 pounds and seven ounces. This weighs 22 pounds, and three quarters of an ounce."

He sat forward.

"You say it is a family heirloom, my Lord?"

Templemere was becoming alarmed.

"So I've been told."

"Well, another thing, it must have been kept very carefully down the years, because this gold looks almost freshly minted, whilst old gold has a particular sheen, closer to orange than yellow. It comes from long exposure to the common air we breathe, or more like what we breathe out, so I've been told. And smoke, of course, of both kinds, tobacco and house warming."

Templemere was now indeed becoming alarmed and he felt a trickle of sweat run down his backbone, but again he recovered.

"Well, on that I cannot comment. It has most probably been kept in a safe or cupboard or some such, but now, if you please, what is it worth?"

Marshfield did not move for a long five seconds, then he brought before him a pencil and paper to carefully go through some multiplication, before checking his work twice. He then looked at Templemere, his face serious, indicating bad news to come.

"I'm afraid, my Lord that, with this bar having questionable provenance, its purity cannot be guaranteed, therefore there is a risk. I can only offer you 13 pounds, on the pound, which gives, at that weight, two hundred and eighty-six pounds, twelve shillings exactly."

Templemere was appalled. He had made his own enquiries as to the price of gold and made his own calculations. He was expecting something in the region of £330. Not only was this insufficient for the dinner-service that he had now ordered to be made, but also he felt that he was being cheated, made a fool of, in some way. His temper rose.

"That's ridiculous! The price of gold today, is pushing up to 15 pounds per pound."

Marshfield sat impassive.

"Fourteen pounds, fourteen shillings and six pence!"

Templemere's temper rose another notch.

"And you are offering me thirteen!"

He subsided in the chair, now resolved.

"I wish to see the Manager!"

Marshfield placed his hands on the desk and pushed himself upwards for Templemere to see that he was surprisingly tall.

"I will go to him now myself, my Lord. His name is Chambers."

"Perhaps you should take the bar!"

Marshfield picked it up.

"If you think it will help your case, my Lord."

Marshfield disappeared back into the further depths of the building, leaving Templemere to sit waiting for a good ten minutes. With that now past and Templemere in darker mood, Marshfield returned with a man of medium stature, cadaverous eyes and face, but in the same dress as was tradition in the highly respectable bank of Campbell and Coutts. Marshfield now carried the bar. Templemere stood and took the initiative.

"I expect to hear that you are able to offer me a larger sum than your man here has offered!"

A pained expression came over Chambers' face.

"I'm afraid the answer is no, my Lord."

Templemere took a deep breath as if to let loose a tirade, but Chambers held up his hand which restrained him before he could utter one syllable.

"If I may explain, my Lord. You see, a Standard Gold Bullion Good Delivery Bar must have a certain purity, that being very high, ninety-nine and a half percent in fact. Very high! You see, the quality of this bar cannot be guaranteed. There is no provenance anywhere upon it. In fact, we have both come to the conclusion that it is continental, in fact exactly ten of Napoleon's standard kilograms. For that reason, my Lord, we find it impossible to trust it. I can only offer my apologies."

The mention of Napoleon renewed the trickle of sweat down Templemere's spine. The further this conversation went, the greater the suspicion that could alight upon him. He reached forward and picked up the bar, to then open his satchel and drop it in. As he turned to leave, Marshfield held up his hand and Templemere stopped.

"My Lord, there is a place where you may be able to obtain a better price, that of course being Hatton Garden. I'm sorry that we could not give greater satisfaction, my Lord."

Templemere turned on his heel and left, neither shaking hands nor wishing either 'Good-day'. Outside he hailed a cab and shouted up to the driver, the destination; Hatton Garden.

Jean Dulongue levered himself off the hitching post when Templemere emerged from the bank. He was the son of a French immigré, their whole family needing to flee France at the time of 'The Terror', in 1793, when, as successful merchants in Nantes, which had taught him useful English, they had been accused of 'speaking against the Revolution'. To be brought before 'La Comite de Citoyens de La Révolution', meant certain death, because any accused were required to prove their innocence rather than require anyone prove their guilt. Therefore, as a prosperous family, 'Aristos', and thoroughly envied, they were therefore automatically guilty, and so, warned by a friend, they had fled into the night, wearing only what they stood up in. So, in his late twenties and now speaking perfect English, he was one of four agents required to watch and follow My Lord Frederick Templemere, all assigned by Colonel John Waters. He had been withdrawn from the stress and tension of duty in France, but now he had had almost four months of what was becoming very tedious. However, now at last, something was happening perhaps. He had followed Templemere before to his bank, nothing unusual about that, but the heavy satchel and the shout of 'Hatton Garden' to the driver when he emerged, aroused his interest. He mounted his horse and followed the cab.

The cab stopped in the middle of the long street and Templemere got out, to pay the driver and then stand and wonder what to do next, as the cab drove off. Templemere walked up the street, then back, wondering which establishment to choose. Eventually he chose one that he surmised had no Jewish nor foreign connections, this entitled 'Robson and Son' which seemed English enough to him, so he entered the door to be immediately confronted by a staircase which led up to a gloomy landing. He ascended to be confronted by a very solid door, with a speak-hatch just above centre and a door-knocker below. He used the latter and then was required to use the former when it opened and the lower half of a wrinkled and unshaven face appeared.

"Yes?"

Templemere needed to bend his knees slightly.

"My name is Lord Templemere. I understand that you buy gold."

"Yes."

"Well I have a gold bar that I wish to sell. Are you interested?"

"Show me."

Templemere reached inside the satchel and pulled out the bar, then, using both hands he brought the bar up to the hatch and turned it over. Immediately, the full door opened to reveal a figure whose age was very difficult to determine, the stature was straight and upright, while the head was topped by thin wispy hair and the face appeared ancient, the skin lined and sallow, but the eyes were quick and piercing. However, the voice grated, seemingly as ancient as the face.

"So sorry to delay you, my Lord, but we have to be certain that those who come up here have genuine business. That none have evil intent, if you understand. As a dealer in gold, we cannot be too careful."

The room smelt of parchment, of which there were rolls on the shelves all around, and of dust and body odour. The Templemere studied the man, this merchant with his ill-fitting clothes and unshaven face, Templemere trying hard to hide his contempt all the while, because, after all, from this man he hoped for a good price. However, the brief examination of the man and the room was terminated by the man holding out his hand for the bar.

"May I, my Lord?"

Templemere handed over the bar which the man immediately weighed in his hand, before taking himself and the bar behind a large, probably antique, table. The bar was placed on a green baize cloth and the man looked up at Templemere.

"It will take me some time to complete my calculations, my Lord, may I offer you some refreshment, a glass of sherry perhaps?"

Templemere was annoyed at the words 'some time'. Surely, one weighed the bar and worked out a price?

"No!"

The man was still studying the bar, presumably looking for the hallmarks that were missing.

"Then may I invite you to sit, my Lord? There is a comfortable chair behind you."

Templemere turned to see an armchair, evidently as antique as the desk and this plain to see from the extent of the wear in both the upholstery and the woodwork, all worn, cracked and pock-marked. Templemere ignored the invitation, in any case he was now fascinated by what the man was doing. Before him, he now had a small tank inside a large one, the inner filled to the brim with water. He then carefully lowered the bar into the water so that that it spilt over the top of the inner. The spilt water was then carefully poured into a long, thin, glass measuring jar and the height of the water carefully noted. Templemere had enough acumen to realise that the volume of the bar had been measured. The bar was then carefully dried and weighed on some ancient scales and then came some tedious long division, a process for which Templemere had consistently held absolute contempt. The calculation being proceeded through was the weight divided by the volume, which added to Templemere's impatience. The answer, with several decimal places, was finally arrived at and then found on a chart on the wall behind the desk, alongside of which was another number, which produced from the man a loud 'hmmmm' and then a scratch of his ear. He turned back to Templemere.

"I have calculated the weight in each cubic inch, my Lord. This indicates the quality and it is not of the best, but still reasonable. I can offer you 14 pounds sterling to the pound."

Templemere's level of elation rose several notches, but he felt that he could bargain and did so.

"Fourteen pounds, five shillings!"

The man studied Templemere for a good five seconds, then he wet the end of his index finger and rubbed it over the surface of the bar. The smear dried quickly.

"Where did you get this, my Lord?"

Templemere immediately took umbrage.

"What's that to you? You know the quality, we only have to agree on a price!"

The man looked down again at the bar, then back at Templemere.

"Fourteen pounds and the half-crown!"

Templemere stared at the man for two seconds, his best aggrieved look on his face, but inwardly he was very content. This was a far better price that Campbell and Coutts had offered.

"Very well, but it has to be cash. Now!"

The man nodded.

"This can be done."

He reached across his desk for pencil and paper, made the calculation and then checked it, twice.

"Three hundred and eleven pounds, eight shillings and 3 pence."

He pushed the paper across to Templemere.

"Would you care to check my workings, my Lord?"

Templemere shook his head, so the man stood, to then walk across the room and pass through a door that was hidden behind a tall bookcase, this stuffed full of ledgers. Templemere waited for two minutes before the man returned, holding a wad of notes and a small bag of coins. He placed both on his desk, resumed his seat and then began counting out the reassuring Bank of England £10 and £15 notes, then the coins required to make up the full amount. The whole was then slid over the desk towards Templemere, who seized the notes, to fold them and push them carefully into the largest pocket of his ornate waistcoat, the coins into the smallest. Then, without another word he left the room, descended the stairs and went out into the pleasant but unseasonable early November sunshine. He hailed a cab and called up "Campbell and Coutts". The cabbie whipped on the horse and Templemere sat back into the upholstery, relishing the thought of banking well over three hundred pounds under the noses of those upstart bankers.

As Templemere emerged, Dulongue remained in the adjacent doorway. He noted that the leather satchel, straining under some weight when Templemere went in, was now folded and plainly empty under Templemere's arm. His destination of Campbell and Coutts meant that, in all likelihood, he was on a mission to deposit money. With Templemere now out of sight, Dulongue turned into the door and climbed the stairs. There he saw the same solid door and speak-hatch and he also used the door-knocker. The hatch opened and the same face appeared.

"Yes?"

The answer was an impressive brass badge pushed through the hatch for the man to examine. Beneath the impressive Coat of Arms of King George III were the simple words, Jean Dulongue. Agent of the Crown. The polished brass shone even in the dim light, but the words 'Agent of the Crown' had their effect.

"What do you want with me?"

Dulongue lowered himself to lean on the shelf at the bottom of the hatch and open his note pad.

"I'll know your name first."

"Alfred Robson."

The words were written.

"That man who just left. What was his name?"

"That's our business!"

Dulongue smiled through the hatch.

"Alfred, this is Crown business. The business of traitors in which you are now mixed up. Traitors can still be hung, drawn and quartered. Did you know that? Hmmm? So, what was his name?"

The answer was clear, but now tremulous.

"Lord Templemere."

"And his business?"

"To sell a gold bar."

"Show me the bar."

Robson went back to the desk and brought the bar to the hatch for Dulongue to see.

"What did you pay? Don't lie now Alfred. Your neck is now in a noose!"

The reply came back in haste, almost shouted.

"Three hundred and eleven pounds, eight shillings and 3 pence!"

The numbers were noted.

"Right Alfred. That bar is now Crown evidence. We need it. I'll give you a promissory note now for the full value, or you can wait for me and others to come back to still give you a promissory note, but take a good look round as well, as we are always inclined to do and who knows what we'll find. Hmmm? Depending on that, and the depth of our suspicions, we may alter the amount. Which do you want?"

Robson was incensed.

"The badge of yours could be forged! I'll wait."

"Fair enough, Alfred, but you do not sell it, am I clear. If you co-operate, then you are an innocent party, caught up through no fault of your own. If you do not have that bar when I return then we will conclude that you have destroyed evidence to protect a ring of traitors and that makes you as bad as them."

Business concerns now arouse in the calculating mind of Alfred Robson.

"I will be paid for the bar, won't I? I paid good money, a fair price, for what I took as genuine gold. I saw no reason to doubt."

"You will, but show me the bar again."

Robson did so, turning it over so that Dulongue could see all sides.

"No hallmarks, Alfred. Did that not give you pause?"

Robson's voice rose an octave. This was becoming serious, he could lose money, but he could lose all to this total stranger with a fancy brass plate that could be a forgery. Such a badge was no great problem to imitate.

"No! That's not so very unusual. It could be a make-up of scrappage and left-overs. And I'll wait!"

Dulongue closed his pad and pocketed his badge.

"As you choose, Alfred, but I'll be back within the hour."

He hurried downstairs, wrote a note which went into an envelope which he gave to a cabbie for delivery to Smith Street. Then he checked the building for no other entrances and then went back upstairs and used the knocker, but he did not wait for the hatch to open.

"Alfred! Are you still there? And with the bar?"

"Yes", was shouted from beyond the dark wood.

"Good man, Alfred. That's wise. My people are on their way. You'd be wise to let them in, no delay now, you'd do well to keep them in a good mood."

All went well and within the hour Colonel John Waters was staring at the gold bar on his desk, with Radipole, General Livermore and Dulongue sat on the far side. Waters looked up.

"So Templemere had a gold bar to trade!"

He looked at Radipole.

"Did you not say a while back, that he was upping the stakes at the gaming tables?"

Radipole nodded.

"I did, and that still applies."

Waters handed the bar to Livermore who examined all sides.

"No markings and the weight is odd, Radipole? Can you say?"

"I can, Sir. The weight is slightly over 22 pounds, but the significant fact is, that it weighs ten kilograms, a measure introduced by Napoleon in the seventeen nineties. The bar is continental!"

oOo

Chapter Eight

"I weren't never so cold!"

A November chill, English weather to those familiar, coursed over the bleak slopes that rose gently above the crucial road from Salamanca to Cuidad Rodrigo. The slopes were the very same as occupied by Picton's Third Division, over two weeks previous, but were now populated by a single Squadron of the 16th Light Dragoons, the 2nd, that of Captain Oakwood. All in the line now wore their long cavalry cloaks with the welcome high collar and the hem down to their boots, but not quite long enough to hide the final inches of their Light-Cavalry sabres. Major Johnson was with them, and all four Officers, including Oakwood, Carr and Peterson, now looked down sadly at the spectacle on the road. It was Johnson who broke the silence.

"Watch, wait and report, is the order and I cannot remember one which I've so gladly obeyed."

The words brought a smile to the faces of the remaining three as they watched what amounted to a whole French Corps marching on the road below, escorting a long line of wagons and carts towards Cuidad.

"You are looking at something well over 3,000 men, gentlemen, which gives us some slight good cheer. Such an escort being now required to get anything into Cuidad must tell us that Sanchez and his boyoes have the whole area between here and Salamanca pretty much buttoned down. One town is cut off from the other, unless Johnny is prepared to mount this sort of effort."

Cornet Carr looked over at him.

"Nevertheless, Sir. Cuidad is now re-supplied."

"It is Carr, which means there's a siege coming. They cannot be starved out now, so don't look forward to too pleasant a Christmas!"

Peterson took up the theme.

"A siege? Do we have the guns now, Sir?"

"Yes Douglas, we do. There's a siege train now, only days from Almeida. Expect a Winter close up to the trenches."

With that he turned his horse to leave.

"Somers-Cocks with Three is next up. Remind him of orders, 'watch and wait'. He's as liable to go looking for a fight as Crauford, who's not so far back at Martiago, but even his Light Division can do nothing against the three we can see down there!"

With Johnson gone, Oakwood gave his own order.

"Stand the men down. Dismount and light fires. At least we can give Three a bit of a welcome when they arrive!"

His men needed no second bidding and soon fires were kindled from the scrub and stunted trees that covered the slope. Thirty miles back from them, as the crow flies, creature comfort was also uppermost in the minds of the 105th, all secure in their billets, barns and stables within Aldea da Ponte, which they had left Alfayates to march to, some days previous. All effort had been made to improve the quality of their stay, this place being their winter cantonment, they were certain. On that day, whilst the 16th sat their mounts and watched events below, continuous hammering could be heard from the interior of a well-appointed stable, obviously once part of a wealthy estate, which had been allocated to the messes of Deakin, Davey and Saunders, this decision having been eased in their direction by several measures of brandy. The stable had been worked on for over a week and was now warm, dry and comfortable. The hammering was being watched, but not supervised, by the farmer, as Joe Pike constructed a shutter for the only remaining bare opening. Some metal hinges and a latch had even been salvaged from a long abandoned out-building, over a mile away. Soon the shutter was nailed into place and the farmer was allowed to pull it closed and use the latch, several times and with much satisfaction. Now fully content, he looked at Pike, smiling happily through an extensive moustache.

"Muito bom, senhor. Muito bom trabalho."

Consuela was standing by.

239

"He says good work, Joe."

Deakin was amused and he turned to Byford.

"Seems like you're not goin' to be needed so much, John, when it comes to turnin' Portuguese into English."

Byford looked up from paying full attention to baby Jed sat on his knee, with Eirin sat close beside him.

"Suits me, Sarn't. I have enough trouble with Spanish, without adding on the oddities of Portuguese as well."

However, whilst trouble was subsiding in the barn, outside in the square of Aldea da Ponte it was rising and from the usual source, this being the deep dislike and rivalry between Nellie Nicholls and Betty Barker, with the husband of the latter never too disinclined to join in, if Nellie's husband, Sergeant Henry Nicholls, was not present. This time the issue was water from the well. Nellie had drawn her water, with Betty some places behind, enough to fill two buckets and she was on her way down the queue. As Nellie passed Betty, she grasped the rope at the back of one of the buckets, tilting it as Nellie passed and spilling much of the water. Nellie looked back and saw Betty not yet fully returned to the queue, which was enough evidence for her. She put down the full bucket and came at Betty with the half full, swinging it heavily against her arm which she had raised to protect herself. The blow now struck, Nellie gave further vent to her anger.

"So why did you do that, now, you ugly baggage? Spill our water?"

Nellie got no further, Betty had her own spleen to empty, now that she stood bruised and wet.

"You Irish cow! You near broke my arm, 'tain't my fault you can't carry a bucket."

Nellie had swung back the bucket again.

"I'll break your gobshite head if you do that again, so I will."

However, at that moment Sergeant Obediah Hill, almost of equal stature to RSM Gibney came running over, just in time to place his own arm on that about to wield Nellie's bucket in a swinging arc.

"Enough! Both of you."

He had heard the argument and knew the issue.

"Nellie, get that bucket re-filled and get on back."

He then pointed to Betty Barker.

"And you hold your place and hold your tongue!"

However, Mrs. Barker now had an issue with Sergeant Hill.

"Oh, so she's 'Nellie' is she? An' wot am I? Not even a missus!"

Hill reared up over the indignant 'Mrs' Barker.

"You hold your tongue, or your mess'll be missin' water this day. And the share out, too."

Betty Barker was intimidated at the threatened punishment and shrank back. Hill had the power to enforce what he threatened and her own husband would be fully forthcoming with his fists if there were no rations arriving simply because Betty fancied starting an argument with another Follower. However, there was no truce when the ration share-out came, this being conducted by Hill again. The hook went into the salt-pork barrel and he intoned the time-honoured words to the Followers behind his back

"Who wants this?"

Betty Barker quickly spoke up.

"Me!"

The piece was a good one that was dropped into her apron and she could not resist a few accusing words in the direction of Nellie and Bridie as she flouted the good piece to enable them to see, her voice gloating and triumphant.

"Seems like your crooked signal scheme didn't come off this time!"

However, a nearby Corporal, well aware of the volatility of Nellie and Betty Barker, came between them and his firm hands on her back, hurried Betty away.

The routine of winter cantonment had quickly established itself throughout all ranks, this now in the form of Lieutenant Richard Shakespeare sitting himself at the table of the Light Company room in one of the larger houses of Aldea and pushing a book before Nat Drake who was busying himself writing a letter.

"The Life and Opinions of Trishtram Shandy. Gentleman. I've read it. What've you got?"

Drake put down his pencil/

"Nothing! My Gulliver's Travels is with him, over there."

The 'him over there', was none other than Major Henry Carr, busy rubbing olive oil into the wood of a pair of Dragoon pistols. Carr looked up.

"I've finished it and passed it onto Maltby. See if he'll do a trade."

Shakeshaft let out a long sigh of not quite despair, this not unnoticed by Drake.

"Never mind, Richard. Get on with your sketching."

There came another sigh.

"I've run out of drawing paper. My book is full!"

"Then your Journal! Flesh that out a bit. We'll give you a hand, we've all got memories of literate merit, I feel sure."

There was no reply, only a blank expression and so Drake turned to Carr.

"Have you written?"

Instead of turning towards Drake, Carr blew some item from the priming pan of one of the pistols.

"I have! Sent off yesterday and I have a reply from the one before. You?"

"Well, I received a letter last week and I'm in the middle of a reply of my own. Here, on this table."

Carr smiled smugly.

"Then I'd say that puts me one up on you!"

The pistols were now wrapped in cloth and Carr stood up.

"I'm for a bit of a wander. Anyone?"

The only reply came from Shakeshaft.

"I need to go and find Maltby, or someone, anyone, who hasn't read this particular piece of popular fiction at least twice."

Accepting that he was on his own, Carr took down his cloak from its peg, swung it around his shoulders and left the room, intending to wander the now familiar streets of Aldea alone. However, he was not long in that solitary state, because O'Hare was also out stretching his legs, also wrapped up in his own cloak. O'Hare fell in besides Carr and smiled at him.

"Some news."

"What?"

"The first of the siege guns are in Almeida. The rest following."

Carr stopped to turn and face him, the memory of the looming and formidable Cuidad ravellins clear in his mind.

"This is serious!"

"It is and he'll have us over there for Christmas, that's how I see it."

Carr's brows furrowed.

"But Johnny's only in Salamanca. Surely he'll come forward when we start digging trenches around the place?"

O'Hare shook his head.

"Not likely. From what I hear he's scattered all over so as to live off the land, as they do. He cannot concentrate enough to bother us. We've got over 40,000 men, us and the Portuguese. The French can't match that and the rumours are of French movements East; troops being drawn off and back to France. Boney's up to something, which means that whoever's in Cuidad are on their own!"

Carr walked forward, staring ahead.

"You been in a siege before?"

O'Hare shook his head as he followed.

"Certainly not for a place as important as Cuidad Rodrigo!"

"Then we're all in for a new experience."

O'Hare merely nodded his head, his face downcast and morose, the thought of a serious and probably deadly siege, had subdued the spirits of even such as him.

However, the mood at that moment in the refurbished barn on the edge of the village was anything but sombre. The food had cooked well in the large fireplace which graced the stable and all were warm and comfortable, with most of the men smoking, mending or making, the latter applying to Tom Miles as he carefully carved a rattle from a nice piece of oak, which brought some grudging looks of appreciation from Nellie Nicholls, this between her own chores of washing and cleaning alongside Bridie, Consuela and Eirin. To add to their contentment, pickets and serious sentry duty were not required, although a night patrol always combed through the streets, to deter marauding or light-fingered locals. However, on this particular night it did not apply to them and they had a welcome guest, one who was kept busy, sat beside the equally literate Byford. Parson's Assistant Sedgwicke was taking dictation for John Davey, whilst Byford was doing almost the same for Joe Pike, in his case it was simply giving advice as Pike himself wrote a letter to his wife Mary. The whole scene was reminiscent of barrack life back in England and all the more comforting for that, the familiar sounds, sights and smells.

However, much of this easy sojourn, for both Officers and men was dispelled the following day, when O'Hare arrived in the room occupied by the Officers of the Light Company, carrying sketches that contained measurements.

"Come over to the table."

He spread the paper, to reveal sketches of wooden structures, both round and square.

"Each Company in the army is ordered to construct some of these for the coming siege, two types, this, and this."

He had pointed in turn to each of the two drawings on the sheet. Above the first was the title 'fascine', above the second 'gabion', the former drawing, including diameter and length, merely a large bundle of branches bound together, the latter a box construction of wickerwork as shown by the specific dimensions for height, width and depth.

"On top, he's going to pay the men!"

From his audience there came an intake of breath.

"Yes. Five pence for every fascine and ten pence for every gabion."

Drake looked over to Maltby, carefully studying the drawings.

"Stuart! Go and find Ellis."

With Maltby gone, Drake tore a sheet from Shakeshaft's Journal, much to his dismay, and made a copy of the drawing. The copy made, O'Hare departed.

"I need to get around the other Companies. I'll leave you to it."

Within 15 minutes, Ellis was in the barn with the Light Company copy, calling all NCO's to the table on which he spread the crude drawings.

"We've got to make these, for the siege that's coming at Roger's Town. As many as we can and we'll get paid. Five pence for this and ten for this."

The mention of money concentrated the minds of Davey, Saunders and Deakin and they followed Ellis' pointing finger. Davey spoke first, placing his finger on the gabion.

"These! 'Tis only a bit of wickerwork."

Saunders placed his finger on the fascine.

"But these is simpler!"

"Yes, but they needs three times the timber. And they'm heavy! You can bet it'll be us as to carry them to this Cuidad place. There's withy beds down by the river to make t'other. Whilst all others will be in the woods hacking at branches, we can do the skilled stuff and earn more money."

He looked at Ellis.

"Do they care which of these we makes? Do we have a choice?"

"At some time they will, because most'll be choosing these fascines. They'm easier, like you said, John."

Davey nodded, satisfied.

"Right! These gabions is no more than five hurdles bound together into a box. Like we made back by Santarem."

Over the next days and weeks, the fields and woods around Aldea were heavily populated with Redcoats wielding mattocks and axes to obtain the wood required to build their quota. Few entered the cold and soggy withy beds alongside the river Aldea, other than the more monetarily motivated members of the 105th Light Company and so over the days, under Davey's expert tutelage, gabions began to appear outside the barn and towards the end, as skills improved, one each day. Jed Deakin, raised on the Somerset Levels, was no slouch himself when it came to making hurdles and so a similar number could be attributed to the Colour Company, the results being surveyed by Captain Joshua Heaviside and commented on in the usual cryptic manner.

"That the man of God may be competent, equipped for every good work. Two Timothy. Three. Seventeen."

His men nearby, those who could overhear, looked at each other, shaking their head with their eyebrows nearer their hairline in puzzlement, but not for long. They were not far themselves from another ten pence. The work progressed well, then, on Christmas Eve, nothing could be seen or at least easily recognised, because it had snowed! Ellis came into the barn and pointed to ten men, each one re-Christened 'you!" They left but soon returned, each with a large, bound bundle, but with Ellis in the lead and prepared himself to risk a small attempt at humour.

"Here! My Christmas present to you all. New greatcoats!"

Miles shuffled forward to receive his. It may not fit, but the routine was to exchange with someone, until a better fit was obtained, but he had something to say first.

"The best Christmas present you can give us, is to say that we'n all stayin' yer till Spring! And what about boots?"

Ellis threw a greatcoat at him.

"Can't say that, Miles, but I can say that there's extra rations for tomorrow. Call that another gift, just from me! And boots comes tomorrow, so I've heard."

Ellis was as good as his word. The boots arrived to be distributed in the same way as the greatcoats and the Christmas Day ration was salt-pork with a generous issue of flour, sugar and dried fruit. As they all sat around to consume the plentiful meal, the door of the barn swung open for an orderly to enter with a pail of rum. Almost immediately, mugs and beakers were being thrust at him, with Tom Miles carefully watching that the Orderly's thumb was not inside the measure to shorten his allocation. The day finished with a rum-fueled sing-song, but the next day, Ellis came again but this time bringing news that was nothing approaching cheerful.

"Get all up together. We're leaving. Tomorrow we're marching out."

All heads were turned towards him and one word came from many directions.

"Where?"

"Somewhere called Zamarra."

"Where's that?"

"Back the way we came to here, back through El Bodon, then back over the river. Same side as we were when we had to hurry back out."

Miles was immediately concerned.

"Will that put us back in that crow's nest place we was in last time?"

Ellis smiled indulgently at him.

"That I doubts, Miles. From what I hear, we're way back from there. If you're luck's in, you could be as cosy there, as you are here!"

However, the full opposite of cosy applied as the Third Division column snaked its way over the icy tracks, with snow still lingering, with the whole column much elongated, as the men carried their siege constructions over the arduous route. As they marched, Davey's reputation became more and more enhanced when it was noted that the heavier fascine needed eight men, a gabion only needed four, one on each corner, but it was not soon when they found themselves again on the Roman bridge over the Agueda. Then they were into the difficult country around Martiago, with no clear tracks to Zamarra to speak of and then a wade through the freezing waters of a tributary to the Agueda. The short day was closing when they entered Zamarra, a town encouragingly similar to Aldea, but all those carrying a gabion or a heavier fascine were ordered into the fields beyond, where they were paid. As Saunders, Davey and the others, walked back into the village to find their billets, the pennies and shillings chinking in their pockets, Saunders spoke his thoughts.

"I suppose this is fair enough, only paying when they'm delivered."

They all had memories of some fascines, very burdensome to carry, being set down beside their route, their carriers fallen out and needing a rest before they could continue, some even leaving the fascine behind, it not being worth the five pence that would be divided over eight men. Their billets, when allocated, were a series of sheds and stables but all there were soon busy bringing them up to some level of comfort, even though much in need of rest. The money went into the Section purse and they began to take off their equipment, when matters took a turn for the worse, Miles lifting his head.

"What the Hell is that?"

Byford thought he knew.

"Irish pipes. They wail a bit more than those from Scotland."

Miles had the last word.

"Is that because Diddykites is all more bloody miserable than even they Jock girlies?"

No-one answered around Miles, but Nat Drake had an answer that was more accurate, when he entered their billet.

"Wallace is forming a choir!

Maltby turned towards him in surprise.

"An Irish one?"

"What else, with his 88th?"

Drake held up his finger.

"Listen!"

They did, for a good half minute, then Maltby gave his opinion.

"They've got a very long way to go!"

The next day it snowed again, but again the order was given 'More fascines and gabions'. Davey and his work-gang set off into the woods, they knew that Zamarra was too high on the plateau for any wet withybeds. He led them into a neglected wood that badly needed coppicing and so they soon returned with plentiful thin branches and saplings to resume work again, but their skills had been retained and a gabion was made each day. However, Miles was far from content, their billets being very close to those of the 88th.

"How're we supposed to get all this done with that Irish racket goin' on day and night?"

Saunders looked up from splitting a branch a little too thick.

"You wants my opinion, I'd say they was getting better!"

"You can say that, but first thing is, you've got to have some liking what they'm singing!"

Davey looked over, laughing.

"And how much singing did you do in that Bristol place you comes from?"

The question seemed to flatten Miles as the memories of the stews of Bristol alongside the muddy Avon, came flooding back.

"Some! But mostly at funerals!"

Saunders had his own memories of his childhood and early teens in Norfolk.

"And of a Sunday as well, so's you'd keep in with the Vicar and then he'd not get you turfed out of your home for not turning up to his Church and listening to his sermons. Just out of spite!"

There was much shaking of heads as the memories of village or town life returned to them all, but they were not required to endure the full performance of the 88th, because that was for Officers and Senior NCO's. 'Senior' included Colour Sergeant Deakin, who was therefore allowed to take his Bridie, but Henry Nicholls, being merely Sergeant, was not included and so Nellie could not go. However, Jed Deakin thought that he had a solution and, after a few minutes searching, he found him whom he sought, inspecting a gabion by giving the joints a severe shaking.

"Sar' Major. Are you going to the 88th concert?"

Gibney's brows came together suspiciously but he answered honestly.

"Aye. I am."

"Well. You know that it's Irish music and I'm taking my Bridie, but Henry's Nellie cannot come with us, him only being a Sergeant, so..."

Deakin got no further when Gibney held up his hand.

"She can come wi' me. That'll be grand. Tha' can tell her so, from me."

Deakin hurried back to convey the good news to the dejected Nellie, but he found the whole room stood to the attention and silent, with Lieutenant Maltby present in the room. All were stood stiffly to attention but that was nothing compared to the cold gaze fixed by everyone on the intruding Officer. Deakin immediately realised that he had returned at the end of whatever had taken place in his absence, because Maltby was saying what made little sense to Deakin.

"I'm sorry that's the case. That is a disappointment."

He then bowed in the direction of Consuela Saunders, turned and left, with Deakin quickly making way to give him room. He looked at Davey and Saunders.

"What was that all about?"

However, it was Miles who answered.

"That slimey, womanisin' bastard just had the cheek to come and invite Zeke's Consuela to the 88th shindig. He's got a bloody nerve, that one! Show up to invite another man's wife to step out with'n. Zeke should've clocked 'im. Be in his rights. We'd all've said he fell over!"

Deakin's happy message to Nellie fell flat in the angry atmosphere, which immediately included Deakin, but a night's sleep and a good breakfast eased the insult that all felt and their continued work on the gabions distracted all minds. The concert was that evening and Bridie and Nellie, in their best, and cleanest finery, stepped out with their escorts to the venue, this being a large barn. Officers had chairs provided, NCO's and their companions were required to stand at the back. In the event, all concluded that the entertainment was not half bad. No-one not Irish had ever heard of any of the songs, with obscure titles such as "The Galway Piper" and "Tarry Trousers", but everyone Irish knew the words and those that could, joined in. Padraigh O'Hare even left his seat to come back and join Bridie and Nellie when they started singing, much to Jed Deakin's mortification, but soon there were too many of like behaviour to make any difference. When they walked back, all agreed that it had been a good concert and a credit to the 88th.

The next day, New Year's Day, the order came to make ready to move, this delivered in person by Wallace in the 105th Headquarters room of the Officer's billets. There was only O'Hare there to greet him while Wallace quickly shut the door against a wind armed with sleet and he spoke immediately.

"He's bringing up everything to start the siege and we can count ourselves lucky!"

O'Hare reluctantly stood up, the presence of a Colonel/Brigadier requiring such, even as good an old comrade as Wallace, the reluctance being caused by the move requiring him to increase the distance between himself and the fire.

"How so?"

"First, Mackinnon is coming back, he's recovered, and second we are to stay this side of the Agueda. And that's not all! We are in a village, somewhere called Serradillo del Arroyo, not five miles East of here."

"And how does that make us lucky?"

"All other Divisions are on the other side of the Agueda, in tents. To get across and get around the town to where he wants his trenches, to the North-west, they'll have to ford it where we did back in September before we came to that mill. I've just come back over it with Picton and Campbell. He's replaced Colville, which is fine, a good Celt. Anyway, back to the Agueda. It's not the easy paddle now that it was for us, there's more ice than water, and it's not one ford, it's two. They're working on that bridge over the leat at the mill, making it stronger."

"For the guns?"

"No. There's a Roman bridge that carries a road running from Almeida to a place called Castillejo something or other. Our gun boys will follow that to get themselves to where will all happen."

"Seems we have much to thank the Romans for!"

"No argument there. Right, I'll leave that with you. I'm off to see Riley and McArdle."

As Wallace departed, O'Hare went to the desk usually occupied by Lacey, to write the Orders, a move that he could feel as a chill, as it took him even further from the fire. At the top of the page O'Hare wrote the date for the movement; 2nd January 1812 and on that day Wallace's Brigade formed their column for the short march East. In a pause between the snow flurries many looked West to the slopes beyond the valley of the Agueda. The whole was bleak and forbidding, but all across could be seen, already there, the long lines of grey tents, marked by the grey/green tracks between each row, these created by many moving figures and all distinctive in the thin covering of snow. Blue smoke from hundreds of bivouac fires drifted upwards to the grey, cold clouds. More dark-coated columns were marching in. Wellington was assembling his army for the first Allied siege of the war that would be conducted in a very purposeful and very determined manner; this one well-armed and fully manned.

oOo

Every head was bent forward, every shako tilted downwards, to provide the best possible protection against the driving sleet that was slanting viciously upon at them from the North-west. There was no conversation, no complaints about 'why us', because each man remained within his own world, intent on protecting wet and raw faces from the relentless stinging ice that added to the general misery. Carr, Drake and Maltby headed the column, it being formed by just one Company, the Light of the 105th. Carr had received the order from Wellington himself, but the General mentioned within the order was Crauford, who had requested

Carr and the 105th Lights for a particular task. Crauford could not order Picton to release them to join his Division temporarily, but it was well within Wellington's power and thus they were now marching across the North of Cuidad Rodrigo to join the Light Division, positioned at the site from where the siege would be conducted. Carr resented Crauford for pulling them away from the Third Division, but, from a career point of view it was satisfying that the request had been endorsed by Wellington himself. Yet Carr would have foregone that, if it meant that he and his men did not have to traverse these frozen fields, with no easy road being available outside of cannon-shot from the walls. Thus, all were now placing their feet carefully into frozen plough ruts and slowly feeling the chill from the ice that attached itself to their trousers from the rime covered remains of last year's crop, despite the protection of gaiters dug out of the depths of their back-packs.

The march from Serradilla to the Light Division assembled in the valley to the North-west of Cuidad, took over two hours and once there, Drake led the company to the far valley side where, at least, the sting was taken from the sleet, if they sat with their backs to it on the lee side of the slope. There they huddled, the tarpaulin cover at the back of their shakoes now lowered to meet their great-coat collars and protect their necks. Meanwhile, no such sparse comfort came to Carr, he needed to go off to find Crauford, but that was soon accomplished, because the figure, now well known to Carr, was pointed out to him by a Captain of the 52nd. Crauford was stood in earnest discussion with a Cacadores Captain and what appeared to be one of his Colonels. Carr marched up and saluted.

"You sent for us, Sir."

Crauford did not seem to mind being interrupted and he turned to meet him, but there was no welcome.

"Carr! You've not met Captain Rafaele nor Colonel Colbourne."

Carr offered his hand to the Rafaele, who took it, but Carr saluted the Colonel. However, Colborne offered his hand which Carr took. That completed, Crauford continued.

"Now, Carr, that big lump behind us is called the Greater Tesson. Everything starts from there, it'll put us on the same height as the city walls, only thing is, the Frogs have built a fort, an earthwork, on top of it, called Fort Renaud. We have to take it, this very night. That's why you're here. We need all the accurate fire we can get to cover the storming party and, not very helpfully, two of my Rifle Companies have been drawn off to guard a pontoon bridge, downstream of here, but not my Cacadores. So, come to my tent and we'll outline the plan."

The tent was not far away and Carr was grateful for some protection from the wind at last. Inside was a small table on which was a large piece of paper, with a square in the centre and the outline of Cuidad's nearest fortifications included at the top. As they entered, another Portuguese Cacadores Captain followed them in. Crauford noticed the newcomer, but in his usual summary fashion, eschewed all niceties.

"Ah, this is Captain Gentile! You can all introduce yourselves later. Now, Colborne, what do you have in mind?"

Colborne leaned over the plan, holding a pencil. As he spoke of each Company, he drew a line to show their position.

"Two Companies of my 52nd and the two Cacadores of Rafaele and Gentile, will go either side to encircle the work. Carr, I want your two Sections mixed in with the two of my 52nd, to make their fire more accurate with your Bakers. Whilst you keep their heads down, I'll be coming up behind with two more Companies of my 52nd and one from the 43rd. We are the storming party and we go through you and then over the ramparts."

He began to quickly draw crosses in the area between the square representing the redoubt and the town fortifications.

"Our only Company of Rifles will be spread out across here, between the town and the redoubt, to deter any reinforcements from the town should things get awkward and to sweep up any fugitives when we do take the place. The fewer Johnnies in the town, the easier the main job will be."

Carr looked up from the plan.

"Do we call you forward, Sir, when we think the ramparts are cleared?"

"No Carr. After five minutes, I'll assume you've played your part and then it's my turn!"

"Very good, Sir, but where would you like me, Sir? I've brought three Officers with me, two Lieutenants and their Captain. Remaining with my Company, I feel that I would be somewhat superfluous."

Colborne nodded.

"Very good, Major. Come with me."

Crauford now resumed command.

"Right! To business. Get your men assembled, gentlemen."

They all filed out of the tent and hurried to their respective Companies. Carr soon reached his own huddled mass.

"Up, all of you! In Sections and follow me. Officers to me."

As he hurried to catch up with Carr, Drake smiled to himself, "No longer the usual languid Henry! We are now in the presence of the enemy."

They were heading towards a long row of lanterns that stretched across the hillside and in line with them were the four Companies who would lead, the two in the centre could just be seen as Redcoats in the weak light. Above them was a skirmish line of shadowy figures, probably Riflemen. Three more Companies were assembled further back down in the lowest part of the valley.

"Nat. We are to feed ours into those two Companies of the 52nd, there in the centre, one Section into each. There's an earthwork over that hill and we are to join with them to keep Frog heads down with our Bakers, so that those you can see down there behind, can come up through us, storm over the ramparts and take the place."

"Where will you be?"

"With the stormers. Allocate your Sections and good luck!"

With that, Carr hurried away to the assembly below, leaving Drake to explain to Maltby and Shakeshaft their part in what was to be attempted. As the two Sections divided to blend with their respective 52nd Company, a Rifles Officer came down the slope to Drake, who thought he recognised the tall Officer.

"We've met before, haven't we? Uniacke, if I've got it right."

The Officer extended his hand.

"Yes, and you're Drake. We met when his Lordship decided to take a close-up look at the walls of this place."

"Yes, and we discovered a bit more than we'd bargained for!"

Both laughed.

"Yes we did, and now we're caught up in this. Equally mad, in my opinion, but there it is. Mine will guide you all forward, to make sure you come up to this place correctly and then mine are to disperse around and beyond. Right now, I've five men lying waiting at the point where you deploy to give fire. From there, I disperse either side."

At that moment, Colborne arrived and both Drake and Uniacke saluted.

"All set, Uniacke?"

"Sir."

"Then move out and we'll follow. Your NCOs know the way?"

"They do, Sir."

"Right, good luck to you both."

As the two centre 52nd Companies moved forward, relations within the ranks were nothing like so convivial. The 52nd was a proud Regiment who remembered their achievements at Busaco and Sabugal and thoroughly resented requiring help from anyone, as evidenced by the words of a 52nd Private to Tom Miles, but him not making the best of choices for his audience.

"What are you doing here? Who said you were needed?"

Miles was staring straight ahead as they advanced, not taking his eyes from the back of the Rifleman, 20 yards ahead.

"Don't think it's out of choice! We'n here because we've got Bakers and is more likely to hit what we shoots at and so I says buggery to the sod as said that we has to have 'em! It's because of carrying Bakers that we'n over here now, goin' up this slope in the dark, in a snowstorm, to take on God knows what!"

Wisely the 52nd Private decided it was best to say no more and he returned to face his front. Merely yards before both, with swords drawn, Drake and Shakeshaft were grateful to be following Uniacke, both unsure where the Captain of their 52nd Company was, but then Drake noticed something had changed.

"Snow's stopped. Seems like the weather's favouring the French. That sleet blowing into their faces would have been useful."

"Yes Sir, but at least we can see more!"

Drake nodded agreement, but said nothing as the line advanced on. Joe Pike's head was full of questions, but he had neither Tom Miles nor John Davey either side of him to provide answers, either side was some stranger, who seemed resentful of him being there. He could trust no-one for a sympathetic answer and so he could only trust what he could feel ahead, rather than see, as his boots swished through the frozen stubble, this still armoured with ice. The advance of minutes seemed like hours, then, against no more than starlight he saw the high Church tower of Cuidad Rodrigo and his own Officers were raising their hands to halt. As the line came up, a tall Officer gestured with both arms to take position either side of him and all did, to kneel or lie on the icy wet stubble. The tall Officer was Uniacke, who came back to Drake to whisper.

"You're about 50 yards off. That horizon you can see is their parapet. I'm taking mine around the other side now. It'll probably be us moving that wakes them up and starts thing off. No bad thing, then you'll have a better idea where they are. Good luck!"

"And to you, Uniacke!"

The Riflemen before them eased off to the left and, as Uniacke predicted, their movement around the redoubt awoke the French and shouts of alarm came from behind the ramparts. Within minutes the garrison were firing out into the darkness, which, as Uniacke had said, gave the covering party the line at which to fire. From somewhere came the order.

"Open fire!"

The whole Allied line sent a volley at the muzzle flashes and then for some minutes they maintained a heavy weight of fire at where the ramparts could now be seen. Joe Pike, as did all others, found reloading awkward they were now prone on the ground, but nevertheless the sound of musketry from his line was continuous. Three cannon were fired from within the fort, their flash illuminating the 52nd line, but it made no difference to the volume of fire skimming across the top of the French parapet. It was not long before the weight of French fire began to recede, caused by what was coming at them from out of the darkness beyond. What came next from Fort Renaud, by way of feeble resistance, were live shells and grenades being thrown into the unoccupied ditch before the earthworks, which harmed their nearby Redcoat and Cacadores assailants not at all.

Some yards back, Carr was kneeling beside a Captain Gurwood of the 52nd, his men with their ladders set a few yards back. It was Gurwood who suggested their advance.

"I think we should go, Sir. There's hardly anything from them now, by way of musketry."

Carr nodded in the darkness.

"I agree. It's time."

Gurwood stood up.

"52nd! Follow me!"

Carrying their ladders, they ran forward. Carr could only hope that he was heading in the right direction because the smoke from the firing had turned the thick darkness into a thicker fog. He just avoided treading on the prone figure of a Cacadore as they passed through the firing line, when, after 40 long strides and with great relief, he found himself at the void of the ditch before his feet. The ladders were lowered to rest against their side of the ditch, but many of the 52nd simply jumped down. Carr did the same, but then he was knocked off his feet by a soldier landing immediately behind him. As he scrambled upright, a French shell exploded off to his right and he heard screaming in the darkness. The ladders were brought forward to rest against the parapet and Carr took the lead on the nearest.

"With me! Follow who can."

The order was superfluous. There were many behind him and many more were scaling the bank of the parapet, their comrades below merely pushing them up. Carr climbed and found himself at an embrasure which contained a cannon but no cannoneers. His right hand still holding his sword, he looped that arm over the barrel and levered himself up, to find himself stood within the cannon's embrasure, but almost immediately, he was not alone. Soldiers of the 52nd were joining him, but the first task was to secure the parapet before penetrating any further. He could not hear and he certainly could not see, any sign of resistance, but nevertheless, he directed each alternate man as they arrived either side to secure their foothold on the first line of defence. Content with that, Carr gathered the next arrivals.

"With me. Come on."

Descending from the parapet was easy, there was no inner ditch, merely a two-foot drop. So far, they had seen no French, but Carr advanced on across the fort's interior, his outstretched sword matching the bayonets of the 52nd either side. Some blue uniforms disappeared into the darkness, but then Carr realised that he was at the far side, where he found Gurwood and some of his Company scrambling over a wrecked gate. Carr lowered his sword.

"I'd say this was done and done very nicely. Who wrecked the gate?"

"No idea, Sir. We heard an explosion and found it in pieces. Most convenient of whoever, I'd say."

Carr laughed and then he did sheath his sword.

"Right. Get your men together. When the French find out that we are in possession, this will not be a healthy place. I'm off to find your Colonel."

Carr hurried back to what seemed like the only building in the fort and there he found Colborne.

"All done, Sir?"

"All done, Carr. Most of them either crawled under their guns or hid in this guardhouse. We've got about 50 prisoners."

"And our losses?"

"About half a dozen dead and twice that wounded. They're being carried back now, but it's a nothing price to pay to capture a place like this. Unioeke tells me he scooped up a few fugitives, but a couple got through, so it won't be long before Johnny's conveying his full resentment for what we've just done, so I've ordered us out."

"Very good, Sir. With your permission, I'll take a tour of the perimeter and check none of ours remain."

"Do that, Carr, but not too long. You know why."

Carr went to the nearest parapet and began his circuit. He came upon one French body, then continued around to find only one more, him slumped over one of the cannon. On the Cuidad side of the work, he could hear the faint sound of shouting from the town ramparts and so he hurriedly completed his circuit and then departed through the wrecked gate. He jogged back, probably just in time, because from the town walls came an eruption of cannon-fire and solid shot began to hit the earthwork and then came shells, dropping out of the night from howitzers somewhere over on the left. He continued on back, some 200 yards, then, very surprised, he came to a halt. There was a dense line of Redcoats and Portuguese, stretching either side into the night, all with picks and shovels, digging the first parallel, which was already three feet deep. Spent cannonballs from the French bombardment rolled into their ditch, to be quickly lobbed out. Carr stood for a moment to shake his head and speak quietly to himself, "Wellington is wasting no time!"

oOo

"Well that didn't last long."

Deakin took one last, miserable look at Serradilla with its solid buildings and good roofs slowly disappearing below the horizon as they descended the good road which, in peaceful times, would have led directly to Cuidad. However, within sight of the city walls they were forced off right to march in a shallow valley which conveniently curved around the North of the town. There was little cheerfulness anywhere throughout the whole 3rd Division column, from the experience of the 105th Light, all now knew of the bleak uplands that were their destination, from where the siege would begin and end. Amongst the Officers the words most included in their sparse conversations were "concentrating his forces", within the ranks the two words most used were "bloody cold!" Eventually, they turned left up the valley side to cross the main North-West road out of Cuidad and there to see for themselves the extent of the army Wellington had assembled to conduct the siege. As far as the eye could see, the camps of three whole Divisions were before them and they would be the fourth, their ground being off to their right beside the main road. However, what sank all spirits, sending necks further down into collars and mouths to be set in grim resignation, was the sight of the bleak, wind blasted plain that all the tents seemed to be perilously perched upon, this view stretching out to be swallowed by the grey reaches of the snow and sleet that filled air. In the centre was the gun-park, the squat naval cannon and their attendant carts and limbers all neatly lined up, ready and speaking of a ferocious conflict to come.

As they marched on, now along a good road to their camping ground, Deakin knew what he was looking for and, when they swung off the road, what he wanted was in sight. As soon as their tents were pitched, he called to all those within the two messes that he controlled and the children.

"You lot, with me!"

They followed him to the barn and stable that he had seen and there he saw what he wanted.

"Right, good. Decent straw. Bundle up all you can."

The straw was gathered and taken back, to be strewn thickly across the bare stubble inside their tents. Deakin gave a final examination and nodded his satisfaction at the extra comfort it would give. The women had their fires going and, with no orders to the contrary, had now begun to cook food. As he emerged from the tent, Bridie came and put her arms around him.

"Oh Jed, this is such a shame to be leavin' where we were and setting up in such a place as this. 'Tis no better than a bare mountainside, so it's not!"

Deakin embraced her and kissed the top of her head.

"I know Bridie, but this is what we gets, us, livin' this life. We just have to make the best of it. There's bedding in the tents now and woodland is not too far. We just have to make the best of it, like always."

Resignedly, Bridie detached herself and went back to the task of preparing food whilst the men went off to gather wood. A decent fire would make all the difference during the coming days ahead.

In the Headquarters tent of the 105th, Lacey sat at his table untying the ribbon on a roll of orders, as Carr and O'Hare sat watching and waiting. Lacey spread the thick paper over the table and quickly scanned the contents.

"It's a list of duty in the trenches. The Third Division go in on the night of the 11th, 11 o' clock, and come out on the night of the twelfth, at 11 again. We relieve the 4th and get relieved by the Light. We go back in sometime on the 14th, relieving the 4th again and sometime on the 15th we are relieved again by the Lights."

Carr pulled the paper to himself for a good look and saw a whole elaborate timetable. O'Hare looked at Lacey.

"And after?"

"My guess is that by then the breaches will be practical, if I'm any judge of the artillery we saw on our way here."

"What's today?"

"10th January."

O'Hare sat back.

"Right, so eat, rest and stay warm until our turn in the parallels, almost all of tomorrow night, the whole day after and then almost to Midnight thereafter."

Then a thought.

"Although, it will be and long gone, Midnight, by the time we've marched back."

When the news spread, the men of the 105th had decided much the same thing themselves and so throughout that day they sat, slept and ate. However, what the veterans could hear and interpret gave them little comfort, which included Deakin sat smoking with his friend Halfway.

"You hear that, Jed? Johnny's not giving best too easy, nor making life too easy for them lads up there in the trenches."

Deakin knew exactly what Halfway was referring to, the constant rumble of cannon-fire, like distant thunder, from over the hill.

"I'd say that was Johnny. Too soon for our guns, they'm not in yet, 'tis the batteries for them that our lads is now buildin'. What's bad, as I sees it, is that Johnny seems to have plenty of powder and shot, so he feels he can blast away all day long at whatever of ours is in range."

Halfway puffed a while on his pipe.

"Remember that siege of Dunkirk, back in '93, under the Duke of York. That one we had to march off from and abandon, 'cos too many Frenchers was on their way to put a stop to it."

Deakin withdrew his own pipe.

"I remembers, an' I remembers too the looks of them walls and I weren't sorry at all, that we'd not have to go up ladders nor scramble over some pile of rubble to get at a hole in their wall. They called it a defeat back home, but wern't they as would've had to do it."

Halfway puffed at his pipe and found it exhausted and so he knocked out the dottle and ash on his boot heel.

"I remembers all that too, and here we is again, with a man in charge as is a lot more sure of what he wants to do and how to do it, than that Duke what we had then. This 'un has the steel in him. He'll not be walking away!"

Deakin stood up from the box they were both sharing.

"You'm not wrong there, Tobe, but let's get over and see if there's any tea going."

Tea was also fully occupying the mind of the Reverend Albright, as he sat on the tailboards of his personal cart, his feet supported by the steps leading down, the warm liquid in his pewter mug now half drunk. Sedgwicke, meanwhile, was bustling around the camp, tidying, wiping and keeping one eye on the boiling stew. Two more mouthfuls and his tea was finished, then Albright's single track mind could turn to the constant rumble of the French cannon.

"I take it we can expect a different kind of conflict, this time, Private. I mean it will not be a battle as in a field, this time. Nothing like 'The Iliad', when the army of Troy issued forth to do battle before the walls with the invading Greeks?"

Sedgwicke sighed in exasperation. A hopeless line soldier as he may be, nevertheless he had a full appreciation of modern weapons and tactics and the idea that Albright's notions of a siege were rooted in the Classics, both shocked and depressed him.

"No Sir, not like that. The French will do their best to frustrate our efforts in various ways, in the hope that we will simply give in or they hear of a relieving army on its way to chase us off. For us, it's a question of making a big enough hole in their wall for us to get through. Or rather a breach as they call it, which will be more like a cleft, made with a giant axe, than a hole. It will be a very bloody affair if we succeed and history teaches us that in many ways what comes after is worse, when the victorious soldiers get inside the town. Rapine, looting and murder are the most common outcomes."

Albright looked shocked.

"Surely not the Christian soldiers of a British Army?"

"We can only hope so, Sir."

"Then we must pray and hope that mercy and understanding remain uppermost in our soldier's hearts."

Sedgewicke sighed again. His own regard and feelings of affinity towards the men in the ranks had grown over this years, but to expect that was too much. Nevertheless, Albright was his superior.

"Amen to that, Sir. Yes, Amen."

oOo

The light was fading by various degrees as the clouds of various shades and densities passed across the sun now almost touching the horizon. The Third Division was formed into Brigade columns preparatory to marching forward the three miles over the fields to climb the back of the Greater Tesson and, when on the far side, to relieve the 4th Division for the first time. The constant rumble of the French guns firing from the walls did nothing to lighten their mood, but that of Lacey and O'Hare was lifted somewhat by a welcome sight coming towards them as they stood at the head of their Brigade column. General Mackinnon was heading their way and the Scot's face split into a wide grin as he held out his hand to both Lacey and O'Hare.

"'Tis guid to be back, lads, I can tell ye!"

The health in Mackinnon's face was plain, even in the gathering gloom. It was Lacey who put it into words.

"You look well, Sir. Autumn in Lisbon must agree with you!"

"Lisbon, be damned! A few weeks in the cold and damp of a dreich Scotland is what set me to rights. And a guid few drams of some decent stuff!"

Lacey and O'Hare laughed, even more at Mackinnon's next words.

"And I brought some oot wi' me. So, we'll have to sink one or two when all this is done!"

Lacey nodded agreement.

"We'll look forward to it, Sir, but you've not returned at the best of times."

"Nae need to tell me that, Lacey, but we get on wi' it, what else? An' for us, this begins wi' a three mile walk as I see it, afore we can turn one spadeful."

At that moment one of Picton's Aides rode up, to halt and salute.

"Please to bring your men forward, Sir."

Mackinnon nodded.

"Very good, we'll move out directly."

The orders were given and the columns moved out, all carrying the wooden bundles and wickerwork that they had been tending since Zamarra, these at last to be released from their care and put to good use. The wind at their backs gave some small aid as they trudged forward over ground thankfully not muddy, but frozen hard. The two Brigade columns kept pace with each other, that of Campbell's on the left of Mackinnon's. After a mind numbing 30 minutes of marching through the full dark, they began to see the flashes of the cannon fire from the Western and Northern walls of Cuidad as the French defenders did their best to both nullify and frustrate the efforts of those whose clear purpose was to eject them from the Spanish town. Once up the rear slope of the Greater Tesson and onto the flat plateau of its full height, an Officer of Engineers came to the head of Mackinnon's column.

"I'm Captain Palfrey, Sir, Corps of Engineers. If you please, Sir, our Colonel Fletcher has allocated to you the far right of what we call the First Parallel. To improve that and work on Battery Number Three which is just below it."

Mackinnon continued to march. It was too cold to stop.

"As your Colonel of Engineers chooses. We are at his disposal."

"Very good, Sir. I am to guide you there and remain in an advisory capacity, you understand."

"Aye laddie, I do. Ye're here to tell us what to do, but we've nae complaint. This needs doin' right and it's the likes of yourself as knows the best way of it."

"Yes Sir, and so if we could tend over to the right somewhat."

The gun flashes became more individual the nearer they came to the walls and soon another column came looming out of the dark to pass them going in the opposite direction.

"Those are the Fourth, I take it?"

"Yes Sir. General Kemmis' Brigade."

They marched on. Despite the darkness, the French were maintaining fire, concentrating on the where they thought the works vital for the siege were, even if they could not be seen. Scattered earth, thrown up as French round-shot hit home, bounced against them and between their feet. The 105th were at the head of Mackinnon's column and the Captain Palfrey came up to Lacey.

"Please to take yours down the sap from the first parallel into Number Three and work there, Sir. There's only one sap leading down for now, and the other two Regiments of your Brigade will be in the parallel above you, making repairs and improvements there."

"What do you want us to do with our handiwork, our fascines and gabions."

"We'll use the fascines for shelter from French fire, Sir, for now, and the gabions, well, some to add and some to replace what's been destroyed."

Round-shot was regularly singing above them or hitting the parapet of the first parallel as the Engineer led them down into it. After a short distance, they were directed to enter the narrow entrance to the sap that zig-zagged its way down to the site of the battery, now named number three. However, once on site at the battery, Lacey gave his verdict.

"Well, this is a proper pickle!"

Even in the poor light provided by the gun flashes from the walls, he could see, as could anyone, that counter fire from the walls had been particularly effective. The parapet of the battery had been almost levelled in some places, but what was worse was that the gabions placed before it by the Fourth and First Divisions were almost wrecked, the soil that had been shovelled into them, spilling out from gaping holes in their wickerwork sides, their neat, square shapes gone completely. O'Hare took one look and then, as the wind from a passing round-shot sounded in his ears, he gave his orders, these born of both experience and common-sense.

"Get those fascines out front and anchored down. Without some protection, we'll not manage a shovelful!"

As the heavy bundles were rolled over the top of the parapet, there came screaming from over on the left. The 105th had suffered its first casualty and O'Hare heard clearly the order to "Get him back up."

Some fascines were already in place beyond the parallel and seemed to have resisted the impact of shot hitting them, this noticed by Drake as Four Company rolled their own number down a few yards to add to what was already there and thus create an effective screen from the incessant cannon fire. On the French side, the branches of these originals must be badly battered, Drake concluded, although he dared not look, but the density of the fascines had held the balls within their interior, witnessed by the lack of exit damage on his side.

"Well that's one thing we've got right at least!"

By now the ten Companies of the 105th had picked up the tools left on site by the 4th Division and were shovelling from the bottom of the trench to repair the extensive damage to the parapet. All were working vigorously to keep warm, then Palfrey came up to Drake.

"I'm afraid there's more to it than just digging downwards to create a parapet from the soil dug up from the bottom of the trench."

"How so?"

"Fletcher and Wellington want the parapet 18 feet wide."

Drake's eyes widened so that Palfrey could see the whites even in the dark.

"18 feet!"

"Yes, I'm afraid so, which means digging from the other side of the parapet. What we call an exterior ditch."

"A nice term indeed! You mean the French side, with not much more than bundles of sticks to give protection!"

"No, we'll have to use some of your gabions to give better protection."

The nearest fascine jerked back against its ropes from the impact of a cannon-ball, which did not interrupt Palfrey at all.

"Yes, that's right. So that will be the first job, getting the gabions filled to create protection, the fascines will be needed when we get up to Johnny's walls and have to cross ditches, but many are already so badly damaged that they will fall apart if we try to move them."

"Then I say we leave them there. We'll need their protection whilst continuing with our shovelling into the gabions that you say should go out front."

"You've made sense. Many of those fascines are now immovable anyway, and we can easily make some more from the woods behind us. That makes sense, but there is another thing."

Drake sighed wearily, hands on his hips, as Palfrey continued.

"The gabions must be placed to create a gap that coincides with an embrasure. Right now the fascines protect us, but would block any fire from our battery, here."

"So, when the time comes, the fascines must be released to roll down the hill!"

Palfrey nodded.

"Mostly, yes!"

"Right, then I leave this 'gabion location' entirely to you. You are staying, I take it?"

"I am."

Drake then began to walk off and leave Palfrey to his deliberations, but he had one more judgment to make.

"That's about the only thing around here that makes any damn sense!"

They parted company and Drake went off to find his Company and get their gabions carried forward and placed correctly between the parapet and the row of fascines, as Palfrey directed after consulting his plan. As the 105th worked, the night became increasingly bitter and as the cold began to take its toll, some men were unable to continue working because they were shivering so badly. O'Hare came to Lacey.

"We cannot ask the men to do more than six hours in this, especially after a three-mile march. We must split into two watches, relief time at one o' clock. I've known men lose fingers and toes from such as this, from what we call frostbite in Ireland. Wounds from Johnny is one thing, losing men from the weather is another."

"It's called frostbite where I come from and we had it in the Americas. I noted fires further back as we came forward, the men can go back to there. Get that organised, Sections with even numbers out when those gabions are filled. Everyone back in with the daylight."

Through the first hours of their period on duty, the work continued, their eyes now well used to the gloom. It was not long before all Officers began to wield a pick or a shovel, not for any egalitarian reasons but simply because it was too cold to stand idle and wait for their day in the trenches to end. From Lacey downwards, the Officers worked alongside the men, O'Hare making endless jokes about Irish Navvies and Heaviside uttering endless quotes from the Bible about honest labour and the prayer of good works. Close by Deakin gave the now time-honoured reply to each.

"Yes Sir. I'm sure all the lads sees it that way, Sir."

When the vital, protective gabions were filled and all now able to stop French round-shot, O'Hare toured the battery himself, ordering the Sections with even numbers back to recover by the warmth of a fire. At the Light Company, strictly Ten Company, all were now sat down in the exterior ditch with their gabions now filled, when Ellis arrived.

"Orders! We're out for a spell. Until one in the morning. Get back and get warm. There's fires back over."

The Light Company needed no further bidding, but downed tools and sped back over the First Parallel, ignoring the comments of the 88th working there, to then see the welcoming fires back beyond Fort Renaud, with many 105th already gaining comfort from their warmth. They were quickly joined by other huddled figures from their Regiment and Davey, Saunders and many others pushed their water bottles close to the flames to at least warm the liquid within. However, better succour did arrive, because Picton, as much in the cause of effective effort in the diggings, as any feelings for his men, had ordered a bean broth to be brewed and this was poured into their mugs by touring Orderlies. The mugs warmed their hands and the broth their lips and stomachs, but few felt the need to start any conversation, rather to stare instead into the comforting flames. In addition, many had tightened a scarf so tight under their jaw that speech was very difficult. Some even managed two hours' sleep, before their time out was curtailed by the watch of Major Carr and then by the arrival of the odd number Companies of the 105th, who came hurrying back and demanded their turn at the fires which sent the previous occupants back to the picks and shovels.

With the arrival of dawn, Colonel Fletcher himself came into Number Three battery and spoke to O'Hare.

"Get your men out of the exterior trenches. Digging there caused too many casualties amongst the 4th with the arrival of daylight and more accurate fire from the walls."

He looked around and what he saw were wooden gun-platforms in the embrasures and splinter-proof screens around the magazines for each embrasure.

"But yours have done well! You should tell them so."

However, still working, ten yards down the trench from them, Zeke Saunders and John Byford were pegging timber against the side of a gun embrasure to provide a clear space for the gun-barrel when both heard a plop and a hiss behind them. Byford was the first to turn to see a live shell, the fuse fizzing ominously. Byford, on his knees, had not the purchase to do any more than seize the heavy shell and lob it up onto the top of the parapet, where Saunders managed to push it further out with the length of timber he was holding. They then ducked down as the shell exploded above them and both were covered in earth as the side of the trench caved in. They shook themselves out of the debris, their ears ringing, but there was now a large hole in the parapet and the wooden revetment along the side of their section had lurched forward into the trench for at least four yards. It was Saunders who made the first comment.

"Well that's three hours work all gone for nothing!"

Fletcher and Lacey came hurrying up, but the former seemed more concerned about the damage done to the battery, his face twisted with frustration and anxiety.

"They did this yesterday, as soon as daylight shows them where our batteries are. They drop shells from the San Francisco Monastery far down over on our left, they must have a howitzer or two in there, with those on the walls spotting for them and with that they can wreck half the work we get done. I'd say best to get all your men into here, Colonel, and allocate some for 'shell watch' to throw the damn things down the hill if they can, or warn those near to lie flat. It was bad yesterday and it'll be the same today. The only good thing is that they give them a long fuse. They want them to explode inside the works, not up in the air. That usually gives the extra seconds to get them away."

A few seconds! Lacey looked aghast at the idea of his men picking up live shells to throw them anywhere, but the destruction they could cause was there in front of him and completing the batteries so that they could at last begin to make a breach was, after all, why they were there. Throwing out destructive shells was part of the task and to this end he felt he could only ask the men himself and so he toured the battery, allocating the task of 'shell watch and disposal' to the biggest and strongest. Thus, Saunders and Solomon, with several others of the Regiment, mostly Grenadiers, stood on watch, most often looking up at the sky, watching for the black speck, easily seen against the light grey clouds, arcing up and over from the left. Nevertheless, this did little to ease the tension in the backs and shoulders of those still required to work, these continuously bent over their picks and shovels or sawing and pegging timber into place, as round-shot thudded into the gabions below them and shells descended from the cold clouds above. Fortunately, those in the Light Company were only called upon to give warning of a shell seen easing its way either left or right during its journey, always to land outside the trench on one side or the other. No more 'handling' was required for them, yet throughout the morning, elsewhere, the incessant shells caused significant destruction and casualties within the 1st parallel and the batteries.

Fletcher continued to tour the works, both the parallel and the three batteries, and he came again to Lacey at Noon.

"Your men are working well, Colonel, but I am concerned that damage from the bombardment should be minimised to enable better progress to be made during the night, without having to spend too much time on repair. I must therefore ask that the Midday meal be taken here, so that the works not be abandoned and then these damn French 'fizzers' can be thrown out before they blow anymore good work to pieces."

Lacey's state of mind had not changed, regarding the idea of actually handling a shell about to explode, but he could not argue. If it exploded in the trench it would destroy lives, as well as works of earth and timber.

"Very good, but does Picton know?"

"He does, yes, and he approves, to the extent that he has ordered food to be cooked and brought forward to his Division in the trenches."

So it was, that for their Midday meal, the men of the 105th sat in the bottom of their trenches, warming themselves from fires made from off-cuts of timber, listening to French guns and the sound of shot hitting the gabions they had carefully constructed and fascines further out. Now all were 'watchers', eyes quitting examination of the sky only to guide their spoons out of their dishes to their waiting mouths. It was Davey who spotted the black dot which worryingly did not deviate in any direction, which meant that it was coming straight for them.

"Here's one!"

All looked up. Would it land in their trench or shift just enough to one side or the other to explode outside the trench? All put down their dishes to keep their hands free, but the shell dropped six feet away on the parapet. No-one could reach it and so they ducked down to wait for the explosion. It came and they were showered in dirt, which was when Tom Miles began swearing.

"Bastards! French bastards. God damn them bastard Frogs to Hell and worse!"

He was now busy spooning lumps of soil out of his precious hot stew. Despite his best efforts at protection, several lumps had bounced in.

"Just they wait until I gets in thur. Thur'll be a reckonin' an' that's a fact. Bastards! Shite-auk, muckrake, stinkin' Frog bastards!"

When all the soil was gone from his dish, there was very little actual stew left, but all around him scooped up a small spoonful from their own dishes and he soon had a decent portion again, but the foul invective towards the French nation in general continued between mouthfuls.

Work was resumed and progress was made, although a quarter of the effort, so O'Hare calculated, had to be spent on repair, but the smile broadened on Fletcher's face as the daylight dimmed at 4 o' clock and the bombardment lessened, in both accuracy and intensity. With the fall in the light, so fell the temperature and, with the five hours they had left, Lacey ordered 'stand down' again by alternate Companies, even numbers out first. Taking their turn first, the Light Company traipsed back to the nearest fire, all, at Davey's command, picking up any spare wood to add to the fire that they had decided to aim for. Sat beside the merry flames, Byford decided to do some research. Looking around, he asked the question.

"Which would you rather, a set-piece battle, or this?"

It was Miles who spoke first, speaking from instinct, because for him the question required no thought.

"Bloody silly question! They'm both damn horrible! Nothin' to choose between either. That Talavera, where we was starvin' and dyin' of thirst, with acres of Frogs comin' at us. And that caper in Fuentes, back over yonder, in and out of them buildings. Don't see much of a difference between that and what's comin' up here."

Saunders gave a more considered opinion.

"Well, with this, it is two days out and one under fire, but that day isn't so bad as a full set-to. If I had a choice, I'd settle for this, rather than going up against the Johnnies so close you can shake hands, like Fuentes and Corunna!"

It was Bill Turner, who rarely said much, who had the last word before they lay back for an hour's sleep.

"Ah, but as I understand it, at the end of this two days off and one on, we've got to clamber up into some breach and shake hands with the Frogs at the top. Given the choice, I'd rather stand in the line and just fire off my ten. From choice, I'd take my chances there."

They lay back for some sleep, their feet warming at the fire, but all too soon odd number Companies came back in the shape of Grenadiers in their case and they were called forward to spend their final two hours in the battery, now almost finished. At 11 o' clock, in the deep blackness of the night, the 105th were ordered to move back. Tools were dropped where they stood and then they obeyed the order to form up, then march off, without one backward glance. Drake remained in the trench, feeling that something should be said during the hand-over, something which may help to prevent injury. He did not have long to wait, as the men of the Light Division came down to relieve them and endure their own second stint in the works. A Captain of the 43rd came up to him.

"Selway, 43rd. Good of you to wait. Anything we should know?"

"Drake, 105th. Yes. Johnny will rain fizzing shells down on you during the daylight hours, now that we've a decent row of fascines and gabions between us and the city walls. Set some men to watch for their arrival, coming down. It'll save lives and preserve the work you've done. If they land in the trench, you've got a bit of time to lob them out, if you've got your wits about you. The fuses are a bit too long, so we've been told."

Selway's voice, coming out of the dark, conveyed his amazement.

"I'd rather put a bet on The Derby. A bit of time! How long?"

"Two, three, seconds. Our men managed it!"

It was at that moment they realised that they could see each other's faces. Drake looked up to the source of the light.

"Well, that's new. Seems that Johnny's built some kind of catapult, or two."

The source was a fireball descending from the sky above them, which then landed several yards away, but still close enough to illuminate their completed workings. Drake stood and watched fascinated, as others arced over the town walls and down onto the top of the Greater Tesson, but there was no resumption of the shells. Just prior to leaving, Drake turned to Selway, now stood amongst his men, all busy with pick and shovel and under the supervision of a Captain of Engineers.

"Anything new, sort of in the offing, have you heard?"

"Well, he wants to start a second parallel on top the Lesser Tesson, which means us working out in front of the gabions and such, to drive down the sap that will connect with it. That may be us, or it may be the 1st, who take over from us. On top of that, the Convent down over on the right, called Santa Cruz, it's full of French, as you probably know, and they'll have a clear sight of any of us working our way down to connect with this second. I'll not be surprised if some effort is not made to capture the place sometime and turf them out!"

Drake grinned.

"Convent, is it? We thought it was a Monastery."

Selway was not amused.

"Monastery you thought! What's the damn difference? There's no prayers being said in there now."

"Right, well, if it's you, good luck with that."

"It won't be us, of that I'm sure, it'll probably be during the time when the 1st is in, but there is one further thing, the 52nd are dragging guns forward to go into these batteries. Tonight, the siege begins proper with a few testing shots, which may deter Johnny from lobbing over his fireworks. With them up in the sky, we'll be able to see his walls at night same as he can see us."

Drake offered his hand.

"Well, good luck Selway. May even see you up on the walls one night, you never know."

Both laughed and Drake hurried back, meaning to catch up with his 105th, now departed this quarter of an hour.

oOo

Back in their camp, despite the late hour, the priority for the 105th was hot food consumed around a decent fire, but evidence of the siege was never far away, because a simple look up in the direction of the town saw the horizon of the Greater Tesson sharp edged from the cannon fire and French fireballs. However, the companions of Deakin, Davey and Saunders would not allow this to distract them as, despite their exhaustion, they ate their first good meal in 24 hours, but Bridie, sat next to Jed Deakin, could not take her eyes away from the sight.

"Oh, Jed, it looks horrid, does it not?"

Deakin patted her forearm.

"Now don't you go worryin' too much. These things always looks worse than they turns out to be."

However, he was not too convinced by his own words as the cannon fire intensified with a new deep crash. "Them's Navy 24's! Ours." he said to himself, but he said nothing to Bridie. The following day was spent in the minimum of movement for the 105th, eating, sleeping and keeping warm, but there was one common activity amongst them, siege veterans that they now counted themselves to be, many made knee-pads from twigs and coarse grass that would enable them to dig on their knees in the greater safety of the trench floor. Bill Turner was able to provide the design that was generally adopted by the Light Company. Meanwhile Carr and Drake added letter writing into their sojourn and Shakeshaft included the upkeep of his Journal. The following day, the 14th, Carr decided that he was restless, bored and had slept enough, despite not yet having the motivation to get off his cot bed and he looked generally jaded when O'Hare decided to come into his tent and sit in the only chair. He came straight to the point.

"They've set up some tents on the Tesson, in the redoubt captured by you the other night, for Officers of Majority rank and above to sit and watch events. To keep abreast of things, as it were."

Carr lifted his head off the pillow to support it with his right forearm.

"Do we not have duties here?"

"None that I can think of. The men are sheltered and well fed, all getting ready for another effort in the trenches tomorrow. I think a wander up to take a look at what we'll be walking back into come 11 o' clock tomorrow may not be a bad thing."

"Tomorrow? So, it's 11 o' clock morning daylight, not 11 o' clock tonight!"

"Yes. No longer a night-shift. The holes in the ground are deep enough."

Carr swung his legs off his cot bed and felt beneath for his boots. He pulled them on and stood, as did O'Hare. Carr was still buttoning his greatcoat as they began their walk.

The three miles took three quarters of an hour and then they were walking over a wooden bridge that had been laid over the ditch that Carr remembered only too well when he had attacked the redoubt, to then enter, via a new entrance pierced through the parapet of Fort Renaud.

"The Peer has made this his forward Headquarters, in the guardhouse over there."

Carr turned his head left to see that the door which had been smashed open six nights ago, was now fully repaired and frequently opening and closing as Staff passed in and out. Carr and O'Hare took themselves to the parapet at the rear, this being nearest to the town, to stand beside an Officer of Engineers. Carr wasted no time.

"Who's in now?"

"The 1st Division, but the 4th will be taking over within the hour."

Any continuous conversation was difficult because the cannonading was incessant from the continuous bark of the guns from the walls and the heavier, less frequent crash of the Naval siege guns now deployed in the three batteries, all served from within the first parallel. Carr took the trouble to count them and found 27 in all. It was not yet a full bombardment, because each gun as yet fired a ranging shot only, some of which were too high to hit the fortification and instead hit the tall church tower behind that point of the main wall. This section had evidently been repaired from some previous siege and was now the object of their own bombardment. Carr continued the effort at conversation and pointed at the Church.

"Will that be the main breach?"

Carr had to shout his question once more before an answer was forthcoming

"Yes, it's where the French got in, the Summer before the one just gone, of 1810. We think it to be badly repaired and it is the furthest North-west point of the walls and cannot be supported from the adjoining walls. They are almost at right-angles to each other."

He paused to allow the roar to die away of another 24lb cannon firing a ranging shot.

"But first we have to batter down the faussebraie in front to give ourselves a clear shot at the walls proper."

Carr looked at him, thoroughly bemused.

"Faussebraie?"

"Yes, it's a kind of intermediate wall outside the main, to protect the main itself. The ravellins stick out from it and there's a ditch back of it. The main one."

Carr nodded, not wishing to explore any further the dry intricacies of 18th Century fortifications, which usually had French names anyway, as did this one.

"And what's new from two days ago?"

"The second parallel is well advanced on top the Lesser Tesson and, more important, we captured the Santa Cruz Convent last night. Some KGL and a Company of Rifles. With that cleared, now we can really push on and make the second parallel and get some guns in. Then we'll start to do some real damage!"

This had been spoken with Carr's ear practically alongside the Engineer's head, but now Carr turned to O'Hare and the pair walked a little way to the site of the gate of Fort Renaud, now an empty gap in the far Western wall, from there to watch the hit of the ranging shots from the individual guns. When one had zoned in on the fortifications beneath the Church, the next began their own gun-laying. The pair were distracted by the two Brigades of the 1st Division marching out of the parallels and Carr looked back to see no sign of the 4th who should be taking over, but then there came complete uproar from the parallel on the Lesser Tesson and the siege-guns in the three batteries beneath them stopped firing. The change in the sounds carried its own warning.

"Something's happening. Something bad!"

He jumped down from Renaud's parapet and ran out through the gate. He heard O'Hare shout "Sortie" from behind and then he was well ahead of O'Hare and running to the first parallel, to then look down and over to see that the second parallel, lower down but on top of the Lesser Tesson, was full of French soldiers, all doing their best to pull down revetments and over-turn the smaller gabions. The gun- crews in the three batteries below them were now running back up to the plateau, abandoning their guns. A British General was in the first parallel, trying to stem the flow of retreating gunners, these running back because many French had now spilled out from the second parallel, were over the dividing valley and climbing the steep slope towards the batteries, all encouraged by sword waving French Officers. Carr ran up to him.

"Sir. What would you have me do?"

The General pointed to a Company of Redcoats gathered in a sap that led back from the first parallel, who had obviously readied themselves to leave, because they had all their equipment about themselves, but they had halted with the arrival of the French.

"Hold the batteries with those. I'll get some more."

With that he was gone, leaving Carr to study the Company for a moment, all stood in shock, their Captain plainly unsure as to what to do. They had been ordered to leave, but now the French had arrived. Carr ran over, shouting and pointing at the Captain.

"You! Get your men into the batteries, now, and give fire!"

The sight of an angry Officer running at them and shouting orders, jolted all in the Company out of their paralysis and they all ran back down the sap, over the first parallel and into the batteries, where, to Carr's admiration, all quickly loaded and began to send musket balls at the advancing French. However, Carr did not need to look closely to see that they were faced with perhaps three hundred, whereas the Company were only about 70 strong. He stood in the way of a party of gunners who were running along the first parallel. He held his sword out before him, one hand on the point, the other on the hilt, this as good as any order to stop and they did.

"Get down into that battery and get a gun loaded. Or two. With anything. Fire it at those bastards who are coming up here to wreck everything we've done."

The gunners ran down the sap to Number Three battery, that which had been worked on by the 105th themselves and they set about loading two guns. Carr followed them and pulled a Bombardier around by his shoulder.

"Any grape?"

"No Sir. Only solid."

"Put in three! In each."

"Yes Sir, but we can only depress that far down by taking off the front wheels."

"Then do it!"

That order given, Carr returned to the Company of Redcoats holding the battery parapets. They were men of the 24th Warwickshires, this confirmed by their broad Midland accents and all were plainly veterans as they fired and reloaded furiously and now other groups were coming into action to add their weight of fire. Carr looked down the slope. There were fewer French now attempting to reach the batteries but those in the second parallel on the Lesser Tesson were furiously wrecking the whole, infuriatingly using the tools that the 1st Division had left there prior to leaving. Carr looked behind to see a horizon empty of troops, but other Officers, including O'Hare, had matched his own response and were encouraging other men of the 1st Division or were firing pistols themselves, then both cannon fired, the unprotected naval roar of the 24lb calibre barrel numbing Carr's senses. When the smoke cleared sufficiently, there were only two smashed French bodies, but the inclusion of cannon against them, and from above, seemed to have a good effect. Their advance up the slope ceased and then came further relief; the same General reappeared beside him and the batteries were now full of extra Redcoats, all kilted Scots.

"Sorry Sir, but I could do nothing about those over there!"

The reply came in broad Scots.

"Never mind, laddie. Ye held them awa' the guns. Nae other thing matters."

The General stood back to shout at a Scots Officer, a Major and then point to the lower height of the Lesser Tesson.

"Farquarson! Lead them on. Clear oot yon scallywags!"

The Major drew his sword, climbed onto the parapet and yelled one word.

"Advance!"

The men of the 24th and the newly arrived Scots surged forward, but the French had gone, many clearly seen taking the tools with them, this eventually confirmed by the Scots and Midlanders from the top of the Lesser Tesson. The retreating French were finally seen climbing the slope opposite, this leading up to the town walls about 500 yards distant. The General placed his sword atop the battery parapet.

"A bad business, this laddie. Fior dhroch! Yon's a mistake we must no make again."

"No Sir, but I'd best get back, Sir. My Division take over at this time tomorrow."

'What's your name, Major?"

Carr sprung to attention.

"Carr, Sir. 105th Foot."

"Well done Carr. I'm General Graham."

"Sir!"

Carr saluted and left, to soon be joined by O'Hare.

"Well, we did not bargain for that! I for one had hoped for a mere gentle excursion to see what our gunners were up to and bit of knowledge about what tomorrow may bring."

O'Hare nodded.

"And it's worse than what you saw. The French have recaptured that Santa Cruz place. They'll have to be cleared out again."

For the pair, it was a weary walk back to camp, the desperation and excitement caused by the French sortie seemed to have sapped all the energy from their legs. At last they slumped down in the 105th Headquarters tent to find that the repercussions of the French sortie had arrived ahead of them, Lacey sat looking at the latest missive from Wellington's Headquarters. He dropped it onto the table and looked at both.

"Seems that your little episode today has caused a change or two. They want us up there at first light and ready for any French jokery, then into the works the moment the 4th have managed the out!"

O'Hare picked up the order paper.

"Any change in timings?"

"No. 11 o' clock remains standard now that the 1st parallel has been finished, which has to be better than going in during the pitch dark, as for our first time digging."

However, something close to full dark certainly applied at 7 o' clock in the gloomy morning as the Third Division left their camp for the three miles' tramp to the First parallel, carrying timber and metal spikes. Again the cold was bitter, carried on a wind that speared them as would a lance, sharpened with sleet and rain in equal measure. As if to emphasise their predicament and give each of his near companions a chance to share their woes, Joe Pike felt inclined to pass on what he had heard the previous day to all those who could hear above the keening wind.

"I heard that three Portuguese sentries froze to death the second night in the trenches."

However, it had little of the impact that he had hoped, especially from Tom Miles.

"Well, you can keep cheerful stuff like that to yourself, seein' as we'n all heading up to the exact same spot. 'Cos I'll tell thee one thing, I ain't never been so cold as on this caper. Froze to death don't shock I one bit!"

At last, with full daylight, they were climbing the back of the Greater Tesson, which enabled them to see the huge accumulation of stores in the Engineers park, but this generated only a feeling of envy as coal braziers glowed there in the poor light of a day still marked by rain and sleet. Ten minutes more and they were within sight of the siege works and the order came to halt, which caused all to huddle closer together, now that there was no requirement for room to swing arms and feet. Ellis came down the outside rank of the Light Company.

"Fall out and make a brew. We're in within the hour!"

This had Miles' approval.

"Now that makes sense! A drop of hot tea whilst we'n stuck yer, waitin' to go back into them freezin' holes what they calls siege lines."

However, whilst their men made fires from the kindling that they always carried with them, there was little respite for their Officers, but their servants did make tea for them. Mackinnon was with his Senior Officers, all gathered around a small table inside the Renaud.

"Santa Cruz has been abandoned by the Johnnies without a fight an' the San Francisco over on our left with the howitzers, has now been captured, so nae need to watch for nasty black shells comin' oot the sky. The guns in our three batteries began proper yesterday evening an' they carried on at dawn. I dinnae need to tell ye, because that's what ye can hear now."

He emptied a glass of spirit, which was immediately refilled by a Scottish Orderly, but that was left untouched as Mackinnon continued.

"The Fourth repaired the second parallel after Johnny's little jaunt, but the Engineers want that deepened, an' also the zig-zag that joins the two up, especially down the side of the Greater Tesson between the two hills. The Johnnies are lacing the whole with grape. The zig-zag is for us, Campbell's are up on the Lesser to deepen that parallel."

His attention finally turned to the glass of Scotch, which he raised, but then replaced on the table untouched.

"Now the Fourth have lost a lot o' men, yesterday and this mornin'. Tell your lads to keep their heads doon, to work on their knees is best. Wellington's orders are that all guns are for breachin' work, none for counter-battery fire an' so Johnny can blaze away unhindered at our lines an' he's takin' full advantage."

The Scotch was now given full attention and despatched.

"Reet, 10.45. Take your lads up!"

The simple order was passed on and all Mackinnon's men rose from their small fires and shuffled forward. It was not long before they passed a Battalion of the Fourth Division coming out of the parallels, with many wounded and also with many bodies being carried in blankets. In the 105th, no-one spoke, this message of the danger they were walking into was obvious, such that they could even forget the flurries of snow now descending in random clusters from the leaden skies. Campbell's Brigade went in first as they were to go furthest, up to the second parallel, then the 74th took the lead and, as the summit of the Greater Tesson was gained, all could see the continuous smoke from the battlements of the town as the defenders served their guns in relays to prevent progress in the siege works before them. The Colour Company were the first to enter the first parallel and, once in, they turned right to get to the far end of it, where the zig-zags to the second parallel began. Once down in, Heaviside inevitably found a quote.

"I send you forth as sheep in the midst of wolves: be ye therefore wise as serpents, and harmless as doves. Matthew 10. Verse 16.

However, Deakin, as anxious as any, did not give the standard reply on this occasion

"None too sure about the last bit, Sir!"

Here, the parallel was deep and few had to lower their heads as they walked in pairs, until ordered to halt, but still in the first parallel. Carr continued on to the end, where he came to the entrance to the first of the three zig-zag communication trenches, two down the Greater Tesson and one up the back of the Lesser. The 74th had only just gone down, yet wounded and dead were already being brought back out. A Captain of Engineers was waiting at the corner, far enough back in the first parallel to keep within its protection. He spoke to Carr, now stood with Heaviside.

"This first zig-zag has a bad line, Sir, it should be more on the contour, on a line away from the walls. The Johnnies can enfilade it almost along the full length. It's the nastiest place in all the siege lines, Sir, which is why we need it deeper. We hope to mount some gabions above on the right, which will make all the difference, Sir. This was started at night and a mistake was made with its line."

Carr looked around the corner for himself and it confirmed the worst of what the Engineer had said. The walls of Cuidad could be seen as he looked over the parapet, their line at a significant angle to the trench, almost perfect for sending grapeshot ricocheting down its length. As he looked, a charge of the same splintered the wood of the revetment at the back of the trench, five yards down, causing him to dart back. He returned to the Engineer.

"What's this 'hope'? That trench is a death trap. What gabions have you?"

The Captain's face changed to one of unease, now that he was confronted by this very angry Major.

"Medium sized, Sir, and enough timber to span across to brace up the gabions when we finally get them up there, Sir, where they can do some good."

"Let's hope that 'good' is the final outcome, Captain. So where are these materials that you hope to so gainfully employ?"

"Back in our park, Sir, but I understand that your 88th have been sent back to bring them forward."

"Good for them, so, meanwhile the 105th are employed how?"

"Deepening the trench, Sir, and the earth from that, can be used to fill the gabions, when night falls, Sir, if your men can just get it over the parapet."

Carr's face darkened.

"Meanwhile, my men are required to work down in that death-trap!"

The weak reply was spoken in a tone equally weak.

"It is safer the further you go down, Sir, towards the lowest section."

"How much?"

The Captain had no answer, which told Carr all he needed to know concerning the relative amount of danger between upper and lower levels. Carr entered the trench to look along its full length. It had revetments either side and walking boards beneath, but it plainly was not deep enough. It was serviceable enough by night, but during the day it was indeed a death-trap. Guns from the town walls could enfilade along the whole length, in fact, from where he was standing, he could actually see an embrasure in a ravellin beyond the main breach, practically in perfect line with the trench. Yet their orders were to deepen the trench and fill the gabions. He withdrew back into the first parallel and pointed over the parapet.

"Right, we start there! With them!"

Level with him and some way across the slope were the three batteries, now pounding the town walls, but just beneath number three were the fascines that they had placed there themselves when building that battery. All were damaged, but many still reasonably intact. They could surely be rolled down and block off the end of the first zig-zag from that dangerous embrasure. At that least, he told himself, they could do. He then went back along the parallel, where the 105th were still waiting, to find Lacey coming towards him.

"What's the hold up?"

"It's this, Sir. If we work in this first zig-zag link we'll take heavy casualties. It can be enfiladed badly from the walls. As a start, I suggest we roll down some battery fascines to the far end of this link to at least hide us from sight. Then, there's nothing for it but to dig, to get as much earth up above us as we can, to lessen the grape-shot coming in."

Lacey's face showed his deep concern.

"This should be happening at night!"

"Yes Sir, but orders are orders."

"Right, you get your fascines where you want them, I'll get things moving here."

Carr saluted and ran back along the parallel where he came to the Grenadier Company.

"Charles! I need your Grenadiers."

"For what?"

"A bit of removals!"

This was spoken on the run but the first Section he came to was D'Villiers.

"Royston. Your Section with me."

He continued, with the Grenadiers following, as he led them down to the top of the sap that led down to battery number three. Round shot from the walls was thudding into the thick battery parapet as the gunners toiled at their heavy pieces. Carr turned to D'Villiers, both stood on a fire step, to look over the parapet with great trepidation.

"You see those fascines there? We have to get them down to the end of our link to take away Johnny's sight line or we'll lose a lot of men. To allow those first three to roll down to the bend for the second link should do it. They only need to be there, blocking the sight line. Tell your men to keep this side of their fascine, which will keep them safe. Your first 18 men, six each fascine. Any casualties will need replacing, get Sergeant Bennett onto that, to feed men forward"

D'Villiers swallowed hard.

"And when we've got them there?"

"We jump into the trench. Come on!"

Carr ran down the sap and into the battery, ignoring the astonished faces of the gunners, then up onto the wide parapet. A cannonball sent a shower of earth back over him as it buried itself in the soil, then he was at the first fascine as some Grenadiers arrived.

"Cut it loose and allow it to roll, but hold the branches to stop it rolling too fast. Stay hidden behind it!"

He arrived at the second and gave the same instructions, then at the third to find D'Villiers beside him with a Corporal and five men.

"Well done, Royston!"

Carr drew his sword.

"Hold on, don't let it roll away from us."

He slashed at the mooring ropes as French shot sang overhead and the fascine began to move, but the Grenadiers held onto the branches within and their weight prevented further roll. They gingerly released their hands and the fascine began to move, its bulk and weight very reassuring as the French counter-battery fire sent shot that hummed both above and to the side. The fascine shuddered as a shot hit, but it was rolling slowly down the slope and under control. Carr looked to the right as they progressed on, to soon see the first zig-zag link and that the Grenadiers with the first two fascines were now down within it and that their fascines had been swung sideways across the join of the two links. They allowed their own to bump into the two already there and then, almost hysterical with relief, they jumped into the trench and ran back up. At the top Carr turned to survey their work, to see, to his great relief, that the view to the most dangerous embrasure was now blocked.

Soon, the trench was full of working men, all shovelling from the bottom to throw over the top, the walking boards now lifted and leaning against the revetment at the side. All were working on the 'safer' side as grapeshot continued to splatter the timber revetment on the far side. The work continued until the Midday meal, when Bill Turner of the Light Company stopped Ethan Ellis on his way down the trench to his own work area.

"This is all wrong!"

"What's all wrong?"

"This! The way we're doing this!"

"Why wrong?"

"Look!"

Turner took a spadeful from the bottom of the trench and threw it up over the top. Within two seconds most of it had fallen back down. Turner leaned on his spade in triumph.

"Throwin' up any more will be a waste of time. You've got piles up there now, with a steep slope back down to us, so what we throws up, just rolls back down. 'Tis a waste of effort! 'Specially with so much being knocked back down with this grapeshot and all."

"And who are you to speak about such?"

"I was a navvy on the canals. Then we did it different."

Ellis looked at him carefully for three long seconds.

"So, you've got a better notion of what to do?"

Turner nodded.

"I have! And it'll make filling them gabions easier, when the time comes."

Ellis nodded.

"Alright. Come with me."

They both climbed the link to find Major O'Hare, watching anxiously as French fire continued to shatter the rear revetments.

"Sir. Turner here worked on the canals and thinks he knows how we can do this better."

O'Hare looked at Turner, who immediately began his explanation.

"We needs shovelling platforms, Sir. When we had to lift soil up a big level, one would shovel up onto a platform for the next man to move it up to the next above. We could use those walking boards, Sir, one edge on the top of the trench, the other held up by something like pit-props, Sir. That'll hold more soil up there and give us more to fill the gabions, come night. No-one'll need to be up on the platforms, Sir. They'll just hold the soil up there."

O'Hare grinned at him then turned to Ellis.

"Make sure he gets an extra rum ration! Now, no more digging, everyone back to get a pit-prop or the like. No more digging until these platforms are in place. Well done, Turner. This'll get you a stripe!"

At 10 o' clock the following morning Colonel Fletcher arrived to find Mackinnon's Brigade of the Third Division all asleep apart from sentries, the 88th in the deepened first parallel, the 105th in the first link down, the 74th in the second link down. As he entered the first link his face turned from deep disapproval at the sleeping figures, to one of deep satisfaction.

"My word, Lacey, damn fine job! Damn fine job indeed! There's no more work required here. We can now give full attention to the second parallel."

He progressed on down, needing to visit the second parallel up on the Lesser Tesson, where the men of Campbell's Brigade were still working. As he passed through the men of the 105th, now stood awake and brushing off the night's fall of snow, he looked approvingly at the solid rank of gabions above him which now protected any passage of where he stood. At the end of the link, where he would begin to pass through the 74th in the second, Fletcher turned to shake Lacey's hand.

"I'll make remark of this to his Lordship, Lacey, be certain of that."

Lacey nodded, but did not smile.

"Please do so, Colonel, but all I ask is that the 105th are not earmarked for any extra pioneering duties beyond what we could normally expect as our fair share."

It was Fletcher who grinned.

"No more than your share, Lacey, as you say. I'll see to that. In the main, all is going well, in fact I'd say you've done your turn at digging. It'll not be long now. Today's the 16th. I'll be looking for the 19th for the final assault and I'll tell him so!"

The 105th whiled away the final minutes, with Carr and Lacey in the sap that connected the third battery with the first parallel, Lacey being concerned about another French sortie, but none came and the order was given for the Third Division to file out, so that the Light Division could take over. However, on the long trek back, seemingly longer than the trek to, 24 hours earlier, there was no feeling of triumph. Men had been lost, both killed and wounded and all were utterly weary in both body and spirit. Despite the daylight, the cold had not abated, nor the wind that had blown them there, but now it sent its blessings of rain and sleet directly into their faces.

oOo

Inevitably, the conversation between Fletcher and Lacey had been overheard and was soon circulated around the 105th, some with full belief, others with scepticism, such as with Jed Deakin.

"Are you tellin' me that Officers never changes their minds!"

However, with pick and spade service in the trenches now far less likely, mostly the days were concerned with eating, sleeping, keeping warm and taking turns to unload the supply wagons that arrived each day, the six attached to Davey and Saunders taking their turn to unload a wagon, with Bill Turner sporting his new stripe as a seventh. The two Waggoners had stripped off the canvas and three of the seven were up on the cart where Davey felt the need to at least be civil.

"Where've you brought this from, mate?"

The Waggoner wheeled over a barrel of salt beef.

"Oporto. The place is crammed. You wouldn't believe the stuff that's being brought in through there. Everything you could think of. There's effort going into this, I can tell you."

"What about the Dons on the way over? Any trouble with them, bunch of thieves they can be?"

The Waggoner shook his head.

"Not a bit! Viva Ingleses all the way, whatever that means."

They all grinned.

"You off back today?"

"No. Day after next. The horses needs a good rest and feed. 'Tis a week's journey up from the coast, although the roads is all good. I'll say this for that Wellington, he don't spare on the backup, there's Portuguese work gangs all along, easing the journey for the likes of me and Ted, here."

Davey nodded his appreciation.

"Well, when this is unloaded, you'm welcome to come and have a bite with us. You and your mate."

He pointed to the rows of tents just ten yards away.

"Second rank, fourth tent."

Both Waggoners grinned and then Ted went to a sack, it suspiciously wounded and open, therefore with contents accessible.

"Yer. Give us yer haversacks!"

All were passed over and each received three brimming handfuls of good tobacco.

Had they known the subject of the conversation coincidental in the 105th Headquarters tent, the atmosphere at the waggon-park would not have been anything like so genial. Crauford himself was there, talking to Lacey, O'Hare and Carr, the General being his usual brusque self.

"I need your Light Company, to add to my Rifles with their Bakers. We've dug rifle pits in front of the second parallel to take shots at the gunners on the walls who are disrupting our own battery fire. It's reduced their fire, but casualties amongst my Rifles has been high. The second parallel now has its own battery, but they're taking casualties as well. We must make life more difficult for the Frog gunners and we can, with the range down to about 150 yards from the rifle pits. Yours are to take a turn tomorrow and on that night we are over the walls!"

Lacey and Carr looked at each other, deep concern written all over their faces, whilst O'Hare just stared at Crauford.

"I have to ask, Sir, has this been approved by Lord Wellington? Ours were called upon to help take Fort Renaud."

Crauford's face darkened.

"It has and I'll tell you why. He's worried about Marmont and Dorsenne combining and coming to relieve this place. He heard about that on the 15th and today's the 18th. We need to get in sooner rather than later and he's ready to pay the price. Whoever can do the jobs needed will be called upon, however tired!"

Crauford's final words sent a chill through the minds of each of the 105th Officers, but there could be no argument and so Carr asked the next question.

"When do you want ours up there, Sir?"

"Dawn! When else?"

With that, he turned and left, leaving the three to stare at each other, a silence that was finally broken by Carr.

"I suppose I'd better get up there and see what we'll be walking into. I'll take Drake with me."

An hour later the pair were walking over the bridge that led into Fort Renaud. The roar of cannon from both sides of the conflict was absolutely incessant and they took themselves immediately to the far wall to discover the results of two days of bombardment since they had quit the trenches. Below the Church, the faussebraie and the main wall behind had practically disappeared, but heavy 24lb shot were still striking what remained of the main wall. However, when they looked left they could see that another point of the walls that was now being bombarded. There were many Officers stood watching, one of which was an Officer of Artillery and so, curiosity aroused, Carr and Drake went up to him and Carr pointed.

"That's new!"

The Artillery Officer turned and grinned.

"Yes. It's an old Medieval tower that must have been incorporated into the walls. We've built an extra battery just for the purpose of hitting it, number four. As you can see, 24lb shot have turned it into a bit of a wreck. Definitely not built to withstand this sort of treatment, more to withstand stones from medieval catapults!"

"So, who's going in there?"

"Crauford's Lights."

"Which means we're going for two points on the walls?"

The Officer turned and grinned once more.

"No, five!"

He leaned conspiratorially towards an astonished Carr.

"Keep this under your hat, but rumour has five. Three British here on this wall, Cacadores at the Castle on the right there, going over the bridge, and another Portuguese Brigade on the far side of the town."

However, before Carr could reply, the Officer pointed over at the tower.

"Oh! Oh! Something's happening!"

All on the parapet looked over to see a cannon shot hit high up on the tower wall that was now slowly descending into a pile of rubble, with a faint rumble amidst a cloud of dust, then leaving a narrow cleft in the wall. The Artilleryman grinned.

"Well that's Crauford's way in. We just have to make it a bit wider."

Leaving all there to wait for the dust to fully clear, Carr pulled at Drake's sleeve.

"Time to get over and see what we came for."

They entered the first parallel and walked to the far end to turn down into the first link and see that the handiwork of the 105th from three days ago was still well in place. They descended down through the second, to use the stepping stones over the stream at the bottom and then begin their climb up the third link to the second parallel. What could only be described as the noise of intense conflict grew with every step upwards. Within the roar of Allied cannon off to the left and French to the right, could be heard the sporadic roar of the two Portuguese cannon in the battery that was now part of the second parallel. Once in a quick glance over the parapet showed them to be less than 200 yards' distance from the walls and they found Riflemen crouched down beneath the revetment as both grape shot and solid crashed accurately into the parapet above. Almost all there were busy with shovels as best they were able, to keep the parallel clear for Artillerymen tasked with bringing up powder and shot from below to feed the guns. Adopting a hunched walk themselves in a trench no more than five feet deep they came to a Captain of Engineers, drinking water and eating biscuits, seemingly oblivious to the noise, danger and intense activity around him. He was sat at the entrance to a sap that led even further towards the town walls. As they made to cross to him, he held up his hand to halt them where they were and the pause caused them to notice that at the sap there was blood on both the bottom boards and the revetments opposite.

"Not a good idea for the moment, there've been too many casualties here. I'm getting a fascine brought up, tailor made for the size."

Drake was nearest.

"Does this lead to the rifle pits?"

"Oh God no! This is, was, a sap forward that we thought would get us nearer to the walls under-cover, but we lost too many men digging it. Johnny can practically fire down the whole length."

"So where are the rifle pits?"

He directed with his thumb above the parapet.

"Down over and no good place to be, I can tell you, but they have made a difference to Johnny's rate of fire."

He pressed himself back against the wood of the revetment as a shower of soil came over into the trench and two grape shot came through the sap entrance to embed themselves in the revetment opposite. With that passed, he continued.

"But what would make a difference is Him allowing us counter-battery fire, but no. It's all for the breaches."

At that moment the fascine arrived, its size making it visible above the parapet as four crouching Engineers carried it and a charge of grapeshot crashed into the top, splintering the branches there. However, despite the jolt, the Engineers carried it on and, finally, it was turned through 90 degrees and dropped into the sap entrance, hiding the interior of the parallel from French eyes on the wall. Carr and Drake were waved forward.

"Much safer now!"

The pair crawled forward and then knelt by the Engineer, Carr looking up at the parapet, with soil dribbling over the top.

"So how do we get to these rifle-pits?"

"You don't, Sir. Not in daylight, and even in the dark there's a peril, with Johnny lobbing his fireballs up into the night-sky. Ours go down just before dawn and they stay there, until dark. I don't need to tell you what it's like out there."

As if to emphasise his words, a perfectly aimed round shot passed through the top board of the revetment above them, cascading down more earth, and burying itself in the wood half way down the revetment opposite. Steam rose from the still hot ball in the damp earth behind the splintered wood.

"I'd say you were here until dark, Sir, when it's safer to go over and take a look. If that is what you are intent on."

Drake dragged out his watch.

"What's the time now? Three, almost, full dark at four-thirty."

He looked at Carr.

"Do you want to go back down?"

Carr shook his head.

"No! We'll stay. The more we can learn about this Hell on Earth the better."

The Engineer grinned and passed over his water bottle to the pair as more powder and shot, the passage now being much safer, were dragged and rolled up to the guns. The minutes dragged by for the pair sat against the revetment, listening to the commands of the Portuguese gunners and the sound of their two guns, just off to their right, sending shot at the main breach. The Captain of Engineers, whose name was Bellinghurst, spent much of the time waxing lyrical about the effectiveness of the pair of guns and then describing in detail the gargantuan effort that it took to get them up there, from the first parallel to where they were now. Drake, inevitably, with patience exhausted, could not resist a peer over the parapet, but first there came a warning from Bellinghurst.

"I'd take your shako off first and wait. You've about three seconds between impact. They've put at least ten guns on us, but they fire one at a time, to adjust their aim for the next shot. Too high or too low. Use that time."

There came one charge of grapeshot that only hit the top of the far side of the trench and Bellinghurst nodded. Drake raised his head for three seconds before lowering it back to safety, when a solid ball then hummed above. Carr looked at him quizzically.

"Well?"

"The walls are practically on top of us! Just down over are the rifle pits, no time to count how many, but they are on a horribly exposed slope. Everywhere is chewed up with grape. No wonder Crauford talked of high casualties!"

Carr sat back against the revetment.

"Ready to pay the price, is he? You won't get one man in three unwounded out of there! And all head wounds."

Carr's jaw clamped together as he thought further.

"Right! You stay here and wait for the Rifles to come back over. You may learn something extra. Then come back. We're going into those pits closer to midnight than dawn."

With that, Carr crouched his way back down the trench leaving Drake sat waiting for the hours of darkness when the Riflemen would arrive back. Finally, visibility dropped to less than 50 yards, this hurried on by deep grey clouds that brought yet another flurry of snow. The first of the Riflemen came back, two at first, carrying a wounded third between them. Soon the trench was filled with their green uniforms and, as Carr had predicted, many were wounded and several more were dead. The last to arrive was a familiar figure for Carr.

"Uniacke! No surprise to find you here. Mine are next in, to pick things up tomorrow."

The Rifle Captain's face was dirty and haggard as he extended his hand for Drake to take.

"Drake! Well good luck to you with that. It's murderous back there. We didn't fire a shot until we'd built some kind of parapet with loop-holes, but the grape sweeps it all away and we had to rebuild before re-commencing. Several times. What I'd give for a bit of stone to put up inside the soil, but there's none anywhere here."

With that he levered himself into a kneeling position.

"Must get mine back down, you understand. We've wounded as you can see."

He turned to the nearest Rifleman.

"Pass the word, we're moving."

It was a sorry procession that made its way crouching past Drake, many awkwardly carrying bodies in blankets, some wounded, some dead, all comrades to be carried back down and away. With all past, Drake followed, to then hurry through the gloom back to the 105th camp. With the fall of darkness, the silence, now that the guns were quiet, was decidedly eerie.

Once arrived, he found his Light Company already in column, this identified by lanterns, but all burdened in some way, with heavy bundles of pit-props, tools, sacks and long iron spikes. He found Carr close to the column head.

"You've had thoughts, I see."

"We're not firing over the top of any parapet. We have to make some kind of parapet to fire between, definitely not over, instead through a narrow loop-hole."

"For what it's worth, that's what the Rifle Captain said."

"Good! Then we waste no time."

266

After what seemed like a forced march, the 105th Lights entered the first parallel to file down and then up into the second. There they found the trench occupied by men of the 43rd Foot, part of Crauford's Light Division. A Major greeted Carr, in the lead.

"Llewellyn. 43rd. Are you for the rifle-pits?"

"Carr. 105th. Yes. It seems the Rifles have suffered somewhat and so we are the next up to fill the gaps, by Crauford Royal Command."

"Rumour has it that this is the last day."

"I'll not be sorry."

With that he climbed over the parapet and led his men down the slope to the dark shapes further down that were the rifle-pits they were to occupy. Carr went along the row, allocating one file to each and the three men unburdened themselves of their loads and set to work. In their pit, their eyes now used to the gloom, Davey and Miles each held their two spikes and Joe Pike hammered them deep into the ground, with the centre two no more than three inches apart. With that, several fireballs came arcing over from the walls and all three ducked down, Davey giving his opinion as to the cause.

"They must have heard the sound of the hammering. It'll be grape as comes next."

However, the fireballs landed and burnt out, but no more firing came from the walls.

"I suppose they'll not be too worried by a bit of hammering."

"I'd say you're right about that, Joe, so now get that timber over."

The timber they had brought, this being eight raw pit props, was laid across the two pairs of spikes, four on each side, as two pairs, one above another, then on top as much soil as they could shovel, both from the bottom and rear of the rifle-pit. They then filled six biscuit sacks with soil and lay two, side by side, to span the gap, Then two above the pit-props, one each side, then the final two at the gap, but at right-angles to the two beneath. The gap remaining to fire through was a neat three inches wide and six high. No more fireballs arrived and, after more soil on the sacks, the three made themselves as comfortable as they could in the cold that was intensifying atop the Lesser Tesson. When the sky to the East began to reluctantly lighten, Carr arrived to jump down into their 'home'. He went immediately to their loop-hole, through which he could now see the outline of the town battlements.

"We've got a bit of luck, men, of sorts. I've just been told by the 43rd back there, that firing at the breaches will now stop. All guns to concentrate on the battlements for counter-battery fire. Johnny will be getting cannon-balls as well, not just what we send his way."

Miles endeavoured to sound both cheerful and encouraged, but, unsurprisingly, failed dismally.

"Well now, won't that be an enormous help to us all, Sir? Everyone of us."

Now irritated, Carr looked at him, hearing only sarcasm, but Davey came to Miles' rescue.

"Any kind of help is welcome, Sir. We'll keep their heads down, Sir, never fear, them walls is well inside our range."

Carr looked at him, somewhat mollified.

"Have you enough powder and shot? And leather patches? As I understand it, you'll need them for accuracy."

"Yes Sir. Plenty. We picked up extra before we left camp."

Carr nodded and then stood to climb out of the pit, but he gave a suspicious look at Miles before leaving.

"Very good men. Now do your best, especially you, Davey. You're one of our best marksmen."

With that he was gone, leaving Miles and Pike slumped down against the pit sides, hoping for a moment of sleep and Davey peering through their firing slit, waiting for the full dawn. The light began to grow and unlike the previous day, this one would be reasonably sunny, then the thought occurred to him. "You Frog gunners, the sun's right behind you!" He slid his Baker through the loop-hole, fully cocked the hammer and checked his sights for maximum, before lining the weapon up on the nearest embrasure which was silhouetted against the newly bright sky. The gun was run out and Davey sighted carefully just to the right of it, taking the first pressure of the trigger. A human shape appeared and he fired. Smoke obscured all, so he had no way of knowing if his bullet had found its mark, but then, perhaps in retaliation, the cannonading started from the walls, sending regular charges of grape-shot at their line. However, reassuringly nothing came through their firing slit, although there was an almost endless shower of dirt and grass as the grape-shot ripped up the already much disturbed turf and soil. Davey sat back to carefully reload his weapon and at that moment their own guns opened fire on the town battlements. With that Davey returned to the firing slit to discover the outcome, at the same time pulling Miles up to observe as well. Miles came reluctantly, but peered through as Davey asked his question.

"What're they firing, Tom?"

Miles soon worked out what the spattering against the stonework signified.

"Grape! Hoping to get something through the embrasures."

More soil tumbled into the pit from the French counter-cannonade and Miles pulled back.

"I'm not getting my head blown off in yer! What damn difference will it make if we sends a few in alongside them guns, where perhaps we hits some gunner? Next to none!"

Davey shook his head.

"We has to try, Tom. Rumour has it we're over the walls tonight, and if we knocks over even a couple of them good Frog gunners, then we might just save the lives of a few lads tonight. We has to try."

Miles looked at him. Davey was a Chosen Man, the rank above himself. He could make it an order, but he had not. Miles rolled over to peer through the firing-slit for three seconds, then roll back. He looked at Davey.

"Right opposite, on a wall down before the main, there's four embrasures as'll cover the way to the main breach. They'm just below us, I'd say. Them's the ones for us, but I'm only a count of three at that loop-hole then I'm pulling the trigger. I'm not sittin' there waiting for some gunner to show himself. The Frogs is altogether upset with us being here and makin' that well known."

Davey took himself to the gap and peered through to see that Miles was correct and what was more, the four embrasures were receiving very little attention from their own gunners, these concentrating on the higher battlements above.

"Fair enough, Tom. Count of three and fire. I fancies keeping all of my skull together as well."

Thus, they began, taking turns to fire and then very carefully reloading to await their next turn. With the arrival of Midday, their shoulders began to hurt from the recoil and they decided that their weapons needed cleaning and it was time to eat what Bridie had prepared, this being dough-cakes filled with chopped boiled pork and the inevitable herbs. As they sat eating, they wondered about their companions to either side and, despite the noise of the guns, Davey shouted to the right.

"Zeke! Zeke! You all alright?"

The reply came back.

"Len's face've changed a bit, but I'm alright, so's John."

"Any change is for the better! We're firin' at the four on the same level. You?"

"Same! But there's plenty down in there still running about."

Davey turned in the opposite direction. Ellis was in the next pit.

"S'ar'nt! Are you alright?"

A growl came back from six yards away.

"Look to your front and keep firing."

Davey grinned.

"I'd say that means he's alright."

As if predicting somehow that this was the last day before the assault, the firing from the battlements intensified, with both grape and solid now arriving and Miles drew the inevitable conclusion.

"They must have plenty in there to work them guns. You think we're doin' much good?"

Before Davey could answer, a solid ball took back the bag of soil to the right of their gap, breaking it open and showering all with soil, Joe Pike receiving a portion full in his face. Davey lurched over to him to lift up his head, his face held in his hands.

"Joe! Can you see me?"

The skin of his face was red and cut in many places from the impact of the soil, but one blue eye blinked, whilst Pike kept the other closed. Davey turned to Miles.

"Tom! Get me some water."

Miles poured some in his pannikin.

"Hold it up under his eye."

Davey placed his thumb gently above the eyelid as the water arrived.

"Joe. You've got to let me take a look. You probably got soil in there."

Pike lowered his hand and Davey gradually raised the eyelid. The eye was red and the socket contained soil, which Davey washed away. He then placed his hand over the good eye.

"What can you see, Joe?"

The single eye blinked.

"You. But you're a bit blurred."

"Right. Where's your kerchief?"

Pike pulled it out of his pocket, whilst Davey folded his own into a pad. This he made wet, placed it over the eye and bound it in place with Pike's own. Then he looked anxiously at his young messmate.

"I'd say you're in for a black eye, Joe, but keep that pad on."

Miles had been making his own observations.

"That's the least of it. Shame it's not your right eye, Joe, the one you sights with. If 'twer, you could spend this night comin' sat in the Surgeon's tents."

Davey's jaw came grimly together. He was angry at the wound inflicted on Joe.

"We've three more hours in here and I'm not leaving with one cartridge. Not one! They Frogs down over have got some coming and when I leaves here, my box'll be empty."

With that he picked up his newly cleaned Baker and went to the firing slit to send a carefully aimed shot through the far-right embrasure of their four, this time after a count of four. He then rolled back with his still smoking rifle.

"I'd say I got one with that. Saw an arm go up!"

Miles grinned as he went to the slit himself.

"He was probably giving you a V sign."

"Do Frogs do that?"

"I don't know, but if I sees one, he'll struggle with just one finger!"

Miles got his shot away and it was encouraging that Joe Pike now came forward, to receive a welcoming slap on his shoulder from Davey. That delivered, Davey reached for the spade.

"Right, we'd better get this mess back over, where it might do some good, and a bit more besides."

The parapet was repaired after a fashion and, because of what had happened to Joe, when not sighting forward to fire, they kept to the parapet side of the pit. Here they were under cover, despite the soil that would roll and tumble down onto them.

"How much longer, John?"

Davey stared into the single blue eye, with the red kerchief covering the other.

"Another hour. You got anything left?"

Pike knew exactly what he was referring to, food, and he shook his head.

"All gone! Water and biscuits."

"How many more cartridges?"

"Five."

"Same here. Tom?"

"Six!"

"Well, we sends them across, then that's that. We can't do no more."

As the growing dark brought the prospect of respite to those in the rifle-pits, so it added to the level of anxiety of the rest of the 105th, now under orders to march at dusk. Mackinnon was sat at the table in the Headquarters tent with a plan of Cuidad spread on the table. The seriousness of his tone and manner matched that on the faces of O'Hare, Lacey and also Carr, who had arrived back from the second parallel an hour previously.

"Picton's are to go for the main breach, led by us, in the order of yours, Lacey, then the 74th an' lastly the 88th. Ye're the Brigade Major, O'Hare."

Startled, O'Hare looked up from the plan, the emotionally charged circumstances overcoming his usual military deference.

"I am, Sir? Well, thank you very much, Sir!"

"Dinnae thank me, Picton's orders."

He returned to the plan, pointing with a dirk as he talked.

"We know there are two ditches, one before the faussebraie, the other, the main ditch, between faussebraie and the main wall. We've got the main breach."

The dirk first stabbed down onto a small gate midway between the main breach and the Castle.

"Campbell's go at it from our right, opposite the Santa Cruz Convent, here at this gate. Once on top of the faussebraie, they sweep left, clearing the top and also the main ditch, which will bring them over to us, here, at the main breach."

The dirk was now transferred to the site of the main breach.

"To help us attacking here, 180 Sappers will throw hay bags into the ditches afore we arrive, an' our column will be led by 300 volunteers from the whole Division, the Forlorn Hope. I said nothing to you and yours about that because ye've got lads up in the rifle-pits and ye've done your share of that kind of work. Our reserve for the assault are Power's Portuguese, the 9th and 21st Line."

He now took a pull from a whiskey flask, open and waiting atop the table.

"From our left will come some Rifles of the 95th, doing from there what Campbell's Brigade will be doing from our right. They will join our efforts at the main breach."

He took another pull from the flask. His next words proved that he needed it.

"This'll be bad. Johnny's given up trying to repair the main breach, we believe. Instead he's been doin' some work that we cannae make out and he does no want us to see. He's screened it, and enough stays there, despite our bombardment, to block our view. He's very ready!"

He sat back and looked at each in turn.

"Right. To continue. Lastly, Campbell's 83rd will be in the second parallel to keep fire onto the walls and our own guns will fire as long as they can, to gi' us support but stop afore they knock any of us over."

Lacey looked straight at him.

"There'll be a mine in the breach?"

Mackinnon stared straight back.

"Almost certain!"

He pushed the flask in the direction of the trio and they all drank, then Carr looked at Mackinnon.

"I've been told we'll be trying at other points, Sir."

"Yes. Three."

Mackinnon immediately moved the point of the dirk leftwards onto the lesser breach, the site of the demolished tower.

"Crauford's going in there with Vandeleur's Brigade of his Light Division."

Then he placed the dirk on the far end of the bridge over the Agueda to run it along the line of the bridge to the Castle.

"And two diversions, unless they find otherwise an' can get themselves in. One, O'Toole an' some Cacadores across here to try the Castle"

He then moved the point to the far side of the plan.

"And two, Pack's Portuguese Brigade, 1st and 2nd Line, here, tryin' the back door. With any luck, they'll drag some Frogs their way, awa' from us."

Then Carr's finger went onto the plan, at a point just before the main breach.

"This ravellin, Sir, part of the faussebraie. Where it hasn't been lowered by our bombardment, either side, it's as high as the main wall."

Mackinnon nodded.

"Aye, laddie. That's so."

"Well Sir. As additional covering fire, that would be a good place for our 105th Lights, with their Bakers. They'd be just the other side of the main ditch and from there, they couldn't miss any French defending the main breach."

Mackinnon looked up.

"Lacey?"

"It makes sense to me."

Mackinnon nodded.

"To me an' all, and seems right, seein' as your Light lads've just spent a day in the pits. Seems only right to spare them the breach!"

Mackinnon began to roll up the plan.

"Anything else?"

The three shook their heads.

"Good. We leave here now. The whole starts at seven!"

270

As he pulled aside the tent flap, which allowed in the sound of singing. He stopped to listen, as did the three remaining inside. They needed no-one to tell them that the singing was of the popular Wesleyan hymn 'Rock of Ages'. The orders to march to the assault line had reached the Reverend Albright and word of a service to be given by him had spread amongst the men. Without orders, Colour Sergeants Deakin and Bennet has assembled the drums to create an Altar and both Colours were now draped over. Whilst the four had been debating their orders, the service had been progressing, almost to its conclusion, however, the four Senior Officers felt it right to go over and stand with their men and their Followers. They left the tent and walked over and once there, they joined in with the Lord's Prayer, the familiar words intoned solemnly from over 1,000 anxious throats, many of the 88th and 74th also attending. They all knew that they were going up into a breach and they all knew the risks that involved. Finally, Albright raised his hands to the grey Heavens and shouted skywards with all his might.

"May the Good Lord bless you and preserve you. To cause his Light to shine upon you and welcome you unto his House should this be your final day on this earth. You, that are now Blessed by his Forgiving Countenance. In Jesus Christ Our Lord's Name. Amen."

The same mouths spoke a heartfelt Amen and the ranks broke up, for Heaviside, unusually for so Presbyterian a man, to then walk up and silently shake Albright's hand. Deakin and Bennet came forward to retrieve their Colours and each sent a solemn nod in the good Reverend's direction, then came the Drummerboys, in a much lighter and irreverent mood, but Albright looked benevolently upon them, all the same. Sedgwicke was packing the Cross and candle-sticks into their case and he looked over at his Reverend Albright, now stood isolated and somewhat at a loss for what to do next.

"Well done, Sir. The men appreciated that, of that you can be sure."

Albright turned to him, smiling slightly.

"You do think so?"

"More than think, Sir. That I know."

oOo

Chapter Nine

The First of the Keys

Drake found Carr waiting for him as the Light Company filed out of the first parallel, ending their journey from the rifle-pits.

"It's tonight, at seven o' clock."

Drake's voice betrayed his shock, even horror.

"Seven! That early! Do we get a chance at a bite to eat? We've just spent a day in the second parallel. The rifle-pits, what's more!"

Carr fully felt the anger in Drake's words and he knew that he was right. He tried to deflect the anger with humour.

"You and your stomach! Morrison will be coming up and he'll have something."

This had little effect.

"And the men?"

"The Followers as well. They'll be needed to care for the wounded and they'll bring up something, I shouldn't wonder. Order are orders, Nat, but at least yours will not be into the main breach. I've persuaded Mackinnon to use you otherwise. Perhaps there's still enough light left to see where you'll be. Come on!"

He motioned Drake to climb with him to the top of the parapet. There was still just enough light for the batteries to continue firing and the flash from their muzzles helped.

"Look. Before the Church where the breach is, there's a ravellin. We want you and yours up there giving covering fire into the breach as we go forward. Maltby's on the far corner left of the breach, Shakeshaft's the other. The 105th go in after the Forlorn Hope."

The mention of the fatal words calmed Drake down.

"There'll be a mine?"

271

"When is there not?"

Drake stood studying the dark area before the Church, now a clear silhouette against the night sky.

"Right. I know it. We've looked at it all often enough. So, talking of who does what and where, Maltby's volunteered for the Forlorn Hope."

Carr turned violently towards him.

"What! He has? I thought we were being kept out of that?"

Drake shrugged his shoulders.

"That may be so, but he heard about it and volunteered. You know how it works. To volunteer for and survive a Forlorn Hope is a certain route to advancement. So, that's that. What can we do? Anyway, where's the Battalion?"

Carr shook his head, there was nothing more to be said on the subject of Maltby.

"Coming up behind, probably at the far side of this Fort Renaud by now. Let's get back. There may indeed be some food."

The Light Company were formed up close-by, a two-deep line of Sections, each Lieutenant at their head and Sergeant Ellis at their far right. Drake took a step forward.

"I'd best tell them now. What we want them to do."

Carr followed him.

"No! I will. I'll be with you at the breach."

He walked over and began his detailed explanation of their task and the reason why it had to be done. The words were received in silence and the silence continued after he had finished, each man busy with his own thoughts.

The rest of the 105th had now arrived on the far side of Fort Renaud, all sat on the cold turf, drinking lukewarm tea. Few felt that they had time for the water to boil fully on their small fires of portable kindling. Mixed in amongst them, close beside their menfolk were the Followers, even Nellie Nicholls sat with her arm through that of her husband Henry, him occasionally patting her hand. Deakin looked at Bridie.

"Well, there is one thing, love. The Colours stays behind. There's no point tryin' to scramble up a pile of rubble an' at the same time carry a Colour. Your Patrick will be stayin' back, him and Rushby, more with you than with me!"

This made little difference and she pulled at his arm.

"And what am I not seein' before me now, to tell me fully what's what? 'Tis full of danger, for certain. You've not yet taken one step and there's Joe, already, with perhaps one eye out of his head! And what about you? I've heard you say that goin' up into these breach places is about the worst thing a soldier can be called on to do!"

He held her close and kissed her.

"I did? Well, I was probably drunk or something and anyway, so I've been told, the gunner-boys have done a good job on this one. This is one of the easiest, not one of the worst!"

Before she could reply, the drums beat out 'Fall in', and all swallowed the last of their tea, either hot or warm and ran to their assembly area, sharing last kisses and then hands extended both forward and back to prolongue the last touch.

Carr was stood waiting at the head of the 105th column, where the Light Company were, because, for the assault they would need to go down first, to quickly get onto the surface of the ravellin. Lacey was stood not far off, with O'Hare, who spoke his own concern to Lacey.

"My biggest worry is not the conduct of the men, but getting lost. It's a maze of walls and ditches down there!"

"You're not alone in that, but that Church is the key. Just keep that in front of you."

They detected movement before them, even in the dark, plus the sound of marching feet and a strange rustling, which O'Hare recognised.

"Ah, that'll be our volunteers and the hay bag boys. Not long now. Can you see the time?"

Lacey pulled out his watch and quickly replaced it.

"No!"

At that point, Mackinnon arrived.

"Cannae be long now!"

"Sir. Are you sure you should be part of this. You've just returned from illness."

"Aye, I think I should, Lacey. Be at the head of ma' lads."

He turned to the three each in turn.

"Good luck, Lacey. Good luck O'Hare, and to ye Carr."

That trio then shook hands with each other and then without orders, Mackinnon walked forward, issuing his own orders

"It must be time or dammit near enough! We've some ways to walk and what's five minutes with a jaunt like this?"

Mackinnon was correct. The Sappers and Forlorn Hope had moved off and soon his own Brigade were over the first parallel to descend through the batteries, all fully manned with lighted matches burning in their buckets of sand. "Good luck" sounded softly either side as they passed through the gunners, then they descended the slope and into the valley between, to splash through the stream at the bottom and begin to ascend to the hard, dark edge that was the top of the Lesser Tesson. The second parallel was full of Redcoats and it was not long before the 105th and the 83rd recognised each other. Military memories last over centuries but this was no more than two Summers ago when the 105th and the 83rd had stood side by side to hold the centre of Wellington's line at Talavera. This time "Good luck to you, boys" was delivered with a soft Irish accent, with "Give 'em blazes, now", added on many occasions. They were half way down the back slope when the night erupted over to their right. The voice of Mackinnon came out of the darkness.

"That's Campbell. In a mite early I'd say!"

Lacey shouted the command backwards.

"Open order! Double forward!"

The 105th split from their single column of Companies and quickly spread out, as did the 74th and 88th coming on behind. At that point fire balls shot up into the sky and every gun on the walls that could train on them opened fire. Not far behind the main walls rose the Church tower, eerily illuminated by both the descending fire-balls and the livid flash of the cannons, both French and Allied. All around them the heavy charges of grape flew past or churned up the soil, both clods of earth and spent balls bouncing around them, but from all sides came screaming as the first casualties fell. All hunched forward and ran faster, hoping to quicker reach the foot of the Citadel slope and get under the elevation of the guns. It was the Battalions following that were suffering most, the 74th and the 88th, these arriving last onto the open slope after leaving the second parallel and so they spent more time under fire. From behind them, their own guns opened up in earnest, now sighting on the flashes on the walls, but the intensity of the grapeshot assaulting them did not slacken and Mackinnon's Brigade began to suffer, the sounds of screams and curses continuous out of the darkness all around.

Running forward, sword in hand, Carr heard a heavy grunt behind him and the thought crossed his already swirling mind that back there were, O'Hare, Drake, Ellis and all the Light Company. Then something glanced off his left shoulder, the blow taking away his balance and he staggered before returning upright. It was Ellis who came to him.

"Are you alright, Sir?"

"I am, Sergeant. Thank you. Let's get on."

The fireballs descending from the night sky were incessant, but, beside illuminating targets for the guns of both sides, they showed the way and now they were crossing the road between the Lesser Tesson and the Citadel slope and then they began the climb. On the slope, they were out of line of sight from the embrasures on the high walls and no grapeshot assailed them, but French fire and also solid shot from their own guns hummed in both directions overhead. The climb was steep, then, much sooner than they expected, they were at the ditch, which was empty! It should be full of hay bags and they were now within sight of the walls and a blast of grape threw back three men as though they were rag-dolls. They were halted at the deep ditch, with no easy means to jump down the severe drop, plus the hay bags could be needed for the main ditch. Carr filled his already heaving lungs.

"Down! Lie down!"

All quickly did, as multiple charges of grape sailed just above their prone bodies. Shakeshaft came up to him and lay alongside.

"Were there not meant to be hay bags down in there. Sir?"

Carr had to shout above the incessant cannonade.

"Yes! Obviously they've got lost. And the Forlorn Hope."

Then his attention was drawn to the depression blasted in the top of the ravellin in front of him, suddenly it was full of Redcoats who must have arrived by running along its surface from the right. The main ditch must be full of Redcoats also, he thought; all from Campbell's Brigade who had arrived too early. By the light of the fireballs on the ravellin he saw the unmistakeable figure of Major Ridge of the 5th. Carr looked right and saw Saunders.

"Corporal! Lower me down."

With hands overlapping wrists, Saunders swung Carr down alongside the ditch wall and he dropped the last four feet. He then ran the final yards across the ditch to scramble up the rubble that had once been the point of the ravellin. There he knelt beside the kneeling Ridge, both gaining some protection from the hollow taken from the top surface by the bombardment.

"Major Ridge. We seem to meet in the oddest circumstances! Mackinnon's are stuck above the ditch, with no sign of the sappers or Forlorn Hope. What do you propose?"

"Nothing for it but to make an attempt. The 5th and 94th are still arriving, when I've got enough I'll give it a go!"

Carr nodded, but Ridge was now looking back to where Carr had come from, away from the wall.

"But what's that?"

Drake and Shakeshaft, above the ditch, knew exactly what it was, the second that they were trodden on and hay bags began to descend into the ditch before them, to be followed by Redcoats descending over the edge like a waterfall. The Forlorn Hope had arrived, but, merely yards back down the slope, O'Hare was worried that his own men would be carried forward by them and he shouted to be heard, even above the constant noise of cannon.

"One Oh Five! Hold here."

The order was passed on and O'Hare hoped it would be obeyed and then Lacey arrived.

"Where's Carr?"

"I saw him drop down into the ditch."

"Right. I'll hold the men here. You follow him."

O'Hare rose up and ran forward, a crouching run, holding his sword across his chest. He came to the ditch and jumped to land on a hay bag and slide down onto the stony soil of the ditch floor, where he saw Carr, now back down in the same ditch, and he ran up to him. Carr wasted no time in elaborate explanation.

"Major Ridge of the 5th is leading his own, the 94th and the Forlorn Hope to attempt the breach. That rubble you can see there marks the breach, on the other side of this ravellin. Ours should be held as the reserve in this first ditch and our Lights should now be up there, on top."

He pointed to the top of the ravellin, at that moment sheltering them both, but not those up on its surface and a body, shattered by grapeshot, fell from above to land but yards away.

"Agreed! I'll call ours forward. You wait here and make them hold."

O'Hare ran the few yards back to see Captain Heaviside peering over the lip of the ditch.

"Joshua! Pass the word. All into the ditch."

Whilst the 105th descended onto the hay-bags, Carr had the chance to look over at the force assembling at the slope of rubble and earth that marked the route over the ravellin to the main breach and he noticed an Officer with lurid green facings that matched his own. It must be Maltby, waiting to be called forward. This was an Officer that he had never much liked, but here, well, this was different and he called out.

"Stuart! Good luck! See you inside."

Maltby smiled and raised a hand, but then the Forlorn Hope was called forward and Maltby ascended the slope of rubble as part of the select group. Immediately, Carr found himself to be horribly in the way as the Light Company 2nd Section began to pile hay bags against the back of the ravellin and begin to scramble upwards onto the back slope. On the opposite half of the ravellin, 1st Section, led by Drake were pulling and pushing each other up the same awkward slope and it was Davey and Miles who got first to the top, with Pike just behind. There were bodies of Redcoats aplenty on the surface, many badly wounded. Crouching just beneath the top of the slope, John Davey looked forward and from there he could see across the main breach to the parapet on the far side, and what he saw there caused an outburst of the kind of bad language that he rarely used.

"Jesus Christ and all the Saints!"

From his angle on the left he could clearly see a parapet that the French had built to defend the right-hand side of the breach and there was a cannon pointing down and out to the summit of the breach slope that had to be crossed by any assault. The parapet was not high and so he quickly brought up his rifle, sighted on a figure behind the gun and fired. The smoke hid all, but then he heard Drake giving orders.

"Rotate by files."

He knew what that meant and so he dropped down beneath the summit to reload. All the while the embrasures in the main wall on his side were belching flame and smoke, but their aim was over to his left, because the angle of those embrasures only allowed that line of fire. For a moment he wondered why, then he realised that the whole section of the parapet opposite him had been battered into oblivion and those embrasures built to defend against him were now thankfully gone, the terreplein behind badly exposed. He finished re-loading, then Tom Miles was back down beside him to reload himself, whilst Joe Pike eased himself up to the edge to find his own target. Pike, sat himself on the slope just below the edge, but he was having trouble controlling the balance of his own mind. His eye hurt and the noise and tumult from all around was more than he could make sense of. Besides the roar of the French cannon, solid shot from his own side were crashing into the French positions at the breach and the yells of hundreds of voices raised in fear and hatred assaulted both his ears and one good eye. Then John Davey was yelling at him.

"Joe! You going to take all night?"

The harsh words brought him back to reality and, as had Miles, he sighted on those around the cannon and fired, then he slid back down for Davey to take his place. Miles had already reloaded and as he crouched down in shelter, he looked up at Davey.

"John! Just in case I don't come out of this, I just wants you to know that you are easily the worst chiselin' kind of muckrake that I have ever come across!"

Despite the stress he felt, Davey managed a choked laugh as he pulled the trigger. Then he heard the cheer as the first assault on the breach went forward. The immediate response was an explosion from the main breach, probably charges of gunpowder, then some cannon fired together from the walls, both those he could see and those he could not, from his angle on that side. The roar, the flash and the smoke were added to by ranks of French muskets. When the smoke cleared, there were no Redcoats to be seen and his spirits sank at the obvious failure, then a solid shot from the parallels smashed into the main parapet on his side of the breach, dislodging several blocks and widening the breach gap. Resolved that this was just the beginning, he sighted on a figure waving a sword and fired, to then slide back down for Miles to come up.

Every sense within Miles spoke of hitting a target, but at the same time minimising the danger to himself and so he eased himself further forward to lie behind a body on the scattered rubble and soil to wait for a target. Then a voice came from above and to his left.

"What be doin' down there, Bloodyback?"

Miles glanced over left to see the green trouser-leg of a Rifleman, who must have somehow arrived from that direction.

"Keepin' my bloody head on my shoulders and you'd best do the same. With all the stuff the Frogs is sendin' across yer, stood up there, your 'ead's very like to get blowed off!"

"Nah! We needs to see who we shoots ...."

With the sentence unfinished, the Rifleman collapsed to a kneeling position, before toppling over, his shako tilting down into the space where the right side of his head once was.

"Told you!"

Miles then found a target on the far parapet and fired, to then roll backwards as musket balls and grape shot continued to hum viciously overhead.

Carr had placed himself up on the rubble of the safe side of the ravellin. He had seen the first attempt go forward, had felt the blast of the explosions and then heard the fearsome discharge that must have gone straight into the faces of the attackers. He was certain that the first attempt had failed and so he looked back down and rightwards into the shadows of the first ditch to see the men of his own Regiment stood waiting, then he looked down left, to see that section of the first ditch also full of men, the light of the fireballs enough to see the yellow on their collars. The 88th had come into the ditch alongside the 105th and, as if to confirm that, Wallace appeared alongside him, his prominent ginger side-burns highly visible alongside the brass chinstrap pulled well back.

"Sir."

"Carr. What do you know?"

"Sir, if we're called up, this is the route forward."

Wallace raised his head, so that he could see for himself what Carr then quickly described.

"Cannon and muskets cover the beach. They've just stopped our first attempt."

Wallace nodded and quickly decided what to do.

275

"We let the second wave go in. If they're through, all well and good. If not, we go before the cannon can reload. Either we support what's successful or it's our turn to try."

At that point, O'Hare came to join them and Wallace slapped him on the arm.

"O'Hare! Mad as ever I see."

"As you say, Sir."

A minute passed, then another, for the three to then hear the cheer again. Ridge was leading his men for another attempt, but Carr knew that the result would be the same, despite Wallace's optimism. However, about one thing Wallace was right, the 105th would be into the breach whatever the outcome, either to support Ridge or to mount a third attack. He slid back down the rubble to look into the faces of the nearest 105th stood waiting. One was Captain Carravoy at the head of his Grenadiers, with Ameshurst just behind him. Carravoy's jaw was working up and down and his hand continuously rising and falling to pull at his collar.

"Grenadiers! 105th! In a moment, we are going through that breach. The Frogs think they've kept us out, but there's no Frogs born who can hold back the Fighting Rag and ………."

The next words were drowned by the French response to the second attack. It was the same roaring discharge from both cannon, as had shattered the first wave. Carr rose up to stand on the ravellin slope.

"Come on, boys. This for Old England!"

The Grenadiers surged up to follow Carr, who immediately found Ameshurst at his left side and Sergeant Ridgway beyond him, O'Hare was just in front. The 88th Connaughts were coming over the ravellin simultaneously, but seeing them was irrelevant, hearing their eerie moan was proof enough. Once across the top of the ravellin, it was barely any kind of jump down onto the rubble that had been blasted out of the main breach and the ravellin itself, but it was impossible not to land on dead and wounded Redcoats who had been blown back into the ditch by the previous French discharges. However, the sheer quantity of loose stone and soil from the bombardment practically bridged the main ditch, as Wallace, O'Hare, Carr and their Grenadiers, clawed their way up to the top of the breach, Carr using his free hand to grasp blocks of loose stone for leverage, but once there, they could go no further. They were confronted by a drop down of almost 20 feet and the bottom of this hollow, 100 feet wide, was covered in planks and beams all studded with spikes, bayonets, knives and swords, making the hollow impossible to cross.

The hollow had been gouged out from the wall centre, the front being the remains of the main wall on which they stood, whilst on the far side there remained a width of the original wall, forming the back of the treacherous hollow. The surface of its narrow terreplein was now very much crowded with French soldiers, all furiously loading and firing their muskets. Equally crowded were the parapets at the top of each side, each with a cannon, but what was astonishing was that the French had completely removed the wall either side of the rubble from the bombardment. They were stood on the stump of the front of the main wall, six feet lower than the side parapets, with a six-foot gap each side cutting them off from the rest of the wall, but they were up there and so Wallace wasted no time.

"Present!"

Every musket beside him and behind him came to the horizontal. He relied on the men to choose their own targets.

"Fire!"

A volley the size of a Company crashed out, then they heard Wallace again.

"O'Hare! I'm going left!"

What Wallace hoped to do, O'Hare could not fathom, but it was clear that they had to get off the isolated block of wall they were on and over the cuttings or be blown away.

Back on the ravellin, Drake could see the mass of Redcoats at the top of the breach, but now brought to a standstill and assailed from both front and side by musket fire. Also, the reloading of the more dangerous cannon was plain to see. He rose up and started forward.

"Come on! They need our support."

The Section rose and began to cross the surface of the ravellin, with many Riflemen of the 95th swelling their number. Drake led them to the edge of the ravellin, which gave no more than a 15-yard gap over the main ditch to the parapets crowded with French, where he immediately noticed Redcoats, all with yellow facings and cuffs, all doing their best to climb and scramble up to the parapet above them. Some were stood on others' shoulders and pulling themselves up the ragged stonework. With extraordinary courage or simple battle madness, other Connaughts were leaping over the cutting on their side, whilst their comrades fired from the stump of the wall to keep back the French. Those crossing or climbing had discarded their muskets and had their bayonets between their teeth as they clung onto the rough surface. Two jumped over to gain purchase on the shoulders of their fellows clinging to the stonework, then they were over the parapet and amongst the French, more quickly followed. Others hauled up and then pushed up to the top of the parapet. Drake gave the immediate order.

"Firing line! Rapid!"

Miles looked over the gap to the main wall and even in the intermittent light of gun flashes, he could also see the yellow facings of the Connaught Rangers.

"Diddykites! Don't seem right to be giving them a helping hand!"

Nevertheless, with his first shot he shattered the head of a French Officer waving his sword, then Davey brought down a gunner loading the cannon on that side. Within a minute, the Connaughts were along and over the parapet, bayonets rising and falling in maddened hands, the breach was taken, at least on that side. Drake called his men off to the left.

"This way! They may need support against any counter-attack."

He feared a French effort from the left to recapture the breach and, at least, they could give some support across the main ditch, at least, pouring fire into its flank. Then Saunders pointed up to the area of wall where the Lesser Breach was.

"I'd not worry, Sir. The only attack coming from down there will be from our own lads."

Drake looked for himself. The parapet there was indeed covered with moving figures, seen in silhouette from fires and gun flashes, all fighting their way onto the terreplein, but soon all such movement stopped. Crauford's men of the Light Division had captured their wall and the fighting had ended, but the first of them were leaving there already, hurrying down towards the main breach. Drake thought that they were being led by a tall figure, very similar, at least, to Uniacke.

On the opposite side of the breach, Carr looked around desperately. His own men were falling around him and, but yards away, across the cutting were distorted French faces, hands busy firing and loading their own weapons. A glance over to the ravellin told him that Shakeshaft had brought Two Section to the edge of the main ditch and they were firing across, bringing down French as well as they could. Then RSM Gibney was tugging at his sleeve.

"Sir! What's this lot here?"

Gibney was pointing at several planks that were down in the cutting on their side, propped against their wall and just reachable. Carr allowed his sword to fall onto its cord and he held out his left hand.

"Hold me!"

Carr lowered himself and Gibney knelt to grasp his left hand by the wrist. They were kneeling down amongst many feet and legs, as men of the 105th sent fire across the cutting, but suspended by Gibney, Carr stretched down to grasp two planks that were with reach and he passed each back up. With both held by Gibney, Carr gave his orders to those around.

"Load and await my orders."

Carr gave his men the 20 seconds they would need, but more fell from French fire.

"Present!"

A dozen muskets came to the horizontal. The target was obvious.

"Fire!"

The muskets crashed out and, in the smoke and gloom, he and Gibney placed both planks over the gap. The parapet had been momentarily cleared by their fire and so Carr recovered his sword and stepped forward.

"Come on, boys! It's our turn now!"

No more than two footfalls on the planks took him onto the parapet where a French face appeared in the thinning smoke, which Carr, from his higher point, kicked as hard as he could. The French had recovered and were firing at all who were following him over the cutting. Once down from the parapet, Carr and Gibney found themselves fighting at the cannon, Carr with his sword, Gibney mostly with a musket butt. A desperate French Officer came at Carr pointing a pistol. Carr swung his sword at the barrel and hit it just as the Frenchman pulled the trigger, but there came only a weak fizz from the pan. Carr's blow had dislodged the priming, but the Frenchman still came on for Carr to deliver a vicious blow into the side of his head using the sharp pommel of his sword. A Grenadier then buried his bayonet up to the socket in the man's midriff. Gibney was now forcing a gunner away from the cannon with a levelled bayonet and more Grenadiers were arriving across the two planks, all of them fighting their way along the parapet past the cannon embrasure. Ameshurst arrived beside Carr.

"Simon! Where's your Captain?'

A weak voice came from behind.

"Here!"

Carr turned to see Carravoy sat on the parapet, holding his left side.

"Charles! You're wounded. Stay here. I'll take the men on."

Carravoy managed a weak nod, then Carr found Gibney beside him.

"Sar' Major. Stay here and look after the Captain."

By now Ameshurst had led his Grenadiers some way forward so that they now held a good ten yards of the terreplein beyond the parapet. The 105th had taken the wall on that side and the French were falling back, the sounds of conflict from the breach itself even fading away, the Connaughts had driven the French off the back wall. Carr looked along the length of the terreplein, now significant from the number of abandoned guns either in or out of their embrasure. The wall curved leftwards to reach the Castle, which he remembered was being attempted by a Portuguese Brigade coming across the town bridge. His duty was to support that effort because it may not have succeeded. He looked for Ameshurst.

"Simon! Where's One Section and Royston?"

"Following Sir. Of that I'm certain."

"And Major O'Hare?"

"He's now leading our men into the town, Sir."

"Right, with me. We're to clear this wall as far as the Castle. Portuguese are there and may need our help to get in. The more the better."

It was at that moment that there came a huge explosion at the breach behind them.

Even some way up from the breach, along the faussebraie, the blast knocked Drake and his men off their feet and, without thinking they covered their heads with their arms, as rubble, stones, dirt and body parts descended all around. Drake was one of the first to recover and he pushed himself to his feet, using his sword. His first thoughts were of a counter-attack and, even in the darkness, he could see that those of Crauford's Division that had been coming down the terreplein towards them could no longer be seen. The men with Drake, those who were able, both Rifles and 105th were now on their feet.

"With me! Back to the breach."

From the back of the ravellin the distance down into the main ditch was a mere five feet and Drake was the first to make the drop. All his men followed and soon they were at the breach, which was now a yawning gap where the wall had been, the stonework now blasted down and what remained hidden behind loose rubble. The stench of gunpowder smoke, scorched stone and flesh was sickening but he led his men into the wide gap to see that there was now a section of the whole wall so completely gone as to be sufficient for him to see right into the town. Under his feet were all kinds of dangerous obstructions protruding upwards, but almost all were avoidable, these being covered in rubble or having been blasted skyward, some were even lodged on top of the ruined left-hand parapet above him. Shakeshaft appeared beside him, having brought his own men down from the ravellin, such as had survived the explosion.

"What to do?"

Drake pointed with his sword at the left parapet above.

"Get up there! There's some of ours further along. We should link up."

He began the climb himself, it was steep but not impossible, the smell of smoke and gunpowder still strong in the easier slope of gravel and rubble that now defined the sides of the breach. He was grateful for some stone blocks lodged there and eventually he reached the top and pulled up some of his own men. When enough were there, he led them on towards the site of the Lesser Breach, but the sights on the terreplein there were immensely distressing, there were so many dead and wounded Riflemen, all with their uniforms blown to shreds and hanging from their bodies. One was being raised up by his comrades and the purple sash around his waist signified that he was an Officer, but he could not support himself and he sagged back to the stone of the terreplein. The area was now full of newly arrived Riflemen and men of the 52nd, all having run down from their breach, and Drake held up his hand for his own to halt. He looked over at the Officer and despite the bloody and blackened face he thought he recognised him. He spoke to a Rifles' Sergeant also stood watching, but almost in tears.

"Is that Captain Uniacke?"

Between sobs, the man answered.

"It is, Sir, and like not to live. All burnt he is and, what's more, he's lost an arm, torn out the socket."

He took a deep breath.

"Too eager, Sir, he were, and too brave, wanting to get to the Main Breach and help out if wanted. 'Tis a tragedy that's full hard to bear!"

"He was a good and gallant Officer."

"That he were, Sir, and thank you, but that's not all, Sir. I'm hearing that General Crauford is wounded too, very bad."

Drake sheathed his sword and motioned his men back to the main breach, his head full of grave thoughts regarding just what the price was to capture a town. Soon, they came to some stairs down and descended into the street below, now full of Light Division soldiers.

Six of Drake's Company, including Davey and Saunders, had been the last off the ravellin and so were the last to arrive at the breach, which was now surprisingly deserted, at least of those alive and whole. The main ditch was now full of rubble to a depth of over three feet and contained many bodies, many with the green collars and cuffs of the 105th. Where possible they were examined and Len Bailey was the first to speak.

"Here's one as'll not be missed!"

They turned to him, now pointing at a body half buried and slumped against the ravellin wall, the face and shoulders that could be seen, much blackened and scorched.

"Maltby!"

All turned away, to begin their own perilous scramble over the surface of the breach, Saunders speaking the thoughts of all.

"No loss there, 'cept we'll be getting a new Lieutenant."

By now, Miles was stood looking around.

"What do we do then? Now? All the lads is into the town, after the pickings. We'll miss out!"

Saunders looked at him gravely and pointed upwards.

"Drake's up there. If we don't follow our own Officer, you know what that means!"

Miles nodded resignedly, sighed, hefted his Baker rifle and then walked forward, but he stopped, staring hard at a fall of shingle and gravel, the filler from the main wall. He had seen an arm protruding, with the same lurid green cuff as his own.

"There's a Wessex lad here!"

Then he looked closer in the poor light. The badge on the sleeve told him everything. His next words were at the top of his voice

"Oh Jesus, 'tis is a Colour Sergeant. Could be Jed!"

All ceased their climb and dropped their rifles to begin scooping the shingle and rubble away as best they could, but more kept descending from above. Joe Pike spread himself above the prone body which helped, but not as much as they needed. They were furiously digging with their hands when a Captain of the 94th came hurried over.

"You men! I need you all over here."

It was Miles who was nearest and the quickest to anger.

"Why?"

The Officer's face contorted in rage.

"You do not question my orders! I want you over there, now! There is an Officer who must be dug out."

Miles stopped shovelling the gravel and looked over to where the 94th Captain was pointing. Miles did not need a second glance. The body was not under light shingle and filler, but under heavy stone blocks, some a foot square.

"He's dead! Not worth diggin' out, that's certain. This 'un 'ere may still be alive."

Miles resumed digging and so it quickly dawned on the Captain that no-one was going to obey his order. He took a deep breath, now in an even greater rage.

"I am giving you all an order. You stop what you are doing and dig out that Officer."

Miles did not even look around again.

"He's dead, this 'un may not be. We stays yer. Sir!"

What happened next was a blur to those around. The Captain, now almost beside himself, drew his sword and raised it above Miles. Miles, hearing the sword leave the scabbard, immediately picked up his Baker and swung the bayonet around to threaten the Captain. The sword remained aloft, but did not descend and the bayonet was not thrust forward. The anger on the face of the Captain had turned to shock, as much from the determined look on Miles' face, as the fact of being menaced by a bayonet, but it was Miles who spoke first, his voice now a hiss, thick with menace.

"This could be our Colour Sergeant and we'n goin' to dig 'im out and give 'im a chance. Yours is dead, I'm tellin' thee. Dead! Diggin' for him be to no purpose!"

The Captain lowered his sword, but the bayonet was not, not until the Captain walked away. It was plain that his orders were not going to be obeyed. Meanwhile, most of the body had been uncovered, although face down and the left arm still trapped. The back of the right leg was red and blistered, there was no backpack nor any other equipment, but the back of his tunic was still badly holed from the blast. Davey lifted the head as best he could.

"'Tis Jed!"

Whilst the others dug furiously to free the trapped arm from more substantial stones, Davey poured water into a cupped hand and washed the face as best he could. There was no reaction, but now Deakin was free and they turned him onto his back, for Davey to clean his face, which was not burnt. Bailey spoke first.

"Explosion was behind him. Took off all his kit, what saved his back."

Saunders was not interested.

"What do we do? He could still be alive!"

They all stared, while Davey washed out Deakin's mouth and brushed some gravel from his nostrils, then a voice came from behind.

"Get some breath into him."

Saunders turned around to look at Byford.

"What?"

"Get some breath in him."

"How?"

"Blow into his mouth. Get his chest working. You'll need to hold his nose."

Byford obviously meant him and so Saunders looked down at Deakin, knelt, held Deakin's nose, pulled the jaw down, took a deep breath and exhaled all into Deakin's mouth. Now under pressure from the immense lungs of Zeke Saunders, Deakin's chest rose up like an inflated bladder and Saunders stopped. Byford came down to kneel beside the prone figure and pushed down on the chest. He looked at Saunders.

"More! You blow in, I'll push down."

Saunders took another deep breath and covered Deakin's mouth with his own to again empty his own lungs into Deakin's. When the chest was at maximum, Byford pressed down. They repeated for a minute, with no response, then Deakin's chin and throat twitched. Davey slapped Saunders on the back.

"Keep going! That's good."

Keep going they did, until there came a weak cough. One more exhale from Saunders and then they turned him onto his front for Byford to press down onto his back with the same rhythm as fast breathing. The response was one stronger cough, then several. Then, to the relief of them all, Deakin raised himself slightly on his elbows and opened his eyes, to begin coughing. Miles bent down to stare at Deakin's face.

"Jed! Can you hear me?"

The eyes opened further and the voice came in a croak between fits of choking, but clear.

"Miles! I must be in Hell!"

All started laughing, except Miles, but they rolled him over and Saunders found his own water bottle.

"Here, Jed. Take a drink."

Deakin took a long swallow, then another, when Miles found his own.

"Here, Jed, take another drink. Summat a bit stronger!"

Deakin took a swallow of the brandy, coughed, wiped his mouth and then drank again. Pike seemed more relieved than anyone.

"Lord, Jed. We thought you was gone!"

Davey nodded.

"We did, Jed, but your leg's bad. Burnt some. Do you think you can stand? Walk a bit?"

Deakin reached up with his arms for help and he was hauled upright to gingerly try his right leg, with nothing remaining of the trouser leg below the knee. He nodded, before speaking weakly.

"With a bit of help, boys, yes, I can get back. I heard a big bang, then came a whack, then nothin'."

Saunders and Bailey supported him either side and they began to carefully pick their way over the treacherous surface. The rest followed, then they heard a sharp and recently familiar voice from behind.

"Him! That one! I want him arrested."

Before he could turn, Miles' arms were seized and he was pulled to one side, those arresting him being two Provosts, whilst the voice came from the 94th Captain. Miles' arms were tied behind his back and he was pulled out into the main ditch and forced downwards to sit with his back to the wall. He called over to the group, now halted by the new events.

"'Tis alright boys! It'll only mean a few on the triangle!"

The Senior Provost looked hard at him.

"You reckons! From what I've heard about you, threatening an Officer with a brummagem; that'll mean the rope!"

The accusing Captain arrived to stare down at Miles, who stared back up and indicated with a tilt of his head.

"See him there, Sir, held up in the middle? He's the one. We got him out. Alive he be! His Missus back in camp would never forgive us, had we not tried. So how's yours then, Sir? Not so dead as he was afore?"

The Officer scowled, and stared down with outrage and indignation, but he said no more and left to enter the town. The 105th group began to move away, ushered on by Davey, who thought it best that they all leave as quickly as possible. The original order to move had been meant for them also.

"There's nothing we can do, best get Jed back."

They moved on, over the rubble to where the ditch was clear, then Davey had another thought.

"Back during the fighting, Tom spoke of not getting through this. I never thought the cause would come atop the steps of some gallows."

None replied, each had their own thoughts. Meanwhile from the town behind them came the sounds of mayhem, violence and chaos. Cuidad Rodrigo was now in the hands of hundreds of victorious and celebrating Allied soldiers, all very grateful to still be alive and determined to celebrate that wondrous fact.

oOo

Chapter Ten

South Again

Carr called a halt. For 200 yards, he had been following the backs of the fleeing French, but they had a head-start, and so now he had no choice but to wait and allow a force to build up behind him and for these reinforcements to scramble up the blasted right-hand side of the breach or cross the planks took time. Thus, the French were some way ahead and by now were all over a barrier that blocked a narrow part of the terreplein, with the Castle some 200 yards beyond them. Carr concluded that this barrier must be part of some kind of defensive plan if the breach was taken, behind which a last and very desperate stand could be made. Carr heard shouts and cheering from beyond the wall, so, whilst his men gathered behind him, he looked over to see what looked like Mackinnon's Portuguese reserve pouring into the town through a gate that was beneath the barrier. He went to the inner side of the wall to find out if there were any internal steps up from the road they were on, by which these eager Portuguese could attack the barrier, but he could see nothing. Therefore, alone, he was faced with an obstacle that was now substantially manned and he saw no reason to sacrifice the lives of any more 105th, especially as he had something that would be much more effective than any frontal attack and it was very near at hand; a heavy cannon, abandoned at a nearby embrasure. Alongside there was plenty of powder and shot and even burning matches. Ameshurst was alongside him.

"Ever fancied the artillery, at any time, Simon?"

Ameshurst followed Carr's gaze towards the heavy piece and sprang over to the position himself, to unhook one of the breaching ropes that linked the gun carriage to the stone of the embrasure. He was not alone for more than three seconds before more Grenadiers joined him and the gun was hauled backwards to be then swung around and pointed at the barrier. The rammer had been abandoned nearby and the barrel was soon loaded with grape shot and elevated to point menacingly at the barrier, this still thick with French.

Ameshurst's Sergeant Ridgway now stood ready, close to the touch-hole with a smouldering match. The whole had taken about three minutes. Carr turned to Ameshurst.

"How's your French?"

"Passable!"

"That's better than mine. Tell them to surrender or we fire."

Ameshurst grinned and walked to within 100 yards of the barrier. He had a white handkerchief on the end of his sword.

"Cession ou nous tirer!"

The result was all those behind the barrier running back towards the Castle. Ameshurst turned and held out his hands in a gesture of incomprehension, but Carr was already leading his men forward. Now abandoned, the barrier was no obstacle and with one leap onto the top, they were down, over and running towards the Castle. Ameshurst was in the lead with Ridgway and his usual 'body guard' attendants and it was not long before they came to a Plaza in front of the Castle and there stood approximately 50 French, all with their muskets down on the cobblestones at their feet. Ameshurst was not far ahead, well within shouting distance for Carr.

"Simon. Get those lined up. We'll soon be marching out."

He pointed to the open Castle gate and door.

"I'd best see what's going on in here."

He motioned to a group of Grenadiers to follow him and they did, as he strode through the gate and up the steps to enter the door, his sword at the ready. Inside, there were as many red coated British as French, some British with pale buff cuffs and collars and others sporting bright yellow. However, regarding these two Regiments, Carr kept his thoughts to himself, they were 'Crauford's 52nd favourites' and the 'Devil's Own" Connaughts'. One Lieutenant of each was present, each with what could only be surrendered swords, held in a bundle beneath their arms. One Lieutenant was Gurwood whom Carr recognised from his time with the 52nd during the capture of Fort Renaud. Gurwood saw Carr and saluted and indicated an evidently very Senior French Officer stood beside him.

"Major Carr, Sir, may I introduce General Barrie, the Governor of this town?"

Carr came to full attention and saluted.

"Sir!"

Barrie plainly appreciated the degree of respect and smiled as he returned the salute. Gurwood then raised up a very intricate sword for Carr to see.

"I've just accepted the General's surrender. This is his sword."

"Very good, Lieutenant. I'll leave you to conduct the General safely back. As he has surrendered to you, he is now your responsibility."

On hearing the words, the other Lieutenant of the 88th, turned, frowning.

"Mackie, Sir. 88th. Perhaps I should be the one, Sir. The General surrendered to me, some time prior to the arrival of the 52nd, here."

Carr was tired and lost patience.

"Regarding who received what from whom, I care not, but I am charging the pair of you to get the General back safely to Lord Wellington, who is probably in Fort Renaud. For your stories about all this, I care nothing! Argue about it in the future."

He turned to General Barrie once again and saluted, which produced a tired smile from the captured French Commander. Outside, Carr took stock. The first fact that hit his senses was the sound of riot and chaos coming from further in the town, the second that Ameshurst had his prisoners well under guard with what looked like the greater amount of his Section, over 50 men, guarding about 50 French. These latter needed to be escorted from the town and so Carr searched his memory for the plan of Cuidad and remembered a gate that led North, the Salamanca gate, probably the best way back to the Allied lines, it led straight onto the far end of the Lesser Tesson. However, this required leading the prisoners and his own men through what was obviously going to be a scene of pillage and gross indiscipline. He rejected the nearer 'Portuguese Gate' which would now, more than likely, be filled with Allied soldiers entering the town.

He looked at Ameshurst's Grenadiers looking at him, so he walked over so that all were within earshot. He had no choice but to appeal to their feelings for their Regiment, so he took a deep breath.

"Grenadiers of the 105th! It is our duty to escort these prisoners to safety, to escort them through a town that is now full of soldiers intent on stealing what is not theirs and getting drunk. As we march through, and march we will, you must ask yourselves what matters to you. The honour and standing of the 105th or taking part in theft and drunkenness? What matters, the reputation of ourselves as the best Regiment in Wellington's army, or falling drunk in the street, with pockets full of worthless trinkets that you'll throw away after one day's march?"

He allowed the words to sink in, but there came no reply, either of rejection or adherence to his appeal.

"Right. Get the Frogs in a column of twos, yourselves in twos either side."

Ridgway and the Corporals began shouting orders and the French were pushed into formation and the Grenadiers fell in on either side. Carr then had a horrible thought and he went to Ameshurst.

"Do you know the way from here to the Salamanca gate?"

"No!"

"Perhaps one of the Frogs does?"

"I'll ask."

He turned to face the column of prisoners.

"Qui connaît le chemin jusqu'à la porte de Salamanca?"

A tentative hand was raised, two files back in the French ranks. Ameshurst called him forward.

"Conduire!"

The Frenchman walked forward and the column followed. Soon they were in streets full of screaming and panicked civilians, but few Redcoats or Portuguese. However, those soldiers that they did see were already taking long pulls at various types of bottles and shouting insults at them when their mouths were free. Without orders, Sergeant Ridgway and Amehurst's unofficial bodyguard ran forward to lever the miscreants away from their column with horizontal muskets, but worse was in the main Square which the Frenchman led them through, although only across one far end, mercifully narrow. The whole Square was a mass of rejoicing soldiers, each with a bottle and each intent of achieving a state of extreme intoxication. However, the sound that was growing in volume was the terrified cries of trapped civilians and of doors and windows being smashed open. Carr dropped back to the rear of the column from where he could observe, hoping that Ameshurst's men would hold their line, but his jaw clamped together grimly, but in pride, when the discipline of the Grenadiers revealed itself as they marched on, ignoring the invitations to break rank and 'take a drink'. Some even held up their cuff of lurid green, pointing to it, as though that were enough justification. Within five minutes they were through the inky blackness of the Salamanca gate to turn left and march alongside the base of the town wall, where what greeted them was another sight, different and more distressing. They had no choice but to pass over the route of Crauford's attack, all strewn with dead and wounded, the latter now thankfully receiving attention or being helped to where Surgeons were operating.

Now inside the town, Lacey and O'Hare were in a far different frame of mind to the now much relieved Carr. They had led their men inside, and far into it, expecting combat from final pockets of resistance. The 105th Officers had kept the men in column and Lacey knew that he had barely seven Companies with him, but the clear objective of reaching the far wall of the town had held the Battalion together. Carr had taken off the Grenadiers, the Lights had departed for their duty on the ravellin and he feared that the Colour Company had suffered worst in the explosion, also he had not seen Heaviside since they crossed the first ditch. However, he felt it right to penetrate through the town, until he was certain that all French resistance in their area had been extinguished. With O'Hare at his side and both with drawn swords, they progressed up the narrow street choosing what they considered to be the most direct route to the wall furthest away from the breach. The sounds of soldiery out of control were growing all around and his concerns grew for his own command, he knew that the temptations were huge, especially after 11 days in the freezing and dangerous trenches. He peered forward into the gloom; he had detected figures in the light of the half-moon and concluded that they were French.

"First three. Make ready!"

The column halted and the first three ranks raised their muskets to the vertical. The figures came on, but Lacey could soon see that this was no organised assault or charge, this was running in panic. He waited and the figures came on apace, then, even in the poor light, he could see that they were indeed French but the looks of relief on their faces, presumably on seeing the red uniforms, was almost piteous.

"Nous rendons! Nous rendons!"

Most surprisingly of all, many fell on their knees before Lacey, who looked at O'Hare.

"Get these back behind us."

O'Hare turned to the first rank.

"First rank, secure the prisoners."

Soon the Frenchmen, 40 and more, were cleared and led back under the command of a Corporal, and so Lacey led his men on, but soon other figures appeared at the end of the street.

"First three. Make ready."

His men responded again as Lacey did his best to identify who was coming towards them. A Sergeant stood beside him and spoke, perhaps helped by younger eyes.

"Sir. Them looks like Portugee!"

Lacey strained his own eyes and saw the odd shaped shako that was worn by some Portuguese Line Battalions. He wanted no accidents.

"Order arms."

The muskets were immediately lowered, butts on the ground. O'Hare was near and could suggest a reason.

"That so called diversion on the far side must have got over."

Lacey nodded and sheathed his sword.

"Yes. Now we must make sure that they do not shoot at us!"

O'Hare walked forward

"I'll do that!"

He raised his own sword above his head, his left hand holding the point, his right on the pommel. Several times he shouted "Ingleses". Lacey saw some Portuguese muskets come to the 'present' and his pulse skipped a beat, but a Portuguese Officer threw up the muskets with his sword, saluted O'Hare and then led his men off left down another street. O'Hare turned and walked back.

"Now we just have to get ourselves out of this!"

Together they walked back down the column, ordering 'about turn' and soon, what they had with them of the 105th and their prisoners, were marching back the way they came, but the further they went the greater the riot and chaos. All French forces had surrendered and therefore the invading Allied troops saw no reason to remain as disciplined soldiers under orders. Now, they were thoroughly disorganised and therefore, left to their own devices, with Officers the exception, all were taking advantage, breaking into shops and houses and generally abusing and molesting the horrified civilians who ran in all directions seeking safety. The Town Square was a madhouse of drunken, cavorting soldiery, an uproar of noise and mayhem from both British and Portuguese. Lacey, O'Hare, other Officers and NCOs supervised the crossing of a narrow end of the Square and Lacey looked along his column to see, to his great relief, that his men held their ranks. Satisfaction for his men now huge within him, he looked right to see that, off this street that led back to the main breach, was a small Plaza, but even that was filling with soldiers intent on drink and plunder. Despite the dark, O'Hare could see that Lacey's mouth was a grim line as he turned to him.

"Get the men formed to hold that Plaza, prisoners in the rear. Four deep here and as many for any other entrance. Any civilians, let them through. Send out Gibney, Hill, Nicholls and any others you trust to drag in any of ours that are out in that main Square. We don't have the Grenadiers nor the Lights with us. Some may be out there in that mob, so you stay here, I'll go out with them."

O'Hare placed his arm on Lacey's sleeve.

"Don't! For the Love of Heaven, don't! There'll be plenty out there that'll now be drunk enough to kill any Officer they see, never mind one that starts giving them orders. Whatever is possible to be done, Gibney and those will do it. Stay here and encourage the men. There'll be some as are tempted, you can be sure. Sorely tempted!"

Lacey nodded sadly at O'Hare's good sense and soon orders were being shouted and, much to Lacey's satisfaction, with very few exceptions who immediately ran off to join the celebratory chaos, the men of the 105th obeyed and formed ranks across the mouth of the small Plaza. It was not long before civilians saw them, the ordered ranks of Redcoats ranged across one side, seeing them as a source of refuge and they ran towards them and any Redcoat or Portuguese who saw no reason why he should not pursue a female through those ranks found himself prostrated on the ground, battered senseless, with no more need for any drink. It was the same for those now penned in the square, who were initially very resentful of their confinement, until Four Company rounded them up and drove them into a house at bayonet point. Meanwhile, NCO's of the ilk of Gibney, Hill and Nicholls roamed the Square and the streets, looking for any drunk with the very distinctive green facings of the 105th and any they were found were cuffed into a state of submission and dragged to the Plaza to be thrown in through the solid ranks.

Lacey and O'Hare walked up and down the front rank, encouraging the men as best they could to remain steady, mostly beginning with 'this is as much a test as any battle', then came a series of words that began with 'remember' and then finished with the name of a 105th battle honour, Corunna being mentioned most, and sometimes the reply came back, "You'll not hear 'Brighton Camp' today, Sir". Much encouraged Lacey felt his own feelings swell up at the memory of his men marching forward once more into the desperate conflict to hold the vital village of Elvina outside Corunna, whilst singing their Regimental song. He was pulled out of his reverie by the sight of Picton, mounted on a horse, top-hat in place and wielding the barrel of a broken musket, using it to lash out at every drunk he saw. It was not long before he noticed the line of 105th with Lacey stood before it. His face was puce with anger, his mood in no shape to grant anyone any credit.

"What's this Lacey? Your gang of thieves got hold of some wine cellar to keep for themselves? You keeping a hoard of booty back there?"

Before Lacey could answer, there came a shout from the rear rank,

"You go take your bad mouth and use it somewer' else, Picton! We holds this. There's nothing here to trouble you, old cock!"

Lacey saluted.

"Sorry about that, Sir. As was said, we're holding this Plaza as a refuge for civilians. We already have almost 200. Plus some prisoners."

Picton's face subsided from livid anger into a mere deep frown as he looked down at Lacey, then at the ranks of the 105th, none of which contained a respectful face looking at him. He then looked beyond the ranks at the civilians now thronging the high steps of the Plaza buildings. Picton then spoke with a scowl, almost through clenched teeth.

"Wellington's bringing up the 5th Division. You'll all be out by morning!"

With that he rode into the Square, with a heavy Dragoon escort, to renew his vicious and passionate swinging of the dismembered musket.

On past midnight the drunken celebrations, thievery and violence continued, but with the arrival of the small hours the noises of outrage did subside and, to the surprise of many, with the arrival of daylight the rioters began to obey their Officers and they dragged themselves, certainly not progressing in any soldierly way, back to the battlements. Stood at 'order arms', the 105th looked disdainfully at the ridiculous cavalcade passing them by on its way to place themselves back under orders. If anything, the looks given to the solid and ordered ranks of the 105th were more than sheepish, many did feel ashamed and said nothing to the 105th, who did not hold back, utterly secure in their own superiority. From somewhere came the comment that most felt.

"You all looks like a bunch of whores and tinkers come the back end of May Day!"

The comment brought laughter, mostly because it was true, several ridiculously sported looting women's clothing, even some Riflemen, but many, 'old sweats', now wore superior French boots and breeches, which brought no comment, only understanding. Lord Wellington arrived from the direction of the Salamanca gate and halted at the ranks of the 105th, who immediately presented arms on O'Hare's orders. Wellington halted at Lacey and studied the ordered ranks, before looking down.

"Ah! My old 'Rag and Bone Boys'. Well done, Lacey. Hold here until this rabble have been marched away."

He looked disdainfully at the colourful parade going past his right boot, none of whom dared to look up, then he turned back to Lacey.

"What are you casualties?"

Lacey took a deep breath.

"No accurate figure yet, Sir, but I estimate between 40 and 50. I know of two Officers dead and one missing."

Wellington nodded.

"We've suffered, Lacey, there's no getting away from it, and of men we would prefer not to lose. Mackinnon's dead, the explosion at the breach got him, and Crauford's not long to live. A bad wound, hit by grapeshot through the spine. He'll not last."

"A great pity, Sir. For them both."

"Indeed, Lacey, indeed, but that's the game we're in. Now, when it's clear, get your men back to camp and await orders. You'll not be here long. The 5th are coming to relieve you."

Wellington walked his horse on as Lacey and O'Hare saluted, then, now alone, Lacey looked at O'Hare.

"Mackinnon! That's a great tragedy. He'd not been back a week!"

O'Hare nodded sadly.

"Yes, he was a good man and a good Officer to serve under."

Lacey took a deep breath.

"Right, the last of the revellers are passing. Time to get ours back. There's a gate opposite the Santa Cruz Convent."

He did not want to use the main breach and so they exited the town through his choice, the smallest, but it was the most direct. Their march back to camp, once they were clear of the fortifications and then matching up the slope to the second parallel required fixed and steadfast eyes forward. They were marching over the ground that they had advanced down over the previous night, which took them past the Third Division casualties, all the dead still being collected into several mournful, blanket covered rows, many showing arms with bright green cuffs protruding from the blanket edge. The seriously wounded had been carried back to Fort Renaud and were being treated in and around there, so when they arrived, Lacey took the trouble to investigate the piteous ranks of those least likely to survive and he came back to O'Hare, much saddened.

"Sixteen!"

O'Hare looked carefully at him.

"Heaviside?"

Lacey shook his head.

"No, not there, so, either dead or slightly wounded."

"So, there's hope."

However, hope was in short supply back at the mess fires of Davey and Saunders. Deakin was sat groggily on a box, Pike was away, hoping for a Surgeon to look at his eye, but the story was the arrest of Tom Miles and hope all but died with the verdict of Ethan Ellis, when he heard the story, whilst drinking tea.

"Pointing a brummagem at the throat of an Officer, that's much the same as mutiny!"

It was Bridie who answered, now that she was content with the immediate lifespan of her own man.

"But did he not do it, so's you all could dig out Jed here, and save his life?"

Ellis nodded and spoke carefully.

"He did, Bridie, but he mutinied against an order. It doesn't look good. I'm sorry, but that's how it is."

Davey looked up.

"He'll get a trial?"

Ellis' face became non-committal.

"He'll get something, but I wouldn't call it a trial like a Court Martial. He'll be brought before Picton or somesuch. Someone like Daddy Hill or Graham would be better, but Picton's most likely, and you know what he's like."

"Will someone speak for him, bring witnesses?"

"Yes, that'll be Drake, but t'other side will be there too. Whoever that Officer was."

"Will reputation and past service count?"

"It could, but that's a two-edged sword with Tom Miles."

Many nodded their heads as Ellis finished his tea.

"Right. I'll get on round. Word is we're moving back to Zamarra, according to Bert Bryce."

It was indicative that even that thought did not cheer them up, then Saunders spoke, in a manner at least positive.

"Well, we can all get our story straight, so's Drake's got something to say. That bugger did raise his sword as though he were like to strike down on Tom. Hasn't a man the right to defend his own life, even in King George's army?"

oOo

Joe Pike had never seen a magnifying glass but here was one making the eyeball of a Surgeon look huge, whilst the same eyeball studied the injured left of his own. The examination complete, the glass was lowered.

"Now cover your right-eye."

Pike did, with his hand.

"What is your vision like?"

Pike had never heard the word 'vision' before, but it must mean something in relation to 'what could he see?".

"It's like there's a mist, Sir. Not thick, but there."

The Surgeon nodded.

"I'd say you've a scratch on your eyeball, if I can put it like that. Your vision from that eye, may improve, but I doubt it will return to what it was. You have to hope. Keep it covered for another week, it's best not to let it dry out, nor for something to go in there that shouldn't."

He studied Pike intently.

"You're a marksman, are you not?"

"Light Company Sir, yes Sir, but I sights with my right eye."

The Surgeon nodded.

"So, when in battle, cover it. I'm sure someone can make you an eyepatch."

With that the Surgeon rose and walked to the next patient, leaving Pike to re-cover his eye, button his jacket and leave the tent, passing Reverend Albright as he did, this worthy now on his way in and accompanied by Chaplain's Assistant Sedgwicke. Deciding that Albright could be abandoned for a minute, Sedgwicke stopped Joe, knowing him to be part of the Deakin and Saunders group.

"Private Pike! Something's happened to your eye, obviously. I hope it recovers."

Pike smiled.

"Surgeon says it might, Parson. We can only hope."

Sedgwicke nodded.

"Indeed, but I hear that Deakin suffered somewhat?"

"Yes, Parson, he got buried, but we dug him out and he's like to recover."

Sedgwicke smiled. The welfare of Jed Deakin, who had always been kind to him, was a matter of personal concern.

"I'm pleased to hear that. Please pass on my best wishes to him and to Bridie. And to Nellie, of course."

Pike stepped away to leave.

"Yes Parson. I'll do that. Goodbye."

Sedgwicke hurried after Albright, who was stood puzzled as to why Sedgwicke was no longer in close attendance, but was mollified when Sedgwicke hurried up to him.

"We must find the Officers first, Private. I'm sure they will be in a separate area."

Albright took a few paces to gain a better view for his search and when he saw beds with swords and pistols beside them, he considered his quest to be over. He turned to Sedgwicke.

"What fruit do you have?"

"None, Sir, bar these apples."

He held up a small canvas sack.

"They came up with the last supply convoy, Sir. I suspect them to be English."

Albright tilted his head forward, as if to give gravity to his next words, this also afforded by the pulpit tone to his voice.

"We will assume them to be so, Private. I'm sure that it will be a comfort to be given fruit grown and nourished in our own Mother Country."

Whilst within himself Sedgwicke was aghast at such a naïve belief within his superior, there was only one reply he could give.

"Yes Sir. I'm sure that fact will be very comforting, Sir."

Albright bowed, a gesture which acknowledged his servant agreeing with his good sense, but then he saw a heavy Bible on a table beside a sword and pistol and there, he felt certain, terminated his search for Heaviside, the most significant of the 105th Officers wounded or missing. The Officer's tunic, with bright green collar and cuffs, confirmed all. The figure in that bed was lying on his front with only some thin muslin spread over his back, despite the cold.

"Captain Heaviside. I'm hoping that is you."

The figure shifted his body slightly to improve the angle at which he could hold his head.

"I am Heaviside. Who may you be? I'm afraid I am unable to see, being forbidden to turn my head too far."

Albright went to the head of the bed and knelt.

"It is I, Reverend Albright. We are wholly pleased to see that you are still alive, if not, ahem, whole and hearty."

"Alive is true, Reverend, I thank you for your concern."

Thus encouraged, Albright turned to Sedgwicke, palms cupped to receive some apples, which he placed on the bed before Heaviside's face.

"We have brought you some fruit. Apples only, I'm afraid, but they are English."

"The fruit of the Righteous is a tree of life and whoever captures Souls is wise. Proverbs 1. 16."

"Just so, Captain. Just so."

Sedgwicke was disappointed that his Superior could not reply with his own quote and so he spoke up with his own and never mind the consequences, at least not for now.

"He is like a tree planted by streams of water that yields its fruit in season, and its leaf does not wither."

They both saw Heaviside grin, albeit only from the side.

"Ah, Private Sedgwicke. Remaining steadfast to The Word, it seems. Psalms One."

Sedgwicke leaned forward, to ensure being heard.

"Yes Sir. Constant in that, as always."

Albright was suddenly thoroughly put out by this sudden burst of affinity between this noble and devout Captain and his own mere Servant. He looked angrily at Sedgwicke, before turning to Heaviside.

"Your wounds Captain. I do hope they are not too severe."

Heaviside lifted his shoulders to turn his head.

"My back is burnt and they spread it with goose-grease, my left arm is probably fractured and I have what they now call 'concussion' in my head. All from being blown up."

"I do trust that all these injuries you describe can be considered minor and that you will soon return to your duties."

"As our Lord disposes, Reverend. We are in his hands."

Albright nodded vigorously and brought his hands together.

"Indeed so, Captain. Indeed so. Shall we pray together, Captain?"

The reply shocked Albright.

"Being of a full Presbyterian disposition, Reverend, I would prefer not. There is a Scottish Major and a Captain in the King's German Legion not so far away and we pray together according to our own interpretation of the Faith.

"Not even the Lord's Prayer."

"Even to that, Reverend, we have our own words. I must refuse."

Much put out Albright stood, his face almost in shock.

"Then we will leave you, Captain, but I will pray for you, nevertheless."

"I thank you, Reverend, for that. Now I must bid you good-day."

Albright then stood and quit the bedside, but Sedgwicke felt able to delay for a short while, whilst Albright searched for another green cuff or collar.

"Sir, it may please you to know that Colour Sergeant Deakin was also injured at the breach, he was buried, but the men dug him out and he will probably make a full recovery."

Heaviside waved his good hand in acknowledgment.

"That I am pleased to hear, Sedgwicke. Colour Sergeant Deakin is a man of the highest standing. I would be saddened to hear of his death. A good man obtains favour from The Lord. Proverbs 12. 2."

"Indeed Sir, yes. A speedy recovery to you, then, Sir."

"Thank you, Sedgwicke. I certainly do not relish the thought of remaining in this position for too long!"

Sedgwicke nodded agreement, although Heaviside could see nothing of him, then he rose up and hurried after Albright, who had strayed amongst the Officers of the 88th and was now confused.

The rearrangements of the command structure of the Colour and Light Companies were more or less made whilst standing still on the road out of Cuidad. Lacey put his ideas to O'Hare, as they formed a column waiting within what was once again Wallace's Brigade, since the death of Mackinnon.

"Rushby to replace Maltby and command Lights One Section. Lieutenant Farquarson as acting Captain for Three whilst Heaviside's laid up, but Rushby moving up means we need another temporary Ensign. Who's the strongest amongst our drummers?"

O'Hare grinned.

"Our adopted French drummerboy!"

"You mean the one we dug out of that alley in Elvina? Who wouldn't let go of his drum?"

"The same and he now beats it for us. He's still got it."

Lacey nodded, slightly bemused.

"Make it so, until something permanent is arranged."

Thus, Henri Rasenne, a native French boy, was, pro tem, elevated to the Commissioned ranks and called forward to at least carry the King's Colour on the march. The ex-French Drummerboy was a good friend of Patrick Mulcahey, who carried the Regimental Colour and they both grinned at each other as they took their places. Colour Sergeant Harry Bennet was not taken at all by a French accent carrying his King's Colour and he complained to RSM Gibney.

"Don't seem right. An ex-French prisoner carrying one of ours. And he still keeps that French drum as we captured with him, back in Corunna."

Gibney gave him hardly a glance.

"Happens he's got two arms, two legs and a pair of eyes as works, and that'll do, at least for now."

The opportunity was taken for the Roll to be called for the whole Brigade, each Senior Sergeant calling out names in flat, unemotional tones, to receive an answer or none. The return for the 105th was hurried up to O'Hare who quickly did the maths, then he turned to Lacey, stood waiting anxiously.

"48. Three Officers killed and 13 men. 4 Officers wounded and 27 men."

Lacey nodded sadly. That was more than half a Company.

"And of the wounded we can expect to get back something under half."

O'Hare nodded.

"Past experience tells us so."

The order finally came to march and there was no more conversation on that subject and so, depleted and minimally reorganised, the 105th marched off and around Cuidad, taking a road that passed across the Northern wall of the town and would lead directly to Almaraz, precluding the need to make any crossing of the now raging Agueda, neither by bridge nor by ford. However, one Officer was not with them, this being Major Carr, because his presence was required at the funeral of General Crauford. This event decided upon and arranged by the Officers of his own Light Division and their earnest request was that he be buried in the Lesser Breach before it was closed up and repaired. Therefore, now, in obedience to that request, a knot of Officers stood around the body, wrapped in Crauford's own boatcloak. Meanwhile, the Third Division, all with arms reversed, passed by at the foot of the glacis slope, on which Crauford had been mortally wounded.

The ceremony was short and poignant. Carefully, via many hands, the body was passed up and laid in the bottom of the cleft, over which his men had fought their way to be the first into the town. All was silently observed by the men of the Light Division, with all Senior Staff, including Wellington, present with heads uncovered. With the body in position, there was no hymn, merely a psalm and a prayer spoken by the Senior Chaplain of the Light Division. All spoke 'Amen" and stood to watch as buckets of wall filler, gravel, shingle and fine rubble were passed up and the body was covered, a small wall repair to the base of the cleft holding all in place. That done, many bowed in that direction, then all replaced their hats and left to their urgent duties. Carr joined onto the Third Division column, joining with the 5th Foot of Campbell's Brigade and he enjoyed some pleasant conversation with their Major Ridge.

The 25 miles to Zamarra were completed in one continuous march but it was joyous as well as somewhat tiring, because the local population were now well aware that the French had been forced back to Salamanca. Even there, according to rumour, their numbers were reducing as French Battalion after Battalion marched Eastwards and so, as they passed through villages and hamlets came shouts of "Viva Ingleses" and "Ingleses Valiente". Once in Zamarra, familiar faces greeted well known 'Soldados Ingleses' and many were able to settle into their old billets, including several of the 105th moving back into the barn that they had refurbished themselves, the farmer being more than happy to accommodate them, hoping for further repairs. Soon, the doors and windows were shut and rations were boiling nicely, when Ethan Ellis arrived and simply stood in the centre to make an announcement.

"Miles is being brought up before Picton day after tomorrow. Drake wants three as'll tell the story. Picton won't allow no more as it will favour Miles. So, I'd say, Zeke, John and Jed. Shall I tell him that?"

Deakin spoke first.

"You can, Ethan. We three be as good as any, better'n most."

"Right. You three get to Headquarters straight after breakfast tomorrow."

Then Davey spoke up.

"Who's the Officer of the 94th?"

"Captain Dunnage."

"Who's he bringing?"

"That I do not know, but Drake's drummed up two more as may, or may not, help. Independent he calls 'em; Gibney and Carravoy!"

All around shared looks of deep concern. No words needed to be spoken, because all knew that Tom Miles dwelt not at all within the affections of either.

The next day, the Court was convened at 9.00 am and dealt first with defaulters who partook too rigorously in the events within Cuidad during the night of its capture. Meanwhile, in a small room, Drake was sat with Rushby, the Light Company's new Lieutenant and Miles' own, if he came out of the trial with his life. Drake sat studying the list of cases.

"Curious! None here are charged with 'looting', which is, of course, a death sentence. Rather all are up for 'disrespecting an Officer', or 'gross misconduct'."

"What will that mean? Punishment, I mean."

"Stoppage of rum or a dozen or even just half that, on the triangle."

He then looked again at the final case, that of Miles, charged with the worst possible, 'mutiny'.

So they sat, whilst in the main room Picton dealt impatiently with the defaulters, quickly dispensing lashes or rum stoppage as Drake had predicted. Then a Clerk Sergeant entered.

"Yours is coming up now, Sirs."

Both stood to go out into a corridor, where they found their other witnesses edging forward to enter what was the largest room in the building and crammed with chairs of all description, but leaving a central walkway down to the front of the room. Once inside and seated, Davey, Saunders and Deakin looked over at Miles, who grinned back at them, when he was able to lean forward to see around the huge Provost who was guarding him, although he was bound both at the wrists and hobbled at the ankles. Picton sat at a table raised on a platform, glowering at the delay caused by the change of personnel, which wasted his time, rather than the arrival of the most serious hearing. Now that all were seated, the Court Officer, a Major in the 77th, came to stand before Miles and all fell silent.

"State your name and regiment".

"Private Thomas Miles. Light Company. 105th Foot. The Prince of Wales Own Wessex Regiment."

"Private Miles. You are charged with mutiny, in that you did threaten an Officer on the night of 19th January during the taking of Cuidad Rodrigo, namely that you threatened him with a bayonet affixed to a musket. How do you plead?"

Impatience came across Miles' face.

"Yes, I did that right enough. He were threatening I with his sword, like enough to clobber me with it. He wanted I to go dig out a dead body, when we were digging out a live 'un, so....."

At this point Picton exploded.

"Miles! This Court needs you to say guilty or not guilty! Say one or the other."

At that point Drake stood up.

"May it please the Court, Sir, in that, as Private Miles has made no allowable plea, that I enter 'not guilty on his behalf?"

Picton's face showed no improvement.

"You may. If it'll speed things up!"

Drake nodded in the direction of the Court Officer who turned to a tall Captain sat nearby.

"Captain Dunnage. You wish to address the Court?"

Dunnage stood and came forward to stand before Picton. He was plainly an Officer of independent wealth, this obvious from his immaculately tailored tunic and breeches made of the finest cloth, the ornate hand guard on his sword and, not least, the mirror finish on his sturdy black boots. Dunnage placed his shako under his right arm and held the grip of his sword in his left. Picton sat back as he began to deliver a speech both polished and well-rehearsed.

"Sir. We were down in the main breach after the explosion and I saw a buried Officer, whom I recognised. I thought it imperative that he be dug out as hastily as possible and the first available men were the group containing Private Miles. I went over to them and ordered them to follow me and rescue the Officer.

Twice they disobeyed my direct order and Miles here, threatened me with a fixed bayonet. They all continued to do what they were already doing, which was to dig out another buried body. I was completely ignored, Sir, except by Miles, who threatened my life when I gave him a direct order."

Picton sat forward.

"And that's it? Twice refused an order and threatened you with an attached bayonet?"

"Yes Sir."

A nod from Picton signalled that he need say no more and he turned to Drake as Dunnage returned to his place.

"Captain Drake!"

Drake stood and walked forward.

"Thank you, Sir."

Drake pulled himself upright and began, looking directly at Picton.

"I have some questions for Captain Dunnage, Sir."

Picton waved his hand in agreement and Drake turned around to face Dunnage, who was now stood before his chair.

"Captain Dunnage. You drew your sword, did you not, when the group refused to follow you?"

"I did not! My sword was already out. We were attacking the main breach."

Murmurs of approval came from around the room.

"Did you raise your sword over Private Miles? Such as to threaten him?"

"No!"

"And your sword was not held nor carried in any way such that Private Miles could justifiably feel threatened?"

"No!"

"And so, in your opinion, why did Private Miles threaten you with a fixed bayonet?"

"To force me to leave, so that they could continue with digging out their own body."

"And your body, an Officer, the one your wanted them to dig out. Did he survive?"

"No."

"He was killed. How?"

Dunnage's jaws came together, as though he wished to utter no words as answer, but the silence defeated him.

"Crushed!"

"With what?"

Again the pause.

"Blocks of stone."

"So, I put it to you, that, although you gave a direct order, it was in a hopeless cause. Your Officer was obviously crushed under blocks of stone. What could you see of him?"

Again the pause.

"His boots!"

Drakes expression became incredulous.

"His boots! All you could see of him, under the blocks of stone, were his boots? And that was enough for recognition?"

"Yes. They were the same as mine. Brady of Bond Street was on the sole. Their trade-mark. They were made at the same time for both of us. Recently shipped out."

Drake nodded.

"And finally, just to make it clear for the Court, at no time did you raise your sword in a threatening manner?"

"No, I did not!"

With the repeat of what he had already heard, Picton had heard enough.

"Dismissed, Dunnage."

He looked at Drake.

"Captain you have more?"

"Yes Sir. Firstly, the man Miles and his group rescued, is here now. Colour Sergeant Deakin, please to stand."

Deakin rose and came to full attention before peeling off an immaculate salute in the direction of Picton.

"Sir!"

Picton raised his hand about nine inches in acknowledgment and Deakin sat down.

"Sir. May I call forward Corporal Ezekiel Saunders of the 105th Light Company?"

"You may."

Saunders came forward to be immediately presented with a Bible, whilst Dunnage, as an Officer had not. For him, taking an Oath was considered superfluous and so Saunders swore the oath, to then state his full name, rank and regiment.

Drake turned and smiled at Saunders.

"In your own words, Corporal, describe what you saw."

Saunders drew himself up to his full, not inconsiderable, height.

"Well, Sir, being the furthest from the breach, being as we were on top the ravellin under your command, we were the last in there and most had gone on, into the town. Miles, here, saw an arm sticking out from a fall of shingle and gravel and the arm had a Colour Sergeant's badge on it and green cuff and so we began digging. An Officer came over and told us to stop and follow him to dig out an Officer. Miles told him that his Officer must be dead, under the stone blocks, whilst our man could still be alive, so he told him we were staying there. The Officer gave the order again and Miles said the same. Then the Officer raised his sword above Miles, who picked up his musket with bayonet and swung it, sort of 'en garde', at the Officer. The Officer then went away, Sir."

"If you were you Miles, at that point, what would you think?"

"That he was about to bring that sword down on me, Sir."

"Very good. Now the sequence. Sword raised first, or bayonet first?"

"Sword first, Sir. Most definite!"

Picton now sat forward.

"Saunders. Are you not in the same Section as Miles here? The same mess, even?"

"Yes to both, Sir."

Picton sat back.

"The Court can make up its own mind regarding your inclination to bend the truth in favour of your messmate!"

Saunders looked straight back at him.

"I've just took an Oath, Sir, with my hand on the Holy Bible. That should be enough to cause any man to tell the truth!"

Picton's face darkened at the challenge to his own opinion and his next words were barked out.

"Dismiss!"

Saunders came to full attention and saluted, which was left unacknowledged by Picton, but Drake continued.

"If you please, Sir, I wish to call Regimental Sergeant Major Cyrus Gibney of the 105th Foot."

Gibney's massive frame passed that of Saunders in the gangway, to arrive before Picton and take the oath and identify himself, as had Saunders.

"Sar' Major. Where were you when this incident happened."

"Sir. I wer' up on right top edge of the breach. Major Carr had left me there to care for Captain Carravoy, who were wounded, Sir. And I wer' left to bandage him up and when it wer' done, I looked down over, before moving off, an' I saw what wer' goin' on. I said to meself that it could all turn nasty."

"And you saw, what? In your own words."

"Well, ah could hear nowt, Sir, owin' to all that noise in the town, but I saw them lads diggin' out Deakin there. An Officer came to them and spoke, for about half a minute, then he raised his sword and then Deakin pointed his brumm ...... ah mean, bayonet at him, Sir. Then the Officer left, Sir."

"Would you say that Miles was menaced by the sword?"

"You'd have to, Sir."

"And please state again the order, sword first, or bayonet first?"

"Sword, Sir."

Drake nodded.

"And you saw this, despite giving Captain Carravoy the attention he needed.

"That's right, Sir. I wer' stood looking over the Captain's shoulder. Pullin' over his tunic, havin' done wi' the bandaging."

"And your opinion of Private Miles is what?"

Plainly aggrieved, Gibney turned to look at Miles, who continued to stare straight ahead.

"Too much to say for hisself, Sir. Always! He questions orders as doesn't come from an Officer, but is good in a fight, right enough. Ah'd be happy enough to have Miles stood alongside when it comes down to muzzle to muzzle with the Johnnies, and that's the truth."

Drake looked querulously at Picton, who had heard enough and waved Gibney away, but not before Gibney had come to full attention and wheeled off a salute of his own, which Picton did acknowledge. Drake then proceeded.

"Sir. My final witness is Captain Carravoy, as mention just now by RSM Gibney."

Carravoy was stood at the back and came forward to stand before Picton and state his name, rank and regiment. Within him were mixed emotions. He was in a dilemma, he was either to contradict the word of a fellow Officer and support the testimony of a mere Private, or to distort the truth and support Dunnage. Alongside that, there was his own reputation and standing within the Regiment. Miles was 105th, after all, and Carravoy's testimony would spread throughout the ranks. Thus, he stood before the glowering Picton, not in a happy state, but then Drake, the despised Drake, began addressing to him.

"Captain. As RSM Gibney has stated it, you were having your wounds dressed by him, at the top of the breach, on the opposite side to where this incident took place?'

"That is correct."

"So please tell the Court what you saw."

Carravoy took a deep breath, he had been pondering the niceties of what he could say for some time throughout the morning, despite what he had previously said to Drake the day before.

"I did not see everything, being concerned for my wound. I saw Miles and his group arrive and begin digging on the far side, then I turned away to be bandaged, then I turned when I heard shouting and saw an Officer speaking to them, then my attention turned away again. The last thing I saw, when I had been attended to, was Miles pointing his bayonet at Dunnage, then Dunnage leaving."

Drake was annoyed. This was a step down from what Carravoy had previously stated to him, but he resolved to make the best of it.

"Where was Dunnage's sword when Miles pointed his bayonet at him?"

"Hard to say."

Now Drake was annoyed.

"But, Captain, if you saw the musket and the bayonet, pointing up, you must have seen the sword. Where was it?"

"Hard to say. I was wounded."

"Was it being carried normally?"

"Hard to say. It was dark and I was in pain."

Drake's jaw came together.

"But can you at least say if RSM Gibney was in a good position to observe events?"

"Yes. If he was looking."

"He stated that everything was in front of him as he applied the bandage. Indeed, when he had finished, the episode had not then played out."

"I suppose that is true."

"And you did not look?"

"No."

"Not as much as he did?"

"No."

"Thank you, Captain."

Picton leaned forward.

"Captain!"

Carravoy came to full attention.

"You say you could not see the sword. Therefore, is it reasonable to assume that it was not raised, but lowered?"

Carravoy took a deep breath. This was the vital question.

"It is possible, Sir, that the sword had been lowered just before I turned around."

"You turned to see Miles still pointing his bayonet at Dunnage's throat!"

"The bayonet was still raised. Sir."

A nod and a wave of his hand, told Carravoy that he was dismissed and he gratefully hurried to his seat.

Drake turned to Picton.

"I have another witness, Sir."

Picton glowered.

"Will he say anything different to what has already been said? Another messmate. Will he add anything?"

"Probably not, Sir. He will corroborate what has already been said."

"Then no."

Picton looked up at Dunnage.

"Captain. Have you anything to say, before the defence makes their final statement?"

Dunnage stood.

"At no time did I raise my sword to threaten anyone. I gave a direct order, twice, and both were ignored. Then I was threatened with a bayonet."

The response was a guffaw from Miles which Drake hoped that Picton did not hear and so he quickly began his own statement, after Dunnage had resumed his seat.

"Sir. It is clear, I believe, that Private Miles acted in response to an extreme threat, a threat that could easily have ended his life, this being a sword raised above him. Whatever the difference in rank, everyone has a right to defend their own life, which is what Miles did. And it was, Sir, a reasonable response to a threat to his own life, it was a defensive posture only. He went no further, there followed no thrust with the bayonet."

Drake paused to allow that to be absorbed.

"Miles is not the best disciplined soldier, but his record with the 105th, is much to his credit. He fought at Maida, during the Sicily campaign of Sir John Stuart's, and defended the castle of Scilla. He was the first into the French line at Rolica, at least on our left flank and he fought at Vimeiro. He served well during the retreat to Corunna and was with his Light Company holding the farmhouse that broke up the French attacks on Elvina during the battle which followed that retreat. He was one of the first over the Douro at Oporto and was wounded at Talavera. He fought alongside me, in my Light Company, for the two days of Busaco. He was in action at Sabugal, Fuentes de Onoro, and the recent siege of Cuidad. In the light of this record and the reasonable possibility in his favour that he acted to defend himself, I ask that the Court view the charge of mutiny as altogether too extreme. Sir. Disrespect, is surely the most he can be found guilty of."

Drake sat down as Picton leaned forward, forearms flat on the table, his face plainly showing his irritation. Almost unprecedented in a mind that operated on such black and white principles as his, he could see no simple way through. Instant obedience to orders, any orders, was all that could ever satisfy him. He looked at the defendant.

"Miles!"

Miles came to full attention.

"Sir."

"The charge is mutiny, Miles. You know what that means if I find you guilty. It means the rope!"

"Yes Sir, I knows that."

"Will you accept my verdict or should all go before a Lieutenant General and be heard again?"

"Your verdict, Sir. That'll do for me."

Picton sat back, now he had no choice but to think. Instinctively, he detested disobedience and Miles, obviously not the most disciplined soldier, had ignored a direct order twice and no Officer had supported his story about being threatened by a sword. However, he had acted to successfully save the life of a comrade and any death sentence had to be confirmed by an authority higher than himself. Wellington probably would not and 'Daddy' Hill, or Graham definitely would not. In addition, here was a veteran soldier who had held his place in the face of the enemy many times and there was enough testimony to say that he had been threatened with a weapon, therefore enough that his life should not be forfeit. He sat back and picked up the hammerless pistol that served as a gavel.

"One dozen! Laid on!"

The pistol came down with a crash and then Picton stood and exited through a door behind him. As he was led away, Miles turned and grinned at his three, tilting back his head as he did so, in a "that'll be alright" gesture. The room emptied and Drake and Carravoy left the building together, but Carravoy could not meet the fierce gaze that he knew was turned upon him by Drake. The three, Davey, Deakin and Saunders were required, as 'rank' to leave only after the higher personages had left, and so they stood together waiting, Davey the most concerned.

"One dozen, Jed, on the triangle. That's bad!"

Deakin looked at him.

"Well, perhaps, but then, you sees, there's triangle, yes. On the other hand, there's triangle!"

Utterly bemused, Davey followed Saunders and Deakin out of the building.

oOo

Whilst that trial was ending, another was just beginning, but with nothing like the formality of Picton's Court, this with a great deal more emotion, of both fear and jubilation, and the verdict already decided, so it would appear, with a garrotte frame prominent in the midst of all there present. Almost as prominent as the frame, Julian Sanchez stood in the Square of the village of Vilar Formoso and all around the sides of the Square, sometimes six deep, stood the local population who had made the journey from some miles around. Their conversation changed to growls of anger as the accused were brought in, all 'afrencados', those accused of aiding or collaborating with the French. There were four; two were obvious traitors, still wearing their French uniform, they had been captured by the Portuguese and handed over to their allies, the Spanish guerrillas. Another was an unmarried mother with a babe in arms, the father a Spaniard now dead. Shunned by all as unmarried with a bastard child, she had taken up with a French Corporal, the pair spending their last days together in Cuidad. So now, whilst he was being marched off to the coast as a prisoner-of-war, she had no choice but to return to her village to hope for mercy from her family, but they remained as hard-hearted towards her as they had at the time when she became pregnant and had then disowned her. Once back in the village and infamous for her French liaison, she had been pounced on by the guerrillas. The fourth was Fra. Pedro Estaves. He had been pointed out to Sanchez by the locals, suspicions about him having been aroused because, while the Allies and French confronted each other either side of the Agueda, he had passed over the bridge at Barba del Puerco too many times to the French side that could be justified, when his Parish was entirely on the village side of the Agueda. Further, it was evident, that while his Spanish flock around him endured near starvation during such lean times, he lived well, with no need for any frugality. A conversation with Colonel Waters about information reaching Massena during the Easter past and the suspicions of the local people, were enough for Sanchez to send his men to the Chapel above the Agueda gorge and drag him forth.

Waters stood at the edge of the crowd as the four were herded forward. Beside him stood Radipole, as much for his own experience as for any help he could give, but his powers of clear thinking had proved more than useful. They watched, jaws tightening and breathing uneasily as the two soldiers were summarily despatched by the gruesome garrotte, each remaining in the frame for a good three minutes as the screw remained fully tightened and the rope bit into their throats, their tongues protruding and their eyes wide open and bulging. All the while the crowd cheered, the joy at their execution being the final sound that each soldier heard. The body of each was cast into the dust and, with both now dead, a team of mules was brought in and the pair were dragged together from the Square at a pace slow enough to allow many to spit on the dusty corpses, both still wearing the hated uniform.

Then came the woman, still clutching her child. Sanchez spoke the 'charge' against her, then many screamed from all sides, the most frequent word being 'afrencado' or 'puta Francesa'. With each shouted accusation, her shape and demeanour sunk down further and several times, as if these were their final moments together, she looked into the face of her child. Sanchez walked forward and raised his arms to call for silence.

"Hay alguien que hable en favor de la mujer?"

Waters turned to Radipole.

"He's asking if there is anyone who will speak in her favour."

Almost immediately a man stepped forward. A big man, clearly able to back up with brawny arms and fists, whatever came from his mouth.

"Para evitar que el niño viva. Vivimos en tiempos difíciles. Fue su unica manera de salvar la vido de su nino!"

Growls of disapproval came as response to his words, but he dismissed all with a contemptuous wave of his hand as he walked back to his place. Waters again leaned towards Radipole.

"He says she took up with the Corporal to save her child's life. These are difficult times."

Radipole looked concerned.

"That should keep her out of that hideous contraption, should it not?"

Waters turned to him.

"Spain and its people have suffered appallingly during the occupation, Radipole. Revenge is the uppermost emotion now, not mercy."

However, at that moment, one of Sanchez' Lieutenants walked to his side and spoke softly to him. Sanchez grinned and raised his arms once more.

"Hay alguien aquí dispuesto a asumir esta mujer y garantizar su buena conducta?"

Waters grinned.

"He's asking if anyone will take this woman on and guarantee her conduct."

Radipole let out a sigh.

"Here's hoping!"

This was not in vain. A man, tall, mid-thirties and with all the decorations and trophies of a veteran guerrilla, French breeches and boots and a multiplicity of ribbons, buckles and buttons, walked forward, carrying a big stick. He walked up to the woman, whacked her on the rump with the stick and pushed her out of the centre of the Square. Hoots of laughter came from all around, whilst the expression on the woman's face changed from resignation of imminent death to one of bewilderment, followed by one of questioning, as she looked at the character who was now to be her man. To more laughter, the pair disappeared through the crowd, the guerrilla's hand between her shoulder blades, the baby held close.

Then came Fra. Estaves. He was placed in the centre, but this time there was silence, Estavez was, after all, a Man of the Cloth. Sanchez spent some time describing the reasons why the Priest had been accused as 'afrencado', and Sanchez last words to him were for Estavez to explain why he made all the visits over the Agueda, why he had been seem talking to French soldiers in San Felices, way over on the French side, and why he was not as starved and thin as everyone else was, this last bringing forth laughter from the crowd.

Estavez stood terrified and silent and the seconds passed to become a minute. All waited, but nothing came, finally Estavez fell to his knees, hands together pleading, his voice broken and weeping.

"Yo confieso! Pido misericordia."

Sanchez walked forward to stand over him.

"Confesar lo que?"

"Dio tres mensajes a los franceses a la Cuidad. De la Capilla en Barca del Puerco."

Involuntarily, Waters gripped Radipole's arm.

"He's just confessed to giving three messages to the French in Cuidad! Using the Chapel at Barba del Puerco. That's the only usable bridge over the Agueda."

With that Waters barged through the crowd to go and stand just behind Sanchez. His words to Sanchez were urgent and overheard by the Friar, who immediately raised his head to see Sanchez nod agreement.

"Le prometo una muerte rápida si da los días o meses."

Hearing the promise of a quick death rather than the gruesome garrotte, if he gave details of when, the Priest shuffled forward on his knees.

"Si, si! Enero, Marzo y Abril."

Waters heard the word for April. He was now addressing Estavez.

"Quando en Abril?"

"Dos días después del domingo de Pascua. En La Feria de Abril."

Waters was taken aback. Estavez was saying that he had picked up the letter two days after Easter Sunday. The four of the Lords Committee had been with Wellington during that the Easter weekend and they had departed three days after that Sunday. It would take but a moment with a calendar to confirm, but if Estavez was saying two days after Easter, that was the day Templemere went for a wander, as Waters put it to himself. They had all departed the following day! So, had the Friar read the note?

"Lieste la nota?"

"No! Que me ordenó de no romper el sello."

He had been ordered not to break the seal. Waters took a deep breath. This was crucial, then he remembered his promise to Estavez and he drew out his own pistol and offered it to Sanchez, who shook his head.

"No cumplir promesas a la escoria de Afrencado como este!"

Estavez heard the words and began to wail for mercy, the sound of which intensified as two guerrillas came to drag him towards the garrotte frame with the burly executioner stood ready and waiting. Waters was plainly not happy with this outcome, but he returned his pistol to its holster and walked away, speaking softly but still audibly, for Sanchez to hear.

"The day will come when you will need to keep your promises, Juliano. Whoever you make them to!"

It was the following day, when Waters and Radipole were long gone to the coast, that the triangle was set up in a field just outside Zamara. The 105th had no halberds, their Colour Sergeants carried muskets as a battle honour in recognition of their service at Maida and so the halberds that always formed the triangle were borrowed from the 88th. The Battalion was paraded around three sides of a square, the triangle a feature of the fourth side, with the Battalion Drummers paraded just behind it. The Followers were arranged behind whichever part of the square they chose. With all stood 'at ease' but in place, Miles was brought into the square, after a short walk from the nearest houses of Zamarra. He took himself to the halberds and stood before them, waiting. A drummer approached and freed his wrists to enable Miles to take off his own shirt. His back showed several scars from previous floggings, but there was something noticeable about the sheen on his back, as remarked on by Lacey to O'Hare.

"What's that, spread over his back?"

O'Hare folded his arms and grinned a little.

"Oh, nothing at all! Dismiss the thought. Would it not be natural for a man to sweat up a little before a flogging? 'Tis perspiration, nothing more!"

Lacey's brows came together, whilst O'Hare pursed his lips, to prevent himself grinning any more. By now, Miles had offered his wrists to be rebound together and then a line was attached to the binding, thrown over the join of the halberds and Miles was hauled upright by three Bandsmen, with both arms stretched upwards. That done, Miles, who well knew the procedure, had spread his legs to the front two halberds, for his ankles to be lashed to each. He then opened his mouth for the wad of leather to be inserted between his teeth and for the attached strings to be tied behind his head. Lastly, he pressed his chest up to the halberd crosspiece, this half way up and parallel to the ground, which would prevent him from leaning forward and riding the blow. Then the Battalion Drum Major came forward carrying a linen bag, to first inspect both the lashings and the frame. Those studying carefully would have noticed that they exchanged a few brief words, then he walked to his position and, from the linen bag he pulled out the cat o' nine tails, which he combed out to separate each strand. He then positioned himself to administer the flogging, the 'cat' thrown out behind him, his arm back, ready for the first. RSM Gibney, stood not far from the halberds, drew in a deep breath.

"Battalion! Atten shun!"

The whole of the 105th came to full attention and the Drum Major turned his head to look at Lacey who nodded. The long drum roll began and the 'cat' whistled through the air to land with a flat slap on Miles' back. He was thrown forward against the crosspiece, then he sucked back into his lungs the breath that had been beaten out, rolled his shoulders and stood waiting for the second. This came, causing the same effect. On it went, up to seven, when Surgeon Pearce stepped forward to examine, not Miles' back, but whether he was still conscious and if the punishment could continue. Miles turned his head to look at him, nodded, and then Pearce turned to nod at Lacey. At this signal, the Drum Major continued, up to the twelve and it was only on the eleventh stroke that blood began to flow. After the final blow, Miles raised himself to his full height and the rope over the halberds was released, as were his wrists and ankles, then he took some time to gather himself by leaning on the halberds. Gibney ordered the parade 'at ease' followed quickly by 'parade dismiss', and Lacey looked at O'Hare.

"Didn't Picton order 'laid on'?"

O'Hare folded his arms again.

"Oh he did! For certain! And had he been here, he would not have been disappointed, of that I'm sure."

Meanwhile, Miles remained leaning on the frame.

"Throw some water on me back, mates. It needs coolin'!"

A bucket of water, then a second, was thrown by two Bandsmen and Miles at last pushed himself away from the frame to support himself. That done, unusually within the ritual, the Drum Major walked behind the halberds, which Miles noticed, for him to then send a nod in the direction of his erstwhile tormentor. This was acknowledged in the same manner and the frame was dismantled to leave Miles stood upright, flexing his arms. As the parade was dismissed, Bridie, Nellie and Consuela came running forward followed by Davey, Deakin et al. Bridie held the muslin and Nellie the bucket full of very salty water and Miles now lay face down for the muslin to be applied and salt water tipped over. The salt stung and Miles clenched his teeth, as the ritual but vital aftermath of any flogging was carried out. Then he stood, the muslin still applied, this now stained pink from the several cuts, but Miles could walk unaided and slowly they took themselves to their billets in the barn. There Miles sat, unmoving whilst Nellie, of all people, brought him some tea. Deakin came to sit near.

"That's one we owes that Drum Major."

Miles looked at him, because he preferred not to nod.

"No need! There's no debt, as he told I when the lashings was goin' on, an' that goose-grease helped. Helped all to slide off without doin' too much harm."

Then Miles did nod, seemingly satisfied.

"Ah well. I've had a worse dozen, an' that's a fact!"

The muslin remained in place for the rest of the day and also the following night, then more bathing in salt water was applied first thing the next morning. Secondly came a thorough, but careful use of a towel, which caused the cuts to stop bleeding and to dry, which would begin the process of healing. Lastly, goose-grease, which had cost both billets all of their tobacco, was applied to the welts that were sore and striped, but not an open wound.

Thus the 105th settled into cantonment routine and adding to their creature comforts, however, the Officers of the Light Company were not quite sure how far that could go, this being the question prominent in the mind of Nathaniel Drake, now stood looking at the few sticks of furniture that provided comfort in their own billet. Carr was present, lounging on his camp bed, somewhere between sleeping and waking, but it was to him that Drake addressed his comments.

"Do you think we should get someone in to add a bit of, ah, security, to these odd chairs and whatnot. I fear that one of these collapsing under me would do me more harm than the French did before Cuidad."

Carr did not open his eyes.

"Perhaps the worst, but leave the rest."

Then he rolled over and was soon asleep. Drake examined all, to identify the worst, this piece having several joints that had parted company. He took it to the doorway and placed it outside.

"Morrison!"

"Sir."

"See if you can get this fixed!"

Morrison hurried from his own small portion of home that existed in the passageway and picked up the chair, but Drake had already closed the door to now choose a safer chair and sit at the table. He then noticed Maltby's chest awaiting collection by the wall, with the new addition of Rushby's alongside, stating as its owner, 'Ensign Stuart Rushby'. At that moment, the same entered the room, brimming with news.

"The siege train's moved off, going South. With many French heavies from Cuidad tacked on."

Drake looked over at him, but not with any pleasure at the news.

"That means Badajoz. And that'll be twice as bad as this performance here."

Rushby was somewhat deflated.

"Well, there is something to cheer us up. Wallace is organising another Irish concert with his 88th. Pipes and dancing and whatnot. The Highland 74th are doing something and the Colonel thinks that we should too. He was thinking Morrismen. Being Wessex, we should be able to dredge up something, shouldn't we?"

Drake allowed his forehead to fall on the table.

"Bloody Wallace and his bloody 88th! I've not got over that last drone, before we left here for the lines."

At this point Carr did roll over.

"Don't be too hard on Wallace, he's doing his best to lift his Brigade after Cuidad. His 88th lost 34 and the 74th lost 21. I know we lost the most, but they took their share."

Drake was somewhat chastened, but not thoroughly.

"Well, it's not their efforts at the breach that I include in that, not at all. It's simply Irish music, if that's the flattering term that can be applied."

Rushby frowned.

"Well, I find most of it jolly enough, and some Highland dancing. You'd have to pay a price, back in London."

Drake guffawed.

"Not me! They'd have to pay me, to sit through such as that."

Rushby laughed, then changed the subject.

"Do you think we'll get any replacements before we try Badajoz?"

Drake shook his head.

"Not a chance!"

At that very moment, there was more head shaking in the barn on hearing words from Ethan Ellis that echoed the earlier words of Rushby.

"Colonel wants any as can Morris dance, up to the town square. There's to be a bit of an entertainment, with the 88th and 74th. Any here?"

It was Deakin who answered.

"Not here, Ethan. All we've here is criminals and long servers. None as've ever been part of any Morris caper."

At this, John Davey sat upright.

"Hang on, now. I've done a bit, afore I was took for a poacher. Being up with the Morrismen gave you a turn at the barrel, put up by the local Squire."

Deakin laughed.

"Ah! Which he regretted when he found you up before him, for the sake of two brace of pheasants!"

Ellis permitted himself a small chuckle, then to business.

"Right, up to Headquarters. All is to happen come three days' time."

He turned to leave, then he saw Miles, lying flat on his stomach.

"How's the patient?"

It was Miles who answered.

"Doin' fine 'till you showed up!"

Ellis nodded.

"Hmmm. Getting better!"

With that he left, followed by Davey.

In the event, Drake's taste in music was given a minor reprieve. The performance was set back to the first week in February, for the evening of the 4th. When the date arrived, he was cajoled into attending, and he assented, "Marginally better than staring at a blank wall!" At the finish, even he could feel that the performances with the different Celtic and Gaelic pipes could be described as 'accomplished', and that of their own Morrismen, to the accompaniment of a 'squeeze-box', was also very praiseworthy. The group managed two rather complicated dances and so the 105th were not in any way outdone by measure of quality. The following day came the order to be ready to march South and thus, on the 6th, the Third Division set out on the road South, all relieved to hear that it was to be the easier route of Sabugal and Castello-Branco, on the Portuguese side of the Sierras that separated the two countries, not over the dreaded Sierra de Gata.

On the 5th, the day before they marched out, Deakin had required Miles to stand up straight before him, so that he could examine his back. It was not long before he shook his head.

"Thy back could wear a tunic, but carry no load. That could be spread about over the lads, but perhaps we don't have to straight away, if we can work a trick. Two days without that will help us all. I'll see what we can come up with!"

Thus, as a result of Deakin's 'trick', when the 105th formed up on the road through Zamarra, Tom Miles was following his kit into the rear of the Reverend Albright's cart. Deakin had had a word with Sedgwicke, who went to his Superior, to explain, albeit half-truthfully.

"Sir, it is generally the case that any man recently flogged is excused the wearing of a heavy pack and equipment on the march, because, after all, it makes sense that he should heal quickly and become an effective soldier once again. Could he not ride in the back of our cart for one day, at least?"

The Reverend nodded sagely.

"It is surely the case, that this man has borne his chastisement and that we should now aid him back to the path of righteousness and to walk forgiven in the sight of The Lord."

The cart jerked forward when Sedgwicke whipped up the mules and Miles braced himself against his pack, this also cushioned by his blanket, his feet firm on the far side boards as he looked out of the canvas opening to see the buildings of Zamarra passing by, the citizens waving their thanks and farewells. As the day wore on, Miles eased his back contentedly against the blanket, he had no complaints, only thanks, that he was being spared the effort of marching with a heavy load on a raw back and shoulders. Then the Reverend Albright came back from the front seat.

"Would you count yourself as a Christian Soul? Would you, soldier?"

On hearing the questions spoken, Sedgwicke, occupied with the mules, felt his stomach sink far below his belt. He had known Tom Miles over several years and well appreciated his inclination to say exactly what he thought to any question, from whatever source, but his apprehension lifted slightly on hearing Miles' reply.

"Well now, Reverend, if you could give me some idea of just what that might mean, then I'll try to tell you just how much I measures up to it."

It took a while for Albright himself to think of a definition of his own and so the reply emerged more as a string of possibilities, rather than any cogent definition.

"It means that you live your life within God's grace, fearing him and his Wrath when you behave sinfully, that of course, but it also means doing your best to live according to his Word, as taught to us in the Bible."

There came a pause as he sought for a few more stock phrases.

"That you fear for the good of your Soul come your judgement at the Gates of Heaven and that in any times of peril and hardship you bear such with fortitude, trusting in God as your Saviour and that your welfare lies within his Dear Hands, as all good Christians believe."

Miles took a deep breath.

"Well, Sir, I can't say as I does much to show myself a Christian, I'm not one to pray every night, nor anything such as that, but I'll join in with the others when there's a Service as before a battle or such. That as much to stand with my mates, stood together, sort of thing, because there's one thing I knows, Reverend, which bein' that my welfare rests with that, there."

He pointed to his perfectly maintained Baker rifle, propped beside him.

"When we'n out front before the line, how good I am with that and how good my two file mates is with theirs, that's where my welfare lies. If they and I puts the Frogs down, then we all stays alive. Each caring for the others, so to speak."

Albright's brows came together.

"Do I take it that you have more faith in your fellow man than in the Lord, your Saviour?"

Sedgwicke's stomach sank another two inches.

Miles looked at Albright carefully, almost indulgently.

"Well Sir, how it strikes me is that what happens up in Heaven, as is recorded against my name, in the balance, as I've been taught, is one thing, but what happens down 'ere is another. Down here what we lives through is closer to Hell than anything to do with Heaven and when we has to face up to the Johnnies, I knows for certain that they has nothing like my welfare in mind. In fact, just the opposite, Sir, but is they all part of God's plan? So, Sir, my faith has to lie with John and Joe, same as they has it in me."

Such a blunt denial, and the clear disparagement of anyone who had more faith in concepts spiritual, than human actions temporal, set Albright back for a good few seconds, but he soon found another tenet of his own beliefs.

"The Lord is all knowing, all seeing, ever present and all powerful. To place your future within his good grace is truly the one and only way to salvation."

Miles was slowly becoming impatient with this man, who plainly came from a world utterly different to the brutality and perils of his own.

"I have to tell thee, Reverend, that salvation to me has two meanings, followin' the Commandments, right enough, but staying alive as well and whatever that takes. Seems to me, Reverend, that them as believes such as you've been talking about, should be more than happy to put themselves in harm's way, 'cos the Lord is takin' all good care. Well, I've been wounded twice, and I do thank the Good Lord that I'm still above ground, but I knows one thing, that it could well be that both bullets as hit I, were maybe not too well aimed for fear of shots comin' from my two mates, all workin' alongside me."

300

Sedgwicke could hear the impatience in the voice of Miles and the astonishment in that of Albright and he was convinced that this would not end well, but salvation came, coming nearer as their cart progressed along the road. At the beginning of Aldea de Ponte there was an ornate and well maintained Calvary, the crucified figure of Christ new painted and the roof overall new and solid.

"Look, Sir, Mr. Albright. Is that not an uplifting thing to see?"

He slowed the cart to a mere creep forward, as Albright came forward to look for himself, to see a British shako placed at the foot of the crucifix. Albright's hands came together in delight.

"It is Private, indeed it is. That those whom we have saved from Godless men, regard our artefacts to be worthy of inclusion in the representations of the Faith that upholds them."

"Yes indeed, Sir, now perhaps you would like to sit up here now and acknowledge the thanks of the people of this town, the same that saw fit to include that symbol of our efforts within their Holy Shrine."

Smiling beatifically, Albright climbed over the driver's seat to take his place and, indeed, to wave acknowledgment of the plaudits from the people of Aldea de Ponte, whose homes they had stood to defend but three months ago. Miles, however, as the cart passed by, turned his head to see what had been so remarkable and when he saw, he let out a snort of disgust.

"And what happened to the head of the poor bugger as used to wear it?"

oOo

On the far side of the Sierra de Gata, all of Wellington's cavalry were set to watch his flank, as if those bleak mountains were not enough protection. Anson's Brigade, the 14th and 16th Light Dragoons were now halted on the far side of the range summit, therefore now in Spain proper. The village that they were in had a name almost unpronounceable to all, Descargomaria, but most had tried as they entered the frozen collection of low buildings, forming a village huddled and clinging to a coll on the Eastern slope. The inhabitants had made no protest at both horses and men being crammed into every building, both domestic and agricultural, for they well understood that it was too great a risk for the horses to be left out, exposed on the bleak hillside, there to be rendered frozen by the chill East wind.

Thus, with the horses downstairs, amidst the domestic pots and furniture, the men crowded the attic in the roof-space, where they could sleep warm, and grateful, that all that disturbed them of the hard wind on the other side of the tiles and slates was the odd draught and a low shriek as the current swirled around some obstacle. However, not all slept, at least not yet, because Withers was passing on the orders received from Anson to his Majors and Captains. As an aid he had a map, spread on a board which was supported by his own knees. His finger traced their required route, as specified to Anson by Stapleton-Cotton, Withers pronouncing the village names in the best English way that he could.

"We go through Cadalso, Pozuelo, then halt at Montehermoso. From there we do what's important, because our main job is to see what's in Plasencia. That's an important town and, if Johnny's still in our vicinity, he'll be in there and Cotton wants that found out. Slade, Alten and De Grey's Brigades are further South investigating Trujilo, Miajades and Merida. The Peer wants word of any Johnnies still in the Tagus valley before he begins at Badajoz. Preferably none, as you can imagine."

Major Johnson leaned forward, the better to study the map.

"Two days to get here, two more to get down onto the plain. We'll have to buy fodder from those villages. What's on our mule train is almost gone, used to get us here."

"I know and we've Spanish coin for that. You know Wellington's orders; 'pay for everything'. He doesn't want the Spanish rising up behind us, as they did for the French."

He rolled up the map.

"Right. Eat, sleep, then off and get further down. The quicker we are further down, all the better. How these people live this far up here beats me!"

So it was the following day that the march continued, with all riding in pairs, their cavalry cloaks fully spread and dropped to boot level. Carr and Peterson, being so far from the enemy, or so they thought, saw justification enough to ride together away from their Troops, Peterson beginning the main conversation, simply and bluntly.

"He's going for Badajoz!"

Carr looked at him, his eyes just above the high collar of his cloak.

"And that's significant?"

301

"Yes! That's the toughest, bar Elvas, that's impossible, but we hold that, just six miles down the road from Badajoz which is still held by the French. Somewhat remarkable, don't you think?"

"Not really, it strikes me that no-one in this austere and desolate country starts anything unless there's a very good chance of success, or unless absolutely ordered to, as I suppose Napoleon's Generals are."

Peterson nodded inside his own high collar.

"I would suspect that you are correct in that, but when it comes to breaking into cities, be grateful that you are riding that nag and not amongst the infantry, who have to do the job."

Carr demonstrated mock umbrage.

"I resent that, or at least my latest mount does. I've grown rather fond of her and have given her a name, 'Jenny', which I like. My first affections were in the direction of a girl called Jenny, and I think that to be rather appropriate."

Peterson laughed.

"So, it's appropriate for a horse that you've got affections for and thereby you bring it up to the equal of this 'Jenny'!"

Both laughed as a flurry of snow, swirled and curled around the close formed column, but all progress was now downward and the following two nights were spent in Wither's named villages. Whilst the distances were short, the roads were poor and always covered in snow up to the horses' knees, therefore Withers often ordered 'dismount' and the horses were led carefully forward. As they entered each village, the citizens scurried away in fright, certain that the two long columns of riders were French, but all minds were set at ease when their guide went forward to ask, loudly, for fodder for the horses whilst holding a bag of coin above his head. The last leg of their journey was to Montehermoso and this was the easiest, a straight, undulating road with a minor blanket of snow that barely covered the horses' hooves. They entered the village to find Anson already there, in the village square consulting with many horsemen, these obviously guerrillas. Withers turned to Johnson.

"Hold the men here. I need to see what Anson has in mind."

The column of the 16th halted and Withers rode forward, the guerrillas parting to allow him through.

"Sir!"

Anson turned to meet him.

"This is Mateo, the local Commander."

On hearing his name, the guerrilla stood in his stirrups and essayed a bow.

"Buenos dias, Senor."

Withers nodded his own acknowledgement as Anson continued.

"He says that there may still be French in Plasencia, but there is another village a short way up, just before it, but over the river Alagon. This village, Carcaboso, is just before yet another river, the Jerte and just beyond that is Plasencia. If there are significant French in there, those rivers will protect us."

He looked again down the road out of the town that would be their future way forward.

"The 14th will stay here. Withers, yours and I will go forward into this Carcaboso place and then we'll make up our minds about Plasencia."

'Sir!"

"Right, you go on with these irregulars and hold at Carcaboso. I'll talk to Dodds first with orders for his 14th, then I'll catch you up."

With that, he wheeled his horse and cantered off followed by his two Aides. With that Mateo rode up to Withers.

"I lead, yes? You follow. Is not far."

Withers nodded and Mateo led his band of 40 or so out of the village using the main road. Withers waved his column forward and as they passed it, Carr pointed out to Peterson, the road sign which stated; 'Carcoboso 4. Plasencia 7.'

"What do those numbers mean? Not miles I hope."

"Spanish Leagues perhaps, but at least it means that we're on the right road."

The road was again straight and level until they were required to dip down to the bridge that crossed the Alagon, a substantial stream now surging between the buttresses, the fierce current swelled with meltwater. It was not long before Anson galloped up to overtake them and again they found themselves on a road even more straight and level than previously. Thus, within what seemed a short time, they entered the village of Carcaboso, where Mateo found some inhabitants and engaged them in urgent conversation, before coming over to Anson and Withers.

"I am said that there are French in Plasencia. Maybe many."

Anson looked at Withers, plainly concerned, then back to Mateo.

"Many? Has he no idea?"

Mateo then shouted back to the man, who held up the fingers of both hands, twice, then he shrugged his shoulders before indicating ten more. Mateo turned back to Anson.

"He say viente, around. Perhaps treinta."

Anson turned to Withers.

"Thirty! Get your Captains up here. They need to know what's to happen."

The call went back down the column and so Tavender, Oakwood, Somers-Cocks and Myers soon arrived, then Anson looked at Mateo.

"This next river, can you cross it and get behind Plasencia?"

Mateo nodded.

"Senor, no need. Plasencia is this bank of Jerte, but long way round. Is big bend, as you say. Is small river into the Jerte between, but easy to cross. This road has bridge over Jerte up to Plasencia."

Immediately concerned that the main river did not give the protection first described, Anson continued, indicating an encircling motion with his hand.

"Can you get around Plasencia with yours while I'll send a Squadron forward to the bridge to come up to it from this side?"

Mateo nodded vigorously, whilst grinning with his white teeth.

"Si Senor, yes, but to come in behind we must ride wide. Follow big bend of Jerte."

He gave a full sweep with his arm.

"Wide, to not be seen!"

"How long?"

Mateo thought.

"One glass of sand!"

Withers leaned over to talk to Anson.

"I think he means an hour, Sir."

"Perhaps we should send a Squadron with him?"

"That will do no harm, but a whole Squadron, Sir? Mateo has 40 and one Section will double that, making 80 men! It's only to take a look."

Tavender had, as had the other three Captains, heard all.

"Cornet Carr, of Captain Oakwood's, has had much experience with guerrillas, Sir. Perhaps even with this band."

Anson looked at Withers, who nodded to confirm, then speak confirmation.

"True, and as good a choice as any!"

"Right, Captain Oakwood. Tell Cornet Carr of his mission, with his Troop to accompany Mateo here, on the wide sweep to Plasencia. Captain Tavender!"

"Sir! This spoken with a tone of triumph.

"After one hour, you cross the river Jerte at the bridge and get into Plasencia from this side. If Carr is in trouble, you go in to occupy the French and give him a chance to pull back the way he came. Clear? We will hold here."

Tavender saluted Anson as Oakwood turned his horse and trotted back to Two Squadron, where he found Carr and Peterson together.

"Carr, your Troop are off with the guerrillas, to get around the back of this Plasencia place and see if any Johnnies are in residence. It's you, because Captain Tavender made Anson aware of your experience with the irregulars. So, you have him to thank for it!"

Carr looked at Peterson with a wry look on his face, but there was no look of such understanding nor accommodation on the face of Sergeant Baxter, nor Corporal Makepeace, the former voicing the opinion of both.

"That bastard Tavender! Because of his down on Carr, we're to go around the back of some dung pile into God-knows-what with a bunch of ragged-arsed irregulars for support! We could be cut off by a whole Brigade of Johnnies!"

Meanwhile more information was forthcoming from Oakwood.

"Tavender's whole Squadron will be supporting you from this side. At a bridge. They move forward up to Plasencia after one hour. Do you have a watch?"

"Yes Sir."

"Then take your men forward."

Carr looked behind him to see whom he needed.

"Sergeant!"

"Sir!"

The Section trotted forward alongside the column and, when at the head of the 16th, Carr gave Tavender merely a glance but enough to register the look of satisfaction on the latter's face, however, Tavender himself noticed the glowering look on the faces of both Baxter and Makepeace. Up with Anson, cheerful expressions greeted Carr, especially Mateo.

"Hola! Senor Carr. See you again is good. I see you are well!"

Carr waved and grinned a reply, but much more demonstrative were the guerrillas when they saw Baxter, Makepeace and Spivey. Especially the last, when they saw him, they pointed, before slapping their own foreheads in memory of the vicious head-butt that he had delivered on one of the French Hussars alongside the river Gevora, back in the Summer. Anson leaned forward.

"Seems you all know each other, Carr!"

"Yes Sir, we've met before."

"Right! Mateo leads, you follow. Captain Tavender will be on the outskirts of our side of the town in one hour. If you need support he'll come in to distract any French attention you may get and you can withdraw the way you came."

He leaned forward for added emphasis.

"You are going to take a look Carr, not to engage. Our business is to find out and then get back to tell the tale. Am I clear?"

"Yes Sir. Absolutely."

Anson sat back.

"What time have you got?"

Carr pulled out his watch.

"12:20, Sir."

"Very well. Off you go."

Anson looked over to Mateo and waved him forward, for his men to then canter after him, many still slapping their foreheads when they saw Spivey, which at least brought a grin from him and his companions. In a double column, Carr led his men to follow.

The ride was along a shallow valley and, as more of the distance was covered, Carr's admiration for the irregulars grew. Always there were two scouts, out front left and right and also two outriders, to their right, the Plasencia side, who regularly rode to the ridge to scout, but never remaining for more than brief seconds. They came to a wide stream and at that point Carr looked at his watch to see 12.45, but the stream was crossed by a rustic bridge of stone slabs, cartwheel grooves deep in the stone. They cantered on and Carr was conscious that their wide sweep outwards was ending, as they now tended markedly right. Their route was across dry, dusty slopes only fit for stunted olive trees, but soon after the stone bridge Mateo halted his men and Carr rode to the front. The halt had been called just below the brow of a hill and Mateo dismounted and gestured for Carr to do the same. Another guerrilla dismounted and with the reins of the three horses in the hands of a fourth, the three walked carefully up the slope, just enough to see over. Mateo pointed and Carr saw for himself a town built on its own hill.

"Is Plasencia. Has murallas, how you say?'

"Walls!"

"Si, walls, around all."

Carr was now very worried and would have spoken out but Mateo was busy with a stick and he drew a roughly oblong shape in the dust.

"Is two doors this side."

He marked both in the side they faced, one in the centre, the second closer to the left-hand corner.

"Is Plaza here and road to Plaza from both."

He marked the plaza then drew the two streets to it from the gates.

"I think is best, half yours on foot, half follow with horses. Same for me. With horses out quick run if many French, si? Keep horses outside gate."

Carr nodded. Mateo was making sense, but this had now become more than just a 'look'. They had no choice, this was a walled town, they had to enter if they were to discover anything useful and factual. Now Mateo had drawn the course of the river alongside a section of the wall.

"The river here, there is another door at the bridge over, but we not use, your camaradas will come to the bridge. We go in here and here, these two. We both get to plaza. French at plaza if in Plasencia."

Mateo had indicated the central gate for the 16th, then he looked at Carr, looking questioningly at him.

"Agreed Mateo, but careful, si?"

Mateo replied slowly and purposefully.

"Si, Senor Carr. Careful, si, mucho!"

Within minutes Carr was back with Baxter.

"This place has walls Sergeant. This is no ordinary town."

Baxter practically exploded.

"Walls, Sir! Walls! No-one said nothing about no walls. If there's Frogs up on them walls then we're dog meat! All they've got to do, is sit up there and wait. Sir!"

Carr nodded, his face as serious as Baxter's.

"That I appreciate, Sergeant, but we cannot go back saying that we could not find anything out because there were walls and we dared not enter. If the walls are unmanned, we must go in. So, we walk forward, half of us in front, the other half leading all the horses. Please see to it."

Minutes later, Carr was on foot and leading his men forward, all with carbines loaded and ready, with half the section leading the horses immediately behind. He drew out his watch to see 1:20. They were late, they should be in the town by now. The hill was not steep at first, but it became steeper as they climbed closer to the town. All seemed deserted and the details of the walls became clearer, Moorish crenellations and imposing flanking towers jutting from the walls. Within musket shot Carr raised his hand to halt. Baxter was alongside him.

"Can you see any life on those walls, Sergeant? We're within range."

Baxter had been studying the walls intently for the past few minutes, but he gave the only answer he could.

"No Sir, I've not seen a soul, but this I don't like. Going in through them walls with just one way back out. This has to be done real careful, Sir. I don't like what I've heard about Frog prisons."

"I hear you Sergeant, and careful is the word. Give Makepeace fifteen men to remain at the gate and hold it, in case we need to pull back quickly. The horses can stay with them, but outside the gate."

Baxter nodded.

"Very good, Sir. Makes sense to me."

Then he was gone, to return in two minutes, when they continued forward, Baxter giving the first opinion spoken as he constantly studied all above them on the walls which loomed higher above them as they came nearer, all also looking to either side where buildings nestled against the grey stone of the intimidating defensive walls.

"The place looks like no-one's home, Sir. Much like any town that was ever in French hands."

They reached the gate, where the horses were tethered to some useful posts in the ground and rings in the walls. Makepeace and his men remained at the gate and Carr and Baxter led the rest on, taking the major road which reassuringly followed Mateo's plan. On either side, the houses stretched high and upwards, all adding to the sense of enclosure and confinement, but they eased their way inwards, one line each side of the street, both hugging the sides of the buildings. Thirty yards further, there came the sudden eruption of gunfire, from the direction of what they took to be the plaza, but it lasted little more than a minute. The ensuing silence was nerve-racking and Carr could only consider to himself the alternatives, that either all of Mateo's men had been massacred or captured or that Mateo had captured the Plaza. He called across to Baxter, leading the other file.

"We must go quicker. Either Mateo's taken this place or it's full of French and we'll have to leave, quickly, but we've got to know, one way or the other."

Carr hurried forward and Baxter kept pace. It was not long before they could see the Plaza at the end of their street and, to his great relief, he saw a knot of light blue French uniforms in the midst of many brown and green clothed guerrillas.

"Come on!"

They hurried forward to soon enter the Plaza. Here, they were greeted enthusiastically by the guerrillas and plainly with relief by the group of French, whom Carr soon identified as Hussars. Five dead Hussars were in the Plaza, being immediately stripped of anything useful and their horses were being examined by other guerrillas, but three were loose, skittering around the plaza, out of control. Mateo was waving his arms triumphantly.

"Senor Carr! Is good. These, all."

Carr approached. The Hussars were kneeling, all plainly in a state of dread, and already, their thick brown pelisse jackets were being pulled from their shoulders and the military insignia being ripped off. Their black shakoes plainly displayed the number two, meaning that this was an elite Regiment. There were eight in all and many were already in tears and gazing up pleadingly at the newly arrived British Dragoons. They knew that these English were their only hope of salvation, which was already being voiced by one.

"Nous sauver de ces guérilleros, cher monsieur, je vous en prie!

Suddenly, a guerrilla came running out of one of the houses of the Plaza, and he went straight up to Mateo and began talking, angrily describing something concerning that house, his arm pointing back in a very animated fashion. Mateo's face grew darker as the description continued, its termination being marked by Mateo lashing out with his boot into the side of the nearest Hussar, then whipping another several times with his riding crop. He then stalked rapidly over to the house and entered, whilst the guerrillas, who had heard all, came closer to surround the Hussars, their muskets levelled down at a menacing angle. Many Hussars began to pray. When Mateo emerged from the house, his face was as black as thunder and he drew his knife, as did all the other guerrillas. Carr ran forward.

"Wait! Wait! What can these tell us? They have information. They must be questioned."

Mateo at least halted at Carr's pleading, although his anger remained wholly unabated. It was noted by Carr that this time his name was not used, instead his rank.

"The last time, Teniente, I give to you, this time no! These dogs must die!"

At that moment, aided by several guerrillas, the subject of Mateo's anger emerged from the house, six women and teenage girls, all doing their best to hold together the torn remnants of their clothing. What the Hussars had been surprised in the act of doing was now completely obvious. Mateo gave them a careful, immensely angry look and he then turned back to Carr.

"These must die, Teniente! Either Ingles way or Espanoles, but die they must."

Carr could see that it was useless to argue and even his eyes were drawn to the huddled and weeping female figures hurrying out of the Plaza. If the Hussars were killed the Spanish way, then the clinical term 'executed' could not apply, it would obviously be utterly gruesome and bestial, this well known to the French Hussars, all of whose faces now contorted in anguish and several began to sob. Carr looked at Mateo.

"We would want the English way."

The reply was fierce and brooked no argument.

"Then you do! If us, we kill as these deserve. For you, Teniente, I give choose and you do."

Carr was horrified. Himself and his men would need to be the execution squad. He turned to look at Baxter, a look that conveyed his feelings of helplessness, but Baxter simply nodded, twice. However, inhuman as he felt it to be, Carr knew he had to get some information if he could. Again he looked at Mateo.

"One question."

Mateo nodded and Carr walked to a Hussar that he took to be something like a Corporal.

"Nous pouvons vous donner une mort rapide, si vous me dire où est votre regiment."

The Corporal stared back, perhaps his hopes of being made a prisoner of war were now dashed, but he said nothing, and so Carr added the threat. A quick death for an answer, or be killed by the guerrillas.

"Ou la guérilla va te tuer."

The Corporal looked at his comrades, many of whom nodded agreement, one even speaking his agreement.

"Dire l'anglais!"

The Corporal looked back at Carr. One word was a small price to pay to keep out of the hands of the guerrillas and die quickly, especially for what they were plainly guilty of.

"Navamoral."

The town meant nothing to Carr, but it was information and he could expect no more. He looked at Mateo.

"Best to use your muskets. We have only light carbines."

Mateo nodded, then Carr turned to Baxter.

"Two lots of four?"

Baxter shook his head.

"No Sir, we can do this in one. Sixteen lads in two ranks. All in one go. 'Tis best I think."

Carr nodded.

"Right. Choose your men."

Carr was mildly surprised that many immediately walked forward to take a musket from the nearest guerrilla and load it with a cartridge provided with it. Meanwhile, Carr motioned the Hussars to stand and move to a convenient plain wall. As they walked many pitifully shook hands and exchanged looks of farewell. The Corporal spoke to Carr as they walked over.

"Merci m'sieu. C'est la guerre, non?"

Carr made no reply, he still held the image of the ravaged women and girls in his mind. The Hussars reached the wall and lined up, those still with a pelisse took them off. The thick cloth could cause only a mortal wound and a slow death. Carr's sixteen formed up quickly before them and Carr walked forward to give the orders, but Baxter came to stand beside him.

"I'll do it, Sir. Seen it before."

Carr nodded his agreement and took one pace back. Baxter then began by walking along the French line, giving each man his target, before halting at the far end.

"Make ready!"

The muskets were raised vertically in the air.

"Present!"

They all came down level. Some Hussars sobbed, two cried 'Vive la France!"

"Fire!"

In the confined Plaza, the sound of the crash was appalling, but even with the ensuing smoke Carr could see that it had been done well. Each Hussar had been hit by two half-inch musket balls at close range, flinging them back against the wall to lie perfectly still and lifeless. He could only stand and stare down at the worn flagstones of the Plaza, whilst his men returned the weapons. Baxter came to shake him out of his mood.

"Best we get out of this, Sir. Best leave this lot to it."

Carr said nothing but he could only agree. The bodies were already being stripped and the horses gathered together. Mateo was on the far side of the Plaza and Carr felt no urge to go over and bid farewell. Instead he turned to the road that they had entered by and his men followed. At the gate, Makepeace had held his place with the horses and they had all mounted when Carr said his first words.

"Captain Tavender should be at the river gate. We can ride around to find him."

What he did not say was what he was thinking, that by now, with the firing, Tavender should have entered the town to give support. Three minutes along the base of the wall brought them to the bridge gate with the bridge itself 100 yards below, but at that point Carr's whole Section came to a halt, all astonished. On the far side of the bridge were Tavender's whole Squadron, seemingly halted on that side by the bridge now blocked by a large assortment of wooden furniture. At this point, Baxter lost patience and, with the solution being obvious, he felt he had enough authority to act upon it. He urged his mount forward.

"Come on, lads."

All followed and then dismounted at the bridge, to then begin flinging each item into the river below. Carr sat watching, picking out Tavender on the ridge above, then after ten minutes, the bridge was clear. Baxter walked up, came the attention and saluted.

"All clear, now Sir!"

Carr nodded.

"Thank you, Sergeant. Then I think we should cross and get back to the Regiment."

"Very good, Sir."

More saluting, then all were mounted and they rode over the narrow, probably Medieval bridge, their horses' hooves clattering on the worn cobblestones, to see below them many items of furniture being carried away by the strong current. Tavender was nowhere to be seen and so Carr could ask no questions of him, but Baxter took the opportunity whilst One Squadron formed on the road, riding up to a Sergeant acquaintance of his, one Sergeant Ned Shelby.

"What held you up, Ned? That place could have been full of Frogs. Why didn't he bring you in, 'specially at the start, with all that firing going on?"

"He ordered find a ford instead."

Baxter was aghast and then angry.

"Find a ford! With the way that river's runnin'? It didn't take ten minutes to chuck that lot over and clear that bridge!"

Shelby inclined his head in agreement.

"You'm right, Sep, but that was what he ordered. Said something about being exposed to fire from the walls."

Baxter looked back at the walls, noting them to be around 150 yards away, far too far for accurate musket fire. He was seething and his anger did not abate all the way back to Carcaboso. Whilst Carr gave his report, Baxter went to the picket lines that had been established there and attended to his horse, his mind full of angry thoughts towards Captain Tavender. They were spending the night in Carcaboso and there, around their mess-fires, the story was told of capturing the Hussars, their execution and of Tavender failing to clear the bridge which could have meant the loss of a whole Section, had the French been in Plasencia in strength. Dawn came, breakfast was eaten and then came the order to mount up. Tavender went to his own mount to check that his servant had done all correctly, when he noticed that the strap on his saddle pouch was unbuckled. He lifted the lid to see a piece of paper, which he drew out and opened, to then read what was written there. The writing was crude, as for a child, but it was blunt, simple and to the point, "Cornet Carr is none of your doings. You keep pushing him into bad places and one day you will find yourself with Frogs front and side and all on your own." Tavender read the note twice more before looking around, to see no-one looking at him reading the note, but the warning was clear; that if he continued to volunteer Carr and his Section for dangerous missions or similar, the next time they were in combat, his men would desert him. Worried and somewhat chastened that his ambitions had been exposed, he mounted his horse.

oOo

The gold bar was once more on the desk, but none of the three paid it any serious concern. Livermore was concentrating on the report that he had received from Waters the previous day and he needed some clarifications and substantiations before he would treat it as solid and even condemnatory. Waters sat waiting on his side of the desk as Livermore now looked up from the paper.

"So, this Friar, would he not have said anything to save his skin?"

Waters sat back, bringing his hands together, fingertips equipoised.

"Yes, of course, but he quoted an exact date within the time when we were there, and within those days Templemere went off on his own. If he were trying to save himself, he could have quoted any old date, but what he said matches with what we know."

"Why not the other two, Hopgood and Mahon?"

"Well, you are the best judge of those two. You were there. What were they doing the days between Easter Sunday and the day you left?"

Livermore sat back.

"I hear you. They were about as much use as a beeswax kettle! Both loafing around, eating and doing their best to bed the daughter of the house. Neither spent any appreciable time away. I can't even remember their horses being saddled!"

He then sat forward; he had another detailed concern.

"So, this note that the Friar said he received. Did he know the contents?"

"No. He was ordered not to open it."

"But he took it to Massena?"

"He took it to Cuidad. Same thing."

"And soon after, Godinot marched to join Soult. Then we got Albuera and how we staved them off, God only knows!"

There came a silence that lasted for some time, as though each were waiting for the other to continue, In the end it was Livermore.

"Right! So, what have we got. Start with Hopgood and Mahon."

With that both Waters and Livermore looked at Radipole, who was able to answer without notes.

"No change. Mahon is from a French refugee family but we have seen no suspicious conduct. He spends almost all his time with Hopgood around the concert halls, their club, the gaming houses and a particular brothel. Their few acquaintances are men of a similar ilk. Both attend the House of Lords on occasions, for no particular reason and there has been no discernible change in their pecuniary circumstances. The one change is that Templemere spends much less time in their company."

Livermore nodded.

"What of him?"

Now Radipole did draw out a piece of foolscap paper from a folder.

"He is now moving in higher social circles and seems able to finance such. He has ordered a new carriage and made enquiries about a new town house in a more fashionable area, between Chelsea and Belgravia. He is more often at the gaming tables and playing for high stakes. The same for the races. None of this has been financed by sales of any part of his estates in Hampshire. In fact, he is spending less and less time there. It is reasonable to conclude that he is now more moneyed than he was before."

"Has he converted any more gold bars?"

"It's hard to say. Certainly not any more in Hatton Garden, although he did call there, but left with his satchel still full of weight. Perhaps the word has passed around that it is safer not to do business with him. As a possible alternative, there have been various callers to his Hampshire residence, any one of whom could have been an agent or a factor of some kind."

Livermore looked at him.

"That's all?"

Radipole nodded and Livermore then looked at Waters.

"So, what we have, is what we've just heard, all added to the French gold bar and him being out of our sight the day before our Friar picked up the note."

He paused to stare hard at Waters.

"What do you think?"

Water's chest rose and fell, whilst he thought during the heavy silence.

"We have no evidence that could bring a conviction, but there is much that stands against him. Chances are he is a traitor and will do such as this again, if paid enough. So, do we take that chance, that he'll sell information again and we'll get another Albuera?"

He paused and the silence became thunderous, until he continued.

"For my money, he is a risk to our security, which I consider too poor a chance. Our efforts against Napoleon could well be compromised by him; there is a lot that points that way, at him. He's too great a risk."

He sat back and looked at both in turn, before giving his decision.

"He needs to be got out of the way, taken out of the picture, one way or the other."

Livermore looked again at Radipole, but there was no reaction, so he turned back to Waters.

"You'll see to it?"

Waters nodded, at which Livermore stood up, recovered his hat and cane and left.

oOo

Chapter Eleven

"It can't get no worse than this!"

"Is this safe? Do you think?"

Drake was examining with a jaundiced eye the now vacant pontoon bridge that was their way across the River Guadiana, the crossing directly South of Elvas. The strong March current had created a distinctive, almost alarming, curve in the line of boats and platforms forming the bridge, such that only one battalion at a time was allowed upon it, and now it was the turn of the 105th. Carr did his best to be reassuring, but no words could compensate for the surging current and the boats swinging erratically both left and right as the current pushed them downstream and the spring of the mooring ropes brought them back.

"Oh, I do believe that we can trust our Engineers! However, if you do have a fear of rushing water, then close your eyes, hold onto the tail of O'Hare's horse there and count 100 paces. That will get you across, I feel sure."

Drake's face compressed into a concerned frown.

"If those words were spoken in the hope of dispensing comfort, I wish you'd not have bothered. I think I prefer to see what's going on. In any case, here we go."

The Engineers had waved them forward but the contrast between the firm bank and the animated bridge was particularly marked and each man of the 105th found themselves with their legs straddled far apart in order to keep their balance, some even linking arms. What certainly did not help the ease of their passage was the need to carry so many gabions and fascines that had been constructed by the Elvas garrison, ordered to make them since the end of the Cuidad siege. In similar fashion at the rear, Sedgwicke found it sensible to dismount and walk between the heads of the mules, who, presumably being four legged, seemed to cope with the uncertain surface quite well. Not so Battalion Chaplain Albright who, with great anxiety, also dismounted and walked behind the cart, his hand on the tailgate for extra security. The Followers came over last, and were the noisiest, many voicing their anxiety over so perilous a crossing, all linking arms to aid their balance as they gingerly placed one foot before the other.

However, within minutes, the reducing distance to the far bank of the Guadiana sped their last footsteps, then they all were over and grateful for the solid ground beneath their feet. However, any gratitude was short lived, the rain, hitherto merely a nuisance, intensified to not quite a downpour, but nevertheless, it was driving, stinging rainstorm, slanting down on a bullying wind that sent uncomfortable entry of water down collars and into the cuffs of arms necessarily upturned to carry the burdens required for the siege.

Drake, now on terra firma, ever the optimist and marching alongside Carr, shrugged his pack into a more comfortable position and strode on, searching for reasons why the Badajoz siege would be a less onerous affair than the siege of Cuidad. His thoughts began with the massive artillery park that they had passed by, all the guns and transport in ordered ranks under the arches of the always imposing Elvas viaduct.

"One thing! At least this time we've more guns, 52 an Artillery Officer told me. And better, all 18 and 24 pounders. That'll speed things up."

Carr pulled the scarf a little more forward to cover more of his face against the almost horizontal rain, the cloth being incongruously wound around both his chin and the top of his shako.

"True, but this time we've got less men. 27,000. He's had to send 19,000 South-east to Cordoba to watch over D'Erlon and Soult and also, he's sent Hill with 14,000 towards Merida. He's had cavalry reports of the French there and at Navalmoral."

"So how many did we have at Cuidad?"

"29,000."

"Well, that's not so different. And with better guns, and we've now learned a trick or two about this siege business."

"One can only hope so, but here, so reports state, the garrison is 5,000, whilst at Cuidad it was under two!"

Now somewhat deflated, Drake lowered his head into his collar which he pulled up a little higher, his head sinking a little lower, matching his spirits.

Just ahead, but mounted, Lacey and O'Hare rode side by side, but O'Hare was upwind, needing to continuously push down his cloak, this blown up and sideways by the wind, thus soaking his right knee, but memories were uppermost in his mind of the previous occasion they had marched this route.

"Was it not around this point that last time we were greeted with cannonballs from one of the outlying Forts?"

Lacey nodded, causing large droplets of rain to fall from his bi-corn hat and onto his gloved hands holding the reins.

"It was, but I'd bet against it now. In this muck we cannot see them, nor them see us."

He adjusted his cloak forwards, over his saddle.

"Whatever, it'll make little difference. They know we're coming and doubtless will have made the best of preparations."

O'Hare nodded, releasing more droplets.

"What is different from last time, is the weather. There'll be no worry about thirst and heat this time. Nor even the concerns of an early Spring."

At that point, his horse lost its footing slightly on the soft, ploughed field and skidded sideways. O'Hare brought the animal back under control and from that point each concentrated on the route ahead, the ground underfoot becoming more and more churned as the rain soaked into it and the thousands of feet ahead of them did their own damaging work. However, it was a level plain that they were crossing, albeit with no track and so they held their place in the column, the monotony being broken, unpleasantly an hour later, by all those on foot being required to wade a stream that was knee deep. Then they were climbing out of the stream's valley, with a low height on their left. After five minutes the whole column halted and their new Brigadier, Kempt, came riding back down to them, followed by an Aide de Camp.

"Lacey! O'Hare! This is it, we're here. The other side of that rise is the first outlier, Fort Picurina. We have to start with that and we start tonight with a parallel. Yours'll be taking a turn, so get yourself settled and get some food inside them. We'll be working at night, as usual."

Kempt began to ride off to his next Battalion, but when he came near them, just before passing the rear of the 105th column, despite the close covering cloaks and hats, he recognised Carr from the Maida campaign, now almost five years previous. He reined in his horse.

"Carr!"

Carr sprang to the attention and saluted whilst Kempt looked down.

"Pleased to see you're still alive. And a Major I see."

"Yes Sir. Pleased to see you also, Sir. A long time since Maida."

The answer was no more than a nod, as Kempt and his Aide rode off and the 105th dispersed rightwards to set up camp upon the vacant space. Within minutes the welcoming shelter of their tents was established and fires were burning under the sheltering awnings. There was no ration issue and the men and Followers ate what was in their packs, whilst the Sergeants spread the 'good' news, Ellis arriving at the messes of Deakin and Davey.

"Eat and rest. Come Midnight we're all on the tools."

Miles looked resentfully at him.

"Farmwork! We ain't been yer five minutes."

Ellis turned on him.

"What did you expect. Miles? Two week's rest and recreation. It's a siege, another one, and it won't work unless we dig, and that includes you, and you work! Just like the rest and I don't care if your back's healed or not, because if I see you shirking, it'll be another haul-up on the triangle."

No-one replied, Ellis was clearly as annoyed as they were, caused as much by the duties the night would bring, as much as by Miles. Sleep came easy and deep, so it was with befuddled heads that they made their way, following lanterns, over the slope of the rise, to pass by the soldiers of the 74th making their way back. Conditions were more difficult than anything at Cuidad as the weather worsened with heavier rain and the wind now at gale force. Any conversation was impossible, orders and instructions had to be shouted two or three times, but the parallel slowly deepened. The earth was still firm despite the immediate surface being churned quickly to soft mud by their shifting feet. A reluctant dawn found them still working, but the weather had cleared somewhat during the night. O'Hare and Carr stood on the top of the newly constructed parapet, looking down the slope. Below them, some 300 yards below, was a low, odd shaped fortress, the red brick clearly defining it, even in the damp gloom. It was Carr who voiced his opinion.

"Sort of like the jutting front bit of a knight's helmet!"

O'Hare nodded.

"A good enough description for me, Henry, but I believe the technical term is the apex. Anyway, I'm back off for a change of clothes and a mug of whatever, tea, coffee, soup, I care not."

Carr followed him back, mingling with their own men, all now relieved of trench work. The 88th passed through them, but all in the 105th were too tired, cold, wet and miserable to exchange any word with their most prominent antagonists and so all kept their heads down and passed each other by. However, it was the 105th who felt more gratitude, not only that their eight hours were done, but because at that moment cannon fire started immediately from behind them. Lacey was stood with Kempt, some 100 yards back from the parallel, and he voiced the reason why.

"Seems that seeing us here, and so close, has given Johnny a nasty surprise, Sir."

Kempt grinned.

"An irritation, yes, which he wants to take out on us."

Round shot began to hit the parapet, but the 88th, now down in the trench were easily able to keep up with the dislodged earth and they even increased the parapet height. However, some hours later Kempt had no good news.

"Expect sixteen hours in, eight out. He wants twice the length of trenches and batteries that were dug at Cuidad. We're going from here, all the way over to the banks of the Guadiana, where the Third were last time?"

Lacey looked at him, very concerned.

"Opposite the Castle, Sir, yes, but the men will need hot food, regularly. Sixteen hours in the trenches is no mean effort. And in this weather?"

Kempt's face hardened at the mild criticism.

"We are aware, Lacey. Picton's taken that onto himself, but bear in mind that everything has to come across that pontoon from Elvas. What can be done, will be done, be assured."

With that he walked off to his horse, being held by a Private of the 88th, mounted it and rode off, leaving Lacey pondering the rate of fire from the Picurina fort, which seemed to easily match anything they had endured from Cuidad Rodrigo. 'Sixteen hours!', the thought came back to him and he soon became mindful of the rest he needed for himself. If they came out of the diggings at eight in the morning, they would need to be back in at four in the afternoon. The news of the sixteen-hour day, delivered at 3.30, was greeted with sullen resignation, as Ellis conveyed the order at the same time as shouting some awake and kicking others. His last words were consistent to each mess.

"Well, at least this time we've not got to march three miles in the freezing cold!"

There was barely time to eat before they were called to form up and again march through the returning 74th. An Engineer Captain was waiting for them and Lacey, O'Hare and Carr approached to receive their duties.

"We're starting batteries, now, Sirs. You're in front of the main parallel with the 83rd of General Campbell's Brigade and there you are to construct Number One battery, the biggest to begin bombarding the Picurina. The 88th and the 5th will be starting Number Two battery, some way over to the right. The lines have been pegged out for them. Also, just so as you know, Sirs, we are extending down from where Number Two will be towards their other outlier, the San Roque Fort, quite close to the town and alongside the river Rivellas. Things are moving on."

Lacey looked at him, evidently somewhat irate and wholly unmoved by the effort on the part of the Captain to boost their morale by giving a detailed explanation.

"Will we be breaking new ground?"

"Yes Sir."

"In full view of the Picurina?"

"Yes Sir."

"Then I'll trouble you to confirm that fascines are in place to give us some protection!"

The Captain's face fell at the serious omission being pointed out to him.

"I'll see that they're brought up, Sir."

The three walked back to their men, Carr attempting to look on the bright side, despite the continuous rain.

"Well, we can be thankful we're not working alongside the 88th, with both ours and theirs having spades in their hands."

The response was a lift of each head and a weak grin, but soon they were organising the rolling of fascines forward to anchor them beyond the markers for the battery and there to give some cover from the guns of the Picurina. This was very much needed, because immediately these began to pound the large and solid bundles of branches and brushwood. However, after three hours of work in the unremitting rain, Saunders soon gave his opinion.

"This is damn hopeless!"

They all stopped working and they knew what he meant; the heavy rain had turned the soil to such a liquid mud that it flowed off their shovels before they could heave it onto any point useful, such as the parapet. Davey leaned on his shovel, the rainwater now running out of his sleeves.

"So, what to do?"

They looked at Bill Turner, the ex-Navvy, who had a good answer.

"Well, with this muck, we'd get it into buckets, then into barrows. Had to, we'd not get paid otherwise. For us now, you can get it into a bucket before it runs off the shovel, then we can chuck it into chutes, so's it runs down to where you wants it. The rain'll do that for you. Once you've got rid of the slime, then you're onto firmer."

Saunders nodded at the good sense.

"Right! Dinner's not far, and we uses the time to get buckets. We've got some of our own back in camp, the artillery'll have some and the Engineers and all. Joe! Think about how we can make a chute. Or three!"

The order soon came for all to send back runners to the first parallel and get the food. This was because the batteries were too far forward for the Followers to venture up and be dangerously exposed to the continuous assault from the Picurina. Deakin and Saunders brooked no argument from their womenfolk.

"We needs your buckets! Bring them up when you can, so's we can use them when we restarts."

They both then returned to the diggings carrying the hot stew and biscuits which was quickly apportioned around. Whilst they were eating, some entertainment presented itself, first noticed by Tom Miles.

"Just look at that dopey bugger!"

An Engineer Officer was out and down to their left, presumably marking out another battery, whilst all the time cutting capers before the French in the Picurina who could easily see him, but he darted about, lifting the skirts of his tunic as an invitation to the French to aim at him, all the while carefully pacing out the distance between markers. A soldier with him was hit and screamed in agony, but his comrades dragged him back to find that the bullet had hit the 'cross' of his cross belts and the man was only winded, but Miles again passed judgement.

"Now that's one murderin' sod of an Officer as seriously needs takin' care of!"

The buckets arrived and better progress was made. When they marched out at 4 o' clock, Deakin and Pike went straight to O'Hare, who went with them to the Engineers' park and some timber and tools were obtained. Their 'off-shift' was during daylight and three simple chutes were made, but then Ellis arrived, when they were hoping to sleep, with an immediate question.

"What're they for?"

Miles was quick to answer, this being a clear opportunity for underhand belligerence to an NCO.

"Getting shot of the slime what runs off our shovels and goes no-wer'."

Ellis looked directly back at him.

"Well, you'll not be using them, at least not so much. You remember that parallel before Cuidad, where we shot at the walls from rifle pits just out in front. We're for that again. Come dark we digs the pits out in front of Number One Battery, what we started now. Us and the Rifles. We has to take a few yards alongside them, who takes the rest."

Even Byford was incensed and showed it.

"So, we spend sixteen hours peering out of a hole in the ground and that hole is out in front of the fascines?"

Ellis stared back, a confrontation with Byford was something new.

"Yes and no, but it's not so bad. You'll be sat out there for half a day of daylight, then back digging when you gets relieved. That's your sixteen."

Byford was not at all mollified.

"Half of daylight hours! That's six hours under cannonfire, peering out of a hole. That's a killing order!"

"Then complain to Wellington, I'm sure he'll listen."

With that, Ellis nodded, shrugged and departed, but Miles was already thinking.

"Tobacco! All of you!"

Without argument, the precious weed was handed over and Miles departed to return in under an hour with three tarpaulin wagon covers, bartered from both the Artillery and the Engineers. Davey and Saunders had already gone to the ration wagons for biscuit sacks and so when they returned to the battery at 4 o' clock in the afternoon, One Section waited for the light to fail, then they crept forward through the spaces between the fascines and beyond and there began to dig 10 rifle pits. At midnight, they had a hole big enough for two to stretch out comfortably and a firing position protected by many bags filled with soil. The tarpaulin was stretched over the whole and Miles gave his orders.

"Right! Joe you're first up to keep watch, two hours whilst me and John gets some sleep under this cover. If you sees anything, shoot at it. There's only space for one at the slot anyway. Can't see any Officer comin' this far forward in the rain and under fire to inspect, so I'd say we'n fairly safe."

The two settled to sleep whilst Pike eased his Baker rifle into the narrow firing slit. All the while the rain pounded on the tarpaulin and, with the dawn, the French cannon in the Picurina pounded the fascines behind them and others from the town walls ripped up the surrounding ground with grapeshot. The three messmates replied with rifle fire in shifts, but not so rapidly. Despite being on the same level as the Picurina embrasures and despite the tarpaulin covering, the damp and the rain caused too many misfires and the pan and touch hole had to be cleaned from wet gunpowder and re-primed each time. At Noon they were relieved, to return at a sprint, to eat and then pick up the tools to work in the battery with the rest of the 105th until they were relieved again by the 88th. For the ensuing days, the routine set in, six hours in the rifle-pits, then ten in the Battery. The rain did not stop.

oOo

Shakeshaft came into the tent and sat at the table, his feet on a makeshift stool to keep them out of the continuous rivulets of water that ran from one side of the tent to the other. Drake, dozing on the cot in the corner, levered his head off the pillow using his right forearm, now grateful for some company.

"Are you still keeping up the Journal, then Richard?"

Shakeshaft had already begun writing.

"Of course. Now. Today's the 19th. The two batteries, One and Two, will soon be opening up on the Picurina."

Drake's head fell back on the pillow.

"And we got here, when?"

"The fifteenth."

"Is that all? God, it feels like a month!"

Shakeshaft looked over at him.

"Well, at least rations are arriving regularly. We're getting fed. I've mentioned that each day."

He continued writing.

"That hill in front of us, that hides us from the Picurina. It's got a name; did you know that? I like to include that sort of detail."

Drake looked wearily at him.

"Go on. Do tell!"

Shakeshaft smiled knowledgeably.

"Cerro de San Miguel."

Drake groaned.

"You mistake me for someone who cares more for that, than for a tinker's left boot!"

Whilst Shakeshaft absorbed himself further in his writing, Drake rolled over and said no more. Depression was the mood that had settled over the whole army, no one was dry and the liquid mud which covered every camp of every Battalion had seeped through the leather of even the stoutest boots. The morale of the 105th matched that of the rest of the besieging force and, with the arrival of their 8 o' clock relief by the 4th Division, all of the 3rd Division trudged back to either a camp bed, if an Officer, or damp straw if 'other-ranks'. However, there were three Officers of the 105th who were not yet on their way, although very much wishing to depart. Lacey, O'Hare and Carr were stood with Colonel Fletcher of the Engineers, discussing the work of the 105th as achieved over the past sixteen hours. Fletcher was pointing out a few details to improve drainage when there came a sudden eruption of fighting over to their right.

Carr was the first onto the Battery parapet, despite the cannonfire from the Picurina, to see what he thought must be 1,000 Frenchmen and about 40 cavalry now into the new parallel that led down from Number Two battery and had by now approached very close to the second outlying fort, the San Roque. The French cavalry were over the parallel and chasing men up the hill, whilst the infantry were doing their best to wreck it and a substantial number were advancing onto the battery itself. O'Hare saw enough and said one word, "Sortie", as Carr ran forward. It was impossible to know who the British were, either the 88th and 5th late out of the trenches or men of the 4th Division now moving in and, even as he ran forward, he could see that a counter-attack was being assembled above at the top of the hill, but the French must be stopped before reaching the battery. Last out of their own works were Number Three Company and the Grenadiers, all thankfully now halted by the sound of commotion. O'Hare called out as they parted Company.

"I'll get Carravoy, you get Heaviside!"

Number Three Company were the nearest and Carr quickly came up to them, Heaviside prominent at the rear.

"Joshua! With me to the battery! Load as they go."

Within a second, Heaviside had drawn his sword and he was calling on his men to follow. Just in the lead of Number Three, Carr arrived in the battery to see that the French were 50 yards off and coming on at a fast walk with bayonets fixed, both above ground and down in the parallel. Carr looked both left and right to see almost two dozen of Heaviside's men on each side of the trench and more arriving. He knew that he could trust to the veteran quality of the 105th and he was correct. Although it would have slowed them up, all had loaded at the run. Carr raised his sword.

"Hold your fire! Wait for my command."

He wanted a solid volley to hit the French, not sporadic shots. In addition, to wait allowed more men to arrive which would add to the impact. The time arrived.

"Make ready!"

The muskets came to the vertical. Perhaps many French saw this and several fired back immediately, but to little effect.

"Present!"

Carr gave his men time to settle their aim.

"Fire!"

There came the crash and smoke billowed out across the earthwork. More men arrived and simply fired out across the space, through the swirling smoke. Carr jumped up onto the parapet and Heaviside soon joined him.

"Out! Fix bayonets."

Three Company climbed out to stand both on and before the parapet, prepared to defend all at bayonet point. There were anxious seconds as the smoke cleared, but when it did, there were no more advancing French. The British counter-attack from above had hurtled down the slope, even repulsing the cavalry and they had now ejected all of the French sortie from the parallel to the San Roque. Many were now no more than fugitives, running between the Picurina Fort and the British lines, but not back the way they had come. Heaviside's men sent sporadic shots at these fleeing across their front, but two young men were now somewhat in advance of the rest of Three Company and yelling at the French barely yards away. However, rescue came in the form of Colour Sergeants Deakin and Bennet seizing the waist sash of each and hauling them back to hurl each down onto the battery gun platform. All this happened close to Heaviside and Deakin felt the need to explain to his Captain.

"These two can get a mite carried away on occasions, Sir."

Heaviside nodded understandingly.

"Whatever your hands find to do, do it with all you might. Ecclesiastes 9. Verse 10."

Deakin nodded.

"Yes Sir. Wish that was all there was to it, Sir."

O'Hare had halted his Grenadiers in the rear of One Battery to act as reinforcements for Carr and Heaviside in case they were needed, but now, very obviously, they were not. He pondered what to do, but he quickly made up his mind that it was right to pursue the French running before him in the hope of taking prisoners. He quickly scaled the battery parapet and ran across it.

"Carravoy! With me."

The Grenadiers were quickly over and following O'Hare. There came no fire from the Picurina because the French fugitives were masking O'Hare and his men, but, with the new appearance of the Redcoats, all French from the sortie quickened their pace, many dropping their muskets. The nimble Voltiguers, as they were, soon outpaced the heavier Grenadiers, but then, beyond the Picurina and down the slope, they came to the inundation caused by the French damning the stream of the Rivellas that ran alongside Badajoz. Many French jumped straight in, hoping to wade across to the safety of the town gate they had emerged from, but they found it too deep and were soon in difficulties and almost all drowned, weighed down by their heavy equipment. The late arrivals saw this and ran to their left hoping for shallower water and they began to wade across. At this point the Grenadiers arrived and immediately began to fire at the hundred or more men in the water. Soon the water was red from the blood of the slain as others struggled across to reach the far bank, where, even there, they were still within range. Soon Lieutenant Ameshurst had had enough and he ran to Carravoy.

"Sir! This is murder!"

Carravoy looked at him, his face grim as stone.

315

"Keep firing. These must not get back in."

Ameshurst looked at him, horrified, but then O'Hare ran up. He felt the same as Ameshurst.

"Enough! Withdraw your men. We have prisoners, we've done enough."

The order to cease fire was obeyed immediately and some Grenadiers even went down to the water's edge to unhook the slings from their muskets and throw them out to wounded Frenchmen and haul them to the bank, where they lay exhausted, but immensely thankful. O'Hare now took stock. Fort Picurina was just above them, unseen over the slope above, but a sortie from there could easily come down upon them, they were now so far forward from their own lines.

"We get back, along the stream, not straight back up. Get your men assembled and the prisoners."

Their return was uneventful, bar two prisoners dying of wounds, and when O'Hare did arrive back, having taken the long route, the morning was well advanced and it was then that Kempt came to the Headquarters tent of the 105th, him as wet, muddy and weary as anyone. He had suffered like them whilst taking his turn supervising the works through the past four days of the siege so far. He dropped his shako on the table and sat. The three there with him, Lacey, O'Hare and Carr, said nothing, but simply waited for him to decide when to start. He was blunt and to the point.

"We're losing too many men. This French Governor, Phillipon by name so we're told, is as sharp as a packet of needles! He's got his men well onto their task, you can hear now for yourselves just what we're getting from the town and the Picurina. It's murderous whilst we dig and always two-thirds of our army is out there exposed, with all that the Peer wants dug."

He did not pause to allow the three to listen to the ongoing bombardment, they all knew well enough the casualties that the 105th had suffered. Kempt quickly continued.

"Our telescopes tell us that Phillipon has that big square church tower in the centre continuously manned and they know what to do. They save their most intense bombardment for when the reliefs are in the trenches at the same time as those they are relieving. Their cannon then make good practice amongst the crowd, so now Reliefs only go in, when all those relieved are out."

Carr's brows came together.

"That means for some minutes the trenches are unmanned and you saw what happened today, Sir."

Kempt nodded.

"It's a risk, I know, but casualties are too high. Picton himself, nearly went skywards yesterday when a shell landed but yards from him."

He picked up his shako, prior to wearing it.

"This is turning into the most damnable, bloody, and God-awful business that I've ever heard about or read about, never mind been involved in!"

He stood and so did the three who saluted as he left. They looked at each other, then O'Hare and Carr departed, sleep was the only thing on their minds.

Sleep was totally uppermost in the minds of Davey, Saunders and their companions. Their tents were now drier thanks to deep ditches dug all around the outside, but sometimes even these overflowed, as they had once again from the continuous rain, which found the Nicholls and Mulcahey children bailing out into another deep hole nearby. The men filed into the two tents, beyond anger, beyond misery. Sixteen hours, day after day, either deepening and extending the parallels in the mud and rain or in the rifle pits enduring shot and shell, had taken their toll. Each sat, offering their pannikin, eyes blank in red, cold-raw faces as the stew was ladled in by Bridie or Nellie and afterwards, Violet, Nellie's youngest, issued the biscuits, two each. Food eaten, each took some time to clean themselves, obviously there being no shortage of clean water, but lice were becoming a problem, few had the time to keep themselves properly clean. That job done, as best they could, each simply slumped over and slept through the best of the daylight, hoping that they were not called forward to man the rifle pits where casualties were now becoming significant. However, this did not apply to the 105th Lights and the 4 o'clock call brought something different, brought as usual by Ellis.

"We're moving, back down to where we were last Summer, behind that stream and alongside the big river."

They sat up, looking at him blankly, so he continued.

"Well, look on the bright side. That's means a night out of the trenches and a day not in the pits. So, break up your camp and get moving!"

They rolled out of their blankets and dressed themselves in time for breakfast, which was reasonably wholesome, hot biscuit porridge and dried fruit. Speech was at a minimum, it required mental effort and so the tents were collapsed, slung on poles and then carried off, in the direction as indicated by Officers of Picton's Staff. The route took them down the far slope of the Cerro de San Miguel that had protected them all the days of the siege so far, then as they slowly descended, through the rain on their left they could see the walls of Badajoz, familiar from the previous summer, but no longer the bright shade of decorative stone, now a sombre, rain soaked grey. Carr and Drake, marching together, both examined the wall to the right of the Castle as it came into better view.

"Any sign of what was ambitiously called a breach, last time we were here?"

Carr had seen enough to answer with conviction.

"No! Not a sign. All now repaired."

The whole of Picton's Third Division was on the move, both Kempt and Campbell's Brigades. Their own Major General, now making use of a misshapen black umbrella, was perched on the only piece of high ground on the flood plain, which was within the angle where the Rivellas and the mighty Guadiana joined as one, the last now lapping at the most vulnerable points of its banks. Left to their own devices, all Battalions returned to the same ground and positions that they had occupied back in the previous Summer, this requiring the minimum of thought and organisation. After the pitching of tents and the midday meal, the order came for all in the Division to march back towards the walls, part way, to where wagons full of tools were waiting for them and there, Colonel Fletcher's Engineers had marked out the site of three batteries, numbers four, five or six, each incongruously numbered by a board rapidly losing its whitewashed number, it positioned forlornly amongst the mud and the sodden, limp flags. O'Hare took himself up to one of the Engineers.

"105th. Where do you want us?"

The Engineer lifted a small piece of tarpaulin that protected the small board he was holding from the rain.

"Number Four. Opposite the San Roque."

O'Hare looked over. To bring themselves opposite the San Roque was another 500 yards further over left and O'Hare waved for the Battalion to follow him. There was no let up from the rain and, even in the poor visibility of the fading March day and the incessant cascade from the slate grey skies, they were soon noticed by the gunners both on the town walls and in the San Roque itself. All too soon, shot passed amongst them from the heavy cannon of Badajoz and shells from the howitzers in the San Roque lunette fort causing casualties as they dug furiously. It was the eventual fall of night which protected them and so, knowing that only being deep within the ground would give them any form of protection, Picton's whole command dug energetically into the soft alluvium. However, the task remained as arduous as ever, the rain quickly turning the earth they had to tread upon into liquid mud. The chutes, now universally adopted, at least throughout Kempt's Brigade, did good service, but with the dawn nowhere in the parallel nor in any of the batteries was the trench more than chest deep, however, there was a parapet of some description. With the daylight, the attentions of the French were renewed and casualties began to mount, not so much from the round shot because now only heads showed above the earthwork, but the high angle shells from the San Roque were altogether another issue. O'Hare went to Lacey, to find him equally worried.

"We should have a shell watch like we did at Cuidad. At least we may have the chance to throw the thing over or simply lie flat."

Lacey immediately nodded agreement.

"Yes. In shifts. A good excuse to rest for some of them, if nothing else, and this cannot go on all throughout the daylight hours. If we are to continue at night, they must have rest, they've been at it since four yesterday afternoon, and now it's eight in the morning and this rain has simply not stopped. They must have some rest and soon."

"We can only hope. Meanwhile, I'll get the Sergeants to identify those for shell duty."

It was Gibney who came to decide who would be the watchers amongst Light Company One Section. He looked around.

"Saunders, Davey, Byford, Bailey."

His piercing eyes fell on Joe Pike.

"Pike! Thee's no use. Only one eye!"

Pike looked up from ladling liquid mud into a bucket.

"It's alright unless we're in bright sunlight, Sar' Major!"

All around collapsed with laughter, even Gibney's extensive whiskers splitting into a wide grin.

317

"Alright! Thee's in. Solomon! Thee an' all. That's six, so for th'next hour, three on, then next three. Saunders, thee to choose who. Hour shifts, then back to diggin'."

Despite the deep grey of the skies, the black shells were not difficult to pick out and to cope with those that would land near, there was no alternative, but to kneel in the liquid mud in the bottom of the trench and shelter behind the parapet. However, eventually they saw one that was not moving to one side or other in its descent, its trajectory was straight down onto them. Byford, on watch, cried in alarm.

"Down! Down! Lie down!"

All flung themselves down onto the chilling slime at the bottom of the trench and waited, their bodies stiff with fear. The shell landed squarely in the bottom of the trench, merely feet from Tom Miles head, and it buried itself into the soft mud. He brought up his knees and rolled back along the trench, desperate that the final seconds of the fuse would save him. The shell went off with a roar and he was blown along the trench to cannon into Joe Pike. The air above was now full of descending mud but Pike, his ears ringing, wiped the mess from his own face before looking at Tom Miles. He could see no life, he was either dead or unconscious. In shock, he said nothing, then Davey and Saunders hurried to his side and they dragged Miles to the side of the trench. They propped him up, but his head simply hung forward, lolling to one side. Saunders turned to Solomon.

"Get George here, quick. Tell him Tom's been blown up."

Solomon took one long look, then hurried away. Meanwhile, Davey was doing his best to examine Miles for any wound, but first washing away the mud that covered Miles' face and hair, the rain and his own canteen being effective in equal measure. The face and head now clean, he looked carefully.

"Nothing, no sign of blood. Nothing."

Byford was stood over both.

"A shell fragment would have caused injury and bleeding, but he may have been hit by a flying stone, or one of the tools, even."

Davey's face grew more anxious at the possibility and he examined Miles' skull carefully, grateful that they had all cut each other's hair because of the lice.

"There's no lump, nor anything like that."

He drew back from his examinations.

"Zeke. Let's get the jacket off him. See what's there."

After scraping away the mud from each button, the jacket was removed and Miles body examined all round. Again, Davey shook his head.

"Nothing, but like you say John, he could have been hit by something."

"Then get his shirt off. There'll be a mark."

The shirt was pulled over Miles' head, but again no mark of impact was found on the protruding ribs and backbone of Tom Miles, the new and old scars from the lash plainly visible. Then Byford knelt before him and felt for a pulse, both in his wrists and at his neck. He made a face, plainly uncertain.

"There might be something. I cannot be certain, but there doesn't have to be a mark or injury. He's been blown up, that could well be enough."

Davey pushed him aside.

"I won't ask enough for what, but for now we keeps him warm. Get his jacket back around him and some greatcoats as well. George shouldn't be long."

Davey was correct in that, and the first thing that Fearnley did was to hold a mirror to Miles' nostrils. The incessant rain confused everything and so he wiped the glass dry and then tried again under a greatcoat. There was a faint mist. He turned around to Davey and Saunders.

"Well, he's not dead. At least not yet, but who knows what being blown up can do to your insides. What helps and can give some protection, like, is a tight uniform, cross-belts and all, but we has to get him out of this cold and rain and under cover."

Without another word, Saunders hoisted Miles over his shoulder and, with the aid of Solomon and Bill Turner, Saunders and his burden were hauled up over the slippery slope that was the side of the trench. Once out, Saunders began trotting the distance back to their camp, Solomon taking a turn, with Saunders supporting Miles' head. Five minutes brought them to their tents and Miles, once inside was laid down on blankets quickly spread out by the doubly anxious Bridie and Nellie, who looked at Saunders.

"Is he like to live?"

Saunders took a deep breath.

318

"That I don't know, he's been blown up, but get him out of those wet clothes and into dry blankets, or he's just as likely to die from an ague or somesuch. If he comes to, get some hot food into him."

There was no objection from Bridie or Nellie at the task of stripping a man to his bare skin, in fact Bridie began straight away. Saunders could now see that all that could be done, was being done.

"We'd best get back. Any sign of malingering could cost my stripes!"

Saunders and Solomon hurried back, but they did not reach the part completed battery and parallel. The 105th had at last been relieved and they were on their way back then, after a meal, whilst the rest slept, many took a shift to watch over Tom Miles. All sat hoping for a sign of life, other than the faint mist on George Fearnley's mirror, when he called around, anxious for news himself. All knew the belligerent and abrasive nature of Tom Miles, but their years of service together and shared dangers more than countered any possible ill-feelings generated by Miles' aggressive temper and, besides, over the years they had learned that his tetchy outbursts were nothing to be taken too seriously anyway, if anything, often a source of humour. Despite all, he was an old comrade!

The return to work at 4 o'clock in the afternoon arrived as depressing an event for the Senior Officers of the 105th as it did for their men. Kempt arrived at their Headquarters tent to find the Colonel and both Majors ready to leave for the trenches, knowing that he would order them to do so anyway, if he had any doubt over their intentions. In the event, he brought bad news.

"Johnny's brought two guns down from San Christobal and they're enfilading the trenches close to the Guadiana, Batteries Five and Six, those two especially. Picton's sent my Rifles down to there, to see what can be done, but I want your Lights to relieve them. The Rifles cannot stay there all night. Can I leave that with you, Carr?"

The salute from Carr began an order chain that moved onto to Drake and then to Rushby, which resulted in One Section trudging head down through the rain to the near bank of the Guadiana, with Rushby and Ellis at their head. Once there, they found that the waters of the Guadiana were now alarmingly high, up through an extensive reed bed which stretched some way out to the main current and at the edge of these reeds they found men of the 60th Rifles, mostly sat, but a line of sentries were standing on watch. A Rifles Officer rose to meet Rushby and introductions were exchanged.

"Kenwood, Captain, 60th Rifles"

"Rushby, Sir, 105th Foot."

"I'm afraid you're here on a false errand. We've driven them off! For now, that is, but they had such a good position that I suspect they'll be back come tomorrow. If we can build battery positions, so can they."

Rushby nodded wearily and the movement allowing rainwater down the back of his neck.

"So, you're still here in case they come back? Sir."

Kenwood grinned.

"We were! Now you are. Assuming you to be our Relief, I'm taking mine out of here."

Rushby had no option but to nod agreement and, with that, a few signals from Kenwood saw the Rifle Company rise from the bank and march away. Rushby looked at Ellis.

"Sat here all night out in the open, being rained on and listening to the Guadiana gurgling its way past, that's a misery I mean to avoid. Did you see anything that looked like shelter as we came across?"

Ellis had been thinking of nothing else during the march across and he had seen what looked like a roof in the low trees to his right, probably, he reasoned, where cultivation began, away from the risk of flood. He pointed upstream but away from the bank.

"Yes Sir. There's something in those trees over there, that'll at least keep the rain off."

"Right. Sentry by files. Two hours on, three files together, 100 yards apart. Let's see where that takes us."

Rushby stood examining the far bank for half a minute, then he left to examine the 'roof', whilst Ellis made his selection during which he attached himself to Pike and Davey, to make up a three. When the rest of the Section marched off, these three stood together, Pike the least happy, he was as wet as anyone and aching in more than one place after his collision with Miles. His own irritation, normally held deep within him, now surfaced for this occasion.

"So, no digging, but all of us stood here, in this, for sixteen hours!"

Ellis looked at him.

"You taken over from Miles with the complaining duties?"

Pike made no reply, he simply let out a deep sigh and Ellis relented.

"Come on. We'll take a stand here. Two hours on, then we're out of it."

They walked to the edge of the water, now lapping onto the bankside track and, whilst Pike and Davey sat, Ellis looked over at the blank, empty slope that was the far bank and led up to Fort San Christobal. The upper works were visible above and to the left, but soon his attention was drawn to events behind him, the flash, smoke and roar of ongoing cannon fire since dawn, from the battlements of Badajoz and the San Roque, whilst there came no reply from his own side. This depressed him more, the obvious fact that his own comrades once again endured seemingly endless labour in the rain-soaked trenches, with no mental succour at all from the knowledge that, at least, some measure of retaliation was being sent back, but so far there was none. There was no alternative for those labouring but to stand in ankle deep mud, wielding a shovel or a pick and hoping that a ball or a shell sent their way by the French did not have them in its direct line. 'Your name on it', as was increasingly being said.

At 10 o' clock at night, Rushby was convinced that he was being shaken awake by his elder sister, but soon her sweet tones changed into the harsh, battlefield voice of Sergeant Ellis. It was too dark to see inside the hay store, which was what the 'roof' had proven to be.

"Sir! I think you should come down to the sentries. I've just been relieved and we're sure something's going on, Sir. On the other side."

Rushby raised his arm to indicate that Ellis should pull him up. He was wholly stiff from even two hours on the uneven boards and was unsure which limb to trust to raise him up. Once on his feet, he and Ellis hurried down to find Zeke Saunders at the picket line, who wasted no time before explaining.

"Sir. In the last of the light I'd swear I saw a fair old gang of Johnnies come down the slope some and start work, Sir. Then full dark came and I could see no more, Sir, but I could still hear voices, Sir, from time to time, even above the noise of this river."

Rushby felt a little annoyed at him being told this almost in the middle of the night, just before dawn would have been just as effective, but he could not complain. His men had done their duty and made him aware as soon as they had some serious concerns.

"Very good. Ellis, warn the change that will be taking over just before dawn, when we will be able to see what's what. If there is something, I want to know. Immediately!"

With that, all that were no longer needed there, returned to the barn, including Rushby and it was Ellis again who shook him awake, this time at first light. In fact, Rushby was already half awake, having been woken by cannon fire, this being very obviously local, but Ellis reported.

"In the night, Sir, they built a battery, like we thought. Only two guns but they've started already. You'd best come, Sir."

Rushby stared at him as the words sunk in, then he reacted.

"I want everyone down there. See to it."

Whilst Ellis began his waking activities, always in the form of a kick or a push, Rushby hurried down to his sentries, but, even as he left the shelter he quickly came to understand what was happening. To his ears came the regular report of probably two cannons and he could see the smoke from each discharge, drifting in clouds back up the slope to the San Christobal, the battery about half way down to take advantage of the elevation. He broke into a run to be met by Saunders and Davey.

"What can we do to slow their fire?"

It was Saunders who answered.

"Not much more than put shots through the embrasure, Sir. 'Tis well built for only two guns and all we can see is the shakoes of the gunners, Sir. They'm sunk well down and a bit higher than us here."

Rushby had no answer. This was his problem, but he had no solution. What he did know was that the two guns could send their fire perfectly along the line of the parallels and batteries that the Third Division were digging and that every shot in line with the workings would cause casualties. He gave the only order he could.

"Right. When the Section comes up, I want everyone sending fire at that battery. I must make a report."

Saunders saluted.

"Yes Sir. If anyone puts their head over that parapet, we'll put a ball through it, Sir, never fear."

Only marginally reassured, Rushby hurried away, back to the workings for the batteries, whilst each ball from the two guns made him crouch a little lower as they hummed overhead. He did not get as far as the nearest battery, number six, before he saw a group of Staff galloping towards him, with the unmistakable figure of Picton in the lead. Rushby stopped, came to attention and saluted as Picton reined in his horse.

"Lieutenant Rushby, Sir. 105th Foot."

Picton glowered down at him as though Rushby was personally responsible for the cannon himself.

"What's happening up there?"

"They built a battery overnight, Sir, and they've installed two guns."

A cannonball passed uncomfortably close overhead. Picton did not flinch.

"What are you doing about it?"

"I have my whole Section, Sir, with rifles, 44 men, firing into the embrasures, but the gun positions are deep. My men can see little to fire at, but they are sending shot through the embrasures anyway. Sir."

Picton seemed slightly mollified, but he continued to stare at Rushby, then his eyes elevated to the sight of the French cannon smoke, drifting up the San Christobal slope. He turned his horse.

"Do what you can!"

With that he was gone and Rushby saluted his back, then he turned himself and jogged back, to find his men firing at maximum rate at the battery, just over 100 yards across the river. Rushby went up to Ellis.

"General Picton wants us to keep firing, Sergeant."

"That we'll do, Sir, for all the good it'll do. Their fire hasn't slackened one shot!"

"Agreed, but orders, Sergeant. Orders!"

Ellis saluted and departed to load his own Baker Rifle. They plied the French earthwork with shot for the next hour, until they were relieved by the 60th, Captain Kenwood again, very curious.

"What are you doing?"

Rushby pointed across the Guadiana at the very obvious earthwork.

"Johnny's built that battery, Sir, and Picton wants it kept under fire."

"Did he say anything else?"

"No Sir, just keep sending fire their way. So, if that's all, Sir, I'll get mine back."

Receiving the nod from Kenwood, Rushby led his men in a wide sweep to avoid the line of fire from the battery and thence back to camp. Once back in their tent, Pike and Davey found Tom Miles sat up, wrapped in blankets, but his head down over his chest. Both knelt down beside him, Davey with his hand on his shoulder.

"Tom. How're you feeling?"

The head was raised for the face to reveal the results of being hurled down a trench, one eye almost closed with swelling and severe abrasions on that cheek.

"Like I been thrown off a cliff! God awful headache. Perhaps I landed on me head!"

Both smiled at the weak humour, as Davey bent lower.

"Have you eaten anything?"

Miles shook his head.

"Don't seem to want nothing."

"What did George say?"

"'Twern't George. He got the Surgeon to call in and he said that all of me's had a batterin' and loss of appetite, as he called it, was pretty much usual."

Both Pike and Davey sat back, mildly reassured.

"Well, we'll get something now, for ourselves. We've been up and down all night."

The pair left to go to Bridie and Nellie and the former spooned out some good beef stew. They returned to Miles and sat with him, both eating the rich broth of salt beef, biscuit and vegetables. Miles studied the two, busy eating.

"Well, perhaps I could get down a spoonful or two. Wouldn't hurt."

These were given from each plate, which Miles seemed to relish, then he rolled over and slept. It was not long before Davey, Pike and many others joined him.

oOo

Their rest was far too short. At four in the afternoon they were roused for their time in the works for the parallel and Battery Four. O'Hare and Carr accompanied their men out to the workings and they first approached the Engineer Major there, both noting that it was not Fletcher. After introductions, during which the Engineer introduced himself as Major Burgoyne, Carr asked the obvious question.

"Where's Fletcher."

The reply was instant and spoken with humour.

"During that sally of Johnny's from the San Roque, day before yesterday, a Frog bullet drove a dollar piece into his thigh. He's confined to his tent, but still giving orders."

O'Hare and Carr, now feeling the rain everywhere about their own person, only nodded, so Burgoyne continued.

"One good thing though. Those two French guns firing from the San Christobal, well, the Peer ordered Leith over on the far side, to do something and he sent a Brigade headed by cavalry along the far bank and they captured the guns. Good thing too!"

More nodding from O'Hare and Carr, but this time the former spoke.

"Any instructions for the digging?"

Burgoyne shook his head.

"No. Just follow the flags. And keep your shell watch, of course. They're still coming over!"

Now Carr nodded agreement, but his words were ironic.

"Thank you. That advice is a great comfort."

The work gangs of Davey and Saunders descended carefully into the trench, now empty of the 4th Division. They knew that eventually they, themselves, would be covered in mud, but later rather than sooner was preferred. They picked up the wet tools, their handles slippery with mud and began to dig and build up the parapet. Cannon shot from the town walls buried themselves into the parapet or buzzed overhead, but the danger was the shells from the San Roque. However, not once did they have to flatten themselves in the bottom of the trench and only occasionally were they required to kneel against the parapet, choosing the side on which the shell was going to land. They were almost two hours into their shift, when Zeke Saunders decided that things were definitely taking a turn for the worse. The rain was now so heavy that it washed the soil from his shovel. When he replenished it, the same thing happened and the trench was rapidly filling with water. He looked at Rushby whilst allowing the liquid mud to slide off his spade. No words were needed and so Rushby hurried over to O'Hare and Carr, both standing utterly miserable.

"Somewhat Biblical this, Sir. The rain I mean. It's making digging impossible!"

Carr turned his head to point his hat towards him, copious water now issuing from the peak.

"Understood you first time, Barnaby."

Carr took another look at the trenches, water pouring in from all directions.

"Get your men out. Plodding about down there does more harm than good."

"Back to camp, Sir?"

"No, the rain may relent. Just get them out."

Eventually, Burgoyne agreed, when it was put to him, and the order soon applied to the whole of the Third Division. Digging was abandoned, so they withdrew to whatever cover there was from possible cannon fire, but Carr soon noticed the change, which he remarked to O'Hare.

"No fire from the walls, have you noticed? Seems that even Frog gunners can't work their pieces in rain such as this."

"Which we will call the faintest of Blessings!"

The tone of conversation was only marginally bleaker for the men crouching down, some way back from the diggings, most sitting on anything that kept them off the sodden earth, with their greatcoats draped over their heads. Deakin was sat with Halfway and before dozing fitfully whilst leaning against each other, Halfway spoke his mind.

"This has to be just about the most miserable damn business I been through in all my soldiering days! I don't see how it can get no worse! When we finally gets in, there's going to be a reckonin' from the lads, a bad reckonin', you mark my words."

"I hopes not Tobe. Cuidad was bad enough. Worse than that will be a worry. But it can't get no worse than this!"

It was in the small hours of the morning when Burgoyne finally came to O'Hare and Carr, with news both welcome and unwelcome.

"Get your men back to your camp, digging is being abandoned. The Guadiana's burst its banks and flooded the workings of Five and Six. It'll be in yours soon."

322

Carr and O'Hare needed no further bidding and within minutes the 105th were trudging back to their tents, cold, wet, miserable and increasingly angry, with everyone, not just the French. The only consolation was a decent meal before they stripped off their wet clothes and hung them up inside their tents in the non-hope that they would be at least merely damp when the time came to put them on again in the afternoon. When the time did arrive, at least there was another hot meal waiting and all kissed Bridie, Nellie and Consuela in gratitude for their efforts to keep them fed during the incessant wet and cold. When they finally entered the trenches again, the work first involved using anything that could be used to bail out the flood-water, all this watched by an increasingly depressed Burgoyne, which he conveyed to Carr and O'Hare.

"It's not better up on the San Miguel heights, only different. The mud for the parapet is so loose it has to be shored up with sand-bags, which Johnny seems to be very good at blowing away, and the rain's even washing the soil out of the gabions."

Carr smiled wanly.

"That may be a comfort to us, but not much, so I'll say for now we're happy to stick with what we've got."

The last few words were very apposite for Colonel Lacey sat with his Storesman, Corporal Len Timmins, both compiling reports on supplies of all descriptions. The news arrived in the form of Sergeant-Major Gibney, who delivered his bad news whilst stood rigidly to attention.

"Sir. Beg pardon, Sir, but there's no rations. The pontoon's broke down at Elvas and nowt can get across."

Lacey, his face drawn into a deep frown, looked across at Timmins.

"What do we have in reserve?"

"What we always try to keep something back, Sir. Some barrels of salt pork and some sacks of flour, Spanish beans and biscuit."

"Enough?"

"Should be, Sir, but in all this damp, I can't speak for the quality."

"And rum?"

"Enough of that, Sir, yes, but that's usually issued before combat, Sir."

The evening ration was issued, this being the salt pork, but the accompaniment that was tipped into the pans of Bridie, Nellie and Consuela brought a look of disgust to their faces. The beans and biscuit all had signs of mould and the flour was now more a paste than a powder. Nellie looked at Bridie.

"And what do we do with this?"

Bridie pulled out some beans and biscuit to closer examine the blemishes.

"Pick out the best, clean some as best we can, throw it all into a pot and give it a good boil. Yet I doubt there'll be enough, and just when 'tis needed, too!"

At Midnight, the men took their meal by coming out of their trenches a short way back, hoping to find a drier place to sit and eat and so, under lantern light, the food was issued. John Davey was the first to notice the small portions.

"Are we on short rations, Bridie?"

Bridie nodded, whilst half filling Joe Pike's plate.

"So we are. There's nothing coming up. That pontoon thing's broke what gets all across the river, so nothing's arriving!"

The short meal meant a short break and so digging was soon resumed, which greatly added to the disgruntled mood, but a half rum ration did somewhat lift their spirits. The return to camp found no welcoming food awaiting them, only a thin biscuit porridge, and with that eaten, or drunk in some cases, they made ready for sleep. At the same time, Lacey called an Officers' meeting in the Headquarters tent, Captains and above and he gave his usual order in times of hardship; brief and to the point.

"First, your men! If you do nothing more than listen and give them some encouragement that progress is being made, that will do some good. But, get around your Companies and at least convince them that you are concerned. The pontoon will be repaired and we will be fed again."

It was Captain Reginald Charters of Two Company who spoke what many were thinking, speaking in a hushed tone, almost desperate.

"Could this be abandoned, Sir?"

Lacey's face darkened at the gravity of such a question, but he was not going to tell a lie.

"It could. Everything's behind schedule, but this is his chance to take what he calls 'The Keys' and we've got one, that being Cuidad. The French are way off and scattered and we're here, concentrated. I cannot see any abandonment. No!"

When Drake arrived at the tent of Davey and Saunders, on his rounds, his first attention was drawn to Miles, now sat scraping the mould from a damp biscuit with his clasp knife.

"Miles! We've missed you. Are you any better?"

The pleasantry was lost on Tom Miles who stared back blankly.

"Bin better, Sir, but worse just lately. Poor commons don't help. Sir."

Drake could only nod in sympathy, but Saunders tried to be at least cheerful and appreciative of Drake's calling on them.

"Well, there is one thing, Sir, with all the rain, it keeps down the wildlife, Sir. The lice is less of a problem."

Pike felt the need to add some cheer.

"Yes Sir. They can drown as can anything else."

This brought a half smile to Drake's face.

"Well, if it helps, none of us are getting fed too well and we all could do with a change of clothes. To get into something clean and dry. Things will get better, of that I'm sure. Our Engineers will get the pontoon back in service, be assured."

With that he left to visit the rest of the Company and the whole tent settled to sleep, that is until an appalling downpour hit the tent at around Noon, filling their drainage ditches around it to the extent that water began to run through the tent, and the accompanying squall pulled out some pegs from the soft earth that held the guy-ropes causing the tent to partially collapse. When all was restored and a new drainage channel dug to relieve their own flood, sleep was impossible and so, in soaked clothes, they all huddled together, sat on whatever would raise them above the soaked straw. To be called for parade at 4 o' clock was a relief and they filed down to the trenches. 'Breakfast' did not take place. The three women had come back empty handed. The biscuit was all gone, the flour now mouldy and the Spanish beans had actually begun to sprout. Nevertheless, Joe Pike ate them raw, which caused a painfull stomach ache, and so no-one followed his example.

That night, under the ecumenical cart, Chaplain's Assistant Sedgwicke was finding it extremely difficult to hold to the tenet of maintaining affection and regard for your neighbour, in his case the neighbour being his Superior Officer, the Reverend Albright. As Sedgwicke shifted his position on the roughhewn logs that now proved so ineffective at keeping his bedding out of the flood of water that poured under the cart, Sedgwicke fought inside himself to hold down the resentment, even hatred, that he felt for the one sleeping dry on the floor of the cart, protected by a stout tarpaulin. There was certainly space remaining there for a frame as slight as Sedgwicke's but all hints that, perhaps, under such weather conditions, they might share the cart, had been either ignored or not understood. The one consolation was that Sedgwicke had his own store of decent food secreted away and that, tomorrow, Albright would have to be satisfied with thin porridge gruel. However, whilst this provided some spiritual comfort, Sedgwicke's physical situation grew steadily worse, as the wind whipped in through the open side of the space beneath the wagon. Inevitably, the resentment grew in direct proportion to the wet seeping in through Sedgwicke's blankets, as Albright snored above him.

The one consolation for all in the 105th was that, at 7.00 that morning, they finished their battery and Burgoyne arrived, in good mood, to speak to O'Hare and Carr.

"Right. That's the mud pie, now to get the guns in! That'll be your job. They're 100 yards back on the only road to here. One Company to a gun should do it. If you can get them up to the two entrances, the gunners will do the rest."

Carr looked up at the sky, now amazingly much lighter and not depositing rain down on them.

"Yes, and just when we could do with some rain to hide us, if only a little."

Burgoyne ignored the complaint and walked back, whilst O'Hare and Carr sent around the order to fall back to the road. Drake took his Company to where he was bid, to a Naval 24 pounder, now mounted on a sledge, because the shipboard wheels would never have turned in the hopeless mud. Drake remembered, "First your men", and so, in that spirit, he picked up the attached rope and behind Saunders, with Solomon leading on the other, they hauled their burden forward. Carr's anxiety had been well founded, because the French, through their own telescopes could see what was happening and the shot and shell began to arrive. The men on both ropes, slipped and slithered, always under fire. At one point, Drake's own line all fell sideways entirely, but, with the Gunners pushing from behind, the gun was propelled forward, all the quicker when some momentum was gained on the slippery surface angled slightly downward through the sap from the parallel to the battery. All strained at their rope, Drake as much as anyone, despite his non-muscular frame. The French fire continued, but it was spread over the whole parallel, and to his relief Drake heard screaming behind him only once. Thus, the gun was delivered, with two casualties and the Gunners took over to wheel their charge off the sledge and onto the wooden gun platform. Their task complete and now relieved of duties, Drake quickly pulled his men back, carrying two bodies, one badly wounded having lost an arm, the other dead, having lost his head.

Whilst their men returned to their camp, the Officers of the 105th Light Company stood to watch the new developments, informed by Colonel Dickson of the Artillery who was now making his rounds. Once they were delivered, the installation of the guns happened remarkably quickly and so, now that all was in place, Dickson sounded almost buoyant as he spoke to them and not just from the fact that the rain had stopped. The guns had been installed and mounted, even though under fire, but with minimal casualties. The siege could begin.

"We'll soon get all of one to six going. One and two are on the Picurina, three on the San Roque, your four, here, will enfilade the Santa Trinidad, five the same to the Santa Maria, six to the San Roque. It's begun."

The bemused look on the faces of all four, including Carr, brought more explanation from Dickson.

"The San Trinidad is that huge bastion on the far-left corner, from where we are here. That's where the main breach will be. The Santa Maria is the next one beyond that, around the corner. That big one opposite, between the Trinidad and the Castle, that's the San Pedro. We're leaving that alone."

They thanked him for the information before he walked on, but any more conversation was impossible, because now the gunners in their battery, with six 24lb cannons and a 24lb howitzer opened up with all the pent-up energy and frustration of the past days, the gunners working with a will and enthusiasm that kindled mild optimism in them all. As they walked back for the little time there was left to eat and get some sleep, Drake turned to Lieutenant Shakeshaft.

"Well there you are Richard. A notable date for your diary. The guns opened up, when?"

Shakeshaft smiled and nodded at the thought.

"Yes. 24th March."

oOo

The optimism turned to apprehension, especially with Carr, when Kempt arrived late the next morning at the 105th Headquarters tent. He wasted no time on pleasantries.

"The Picurina is under bombardment as we speak, but Wellington wants it taken now, that being tonight. We've wasted too much time with this weather and casualties are higher than expected. Besides the ague, Surgeons tell of men unable to walk because of swollen feet, caused by being perpetually cold and wet, so they say. On top, a French army is moving towards us, although still a long way off and we are not certain where. Wellington wants the Picurina, which will involve all my Lights and those of the 77th and 83rd from Campbell's. They'll combine with some from the Light Division. You're one of the Majors from mine, Carr, so get up there now. You'll be part of a column with a Major Shaw of the 74th in overall command. He's got your orders."

Almost in shock at his sudden inclusion in what sounded little better than the exploits of a Forlorn Hope, Carr nevertheless rose and hurried to Wellington's Headquarters behind the Cerro de San Miguel. Within an hour, he was on his way back, having heard Shaw's overall plan. He took himself immediately to the tent of Drake, Rushby and Shakeshaft to impart the news. Before he spoke he looked carefully at each.

"There's going to be an attempt on the Picurina. Tonight, and we're part of it. A sort of reserve to the Forlorn Hope, whatever that may mean or bring. They're the ones with the ladders, them being a Company from the 74th and one from the 88th. There'll be carpenters, sappers and miners along with us, 24 of them in all."

He allowed that to sink in, but not long enough for questions, because he quickly changed the subject.

"Have rations come up?"

Drake nodded.

"Yes, they got the pontoon repaired last night. We've plenty of everything. It includes some cheese!"

Carr's eyebrows lifted.

"You don't say? Cheese! Right, so, get them fed, including cheese! Midday meal is practically now and then another late evening. The attack goes in at nine tonight."

The anxiety grew on their faces, but Carr did not intend to let them brood for the remainder of the time that they had. He pulled out of his pocket a plan of the Picurina which he had copied from that shown the assembly by Shaw. They all drew up chairs and stools to the small table and looked expectantly at Carr. So, for the next hour he described Shaw's plan and, for the next hour after that, they asked questions and made suggestions. Then, feeling more assured, they slept, but first they sent Ellis to order their men to do the same. None expected to sleep during the coming night.

Thus, it was, that a well fed and rested, 105th Light Company found themselves marching on the road to the Cerro San Miguel, but they were not alone, ahead were Kempt's 60th Rifles, and his Light Companies of the 74th and 88th. Behind them came those of the 77th and 83rd from Campbell's Brigade. There was no talking, the rumour had circulated and here was the confirmation; they were marching to get behind the Picurina to mount an attack. The daylight was dying as they arrived to form up and wait at the rear of the San Miguel, when Shaw came immediately to Carr.

"Is all well?"

"It is."

"Right. Now's your chance to explain to your men. Their knowing how we expect to do this thing cannot do any harm."

With that, he was gone and Carr called for his Officers and Sergeants, giving them the task to pass on the plan. It was Rushby who arrived at the group of Davey and Saunders. They sat with their muskets leant back over their shoulders, most with hands folded over the trigger guard. There was no air of enthusiasm, they all knew that they were to be part of some type of dangerous assault, but Rushby began as enthusiastically as he was able.

"We are to assault the right wall of the fort here. We are in reserve to the 74th and 88th, who will be carrying the ladders. Others will be attacking at different points, like Captain Powis and his 83rd Lights on the point, so, when we get in, you can expect to find others, like us, arriving from different directions."

Their faces remained blank, the one question came from Tom Miles.

"Any plunder in there, Sir?"

Rushby smiled weakly.

"Pleased to have you back with us, Miles, but the answer is, I doubt it, other than what can usually be gleaned from any battlefield."

With that, he stood and walked off to check that all other groups had been told. Miles looked at Byford.

"What's 'gleaned', Byfe?"

Byford chuckled, as did they all.

"It means picking up the leftovers from a harvest. The ears of corn left lying on the ground. So, for you and Len it means obtaining only what you have to look carefully for and then gather unto yourselves."

Miles was not content.

"Leftovers after they Diddykites and Scots bastards've got in first!"

They all ignored him, Miles was back to something resembling normal and they settled back to sip their issue of rum which they had been given immediately on arrival. Then they dozed fitfully, this being a chance for more sleep, but at 7.30, when it was full dark, the sounds of movement came to them through the darkness, two groups changing position. Drake stood waiting with Ellis.

"That'll be the 74th and the 88th going forward. Which means we're next."

However, he was wrong, there came no order to move, what did arrive was Kempt, whom, in the total darkness, was only recognised by his voice.

"Where's Carr?"

The answer came from the darkness some way off from them.

"Here Sir."

"Carr, I want you with the first wave, with Shaw's. He's in the first parallel, where you start from."

"Sir!"

Then more from the darkness, but still Kempt.

"Drake!"

"Sir."

326

"Wait here until you are called forward. If at all."

Carr then departed for the parallel and the 105th Lights remained where they were as the minutes ticked by. Carr found Major Shaw in the furthest parallel forward with the Light Companies of the 74th and 88th now spread along its length. He was surprised at the silence, there was no cannon fire at all. All that was distinguishable were the exchanges of the French sentries up on the walls, a regular intonation of, "Tout va bien dans la Fort Picurina". Carr spoke quietly to Shaw.

"I had no idea we are this close!"

Shaw was looking at his watch in the negligible light of a covered lantern

"Close, Carr, yes, but not close enough."

"How much damage has the bombardment caused?"

"Nothing for us, some on the apex point for Powis and his 83rd."

He studied his watch regularly, whilst Carr stared into the darkness, thinking over what he knew of what lay ahead and it was no comfort at all; an open glacis, then some kind of palisade above the ditch, the ditch itself and then an undamaged wall on the far side. He looked along the parapet and there was just enough light for him to see the ladders laid along the top, then Shaw was moving, out of the trench and crouching as he ran forward.

"Come on!"

Within half a minute the trench was empty and they were all running forward over the exposed space. The single sound of their running feet lasted not a minute before they heard the alarm from the Picurina walls, shouted many times and from many points, "Alarme. Se tenir. Nous sommes attaqués." Almost immediately the walls erupted with a deluge of fire which was added to from the walls of the town itself. Two men at the forward end of a ladder were soon felled and so Carr seized another man and they both picked it up and continued forward, but the carnage amongst this first wave was appalling, this only revealed when the French threw burning torches across to land onto the end of the glacis at the ditch. Carr estimated that barely a half had managed to arrive at the ditch to then find progress denied by a stout wooden palisade which the Sappers with them immediately began to hack at with axes and crowbars. With little success, but it did give some cover from the musket fire from the Picurina walls and aid came ironically from the walls themselves; a double charge of grapeshot, aimed too low caused the heavy balls to badly damaged a section of the palisade over about two yards.

"Here! In here!"

Men rushed to him and they pulled away enough of the timbers to make a large gap, then they were through. Carr saw the ladders being flung into the ditch from beyond the palisade and, all along the palisade, men pushed and pulled each other over the rough timber uprights. However, once over, Carr fully realised that there was nothing like two Companies following the ladders down into the depths of the ditch, more like just over one. Once down in the ditch the crack and roar of the French defence continued above them, but the survivors were placing their ladders against the far side to climb and attack the parapet, at which point came a torrent of angry expletives, in both English and Gaelic. The ladders were much too short to reach the parapet from within the very deep ditch.

Meanwhile, Drake was sitting with his men, alongside Shakeshaft, each saying nothing because the only possible topic of conversation would be on the sound conveying the intensity of the French defence and that was too courage sapping a topic to discuss. Their silence was broken by Kempt himself arriving. It was clear that things were not working out well, because he shouted but two words, "Follow me!" They all rose, not to follow the 74th and 88th, but instead to move left, further across the face of the Picurina. Drake felt justified in asking at least one question as they jogged over the summit of the San Miguel.

"Sir, may I ask where we're going."

Kempt was fairly breathless, but he answered.

"The attack has been stopped everywhere. I'm leading you to have another go at the wall's apex, where Powis and his 83rd have been stopped. At least we've managed to batter some kind of breach there."

Drake said no more, his immediate thoughts were of Cecily and their child.

As Drake made his run, Carr looked up at the parapet, too high, but at least grenades and lighted shells were not raining down on them. The men were sheltering under the French side of the ditch, beneath the main wall.

"Pick up those ladders and come on!"

His orders were obeyed and they ran around towards the rear of the fort, but they had not gone 30 yards before they were halted by another palisade stretching right across their floor of the ditch. The sappers immediately got to work and, as they hacked desperately at the woodwork, the ladders were raised again to the walls there, but they did not need to be fully placed against the wall to see that again, at this point they were too short. He looked around at the men again crouched beneath the wall and desperation began to grow within him. They were trapped down in this very deep ditch and, even if the Sappers broke through, there was no guarantee that the walls would be any lower further on. Then an Engineer Sergeant came up to him.

"Sir. I believe the ladders would span across this, Sir. It's deep, but none too wide. If we could get some ladders back up, Sir, and drop them across, we'd have a chance, Sir. It'd be a bridge."

Carr stared hard at him. The Sergeant was suggesting that they cross over the ditch on a kind of bridge, in full view of the defenders as they crawled over. It was insane, but what else? In the light of the French torches still burning above Carr simply nodded, then he turned once again to the men below the wall.

"Get these ladders back up to our side."

The men needed no further bidding to make immediate efforts to get out of the ditch and the ladders were raised to again prove to be too short also for that side, but not by so much. All were placed and men began to climb but many quickly fell victim to French musketry fired from the embrasures of the walls behind, shot in the back, to fall dead or wounded down the 30 feet below them. Carr was one of the first up, pushed up by an 88th Sergeant. He had felt something skim his shoulder and a quick look revealed one epaulette now hanging by some threads, but he immediately picked up a musket and began to load and fire, using cartridges from a dead Connaught Ranger. For the moment, there was nothing more to do, as men scrambled over the edge of the ditch, pushed up by comrades below. However, despite the casualties, many reached the top and, the veterans of the 88th and 74th quickly took shelter behind the damaged palisade and began to answer the fire from the three embrasures opposite and soon more and more men were answering, each capable of a higher rate of fire than that coming from the French manning the walls. The French fire fell off and three ladders were dragged up from the depths at which point Major Shaw arrived, plainly distraught at what had so far been a complete failure. Not one man had reached the French parapet. He seized Carr by the arm, his face desperate, his eyes wide, but his voice firm and determined.

"What can we do?"

Carr was about to answer when Shaw was struck by a bullet, just in from his right shoulder and he fell clutching his wound. If he heard, Carr knew not, but he said it anyway.

"Our ladders will reach across. I'm going to try that. A kind of bridge."

Shaw gave a kind of nod, but Carr's mind was wholly elsewhere, because the Engineers had already dropped two ladders across the ditch and a third was being added. He seized the sleeve of a Highland Sergeant.

"Get some men and stay here, at this palisade. I want continuous fire through those embrasures if we are to stand any chance of crossing on those ladders."

Whilst the Sergeant bellowed his own orders and seized men to fling them behind the palisade, Carr ran to the three ladders where an Officer came up to him.

"I'm still here, Sir. Captain Oates. 88th."

Carr nodded an acknowledgement, then he drew his sword to shout above the din.

"Connaughts and Highlanders! I've damn well had enough of this. I'm going over and I'm getting into that place to settle accounts with these Crapaud-bastard Frogs. Follow me who can!"

He stepped out and the three ladders swayed and dipped alarmingly but they held. Carr dared not look over to the parapet, being too concerned for his own balance, but he could hear the weight of fire now organised by the Highland Sergeant and it was definitely quelling the fire from the embrasures both in front and to each side. Then the ladders swayed and dipped under his feet. Men were following him over and he heard an Irish voice from behind.

"Don't stop now, Sir. Them as walks tightropes, they always keeps goin'! Sir!"

Meanwhile, further over at the apex, Kempt led the way to the head of the glacis, with Drake just behind. Once there on the horribly exposed surface, they saw the full extent of the casualties, but they were mildly encouraged that further forward they found many 83rd still alive, guarding their ladders and doing their best to return fire. The French fire had slackened, presumably because they had halted the attack and seeing so few Redcoats now advancing forward, they were saving their ammunition, but there could be no doubt that they were ready to react again. Kempt seized Drake's sleeve.

"I want your best marksmen on the edge of the ditch sending fire through the breach. I'll take the rest down into the ditch with the ladders. Powis led these, he may still be alive."

Drake now turned to his two Lieutenants.

"Richard. Barnaby. Spread yours either side of here. Fire in through that breach, there may be a cannon there, and across the top of those embrasures either side as well. The cannon in them can't bear on us, but they can be used as cover for the Frogs. Keep their heads down."

The weight of French fire was now renewed, they had been seen, but both Sections of the 105th Light began answering and the French reply did not reach any impossible intensity, from neither cannon nor musketry as Drake's men poured fire across the top of each embrasure and in through the breach itself. Kempt had disappeared into the ditch, taking all of the 83rd still alive and unwounded with him. Drake may have taken a breath, but he thought not, being so concerned with anxiety for Kempt and his men, as he watched the ladders being set up to just reach up to the bottom of the breach and it was Kempt himself who was first in, followed by an obviously vengeful 83rd. He witnessed a brief struggle on the far side and then French fire slackened and fell away as the ramparts were cleared. He stood up.

"Come on! We're needed inside."

He shinned down the nearest ladder on his side and then climbed the first he came to on the opposite, to reach the breach and scramble through over the dead and dying, both red and blue, followed by his whole Company.

Carr had reached his embrasure, to find it half blocked by a cannon. He squeezed past the barrel and was almost through, when a musket went off beside his ear, fired by the following Connaught, setting his head ringing. He carried on through the smoke to find himself standing on the body of a dead French gunner, before discharging his own pistol at the first blue uniform he saw. Connaughts and Highlanders were arriving, but not moving on into the fort yet, first crowding around Carr to consolidate their lodgement, quickly bayonetting the few defenders there or casting them off the wall. Carr shook his head to clear it and quickly decided.

"We go left into the fort."

A newly familiar voice spoke up behind.

"As you order, Sir. Captain Oates again."

He had not drawn another breath before he collapsed against the parapet with a bullet wound in his thigh, the wound bleeding copiously. Immediately the cry was taken up by the Connaughts.

"He's down! The Captain's down. The bastards've got the Captain!"

Without orders, the Connaughts surged along the parapet's walkway, a charge which Carr decided would be useful to follow, but the trail of the Connaughts' progress was marked with many dead Frenchmen; the Irishmen were obviously taking no prisoners. Carr looked back to see who was following and reassuringly found the walkway crowded with red uniforms, but the maddened Irish were now far ahead, murdering any Frenchman they found in their way. They were halted by a bellow that could only have come from Kempt, who then noticed Carr.

"Major! Get these down to the back gate. Stop any reinforcements from the town."

By sheer good luck, Carr was close to a set of steps and a small jump down took him onto the uppermost. The interior of the fort was almost full dark, but he had no choice.

"Come on. Follow me."

All who heard jumped, or ran, down the steps and Carr could hear Kempt sending extra men after him. He ran forward, using all his senses to ascertain what was ahead, but what came to his ears made no sense at all, not so much as what caused them, more concerning what he could expect on arrival. Amid the sounds of conflict came the unmistakable sounds of many axes biting into wood. However, when this fell away there came the continuous sounds of hand-to-hand conflict. Carr ran on and to his surprise he found himself staring at the backs of large French Grenadiers, their bearskins and wide epaulettes unmistakable, even in the gloom. He could not bring himself to stab the nearest in the back, and so he dealt him a blow on the back of his neck, but not so the Connaughts, nor the Scotsmen, who killed several from behind before the Grenadiers' line broke and they surrendered. Carr pushed through them to confront the first Redcoat of any rank, who immediately came to the attention and saluted.

"Captain Holloway, Sir. Royal Engineers."

Carr offered his hand, but it was taken by Holloway's left.

"Carr. 105th, Well done Captain, you found a way in! But you're wounded."

"Yes, Sir, but I'll live. There's some more of us under Lieutenant Gipps just outside, there to hold off any attempt to re-take this place, Sir. They are in a communication trench."

"Right. Detail some of yours to take these prisoners back, but get the rest of yours up on the walls at the back here! If an attack comes, it'll come from the San Roque. It's only 400 yards away. I'll get mine out to meet this Gipps of yours."

Holloway saluted, but Carr had already turned away. With such a mixed force, he had only one choice of words.

"All mine! With me!"

He ran forward and, by the light of gunfire from the town, he could see the remains of a palisade that blocked the rear entrance, recently hacked down, but once through and down the slope they were in a communication trench that ran straight to the town walls. Carr immediately gave his orders.

"Man the right side. Load and wait."

Leaving the NCOs to distribute the men, he ran on to find two Officers in conference. They turned to meet him, but one was leaning heavily on the parapet. It was he who answered Carr first, but with a voice which showed the severity of his wound.

"Gipps, Sir. Royal Engineers."

Carr immediately pulled the nearest two soldiers from their parapet.

"Get the Lieutenant back to our lines."

The two seized Gipps' arms and practically carried him back up towards the Picurina. The second Officer introduced himself.

"Lindsay, Sir. 88th."

"How many men have you?"

"About 200, with Gipps'. To hold any counter-attack."

"I have another 100. About! Hold here and see what happens."

What happened was that the guns from the San Trinidad and San Pedro bastions sent a deluge of cannon fire at the Picurina, now they realised that it had fallen. The shot hummed continuously over their heads to batter the back wall of the Picurina, but many balls entered the interior over the wreck of the palisade at the rear gate and caused casualties. Kempt, still inside, did not hesitate and he yelled at Drake.

"Out! Out! Back the way we came!"

Within a minute, both British and their prisoners were back onto the glacis, with the fort now protecting them, but Kempt was not finished, there was yet another task. He knew which Regiments were involved, but not what he had with him and they had to be pulled together. There was nothing else for it. other than to shout and hope for the right response.

"If you can hear me! Follow me!"

Men came quickly to him and he led them rightwards, into another French communication trench that linked the Picurina to the San Roque and he gave the simple order.

"Hold this trench. Watch to your right front."

His direction was perfect, because, by the light of the French guns in the town, they soon saw a whole Battalion of French emerge from the San Roque and advance rapidly at the Picurina. Kempt raised his voice above the din.

"All Officers! Fire as you choose!"

The San Roque counter-attack was passing across their front and, as they came within effective range, Kempt's men opened fire and the French advance faltered, but continued. However, it halted completely when they were met by fire directly from their front. Drake was close by and Kempt drew his own conclusion.

"I assume that's Carr down there!"

"As it was you that sent him there, Sir, I think we can assume so."

The French attack was melting into the ground and soon the survivors fell back to the San Roque. Kempt sheathed his sword.

"I think, Captain, we can assume that that, is that!"

"Yes Sir, as you say."

However, behind Kempt, Drake could see what his Brigadier could not, that the Picurina was now being battered to pieces by intense cannon fire.

oOo

Joe Pike and John Byford stood together on a bank a little way behind Number Four Battery, both with bandages about them covering wounds gained from the assault on the Picurina. Byford, perhaps more poetic, but certainly more cerebral than his comrades, had reasoned to himself that the events now taking place before Badajoz were such that he would probably never see the like again in his lifetime. Therefore, with the Midday meal inside him, he had decided to wander forward from their camp and Joe Pike had taken it upon himself to tag along. Byford was one of the few who would tolerate his naïve and unworldly questions, but there were few questions that needed asking to explain any further the sight before them and its incessant warlike sound, all was only too obvious. On both sides, from both the walls and the parallels, cannon fire roared out constantly, insistently commanding all of their senses. From the walls came the continuous blasts of cannon smoke, ten to fifteen yards out beyond the muzzle, whilst at that central point dwelt the flash from the muzzle and then the orange flame. All was answered with equal intensity from their own side, from what seemed to be a ring of batteries from where they stood, circling further round to the far side of the town. The smoke from both conjoined to form an immense cloud that drifted upwards and slightly sideways on the faint breeze. However, what was different on the town side were the persistent sprays of rubble thrown into the air from the far side of the San Trinidad bastion. Although they could not see the breach wall from where they were, because it was on the far side from them, the effects of the bombardment upon it were obvious, dislodged bricks and blocks from the wall being repeatedly thrown up into the air. They stood to study the scene for some minutes, before Byford made his comment, half to himself.

"This is a scene from Dante's Inferno!"

Joe Pike had heard and turned to him.

"What's that, John?"

"It's a book. About Hell! And this Hell contains innocents, not the Souls of the condemned."

Pike then added his own, perhaps more prosaic comment.

"If you saw this from a long way off, or from up in the sky if you could, you'd think the whole place was just a pit of madness!"

Byford smiled and nodded in his direction, but, with that and both having seen and heard enough, they returned to camp, to be greeted by Davey.

"What've you two been doing?"

It was Byford who answered before crossing their camp to sit next to Eirin.

"Taking a look and a listen, at what both sides here think of each other!"

Tom Miles, still with a pain in his head, did not fully understand what Byford had said, but the word 'look' was enough.

"I 'd've thought you'd seen plenty enough by now, of what's goin' on around here, without wanderin' forward to see some more!"

Joe Pike now felt able enough to chip in.

"He called it Dantes Inferno!"

Tom Miles turned on him

"Did he now, whatever that might be, but me, I've seen enough to fully judge the murderous business that this has turned into! Plenty enough."

At that point the conversation ended, because Sergeant Ellis had arrived with orders and all faces then turned towards him.

"When it's dark, we're repairing Number Four. That big bastion right opposite us, the San Pedro, our Officers calls it, have done some damage that needs putting right. So, when 'tis dark, form on the road."

Tom Miles continued to stare at Ellis.

"When will the day come when you brings some good news?"

Ellis chuckled.

"If I had some, Tom Miles, you'd be the first to hear it, just to see your face, but I do have some. Tobacco's included in today's rations."

That news removed the sour look from Tom Miles' face but nothing more enlightening was spoken to them concerning their next few hours and later the repairs were completed with no casualties. It was again the very new future that became the principal concern of all in the 105th as they sat idle in their camp during the next two days after the capture of the Picurina. Unsurprisingly, these new developments had arrived first and in more detailed form at the Headquarters Tent of the 105th, with Lacey arriving back from Division to find

O'Hare and Carr sat drinking coffee and reading newspapers three weeks old. O'Hare lowered his newspaper and looked at Lacey.

"Anything to cheer us up?"

Carr answered first, before lowering his paper.

"It's not raining!"

However, Lacey had returned in no mood for levity.

"We've got the Picurina, but little else can be described as going well. The Fourth and Fifth Divisions have finished batteries between the Picurina and the San Trinidad, but at frightful cost, up to 100 killed and wounded. Also, our opponent has fortified the ravellin in front of the San Trinidad even more, that's where the main breach is and he's put men up on it to fire into our batteries and at any workmen. Gun for gun, he's winning the duel. We lost two guns yesterday."

Carr looked glumly at him.

"And the future?"

Lacey held up his hand to count each task off on his fingers.

"Extend the sap to the San Roque. Build a Number 10 alongside our Number Four. Get some Riflemen out before the San Trinidad. Blow up the San Roque dam."

O'Hare frowned.

"The second and third may well have our number on them.

Lacey nodded.

"Certainly the second, but I'll be annoyed at the third. Our Light Company has done as much, perhaps more, than any in the 60th or 95th."

Lacey was correct regarding the second because an order from Colonel Fletcher, still laid up, arrived not an hour later to convey the order to dig a Number 10 Battery. This arrived in due course in the mess areas of Deakin, Davey and Saunders, in the usual manner from Ethan Ellis. After the final words of the grim news, Deakin looked up.

"Have a sit, Ethan. Take some tea and have a smoke."

Jed Deakin took no notice at all of the look of extreme annoyance that now covered the face of Tom Miles, but Bridie soon passed over the tea and John Davey tossed over his tobacco pouch. After the first puff, Ellis shook his head.

"The mood's bad, through and through. All over and I don't like it. Talavera was a bad battle, all starving and thirsty, and so many dead, but there were no evil feelings then, if you understands my meaning. The high jinks in Cuidad was not much more than that, but there's real bitterness here, like some paying out has to come."

Byford leaned forward.

"As though for revenge?"

Ellis nodded.

"Just so, and 'tis across all the Brigade. Across the whole army, I shouldn't wonder."

Tom Miles glowered around the gathering.

"You can count me in on that!"

Deakin withdrew his own pipe from his mouth

"Well, that's one thing, but 'twern't Johnny as brought the rain, an' no-one can expect 'em to open the gates and say "Welcome British army, come on in!". 'Tis their job to keep us out, as much as 'tis our job to get ourselves in!"

At this point, Bridie hit him with a spoon, her green eyes flashing as she gave vent to her own frustration.

"Well, I for one have had enough of this siege business. Living in these holes in the ground, everything all wet and damp each day, and all the noise!"

This was the cue for Nellie to give air to her own concerns.

"And isn't that true, an' all! All this noise keepin' the childers awake an' the constant worry of French cannonballs rollin' through everythin'. Rations, pots, cooking-fire and tents!"

On hearing this, Deakin turned on both.

"Them's French overshoots, spent balls. The youngers knows not to touch 'em. They do, don't they?"

This was Deakin in his most ferocious form and both women nodded meekly, but Deakin had not finished.

"You let's them roll on, you hear?"

Whilst they nodded again, Deakin replaced his pipe, to then quickly remove it, when they heard what Eirin had to say.

"There is some good news! I'm going to have another baby!"

The mood changed instantly, as Bridie hurried over to kiss her sister, whilst anything that easily came to hand was thrown at the embarrassed Byford.

In better mood than for some days, they assembled later on the road, where the tools were waiting for them and they walked forward to find an Engineer Officer waiting amidst the flags indicating the ground for Number Ten. They soon realised that they were nothing like so spaced out as for the main Number Four, but this did not create any feeling of relief, the reason well noticed by Zeke Saunders.

"This is a moon you could read by!"

Tom Miles replied instantly.

"If you could read!"

"Which I can!"

The end of the argument came from Ellis.

"Enough! The sooner we gets this dug, the sooner we'm back off out of it!"

They began with pick and shovel, all expecting a fusillade from the San Pedro walls, however, when the cannon there opened up, nothing came their way. Their target was unknown. Curious, all looked up and over, towards the San Roque and even in the monochrome light of the moon, all could see the intense bombardment striking the area of the new San Roque sap, now fully down from the Picurina. Byford returned to his spade-work.

"Someone's getting it bad. We can only be thankful Johnny's more worried about what's happening there, rather than over here."

The 105's work was completed well before dawn and Kempt's Brigade drew back, but Drake and Carr remained to talk with the artillery Officer who had supervised the work. Drake asked, whilst Carr studied events in the distance.

"What's this one for?"

The Officer pulled his attention away from regarding the completed work, with the gunners finally completing the wooden platforms and gun mountings.

"Lobbing shells onto the ravellin before the San Trinidad. He's got a lot of men up there, who are doing us harm. Time to clear them away!"

"How are things up that end?"

"Very bloody! Johnny must be manning his guns in relays because it's non-stop and his infantry are just as active. Whoever the Governor is of this place, Phillipon so deserters tell us, he should get one of Boney's Legion d'Honneur, if he survives. There's only days left of this!"

That answer absorbed, came the next question.

"Who'll be dragging in the guns?"

"You've drawn the short straw. Get some rest; the call will come."

"Tell me that's an April Fool!"

"It is not. It's you for the ropes!"

The call came, exactly when breakfast should be taken, but they were asleep and so it was a very befuddled and bitter 105th that dragged in the three 24lbs howitzers, but that was soon done and they returned for breakfast. However, again Carr and Drake remained to watch the gunners mount their pieces with remarkable speed and soon the first shell was fired, but misdirected, to land and explode too obviously amongst houses. It took five more shots before the artillerymen were satisfied and then all three guns opened fire together.

The next two days was a period of inactive waiting, all to the sound of cannon replying to cannon, but then new developments involving the 105th arrived, in the form of Kempt himself.

"Bad news. We got onto the San Roque dam last night and set charges, but they were not big enough and so the dam still stands and I bet Johnny's repairing it as we speak and so the inundation across the front of the San Trinidad is still there. Next, more bad news. Johnny's floated a raft across the inundation to worry the San Roque sap. As cover for them, he's built a canvas tunnel out from the San Trinidad gate to get men down to the bank opposite and into a trench. They must be opposed from rifle pits between the water and the sap. Expect your Light Company to be involved, probably tomorrow. Light Division's 95th are opposite the San

Trinidad ravellin and fully occupied there with suppressing fire. Johnny's doing everything to hinder that San Roque sap. He expects our next effort at capture to be that place. Tonight, my 60th dig the pits, so yours go in at dawn. See what you can do."

When dawn finally broke, Carr, looking through the lingering smoke and stood in a newly dug rifle pit, spoke four angry words.

"That is bloody insolent!"

He was not looking at a raft, as such, it was more a platform four feet above the water, the front well-padded, but with loopholes through which the French infantry from within were already sending fire at the workmen in the San Roque sap, 20 yards behind Carr and slightly above. His own men were already aiming careful shots at the loopholes and so Carr switched his attention to the canvas tunnel that stretched down from the San Trinidad gate to a trench that ran along the bank of the inundation. Remaining in their rifle pit, Carr turned to Drake.

"Why hasn't all this been blown away? Four charges of grape would see both in 'Kingdom Come'!"

The evidence of sufficient cannon firepower was humming and buzzing in the region of 30 feet above their heads as Number 11 battery, guns only installed during the night, battered the San Roque, 500 yards to their right, and also the replies that came from the undamaged wall of the San Trinidad opposite, crossing almost at right angles. He looked behind to judge the run back to the battery.

"Let me see what I can do!"

He scrambled out of the pit and ran crouching over the distance to the very active Number 11 battery. Once in, he immediately found a Captain of Artillery.

"What are the chances of a few rounds of grapeshot at that platform and that canvas opposite?"

The Captain saluted, whilst his face became very worried.

"I'm sorry, Sir, but we've strict orders that all our fire is to be for breaching work, against the walls opposite."

Carr was aghast and looked it.

"So, you have been given no orders to destroy that, out there, which is causing us casualties in the San Roque sap which is being built to take advantage of your breaching when the time comes? Is that true?"

"Yes Sir, I'm afraid it is. Breaching only. I've got it in writing."

"So if I gave you an order ...."

The Captain finished the sentence.

"We'd both be in trouble, Sir."

Carr's anger increased.

"Where is your Colonel Dickson?"

"I couldn't say, Sir. Probably at the batteries opposite the San Trinidad."

Carr now had a choice. To desert his men and go wandering all over the siege lines in a quest that may well be denied, or supervise the rifle pits as he had been ordered. It was no choice. He climbed over the battery parapet and ran back down to Drake in their rifle pit.

"Not a chance. Strict orders to pound the San Roque, nothing else."

"That's ridiculous! We should hit the raft, at least. What they are doing to us from that trench over the water is nothing compared to what comes from that cheeky construction. That are much more dangerous, they've a better angle of fire. Almost right down the trench!"

Carr made no reply, instead he began loading a Baker rifle. There seemed little else he could do to influence events, bar add to the weight of rifle fire replying to the raft.

Soon, all of the 105th Light Company realised that they were in a very bad place, as musket fire buzzed over and slapped into their parapet from the trench opposite, but more so the raft, Also, and much worse, grapeshot from the San Roque began to skim across the top of their rifle pits. The British in them were shooting at the French marksmen on the raft and in the trench opposite, who were directing their fire at the battery bombarding the San Roque. In that case, the French Commander of the San Roque decided that it made sense to assail the 105th, who were reducing the fire of those French who were attempting to reduce the cannon fire on him! All in the rifle pits immediately used the tools still there to create a protective bank on their right side to give cover when they came up to their own rifle embrasure and sight on the platform or the tunnel.

The vulnerability of the platform especially to cannon fire was not lost on Chosen Man Davey as he sent a carefully aimed shot at a platform loop hole when a musket appeared through it. It was satisfying to see that the musket fell out and forward, presumably from wounded or lifeless hands. He sat back down to reload.

"Why aren't those Frogs under cannon-fire? 'Twould take but, two, three shots."

At that moment a charge of grapeshot hit their protective bank and all were showered with soil. Tom Miles immediately began cursing, then his villainous mind got to work.

"Them lads back over, in the battery. How much do you think they'd charge to send a few the wrong way?"

Joe Pike was now at the embrasure.

"You mean bribe them?"

"I do, that eel platform out there has to go, or we'll still be here, takin' shots at them, till all this is done. While that's here, so've we got to be, combed through by grapeshot 'n' canister! This is damn dangerous an' some of us will be stayin' in the bottom of these holes, as these'll be their grave! Any coin It takes, we'll get the same back when we gets into the town."

Davey had almost finished reloading.

"Well, we can't do a thing today. There's no chance of a whip round now, nor a cosy chat with any of they gunners back over. All we can do is hunker down till night."

The faces of each showed that they had settled for that, but some help did come for the rest of the day, these being more Riflemen in the sap above. That section had now been finished and they added their fire to that of the 105th Light. When full dark came, all left their positions and climbed back to the San Roque sap to find it being evacuated by three Companies of Rifles, two of the 60th and one of Portuguese Cacadores. They were carrying out many casualties with them and Drake passed judgement.

"If that raft were gone, they wouldn't need to be there. That part of the sap they're in, is already built and has no need to be occupied, but in daylight staying there, they're dreadfully exposed."

At the same time, Miles was in negotiations with two Gun Captains, whose embrasure angle allowed them to train onto the raft.

"How much for a dose of grape onto that monkey platform out there?"

The two looked at each other and the Senior answered.

"Orders say not, only on the fort. What do we say to our Officer, when that thing gets blown apart, right in front of him? It must've been us and then we're on the triangle."

"Not necessarily. There's plenty of shells flying over this way, comin' from a battery over our way. You can see 'em fizzin' across. Just say that it blew up, like. All of a sudden. Must've been a shell fallin' short. Bit of luck, eh? We've not had too much of that over this caper. Perhaps we'n due some?"

The two looked at each other again, then the Senior answered.

"Ten dollars!"

"Eight!"

"Nine."

"Done, but we wants a double charge of grape from 'ee both. Two guns, one shot together, double charge."

"When?"

"When 'tis light enough. You'm the experts!"

"Payment in advance."

"What else? First thing when we comes back here tomorrow."

By now Rushby was shouting Miles' name and he ran out of the battery and carried on running to catch up.

"Sorry Sir. Just doin' a bit of tradin', like."

It was full night when they arrived back at their camp and then two significant events took place, one, the collection was made and secondly, Carravoy's Grenadiers left camp to feel their way, as ordered, slowly along the bank of the Rivellas, up towards the San Roque. Carravoy was irritable, but D'Villiers and Ameshurst were both curious, now that all was in motion and they had the time for questions, after Carravoy's initial explanation.

"Kempt's orders, no less, for us, we are the nearest. Some Sappers are to have another go at the San Roque dam across the Rivellas. We are to meet 30 of them a little further up."

In the dark D'Villiers' brows came together.

"Why does it matter?"

Whilst Carravoy searched his memory for anything that he may have heard in passing, Ameshurst answered definitively.

"Because the water held by the dam is all across the front of the San Trinidad. An acquaintance of mine in the 40th, the Somersets, in the 4th Division there, says it is chest deep in front of the breach. Not good for our men making an attempt there, obviously."

Carravoy became more irritable now that his own knowledge had been found wanting and, feeling exposed, he resolved to take a greater interest, but at that point they saw the Sappers waiting in the gloom. One came forward, obviously the Officer.

"Stanway. Royal Engineers."

The three introduced themselves, then Stanway explained.

"We have as many charges as we can carry and we intend to lay them against the dam. If you could follow to within range of the walls and anything that Johnny sends at us, if we're discovered, could you reply to? Keep their heads down."

Carravoy answered.

"Agreed. Lead on!"

"We're going down to the river bed. A bit more cover alongside the bank. Wish me luck."

"Of course. Good luck!"

Stanway turned away and the Grenadiers followed along the river bank, Carravoy in the lead and Ameshurst and D'Villiers at the head of their Sections. After some minutes, Stanway returned, to whisper to Carravoy.

"The San Roque is 100 yards up, or just over. We're going forward now and into the water. Best you hold your men here."

With that he disappeared into the dark. Carravoy stared forward, straining his eyes to see anything that could indicate the whereabouts of the San Roque, but D'Villiers was at his side.

"Should we load?"

Carravoy turned to him.

"Yes. Give the order."

"Hammer down, pan primed?"

"Yes."

The night-time cannonade, albeit far reduced from its daytime intensity, hid all sound and the darkness before them remained like a thick curtain. Minutes passed with no change, suddenly there came a shout, in French.

"Alarme! Alarme! Au barrage! Tirez! Tirez!"

From what could only be the level of the San Roque parapet, the night exploded in musket fire. Ameshurst reacted first and his Section opened fire, but D'Villiers' was not far behind. There was no return of fire and so, for some minutes the Grenadiers fired at the muzzle flashes. Then there was an explosion, the flash of which lit up the walls of the San Roque, but it also revealed several figures down in the shallow water of the Rivellas, many struggling back towards them. Ameshurst was nearest the water and gave a quick order.

"Sling your muskets! Get them out!"

He led his men himself into the water and soon they were pulling men to the shore, several plainly wounded. One was Stanway, one arm limp, and one leg unusable, him now being supported by a Grenadier. Carravoy trotted down to him as the firing died away.

"The dam! What do you think?"

Although in great discomfort, Stanway answered, his words punctuated by gasps of pain.

"No! Another failure. There would be a huge rush of water past us by now if it were broken. It's still there."

Much later during the night and fully concerned with their own good or bad fortune, in the last of the dark, the Light Company eased their way down from the San Roque sap and into the rifle pits. First, they had passed through the Riflemen already in the sap, all waiting for the dawn, but, again, the sap was full, which brought a remark from Drake.

"The Peer's putting every marksman he can spare into this. It must be important to him."

Carr was close by, but barely seen in the gloom.

"It seems so to him, but really, can this dog-kennel of a Fort be worth all the casualties there will be, especially here? The San Trinidad breach is around the corner and he's got enough guns and men on there, surely? Just leave this damn place alone. When we get the town, it will have to surrender, just like the Christobal."

Drake was not convinced.

"True, but leaving the San Roque, means leaving the dam, which means leaving a flood before the main breach. How can that be left as is?"

"I think he's going to put up with that, but still silence the fort's guns. If I've got it right, they can fire right across the front of the San Trinidad."

"Then good luck to the Fourth. That breach will be their job!"

Just before the two Officers, the rifle pits were being occupied, the last into their's being Tom Miles.

"Payment made and I hopes for their sakes that they Gunner shite-auks keeps their side of the bargain, or my rifle'll be pointing the wrong way!"

Davey was kneeling at the embrasure.

"And that they has enough sense to not make it their first shot and only when shells is passing across."

"Should hope! Gunners is supposed to be the ones with the brains."

Full light brought the resumption of full hostilities; the Riflemen firing at the raft and the trench served by the covered way, the San Roque bombarding the Rifles in the sap and pits and the French raft and trench assaulting the sap. The battery behind opened fire on the San Roque and shells from Number Ten Battery over at the 105th camp, began to sail across the sky above, fuses leaving a trail of smoke. It was in the midst of the worst of the cacophony that the raft exploded, wood, padding and men being flung far back into the fetid waters of the inundation. For the moment, all involved ceased fire and Tom Miles took the opportunity to lift his head over the parapet to see debris scattered over the water, and men, both alive and wounded, struggling for their lives amidst the remains of their platform.

"Seems like they Gunner coves did a good job!"

Back in the sap Drake and Carr stood dumbstruck.

"How on earth did that happen?"

Drake turned towards him, then back to the gladdening sight.

"There's a rumour that some money has changed hands!"

Carr grinned.

"Villainy!"

oOo

Chapter Twelve

The Walls of Badajoz

Captain Tavender yawned extravagantly. It mattered greatly to him that he conveyed to all within earshot his opinion of the complete tedium of their duties as they existed at that moment. The source of the monotony was the fact that his Squadron were holding a ridge just to the East of the village of Merida, this some 40 odd miles East of Badajoz, as the crow flies or as the horse gallops, the plains all around being so open and utterly featureless; which fact did not help his mood. The heavy drizzle did not help either! The mildly satisfying memory of galloping at a tiny French two-gun battery below Fort San Christobal was already fading. The gunners had escaped through the trees, and the prizes had been towed away by the supporting infantry. He studied his watch, then quickly thrust it back into his waistcoat pocket, it gave no comfort of time passing quickly. There were still over two hours to go until relief which would bring the Midday meal, but the afternoon would bring another spell on Watch, albeit shorter. Cornet Smythe's A Troop were with him, and Smythe himself close by, but he, well aware of his Captain's tetchy character, made no effort at pleasant conversation, which would perhaps have enabled the time to pass more quickly for both of them.

Tavender looked back to the village, noting the haze of smoke indicating comforting fires, then out to the horizon, then at Smythe's Troop, all well spread out and all seemingly content with this mind-numbing duty of watching nothing Eastwards, which had been the case since mid-March, the month now being April. The note he had found in his saddlebag still rankled when he recalled it to mind and the sight of the Troopers all lined up, each a possible author, did just that. However, perhaps it was something that entered his subconscious, that caused him to return his thoughts to the horizon, the particular point where the Roman road ceased to blend with the dull, brown fields to either side, before all disappeared into the murk. He pulled out his telescope, but Smythe had beaten him to it and was already focused.

"Something coming, Sir."

Tavender focused carefully. From that distance, what could be seen on the road resembled a brown caterpillar-like insect, but again Smythe spoke the identifying words first.

"Looks like a column of irregulars, Sir. A strong one."

Both retained the use of their telescopes for some time as the column came on at a fast canter, one leader and perhaps 50 following. After ten minutes, Tavender decided that he needed to react, but he needed a second opinion as confirmation.

"Smythe! Definitely not French, in your opinion?"

"No Sir."

"You, a Sergeant and four men. Follow me."

Tavender spurred his horse down the road, placed himself upon it and waited. Smythe came to a halt beside him and Tavender voiced his opinion.

"Some guerrilla crew coming in, demanding food and ammunition, I shouldn't wonder."

Smythe did not reply, he preferred to wait and the withholding of his opinion was justified as the leader reined in his horse just enough to overlap with Tavender's. The guerrilla was dirty and unshaven, a large moustache beginning beneath his nose and finishing as a pair of sideboards covering most of his ears. His mouth was grim, his eyes red and tired, and he plainly saw little need for civility, but perhaps his limited English would not allow it.

"Hola Ingles. We have this taken from caballero francés."

He reached behind him and thrust forward a large leather despatch pouch, dark brown, with a large 'N' etched into the cover.

"We ride two days, no stop, to get this to you."

As Tavender did not reach forward, Smythe took it instead, to the guerrilla's surprise, his eyes flickering from one to the other, then back to Tavender.

"It say, in there, that Soult has moved his men over the Sierra Morena. He tell Marmont this who is far in Portugal. Soult is now only five days from here. Is why we ride all nights."

Smythe looked at Tavender.

"Sir, this is vital. We must get it back immediately! It may mean that the final assault on the town must be sooner rather than later."

Tavender turned his head to Smythe, but said nothing. Then he turned back to the guerrilla, but again he said nothing, and so Smythe now felt impelled to react, in some way.

"Senor, you have our thanks for your efforts."

He offered his hand to the leader, who took it firmly.

"Now you have what you need, Ingleses, we get what we need, in Merida there. Food and sleep."

He spurred his horse forward.

"Adios, Senores."

The guerrilla column followed at a fast canter, past Smythe and Tavender. Smythe looked at his Captain, hoping for orders, but none came and so he spoke the obvious.

"Sir. We should take this to the Colonel."

Tavender at last reacted.

"No need! In fact, a bad idea. This must be got back to Wellington immediately. To search for the Colonel would be a waste of time and he would only say what I've just said."

"Sir, would you like me to take it? I trust my horse for such a journey. Rapid delivery being required."

Something at last happened inside Tavender and the idea of a mere Cornet arriving with such intelligence, when he could be the vital courier himself, was quickly rejected.

"No, I'll take it, with Shelby and the three men we have here. You return to the ridge and take command. Maintain the watch. Send your Senior Corporal, whatsisname, to inform the Colonel of where I've gone and why."

He reached out for the pouch and Smythe handed it over. With no more discourse, Tavender rode off, Westwards, followed by the Sergeant and the three Troopers.

oOo

It was mid-morning of the following day, when Kempt came into the Headquarters tent of the 105th with the simple piece of information.

"We're for the walls! Those opposite!"

The image of the high walls atop the steep bank immediately entered the minds of the three sat there, Lacey, O'Hare and Carr. Lacey recovered first, but 'recovery' was not an accurate word. 'The walls' were their worst fear.

"Not the main breach? Not for us?"

Kempt shook his head.

"No! That's for the Light Division and the Fourth. Us, the Third, we're more of a diversion than an attempt. A Brigade of Leith's Fifth will be trying another diversion, on the opposite corner to us at the San Vincente bastion, as it's called, on the far side of the town. We are for the Castle."

Carr looked at O'Hare, who was now as concerned as anyone and looked it, but Carr turned to Kempt.

"So, the main breach has been judged as practical, Sir?"

Kempt took a deep breath, as though he were not sure himself.

"It has, just! It could be increased to some benefit, as I see it, but Wellington's had news that Soult is but six days away. He's not with Marmont, he's on some Portuguese jaunt, but if Soult arrives and we are still in the trenches, The Peer will have to divert half his force to hold him off. So, we go either tomorrow night, or the night after and either means ladders for us, so get some men off to the Engineers' camp for the timber. That's the men's task now, to make ladders, 30 feet long."

Kempt rose to leave, but, at the entrance, he turned to examine the three troubled faces.

"I know what you're all thinking, nothing need be said, but this is the game we're in!"

With that, he departed and the tent flap closed behind him. Lacey took a deep breath.

"Padraigh! Get Gibney, Ellis, Deakin, Nicholls and Hill onto this. Decide who goes to the Engineers and then get them on their way. Henry, you go to the Engineers, get them to ready up the parcels of timber, or at least try to find out where ours go to get it."

As O'Hare left immediately, Carr asked his question.

"How many ladders? We've 550 men."

Lacey thought for a moment.

"30 men to a ladder is the received wisdom."

Carr did a rough calculation.

"Call it 20 ladders, then."

With that in mind he took himself onto the half mile walk that led to the Engineers' park, that track now well beaten, the park itself astride the road to Talavera la Real, the small village 10 miles East of Badajoz, mercifully unaffected by events Westwards. He soon found a Captain of Engineers himself busy with paper and pencil.

"Captain!"

The paper and pencil came down to his left leg as he came to the attention.

"Sir!"

"Where can my men obtain the material to construct 20 ladders?"

"Just down the road, Sir, there's plenty of 3 by 2! But you'll need a note from your Colonel, Sir."

Carr was immediately incensed.

"My men are on their way, Captain. My presence will have to do!"

"Yes Sir. Well, as I say, Sir, it's just down there. 200 yards."

Carr nodded in his direction and decided to wait. It was plain that his question had been superfluous, because every other Battalion in the Third Division had received the same instruction, some earlier, and their parties of men were already passing him having come from the obvious direction, two or three carrying the long lengths needed to construct the assault ladders. It was noticeable that there was no sign of the usual jocularity or even cheerful banter, only grim men carrying out their prophetic orders. He was stood waiting for the arrival of his own men, when he heard the sound of a horse behind him and then he easily recognised the silky, but insolent, tone.

"Ah, Major Carr. Please to have found you, Sir."

Carr turned, a very disagreeable look quickly arriving on his face.

"Captain Tavender. And what brings you here?"

Tavender paused before answering as he sat forward in his saddle, as though privileged enough to take whatever time he chose.

"Oh, just taking the opportunity to see what's happening. Sir. We are not often back where the main action is taking place.

"Well! Now that you've seen it?"

The invitation to leave was obvious in Carr's tone, but Tavender merely spent time checking the alignment of the reins and patting the neck of his horse.

"Yes Sir, but what impressed me are the walls that you and your men have to get yourselves over."

The clear indication in both Tavender's words and expression, that there was something extra behind Tavender's reacquaintance, disagreeable as it was, was not lost on Carr.

"There's something on your mind, Tavender! Never mind rank, say what you have to say."

Tavender looked into the distance, at the walls of Badajoz Castle, then did some more saddle easing before he spoke.

340

"Well Major, it seems to me, that what you and your men will be asked to do in the next day or two, strikes one as one damned chancy business. Something beyond what one might call 'normal soldiering risk', as we in the military would call it."

Carr remembered Kempt's words and used them himself.

"That's the game we're in!"

Tavender's oleaginous tone revealed that he had arrived at the point of what he wished to say.

"Quite so and with that in mind I would wish to reassure you, that should anything happen to you of an unfortunate nature, if you take my meaning, well, you can go at those walls certain that Jane will be well taken care of. She'll not want, for anything, you understand. You can pass the same onto Drake, regarding Cecily. You can count on me to do the good neighbourly thing, be most assured."

Carr's face darkened, the insinuations were obvious. Tavender would be looking to share the bed of one of the two. However, Carr remained punctiliously polite, his reply measured and carefully spoken.

"I, we, thank you for that, but Lady Constance will ensure that each of our wives, and Drake's child, have a roof over their heads. Of that we can both be certain. Or perhaps three of us, you, I, and Drake."

Tavender spread his mouth to either side, a grimacing gesture which showed that he was very much less than certain.

"Well, there's more to it than that, now, isn't there? I mean as time drags on, and there's little else in your life. I mean, no further children, with both, for example."

It was all that Carr could do, to stop himself from dragging Tavender off his horse and beating him senseless, but instead he clamped his jaw together for some seconds before speaking, his left-hand flexing on his sword hilt. The implication that, in her widowed loneliness, Jane would automatically turn to him was obvious.

"I think we can assume that Jane will take the best decisions, both for herself and for her immediate family. Of that we can be certain."

For a moment, the two shared a hard stare, but it was Carr who broke the profound silence.

"Whilst you are here, Captain, I have an issue of my own, concerning yourself. Some time ago now, back in February, in fact, I received a letter, poorly written, bad grammar and whatnot, but definitely from someone in your Regiment, an NCO would be my guess, saying that you were making a habit of sending my brother into, let's say, situations beyond 'normal soldiering risk' to use your phrase. 'Bad places' was how he put it. So, plainly someone is looking out for my brother and if I survive this and later in this war I hear of my brother's death, then I will investigate. If I find that you were involved, significantly and suspiciously, then you and I will try conclusions, if you understand me. If it costs me my Commission or not, I'll be coming for you!"

The revelation that Carr had been sent a similar note to the one Tavender had received both shocked and surprised him and so he could make no reply. Carr was content for the silence to reign for a few seconds more, then he broke it himself.

"Now, if there's nothing further, especially of military concerns, then both you and your horse are badly in the way! Captain!"

The return of military rank and the issue of an order was obvious and so Tavender managed a rictus smile, then he languidly nudged his horse into motion. Carr turned away, wishing to see no more of the odious Tavender, instead he joined his men of the 105th as they made their way back, each carrying their burden, either timber or tools.

Back in their mess area, the timber descended from the shoulders of Saunders and Solomon with a clatter, but Joe Pike went immediately to the tools and opened the bag. He spoke authoritatively.

"Good! Saws, chisels, mallets, awls, hammer, nails."

He rummaged further into the canvas folds to find the last that he wanted.

"And a rule and a tape."

The others stood and looked at him, awaiting instructions, but the atmosphere was tense, the mood subdued and expressions glum. Here was confirmation that they were for the walls, those which had stood challenging them for almost all of the past three weeks. The timber for the ladders could mean nothing else.

"We can't just nail the rungs to the uprights. They'll soon give with the weight of a man. There has to be halving-joints for the rungs, better to take the weight, because they're stronger. That's what the chisels are for, along with the saws. The nails are just to hold the rungs inside the rebates."

One of his audience was RSM Gibney, who was anxious to hear what the ex-woodworker Joe Pike had to say. He had heard enough.

"Raht, Joe. Explain all to these here, then you get on round and see that all is done as you say. Make sure Deakin, Davey and Saunders here understands, and then they can get on round an all, and see that all starts proper from the off, an' no timber gets cut wrong."

Pike stared back at him.

"30 foot, Sar' Major?"

"Aye, Joe. 30 foot is what's needed, so's we've bin told!"

For the rest of the morning most of the Officers of the 105th stood studying the walls, doing so to the sound of hammering and sawing from behind them. Almost all that was spoken, was spoken in order to be encouraging, so as to possibly reduce the task viewed before them to something less than extremely difficult. Not least from Drake, who spoke with some truth to Carr, Rushby and Shakeshaft.

"French fire from the walls has slackened considerably. They must be running out of ammunition. They've been at it pretty strong since this all started."

Carr turned to him, smiled and nodded. He did not speak the obvious thought, that the French were saving enough to meet the forthcoming assault, so he contented himself by observing the progress behind them of Portuguese gunners hauling several large howitzers over towards the Guadiana. He pointed over his shoulder.

"They are what matter to us. Fourteen 24lbs howitzers going into the last battery, being built closest to the Guadiana. They are to support us with shellfire."

All within earshot turned to see the long column of mules, guns and limbers easing their way along the track behind. They were able to count ten passing by with more already gone and so no-one doubted Carr's number of 14, but then Rushby spoke the question that had been on all their minds since the ladder construction had begun, speaking to no-one in particular.

"Do you think it'll be tonight?"

Carr turned to him and took a deep breath.

"It may be, yes. We'll know this evening when Kempt arrives. It'll be his job to tell us, one way or the other. He'll get it from Picton."

No reply came from any direction and Carr felt impelled to convey what extra he knew.

"This Phillipon has wound his men up to the extreme and they have worked prodigiously throughout every night to repair what we do during the day, or at least lessen the benefit to us. How practical the breaches are, that's up to Wellington, but he'll decided after midday, then we'll know."

There came no reply again and what filled the interval was the full intensity of the breaching batteries before the San Trinidad, albeit almost a half a mile away, hammering away at the wall. The hammering behind them, that of carpentry, however, was fading away. The ladders had been constructed and were now being tested, not least by way of men of the stature of RSM Gibney and Sergeants Hill and Nicholls standing on the bottom two rungs, whilst the ladders were held vertical. There were no problems, Joe Pike's design had held true, and so the men abandoned their ladders where they lay and took themselves back to their mess areas for the midday meal. It was no coincidence that Deakin, Pike, Saunders, Byford and Henry Nicholls took their food sat close alongside their wives. Whilst they ate, there was little conversation, but food now having been taken, there was time for talk, not of the task of getting over the walls, but of the town itself, begun by Len Bailey.

"There's talk that this Badajoz place has no liking for us, the British."

It was Byford who answered, him immediately realising where that sentiment would lead to.

"So, this talk is saying, in effect, that they would rather have the French ruling their lives than their own Government. That we should take ourselves off and leave them as they are!"

Bailey was not appeased.

"Well, that's the talk and it'll have come from somewhere!"

Byford had further argument.

"They will have heard, by now, of what we saw after the French retreat up from Santarem. What they did to the Portuguese. How dreadful that was and yet all this talk that you've heard, is saying that these citizens see the French are their saviours! From what?"

Bailey was now angry. He had no answer to Byford's careful arguments.

"It's what's bein' said and what I've heard. That's the thinkin' what's all over, mostly."

Deakin's face showed that he was deeply troubled.

"Sounds to me like no more'n a good excuse to rob and plunder this place, till there's nothing left. John's right, we knows what the French can do, and does, to get their food and whatever, including torture. On top, there's that irregular war, guerrilla war they calls it, happenin' all over against the Frogs 'cos of their nasty ways. So you'm sayin' that this one place don't think like that, out of all of Spain as've suffered from these Frogs comin' in an' rulin' the place. They here looks on 'em different, you'm sayin'?"

"All right, don't have a go at I. I be just passin' on what I've heard. And, like I say, 'tis all over."

Toby Halfway looked at Deakin.

"There's truth in what he's sayin', Jed. This has been a bad go, worse than bad, and the mood's sour. You can feel it and hear it, all over, like someone's got to pay."

Tom Miles now raised his head.

"And I goes along with that! What I says is that there has to be some reckonin' for what we've gone through here. The killing and the wet and the cold. We'n owed something!"

Deakin turned on him.

"And that reckonin' has to be with the civilians an' not with the French, you'm sayin'? I said back along that it's the Frogs' job to keep us out and the fact that they've made such a good job of it, helped by the weather, is no fault of them as lives inside them walls."

Miles now lost his temper.

"'Tis alright for you to say. You weren't blown up, you weren't in they rifle pits up to your arse in water, an' I got froze and soaked an' done the diggin' an' humpin' just as much as you, whilst the Frogs was throwin' Christ knows what at us. And what about all them lads up at the main, as'll have to wade chest deep through water to get even near!"

Deakin leaned forward, challengingly.

"So, just what have you got in mind?"

Miles paused, he knew that he needed to choose his next words carefully, if they be truthful or not.

"Well, I'd say I was due a bit of coin. And a drink! A good drink! I don't see how that's too much to ask after what we've been through. An' bit of plunder an' all."

Deakin sat back.

"I'll not argue too strong with that. Provided ...."

Then he sat forward again.

"No killin'! No killin' to get it. There'll be enough killin' up on they walls. Enough even for you!"

Saunders now sat forward and looked directly at Tom Miles.

"We've served together for years, Tom. We was in the Norfolks together, with Jed, Henry and Toby here, but I tells you now that if you goes off murdering to get this coin and whatnot, as you thinks is your due, then you'll have me to deal with!"

Miles looked at Len Bailey, but saw no chance of support.

"All right! No killin' of these good citizens, as if I would. Just a few coins. And a good drink!"

The faint humour in the words changed the atmosphere and it changed again with the arrival of the Reverend Albright and all sprang immediately to their feet, as he entered their circle, whilst Sedgwicke remained just outside of it.

"Good afternoon, men."

From all around there came the sound of several "Sirs', whilst arms came up to the salute. Albright stood beaming all around at his small congregation which was expanding as more came to the edge of the circle. He stood in his classic pose of slightly leaning forward, his palms together, his hands held just before his chest.

"I have come that we might share a prayer together. It is not known if our efforts will be required this night, but just in case Our Lord decides in that direction, I thought it best to move amongst you now."

Deakin spoke up, his words not fully echoing his thoughts, but some response was required.

"That's very kind of you, Sir, to put yourself out in such a way. I'm sure the lads all appreciates what you tries to do."

From all around came several words of agreement, which caused Albright to beam all the more and his hands before him conveyed the uplift within him, both clasped together swinging vertically up and down as if in fervent prayer.

"Then let us pray!"

All heads were bowed.

"Oh Lord, in the name of our Saviour, our Lord Jesus Christ we beseech you to give strength and righteousness to our arms during the coming night, that we may free so many of our fellow men from the yoke of Godlessness that, even as we speak, sits heavy upon the necks and shoulders of so many innocents. Bring us victory and look over us, Oh Lord, but if it is thy will that we do not see the light of the following day, then we beg you to take us unto you, knowing that we left this life attempting the path of goodness as taught us by your only Son, Jesus Christ. Amen."

A chorus of 'Amens' echoed that of Albright and after further beaming at his pliant congregation, he turned and left, but Sedgwicke took the two paces up to Jed Deakin and he offered his hand, which Deakin took.

"I wish you every good fortune, Colour Sergeant Deakin, with what is about to happen and please be wholly assured that, should the worst come about, I will take the very best of care of Bridie and Nellie."

Deakin nodded and smiled, even though he knew that Sedgwicke's words were wholly unnecessary. In the event of his death, he realised full well that Bridie would take up with whoever of those still alive looked the best prospect, but he spoke his thanks anyway.

"Well, that's a comfort Old Parson, and I thank you for it!"

With a further smile and a nod, Sedgwicke turned to follow Albright, who was already in the next circle, but Deakin turned to Miles.

"You heard what the Vicar said, Tom, takin' the yoke off of innocents' shoulders, not puttin' one back on, one of misery and pain!"

Miles did no more than incline his head with a 'that's what you think' expression on his face, before he pulled his bayonet out of its sling to further sharpen the point.

The afternoon wore on and the tension grew and wives sat with husbands and old friends sat together. In the Headquarters tent, the three shared some of O'Hare's best Irish, but little was said, each with his own thoughts. They knew that Cuidad had been bad, but Badajoz had all the signs of being very much worse. However, none of this was spoken and it was a relief when Kempt came into their tent and they all turned to him immediately, then he spoke the words that they both dreaded and wished to hear.

"It's off! Not tonight."

Each stared intently at him as he sat down and O'Hare poured a tot of whisky, from which Kempt took one sip before continuing.

"Yes, it's off. He's heard that Soult's at Llerena, three, four days away, and this afternoon it was on, but Fletcher inspected the breach and the French have crammed it with all sorts that makes it almost impossible. So, another breach is going to be made in the curtain wall that joins the San Trinidad and the Santa Maria, the one around the corner from us. He's heard that it's weak and so one can be made in a day."

Carr looked at him, his puzzlement very apparent.

"A fresh breach, Sir? In an undamaged wall?"

"That's it, Major, and he's put five batteries onto it. So, it's not tonight, but definitely tomorrow night. He's worried about Soult and so he should be! He's sent off one of Leith's Brigades around to the South-west to hold some hill down there, Hill is to blow up the bridge at Merida and the 1st, 6th and 7th Divisions and a couple of Portuguese Brigades are to go down to Albuera and we all know what happens down there. What's left, half of Leith's plus a Portuguese Division, Picton's 3rd, Cole's 4th and the Light are for the assault. Tomorrow night!"

The three nodded gravely as Kempt continued.

"You'd better get this clear and tell your own Officers. You going at the Castle, so when you get in you could find Leith's coming at you from the San Vincente opposite from us and Cole's 4th and the Light coming at you from the left. Make that clear."

With that he drained the last of his whisky and was gone. Lacey looked at the others and sighed.

"Well, we've an extra night and a day to prepare ourselves. What we are going to do, I do not know. I was ready to go tonight!"

The news was not well received throughout the 105th, especially by Tom Miles.

"I don't see what difference a day can make. We're all wound up for tonight, and then Nosey says no. Things can't be that much different this time tomorrow as to what they is now."

John Davey was nearest and so he answered.

344

"Listen to the guns, Tom. That's as fierce as any we've heard. That's going to make a difference somewhere."

"Yes, but not here. Them walls will be the same tomorrow for us, as now."

However, the mood eased with ration call, which proved to be more than generous and, on this occasion, there was no need for jealous looks in any direction between Nellie Nicholls and Betty Barker, both well content with the issue. All settled for a good meal, but, that evening as for the previous, there was none of the usual camp activities of gambling, music, dancing, singing or any form of cutting capers.

The next day, all woke to the sound of the guns pounding the curtain wall between the Santa Maria and San Trinidad bastions and as breakfast was taken, most watched the smoke drift Northwards on a soft Southerly wind, but it was noticeable that this was not combined with any smoke from the French defence, their guns were ominously silent. As the morning progressed, Carr grew more irritable and angry and he went to O'Hare.

"It's not good for the men to sit about all day, scratching their backsides and getting on each other's nerves, such that fights break out. What do they know about holding a ladder against a wall?"

O'Hare looked at him puzzled.

"What's difficult about that?"

Carr had remembered what his then Light Company had been asked to do to storm the fortress of Scilla in Southern Sicily, some years previous.

"The French could push it off or slip it sideways, unless there are restraining ropes. I've a mind to do some training with that. Keep them occupied."

Thus, for the rest of the morning, once rope had been obtained from the Engineers and Artillery, those allocated as a ladder party found themselves stood by ropes that could not be realistically employed because there were no walls, however, they were taught their role and many were given mallets and pegs to further anchor their ladder, provided the ground beneath the walls could receive them. Midday found even that activity exhausted and so, after that meal, Drake and Carr took themselves off to wander up to Battery 12 for which they had seen the howitzers arrive the previous day. The effort was not without interest, as, during the afternoon, the Portuguese gunners fired ranging shots and the pair watched as barrel angles were set and adjusted and fuses set in the shells. An Artillery Officer, British, came over to engage the pair.

"Fanshawe. RA."

The pair gave their names, then Fanshawe asked the crucial question.

"Are you for the walls?"

Drake nodded, whilst Carr watched the flight of another ranging shot, the smoke from the burning fuse describing its course to the walls.

"Well, we'll do our best. We'll set the barrels at maximum and hope to drop stuff in behind the walls. We can only hope that will help."

"Are you getting the range?"

Fanshawe nodded.

"I do believe so. With barrels at maximum, we vary the strength of the charge."

Drake extended his hand.

"Well, thanks for your efforts. Whatever help you can give!"

Carr also shook hands with Fanshawe, who then left, but the pair remained for many minutes more to study the flight of several more shells. As they walked back, both indulged in more than one look at the walls, almost half a mile distant, most noticeable being the French flag atop the Castle tower, at that height picking up the best of the breeze and visible through the thinning cannon smoke arriving from batteries bombarding the San Trinidad. Suddenly, some April sunshine broke through the cloud, but it was too far after the Noon apex for the bright rays to light on the front surface of the walls' stonework, instead the town itself, behind, was illuminated, contrasting the walls by throwing them into dark, brooding silhouette.

oOo

John Davey had felt the knot in his stomach tightening all through that afternoon, and not even a good pull at the mess brandy flask had helped that much. As were all the others, he was arranging his backpack, haversack and any other possessions into a neat pile and those who could write were closing the flaps down onto scraps of paper with their names on whilst those who could not write were waiting for their label to be

345

written by the likes of John Byford. Davey's possessions were beside those of Zeke Saunders, these watched over by Consuela. Davey gave a deep sigh and turned to him.

"Zeke, I got a bad feeling."

He pointed to his own pile.

"There's stuff in there, personal like, not King George's, that I wants got back to Molly, Tilly and the babes. You'll see to that, won't you, if you can?'

Saunders gazed down at him, his face understanding, yet trying to be cheerful.

"You'll be alright, as will we all, what with Joe's ladders and Carr's ropes, we'll get over."

Davey sighed again.

"That's for the newcomes, Zeke. Some of us won't, and if one of 'ems me, and you comes through, you'll see that this gets back? I'm countin' on 'ee!"

Saunders nodded.

"Be certain, John, I will if I can, or it could be Consuela if, well, you know. But it'll get back, one way or another. Any of the lads'll see to that, for any of us!"

Davey nodded and patted Saunders on the arm. Nothing more was said between them and it was very similar in the tent of the Officers of the Light Company as each closed down their chest, each with their name stenciled on the top in black letters. When each stood up, Drake spoke the words.

"Everything personal to me is in there. One of us will come through, at least, and if it's me, I promise that your chests will get back to your parents. Is that a pact between us?"

Rushby and Shakeshaft nodded and all solemnly shook hands. Outside the day was dying but there was no let up from the cannonade, this just as intense and assaulting their ears from the direction of the San Trinidad. This was the background to the meeting in the Headquarters tent of the 105th which now contained Kempt, on his way around his three Battalions. He was terse and totally factual, him feeling the growing tension as much as anyone.

"The first wave will be led by Colonel Williams of the 60th Rifles, leading three of his own Companies and all the Light Companies of the Division. The second wave will be; naming from the right, Campbell's Brigade, his 5th, 77th, 83rd and 94th. Your 105th are in the centre, then the 88th and 74th on the left. In reserve are Da Costa's two Portuguese, the 11th and 23rd Line plus his 2nd Cacadores. All ladder parties in possession at 5 o' clock. Assemble on the start line at eight. Engineer Colonel McCarthy will be leading us forward."

He turned to Carr.

"Henry. Williams would like you as his Second. You agree?"

Carr answered quietly.

"Yes Sir, of course."

Kempt nodded and stood up, to offer his hand to all there. That done, he departed, when Lacey looked at Carr.

"You'd better tell our Lights!"

Carr's face became grim as he nodded and rose from his chair. He knew that this news was best delivered by an Officer, to spare the Sergeants the inevitable abuse, and discipline must be maintained as thoroughly and as long as possible. He left and was soon entering the tent of the Light Company Officers to find each sitting on their travelling chest. His face betrayed the bad news he brought with him.

"We, that is the 105th Light Company, are in the first wave, made up of some Rifles and all of Picton's Lights."

He moved on quickly.

"Nat, I think you and I should go around to inform the men, and not leave it to the Sergeants."

Still reeling from the news, Drake rose and followed Carr to the mess areas of the Light Company. The news was delivered with all rigidly at attention, being in the presence of Officers, and then Drake and Carr went on their way to the next mess area who also listened at attention, in somber silence. At their departure from the camp of Davey, Saunders and Deakin, female arms were thrown around the necks of Byford, Saunders, Deakin and Nicholls, even though the latter two were not Light Company.

Back in the Headquarters tent and still able to visualise all the anxious and even angry faces that he had spoken to, Carr sat down, but not for long. Lacey was looking at his watch.

"6.30. Time for inspection. Weapons, water and ammunition. Nothing else. That task is for Lieutenants and Sergeants."

There was something mournful about the bugle notes, on this occasion, sounding 'fall in', something not normally felt, although they were precisely the same as those sounded to assemble to begin a day's march. They caused many heads to rise and last looks to be shared, and then a last embrace, even between Nellie and Henry Nicholls, her telling him, "Not to shame us, now", before a last genuine clasp of each other. The last act was John Byford kissing little Jed, then they were gone into the growing gloom, for Ellis to make his inspection and Drake, Rushby and Shakeshaft to dispense some encouraging words, the response always being one of three, "Yes Sir", or "Thank you, Sir", or "That's kind of you, Sir." There was even no animosity between Ellis and Miles, the former feeling enough kinship at that moment to pat Miles twice on the chest just below his left shoulder and receive a nod and a half smile in reply. Then came the order for the Light Company to march off and they did so, with many calls of "See you soon" or "Good luck", coming out of the darkness.

The start line for the 105th Light was 100 yards back from Battery 6, the furthest right of their main batteries. With his men now in place Carr went forward to find Picton, Engineer McCarthy, and his own Colonel Williams. Picton did not give him a second glance, as Carr introduced himself to McCarthy and Williams. Then Picton spoke.

"7.45!"

What this was meant to convey, no one knew, but McCarthy had some concerns.

"Sir, I feel that I should go some way forward, in order to be certain of the line we should take!"

Picton turned on him, his mouth open in surprise.

"Damn you, Sir. Do you not know? Have you wasted the daylight hours writing love poems! Is it not straight through Battery Six and then on from there?"

McCarthy shrank a little, then he justified himself.

"Yes Sir, that is correct, but there are markers out there for us, which should be found. Sir."

Picton's voice was an angry growl.

"Then you'd best go!"

As McCarthy disappeared into the darkness, an Aide-de-Camp arrived, on horseback, to dismount and salute before Picton.

"Sir! The assault has been postponed until ten."

Already in a foul mood, Picton turned on him, a Major of the 2nd Foot.

"Why? What the Devil for?"

The Major stood his ground. He carried Wellington's authority with him.

"Delay in assembling the attack at main breach. Sir. That is all I can say."

With that he remounted and rode off, leaving Picton to fume. What happened next, both comforting and ominous did nothing to mollify him. McCarthy returned, stating that he had found Major Burgoyne at the battery and the markers had been found. With that said, the battery guns that had been pounding the San Trinidad then fell silent. Williams turned to Carr.

"This is not good. This gives Johnny two hours to refill the main breach with all kinds of nasty objects!"

Carr nodded in the darkness, but still answered.

"Yes Sir. Not good!"

Now Picton was giving orders.

"Allow the men to sit!"

Then another thought.

"Have they been given their rum?"

Williams replied.

"Should be happening now, Sir."

"Go back and check!"

When the order came to sit, the rum arrived and, with their beakers left behind, all had to drink from the communal cup attached to the rum bucket. The Orderly came to Tom Miles and the exchange was as always.

"All the best, Tom. Come the finish, eh?"

Miles took the cup and hoisted it slightly in the Orderly's direction before he drank.

"Yes mate. Come the finish."

The next was Joe Pike whose rum ration was always watered down, which fact was spoken by Miles, but Ellis intervened.

"Leave him be! Time he took his rum like the rest of us."

The clank of the bucket and beaker receded along the ranks and silence fell, which no one felt inclined to break. They heard the Badajoz Cathedral clock strike 8 o' clock, such was the depth of the calm, then the minutes dragged by. Joe Pike began to sing until elbowed into silence. The Cathedral clock continued its passage of time, chiming out for many the final quarter hours of their lives. It was at the chime to mark the beginning of the final quarter of the ninth hour before full 10 o' clock, that Picton gave the order to stand and his whole Division rose in the darkness, for himself to then lead William's first wave forward. McCarthy and Burgoyne were some way ahead, Kempt had now joined Picton who was just ahead of Carr, who barely had time to set one foot inside Battery Six, before there came an eruption of musketry from the direction of the San Roque. That was now under attack, but Carr had barely cleared the parapet on the front side of the battery before the walls before them erupted with their own cannon fire. Immediately shot and grape began to hum and buzz past them on all sides and men began to fall, their cries drowned out by the intensity of fire from both in front and to their left, at the San Roque. Then their own supporting Battery 12 opened fire with their howitzers, from behind and to the right, adding their own contribution to the din. They had not advanced more than a few paces when McCarthy came running back to stand before Picton.

"Sir, I'm not at all sure that we're going in the right direction!"

Picton immediately drew his sword and held it aloft above McCarthy. Kempt immediately sprang forward to place his hand on Picton's upper arm, but Picton had thankfully resorted to words.

"Damn you, Sir. Damn you again and thrice! Do you expect me to halt the whole Division to enable you to perform your duty? Lead on and we will follow, such that both you and I can hope that you have the right of it!"

McCarthy disappeared again, but at that point Picton collapsed, holding his right thigh just below the groin. Two Aides rushed to him and carried him leftwards, but, through the pain, he called back.

"Kempt! Take them on!"

Kempt increased his pace to put himself in the lead and after two minutes McCarthy came running back.

"Sir! I think I have it correct."

Kempt's temper was only marginally less volatile than Picton's.

"You think you have, Sir, do you? Well, I see cannon flash ahead and that's enough direction for me. You do as you will!"

Even though hurrying forward, it took many minutes to cross the space between the battery and the banks of the Rivellas. Shot, shell and grape came at them both from the walls and also from Fort San Christobal on their right, the gunners there adding their flanking fire to that which assailed the advancing Division. At the river, many men jumped into the stream, but soon found it difficult to wade over, it still being significantly deep from the recent rain. Men soon fell, easy targets for the short-range musketry that was now coming from the walls, the water illuminated by burning carcasses of cloth and straw thrown down from the battlements, to roll down amongst the attackers. Then McCarthy came running along their front shouting repeatedly.

"Move left to a mill dam and the bridge."

Carr decided that, if he was going to die, it would be amongst members of his own Regiment and, that if he was going to lead any up and over the walls, it would also be them. He knew where the 105th Light were in the line and he ran over to find Drake at their head.

"Come on! We must do as he says."

They followed the press of men, which was of such density that they soon came to a standstill and the reason was obvious, only a few at a time could cross the dam and the bridge. All the while grape from the walls tore huge gaps in the press of men on the dam and in those stood waiting to cross. Carr saw Saunders and Solomon, two of four carrying a ladder.

"Saunders! Come on!"

The depth of the water below the dam had to be attempted and Carr plunged in, followed by Drake and the ladder party. Being further upstream, the water came above their knees but no more and they brought the ladder across. Many followed, using the same route and on the far bank they found McCarthy calling for all there to demolish a palisade that separated the Rivellas from the dirt path beneath the Castle slope. The palisade was rocked back and forth by many desperate and angry hands, until it finally gave way and came apart. More ladders were arriving as McCarthy jumped over the wreckage of the palisade.

"Up with the ladders!"

Drake was not sure what he meant.

"What, up here, Sir?"

"Yes!"

McCarthy ran on, tackling the slope, and the ladders that were now over the Rivellas were carried up after him. It soon became obvious that the 30-foot ladders were a dreadful burden to carry up such a gradient and even Saunders' party began to struggle. Carr, Drake and Ellis all took a hold and better progress was made, not least from the fact that they were now under the guns up on the wall and out of line with those of Fort San Chrisobal. Those gun flashes could no longer be seen, which worried Carr somewhat but only momentarily. They had a wall to scale and, as yet, there were not enough ladders. McCarthy was stood below the wall, looking left and right as ladders did begin to arrive, their carriers practically exhausted from hauling them up the 100 yards of steep slope. Carr took the opportunity to speak to Drake.

"Have you seen Kempt or Williams?"

Drake was catching his breath.

"No to both."

"Casualties?"

"Heavy, I should guess!"

"Are you alright?"

"Bad bruise on my side from something, but still game. You?"

There was no time to answer. Six ladders were against the wall and men were scaling each, encouraged by McCarthy, but they were all too short and not one man got close to any embrasure, which were some five feet above the top rung of any ladder. All were shot or bayonetted as they tried to lever themselves up the final distance and they fell back down onto their comrades below. Then the ladders were pulled sideways by defenders, using hooks on long poles, all bar one, which the French pulled up into the Castle. Then, equally damaging, cannon-fire came from both sides, pouring grape shot down onto the attackers grouped at the base of the wall. Carr looked to either side to count at least three embrasures, each with an active cannon.

"This shouldn't be happening! We're in the wrong place. We're too far left, there should be nothing either side."

He ran off to look for McCarthy, while more ladders were raised and men sprang at the rungs and began their ascent. Carr blessed his luck that he found McCarthy so quickly and he immediately pointed up to their right. Illuminated by the cannon flash, it was obvious that something had gone wrong.

"Sir! That's the Castle Tower up there on our right. It should be on our left. We are attacking the wrong wall!"

McCarthy looked to where Carr was pointing and realisation also came to him.

"That mill dam took us too far to the left!"

"Yes Sir. We must move!"

At that moment, Williams arrived to stand immediately before McCarthy.

"We're at the wrong wall!"

"I know, we must take them around to the right."

Joe Pike placed his foot on the bottom rung, followed by Saunders. Men were holding onto the ladder ropes and the ladder felt steady. Pike began to climb, followed by Saunders, but Pike being such an athlete, he climbed more rapidly. He reached the top, two rungs down, to be met, although the ladder was short by several feet, with thrusting spears and bayonets so he thrust upwards with his own bayonet on the end of his Baker rifle. The effect could not be seen, but what appeared immediately above him was an angry French soldier, standing on the edge of the embrasure, with a halberd spear of some kind in his upraised hand, preparing to stab it downwards onto Pike's head and shoulders. The spear came down and Pike twisted to avoid the thrust, but his movement was limited by being at the top of a ladder and the point entered his left shoulder, but not enough to thoroughly pierce, instead it slid down over his shoulder blade. In pain and badly balanced, with more thrusts about to connect, Pike fell, but as he left the rung, Saunders seized the cuff of his right trouser and, with his immense strength, he was able to hold the swing of Pike's body, so that Pike collided with the ladder lower down and was able to cling on and lower himself down the outside of the ladder. Saunders looked up, now it was his turn and so he ascended one rung, then another, but someone was shouting his name at the foot of the ladder. He looked down to see Captain Drake.

"Saunders! Saunders! Come down, we're in the wrong place!"

Saunders looked down, then up, then down again and then he descended. Drake was waiting for him at the bottom.

"Get some men and carry this to our right."

With that, Drake was gone into the returning darkness, as men quit the walls and the French guns fell silent through lack of argument. Saunders seized some men and the ladder was lowered and then raised to their shoulders for them to follow the column of men running around beneath the Castle walls. Soon the only evidence of their abortive attack were the hundreds of men lying dead, wounded or dying beneath the highest walls that Badajoz could offer, between the San Trinidad and the San Pedro.

oOo

Carr and McCarthy led the column around to the right, whilst Williams gave himself the task of ordering the last of their command to follow. Once quickly beneath the correct walls they found the area crowded with Portuguese, their Brigadier, Da Costa, hurrying over to meet them.

"We are the first here! It should not be so."

Carr answered.

"Yes Sir, we lost our way. Where's General Campbell?"

"That I do not know, but General Kempt is here."

"Right Sir. Then to business."

The number of ladders now available had trebled and soon many were raised up, to again be found too short, but not by as much and men now swarmed up to attempt entry. Carr watched, soon in near despair, because every man at the top of every ladder was being pitched off, either wounded or dying, or the ladder hooked and hauled sideways, toppling the men onto the upraised bayonets of those below. Surprisingly, there was no continuous sound of exploding ordnance, neither cannon nor muskets, because the whole had degenerated into a crude, medieval assault of men attempting entrance and defenders making the best resistance they could. Down from the walls came rocks and logs, and the inevitable burning cloth and straw carcasses which illuminated the foot of the walls to aid the gunners of Fort San Christobal and those of a small bastion far over to their right. What ordnance there was came in the form of French grenades, but worst of all was the occasional lighted shell which exploded with destructive force, demolishing both men and ladders alike. Their own howitzers from Battery 12 arced overhead but gave no immediate assistance, exploding further back in the Castle. Kempt ran up to Carr, him still looking upwards at the embrasures high above, each with a ladder arriving up in place, or with men fighting unsuccessfully at the top to soon be badly wounded, or a ladder finally being hooked sideways away from any opening.

"Carr! We're getting nowhere! Any ideas?"

Carr looked down at Kempt's anxious face.

"Not so far, Sir, only to keep trying. We must at least hold here these French up above us and hope that things are going better at the main breach."

A ladder was raised just alongside them and Carr placed his hand on one of the rungs.

"If you'll excuse me, Sir. I think it's my turn!"

Kempt nodded, as Carr drew his Dragoon pistol from the sling at his side and began to climb, followed by several Portuguese. The presence of the ladder at the embrasure brought French faces, arms and shoulders over its edge. One grinned, his face ghastly in the light of the burning carcasses beneath.

"You come up, Rosbif, yes? We welcome you to Badajoz!"

Carr's pistol was at his side and so he climbed another two rungs, raised it and fired. The ball entered under the man's chin and continued on, to send a spray of blood and brains up into the night. Carr dropped the pistol, drew his sword and continued upwards, but there were now three defenders above him, one pointing a musket downwards at him. Then came the sound of a shot from below and Carr felt the heat of the muzzle blast on the right side of his neck. The French musket fell down past him, its user having been shot from below by a Portuguese infantryman. There was no time for thanks as Carr climbed another rung, but he was faced with a hedge of bayonets and spears and, from the immensely difficult position at the top of the ladder, it was all he could do to fend off the thrusts from above. Progress into the embrasure was impossible from that height, four feet below the embrasure edge, but French could be seen looking down and over. He dropped down two rungs and shouted down, hoping to be heard in the mixed din of hundreds of raised and furious voices.

"Get some fire on that embrasure!"

If his order was obeyed Carr had little idea, amidst the incessant sounds of conflict, but at least one Frenchman fell back and another fell forward past him. He went upwards to again meet the bristling defence of pointed steel and this time he managed a backhand swipe at a soldier with a bayonet, but now, momentarily, his sword could no longer be used for defence and a sharpened spike was raised above him by a screaming Frenchman. Carr's only hope, and it was remote, was that he could swing over to dodge the thrust, but there were other defenders waiting alongside his would-be assailant to attempt the same. The spear began its thrust, when suddenly there was an explosion beneath him and the ladder descended by six feet. The thrust came down into mid-air as Carr clung on to a ladder now collapsing beneath him and sliding sideways. A shell had exploded at the foot of the ladder, taking off several feet from its length and killing or wounding all those stood at the base and firing their weapons. He jumped and landed awkwardly, feeling a pain in his right ankle and so he leaned momentarily against the wall, his sword now dangling from his wrist by its cord. Carr was very grateful for his luck, but felt great pity and anger for the men who had obeyed his order and were now all dead or badly wounded. RSM Gibney came running up, blood running down between his nose and his right eye.

"Are you alright, Sir?"

Carr nodded in the yellow light of a burning carcass.

"Sort of Sar' Major, but I don't think I'll be marching too well in the near future!"

Gibney almost grinned.

"Ah'll forgive you that, Sir, but I dohn't think this is going at all too well!"

"You're not wrong there, Sar' Major, but we keep going. Where's the Colonel and the Major?"

"Both around, Sir. Doin' their best to keep things 'appenin'!"

Carr reached out to place his right hand on Gibney's shoulder for support, then he tried his right ankle and nodded and smiled, relieved that nothing was broken.

"Thank you, Sar' Major!"

Gibney saluted, then ran off to help with the raising of more ladders. Carr thrust his lucky escape to the back of his mind. He had to, because Williams was running up.

"Any success anywhere?"

"No Sir, and it's best not to look too close."

His words were amongst the most mournful he had ever spoken. The foot of the wall and ten feet from it was almost a carpet of Allied dead, or badly wounded or dying. Instead, Williams looked at Carr.

"I've ordered them to unfix bayonets. Men falling from the ladders are being impaled as they fall."

"That's sensible, Sir. The French are doing us more damage than we can cope with, without doing it to ourselves as well!"

Another ladder slid across the wall in front of them, hooked over from above by the French, the unwounded men jumping off, the wounded or dead from the top falling like puppets to crash amongst those 20 to 30 feet below on the ground, who were already casualties from what was proving to be a hopeless venture. Williams ran off to assemble some more ladder parties.

"Well, good luck, Carr! Keep on keeping on!"

Carr paused to look around, unsure as to what would be worth attempting that had not already been tried and failed so many times. For what had seemed an age, the scene all around had been carnage and mayhem, maddened Redcoats and Portuguese continuously attempting to scale the walls with minimal hope of success, whilst at their feet grew an extending and thickening covering of their own dead, with the wounded crawling away down the slope to escape the missiles and ordnance thrown down upon them. All took place in a light borrowed from Hell, the burning carcasses giving each man a demonic appearance, dancing the steps of insanity in both silhouette and half-light, everyone working like men robbed of all reason to raise a ladder yet one more time. From above came missiles of all descriptions, rocks, logs and heavy furniture, but worst were the shells and grenades which burst to add their own noise and brief flash to the mayhem and then to cause the screams of the freshly wounded. From above also came the taunts of the French, who seemed to now be enjoying the whole experience, taunts of, "Victoire! Victoire! Voutes etes finis Rosbifs", or simply, "Rosbifs! Welcome to Badajoz!".

For Lacey and O'Hare, their feelings were no different to those of Carr, but Lacey felt the failure and resulting carnage more acutely. He had spent what seemed an hour trying to bring order to the ladder parties, as each ladder crashed to the ground, he organised men to raise it again. All effort was in the midst of a mind-numbing mayhem, as men continuously fell from above, inhuman shapes dropping almost 40 feet to add yet more bodies to the spread of dead and wounded all around, which was also added to by the onslaught of deadly objects raining from above. All this in a darkness only punctuated by the brief flashes of French explosions which added to the manic, eerie, spectre of a world gone mad.

Carr decided that it was time he tried again. He went to a ladder and looked around for an Officer or NCO and he saw Shakeshaft, his left sleeve very ragged, but the arm inside still seemed to be working.

"Richard! I'm going up this ladder. Get some of ours back behind me down the slope. They may be able to see a target from back there! This is attrition, we must wear them down as much as they do us. I suspect that there are none too many French up there."

"It doesn't feel like it, Sir."

"No, but we have to hope!"

Shakeshaft gathered half a dozen 105th and 60th Rifles and led them back to where they stood a better chance of sighting on any defender stood in the embrasure. Carr then placed his first foot on a rung, but a hand came onto his right forearm. It was Rushby.

"I think it's time I took a turn, Sir. With respect!"

Carr nodded and stepped back.

"Right, but make no effort to get into the embrasure. Draw them forward and defend yourself. Do no more! Shakeshaft's men behind you will try to down a few. Right now, that's all we can do! We can only hope for success at the main breach."

"Very good, Sir."

Rushby climbed, followed by Solomon. Once at the top, the bayonets and spears appeared again, but Rushby's sword and Solomon's bayonet deflected all, and two of their assailants were shot from below and tumbled back into the Castle, but no more appeared in the empty embrasure. Some canny French NCO was clearly content to leave Rushby poised there whilst he made no further attempt to progress any further and there was no point in losing any more men to dislodge him whilst he remained static. The 'Rosbifs' would soon give up, anyway. Rushby and Solomon remained at the top of the ladder, but Rushby looked down.

"Solomon. Can I stand on your shoulders?"

Solomon climbed the extra rungs, Rushby placed his feet on his shoulders and Solomon climbed some more. Before elevating his head over the lip of the embrasure, Rushby raised his pistol to fire through. The result of that was unknown, but, in the smoke, a Frenchman appeared, too far back to be shot from below. Then what appeared to be the top of a wooden trunk or cabinet was pushed forward into the opening, thoroughly blocking it. Solomon, ordered by Rushby, lowered him to the top rungs, but Rushby clung on to the ladder.

Carr sighed at what he had just seen and spoke the words out loud, "Stalemate. We cannot remain here much longer!". He pulled out his watch, it was gone eleven, they had been attacking the walls for over an hour! He was stood thinking again of anything that could be done that might advance their cause, however minimally, when Brigadier Campbell arrived.

"Carr, isn't it?"

"Sir!"

"Kempt's wounded, but Picton's back on his feet and in command. Mine went too far to the right, but we're here now. Things have not gone well?"

"No Sir. We can only hope that we have worn them down somewhat."

"What else, Major? Now that we're here, I'm leading mine for another attempt. And you?"

"In a bit of a quandary, Sir. Nothing's working here."

"No matter! My Major Ridge is over to the right. He thinks he has a better chance over there. My Brigade are here now to take over, so you get over there with some of yours and give him what support you can."

Carr saluted and, carrying his sword, he trotted across to the right. Shot and grape were still arriving from Fort San Christobal, sweeping along the base of the walls, but he managed to gather Ellis, Davey, Pike and Saunders. With this group, he ran to what was the end of the main wall, this marked by a low bastion which was sending musket fire along the face of the wall they were standing under, but Ridge was sheltered behind a square flanking tower. Carr soon recognised Ridge and ran up to him.

"Ridge! Campbell sent me over. It seems you have a marginally better chance here than a Forlorn Hope!"

In the satanic light, Ridge's grin seemed otherworldly, but his answer was cheerful enough.

"Carr, glad to have you here. Yes, seems that the wall's a bit lower here and this tower gives some protection. I've sent men to get a ladder, two if possible, and my Lieutenant Canch has gone off to get one for himself."

On another ladder, further back, Tom Miles was crawling up, his body as much flattened against the rungs as possible, his mouth uttering every foul word in his lexicon. His rifle was loaded and stood beneath were Deakin, Halfway and Bailey, all with loaded weapons, hoping to see targets. Miles arrived at the top, reached up to place a hand on the edge of the embrasure to then withdraw it and fully cock his Baker. A shape appeared above topped by a French shako and Miles fired for the man to immediately topple forward, then down. Another appeared to be shot from below by Len Bailey and tumble back, but no more came into view, merely an array of sharp points, all bayonets and spears, all above the edge, which indicated the threat still present. Miles reloaded and waited. He rose up to peer over the embrasure and then duck back down. There were several French waiting, but none came forward. For Miles, as for many others, it was also a simple standoff.

At Ridge's flank, the ladders had arrived, two, one made by the 105th, identified by the ropes from the top and halfway. Both were raised, close side by side, up to the sheltered side of the tower and held firm by the ropes. Ridge looked at Carr.

"Well, here goes nothing!"

A voice came from their left, where they could see another ladder against the wall.

"Ready here, Sir."

"With you, Canch! Up we go!"

Carr pulled forward the nearest, largest men, Saunders and a Grenadier Corporal of the 5th.

"Name?"

"Digby, Sir."

"Fix bayonets. Hold them up above alongside the Major. Give him some protection."

Ridge placed his left hand on a rung and pointed his sword above him. From the ladder alongside the bayonets of Saunders and Digby came up beside the sword and the three began to climb, Ridge first, then Saunders and Digby each as close as possible to keep their bayonets at the maximum height, their weapons held by the small of the butt. Carr turned to Davey.

"Are you loaded?"

"Sir!"

"Fall back a few paces. Give yourself a chance to see anyone."

Carr stood back to see men on all three ladders, including Canch a little way over, but Ridge was the highest. He was soon at the top and a defender appeared, to be immediately shot by Davey. A sword came slashing sideways at Ridge but it was blocked by Saunders' bayonet, then Ridge took the large and vital step from the topmost rung onto the front edge of the tower's embrasure. Two defenders sprung at him, but Ridge fenced with one, whilst Saunders thrust his bayonet into the groin of another. Then Digby joined Ridge, to fire his musket into the Castle, whilst standing on the wall, then to hold off menacing defenders with his bayonet. Meanwhile, Ridge, by main strength, managed to send his opponent over the edge of the tower, with a punch to the head, followed by a shoulder barge. Saunders arrived to stand on the man he had bayonetted and was now bleeding to death. He shot the nearest defender attacking Digby and then stood with his own bayonet at the ready, all three shoulder to shoulder in the embrasure. Ridge stepped forward.

"Push forward. Give some room for more to come up!"

It was easier said than done, the three were attacked with desperate vigour, but Ridge's sword, Digby's bayonet and Saunders great strength using rifle butt and bayonet, pushed them back. First to join them were three of Ridge's 5th, followed by Carr and Davey, the latter with a loaded rifle, which he used to despatch the nearest assailant. The embrasure had been captured.

The language of Tom Miles had not abated but even his aggression and ill-temper could not overcome the good sense of not attempting to enter the embrasure. Below him on the ladder were several Connaughts but they also could do no more than wait. Below them, Jed Deakin felt something heavy hit his shoulder and then bounce down. He looked down to see a grenade with the fuse still burning. His first instinct was to stand on the fuse, which he did, and he ground the burning end with his foot down onto the stony soil. When he lifted his foot the fuse was extinguished, but then he had a thought, the fuse was overlong, it had been thrown over too quickly. He picked up the grenade and went to a burning carcass to relight the fuse, which had more than ten seconds remaining. He quickly returned to the ladder.

"Tom! Tom!"

Miles looked down to see Deakin holding a burning grenade.

"Tom. Catch this. Give it 'em back!"

In the event, there was no need for a throw. A Connaught hand reached down and the grenade was quickly passed up to Miles. As it reached him a voice came from above.

"Rosbif! Rosbif! Est tu la!"

Miles hefted the grenade and saw that the fuse was almost gone. He had no idea what the Frenchman had said, but he replied anyway.

"Here! Hold this! You muckrake frog-eatin' shite-auk!"

The grenade was tossed over the embrasure edge and immediately exploded for smoke and blast to pour out from the opening. Miles was instantly at the very top of the ladder, standing on the top of the uprights, then into the entrance, followed by Connaughts, all making a rapid ascent, each pushing the one above into the embrasure. Miles shot the first Frenchman he saw and the next Connaught shot another, before both bayonetted two more, then, in a tight group, with some Connaughts on the top of the wall itself, they rushed forward to secure the walkway behind the embrasure. There were few defenders and many were now falling back. Miles looked over to his right to see a surge of Redcoats crossing the ditch behind the parapet, with what looked like Carr, Saunders and Davey at the front. The Connaughts with him were screaming and cheering and other Redcoats and Portuguese were now up on the walkway. Further over, two of these were Rushby followed by Solomon over their own embrasure, then Miles saw Rushby felled by a bayonet thrust from one of the last defenders, just before Solomon stove in the side of the Frenchman's head with his rifle butt. He dragged Rushby to one side and then joined the charge over the ditch behind the battlement wall. The final defenders were being chased back into the Castle and all that were caught were killed without mercy.

On the far right, Ridge, in the lead, shouted over to Carr.

"Send me as many as you can. I'll form a line beyond the ditch."

Carr waved his sword in acknowledgement and he was still within hearing when he heard Ridge shout, "Come on my lads! Let's be the first to seize the Governor!"

Carr stood on the far side of the ditch and all who crossed it were directed up to Ridge. When the trickle became a flood of men coming over the wall and then the ditch, Carr left to rejoin Ridge in what looked like a wide courtyard. Ridge had assembled his men in a thick line, three or four deep, with himself in the lead. Carr placed himself on the left end of the line and as they edged forward, so did he. Through the gloom and in the light of exploding British shells still coming over, could be seen an equally dense line of French, formed to defend what was obviously the Castle gate, the low towers rising behind them. Ridge's line stopped and he raised his sword.

"Why do you hesitate? Forward."

The line continued forward, all in the line who were not loaded did so as they advanced. They were still moving forward when Ridge gave the order.

"Open fire!"

A ragged volley ensued from the British line to be answered immediately by that of the French. Carr saw a sword go up in the air to his right and he turned to see Ridge flung backwards, hit by fire from the French line. Carr immediately took command.

"On boys, on! Right up to them!"

The Redcoats and Portuguese continued to pace forward, keeping up a steady fire. With the range down to 20 yards the French line dissolved and they fled, in all directions, but mostly through the gate that led into the town. Carr immediately ran forward.

"On boys, on! Get to the gate!"

He ran on, with many immediately behind, but Carr ground his teeth as he saw the main gate swing shut. He and many others slammed their shoulders into it, but it was now firmly barred. Then came a voice from the left.

"Sir! There's a small gate here. We can get through."

Carr ran over to find a small wicker gate, fully open, but the opening was only wide enough for one man at a time. He took a deep breath, pulled the gate back further and stepped through. The result was him seeing a dozen flashes from French firing-pans and he immediately dodged back during the split second before the bullets smacked into the stonework either side. However, one came through and hit a private of the 5th in his left ribs and he staggered back. Carr had little choice, the small gate was obviously no way out.

"Up on the walls, all of you. Give fire!"

Carr followed several men up the steps to the rampart above the gate and each soldier immediately began to fire at the crowded French gathered below. Carr saw a Captain of the 5th ascending the steps.

"Take charge. Maintain fire on those below. More men will arrive."

Carr ran back down to be met by Brigadier Campbell.

"Well done, Carr! You got in."

"Yes Sir, but it was Major Ridge of the 5th who was the first in."

"Where is he?"

"Back towards the wall, Sir. I think he was badly wounded pushing the French back to this gate."

Campbell looked up at the men now crowding the parapet above the gate and each side of it.

"Right Carr, I'll take charge here. You could do a lot worse than get that Frog flag down! While it's still up there, we'll still get our own shells exploding around our ears."

Carr nodded and looked around to see Davey and Pike. He pointed.

"You two! With me!"

oOo

Lacey and O'Hare arrived at the top of a ladder, just in time to see the body of a dead Redcoat being dragged back into the Castle to ease their entrance. Lacey's head was reeling, the two hours of bloodshed and havoc at the base of the wall, was beyond anything he had ever experienced. He and O'Hare had spent the whole of the attack at the base of the wall, organising men to reset ladders as each was pushed away or over, whilst casualties mounted all around. Lacey had scaled a ladder himself, or half scaled, until it was hooked over and he had landed on top of several wounded men which broke his fall, but probably further wounded them. Now actually in the Castle, it was only Picton's grating voice, from the next ladder over, that pulled him back to anything like reality from the still vivid memories.

"Lacey! Lacey! Help me through."

Once through the embrasure, with even the cannon now pulled back, both went over to help Picton enter the Castle. The top of his right leg was swathed in bandage but his irascibility had got him up the ladder and over the wall. Once through, it was O'Hare he leant on, because Lacey was now sat wearily on the parapet, but it was Lacey that Picton directed his questions to, to receive a terse answer, borne of utter weariness.

"Where's Kempt?"

"Wounded Sir!"

"Campbell?"

"He's across to the right, Sir."

"Wallace?"

"No idea, Sir!"

"What's happened at the main?"

"No idea again, Sir. I got in only moments before you."

The implication that Picton was asking ridiculous questions was not lost on him, but he let it pass.

"My impression, Sir, is that it's been utter failure."

Picton stood squarely before Lacey, who rose to his feet and saluted as Picton gave his orders.

"We must get down there and support, take the French in the rear, if needed. What do you have?"

Lacey pointed to the area beyond the ditch.

"Over there, Sir. My Colour Company and my Grenadiers are formed up, what's left of them."

Picton turned to see the two Companies of the 105th formed in column, eight men wide. His face took on the expression that only he could manage; admiring disapproval. He turned to O'Hare.

"Major! Lead those down to the main breach. See what you can do!"

O'Hare saluted and ran over to Carravoy and Heaviside.

"Charles! Joshua! With me. We're going along the walls."

355

O'Hare ran to a small bridge that crossed the main wall ditch and onto the walkway. Holding his sword in its scabbard, he jogged on, to see Simon Ameshurst close at his side.

"Pleased to see you in one piece, Simon."

"Thank you, Sir. I'm leaking a bit here and there, but generally sound."

Before O'Hare could reply, they came to a blockhouse containing a gate, the purpose of which was to split the ramparts into sections. It was a wood and iron bound gate and secure in a low doorway. Ameshurst looked up.

"I could try from the other side, Sir."

"What you can do is get up there and see how many Johnnies are on the other side. We go from there."

Ameshurst climbed a pyramid of his own men to get to the top, but his own 'bodyguard' would not let him stay there alone and soon the top was crowded with Grenadiers.

"No one here, Sir."

"Right. Down and try this gate."

Soon they heard the sound of the efforts that Ameshurst and his Grenadiers were making to open the gate from the far side, but nothing gave. The lock and chains were solid and unyielding. Then came a cry from behind.

"We have two ladders, Sir."

"Right, if we cannot go through, we go over. Pass them up."

The ladders came forward and were soon placed on both sides. Progress over the blockhouse was slow, but soon O'Hare had enough men to continue along the rampart. They came to a huge, but deserted battery, guns and serving equipment still in place.

"This must be the San Pedro!"

However, no one was listening, his men were running on. They crossed the rear of the huge, but deserted bastion, where they came upon a small store and O'Hare pointed.

"What's in there?"

He could see another blockhouse a little further along, preventing further progress, but his men came out of the store with axes and metal handspikes to quickly attack the iron door of the blockhouse and dislodge its hinges from the stonework. The door was pushed down and on they went, but it was obvious where they had now arrived. They could see the rear of what must be the San Trinidad bastion and the walls there were still crowded with French soldiers. No Redcoat was coming over the summit of the breach, all was static as at the commencement of the attack, the French were still there, obviously the defence had held firm. O'Hare looked behind him. His men were strung out along the parapet from the bastion they had just left. They must get off the wall and form up, if they were to have any impact on the solid group of defenders holding the main breach and defending it very effectively. O'Hare could see the French rotating to shoot down over the breach and then retire to reload. Other were heaving and throwing all sorts over the walls, rocks, logs, shells or grenades. O'Hare pointed downwards.

"Off the wall and form up!"

Inside the wall was not high and many jumped down rather than use the steps. With the two Companies formed in ranks of three, he turned to look at Heaviside on his left, then Carravoy on his right, then he waved his sword forward. However, they had not gone ten yards, before a tumult of Redcoats came down to attack the rear of the breach from the right. As his line marched on, O'Hare strained to identify them, but the sight of those arriving immediately opening fire on the breach defenders told all the story that O'Hare needed. The Brigade of Leith's Division had got over the San Vincente bastion, they had now come along the wall to attack the main breach and they had arrived in force. Soon the French defenders were abandoning their posts at the breach and streaming back through the rear of the bastion. O'Hare took his decision.

"Halt. Make ready."

The French garrison of the San Trinidad were all running back towards him, making for the Castle, presumably, or so O'Hare thought, because it was agreed to be the place of their last stand. The fugitives came on and there was just enough light to see the shock, and then horror, on their faces when they found their way back blocked by two Companies of British Redcoats. Those leading skidded to a halt and O'Hare gave his order.

"Present!"

The muskets came down level.

"Volley by ranks. Fire!"

The first rank blasted their volley into the gloom, then came the following two, with the standard 105th three second space between the volleys. When the smoke cleared, there were many French stretched lifeless or writhing wounded on the ground, whilst the rest fled off to the British right, into the depths of the town. O'Hare looked down through the San Trinidad bastion. British troops were arriving up and over from the breach below, but only in very small groups. The breach was now held by Leith's men, many of whom now took it upon themselves to help up the men of the Light and Fourth Divisions and to cross the dense array of obstacles that O'Hare could see even from where he was, all covering the top of the breach. O'Hare saw no point in remaining and he called out.

"Charles. Joshua. Back to the Castle. I'd say that we can now use the road back up!"

For Carr, Davey and Pike, the tower loomed up before them, even in the gloom of near midnight. A shell exploded over to their right and the brief light revealed a door with, amazingly, a French sentry still at his post. The three ran up and all he did was to present arms! Carr seized his collar.

"Les Couleurs! Quel sens?"

The sentry tore himself free.

"Je ne sais pas!"

Carr punched him with the bell-guard of his sabre.

"You know alright!"

However, the result was the Frenchman throwing down his weapon and striking his chest.

"Frappe-moi!. Je suis Francais!"

The brave gesture of defiance moved Carr just enough for him to lower his sword. He turned to Davey and Pike.

"Shove him out the way!"

The two used their rifles on the Frenchman, thus unblocking the door and Carr ran inside to mount the first set of stairs he came to. With Pike and Davey, he climbed at least three flights, then they were on the roof and the flagstaff could be seen in one corner, with the French Tricolour swinging lazily in the smokey breeze. They ran over and Carr seized the halyards whilst Davey untied the ropes around the cleat on the pole.

"My job, I think!"

Carr allowed the halyards to run through his fingers as the weight of the French flag carried it down. He quickly unbent its ties, then came the thought, "What to put in its place?" He turned to Pike.

"Pike! Off with your jacket."

Joe Pike began to undo his buttons but it was obviously painful progress. Davey helped him and when the jacket came off, Carr could see the large cut in the back of the jacket.

"Pike, you're wounded."

"Yes Sir, but not too bad, Sir. Just a few stitches'll put it right."

Carr turned him around to see the back of his shirt, soaked in blood.

"You play no further part in this, Pike. Get back down the wall and get with the wounded. You've lost a lot of blood!"

Whilst Carr tied Pike's jacket onto the halyards via the sleeves, Davey looked over and down to the main breach, easily seen from their high vantage point. It was swarming with British troops.

"Looks like the town is ours, Sir. Every bit of it. At least all that counts!"

"True enough, Davey, but the worry now is what happens next?"

oOo

Miles and Bailey were amongst the first out of the main Castle gate, once it had been unbarred. The French had disappeared and so now a dense crowd of British and Portuguese, a complete mixture of Third Division Regiments quickly crossed the wide road beyond. Few went any further, most began to smash in the doors of the houses opposite and soon there were screams and shouts of uproar, punctuated by musket shots. However, with several others, Miles and Bailey found a narrow street that led downwards, plainly to the centre of the town. As they descended, the houses became more impressive and plainly prosperous and strangely with candles in the windows. Bailey halted and tugged at Miles' sleeve.

"How about one of these?"

Miles shook his head.

"Leave 'em. Nothin' in any but a few trinkets and whatnot as can't be sold for bugger all! There's better pickings down on."

"So, where're we going"

"Every army has a Headquarters with their pay chest in it. That's for us, but we needs to be quick."

He continued his descent at a loping run and Bailey followed, but the houses that they left behind had but a short reprieve, from behind the pair heard the locks of the doors being shot through and again the shouts of both triumph, terror and shattering glass. However, they were not alone, a whole crowd of soldiery were following, all intent on reaching the centre of the town. Some French appeared from a side road, their faces soon distorted with fear when they saw the street above them full of Allied soldiers and they ran in terror, pursued by shots which downed several. Miles caught up with a French Officer and tripped him, for both him and Bailey to pounce on him, but then drag him to his feet. Miles punched him in the side of his head, seized his lapels and then stared into his terrified face from mere inches. The Officer, a Lieutenant, was only in his early twenties and plainly horrified at what he was certain was about to happen, but Miles had other ideas.

"Your Headquarters! Where is it?"

The Lieutenant calmed down when questioned, his life was not about to end just yet, but he did not understand. His face turned to puzzlement.

"Ce qui? Je ne comprends pas!"

Miles shook him violently and the fear returned, but Bailey did know some French.

"Try maison de Phillipon."

The Lieutenant heard and understood and pointed down the street, so Miles hurled him in that direction and then pushed him further. Knowing his life depended on compliance, the Lieutenant hurried on, followed by the pair and soon, after only one change in direction, they were in a square, at the back of the Cathedral with the bonus that their erstwhile companions in plunder had been tempted away by the many sizeable houses on their way down. Both were practically alone in front of an imposing building, with the French Tricolour still in place above the door. Miles looked at Bailey.

"This is it!"

He threw the Lieutenant towards the Cathedral and he sprinted off. There were many wounded French in the space around them and Miles pointed to one.

"Get his backpack! And another."

The first soldier groaned as Bailey rolled him twice to remove the straps, and then he dragged another backpack from a dead body, to throw the second at Miles, next they both entered what was obviously the Governor's Headquarters. From outside the sounds of tumult and disorder grew, but Miles, undeterred, headed for a staircase, then stopped, because he had noticed four crates of wine over against the wall, so he hurried over to them but not to drink.

"We'll chuck these in front the door. They'll slow up any comin' in after us."

That done, he returned to the staircase.

"What we want will be upstairs, most likely. In his Office. We'll have to be quick."

They ascended and barged through the most imposing door, to see an equally imposing desk and behind that a brass bound chest with a lock securing the lid. Miles ran over to it.

"Here's most likely!"

With butts of their rifles, they quickly smashed the hasp free from the front of the chest and opened the lid. Miles' face lit up.

"It's our birthdays!"

Inside were four bags of coins. Miles opened the neck of one to then produce a gold coin with the image of Napoleon stamped upon it. He estimated that each purse had about 50 coins, then he closed the neck, put that purse into his backpack, then another. The second two he tossed up to Bailey for these to be safely stowed in his backpack.

"Now for a good drink!"

They started with two bottles from one of the four crates in the doorway, these now being pillaged by a group of Scotsmen.

Back at the Castle, his head still aching from the stress of the past two hours, Lacey was more than grateful to see Carr.

"Where are our men?"

Carr could not keep the helplessness out of his voice.

"I really don't know, Sir. I only know that Joshua's and Charles' are back here with us, and Drake's are close gathered."

"It's possible that many could be quite near, up in the tower, or in the Castle houses and there's a Square just outside the main gate. Some will be there."

Carr detected the weariness and lack of real hope in Lacey's voice, but he answered as positively as he could.

"It could well be so, Sir."

Lacey turned away from him to look at the two soldiers who were never too far away from their Colonel, Sergeant Herbert Bryce and 'Bugle' Bates.

"Bates! Sound 'Fall In'."

For the sake of avoiding any confusion, as soon as they entered the Peninsula, Bates had been required to compose a call unique to the 105th and he sounded it now, the notes echoing around the surprisingly almost deserted square. The first to arrive from the night shadows were Heaviside's Colour Company.

"Fall in, Sir?"

"Yes, Joshua. Column of fours."

The Colour Company did so and the Grenadiers copied. Then, over the following minutes, the Captains, Lieutenants and NCOs of the remaining eight Companies arrived, as did their men, coming from all directions, the tower, the main gate and the dwellings within the Castle. Within 15 minutes they had what looked like a weak Battalion, but the 105th had responded. Carr was amazed, and whispered to O'Hare.

"I doubt you'd get that from the Coldstreams!"

O'Hare leaned over.

"I suspect you would Henry, but to match them, well, that does mean something. He's certainly put something into ours. Wish I knew what it was. I'd bottle it and sell it!"

Lacey now turned to both.

"Is that all, do you think?"

O'Hare answered.

"Impossible to say. We've left many dead and wounded on the other side of that wall and some may have drifted off some way away."

"Right! Well, let them rest and get some food. They came in here with nothing bar weapons and water. One man in four back to camp, at least then they'll have something for breakfast."

As Carr ran off to give the order, Lacey and O'Hare stood in the Castle Square, listening to the growing sounds of a town being sacked and pillaged. Carr briefly stopped at Drake and each concluded that the other was a scruffy mess, but they shook hands, each grinning with relief at finding the other alive.

"We must write!"

"Yes, Nat, we must."

That said, Carr sped off.

Through the rest of the night of the assault, the 105th slept where they were, the ominous sounds coming from beyond the Castle walls mixed with the disquieting sounds of the wounded, all now within the Castle grounds. All these were gathered together in groups, but few as yet had been seen by any Surgeon, despite all of the Surgeon's in Picton's Division now being present and working both within and beyond the Castle walls and some even beyond the Rivellas, attending to the wounded from their advance to the Rivellas.

At dawn, with the sounds of the despoiling of Badajoz even more riotous than before, Lacey called O'Hare, Carr and RSM Gibney to him.

"What's going on in there is looting, rape and murder. Assemble some men you can trust and get into the town. Find any of ours that are in there and drag them out. Wellington will be sending in the Provosts and there will be executions. Any that you get back here, and come willingly, I'll give them the benefit of the doubt, provided they still have their weapons."

O'Hare looked at Gibney, now with a bandage between his neck and tunic collar.

"You have some names in mind Sar' Major?"

"Aye Sir, ah do!"

"Ten minutes before you go?"

"That should do it, Sir."

In the interim, both Carr and O'Hare looked at Lacey and Carr spoke the words.

"Sir, you should rest."

Lacey nodded wearily, but he changed the subject to one of more major concern, for him.

"Casualties?"

O'Hare shook his head.

"Impossible to say, but we'll call the roll this evening."

"Officers we know of? Killed?"

O'Hare's shoulders slumped down.

"Four I know of, two Captains, Royce and Knowles and two Lieutenants, Phipps and Carter. Rushby badly wounded."

"Rushby! I know his people."

Carr had had enough.

"Bryce! Can't you get the Colonel a cup of tea of something?"

Bryce sprang to attention, down in the parapet ditch.

"Water's just boiling now, Sir."

Carr nodded, regretting the tone he had used.

"Well done, Bryce. Carry on."

By now Gibney had returned with his trusted NCOs, these being Sergeants Deakin, Ellis, Hill, Nicholls and Ridgeway, with ten Corporals and Chosen Men, which included Saunders and Davey. Carr and O'Hare led them forward without a word and they followed. When they began their descent into the town, Davey took the opportunity to get himself beside Zeke Saunders.

"Who of ours is missing?"

"Tom, Len and Nat Solomon."

Davey had another topic on his mind.

"Sorry about being a bit sorry for meself afore we started off yesterday."

Saunders grinned.

"Think nothing of it. I said just the same to Jed Deakin."

Both managed an embarrassed half smile but by now they were out of the Castle Gate. The morning was now well advanced and yet the screams and sounds of violence continued unabated. Immediately beyond the Gate and in the first road down, were the first signs of what was to come. Utterly incapable British and Portuguese soldiers were stretched out on the cobbles, but some were capable enough of staggering back to the Castle, carrying or wearing any type of ridiculous apparel, anything ranging from whores' dresses to a Monk's habit. Some were 105th and after a good cuffing from Gibney and Saunders they were sent on their way under the charge of an NCO. Reassuringly, all had their weapons, bar one, who became a particular object of Gibney's ire. However, what was most distressing was the plight of the civilians that they met, many in despair out in the road, wringing their hands in grief, often alternating between mourning the body of a dead relative in the road or staring in shocked horror at the wreckage of what had once been their home. Several houses were half destroyed by sheer wanton vandalism and those not, were now occupied by drunken soldiers and the sound could clearly be heard of them smashing up the family furniture to feed their fire.

The further into the town, the greater the evidence of outrage of an army on the verge of mutiny. Further down from the Castle the greater the availability of drink so that now the air was pungent with the smell of spirit and wine, as both, in an overpowering cocktail, flowed down the gutters where many were lying there to drink from it. However, what angered those of the 105th most were the growing instances of abuse and mistreatment of civilians, even rape. As their street finally ran out to enter the Cathedral Square, a half-naked female, clutching a child, ran into it, pursued by several Redcoats. No orders were required, the woman was allowed through and then the 105th closed ranks to then batter into unconsciousness her drunken pursuers. A few final kicks were administered before they entered the Square itself, which was the scene of a madhouse carnival, as if for the last day of the world, all run and organised by the released in-mates of an asylum. The square was full of drunken, cavorting Redcoats and Portuguese, although few were now in recognisable uniform, for most had donned some ridiculous looted garment, several even sporting nightwear over their tunics. Every building was smashed open, with not one pane of glass intact, but worse again was the treatment of the town's civilians, many being pushed and pulled and cuffed around the Square, their faces distorted by fear and weeping. Several were forced to give rides to soldiers, carrying the whooping rider around on their backs. Towards them came a naked priest, identified as such only by his ecumenical hat, being whipped onwards by a group of Redcoats from mixed Regiments. The angry Saunders seized one of his tormentors by the cowl of the monk's habit he now wore and pulled him backwards to then seize the loose cloth at the front.

"What's this!"

The drunken Redcoat remained angry.

"Frog sympathisers all! Don't you remember what they were like to us when we got here starving after Talavera? Never gave one damn thing, 'though we was all nearer dead than alive!"

He tore himself away and Saunders let him go. From across the Square shots were being fired and so, with Gibney, Ellis and Deakin in attendance, Carr and O'Hare hurried across to find a dead British Officer, blood now running from a chest wound, but the chances of finding his murderer were nil as the mad crowd swirled around them. O'Hare remembered their mission and spoke quickly to the incensed Carr.

"Remember why we're here. There's nothing we can do against this."

He pointed to the body of the young Lieutenant.

"He tried giving orders and it cost him his life! This will only die down of its own accord. Best to let them drink themselves into helplessness. In that state they'll do less harm!"

He re-studied the chaos all around.

"Best we keep together when we search the streets for ours, but we can split into two to search here. I'll take Gibney and some, you take Deakin and Ellis and others. Ten minutes back to the road we came down."

There came more firing, but now the targets were obvious, as the bells in the Cathedral rang discordantly as the shot hit them. They hurried back to their men and the parties split and searched the Square, many times throwing aside those who accosted them for no particular reason or wanted them to take a drink. The lurid green of the 105th facings at least made their search easy and a handful were found, to be dragged back, some still capable of walking, to their entrance road, where Gibney and Hill threw them to the ground and began to impart in their fiercest manner, their very lowest opinion of them. Thus quelled even further, with three NCOs as escort, they were forced back up the hill, each mercifully being given a musket, of which there were many on the cobbles of the square. Nicholls' words rang in their ears all the way up, making it very clear why they were needed and, sheepishly, each did their best to lodge the weapon securely on their shoulders.

Back in the square, O'Hare looked at Carr, who had remained angry and livid at what he could see but was helpless to prevent.

"Now for the streets, but we keep together."

In a tight group, they scoured the narrow streets that led from the Square. These were not so crowded and the evidence of outrage not so prevalent, merely smashed houses and inebriated, sub-conscious soldiery. In the third street they entered, Saunders tugged at Davey's sleeve. He had seen the green.

"There's two!"

They hurried forward to roll each upright and Saunders immediately recognised each.

"Well, here's two of our lost sheep!"

Bailey and Miles were hauled upright to a sitting position, both in a so extreme a state of intoxication that neither could close their mouths nor hold their heads erect. Davey knelt between the two.

"Seems like you've both had a good drink. An' both still got your Bakers too. That'll save your backs!"

Miles now managed to rouse himself to a state near consciousness, his words slurred and stuttered.

"And that's not all we got on our backs, in these French packs!"

The effort was too much and his head subsided again. Davey pulled him forward and lifted up the flap now exposed and he looked inside, then he allowed Miles to fall back against the wall. He did the same for Bailey.

"Nothin'! There's nothin' in them packs!"

Through the fog of inebriation, shock and horror came to Miles' face.

"There's bags of French coin in each. Two!"

Davey stared down at him, his face indulgent.

"Well, they b'ain't there now!"

Miles was now even further animated and struggled out of the pack slings and that of his Baker to look inside the French backpack, his face becoming horrified and then angry.

"We've bin robbed!"

Davey laughed.

"You've been robbed. Who did you rob?"

Miles was now struggling to his feet.

"Frogs! We robbed the Frogs!"

He looked around to see only prone soldiers, but nevertheless he staggered over to several and searched their pockets, but in vain. Then he collapsed against a wall, his face writhing with despair.

"We 'ad two each!"

By now Ellis had arrived.

"Miles and Bailey! Why am I not surprised?"

He looked at Davey and Saunders.

"They're ours! Get 'em back up. Try to sober 'em up a bit. Least they still got their weapons."

Saunders and Davey hauled both to their feet and began the tedious trek with them back to the Castle. Their return to penury had now dawned on Bailey.

"We was rich!"

Saunders grinned down at him.

"Yes Len! So you say."

They progressed on, both of their charges gradually becoming more sober, but at the Castle they were thrown into the Keep, there to collapse with the other '105's who had also been brought back and there to sleep or vomit.

Lacey was up above the Gate. He had noticed the trickle of his own returning men, some under their own power, some returned under escort, but he paid them little attention. What now occupied him was the stream of Spanish refugees crossing the Guadiana by the Roman bridge to halt on the slopes below the San Christobal. In addition within his despairing view was another stream of shocked despair passing below his Castle wall to cross the Rivellas at the mill and gain the relative safety of the open ground there. Lacey had never felt so low and even ashamed regarding his lifelong trade as a soldier.

oOo

Chapter Thirteen

End Game

Carr and O'Hare looked up at the single figure stood atop the Castle gate, him not watching their return, but studying events down towards the Guadiana.

"The Colonel's taking this hard!"

"I know, Henry. For me, this has been the worst task ever given to any British army anywhere, that would be my opinion and this rape and pillage has come on top. And remember, Livermore pulled him out of retirement back in the year five to run that 5th Detachments, as we were then, a true collection of odds-and-sods, sweepings, survivors and hard-bargains. You were there!"

"I was, and then we went to Sicily. Some baptism!"

The pair were walking slowly away from the Castle gate and Lacey noticed their movement below him and this pulled him back to some measure of reality. Here were O'Hare and Carr who had returned with their search party, containing two dozen or so drunks and pillagers, who needed to be dealt with. His men had not had a decent hot meal for 36 hours, they were tired and there were many wounded. It was time to return to camp, he decided and, very much against his natural instinct, he saw no reason to seek permission from anyone. He descended the steps and called to O'Hare.

"Form fours. We're leaving. Get our miscreants up and moving. Any that cannot, leave for the Provosts!"

O'Hare ran off and the orders rang out for the men of the 105th to rise wearily to their feet and fall in prior to marching off, but Carr had a question.

"Sir, which way? We cannot go out through the town gates, that means passing through all that riot and there we'll lose some. The best way, if we can, is over the main breach. If not, there's another gate further around, past the Pardelleras fort, but that also means entering the town, if only on the outskirts."

Lacey nodded.

"True, Henry. So get down to the main breach and see if was can pass out over there."

Carr saluted and ran off, through the Castle Gate, through a very ornate Square and down to the main breach. There were many soldiers at the top of the battered wall, but inside were a set of steps that led to the breach and the embrasures either side, their guns all still in place. He came to the top and looked over, there to catch his breath, from shock. The breach had been cleared of both dead and wounded, also from the obstacles that were now in several piles down in the ditch. It was these that made him gasp, piles of vicious constructions, not least many planks with swords, spears and bayonets driven up through them, with chains at each end to hold them in place. All would have inflicted wounds enough to incapacitate without any French attention. In the fields beyond were rows and rows of wounded with hundreds of figures amongst them, giving what attendance they could. The floor of the ditch below was slushy mud with several puddles. He studied the slope of the breach and saw that it was very possible to pass over, but all the obstacles, now cleared, would have rendered any assault over it doomed to failure. A Captain came up to him, both his hand and his forehead bandaged.

"Can I help you, Sir? I'm Captain Bathurst, 40th, 2nd Somersets"

Carr turned away from his examinations.

"Yes. We are up at the Castle and wish to leave. This is our quickest route. Who should we ask permission from?"

The Captain looked puzzled.

"That I cannot answer, Sir. Were I you, I would just turn up and see what happens."

However, the Captain's face remained puzzled.

"So, you've kept yours together, Sir? They're not off in the town making merry!?"

"Ours are together and formed up. We are the 105th, the 'Rag and Bone Boys'. You may have heard of us?"

"Yes Sir, I have and I'd like to point out that ours are pretty much up together, also. What's left of us."

On hearing the last words, Carr turned towards him.

"Were you here?"

"Yes Sir. The Fourth came at this breach. Both Brigades."

"And you got in?"

"No Sir, we did not. Total failure. I lost count of the number of times we tried, some say 40, but not one man got to where we are standing now. The breach was utterly impassable from the obstacles you can see over there and the ground below was flooded. They actually had a boatfull of soldiers off to our left to fire along the front of the wall."

"Casualties?"

"A bit early, Sir, but we're hearing almost a thousand dead and wounded from each Division, each that is, both our 4th and the Light."

The staggering number of almost two thousand men lost in one place shocked Carr and he could do no more than stare into space for several seconds, before looking again at Bathurst.

"Two thousand!"

"Yes Sir. Here and the attempt at the curtain wall, next gap up, between the Trinidad and the Santa Maria. It was ours who tried here, the Light up there between those two bastions."

Carr sighed deeply, but time was getting on."

"I must get back. Thank you, Captain, and good luck to you. I hope your wounds heal well."

"Thank you, Sir."

Bathurst saluted, which Carr fully returned, then he hurried back up, to find the 105th already issuing through the gate of the Square, the head of the column advancing towards him. He went straight to Lacey.

"My impression, Sir, is that we can march straight over, but the descent will be a bit of a scramble."

Lacey nodded.

"Very well, lead on."

The ascent of the internal steps and the descent down over the breach slope were accomplished without inordinate difficulty, but many drew their own conclusions from the pile of formidable obstacles still visible and the fields full of wounded they passed between, on both sides of the Rivellas. That done, it was a short march back to their old camps, past the batteries now having their guns extracted by Spanish labourers and Portuguese gunners. Davey made the remark.

"At least we're done with all that!"

It was Ellis who replied.

"And paid a price!"

Lacey had sent warning of the men's final return in the shape of Bert Bryce, so that hot stew would be waiting for them, but Bryce had been assailed with enquiries concerning names that he could not answer for and so the deep fear and anxiety remained amongst the Followers. Therefore, now seeing the return of the Battalion in the distance, their womenfolk and children came running down the track, abandoning their cooking to find their men, yelling names in the hope of a quick response from him that mattered within the approaching ranks. Since the departure of their men, until the arrival of Bryce, the Followers had been stood in darkness staring at the walls of Badojoz. As the assault developed, they had clung to each other in terror, many weeping uncontrollably, staring intently from 500 yard's distance at the Hellish spectacle of explosions, musket fire and burning carcasses in which their men lived or died. The subjects of their deep concern, cruelly unseen and unidentified, had been seen only briefly as frenzied figures within the distant flashes of light, the whole accompanied by the noise of murderous conflict. They had endured this misery for almost three hours, with no way of knowing the fate of those they cared for most. Then, with the sounds of conflict over, they had stood for the remainder of the night, listening to the sounds of shocking disorder coming from within the city, accompanied by the sight of burning buildings beyond the walls.

Now, with the arrival of daylight, and ignoring all discipline, many burst into the ranks and flung themselves into the arms of their men, those who had survived, whilst many collapsed weeping at the side of the track. Arm in arm with those they had found alive, rapturous they progressed back, all grinning with relief, to then remain close to their men and enquire anxiously after their wounds and who was now wounded or dead. After food, the needlework began, Joe having already been sewn up by Bridie and, once all had eaten, George Fearnley was sent for. He admired Bridie's work on Joe then he began the task on Byford, Ellis and Bill Turner, Eirin taking the role of holding their hands whilst stitches were inserted into the wounds of all three. Deakin and Halfway meanwhile submitted to Bridie for their stitching.

In the gloom of the grey afternoon of the 6th, came what could be put off no longer. Lacey sent for RSM Gibney.

"We must call the Roll, Sar' Major."

Within 15 minutes the Battalion was paraded for their Captains to mechanically intone the names, Carr and Gibney taking the places of Captains Royce and Knowles. With each name, there came either the flat, 'Present, Sir,' accompanied by the simultaneous sound of the responder bringing their musket to 'Order arms', or, too often, an unnerving, bleak, silence. Next, the Callers of the Roll went to the lines of their wounded and then the numbers could finally be given to O'Hare, who achieved his own totals, which were handed to Lacey in the light of a candle lantern. He was moved to read them out loud.

"Six Officers killed. Nineteen men killed. Eight Officers and 64 men wounded. Four missing. 101 in all."

Lacey lowered the paper.

"That's two Companies! Almost. That puts us down to a strength of eight!"

There could be no reply and so, with that, both Carr and O'Hare saluted and took themselves off to their tents. However, there was one Officer who could not sleep but was sat outside his cart, wrestling with his conscience, despite the words of wisdom imparted to him by his servant, Chaplain's Assistant Percival Sedgwicke.

"We should go in there, Private, we really should. I'm sure that the presence of a Man of the Cloth and some words spoken as would Our Lord, will do much quell the appalling events which I hear are now taking place. That of which we hear and are also able to hear now, for ourselves!"

Sedgwicke glanced towards the walls, now silhouetted by the fires within, but he soon returned his attention to his Officer.

"Sir, it will cost you your life! There are no words, no prayers nor sermons that can quell what is happening in there now. It would take a full invasion of the most trusted troops and the risk is too great that even those same trusted men would not break ranks and join in. If Wellington is powerless, then so are we."

Albright looked up from his wringing hands, aghast at what Sedgwicke had said.

"Is there nothing, nothing, that can be done to prevent all the suffering, even death?"

"No Sir, there is not and it has been so all through the passage of time."

Albright stopped wringing his hands, instead he began rubbing them on his knees.

"By why, why, should Christian men behave so? Why, we said prayers together prior to the assault!"

Sedgwicke took a deep breath.

"We did, Sir, yes we did and then they went forward and we remained behind. I can only give you my own thoughts, Sir, such as they are."

Albright sat still and Sedgwicke took a deep breath.

"When our men scale those ladders, they count themselves as dead! They continue up to follow their comrades, but they harbour within themselves no hope of survival. Then they are over the wall, still fighting, but they survive even that and find themselves alive, but their minds remain blank and pitiless, no thought for themselves was what got them over the wall in the first place and so there is no return to sanity, as we would call it. Instead comes a desire for the most excessive self-indulgence, ignoring the consequences, either through celebration at still being alive or personal reward for their success. Or both, but that desire, Sir, is a kind of madness, that neither you, nor I, nor the most fervent prayer can contain. Nor, I think, can we have any perception of."

Sedgwicke could see the emptiness in Albright's face, the complete lack of understanding.

"This is soldiering, Sir, and the business of a siege is soldiering at its worst!"

He stood and helped the still distraught, but more understanding Albright to his feet.

"Best get some sleep, Sir. Things will have subsided with the morning, if only because too many of the men in there will be unable to move."

oOo

The following morning Deakin, Saunders et al, found their breakfast being served by Eirin and Consuela alone. It was Deakin who enquired as to why and it was Eirin who answered.

"Gone into the town to get some clothes. They didn't ask you. They knew you'd say no!"

Deakin almost dropped his plate.

"Jesus, have they?"

"Yes! We all needs new clothes, us and the children and we hear tell that there's clothes of all sorts, all scattered about."

"Which gate?"

"The one opposite the river, with the bridge opposite."

Saunders looked over at his agitated Colour Sergeant.

"There's nothing we can do, Jed. We can't leave camp, to go looking for wandering Followers!"

Deakin's jaw ground together.

"Tell me somethin' I don't already know. Them as is still in there, will now be wakin' up and lookin' for more drink and sport, I shouldn't wonder, and what is it that makes that pair look any more British than Spanish? They'n as likely to get picked on as any pair of women!"

As the words were spoken, the pair in question were entering the imposing Los Palmas gate. They ignored the drunken soldiers either slumped on the road or staggering over it, but noticed well enough the prone bodies and shattered figures of civilians slumped in doorways or in alleyways. Nellie was the first to notice and the first to comment.

"Well, hasn't there been some terrible goin's on in this place?"

365

Bridie did not answer, but looked anxiously around as they entered the first street up, avoiding the smashed furniture and the soldiers lurching back into consciousness. In the highest part of the town's shops and dwellings, but still below the Castle, they came to a row of shops, one being a clothes shop, judging by what was now spilling out of the smashed windows and the doorway. They went inside to find four soldiers of the 48th in residence. They were awake and eating Spanish sausage and bread. They looked up and the Corporal stood.

"What do you want? This is our shop!"

Nellie adopted her full challenging posture.

"And just how do you mean? Sayin' that? Your shop?"

"We've been selling what's here and made some good coin."

Bridie now joined in

"Selling!"

"Yes, selling. Seems what's in here is much called for."

He pulled the others to their feet.

"But it's yours now. We're for some more drink. You can take over."

Bleary eyed, the four picked up their equipment and trooped out through the gaping main window, their feet crunching on the glass, leaving the pair utterly bemused, but the question came first to Bridie.

"What do you think? This has all we want, but 'tis stealing really. Out of a shop!"

Nellie looked around. What was still there was very tempting.

"Well, not so much worse than pickin' up what's already out and bein' trampled on in the street and this'll all go soon enough, taken by someone. Either Spanish as've been stripped of their own clothes, or our own men or Followers. They'll be in soon."

Bridie was not convinced, but she nodded.

"A bundle each. That's fair."

"That's fair and we can confess come our next Communion. It'll be five Hail Marys and five Our Father's! That should cover it."

Now grinning, a 'bundle' was gathered by each of good practical dresses, shirts, breeches, hose and some shoes. All the while the sounds grew louder from outside of men searching for drink and whatever else took their pleasure. The large bundles were assembled and closed with dress arms knotted together, making a loop for ease of transport. Bridie took a look outside and was immediately troubled.

"There's a few out there as I don't like the look of. Perhaps we should wait a bit. Perhaps the Provosts will come in an' drive 'em off!"

"And take all this from us and perhaps add our necks to those for the gallows! Best to take off."

"What about puttin' on a red jacket like we did on our way back to Corunna?"

"Good idea, but where to get one? Each has a soldier inside with a sore head!"

Bridie nodded.

"Well, perhaps not, then, but carryin' a musket with a bayonet won't do no harm!"

"Alright."

They went outside and quickly armed themselves from what was lying all around, muskets aplenty, and bayonets were quickly extracted from the belts of still supine soldiers and were equally quickly attached. Holding the weapons across their chests they turned into the street they had come up to find it full of soldiers just emerged from the buildings, evidently in riotous and belligerent mood, calling for more drink, which was being tossed down to them from upstairs windows. Nellie pulled Bridie back.

"Next one!"

Back in the main street they hurried on, looking for a street parallel to the one just denied them. A Scotsman noticed Bridie and lurched over, she being noticeably comely and attractive.

"Spanish are ye! Well, now's the time to show some gratitude."

Bridie pulled away from him

"British Followers is what we are. Of the 105th!"

The Scotsman was not put off.

"Ah well, what's that tae a brae lad like me!"

He lurched towards her, but laid on not a hand, but instead collapsed in a heap, his eyes rolling upwards. Nellie had expertly dealt a fearsome blow to his head with the butt of her musket, just behind his ear.

The pair sped on and did find a street that led downward, but halfway down the street it was Nellie who stopped her face contorted with anger.

"Now what a surprise to find you two here!"

It was Betty Barker who first turned her head, whilst she held an old man against a wall. Neet, her husband, was on top of his wife, one knee holding her down, a bayonet under her chin. It was Betty who began shrieking her outrage.

"On your way! Nuthin' to do with you. Irish baggage!"

Nellie remained in place, legs apart, hands on her hips.

"Let them go!"

Neet looked up.

"Not a chance. These has gold and he's goin' to tell or she gets skewered!"

Nellie swung the musket off her shoulder, as did Bridie. Both were levelled at Neet.

"Let them go, I said!"

Neet Barker smiled contemptuously.

"I got a feelin' they muskets be not loaded!"

Nellie smiled back, with equal contempt.

"What makes you think we don't know how to load a musket? And who'll miss you pair? Two more dead in the middle of all this? To rid this God's Earth of both such as you would be doin' the world a service, God's work, is what I'm thinkin'."

Bridie turned her own musket towards Betty.

'So it would."

The eyes of the Spanish couple rolled in terror from one figure to another, finally alighting on the Barkers. In the pause, Nellie drew back the hammer on her musket to be followed by Bridie. The ominous double click sounded thunderous, even in the bedlam all around. Betty's expression changed and she released the old man.

"Leave it, Neet. There'll be other pickings. These two Irish madwomen is just crazy enough to pull the triggers."

She moved away, but Neet's face turned to anger and he remained astride the woman.

"These has gold! That I'm sure of!"

The response was the bayonet from Nellie's musket pricking his ear. Betty was now certain that her man was about to be killed.

"Neet! Come on! She means it, evil Irish cow that she is."

Very reluctantly, Neet Barker rose, his knee leaving the woman's chest, his bayonet coming away from her chin. He backed away, his face livid, then he turned and made off with his wife, both sending curses over their shoulders.

"This b'ain't finished between us, Nellie Nicholls. Have no fear of that!"

However, it was Bridie who answered first.

"And we'll be waitin'. Have no fear of that!"

The old man came over to help his wife to her feet and then to lean on Bridie.

"Gracias, senoras, muchas gracias."

Bridie patted him on the shoulder.

"That's fine, old one. We'll be getting along now."

He held up his hand to keep them there and then dug his fingers into the interior of a thick and wide leather belt. His fingers appeared holding a gold coin, which he gave to the astonished Bridie, then more digging produced one for the bemused Nellie. That done he helped his wife up the steps of a wrecked house and eased her inside. The last they saw was his face, turned briefly back as he disappeared into the gloom of the open passage.

"Adios. Vaya con Dios."

Bridie pulled at Nellie's sleeve.

"Back! Quick!"

They hurried down the street which joined another at a junction, but a look right saw the large Square of the Los Palmas Gate. They threw their muskets away and hurried through, then along the track at the foot of the Castle walls. The mill dam took them over the Rivellas and then they were in the fields, beyond which was the camp of the 105th. Wounded were still being tended there.

Jed Deakin and Henry Nicholls had been stood watching and waiting for a good hour and it was Jed who saw them appear around the mill building.

"These two just arrived, if I'm not mistaken!"

Henry Nicholls folded his arms, but he was smiling. They watched the pair hurry towards them, noticing the large bundles swinging on their backs. Once sufficiently near, Jed could no longer remain quiet.

"I ought to clout you, so I should. Takin' off to go into such a place as that. You could have been killed. Or worse!"

However, Bridie took no notice but hurried up to him, holding up her gold coin in her fingers.

"Look at what we got, each, for savin' a pair of old Spanish whatnots!"

Deakin frowned and took it and his face changed to wonder. It was a gold Napoleon! Then Bridie swung her bundle off her back.

"And look what else! Good clothes and shoes as'll see us through this Summer's campaigning! There's some for little Jed, too!"

Deakin put the coin in his pocket and then embraced Bridie fiercely, which they held for some time. Nellie looked from the pair to Henry. Her face showing no little outrage.

"Now shouldn't I be gettin' some of that?"

Her bundle fell to the ground and Henry Nicholls, for the first time in a long time, took his wife in his long and brawny arms.

The unwelcome news arrived with the first of the darkness, Kempt arriving in the Headquarters tent of the 105th, where the three were drinking French brandy, as obtained by Sergeant Bryce.

"Wellington went in this evening and got a very poor reception, total disrespect and you know what that does to him. He sent in Power's Portuguese and they just fell apart and joined in the fun. So, tomorrow you go in, with the 1st and 9th of the Fifth Division. Himself named yours!"

O'Hare wearily set his glass on the table.

"I suppose we can count that as an honour!"

"You should! Good as a battle honour, to dwell in the highest esteem of our Commander in Chief. The army has fallen apart and those not involved with the assault are just itching to get in themselves and get their share. There are few Battalions that he can thoroughly trust not to fall apart once allowed in."

Carr was wholly unimpressed and his tone of voice showed it.

"And when we get in, we do what? Sir."

"Any that can walk drive out."

"And those that can't?"

"Leave! They'll be cleared next day."

Lacey leaned forward.

"Where do we start from?"

"Go in through the Southern gate, the Pilar, and join up with the 1st and 9th. Make your arrangements there when you meet."

As darkness fell, the Light Company recovered the last of their missing, this being Nat Solomon who eased himself back into their circle and sat down. Saunders was the first to recover from the shock appearance.

"Where've you been?"

"Wounded!"

"Wounded where?"

"At the wall I got a rock on me head, but thought it not too bad, with only me shako stove in. Once inside I took up with some lads of the 5th and all they did was bust into some house and make themselves at home, with a bit of drink like. They kept out any as wanted to get in themselves; shot some I shouldn't wonder. There's no love lost between the Connaughts and the lads of the 5th, I can tell you. The woman of the house, she had no man, did some cooking for us knowin' we'd protect her and her three little ones. But I keeled over, and was bad for a couple of days. The lads of the 5th left this morning, late, and I crawled out a bit later, with dark comin' on, still feelin' rough. Decent lads, them of the 5th but I could barely understand a word they said."

"Where's this wound? Needs to be obvious, or you're for the triangle!"

He pulled off his shako and even in the poor light of their camp-fire, they could see the discoloured lump on the hair-line above his left eye-brow and the livid cut across it.

"You alright now?"

"I'd say so, yes. I got myself back here."

Saunders turned away.

"Should be enough to satisfy Drake! Don't know about Ellis. Still, 'tis good you've come back at a busy time. We're ordered back in tomorrow for the clear out."

Their march was to be an awkward one, past the 'peak' of the Picurina and then behind the rear of the larger Pardeleras, to get themselves to the imposing Pilar Gate. As they marched, always over on their right was the sight of the town beyond its battered walls, smoke easing its way upwards and over from hundreds of fires, some innocently in a fire grate, but most others more suspect and dangerous. Ellis was marching besides Miles, who saw no reason not to quiz Ellis as to why this was happening.

"Why are we going back in?"

"The purpose, Private Miles, is to get out from there such as you were, the day before yesterday; a nasty, disobedient, drunken, mutineer, as I sees it."

Miles allowed this utter condemnation to sink in and made no reply, as Ellis continued, very much easing what was very much on his mind.

"And any as remains in there, like you was back then, is now very likely to get strung up. If I knows Nosey!"

"Didn't do us much good! Goin' in early and stayin' for a good drink, like."

"Don't go lookin' to me for sympathy! There'll be a gallows in there afore long and you count yourself lucky that we found you and we got you out. You'd still be in there, if I knows you. Thank the Colonel for that!"

Miles changed the subject.

"What about Nat Solomon?"

Ellis continued staring ahead.

"If you shut up, so will I!"

The answer from Miles was a dismissive sniff, as they passed the largest outlier fort, the Pardeleras, now with a Union Jack at its flagstaff. They swung right and entered the town by the ornate entrance of the Pilar Gate on the South side of the town. The last yards were pounded out, scattering many drunken celebrants as they made their way up to the San Vincente bastion. There, Lacey went to the Colonels of the 1st and 9th for a quick discussion and he soon returned.

"The 1st are working towards the Pilar Gate, the 9th to the Palmas, us to the Castle, putting us in the centre."

"That means we get the Square!"

"Yes, Henry, so you keep the Grenadiers and Joshua's together and get straight up there and clear it. Just get them out and on up to the Castle. Any that drift sideways, then the rest of us, or the 1st or the 9th will pick up."

"Yes Sir."

He peered over Lacey's shoulder.

"Seems that we have an auspicious audience, Sir."

Lacey turned to see Wellington and an escort of ten Heavy Dragoons, sat mounted close to the 1st Foot Guards.

"We'd best move off!"

Carr hurried over to recruit Carravoy, then onto Heaviside, his arm in a sling from a dislocated shoulder, but now reset.

"Joshua, I hope you are not in too great a discomfort?"

"No, Henry, I thank you. Better by the day."

Carr nodded.

"Yours and Charles', led by me, are to clear the Square. Probably the worst job!"

Heaviside adjusted his sling and stared forward.

"Learn to do good, seek justice, correct oppression, bring justice to the fatherless, plead the widow's cause. Isiah One. Seventeen."

Carr smiled.

"From what I remember up there, during the day after the assault, there'll be plenty of that."

Heaviside turned to Deakin, just behind.

"Colour Sarn't! Fix bayonets and load. Hammer down."

Carr departed to the sound of bayonet sockets rattling over muzzle ends and he went over to Carravoy.

"Right Charles. Straight up there!"

"Gibney's with us! He asked me, and I acceded."

"Pleased to have him!"

The drive began. Any Redcoat or Portuguese that came towards them was turned around and any stretched out on the road was prodded into life with a bayonet, hauled up and thrown forward. Any that collapsed again were left with simple words in their ears.

"We'll leave you for the Spaniards! They looks on you same as if you was French and you know what they do to them!"

That animated many more and soon there was a reluctant, morose and sickly herd making their way to the Square, urged on by bayonets, boots and curses. The sheer justice and even nobility of what they were doing, freeing the citizens from such drunken oppression, soon dawned on the men of the 105th and they now fully appreciated the full kit inspection they had endured before they marched out. With full packs, shakos, rolled blankets and cross-straps, they looked wholly different from the reeling, disheveled, civilian garbed rabble they were pushing slowly uphill. Thus, they had no hesitation in replying to any complaints, such as that which was hurled at Toby Halfway as they prodded some ludicrous figures onward, all dressed as pantomime Dowagers.

"Who do you think you are? Green cuffed bastards!"

"The 105th, that's us! The 'Rag and Bone Boys', an' if you wants to take us up on any of that a bit later on, feel free, we'll be waitin'."

Once in the Square, there was greater inclination not to move amongst its occupants, plainly the remaining hoards still preferred to laze and lounge on the steps and the pavements, being still reluctant to return to army discipline and give up the easy access to wine and spirits. Many were also in the buildings of the Square, but the men of the 105th entered each and cleared all out. Hearing shots, fatal or otherwise, caused a marked change in attitude to those outside in the Square and soon all were on their feet and shuffling forward. Gibney and others of equal stature, now manned the exits and allowed no one to leave still wearing civilian apparel. This was often done at bayonet point and the pile of civilian clothes and booty grew to an inordinate size and it was not long before some Badajoz civilians came to pick over the pile, to which Gibney and his band turned a blind eye. Also a deaf ear, as curses were hurled by these townspeople at the subdued column that now trooped past on their way upwards. Gibney had his own words of encouragement.

"Tha' came in as soldiers, go out as such. An' ah'll tell thee more, if tha' can find a bundook, tha'd do well. It'll save tha' back."

Carr was grateful that clearing the Square provided nothing like the trouble he had anticipated, there was no riot, and it was a doubly pleasant surprise, when an Officer of the 88th came running across to him, from the direction of the Cathedral. He was merely a Captain approaching a Major, but he was smiling broadly.

"Thank goodness you've come, Sir. It's been the devil's own job to protect the Cathedral, I can tell you."

Carr smiled at the irony of the unintended choice of words, the 88th were known as the 'Devil's Own' but he could not imagine why the fearsome 88th had taken upon themselves such an odd task as the protection of a Cathedral. Perhaps the motive was religious?

"Why did you? For good Catholic reasons?"

The Captain stopped and saluted.

"Why no, Sir. Some Officers and NCOs, a mixture of Regiments, we, well, took it upon ourselves to set up the Cathedral as a sort of refuge, Sir, especially for the women. We've taken some in with barely a stitch on their backs, and children also, and it's been all that we could do to keep them safe, so many wanting to barge in and, well, you know what!"

"And you've been here since we got in? The night before last."

"Yes Sir, pretty much, Sir."

Carr extended his hand, which the Captain took.

"My best to you, Captain. General Kempt will hear of this be certain. You've done well. Tell me your name."

"Geoghan, Sir. Michael Geoghan."

"Duly noted. Now, what would you like from us?"

"Some more sentries, Sir, if you can. If only to reassure those in our charge until this is over. We've not had much sleep, but, as yet, none of those within our care want to return to their homes."

Carr nodded.

"That I can understand! Right, leave it with me. Some of our Grenadiers, perhaps?"

"Perfect, Sir, thank you."

Carr went straight to Ameshurst. He could not see Carravoy.

"Simon. Get some of yours into the Cathedral and remain with them until the town is completely cleared. You are to guard the female refuge there, that's yourself, other Officers, NCOs and any you can trust. They've been holding out for two days, so count yourself as their Relief."

Ameshurst smiled.

"Protecting a female refuge, Sir! Rotten job, but someone's got to do it."

Carr almost smiled but managed not to.

"Away! Follow orders!"

Ameshurst ran off and gathered up Sergeant Fearnley and his 'bodyguard'. As they entered the Cathedral, they were greeted by gasps of alarm when the women saw the Redcoats, but the full and tidy uniform and being led by an Officer was immediately reassuring and the anxiety quickly subsided. Ameshurst stood and looked for a few seconds.

"Right, boys. We are here for a day or so, therefore we must make sure that we conduct ourselves appropriately. Not too much fraternisation!"

By now Carr had gone back into the Square, with the Cathedral behind him. The gradual movement of now compliant, sullen and badly hungover soldiery was slowly coming towards him, prior to leaving the Square and making their shepherded way up to the Castle. Acceptance of leaving was now wholly prevalent, not least perhaps, because a gallows was now under construction at the far end, with Wellington in close attendance. With what he had just heard concerning the Cathedral, Carr was motivated to cross the Square and make Wellington himself aware of the effort made by some of his Officers and NCOs to protect women and children and so he took himself across to stand before Wellington, come to the attention and salute. He could not fail to notice that his Commander in Chief looked tired and strained, his face ashen and drawn.

"Beg pardon, Sir. If I may."

Wellington looked down.

"Ah, Carr! Bad business this."

Carr was entirely unsure what the 'bad business' referred to, either the near mutiny, or the appalling cost of capturing the town, but when your most superior General states a fact, however vague, then there can only be one possible reply.

"Yes Sir."

Wellington perked up a little.

"At least we've turned Soult around. Did you know that?"

"No Sir."

"But now we must get back up North. Marmont's raided across the border. He's in Sabugal, even, and Cuidad is ringed around. We cannot remain here too long!"

Being confided in, although a Junior Officer, by the Commander in Chief, Carr could only attribute to strain and shock on Wellington's part, but he wanted to raise his own subject.

"No Sir, but beg pardon Sir, if I may, I'd like to make you aware that all through this, some of our men, Officers and NCOs made the Cathedral a safe refuge for the women and children, Sir. They are in there now and I'm sure they would appreciate a word from you, Sir, if you have the time. Acknowledging their efforts, which must have been very difficult and at times very dangerous."

Wellington looked down and studied Carr for a second or two, his face quizzical, almost annoyed.

"Make me aware, Carr, you say?"

On hearing those words and the tone in which they were spoken, Carr came to an even stiffer attention.

"Yes Sir. It being something of undoubted merit that is greatly to the credit of our men. I thought it might be something you'd like to know. Sir."

Wellington nodded, now pacified.

"I would, Carr and I thank you. Any chink of light in this godawful business is welcome."

"Yes Sir. Thank you, Sir. I'd best get off now, Sir, with your permission. I'm part of clearing the town."

Carr saluted, which Wellington acknowledged with the merest lift of his riding crop and so Carr departed, feeling the need to rejoin Heaviside and Carravoy. Also, he would appreciate seeing Lacey or O'Hare again, but that probably would not be for some while.

Carr was one of the last into the Castle and, whilst outside the gate, he could hear shouts, screaming and vile insults coming over the walls. Once inside, he could see why. Their charges were being sorted into their Battalions, the largest groups being Irish and Scottish Regiments, the Connaughts being prevalent amongst the former. Kempt was the most vociferous and abusive, with Picton himself not far behind, and eventually, under the supervision of an assigned NCO, if the group did not already have one, the groups were marched out of Badajoz over the main breach. With the last group departed, Carr turned to Heaviside and Carravoy.

"Get ours formed up. Time to leave. We'll use the Las Palmas."

In ranks of three, the two Companies negotiated the twists and turns of the Castle gate and then onto the road that led directly down, inside the town walls and to the gate of Las Palmas. The amount of smashed furniture remaining did not badly impede their progress, but what was disturbing was the way that civilians ran before them in terror or hurried back into their houses, to send black looks or even curses from the relative safety of their smashed windows and demolished doors.

"Ingleses asesinos! Ingleses asesinos!"

Once through the Las Palmas Gate, they were on the open track beneath the walls and, as they appeared on their right, all looked up to the walls which they had scaled but one night previously. However, few studied too long, the memories were too harsh, too vicious, the blood stains too many and all quickly faced their front and marched on. The bridge at the mill took them over the Rivellas and onto the fields beyond. Once in camp they found that the other Companies of the 105th had arrived ahead of them and all went to their own areas for their midday meal. The atmosphere of quiet contentment grew and through the rest of the day and through the evening, the least wounded now returning to their mess groups certainly added to the feeling of good cheer. For the 105th, the bitter memories capturing Badajoz became less sharp edged, but there was neither buoyancy nor elation as all sat and rested with many gaps around their fires, empty spaces, once filled by missing messmates.

oOo

Lord Frederick Templemere was becoming more self-satisfied by the mile. The brand-new coach, delivery taken that very day, was of the latest design, this coming to be known as a Brougham. What was so pleasing to Lord Fred was that the very road that he now travelled was notorious for the discomfort that it inflicted on its users, yet his new coach, well sprung, did a 'thoroughly good job' as he put it to himself, of flattening out the ruts, bumps and potholes now encountered on the outskirts of London. An addition, as insisted on by himself, were several extra lanterns, four extra besides the standard two in the top corners, one either side of the driver's foot shield and two at the back. This was because he wanted to be certain that, even in the dark, as it now was, his approach would be recognised by any of his tenants on the road and they would clear the way for him. Two small lanterns also decorated the interior, as did a splendid brass clock.

All in all, it had been a very satisfying day. He had caused some disruption in the House of Lords by speaking against a Provision for the Poor Bill, had spent a stimulating two hours in Pimlico, taken delivery of his coach and enjoyed a good dinner at his club. Now he enjoyed the steady and rhythmic sway of a ride in his new means of transport and within its quiet confines the thought occurred to him that he had heard nothing more from Livermore, Waters, or the reptilian Radipole. Plainly, suspicion had moved away, perhaps onto Mahon, that all to the good, but no matter, the accusing gaze was no longer focused on him.

This agreeable reverie, sustained by a bottle of claret and several glasses of port, less than an hour ago, was suddenly shattered by the coach being brought to a violent halt followed by shouting could be heard outside. He reached for the door to enquire the reason for the halt, when both doors opened and two men climbed in, one from each side, both all in black and both with faces masked under low top hats. Each pointed a very large Dragoon pistol at him, the eyes of each staring and unblinking in the yellow light of the lanterns, all made more sinister by the masks they wore. They said nothing for at least half a minute, this marked by the elegant ticking of the clock. Despite being in a state of frozen terror, nevertheless, Templemere's aristocratic instinct did assert itself.

"How dare you! What is this?"

The one on the right gave the answer, the thin silk over his mouth moving eerily back and forth as he spoke.

"It will be recorded as a plain robbery, Lord Fred. Nothing more. The work of footpads, but more murderous than most."

On hearing the final words, panic did set in, following utter confusion.

"Recorded as! I don't understand! But I can give you money! We are not far from my estate and once there, I can give you more. Much more than I have with me now."

It was possible that the eyes of both grinned and the man spoke again.

"It's not about money, Lord Fred. You see, we are convinced that you have been rather a bad boy, hobnobbing with the French and letting them know things that are good for them and very bad for us. That's why we are here."

Despite his fear, Templemere was outraged.

"Absolute lies and you've no proof! None at all!"

The man turned to his companion, both now plainly amused.

"Now that speaks volumes, do you not think, Mr. Yellow? Most start by saying, 'I've done nothing of the sort'. Is that not your experience?"

The other nodded.

"It is Mr. Orange. It is."

The obvious code names did nothing for Templemere's state of mind, then 'Orange' leaned forward to tap Templemere on the knee with the barrel of his pistol.

"You see, Lord Fred, this is the dark world of espionage. Spies and traitors and whatnot. We need no proof, just a weight of risk, and in your case the scales have tipped very much against you."

Templemere took a deep breath to protest again, but the barrel was raised to his face.

"Enough, Lord Fred. You've taken French gold! Documents have come into our possession which prove your doings and very bad things have come about as a consequence of your dark deeds. It all makes you a grave threat to The Crown."

The hammer on the pistol was pulled fully back but the muzzle remained pointed at Templemere's knee.

"Now you tell me, Lord Fred, do we put a bullet in your brain for the damn traitor that you are, or do we make use of you, of some kind? Assuming that you have anything useful to tell us!"

Templemere sat forward, suddenly very focused, if still fearful. Plainly, his life depended on it.

"I have! I can name my contact. He called himself Michael Granger."

The pistol was raised six inches.

"You need to do better than that, Lord Fred. If there's a nest of French agents controlling you, we need to know where they are. And his name is no more Granger, than mine's Orange."

Again, Templemere was thinking fast. Plausible lies were called for.

"They took me somewhere, but I was masked."

The pistol dropped a little.

"This Granger. You'd recognise him again?"

Templemere nodded vigorously.

"Oh yes, he climbed into a cab that I was using. He gave me the first gold bar."

"Very good, Lord Fred. Now, the place they took you. Anything special about it? Type of building, anything unusual nearby, special building nearby, special noises, anything you saw, or didn't understand?"

However, before Templemere could answer, the pistol was raised up to face level and the voice became silky and very threatening.

"Remember, Lord Fred. You tell us a pack of lies and you are a dead man. We found you once, we'll find you again. Our reach is beyond anywhere that you could get yourself off to."

Templemere cudgelled his imagination, then he switched to memory, as an idea was formed.

"Well! Out of the window I saw a sign – 'Fink's Hats and Millinery', and, do you know, I do believe that the room we were in was above a bordello! Lots of female giggles and male laughter."

The pistol was lowered.

"Anything else?"

"Well, style of building is such as you get in the better parts of Pimlico. And Chelsea!"

Orange turned to Yellow, who nodded, then Orange turned back to Templemere.

"We will investigate, Lord Fred, and if this doesn't play out, that being something helpful on your 'room above a house of pleasure', then our threat will be carried out!"

The pistol was raised again, and the eyes grinned malevolently, but after three seconds, the hammer was pulled back and allowed to gently fall forward. Then both were gone, out into the night, leaving the carriage interior as though they had never been. The door opened again and, in fright, Templemere turned his head, still expecting to see a pistol, but instead it was his Coachman.

"Don't know what that was about, Sir. Trouble on the road ahead they said. Something military. Do I drive on, Sir?"

"Yes Wilkins. Drive on."

Once safely under his own sheltering porch and his anxiety now quelled, Templemere jumped out before the Footman could lay a hand on the door handle, to then shout up to his Coachman.

"Wilkins! I want this coach ready again at dawn. Ready for a journey. You hear me?"

Wilkins looked down, the reins still in his hands. This night now held little sleep for him.

"Yes Sir. At dawn."

Templemere ran inside, ordering all the servants who were waiting to greet him, to get off to their rooms and to bed, bar the cook, who was shouted out of her room to make some food for now and also some food for the journey. He found the stout leather satchel and two other strong cases and he filled these last with any valuables in the house, the satchel finally receiving the remaining three gold bars from the safe. Too agitated to sleep, he ate what the cook had provided and sat by the fire. Eventually, he dozed in the chair until a footman shook him gently awake.

"Sir. The carriage is outside."

Templemere sat upright and then stood, to reach down for the satchel. The footman reached for the cases, but Templemere stopped him.

"Those are for me. You may go."

Careful to wait for the Footman to bow out of the door, then Templemere, much burdened, made the journey to the coach, the satchel over his shoulder, a case in each hand. He took a final look at the front of his house and then banged on the coach roof with his fist, but the coach did not move, instead the small hatch slid open behind the driver.

"Sir! Where are we going?"

Templemere wanted to shout, but he knew he could not, unfriendly ears may be listening, so he rose and spoke carefully.

"Newhaven!"

There was no reply, but the coach began to move and Templemere sat back. He knew of a Captain who often plied an illicit trade to France, a lucrative enterprise between Newhaven and Le Havre, of which Templemere himself had often taken advantage. From that French port, Templemere was certain, he could take ship to the Americas. Relations between France and that new country were always good and gold and jewelry were currency anywhere. An agent could sell the estates, for a heavy commission.

The coach exited the estate gates, with early workers doffing their caps, but this was ignored. With each mile, Templemere's pulse and breathing eased and the carriage sped through the early day, with no rest for man nor horses. With late morning, the coach rattled onto the cobblestones of Newhaven quay and it was with unbridled relief that Templemere saw the fast cutter of the smuggler against the quayside. He descended from the coach and locked both doors, before shouting up to Wilkins.

"Wait here!"

With that, Wilkins fell asleep, as did the horses, and Templemere entered a small warehouse to find the one he sought and thankfully he was there with some of his crew, all sat idle in a variety of chairs. Templemere wasted no time, walking straight up to the Captain and throwing a gold necklace on the table before him.

"Passage to France!"

The Captain slowly picked up the necklace, went to a window and examined it in the good sunlight, before pocketing it and returning to his seat. Templemere was a good customer and he saw no good reason to do him wrong, future business may depend on it. It may be an odd way to pay, but it may be urgent and Templemere's business was his own.

"With the tide! Two hours."

Templemere nodded and returned to his coach and there he sat waiting, in an agony of impatience, studying the extra detail of the cutter's masts as they were reluctantly revealed by the rising tide, as though they were the irregular markings of an unusual clock. Eventually came relief as the crew boarded, but he was not called forward for a good half hour more, until one of the crew, probably the Bosun, waved him towards the gangplank. Now much burdened, he descended from the coach and walked to the vessel, ignoring the question from Wilkins of, "What now, my Lord?". He had but yards to go, when rough hands halted his progress, one grasped his arm, the other the strap of his satchel. He felt a knife prick his back and he recognised the voice of Mr. Orange, as the strap disappeared from his shoulder, cut from behind.

"I think this should remain here, Lord Fred. Let's call it Dues to the Crown!"

Templemere froze, but the voice, silky and menacing as the previous night, spoke further.

"So off you go, Lord Fred. You can keep your baggage, but if we see you again within these shores, it'll be your end, at least in this life!"

The knife jabbed again and Templemere hurried forward, to clatter over the wood of the gangplank. Once on the deck, he gave a huge sigh of relief and turned around, to see an empty quayside.

Some days later, Livermore met with Waters, Radipole and, this time, Jean Dulongue was amongst them, the erstwhile Mr. Yellow. The first item on their agenda should be very short, Livermore hoped, and for it, he turned to Dulongue.

"Templemere. What of him?"

"Dealt with. Almost certainly."

Livermore brought himself bolt upright.

"Almost!"

"Well, this I can say with certainty. He's gone! Out of the country, very probably to France. He took ship, a known smuggler, out of Newhaven. We ushered him aboard."

Livermore nodded and subsided, somewhat.

"And what he told you?"

"All lies! But it cost him his gold."

Livermore smiled at that point, then he returned to his first concern.

"You said almost!"

It was Waters who answered.

"Yes! Well! Frightened off to France is probably the most sensible way to be rid of him. Instil a bit of terror! He can do no more harm there, and murdering a Peer of the Realm would lead to awkward questions."

He sat back to continue his reply.

"On top, to make it look like a genuine robbery and murder on the road, we'd have to kill the coachman. Hardly fair! The same if we detained him for questioning to find out what he does know. That would come out and we would have to justify it. He knows nothing. Merely a dupe."

Livermore sat back and a rueful look came over his face, then some vexation.

"That I can agree with, but he does seem to have got away with it. The mass graves at Albuera are wider and deeper because of him. He caused Godinot to land on Beresford's plate as reinforcements for Soult. Remember?"

Waters looked at Dulongue and the two shared a conspiratorial half smile, before Waters sat back and answered Livermore.

"Well, you can set your mind at rest over that one, Sir. As we speak a certain device consisting of a clockwork mechanism, some acid, some phosphorous and some gunpowder, has very probably activated itself by now. Not enough to blow up the whole affair, just enough to make a rather terminal hole in the side of their vessel. As for Templemere, they probably cut his throat a mile off the harbour, him with two weighty cases and obviously attempting some kind of escape. We'll know if his earthly remains come floating back to shore."

Livermore frowned, but Waters continued.

"So, have no conscience for the smugglers, Sir! In the year nine an Excise cutter was sent to wait for them when they returned from France and was never seen again. They returned to harbour with a clean ship, but said nothing of the Exciseman or her crew. They've been a thorn in the side of the Service for years."

Livermore smiled, nodded, then turned away, to look encouragingly at Waters' Assistant.

"Right, Radipole. What's next?

oOo

The following day all of the Officer corps of the 105th were sat in quiet contentment, writing letters, nursing newly doctored wounds, until all were summoned to the Headquarters tent, every one, Lieutenants and above. There they found Lacey, stood outside, with Carr and O'Hare in attendance. When they had all gathered, Lacey pulled himself up to his full height, clasped his hands behind his back and began. He was heard in total silence.

"I do not want to keep you long and I thank you for your attendance. I have called you all together, because I am anxious that you hear what I have to say directly from me, rather than from some other source."

He paused.

"I have decided to resign as your Colonel! I feel that I have done as much as I can and can do no more. Our Regiment is now one of the most respected Battalions in Wellington's army and with that achievement, from our humble beginnings in Sicily, I feel that I have done my duty."

He paused again and swallowed hard.

"I have to thank you for the loyal service that you have given to me and to The Colours of the 105th. We have been through some hard and terrible times which I often thought we would not survive, but we did and ourselves now standing here proves just that. I will soon be returning home and who takes command, either permanent or temporary is out of my hands, but if you support him as you have supported me, then I have nothing to fear for the future of our 105th Foot, the 'Rag and Bone Boys!', the best I've served with."

He took a deep breath. Emotion was winning.

'And the best in this army."

With that he turned and went into his tent, for the flap to be quickly pulled down. His Officers stood in stunned silence and then with merely a few words and surprised looks exchanged between them, they slowly dispersed. Carr turned to O'Hare.

"Did you have any inkling of this?"

O'Hare shook his head.

"No, but I know, as well as you, that he has taken this business here very, very hard. You could see it, so could I. Remember what I said yesterday and it's no surprise, he was dragged out of retirement by Livermore back in the year five to run that Battalion of Detachments and get it up to scratch. You were part of it."

He sighed deeply.

"He was in the American Wars. He goes that far back! He's had six extra years, all fighting Napoleon and this business here has just about finished him. Can't say that I'm all that surprised."

Carr allowed his own thoughts to gather, but few arrived, bar one bland statement.

"All the same, it's a bit of a shock. It's as though some fixture of your life, that you assumed permanent, like the sky above, has suddenly dissolved."

O'Hare nodded.

"I can see that Henry, but nothing's forever, you know. Nothing! Not one thing."

They parted company to go to their own tents, Carr preferring to be alone. He had a letter to write and he knew that the conversation amongst the Light Company Officers would be all speculation as to their next Colonel and, to that end, seeking solitude, he took his evening meal alone in his tent before touring the lines and then, surprisingly, enjoying a long and untroubled sleep.

The next day was preparatory for the march North that was soon to come and all that was noteworthy for that day, was information from Kempt which Lacey took to Carr.

"This says that the final stragglers are being extracted from the town today. Those that cannot walk will be loaded into carts and dumped in the Rivellas."

Lacey looked up.

"That's all it says. A bit harsh! Presumably it means that they either recover or drown! Get down there, with Gibney and see if any are ours. I doubt it, but there may be some that we counted as dead. In fact, some of those in the carts may well be dead!"

Carr took one pace back and saluted.

376

"Yes Sir. Sorry to hear that you're going, Sir."

Lacey nodded.

"Yes Henry. Thank you for that, but the time has come. Inevitable, but I have no regrets!"

Whilst crossing the fields down to the Rivellas, Carr and Gibney kept pace with each other, but exchanged few words and soon they were over the remains of the battery redoubts of the previous summer's abortive siege and at the banks of the river. The carts arrived, about ten, supervised by Coldstreamers and any of the occupants that could not dismount themselves were tipped into the river, just below the mill dam. Many Badajoz civilians were up on the walls and laughed and jeered as those thrown in thrashed around in water four feet deep, having been brought back to life by the fact that, suddenly, they were unable to breathe! Now animated, they waded unsteadily back to shore, to the non-Badajoz bank, where several Officers and NCOs seized on any of their own Regiment and frogmarched them off. When the last came ashore to collapse on the muddy bank, Carr turned to Gibney.

"None of ours then, Sar' Major!"

"None Sir, no. 'Appens as they all found their way 'ome!"

The following day was inspection, this left to the Sergeants, with the highlight of this for the Light Company, as always, being the confrontation between Miles and Ellis, the camaraderie between the two during the night of the assault now thoroughly evaporated as Ellis pushed and pulled at Miles' equipment. Last was the Baker inspection and Miles' silence finally broke as Ellis pulled back the hammer to examine the firing pan and touch hole.

"I hear the Old Man's leaving?"

Ellis was testing the sharpness of the flint.

"What's that to you. Miles?"

"Well, we might get a flogger! There's plenty of them still about."

Ellis handed back the Baker. It was perfect.

"We might, yes, and that should worry you, Private Miles, more than most!"

Then he grinned.

"I hear that you had a bit of good luck, then a lot of bad luck, the night we went in. Too much drink, I hear tell. Well, the next time we goes over a wall, I'd suggest that you, Private Miles, should think very carefully about taking The Pledge!"

He permitted himself a small laugh before moving onto Joe Pike and leaving behind the scowling Miles in the midst of his grinning comrades. Throughout the inspection, none in the Light Company were instructed to go off to the supply tents, meaning that none were charged stoppage of pay for any loss of uniform or equipment. There had been no shortage of spares of all kinds, both within and without the walls of Badajoz, from which to replace anything missing and so none found themselves accused of 'loss of King George's property' resulting in loss of pay; all were fully clothed and equipped. As he wandered idly up and down the ranks of his Company, leaving Ellis to his task, Drake was approached by Sergeant Bryce, Lacey's Secretary.

"Sir. Orders from the Colonel, arrived from Division, Sir. I'm informing all Captains. Prepare to march tomorrow."

Drake went straight off to Carr.

"We march tomorrow!"

"Yes."

"Which will be the Colonel's last parade. I assume we'll be marching off without him."

"Yes."

"We must do something."

"Yes!"

That dawn of the 11th arrived as a bright Spanish Spring day and it was Gibney who arrived at Lacey's tent to respectfully knock on the tent post.

"Enter!"

Gibney strode in, came to full attention and reeled off a blistering salute.

"Beg pardon, Sir, but you are needed outside!"

Puzzled, Lacey wiped a few crumbs from his mouth lodged there by his meagre breakfast and he rose from his chair.

"Outside, Sar' Major?"

"Yes Sir."

Lacey buttoned his tunic and came around the table, but Gibney was concerned over one item and he picked it up to offer it to his Colonel.

"Your sword, Sir. Best put it on!"

Still puzzled, Lacey clipped the scabbard slings to his belt and pulled back the tent flap, to be greeted by a huge Irish bellow from Padraigh O'Hare.

"'Tattalion! 'Tattalion. Present arms!"

The whole of the 105th, with many wounded but on parade nevertheless, in perfect unison swung their muskets from 'Order arms' beside their right feet through the positions to achieve 'Present arms' with their bayoneted muskets held vertical before their chests. All Officers were before their Companies, with swords drawn and now at the salute. Both Colours were already uncased and stretched out huge in the steady breeze. Lacey knew the role he needed to play and so, with O'Hare and Carr as escort, both with swords drawn, he progressed along the ranks, each man stock still. He spoke to no one until he came to The Colours, where he grasped a corner of each, in each hand, and stood for a long moment with head bowed, in profound silence, until he stood upright again and moved on, but not far.

Deakin was stood beside Ensign Mulcahey, him now doing his best to hold the bright green Regimental steady in the stiffening breeze.

"Deakin."

Deakin answered despite the awkwardness of the chinstrap.

"Sir."

"Seems a long time ago since we made you a Colour Sergeant back on Camberwell Green. We're both a long way from there."

"Yes Sir. And a long time, Sir."

"Remember Corunna? We were both feeling our age that day."

"You've the right of it there, Sir."

Lacey, smiling, studied the ground whilst recalling the memory, then he looked up.

"And we've carried 'The Old Bits of Rag' to a few places."

"We have that, Sir."

"So, perhaps now they'll give you and Bennet proper halberds."

"Hope not, Sir."

Lacey stepped back.

"Well, Good Luck, Deakin."

"And to you, Sir."

Lacey progressed on to the end of the ranks, and then he returned to the centre to face The Colours once more. O'Hare and Carr, both with swords drawn, now turned to face him and Gibney now took a deep breath.

"'Tallion!"

A three second pause, but the only sound or movement were The Colours being worked by the breeze.

"'Tallion. Huzzas for the Colonel!"

The three rang out, three mighty bellows from everyone in the ranks, all prompted by Gibney. Lacey then drew his own sword, brought it to the salute, paused for three seconds then, shakily, he returned it to its scabbard. He then marched back towards his tent, needing to clamp his jaw tight shut as, from all along the ranks, although it strictly was a flogging offence to speak on parade, came the very frequent cries of "Good luck, Colonel!" Once inside his tent, the tears really did begin to flow as, from somewhere, his men struck up the tune of 'Brighton Camp', which they were still singing as they marched away, to Elvas and once more the North.

oOo

Footnotes

Chapter One
    In 1910, Sir Charles Oman passed through Porto de Mos and he tried to discover if any memory of the appalling tragedy in the Chapel there survived. The Sacristan at once took him to a ruined chamber to the left of the Church and he was told that 200 people had been burned there, 'in the time of the French'. A new Sacristy had been built to replace it in 1814, the original chamber being held as 'accursed'. The description included in Oman's Volume IV comes from the Memoirs of Donaldson, 94th Foot.

    The best account of the French retreat from Santarem can be found in 'Costello. The True Story of a Peninsular War Rifleman, by Eileen Hathaway.' There are dozens of harrowing descriptions of the French treatment of Portuguese peasants as they fell back before Wellington's men. The deeds committed by Massena's starving, defeated and desperate men were probably the worst committed during the whole of the Napoleonic Wars.

    Two French Eagles were captured in March 1811. At Barossa that of the 8th Ligne was taken by the 87th The Prince of Wales' Irish, captured by Sergeant Masterman, to the cry of "Blow me boys, I've got the cuckoo". The second was at Foz de Arouce, that of the 39th Ligne, which was found floating in the river after the 39th broke and ran to cross the river in their hasty retreat from the attentions of the 88th, the 45th and others.

Chapter Two.
    The incident of British soldiers cheering the exploits of their French equivalents actually happened near the village of Gallegos. The ridge and valley are as they were, still farmland.

Chapter Three
    The retreat from Pozo Bello by the Light Division was undoubtedly Crauford's finest hour. Ramsey' battery escaped as described, but Ramsey was killed at Waterloo, as was Picton. Fuentes de Onoro ranks alongside Albuera and Talavera as easily the three mostly costly battles of the whole Peninsular War. Albuera gave rise to the much used phrase 'Die Hard'. When Colonel Inglis of the 57th, wounded from a round of canister, which he believed to be mortal, saw his Battalion being wiped out whilst holding their line, he cried

out the renowned words "Die hard, 57th, die hard!". From them on the 57th West Middlesex were known as the Die Hards.

Throughout the Peninsular War the 88th Connaught Rangers, "The Devil's Own", showed themselves to be the foremost shock troops of any Army. Their repeated ability to defeat many times their number was never better illustrated that at Fuentes de Onoro where a single Battalion, at a crucial point in the battle, repulsed a French column of possibly five Battalions led by Conroux, all advancing up the main road past the Church at the top of the village. There is a Monument at the top, unusual for Spain, but this is changing, especially on the battlefield of Salamanca where there are now many 'Interpretation Boards'.

Chapter Four.
The gorge at Barba del Puerco (now called Puerto Seguro) is utterly spectacular with the Roman bridge at the bottom and the Chapel still there at the top. It was the scene of the amazing defence mounted by a Company of Rifles in 1810, holding off 600 French Grenadiers who had crossed the bridge, and also the route of the French escape from Almeida in May 1811.

Chapter Five
The confrontation in June and July1811 was arguably the most important of the Peninsular War. Soult's failure to attack after the relief of Badajoz allowed the initiative to swing to the Allies and they never lost it, although it did hang in the balance once or twice during the following months.

Chapter Six.
Amazingly, Wellington did inspect the walls of Cuidad himself, sneaking along the main ditch, with Colonel Fletcher. The Santa Cruz Convent has been replaced by the Bull Ring, the Lesser Tesson is now much built on, but the remains of Fort Renaud are still there, if you circumvent the barbed wire.

Chapter Seven.
Marmont's extraordinary lunch out before his lines at Fuentes Guinaldo did actually happen and he was left unmolested by any cannon fire.

Chapter Eight.
Captain John Uniacke's death from the explosion at Cuidad Rodrigo was possibly one of the most tragic. His widowed Mother, his brothers and sisters were completely dependent on his pay and they descended into poverty. He was buried in the churchyard of Gallegos, this allowed by the Priest because Uniacke was a Catholic. The church is still there, but no churchyard in any way close.

Chapter Nine.
A memorial plaque to Crauford can be seen on the interior of the town wall. It is where the medieval tower once was, now turned into a major entrance tunnel to the town. The Lesser Breach was to the left of the pedestrian tunnel, and Crauford still lies in there, undisturbed.

The Church Tower, behind the site of the main breach, still shows the scars of the bombardment of the walls, merely yards in front of the tower. The 'scallop' taken from the point of the ravellin that protected that part of the wall, by the bombardment, remains unfilled and very obvious. A monument to the Guerrilla Leader, El Charro, is also there.

Chapter Ten
Life in the siege lines surrounding Badajoz was miserable beyond description, all added to by the efforts of the very able General Phillipon. At Badajoz, Wellington did not cover himself with glory. For example, why efforts were not made to capture the San Roque, as they were for the Picurina, to enable the destruction of the dam across the Rivellas, remains a big question mark. At the main breach, hundreds of wounded were drowned. Of the 4th Division attacking there, the 40th 2nd Somerset suffered the worst casualties, 236, whilst of the Light Division, these ordered to assault the new breach in the curtain wall

between the San Trinidad and Santa Maria bastions, the 52nd, 43rd, and 95th suffered 320, 341, and 194 respectively. These numbers were unique throughout the Peninsular War. Phillipon enjoined his men to take from Wellington the 'lives of his best soldiers' and they did.

Chapter Eleven.

The sack of Badajoz is probably the reason why the victories of the Peninsular War are not more prominent in British Military history. It ranks with the Amritsar Massacre as one of the worst crimes perpetrated by British soldiers. Our soldiers never thought that the citizens of Badajoz treated them too well. General Phillipon and his two daughters were escorted from the town to the camp by two British Officers who protected them, especially the girls, from the violent attentions of many soldiers.

Nowhere in Badajoz is the Peninsular War commemorated, whilst the opposite is the case in Cuidad Rodrigo. The first point of Badajoz where British entered the town is the leftmost embrasure of the San Vincente looking up from outside, where soldiers of Leith's Fifth Division forced entrance. It is now blocked by shrubs and metal fences as part of an FE College car park. The Castle walls are being returned to their original Moorish style and so Ridge's tower is now much higher. Perhaps Badajoz does remember, but in a different form, because when examining the brickwork of the San Trinidad for signs of the breach, my wife and I were ordered off the grass by a very irate Policeman.

Chapter Twelve

The despoliation of Badajoz continued for three days, from the 7th to the 9th of April. The one point of light is that the Cathedral was held as a refuge for Spanish citizens by British soldiers throughout all that time, probably by men from Walker's Brigade of Leith's Division. They did not suffer as much as Picton's Division and the men of the 4th and Light Divisions did not get in